LANGUAGE, MINORITIES AND HUMAN RIGHTS

International Studies in Human Rights

VOLUME 45

The titles published in this series are listed at the end of this volume.

LANGUAGE, MINORITIES AND HUMAN RIGHTS

by

FERNAND DE VARENNES

MARTINUS NIJHOFF PUBLISHERS
THE HAGUE / BOSTON / LONDON

A C.I.P. Catalogue record for this book is available from the Library of Congress.

ISBN 90-411-0206-X

Published by Kluwer Law International,
P.O. Box 85889, 2508 CN The Hague, The Netherlands.

Sold and distributed in the U.S.A. and Canada
by Kluwer Law International,
675 Massachusetts Avenue, Cambridge, MA 02139, U.S.A.

In all other countries, sold and distributed
by Kluwer Law International,
P.O. Box 85889, 2508 CN The Hague, The Netherlands.

Printed on acid-free paper

Printed and bound in Great Britain by
CPI Antony Rowe, Chippenham and Eastbourne

TABLE OF CONTENTS

Contents

3.1 Afghanistan; 3.2 Albania; 3.3 Algeria; 3.4 Andorra; 3.5 Antigua and Barbuda; 3.6 Argentina; 3.7 Austria; 3.8 Bahamas; 3.9 Bahrain; 3.10 Barbados; 3.11 Belarus; 3.12 Belgium; 3.13 Belize; 3.14 Benin; 3.15 Bolivia; 3.16 Bosnia and Herzegovina; 3.17 Botswana; 3.18 Brazil; 3.19 Brunei; 3.20 Bulgaria; 3.21 Burkina Faso; 3.22 Burma; 3.23 Burundi; 3.24 Cameroon; 3.25 Canada; 3.26 Central African Republic; 3.27 China; 3.28 Colombia; 3.29 Comores; 3.30 Congo; 3.31 Costa

ACKNOWLEDGMENTS

Only the assistance, patience and encouragement from many friends such as André LeBlanc, Stephen Campbell, René Basque, Michel Cyr, Louise Guerrette-Cormier, and Lili Sainte-Marie, the understanding of Elisabeth Thaler and the forgiving smiles of my son Lucas, have made this book possible. I am also beholden to Lise Lorrain for the many hours spent reading the manuscript and offering suggestions. The comments and inspiration of Professor Bruno de Witte, of the Rijksuniversiteit-Limburg, in Maastricht, who supervised my doctoral thesis, the comments and information received from Professor Antoni Milian i Massana, of the Universitat Autonoma de Barcelona, and Doctor Normand Labrie of Toronto, amongst many others, were invaluable. Finally, I owe a great debt to Rosalyn Higgins, Judge at the International Court of Justice, for her unflagging support and faith in my work over the years. Financial assistance from the Foundation from Legal Research of Canada for research on the rights of indigenous peoples is also acknowledged.

F. de V.

1. Introduction

The tie of language is, perhaps, the strongest and most durable that can unite mankind.

Alexis de Tocqueville[1]

The issue of language is fundamental in human society because homo sapiens are, by definition, "language animals". Language plays a central role in terms of economic opportunity and success, as the dominance of one language in a state will be advantageous, in terms of access to and distribution of public resources, to individuals who have greater fluency in the official or majority tongue. Moreover, language is often of essence to the sentiments of community and culture, of tradition and "belonging". As a result, any menace to, disrespect of or attack upon its use or existence may arouse strong emotions and constitutes a potential cause of conflict.

Because individuals most often cannot easily change their language, and because language plays a prominent role as a marker of the community to which individuals have close ties, language becomes a signalling point, like race or religion, identifying those who are "different", hence potential targets for discrimination.

In the last century, states have extended their reach into society, delving more and more deeply into the lives of individuals and communities. Because of the status of language as the principal link between individuals and community life and because of the highly charged sentiments aroused by language as part of the history and culture of many people, antedating even the state, language has become one of the most common differentiating factors used in human affairs, along with religion and race.

The role of the state as a major purveyor of services and employment or economic opportunities, for which individuals compete intensely, has expanded. Formerly, state intervention in the lives of individuals and communities was generally limited to maintaining an internal order, generally for the benefit of the controlling elites, as well as exacting tribute from or exploiting the resources of its people and territory, and defending them against foreign aggression. The modern state by contrast is highly invasive and provides a wide range of services (education, health care, welfare, postal services, etc.) and regulatory mechanisms (i.e. in broadcasting). The state has no choice but to use at least one language in the discharge of its duties. Those whose primary language is that used by the state thereby gain an enormous advantage over others. Amongst native speakers of a language, the common interest fostered by a shared cultural outlook and the psychological bonds born of that language are enhanced by such practical interests like that arising from state preference(s) in language. Language has become highly politicised, being intimately connected to economic and social mobility in today's society. Whilst separation of state and religion has become largely possible, the separation of state and language is no longer a realistic goal in most societies.

All of this serves as background to a fundamental question which I will be attempting to answer: why should human rights be used to protect language? At the heart of this question are a series of misunderstandings as to the nature and effect of human rights, mistakes as to how these should be interpreted, and erroneous assumptions as to the reasons why they should not interfere in a state's use of or preference for a particular official or majority language. All of

---

[1] de Tocqueville, Alexis (1969), *Democracy in America*, J.P. Mayer (ed.), Doubleday Anchor, New York.

these require close examination in order to elucidate how they came into existence and why they should be criticised.

This study also attempts to situate language issues in a broader theoretical context and to develop an analytical framework which takes into account the legitimate needs and interests of the state, and the rights and interests of the individual who speaks a language other than the state's official or majority language.

The principal issue of inquiry here is not that of "collective" or "group" rights, but rather of the proper place and appropriate role of traditional individual human rights in matters relating to language. An attempt shall be made to dispel common misconceptions on how minority and language concerns can be accommodated within the individualist framework of human rights, such as freedom of expression and non-discrimination. A recurrent theme throughout this study is that it is intolerance of linguistic differences and/or ignorance of the very real and serious disadvantages state language preferences have on some individuals which have generated fragmentation and conflict in many parts of the world.

The disciplines of law, political theory, sociology and economics have been examined in an attempt to offer a better understanding of the nature of language issues and their importance in relation to human rights. Thus, a selective approach to relevant materials has been unavoidable, the most practical contributions having been blended in order to arrive at some degree of coherence. In the process, some issues may have been oversimplified and some possibly broad generalisations may have been made. Any comments or suggestions for improvements from those specialists who have a more exact understanding of the various facets of this topic would be appreciated.

This study begins with a review of the historical evolution of state intervention, world-wide. This is undertaken in an attempt to present a general perspective on how attitudes towards language and legal treatment thereof have evolved alongside evolving societies, and also to dispel the erroneous view that language issues are a strictly modern or Western concern.

Thereafter, the most relevant human rights standards generally recognised in national and international law, namely freedom of expression, equality and non-discrimination on the ground of language, and the right of members belonging to a minority to use their language in community with other members of their group, are examined in some depth. An empirical approach has been employed, and concepts drawn from the legal traditions, experience and scholarly research in a wide range of countries and cultures; this, in an attempt to develop a comprehensive analytical framework which may aid in providing an effective response to the increasingly strident language demands in many parts of the world, and which is consistent with the individualistic oriented regime of contemporary human rights.

On a more practical level, the application and the interpretation of these human rights are "tested" in the fields of education, public services, private and public media, and naturalisation and citizenship in order to give a sense of how these rights can be translated in terms of *realpolitik*. This will demonstrate that human rights can help to provide a flexible, realistic mechanism which can adapt to a variety of situations.

Finally, special consideration is given to the situation of indigenous peoples and what appears to be a growing consensus that they are entitled to greater sensitivity and consideration on the part of state authorities in language affairs, amongst other areas, because of their unique legal and political status.

The importance of focusing on language matters and human rights and better understanding these issues cannot be overemphasised. Since the end of the Second World War, violent conflicts have claimed more than 20 million lives. The majority of these conflicts no longer involve war between states, but occur within state borders and involve so-called ethnic divisions, where divisions of language, religion and/or race tend to arise. In a general sense, too little regard has been given to the real consequences of state language policies for individuals and their possible disregard of the central role of language as a community symbol and beacon. As will be shown, human rights such as freedom of expression, non-discrimination, and the right of minorities to use their language with other members of their group may be useful in offering an alternative to more antagonistic, oppressive or burdensome state practices, whilst at the same time acknowledging the legitimate interests and objectives of a state. Whilst the relationship between language and these human rights is more complex than is normally supposed, it is also less antagonistic.

2. Historical Overview of Language and Law

2.1 LANGUAGE AND GOVERNMENTS

2.1.1 *Of Language, Communities and Empires*

> Italy has been selected by God to collect dispersed power, to soften customs and to unite, by the communion of one language, the diverse and barbarous dialects of so many peoples, so that all the races of mankind should have one fatherland.
>
> Pliny[1]

Language as a marker of membership in a community and therefore as a possible red flag for intolerance and discrimination is not a uniquely modern phenomenon. The Old Testament contains a passage in Judges on the people of Gilead seeking out and massacring members of the Ephraimites. These "others" were identified by their accent in pronouncing the initial sound in the word "shibboleth". The passage is one of the earliest written accounts of "ethnic cleansing" aimed at individuals distinguishable by their language.

Despite this and other examples throughout history, it is a truism that language-based conflicts were relatively infrequent until the seventeenth century. It appears that "[w]hen a country was governed by a limited ruling class, it did not matter what language the masses spoke, as long as they kept their place".[2] Although society's attitude towards language has varied according to time and place, it has most often been appreciated as a tool for communication amongst diverse peoples or otherwise perceived as an obstructive barrier.

Alexander the Great, in order to consolidate his control of his vast empire, favoured a fusion of his subjects in Europe and Asia by "Hellenising" the populations. His approach was not to impose Greek by law but rather to encourage his soldiers and officers to marry into the indigenous elites in the hope that their children, brought up under Greek culture and language, would ensure the expansion of those aspects of the Greek social and political community he deemed of primary importance.[3] To a large extent his efforts in this area were successful, since the Greek language survived in many parts of the Mediterranean and Asia Minor until the Arab conquest.

Alexander and his successors adopted a process which was prevalent before the appearance of the Western European concept of the nation-state: most ancient empires and pre-modern legal and political structures sought to a large extent to preserve the administrative, community and legal structures already in place. For example, in the vast Hellenic Empire indigenous personnel were maintained whenever possible, and as a result the language used at the local level remained largely unchanged. Whilst it is probable that with the passage of time the indigenous elites

---

[1] Macartney, C.A. (1968), *National States and National Minorities*, Russell and Russell, New York, at p. 27.

[2] Quoted in Dua, Hans R. (1987), "Comments on Brian Weinstein's Paper: Language Planning and Interests", in Lorne Laforge (ed.), *Proceedings of the International Colloquium on Language Planning*, Les Presses de l'Université Laval, Québec, pp. 60-67, at p. 63.

[3] The ancient Greeks defined themselves linguistically as distinct from the *barbaroi*, or barbarians, whose speech was clearly not Greek.

became more and more Hellenised, the basic concept was not that of imposing the language of the victors on the masses, but rather of ensuring their loyalty and collecting taxes and other resources of interest to the reigning people.[4]

It should be emphasised that initially language was not dealt with under specific legislation; thus, indigenous populations were largely allowed to use their native language in contacts with the official representatives of the Hellenic Empire, and other empires. As a result and because of the preservation of local customs and personnel, along with the varying degrees of autonomy maintained throughout much of early history in many parts of the world, indigenous languages often were not superseded.

The advent of the Roman Conquest brought forth the expansion of the Latin language. Whilst it was the language of the army, of justice and of the bureaucracy, the Greek language was never actually supplanted. The Roman Empire was in many respects a multilingual state: in recognition of the prominence of Greek language and culture, the Roman chancellery was bilingual, administrative documents sent to Asia Minor were translated into Greek, and Oriental courts officially used Greek; at the local level, indigenous languages were also used by the various peoples in the affairs regulated within their communities. Still, Latin expanded greatly in the Western parts of the Empire and largely supplanted indigenous languages there with respect to law, commerce and diplomacy, at least amongst the educated elites.[5] Although Rome appears to have cared little what language her new subjects spoke, or what customs they followed (provided that they did not rebel), Latin did in fact absorb many linguistic groups in Western Europe. This was not the result of any overt assimilation policy but rather a consequence of the centralised Roman administration, the Roman army, and the attraction for many of Roman culture.

Despite the success of the Latin language, it remains that in its earlier conquests Rome left intact the language, customs, and institutions of the peoples which she subdued. Indigenous languages maintained a customary role in private or religious matters within the jurisdiction of indigenous communities. As the story of the trial of Jesus of Nazareth by the Pharisees shows, indigenous law and customs were allowed to co-exist with Roman law. As a result, there survived an institutional tradition of use of the community's language.[6]

In the Byzantine Empire, Greek became the language of the state machinery, but literary languages (Armenian in eastern Anatolia, Coptic in Egypt, Syriac in Syria) were allowed to survive and even flourish. This is especially true in the case of languages associated with religious institutions other than the official Orthodox Church.

It would be inappropriate to equate this tolerance for and legal accommodation of language diversity as a uniquely Western phenomenon. The appearance of Islam and the growing prominence of Arabic in the Mediterranean Basin after the seventh century did not mean that all native languages were set aside. On the contrary, Islam recognises rights for certain religious communities that imply the use of other languages in legal and administrative functions:

> Under the 'Abbasid caliphs, the Nestorian patriarch in Baghdad, and under the later Egyptian dynasties, the Coptic patriarch in Cairo, held a special position of influence and

---

[4] Meuleau, Maurice and Pietri, Luce (1971), *Le monde et son histoire — Le monde Antique et les débuts du Moyen-Âge*, Éditions Bordas and Robert Laffont, Paris, at pp. 263-264.

[5] Ibid., at p. 463.

[6] See Barrow, R. H. (1949), *The Romans*, Penguin Press, Baltimore, USA, at pp. 115-116.

respect. The heads of the communities were responsible for ensuring that the terms of the *dhimma* or contract of protection between the Muslim rulers and the non-Muslim subjects were honoured: peace, obedience and respect... They also had a function inside the community: they supervised the schools and social services, and tried to prevent deviations in doctrine or liturgical practice. They also supervised the courts in which judges administered law in civil cases involving two members of the community, or reconciled disagreements; if they wished, however, Jews and Christians could take their cases to the Muslim *qadi*, and they seem to have done so frequently.[7]

Nevertheless, for those populations that did embrace Islam, the prominence of Arabic grew quickly. Until it confronted a well developed and long established literary language in what was to later become Iran, and with other notable exceptions such as language of the Berbers of Northern Africa, Arabic as the language of revelation was accepted as the language of everyday life in many communities. Since the Qur'an represents Allah's words to the Prophet and was written in Arabic, it was deemed essential for many of those who accepted the Qur'an as the Word of Allah to understand its language, though Persian and other languages also continued to be used east of Iraq.[8]

The Ottoman dynasty, the Safavids in Iran, and the Mughal Turkish dynasties in Northern India towards the sixteenth century, quite apart from granting linguistic autonomy to non-Muslim communities, did not seek to impose the exclusive domination of Arabic on the Muslim faithful:

> The dynasties established by Turks continued to use forms of the Turkish language in the army and palace, but in time they were drawn into the world of Arabic or Arabo-Persian culture, or at least acted as its patrons and guardians. In Iran, Turkish was the language of rulers and armies, Persian was that of the administration and secular culture, and Arabic that of religious and legal culture. To the west, Arabic was the language of rule and Arabic that of civil officials and high culture; later this changes to some extent, when the rise of the Ottoman Empire led to the formation of a distinctive Ottoman Turkish language and culture, which was that of the high officials as well as the palace and army.[9]

Only in the Umayyads Kingdom in Spain does one find that Arabic became the *lingua franca* of Jews, Christians and Muslims alike, although this exception was to be eliminated with the reconquest of the Iberian Peninsula by the Christians.

Chinese policy in the ninth century in its southern regions also acknowledged that a degree of local autonomy, accompanied with the use of local languages even in official affairs, was the appropriate route to follow in some cases. Initiated during the Tang dynasty, the *Du Si* system of local administration for indigenous populations even survived, with the Zhuangs, until 1929.[10]

As for the situation in pre-Columbian America, it appears that a manner of bilingualism was practised by some indigenous governments, with a definite "American" twist: whilst the Incas

---

[7] Hourani, Albert (1991), *A History of the Arab Peoples*, Warner Books, New York, at p. 119.

[8] Ibid., at pp. 48-49.

[9] Ibid., at pp. 88-89.

[10] Poulin, Richard (1984), *La politique des nationalités de la République populaire de Chine: de Mao Zedong à Hua Guofeng*, Éditeur officiel du Québec, Québec, at p. 114.

may not initially have endeavoured to abolish local languages, they "ordered and decreed, with severe punishment for failure to obey, that all the natives of their empire should know and understand the language of Cuzco...in the space of a few years a single tongue was known and used in an extension of 1,200 leagues; yet even though this language was employed, they all spoke their own."[11]

In Western Europe, Latin maintained an important role despite the disappearance of the Roman Empire because of its widespread use as the *lingua franca* of the elites in many parts of the Continent, as well as its role as the language of liturgy, law and administration, and of scientific and cultural knowledge until the Middle Ages.[12] The Church and educational institutions closely associated with it (that is, essentially all educational institutions at the time) continued to promote the use of Latin. But popular languages had already started to acquire a higher profile in the ninth century as they began to take written form, be they Celtic or Germanic speeches (Dutch, English) or offshoots of popular Latin (French, Portuguese, Spanish).

It is therefore wrong to believe that the domination of Latin meant that other languages were simply swept aside in Western Europe. Local languages were not only used in the day to day life of the vast majority of the populations, they were also used in courts by the common folk even if written legal documents would have been in Latin. The use of these languages also began to appear in some churches.[13]

Even as the status of Latin was revived for a period as the language of Charlemagne's Empire and of intellectual life in much of Western Europe, the use of local languages increased considerably as education began to reach ever increasing numbers of individuals. In England, Latin did not seem to have much influence in the legal sphere since the laws (dooms) prior to the Norman invasion of 1066 were written in West Saxon (Old English). After the Norman invasion, the spoken language of the courts came to be French (the language of the upper classes) although much of the written material of litigation was in Latin.[14]

Religion played a considerable role in Europe initially as a factor favouring the expansion of Latin but subsequently providing the impetus for greater use and legal recognition of local languages. As early as the year 813, the Council of Tours, noting that most Christians had no knowledge of Latin, ordered the clergy to preach "in the rustic romane tongue, or in the germanic tongue, so that all could understand more easily".[15] The development of the written Armenian and Georgian languages can be traced to the efforts of Christianity in the fifth and tenth centuries respectively.

Although the history of the Middle Ages differed greatly from that of the ancient world, ancient and medieval political structures were similar in that power remained divided amongst

---

[11] Quote from *Nation-States and Indians in Latin America* (1991), Greg Urban and Joel Sherzer (eds.), University of Texas Press, Austin, USA, at p. 312.

[12] Wolff, Philippe, (1970), *Les origines linguistiques de l'Europe occidentale*, Hachette, Paris, at pp. 132-133.

[13] *Supra*, note 4, at pp. 661-664.

[14] Robinson, O.F., Ferguson, T.D., and Gordon, W.M. (1985), *An Introduction to European Legal History*, Professional Books, Trowbridge, United Kingdom, at p. 237.

[15] Carbonneau, Thomas E. (1981), "Linguistic Legislation and Transnational Commercial Activity: France and Belgium", in *American Journal of Comparative Law*, Vol. 29, 393-412, at p. 394.

a variety of local centres, rather than centralised, which made for rather flexible concessions in areas not wholly under the control of ecclesiastical authorities.

Administrative divisions under feudalism tended to coincide with the divisions of the various peoples. Counties in England, for instance, often mark the limits of the settlements of the different invading groups, each speaking different languages or dialects (Jutes, Angles, or Saxons). Even within the larger areas, which included settlements comprised of different ethnic groups, feudalism maintained a highly subdivided system of delegated authority, so that when the people came into direct contact with authority, it was usually in a small group more often than not sharing a single language. One valley might be inhabited by Celts, another by Germans; but each would be under its own local lord who administered its affairs. The language used in this form of highly decentralised power structure would simply be whatever language was in use locally.

Eventually, the use of Latin in non-religious affairs began to decline with growing urbanisation and social and economic changes in the eleventh and twelfth centuries in parts of Western Europe. These were accompanied by changes in education, responding to societies shaking off the shackles of feudalism for the emerging commercial and labour classes. This was to have substantial implications for many local languages.[16]

By the early thirteenth century, one cannot identify clear "legislation" prescribing any particular language, but in practice various governments were already beginning to impose a local language or the language of the reigning elite in preference to Latin in many of its operations. Legal documents in the south of France were written in the local language, as they were to be written about a century later in the north. Diplomas, charters and finally laws and municipal decrees began to appear in local German dialects in the thirteenth century, and Frederick II promulgated in German his **Law on Public Peace** (*Landfriedengesetz*) in 1235. Municipal charters in Flanders began to appear in Dutch by the early fourteenth century. The use of Spanish (Castilian), Catalan and even Basque in legal documents began in the eleventh century, whilst Portuguese made a later appearance around the twelfth. Under the reign of King Edward III of England, a statute in 1362 provided for English to replace French as the language of pleas.

By the fifteenth century, most legal documents in much of Europe were no longer in Latin,[17] and laws requiring proceedings to be in the "common tongue" were promulgated with increasing frequency. The appearance of local languages in written form and their growing prominence also meant that the elites became less and less inclined towards Latin. Religious congregations for example opened schools reaching larger and larger numbers of pupils where local languages were in use. To this must be added a political aspect: the weakening of feudal

---

[16] *Supra*, note 12, at p. 141:

> *Cette société se laïcise en un certain sens : dans le sens même où le mot laicus perd peu à peu sa valeur d'"ignorant" pour désigner plus précisément les hommes qui ne savent pas le latin. Parmi les rois et les princes se multiplient les exemples d'hommes qui, sans connaître le latin, ou fort peu, possèdent une réelle culture et favorisent la rédaction d'oeuvres en langues vulgaires. Les besoins professionnels suscitent une importante catégorie de juges, de légistes, de notaires, de scribes, qui remplissent en nombre croissant des fonctions primitivement réservées au clergé, et ressentent le besoin de se mettre à la portée de leur clientèle en élargissant l'usage écrit des langues populaires. Un peu partout naissent des écoles urbaines... Ces écoles sont loin d'éliminer le latin de leurs programmes. Mais elles donnent principalement l'instruction pratique en langue "vulgaire" dont ont besoin les fils de négociants et d'artisans.*

[17] Ibid., at pp. 146-196.

society and of the use of Latin appears to be coupled with attempts by a growing number of monarchs to assume greater direct control over their domain and inhabitants, therefore circumventing feudal overlords. Not everyone was pleased with these developments. Whereas in the Eastern Orthodox Church there was a willingness to use local Slavic languages in liturgy, in the Roman Church there was discomfort at the spread of non-Latin religious books: a decree in Toulouse in 1229 stated that "lay people shall not have books of scripture, except the psalter and the divine office; and they shall not have these in the vulgar". This was perceived necessary since, as Pope Innocent III declared, "the secret mysteries of the faith ought not...be explained to all men in all places".[18]

By the fifteenth century the trend is unmistakable: the rulers of centralising states felt the need to directly claim the allegiance of their subjects. Subsequent to jurists such as Marsilius holding that the ultimate source of a sovereign's power is in the people, a ruler could use a common language as natural proof of this allegiance,[19] or impose his language on his subjects in order to strengthen the bond between them.

Finally, two further historical events were to contribute to an ever increasing prominence for some local languages in Western Europe which were to have vast legal consequences for centuries all over the world: the Reformation and the Gutenberg press.

The Reformation has been described as the first minority revolt against the dominance of the elites attempting to maintain the privileged position of a major *lingua franca*, Latin. By rejecting the authority of the Roman Church and introducing local languages into religious services, Germanic and other European nations were to drastically undermine one of the major domains of the Latin language. Luther himself is claimed to have said he preferred to glorify God in German than in Latin.[20] In addition to establishing national churches, Nordic nations translated the Bible into local languages in the sixteenth century following Luther's model.[21]

It became possible during this time to reach the masses directly, through the language used by the vast majority of the populations of Europe, instead of relying exclusively on what remained for most people an unknown and mysterious tongue, namely Latin. As the Reformation and the Counter-Reformation fought over the minds and souls of the masses, there followed the need to translate Bibles and theological documents, and in some cases to create a whole new written form for a number of languages.[22] In Scandinavian countries, once both God (thanks to

---

[18] Innis, Harold A. (1986), *Empire and Communications*, Press Porcépic, Victoria, Canada, at p. 129.

[19] As shows the address of Henri IV of France to the Savoyards round about 1600:
> *Il étoit raissonable que puisque vous parlez naturellement françois, vous fussiez sujets à un roy de France. Je veux bien que la langue espagnole demeure à l'Espagnol, l'allemand à l'Allemand, mais toute la françoise doit estre à moy.*

[20] Hagège, Claude (1992), *Le souffle de la langue : voies et destins des parlers d'Europe*, Éditions Odile Jacob, Paris, at p. 137.

[21] Haugen, Einar (1981), "Language Fragmentation in Scandinavia", in Einar Haugen, Derrick McClure and Derick Thomson (eds.), *Minority Languages Today*, Edinburgh University Press, Edinburgh, at p. 103.

[22] Meillet, A. (1928), *Les langues dans l'Europe Nouvelle*, Payot, Paris, at p. 135. See also Gambier, Yves (1986), *La Finlande bilingue : histoire, droit et réalités*, Éditeur officiel du Québec, Québec, at p. 26.

the Reformation) and his representative on Earth, the King, began speaking Swedish and Danish, these languages were to spread thanks to this newly acquired veneration.

The advent of the Gutenberg press by 1450, with its use of mobile print, marks another major turning point for greater use of local languages as books become easier to make and less expensive to acquire. Whereas the high cost of Latin manuscripts made these inaccessible to most people, both in terms of price and language, the printing press made it feasible to mass produce books, which implied the possibility of printing books for the masses. Of course, the masses would have to be able to read, but education was reaching the population in ever increasing numbers. Thus, by the sixteenth century, the printing press combined with an ever increasing number of people capable of reading were to have an undeniable impact on the greater prominence of local languages, at least in relation to Latin.[23]

2.1.2 *Emergence of the Nation-State and Increasing Legal Restrictions*

We have revolutionized the government, the laws, the habits, the customs, commerce, and thought; let us also revolutionize the language which is their daily instrument. Citizens! the language of a free people ought to be one and the same for all; ...free men are all alike, and the vigorous accent of liberty and equality is the same whether it comes from the mouth of an inhabitant of the Alps, the Vosges, or the Pyrenees... We have observed that the dialect called the Bas-Breton, the Basque dialect, and the German and Italian languages have perpetuated the reign of fantasy and superstition, secured the domination of priests and aristocrats, prevented the Revolution from penetrating nine Departments, and favoured the enemies of France. You have taken away from these stray fanatics the empire of saints by establishing the republican calendar; take away the empire of priests by teaching the French language... It is treason to the fatherland to leave the citizens in ignorance of the national language.[24]

Although the Reformation and the development of the printing press initially seemed to augur well for maintaining and even enhancing the customary and legal use of local languages, the decline of feudalism was to simultaneously signal changes which would ultimately severely restrict the use of less prominent languages.

History shows that in many cases as a king (or queen) tries to establish royal authority over subjects who previously owed allegiance to their feudal lords, differences in language are both inconvenient and obstructive. A local lord or chieftain may be able to share with a population knowledge of the local language, be it Welsh or Provençal, whereas beginning in the fourteenth century the new sovereigns attempt to centralise power and rule through a bureaucracy which more often than not lacks such knowledge. Since language is perhaps one of the strongest symbols of community and shared culture in human society, there begins to appear a sense in a number of states that language diversity is a menace, or at least an inconvenience, that would best be eradicated.

Thus came into being the first clear legislative attempts to eliminate the institutional or customary use of languages at the local level and to force the assimilation of individuals into the language privileged by the sovereign. As the power of feudal lords was broken, a process of

---

[23] Meillet, ibid., at pp. 225-226.

[24] French Revolutionary Barrere, quoted *supra*, note 1, at pp. 110-111.

systematic centralisation began. The unified national institutions which came into being were usually modelled on those of the majority, and the minorities were required to bring their own customs, and even languages, into line. For example, between 1293 and 1327, Sorbs[25] were to see their language banned in Bernburg, Altenburg, Zwickau and Leipzig by German conquerors.

Under **An Act for the English order, habite and Language**,[26] English law sought for many centuries to do away with the Welsh language in Wales. The English Crown then attempted to suppress its presence with legislative measures such as **Concerning the Laws to be used in Wales**,[27] particularly Article 20 which prohibited the use of Welsh in courts or by any individual holding an office or receiving any fee from the Crown.[28]

By the beginning of the sixteenth century, rulers in a number of European states began to advocate the use of local languages in legal matters to the exclusion of Latin where the need for the parties involved to be understood was obviously great. In Catalonia, the Constitution of Carlos I in 1542 left no doubt as to why this was deemed essential:

Perquè los laics que no saben ni entenen la lengua latina millor sapien i entenen lo que disposen, i ordenan en las suas ultimas voluntats, statuim i ordenam que los Notaris no pugan rebre ni testificar testaments, codicils i donacions mortis causa sino en lengua vulgar cathalana.

King Louis XII had already done much the same and prohibited the use of Latin in criminal trials and investigations, making the language of the people mandatory in such proceedings in 1510,[29] and subsequently completed the process by making the "maternal French tongue" the exclusive

---

[25] A Slavonic tribe found today in the eastern part of Germany.

[26] 1537 28 Henry VIII, chap. 15:

[T]he People of the same Dominion have, and do daily use a Speech nothing like, ne consonant to the natural Mother Tongue used within this Realm, some rude and ignorant People have made Distinction and Diversity between the King's Subjects of this realm, and his Subjects of the said Dominion and Principality of Wales, whereby great Discord, Variance, Debate, Division, Murmur and Sedition have grown between his said Subjects; His Highness therefore of a singular Zeal, Love and Favour that he beareth towards his Subjects of his said Dominion of Wales, minding and intending to reduce them to the perfect Order, Notice and Knowledge of his Laws of this his Realm, and utterly to extirp all and singular the sinister Usages and Customs differing from the same, and to bring the said Subjects of this his Realm, and of his said Dominion of Wales, to an amicable Concord and Unity...

[27] (1535) 27 Henry VIII, chap. 26.

[28] Of course, legislators cannot wipe out a language or the people using it by the stroke of a pen. Welsh continued to be used after 1536 in legal and administrative matters, simply because the vast majority of the population could not speak English. Thus, it was necessary to use interpreters constantly and to have mixed juries composed of half English and half Welsh speakers.

[29] The King's ordnance of June 1510 made it mandatory to use the *vulgaire langage du pays* instead of Latin in criminal trials and all inquests, but did not at that time seek to prohibit local languages in such legal affairs. See Delaporte, Vincent (1976), "La loi relative à l'emploi de la langue française", in *Revue critique de droit international privé*, at p. 451.

language of the law by the **Ordonnance de Villers-Cotterêts** in 1538.[30] Although initially a move to restrict the use of Latin because the vast majority of French citizens had no practical knowledge of that language, it also eventually had the effect of curtailing the use of local languages like Basque, Breton and Provençal. However, these so-called dialects in practice were to be maintained in local administration until the advent of the French Revolution and the consolidation of conquests by Napoleon.[31]

Spain's approach was perhaps even more systematic, at least in the initial stages as the Christian sovereigns attempted to consolidate their control over the territories they had reconquered. King Alfonso X chose to replace the Latin of the feudal era with Toledo's variety of Castilian as the standard form of what many know today as Spanish. In the thirteenth century he imposed it in the territories under his influence, with the exception of Catalan which continued to be utilised in the institutions of government and law of Catalonia. Following the disappearance of the last Muslim state in the Iberian peninsula in 1491, Arabic-speaking people continued to represent not only a large proportion of the population in the areas of Granada and Valencia, but perhaps even a majority. Despite the fact that the November 1491 treaty between the Catholic Crown and Boabdil protected the religious and language freedoms of such people, a series of repressive legal language policies were quickly adopted. As of 1501, every Qur'an and other book dealing with Islam was to be burned, except those texts in Arabic dealing with medicine or philosophy. Ten years later, all Arabic language books without exception were to be destroyed. Finally, the use of Arabic, be it in print or in speech, was to be forbidden.[32] Such a trend would maintain itself in seventeenth and eighteenth century Europe, as the absolute monarchs pursued a policy intended to stamp out the feudal nobility and to centralise power in the hands of the Crown. The policy was eventually to succeed in countries such as Spain, France, and parts of present-day Germany, where centralised states were created.

The context in the Americas facing Spanish, as well as English, Portuguese and French colonialists, was quite different and required, at least initially, a modified approach. Although Spain sought with a 1550 ordnance[33] to impose the use of Spanish as the language of instruction of the indigenous peoples, the ordnance was opposed by Catholic missionaries relying on the conclusions of the Council of Trentino (1545-1563) which approved and even encouraged the use

---

[30] Article 111 is quoted in Didier, Emmanuel (1984), *Droit des langues et langues du droit au Canada*, Doctoral Thesis, Université de Paris I - Panthéon Sorbonne, at p. 89:

> ...*d'oresnavant..tous arrests, ensemble toutes autres procédures, soient de nos cours souveraines et autres subalternes et inférieures, soient de registres, enquestes, contrats, commissions, sentences, testaments, et autres quelconques, actes et exploicts de justice, ou qui en dépendent, soient prononcés, enregistrés et délivrés aux parties en langage maternel françois et non autrement.*

[31] *Ethnic Groups and Language Rights, Comparative Studies on Governments and Non-Dominant Ethnic Groups in Europe 1850-1940*, (1990), Sergij Vilfan (ed.), European Science Foundation, New York University Press, New York, at p. 297:

> By the decree of 24 Prairial, Year XI (13 June 1803), Bonaparte finished the matter off: "In one year...public legal documents in the departments of the former state of Belgium, in those of the left bank of the Rhine...and in the other territories where the custom of drafting the said documents in the local language has been maintained, shall all be written in French."

[32] See Le Monde Diplomatique, September 1993, at p. 17.

[33] **Leyes de Los Indios**, 1550, Volume 6, Title 1, No. 18.

of indigenous languages as the preferable route to adopt in order to ensure the conversion of the pagan population. Moreover, in some cases it was easier for missionaries to learn widespread former imperial languages such as Nahuatl. Nonetheless, ultimately the Spanish political authorities were to gain the upper hand and apply a policy similar to the one it had used with Arabic-speakers in the Iberian peninsula. On 10 May 1770, Charles III issued a decree making Spanish the language of instruction for indigenous peoples in the Spanish territories of the New World.[34]

Indigenous languages in Latin America thus moved from an initial position of favour, destined to facilitate conversion efforts and the administration of territories, to an increasingly repressive situation. The case of Brazil is instructive of the legal treatment of indigenous languages. The use of the Tupí language was actively encouraged by the Portuguese authorities as the *lingua franca*. Gradually, this compromise would be replaced by mere toleration of indigenous languages until finally they could be suppressed. As in the Spanish-speaking portions of the New World, this final step came about in the eighteenth century.[35] The only real exception appears to be the use of Guaraní in Paraguay, which despite some repressive measures was allowed to be used and somewhat protected by the state into the modern era, thanks in part to the early efforts of Jesuit missionaries. By the early nineteenth century, Castilian had become the official language of Latin American countries (except Brazil), although not the primary language of most indigenous peoples.

Similar restrictions were to be imposed in Europe as the absolute monarchies consolidated the nation-states over which they reigned, exemplified in the case of the Spanish state when King Philip V of Spain made Castilian the only language of the courts in Catalonia and the Basque country, with subsequent legislation being adopted under Carlos III imposing Castilian as the exclusive language in all schools, thereby further crushing any remnants of autonomy in these areas.[36]

As explained by Professor Sergij Vilfan:

> [The march to uniformity] resulted in the consolidation of the nation-states, together with the subsequent establishment of a centralised order arising out of the middle class revolutions — centralisation appearing from the early years of the nineteenth century as the

---

[34] In practice, the implementation of this decree would seem to have been problematic. See *Les langues autochtones du Québec* (1992), Jacques Maurais (ed.), Les Publications du Québec, Québec, at p. 17.

[35] Ibid., at pp. 17-19.

[36] Lapierre, Jean-William (1988), *Le pouvoir politique et les langues*, Presses Universitaires de France, Paris, at p. 19. See also the decrees of 3 April 1711, 28 November 1715 and 16 January 1716 quoted *supra*, note 31, at p. 68; see also the comments in Milian i Massana, Antoni (1984), "La regulación constitucional del multilingüismo", in *Revista Española de Derecho Constitucional*, Vol. 4, N° 10, 123-154, at pp. 123 and 124 on the practice of the period:

> *En España, desde la configuración del Estado como Estado-Nación, las lenguas españolas distintas del castellano han sufrido persecución y/o discriminación, como lo prueban numerosas disposiciones y el espíritu de declaraciones e instrucciones políticas. Entre las primeras cabe destacar: Real Cédula de 23 de junio de 1768 "para que en todo el Reyno se actúe y enseñe en lengua castellana"; Real Cédula de 22 de septiembre de 1780 ordenando y recordando la obligación de enseñar a los niños en su lengua nativa (que según la Real Cédula era sólo la lengua castellana)...*

hallmark of the structure of the liberal state, the champion of the egalitarian ideal. However, the process was detrimental to the continued existence and the development of the diverse languages that had been in common spoken or written use until that time.

Political unification is indeed a process that entails the imposition of one language — defined as the national language — at the expense of all others; it is one more means of asserting the position of the nation-state to which the process leads. In addition to other philanthropic arguments, the rationalist oligarchical approach includes that of linguistic uniformity...

These ideas, of course, were to gain ground among that section of public opinion that stood to gain from the unifying process. Politico-administrative centralism and the ensuing uniformity were a widespread phenomenon in Europe and Spain was no exception.[37]

The perceived need to create a unitary, centralised state in Revolutionary France and to eliminate the remains of the old system inspired some political leaders to present the concept of equality of citizens in a somewhat distorted way: equality meant that everyone should be treated by legislation as if they were identical, and so the French nation must use only one language to the exclusion of all others.[38] Moreover, languages other than French were perceived as being in some way inferior since only through the French language could the revolutionary doctrines be properly appreciated. In fact, far from being inspired from any real commitment to equality, the language policy initially put into place by Revolutionary France, and subsequently copied by others in search of the perfect nation-state, had more to do with the Jacobins' perception that the non-French cultures of France were inherently hostile to the Revolution.

2.1.3   *Language Restrictions in Modern Nation-States*

As states were to gradually replace religious or private groups in the educational field in the nineteenth century, especially in Europe and North America, a state-operated, universal system, often meant discarding the use of many languages regarded as an inconvenience or even an affront to the new nation. Public education in the Netherlands is a typical case. The move to centralise instruction in the hands of the national government, along the same model provided by Revolutionary France, carried with it the consequence that Frisian was banished from

---

[37] *Supra*, note 31, at p. 67.

[38] See the **Loi portant qu'à compter de sa publication, nul acte public ne pourra, dans quelque partie que ce soit du territoire de la République, être écrit qu'en langue française**, quoted in Calvet, Louis-Jean (1987) *La guerre des langues et les politiques linguistiques*, Payot, Paris, at p. 256, and the *Rapport sur la nécessité et les moyens d'anéantir les patois et d'universaliser l'usage de la langue française*, tabled at the Convention in 1794, quoted *supra*, note 31, at p. 67; and finally Plourde, Gaston (1972), *Options politiques fondamentales de l'État plurilingue*, Les Presses de l'Université Laval, Québec, at pp. 20 and 21 who summarises the various legal steps taken by the French government to impose French as the exclusive language of the new nation because "*Chez un peuple libre, la langue doit être unique et la même pour tous.*" The French Revolutionary government felt the need to create universal schooling in order to promote the principles of the Revolution and a single common language were they to supplant the remains of the old order. In October 1793, primary schools were set up throughout the Republic, and French was chosen as the exclusive language of instruction.

elementary schools. Teachers were advised not to allow the children to speak Frisian nor to speak Frisian themselves.

Former American colonies were to adopt an attitude towards the languages of indigenous and minority communities similar to those of European nations. A Guatemaltec decree issued in 1824 called for the elimination of the use of indigenous languages, and indigenous languages were banned from use in Mexican schools from 1910 through to approximately 1935.[39]

Despite the fact that English was never made the official language of the United States of America after independence (nor of the United Kingdom for that matter), it was the *de facto* language of the government and came to be identified as the "natural" national language since it was the language in which was written the **Declaration of Independence**, in addition to being the language of a majority of Americans.

As in many other countries of the world towards the end of the nineteenth century and up to the Second World War, language considerations remained highly influential in the United States through efforts to create a unifying national bond. Despite the occasional claim that the United States never attempted to suppress people because of their language, contrary to some European countries, the statement simply does not hold up to closer scrutiny. Although there have been times of great flexibility in recognising the need to accommodate large segments of the population having a primary language other than English, there have also been occasional periods of repression in the "Land of the Free". Members of certain minorities, especially Spanish- and German-speaking citizens, as well as indigenous peoples, were sometimes denied employment or the exercise of the right to vote because they spoke a "foreign" tongue,[40] and even faced possible jail terms for the private or public use of their language.[41] Following World War I, seven states made it a criminal offence for teachers to use a language other than English as the medium of instruction except in foreign-language courses — even in private schools. Decrees in Iowa and South Dakota prohibited the use of any language other than English in a public place or over the telephone, and German language schools, social clubs and newspapers were obliged to close.[42] As late as 1921, it was pointed out that World War I hero Marshall Ferdinand Foch risked finding himself in prison in Nebraska if he attempted to address a group of people there. Because of his limited knowledge of English, Foch was expected to speak French when attending public functions, thereby committing a criminal offence.[43] Finally, even the admission of new states appears to have been delayed until the majority of the population was English-speaking.[44]

---

[39] *Supra*, note 34, at p. 19.

[40] The claim that Spanish or even French are foreign in the United States is factually incorrect since both predate the English settlement of the New World. In relation to indigenous peoples, it is English which is foreign to North America.

[41] Baron, Dennis E. (1990), *The English-Only Question: An Official Language for Americans?*, Yale University Press, New Haven, USA, at pp. 108-111.

[42] Piatt, Bill (1990), *¿Only English? Law and Language Policy in the United States*, University of New Mexico Press, Albuquerque, USA, at p. 17.

[43] *Supra*, note 41, at p. 144.

[44] Ibid., at p. XV:

The United States has generally withheld statehood from territories until they contained English-speaking majorities. Louisiana is the one striking exception... Statehood was delayed for Michigan, originally settled by the French. State boundaries in the American Southwest were

Still, as the United States' territory expanded during the nineteenth century, the federal government recognised that in some parts of the country the majority of the population was not English-speaking, and accordingly legislation did — at least initially — provide for language rights in California (Spanish), Hawaii (Hawaiian), Louisiana (French), and even Pennsylvania (German).[45] For example, the **Constitution of California of 1849** provided that all "laws, decrees, regulations and provisions shall be published in English and Spanish".[46] A similar situation existed in New Mexico.[47] The early Louisiana constitutions provided that statutes be promulgated both in English and French.[48]

Despite these early concessions, the trend towards the gradual elimination of "foreign" language rights persisted as the English-speaking population increased in size. US courts in some cases invalidated laws or practices permitting publication or use of a language other than English.[49]

During the same period, the United Kingdom continued its own practice of attempting to eliminate the only surviving language of any importance in the realm by forbidding the use of Welsh in education by an act of Parliament in 1870.[50]

The consolidation of centralising tendencies in the modern nation-state seemed to favour legislative steps in order to curtail the use of languages other than "that of the nation", i.e. languages that were different from that of the controlling majority or elite. But new voices were already being heard in the nineteenth century as the concepts of democracy and of human rights,

---

drawn to ensure English-speaking majorities for Colorado, Nevada, and Arizona. And statehood was withheld from New Mexico for over sixty years because of nativist opposition in Congress to the territory's Mexican American majority population and to the prevalence of Spanish in New Mexican life.

[45] Ibid., at p. 74:

Official state publications were routinely issued in German as well as English, including the minutes of the state constitutional conventions of 1776 and 1789-90. Session laws were published in German as well as English from 1786 to 1856. And German schools continued to exist: neither section 44 of the 1776 constitution, nor article 7 of the 1790 constitution, both dealing with the common schools, prescribes an official language of instruction, though one section of article 7, guaranteeing the rights of religious societies, implies protection for the German parochial schools of the Commonwealth.

[46] "Official English: Federal Limits on Efforts to Curtail Bilingual Services in the States" (1987), in *Harvard Law Review*, Vol. 100, 1345-1362, at p. 1348.

[47] Schmid, Carol (1987), "Language and Education Rights in the United States and Canada", in *International and Comparative Law Quarterly*, Vol. 36, 903-908, at p. 904. In New Mexico, the early territorial legislatures conducted their business in Spanish as a matter of course, and many of the laws were drafted in Spanish first and then translated into English.

[48] **Louisiana Constitution of 1845**, Articles 103, 104 and 132; **Louisiana Constitution of 1852**, Articles 100, 101 and 129.

[49] See for example **McCoy v. City of Chicago**, 136 Ill. 344 [1891] (United States), and **Perkins v. Board of Commissioners of Cook County**, 271 Ill. 449 [1916] (United States).

[50] Lapierre, *supra*, note 36, at p. 22.

and the expanding education opportunities for the middle classes and citizens in general began to spread.

For example, subsequent to the issue of a decree by Prussia in 1818 to restrict the Sorbian language,[51] increasingly loud voices in 1848-49 demanded what was believed to be equal rights, including, in the minds of Sorbs, equal rights for the Sorbian language and culture in schools, churches and courts.[52]

The same was true of the inhabitants of Alsace in France, where it was often complained that it made no sense holding trials or hearings in a language not well understood by many if not most *citoyens* of the area.

The emergence of equality of political rights in the Helvetic Republic of 1798-1803 implied in the Swiss context that German, French and Italian were considered to be of equal status. Despite a brief period of domination of German during an unsuccessful attempt to create a new centralised state, the adoption in 1848 of a new federal constitution which included a large degree of cantonal autonomy also served to enshrine the language rights of the three main languages used by the Swiss population. Article 116 of the 1874 **Constitution** provided the definite form of the arrangement by stipulating that the German, French and Italian languages have equal rights in the civil service, in legislation and before the courts.

Similar measures become more and more common in a number of countries. Article 133 of the **Constitution Act of 1867** of Canada provides that both French and English are to be used in the Parliament and in some courts. Article 19 of the Austrian **Constitutional Law of 21 December 1867** provided for the absolute right of ethnic minorities of the state to maintain and develop their language. Furthermore:

> All the languages used in the provinces are recognised by the state as having equal rights with regard to education, administration and public life. In provinces inhabited by several ethnic groups, the public educational institutions shall be organised in such a way as to enable all the ethnic groups to acquire the education they need in their own language, without being obliged to learn another language of the province.[53]

The case of Belgium is interesting not so much for how language differences can be divisive, but for why disregard of the language of a large portion of a state's nationals can lead to tension and even open conflict. Although a majority of Belgians have Dutch as their primary language, French dominated and was obligatory in many areas of public life; thus, access to higher education and better jobs with the government was limited for those not having a mastery of the language chosen by the controlling elite. Not until 1873 could Dutch be utilised in local tribunals, nor until 1878 could it be utilised as the official language of the public authorities in four provinces. French was to remain the official language in the country's other provinces. By 1893, universal suffrage finally signified that the Dutch-speaking population could exercise the degree of influence in state affairs associated to its numerical importance. A law adopted on 18 April

---

[51] Sorb is a Slavic language currently spoken in a number of communities in Brandenburg and Saxony in the territory of former East Germany.

[52] These demands were not successful as they were followed in 1875 with a general ban on the Sorb language in the schools of Prussian Lausitz.

[53] *Study on the Rights of Persons belonging to Ethnic, Religious and Linguistic Minorities, Francesco Capotorti, Special Rapporteur* (1979), United Nations Publications, New York, at p. 3.

1898 provided that legislation be promulgated in the two languages. The friction between the French- and Dutch-speaking populations escalated to the point that Belgium became in all but name a confederation of territorially-based linguistic communities.

Further east in Europe, the status of the Polish language and its use depended upon the area in which one resided. Individuals living under Prussian or Russian jurisdiction in the 1860s confronted a policy favouring assimilation with the German or Russian majority, whereas Poles in Galicia under the Austro-Hungarian Empire in 1869 were able to acquire the right to use Polish in the internal administrative affairs of their province, as well as its use as the language of instruction at the University of Krakow. The Czechs during the same period secured the adoption of a series of decrees to improve the legal position of their language as well as to obtain control of their own university in Prague. Their efforts did provoke resistance from the German-speaking minority of Bohemia, which reacted violently when the Czech majority convinced the government of Badeni in April 1897 to adopt a policy of mandatory bilingualism for all public officials in Bohemia. The Austrian government had to back down under pressure from a number of German-speaking groups in the Empire, whose resistance may be explained by the fact that complete bilingualism of the civil service virtually excluded all of the Germans in Bohemia, as most did not know Czech.

Russia also underwent various changes in dealing with its territories and the language of their inhabitants. In the case of Finland, the Russian government initially adopted from 1881 to 1887 a series of decrees and ordnances extending the right to use Finnish before Imperial courts, as well as the right to require public services in Finnish from Tsarist government officials stationed in what is today Finland. This policy was finally set aside in reaction to a growing nationalist movement seeking independence for Finland in the 1890s and replaced, intermittently, with avowedly assimilationist "Russification" efforts.[54]

Just as in the United States of America, some Australian states enacted laws which outlawed teaching in "foreign" languages. Australian legislation dealing with education after the 1850s established English as the sole language of instruction. This resulted in particularly dire consequences for aboriginal communities:

> Aboriginal languages fared even worse, By this stage, oppression, genocide and forced assimilation — partly through removing children from their parents — had led to the death of 100 of 250 languages which had been spoken in Australia in 1788.[55]

In contrast to the tendency in nation-states to restrict the languages used by public authorities, other models were still in place in other regions. In the latter period of the Ottoman Empire, the central government maintained control over national matters such as defence and finance, whilst the recognised non-Muslim communities that were *dhimmi*, followers of religions which Islam considered revealed, were given the responsibility of governing themselves in other manners. The millet system was the Ottoman administration's attempt to take into account the organisation and culture of the various religious-ethnic groups it ruled. Thus these communities, in their areas of

---

[54] Gambier, *supra*, note 22, at p. 38.

[55] Clyne, Michael (1991), "Australia's Language Policies: Are We Going Backwards?", in *Current Affairs Bulletin*, Vol. 68(6), at pp. 13-20.

jurisdiction, could use a language other than Turkish:

> The millet system was a socio-cultural and communal framework based, firstly, on religion, and, secondly, on ethnicity which in turn often reflected linguistic differences. Religion supplied each millet a universal belief system while ethnic and linguistic differences provided for divisions and subdivisions within each of the two Christian millets... Language appeared both as a means of communication and as the distinguishing mark of the ethnic subdivisions in the millet, although linguistic differences had limited, if any, political significance until the eighteenth century when the Greek language began to be used as a means to Hellenize the Orthodox millet. The Armenian millet was spared internal schism... because there was no effort to spread that language to other subgroups.[56]

These communities had the right to legislate in education matters, including the language of instruction. In the millet's sphere of competence, individuals belonging to minorities had few direct contact with the Ottoman administration; they dealt for the most part with the minority's courts, schools, and other authorities. As has been pointed out by one author, the millets, originally set up on a religious basis, increasingly became language-based. This was due in part to frequent internal conflicts such as the Serbs opposing both the Bulgarians and the Greeks who wished to impose their language in church as well as in the schoolroom. Tensions attained such a level that it was finally decided to divide the original religious millets on a linguistic basis so that the three millets of the fifteenth century had become fourteen by the twentieth[57].

2.1.4   *Nationalism, Language and State*

The increasing involvement of the state in what had previously been the private affairs of individuals and communities had a dramatic side-effect: many individuals who had generally been free to use their native language, as well as have their children learn that language, now found themselves obliged by the state to submit to the language preference of the majority.

Nationalism became closely associated with the image, some would even say the myth, of a community of individuals sharing a common cultural identity, often expressed by a common language. The Romanian movement of national renewal corresponded with a growing popularity of the language, also tied in the first half of the eighteenth century with the appearance of Romanian books, the rejection of the dominance of Greek under the millet system during the Ottoman empire, and the spread of the ideals of equality and democracy. Many of the same

---

[56] Karpat, Kemal H. (1982), "Millets and Nationality" in Benjamin Braude and Bernard Lewis (eds.), *Christians and Jews in the Ottoman Empire: The Functioning of a Plural Society*, Holmes & Meier, New York, at p. 142; see also Nisan, Mordechai (1991), *Minorities in the Middle East: A History of Struggle and Self-Expression*, McFarland & Co., Jefferson, USA, at pp. 19-21.

[57] Laponce, Jean A. (1987), *Language and Their Territories*, University of Toronto Press, Toronto, at p. 171. The Polish practice of the Kahal by which administrative and governmental power was delegated to the Jewish community would have had a similar effect.

influences can be seen at work with the Bulgarian, Serbian, and other national movements of the eighteenth century.[58]

At the same time, the evolution of the modern, centralised nation-state often signalled a less than tolerant attitude towards individuals having a primary language different than that of the majority. The French Revolution, for example, increased the government's endeavour to enforce unitary linguistic standards upon every citizen, perceived as a consequence of the political and legal aim of *égalité*, i.e. the use of French as the one national language of all citizens. In others words, equality became identified as conformity to the characteristics and preferences of the majority, and an individual could only become truly equal if he or she were no different from the ideal chosen by the state. Since the French state was ferociously secular, religious differences were of no consequence and could be ignored, but the French government had to function using a particular language which became to represent *la nation française*.

The political will to create a new community represented by the state required common symbols, and language was considered such a symbol. Therefore, in a number of nation-states governments adopted measures to ensure conformity with the symbols chosen by the majority, but not necessarily all, of its populations:

> In nineteenth-century French schools, under orders to spread the national language to that half of France which still was not francophone, teachers used punishment to suppress the students' use of their native tongue. In the 1890s children caught using Breton were put on dry bread and water or sent to clean out the school latrine, or were made to wear a token of shame. Tove Skutnabb-Kangas labels as violent the requirement that some minority-language speakers — for example Lapps in Norway, Finns in Sweden, Kurds in Turkey, and Native-Americans in the United States — attend centralised assimilation schools that isolate children from their families and exterminate their native culture and language. She further describes Finnish and Welsh children punished for using their home languages by being made to carry heavy loads or wear collars that restrain head movement. In 1846 Welsh was allowed in classrooms only as a vehicle for teaching English; it was banned completely between 1871 and 1939. American schools were equally zealous to convert everyone to English. When the United States took the Philippines from Spain in 1898, it imposed English in the schools, together with the practice of suspending students or lowering their grades for using a non-English language.[59]

The approach adopted in Communist countries was, at least in theory, quite different from that of many democratic nations, since it was of primary importance to reach individuals at the earliest possible moment and in the most convenient form. Thus, according to Professor Jean-William Lapierre:

> *Les populations allogènes pouvaient être plus aisément alphabétisées dans leur langue, instruites et endoctrinées, par là même plus mobilisables pour la modernisation technique et le développement économique. Celui-ci, par effet rétroactif, favoriserait la mobilité*

---

[58] Weill, Georges (1930), *L'éveil des nationalités et le mouvement libéral 1815-1848*, Librairie Félix Alcan, Paris, at pp. 162, 165, 376, 377, 384 and 385. His book contains much interesting material on language use in Central Europe during the period.

[59] *Supra*, note 41, at pp. 164-165.

géographique, les relations interethniques et les contacts linguistiques, le rapprochement entre les diverses nationalités, la sélection naturelle de quelques grandes langues véhiculaires régionales et finalement la fusion de toutes les cultures sous l'hégémonie d'une langue commune à tout l'Union, qui ne pouvait être que le russe.[60]

Whilst one of the central principles of Communism has been equality of national languages and of minority language rights, as witnessed by the November 1917 **Declaration of the Rights of the Peoples of Russia**, leaders such as Stalin have favoured a stronger centralised state, which in practice has signified a more prominent role for the Russian language as well as discouraging attendance in minority language institutions whilst inviting "voluntary" registration in Russian language schools, an "international" language having greater social and economic potential. Moreover, not all Communist regimes consistently applied the principles of equality of national languages in a generous manner.[61]

There are other less pleasant examples this century of government legal action in relation to language. In 1923 Mussolini banned the use of foreign words on billboards and posters, and eliminated the use of the French language in educational activities, and banished "non-Italian place names" in the Valle d'Aosta region.[62] Even inscriptions on new tombstones were to be in Italian exclusively. As of 5 August 1926, names were only tolerated if they were Italian, and even many family names had to be changed.[63]

Spain adopted similar measures just before the Second World War with a view to creating a purely Castilian nation. These were largely aimed at attacking the use of Catalan and Basque, going so far as to deny the right to register non-Castilian surnames and to threaten exclusion from

---

[60] *Supra*, note 36, at p. 210.

[61] Schifter, Richard (1991), "To Hate All the People Your Relatives Hate", in *Human Rights Law Journal*, Vol. 12, N° 8-9, 327-330, at p. 328:

Romania's Ceausescu decided in the course of his tenure to turn his country's Hungarian minority into Romanians. Instruction in the Hungarian language was eliminated in institutions of higher learning and cut back in secondary schools. Financial support for ethnic Hungarian cultural institutions was cut back. Ethnic Hungarian villages were scheduled to be depopulated as new multiethnic towns were to be built, to which villagers would be required to move as part of a program known as "systematization."

Ceausescu's approach was benign when compared with that of his neighbour, Todor Zhivkov of Bulgaria. More than 12 percent of the population of this country consists of ethnic Turks. As their fertility rate is greater than that of the country's Slavic population, it is a percentage that is on the increase. In the style fitting a totalitarian ruler of his type, Zhivkov went about eliminating his problem of ethnic Turks by turning them into instant Bulgarians. To accomplish that result he sent his army in late 1984 into ethnic Turkish towns and villages to compel all persons bearing Turkish names to change them into Bulgarian names. School instructions in the Turkish language had long ago been ended. Now there would be no Turkish-language newspapers or other publications, no Turkish ethnic dress, and the use of the Turkish language was prohibited.

[62] Decree No. 2191 of 22 November 1925, **Disposiziono riguardanti la lingua d'ensegnamento nelle scuole elementari**, quoted in Calvet, *supra*, note 38, at p. 261.

[63] International Centre for Research on Bilingualism (1978), *Linguistic Minorities and Interventions, Towards a Typology*, Les Presses de l'Université Laval, Québec, at p. 79.

the teaching profession those instructors — even in private schools — who used any language other than Castilian. As it was stated in an order issued 18 May 1938 "[t]he Spain of Franco cannot tolerate aggressions against the unity of its language".[64] Nazi Germany followed the same route of purification by systematically eliminating non-Germanic place names in Pomeria, Silesia, etc...

In his drive to construct a modern Turkish state, Mustafa Kemal (Atatürk) adopted the Latin alphabet in 1928, abolished the use of Arabic and Persian as languages of education in 1929 and replaced them with Turkish. He also decreed in 1931 that the Qur'an would be read in Turkish only, and finally adopted legislation in 1934 obliging citizens to adopt a surname of Turkish origin. His efforts to forge a new nation were in some respects successful, but they have also sowed the seeds of continuing difficulties with the largest minority in Turkey, the Kurds, who to this day are subject to measures restricting the use of their language.

In pre-colonial South and South East Asia, individuals were governed by personal laws — largely the customary laws of the localities where they lived — but also by religious laws of their communities, covering matters such as marriage and divorce, relations between children and parents, inheritance and succession, and various religious practices. According to Professor Yash Ghai of the University of Hong Kong, this ensured a measure of group autonomy as well as the maintenance of the values, culture and institutions of the various communities, including their languages. Furthermore, colonisation did not substantially change this picture as:

> The preservation of regimes of personal laws moderated the consequences of foreign invasions or changes of sovereignty. With the striking exception of the Philippines (where neither the Spanish nor the US recognised indigenous laws), the colonial authorities recognised personal laws for the most part, although they were now interpreted and enforced in a different and more formal legal and judicial framework which had an important impact on their development.[65]

Colonialism in effect responded to very diverse and complicated language situations in a variety of manners. One interesting example is the case of South Africa where the Afrikaners actually practised a policy inspired from the British:

> That the British authorities saw the importance of language is apparent from the steps periodically taken to compel the public use of English. They applied pressure first in the schools: they extended it by proclamation to the courts from the late 1820's onwards, in 1853 they made English the exclusive language of Parliament, and by [1870] they appeared to be triumphing on all fronts. By the middle 1870's the Chief Justice, J.H. de Villiers, could tell an audience that although the time is still far distant when the inhabitants of this colony will speak and acknowledge one common mother-tongue, it would come at last, and when it does come, the language of Great Britain will also be the language of South Africa...

---

[64] *Supra*, note 31, at p. 69.

[65] See the unpublished paper by Ghai, Yash (1993), *Legal Responses to Ethnicity in South and South East Asia*, delivered at the Conference "Ethnicity, Identity and Nationalism in South Africa: Comparative Perspectives", 20-24 April 1993, Rhodes University, Grahamstown, South Africa, at pp. 11 and 12.

For the colonised people themselves, this meant that English language and English cultural traits acquired an economic and social value that was treasured above all else while their own languages and many of their cultural traits were devalued and often despised.[66]

In regions where there already existed a well-established written language, colonial authorities could adopt it in their administrative activities.[67]

The end of the colonial era brought with it a legacy of acute problems for new nation-states in Asia and Africa, including that of how to address the presence of a plethora of languages spoken by groups varying in size from a few thousand to millions of individuals. The drive to create modern nation-states collided in most cases with national borders enclosing numerous peoples and tribes, each having their own language and culture. Some countries in Africa found it extremely difficult to ensure adequate communication amongst the different groups.[68] A number chose to retain the language of the colonial power, already utilised in government and favoured by the controlling elites but at the same time perceived as being "neutral", not being identified with any specific ethnic population.

Even amongst members of the same race, populations using different languages were perceived as a threat to the established order. One story tells of Dominican dictator Trujillo's order that Haitian workers should be removed from the country. Since it was not possible to distinguish a Dominican and a Black Haitian by way of physical attributes, an individual would be asked to say the Castilian word for dog, *perro*. A Haitian having French or Créole as a primary language would have difficulty pronouncing the Castilian double "r", and would either be deported, if he was lucky.[69]

2.2   LANGUAGE AND INTERNATIONAL LAW

2.2.1   *Pre-League of Nations Period*

The treatment of language in international law differs from its evolution in national law in that the former is a relative newcomer. Although at origin dealing with relations between states,

---

[66] Alexander, Neville (1989), *Language Policy and National Unity in South Africa/Azania*, Buchu Books, Cape Town, at pp. 17 and 20.

[67] See the unpublished paper by Ajayi, Jacob Ade (1993), *Historical Perspectives on Ethnicity and Nationalism in Nigeria*, delivered at the Conference "Ethnicity, Identity and Nationalism in South Africa: Comparative Perspectives", 20-24 April 1993, Rhodes University, Grahamstown, South Africa, at pp. 10-11:

> The colonial authorities adopted this Hausa as the language of administration in Northern Nigeria, in which all colonial officials had to be proficient. It also became the *lingua franca* of the Army. In these and other ways, colonial authorities spread the influence of Hausa throughout Northern Nigeria, not only in the Muslim areas, but also among non-Muslims brought under the rule of Hausa-Fulani emirs. The written form of Hausa was thus more successful than written Yoruba in contributing to the growth and expansion of a pan-Hausa culture.

[68] *Linguistic Minorities and Literacy: Language Policy Issues in Developing Countries* (1990), Florian Coulmas (ed.), Mouton Publishers, Berlin, at p. 47.

[69] Calvet, *supra*, note 38, at p. 41.

international law did nevertheless offer some guarantees to individuals belonging to certain communities, as demonstrated by the appearance, at an early stage of Western and Middle Eastern history, of treaties between states which provided for the protection of some religious minorities.

In the seventh century, Arab Caliph Omar entered into a treaty with the Byzantine Emperor, promising to allow freedom of worship to Christians who paid a tax for the privilege, though in essence this appears to be no more than what Islam normally provides for Christians living in the *dar al-Islam* (territory of Islam). A few centuries later, in 944, an agreement was concluded between the Emperor of Constantinople and the Russian Prince Igor, which extended to the Emperor a right of protectorship on the officers of the Orthodox Church residing in Russian territory.

By the seventeenth century, a number of multilateral treaties in Europe dealt with the protection of religious freedom:

> ... since the Reformation, the lot of religious minorities had become a very serious question, no longer the concern only to the states involved, but also profoundly affecting international relations. In this connection it should be remembered that the desire to protect religious minorities had served as a pretext for many interventions by foreign countries... This situation encouraged many European states to stipulate in their mutual relations, especially on the occasion of transfers of territory, the requirement that religious minorities be allowed the right to profess their faith freely without fear of persecution.[70]

Some have advanced that at that time, neither language nor race were of sufficient concern to warrant any real measure of legal protection or recognition in international law.[71] This would appear to be an oversimplification as language does appear in a number of treaties, identifying individuals who were to be the subjects of protection. The 1516 **Treaty of Perpetual Union** between the King of France and the Helvetic state contained a provision identifying those who were to receive certain benefits as the "Swiss who speak no language other than German".[72] The **Final Act of the Congress of Vienna of 1815,**[73] signed by seven European countries, which provided for the dismemberment of the Polish state, also contained certain rights to ensure the conservation of the Poles' nationality. Indirectly, this treaty resulted in Poznan Poles retaining

---

[70] *Study on the Rights of Persons belonging to Ethnic, Religious and Linguistic Minorities, supra,* note 53, at p. 1.

[71] For a background on the history of the protection of religious freedom in international law, see Thornberry, Patrick (1991), *International Law and the Rights of Minorities,* Clarendon Press, Oxford, United Kingdom, at pp. 25-54.

[72] Dessemontet, François (1984), *Le droit des langues en Suisse,* Éditeur officiel du Québec, Québec, at p. 29. The author also mentions an earlier 1515 treaty containing a similar linguistic definition, as well as a 1403 treaty between the cities of Bern and Fribourg which used a German word, *welsche,* signifying someone who speaks a foreign language, in order to identify a potential enemy.

[73] **British and Foreign State Papers,** 1814-1815, Volume II, 1839, at pp. 7-55.

the right to use Polish for official business.[74] To a large extent, a similar approach was taken in regard to the Russian portion of dissected Poland, at least until the Polish revolution of 1830.

Furthermore, the protection of religious rights and freedoms sometimes had linguistic ramifications. For example, in the nineteenth century when the Muslim minority in Greece had largely adopted the Turkish language, a 1881 treaty guaranteeing the free exercise of the Islamic faith and the maintenance of Islamic courts and other community structures also implicitly provided for the continued use of the Turkish language as part of the Muslim religious and community activities.[75] Other treaties were even more explicit in providing that cultural institutions, including minority language schools, were to be protected.[76]

It must be remembered that until the advent of the modern nation-state and the ideal of democracy, there were relatively few pressing reasons to attempt at the international level to protect individuals belonging to linguistic minorities, as most individuals had relatively few contacts with governments. Since governments were largely absent from direct involvement in most areas of individual and community life, any legislative measure involving language tended to be negligible — at least until the state became a major purveyor of employment, education and social benefits — and thus language would generally have been perceived as not warranting international concern.

By the First World War, the evolution in most countries was such that it was no longer possible to neglect language issues because of the increasingly active role of government in modern societies. Some type of international mechanism to respond to these changes, and the mounting tensions which resulted, had to be put in place.

---

[74] Article 1 of the **Final Act of the Congress of Vienna**:

Les Polonais, sujets respectifs des hautes parties contractantes, obtiendront la conservation de leur nationalité, d'après les formes d'existence politique que chacun des gouvernements, auxquels ils appartiennent, jugera convenable de leur accorder.

[75] **Convention for the Settlement of the Frontier between Greece and Turkey**, 24 May 1881, (1881) 158 Consolidated Treaty Series 367, Article 7. See other similar provisions involving Muslims in the **Treaty of Peace between Serbia and Turkey**, Article 7, signed 14 March 1914 in Constantinople, (1913-1914) Vol. 219 Consolidated Treaty Series 320, at p. 322, and the apparent protection of private schools of numerous linguistic and religious minorities in Article 29 of the **Treaty of Peace between Austria-Hungary, Bulgaria, Germany and Turkey, and Romania**, signed 7 May 1918 in Bucharest, (1917-1918) Vol. 223 Consolidated Treaty Series 241, at p. 264.

[76] See for example the case of the Vlach minority, who speak a distinctive form of Romanian, whose schools were protected under the **Treaty of Peace between Bulgaria, Greece, Montenegro, Romania and Serbia**, signed 10 August 1913, (1913) Vol. 218 Consolidated Treaty Series 322, at pp. 335-337; see also the provisions regarding German language schools in Articles 38 to 41, **Treaty between Germany and Romania supplementary to the Treaty of Peace**, 7 May 1918, signed in Bucharest, (1917-1918) Vol. 223 Consolidated Treaty Series 304, at pp. 311-312, and the provisions regarding Turkish language private schools for Muslims living in Serbia, Article 9 of the **Treaty between Serbia and Turkey**, signed at Constantinople, 14 March 1914, (1913-1914) Vol. 219 Consolidated Treaty Series 320, at p. 324.

2.2.2   *The Minorities Treaties Era*

Despite various proposals, no provisions dealing with the protection of minorities, nor for that matter human rights, were incorporated in the establishment of the League of Nations at the end of the First World War, apparently to avoid subjecting all members of the future organisation to such provisions. This provoked a great deal of criticism[77] which led to a compromise of sorts: a number of so-called minorities treaties were adopted and subsequently overseen by the League of Nations. Essentially, these fell into three categories. The first category included a series of treaties imposed upon the defeated states of Austria, Hungary, Bulgaria, and Turkey. The second dealt with the new states born of the remains of the Ottoman Empire and states whose boundaries were altered under the self-determination principle put forward by American President Woodrow Wilson (Czechoslovakia, Greece, Poland, Romania, and Yugoslavia). The third category included a number of special provisions relating to minorities in Åland,[78] Danzig, the Memel Territory, and Upper Silesia, as well as a series of five unilateral declarations made by Albania, Lithuania, Latvia, Estonia, and Iraq upon their admission to the League of Nations.[79]

The first two categories of treaties described above incorporated the right to equality of treatment and non-discrimination, the right to citizenship, the right of minorities to establish and control their own institutions, a state obligation to provide equitable financial support to schools in which instruction at the primary level would be in the minority language where warranted by sufficient numbers, and the recognition of the supremacy over other statutes of laws protecting minority rights. In addition, a certain degree of territorial autonomy was provided for minority groups in some cases.

These treaties were complex documents, sometimes including the recognition of the right of everyone to equality without discrimination — whether belonging to a minority group or not. This particular point is at times overlooked when it is claimed that the minorities treaties exclusively dealt with minority group rights. Rather, in each treaty, general provision was made in order to ensure the protection of life, liberty, and free exercise of religion for all inhabitants of a state, without distinction as to birth, nationality, race, religion, or language.[80] Nationals were to enjoy civil and political rights and to possess equality before the law without distinction

---

[77] See *Ethnic Groups in International Relations*, *supra*, note 31, at p. 13:

> Those decisions, and particularly the atmosphere which accompanied their creation, greatly disappointed numerous advocates of the national principle as the foundation for the building of both the new Europe and the new world. The leaders of the victorious countries faced severe criticism coming from various directions. Thus, the idea of including in treaties the imposition of minority obligations on individual states, whether new or considerably enlarged, should be seen as a kind of compensation for the unfulfilled hopes evoked by the idea of national self-determination.

[78] The case of the Åland Islands is interesting because the arrangement has survived to the present day and provides a precedent on the potential importance of self-determination and autonomy arrangements for linguistic populations.

[79] See *Study on the Rights of Persons belonging to Ethnic, Religious and Linguistic Minorities*, *supra*, note 53.

[80] As in Article 2 of the **Polish Minorities Treaty**. This treaty preceded the others chronologically and served as a model for most of the subsequent instruments.

as to race, language, or religion. These rights and freedoms are obviously individual, regardless of minority status.

Specifically on the issue of language, it has been pointed out that:

> As regards the use of the minority language, states which have signed the Treaties have undertaken to place no restriction in the way of the free use by any national of the country of any language, in private intercourse, in commerce, in religion, in the press or in publications of any kind, or at public meetings. Those states have also agreed to grant adequate facilities to enable their nationals whose mother tongue is not the official language, either orally or in writing, before the courts. They have further agreed, in towns and districts where a considerable proportion of nationals of the country whose mother tongue is not the official language of the country is resident, to make provision for adequate facilities for ensuring that, in the primary schools...instruction shall be given to the children of such nationals through the medium of their own language, it being understood that this provision does not prevent the teaching of the official language being made obligatory in those schools.[81]

The treaties thus included two principle types of measures: firstly, individuals belonging to linguistic minorities, amongst others, would be placed on a footing of equality with the other nationals of the state; secondly, the means to preserve racial peculiarities and national characteristics of minorities, including language, would be ensured.

The Permanent Court of International Justice, which was called on to interpret the provisions of these treaties, stated in one of its key opinions how the two type of measures interact:

> These two requirements are indeed closely interlocked, for there would be no true equality between a majority and a minority if the latter were deprived of its own institutions and were consequently compelled to renounce that which constitutes the very essence of its being a minority.[82]

As a result, nationals belonging to linguistic minorities were to enjoy the same treatment in law and in fact as other nationals. In particular, they had an equal right to establish schools and institutions at their own expense. Such schools were distinct from state schools where the minority language was the language of instruction. Finally, in those towns and districts where the minorities constituted a considerable proportion of the population, they would be assured of an equitable share in the enjoyment and application of sums provided out of public funds under state, municipal, or other budgets for educational, religious or charitable purposes.

Although implementation of the treaties did leave much to be desired, the principles

---

[81] *Study on the Rights of Persons belonging to Ethnic, Religious and Linguistic Minorities, supra,* note 53, at pp. 18-19.

[82] **Advisory Opinion on Minority Schools in Albania,** (1935) Permanent Court of International Justice, Series A/B, No. 64, 3, at p. 4, also known as the **Minority Schools in Albania** case.

involved were relevant at the time and are still relevant today:

> The League, even though "of nations" was an organisation of autonomous states. Therefore, the organs of the League, particularly the Council and the Secretariat, considered the minorities' problem mainly from the viewpoint of its members, and not the minorities themselves. The lack of understanding of that basic issue often resulted in disagreements. Such were most fully expressed in criticisms of the League as an organisation that avoided any effective actions relating to the minorities position. Expectations raised by the constitution etc. envisaged the organs of the League as ideally actively engaged against any given state considered "guilty" of violating certain minority obligations.[83]

Because only a small number of states were subjected to the minorities treaties, and thus could with some justification claim to be treated as "second-class nations" by the international community, there soon appeared a gradual disenchantment with the League of Nations' minorities system.[84] This was accompanied by an inexorable movement declaring the need for universal protection of basic human rights, which came about as a result of the ravages and human rights violations committed during the Second World War.

Following the war, a study by the United Nations Secretariat concluded that the engagements entered into by states after World War I under the minorities system had ceased to exist, except for the Åland Islands agreement.

2.2.3   *Post-World War II Developments*

The rhetoric was seen to shift after 1945 to one emphasising universal protection of individual rights and freedoms. The approach was such that whenever someone's rights were violated or restricted because of a characteristic such as religion, race or language, the matter could be addressed by the concept of protection of the rights of the individual, particularly the principle of non-discrimination. As pointed out by Warwick McKean:

> Throughout the discussions on human rights at the United Nations Conference on International Organisation, the minorities treaties were not referred to, but a considerable amount of influence was brought to bear in favour of a "new covenant" and a fresh approach.[85]

In language matters, this fresh approach can be seen in the widespread commitment towards individual rights. The **Charter of the United Nations** solemnly proclaims, in a series of

---

[83] *Ethnic Groups in International Relations: Comparative Studies on Governments and Non-Dominant Ethnic Groups in Europe, 1850-1940* (1991), Sergij Viljan (ed.), European Science Foundation, New York University Press, New York, at p. 32.

[84] For an excellent description of the background on the minority protection system after World War I and the basis and debates pertaining to the disenchantment with the system see ibid., at pp. 14-45. See also *L'Europe centrale et ses minorités : vers une solution européenne?* (1993), André Liebich and André Reszler (eds.), Presses Universitaires de France, Paris, at p. 45.

[85] McKean, Warwick (1983), *Equality and Discrimination under International Law*, Clarendon Press, Oxford, United Kingdom, at p. 53.

provisions, the principles of universal respect for human rights and fundamental freedoms, equality and non-discrimination. Article 1(3) provides that one of the purposes of the new organisation is "[t]o achieve international co-operation...in promoting and encouraging respect for human rights and fundamental freedoms for all without distinction as to...language". According to Article 13, the General Assembly in the exercise of its functions may initiate studies and make recommendations for the purpose of assisting in the realisation of human rights and fundamental freedoms for all without distinction as to language and other grounds. Pursuant to Article 55, the United Nations is to promote universal respect for, and observance of, human rights and fundamental freedoms for all without distinction as to language.

Still, these **Charter** provisions have retained one of the main components of the inter-war international system for the protection of minorities — the principle of non-discrimination — though with one major difference:

> There is, however, a very important change in approach in comparison with the past; since 1945, this principle has been included in the context of the protection of the human rights and fundamental freedoms of all human beings, and not the context of measures designed especially to protect minorities.[86]

Other international instruments incorporating provisions related to language came into being at an increasingly frequent pace. On 10 December 1948, the United Nations General Assembly proclaimed the **Universal Declaration of Human Rights.**[87] Article 2(1) provides that "everyone is entitled to all rights and freedoms set forth in this Declaration, without distinction of any kind, such as...language". Pursuant to the International Labour Organisation **Convention No. 107 of 1957 concerning Indigenous and Tribal Populations,**[88] protected indigenous populations have the right to be taught in their mother tongue or, where this is not practicable, in the language most commonly used by the group to which they belong.

The European **Convention for the Protection of Human Rights and Fundamental Freedoms,** signed at Rome on 4 November 1950, contains a clause on non-discrimination. By virtue of Article 14, the enjoyment of the rights and freedoms set forth in the Convention "shall be secured without discrimination on any ground such as... language".[89]

Article 1 of the **American Convention on Human Rights** is patterned on Article 14 of the **European Convention** and was adopted on 22 November 1969.[90] The provision on non-

---

[86] *Study on the Rights of Persons belonging to Ethnic, Religious and Linguistic Minorities, supra,* note 53, at p. 27.

[87] General Assembly Resolution 217 A (III), UN GAOR, 3rd Session, Resolutions, Part 1, at p. 71 (1948).

[88] United Nations Treaty Series, Volume 328, at p. 249.

[89] Council of Europe, European Treaty Series, No. 5.

[90] (1969), Organisation of American States, Treaties Series, No. 36, at p. 1. Entered into force on 18 July 1978. Article 1 provides as follows:
> The state parties to this Convention undertake to respect the rights and freedoms recognized herein and to ensure to all persons subject to their jurisdiction the free and full exercise of those rights and freedoms, without any discrimination for reasons of...language...

discrimination in the **African Charter on Human Rights and Peoples' Rights** adopted on 27 June 1981, is also similar.[91]

In the two United Nations covenants on human rights adopted on 16 December 1966, language is again specified amongst the impermissible grounds of discrimination. Article 2(1) of the **International Covenant of Civil and Political Rights** provides that:

> [e]ach state party undertakes to respect and to ensure to all individuals within its territory and subject to its jurisdiction the rights recognised in the present Covenant, without distinction of any kind, such as...language.[92]

In recognising the importance of language as part of the due process of law, this **Covenant** also provides in Article 14, Paragraphs 3(a) and (f), that in connection with any criminal charge an accused is to be "informed promptly and in detail in a language which he understands of the nature and cause of the charge against him" and is to have "the free assistance of an interpreter if he cannot understand or speak the language used in court". Article 26 of the **Covenant** also provides that:

> [a]ll persons are equal before the law and are entitled without discrimination to the equal protection of the law. In this respect, the law shall prohibit any discrimination and guarantee to all persons equal and effective protection against discrimination on any ground such as... language.

Finally, another highly influential provision in regard to language matters is Article 27 of the **Covenant**, which provides that:

> [i]n those states in which...linguistic minorities exist, persons belonging to such minorities shall not be denied the right, in community with the other members of their group, to enjoy their own culture...or to use their own language.

As regards the **International Covenant on Economic, Social, and Cultural Rights**, Article 2(2) provides that:

> [t]he state parties to the present Covenant undertake to guarantee that the rights enunciated in the present Covenant will be exercised without discrimination of any kind as to... language.[93]

The **Convention Against Discrimination in Education** of 1960[94] prohibits, under Article 1, "any distinction, exclusion or preference" based upon language or other grounds, which "has the

---

[91] (1981), Organisation of African Unity, OAU Doc. CAB/LEG/67/3/Rev.5. Article 2 provides that: "Every individual shall be entitled to the enjoyment of the rights and freedoms recognised and guaranteed in the present Charter without distinction of any kind such as...language."

[92] (1966), United Nations Treaty Series, Vol. 999, at p. 171.

[93] (1966), United Nations Treaty Series, Vol. 993, at p. 3.

[94] (1960), United Nations Treaty Series, Vol. 428, at p. 93.

purpose or effect of nullifying or impairing equality of treatment in education". The **Convention** makes it clear, in Article 2(b), that it does not constitute discrimination to establish or maintain, for linguistic reasons, separate educational systems or institutions.

The **Convention** also provides in Article 5(1)(c), that it is essential to "recognise the right of members of national minorities to carry on their own educational activities, including the maintenance of schools and, depending on the educational policy of each state, the use or the teaching of their own language", provided that "this right is not exercised in a manner which prevents the members of these minorities from understanding the culture and language of the community as a whole and from participating in its activities, or which prejudices national sovereignty".

A number of peace treaties concluded following Second World War II included provisions in which language also figured more or less prominently. The treaties signed with the Allied and Associated Powers in 1947 provided that each state concerned should take all measures necessary to secure to all persons within their jurisdiction, without distinction as to language, the enjoyment of human rights and freedoms, including freedom of expression, of press and public opinion, and of public meeting.[95]

Three states were required to undertake that the laws in force in their countries would not, in their content or application, discriminate or entail any discrimination amongst persons of the nationality of the state, on the ground of language, whether in preference to their persons, business, professional or financial interest, status, political or civil rights, or any other matter.[96]

In addition, many countries in Europe and Asia have more recently concluded, especially since the demise of the former Soviet Union, bilateral agreements dealing with some of their linguistic minorities, at times providing for the protection of language and cultures, and for the maintenance of minority schools.[97]

Finally, in the last few years, international and regional treaties, declarations and other instruments in which language rights and freedoms, and even recognition of a degree of autonomy for territorially-based linguistic communities, have proliferated.

Amongst the more prominent are the **UN Declaration on the Rights of Persons Belonging to National or Ethnic, Religious and Linguistic Minorities**, the draft **UN Declaration on the Rights of Indigenous Peoples**, the **Vienna Declaration on Human Rights**, the Organisation on Security and Cooperation in Europe (formerly the Conference on Security and Cooperation in Europe) **Document of the Copenhagen Meeting of the Conference on the Human Dimension**, the **Déclaration d'Athène sur les droits des minorités**, the **Declaración Final de Lenguas Europeas e Lexislacions**, the International Labour Organisation's **Convention (No. 169) Concerning Indigenous and Tribal Peoples in Independent Countries**, the **European Charter for Regional and Minority Languages**, the **Central European Initiative Instrument for the**

---

[95] **Treaty with Italy**, United Nations Treaty Series, Vol. 49, at p. 3; **Treaty with Romania**, United Nations Treaty Series, Vol. 42, at p. 3; **Treaty with Bulgaria**, United Nations Treaty Series, Vol. 41, at p. 21; **Treaty with Hungary**, United Nations Treaty Series, Vol. 41, at p. 135; **Treaty with Finland**, United Nations Treaty Series, Vol. 49, at p. 203; **Austrian State Treaty**, United Nations Treaty Series, Vol. 217, at p. 223.

[96] Article 3(2) of the **Treaty with Romania**, Article 2(2) of the **Treaty with Hungary**, and Article 6(2) of the **Austrian State Treaty**.

[97] Most of the provisions of these treaties are included in the Appendix.

Protection of Minority Rights, and the **Convention-cadre sur la protection des minorités nationales.**[98]

Although by no means exhaustive, this list does give an indication of growing international recognition of the importance of language as a human rights matter and of its profound relevance in many of the contemporary efforts to find peaceful solutions to conflicts and tensions.

2.3   SUMMARY

Because language is a fundamental human characteristic which at the same time signals one's membership in a community, it has throughout human history been intimately associated with competition between communities or individuals. Whilst in ancient times most rulers probably regarded the users of foreign languages as strange or inferior, true barbarians, this intolerance seldom extended into prohibiting local languages or other forms of oppression by public authorities. Until the appearance of an increasingly centralised state in Europe a few centuries ago, most empires and government structures tended to adopt a rather benign attitude towards the language used by the peoples under their control, as long as these showed proper obedience to authorities and provided the requested taxes and resources. In some ancient empires it was seen as useful to have the elite or even much of the population understand a common language, but this seldom, if ever, meant exclusion of local languages from private or public affairs.

All this began to change dramatically after the fifteenth century with a gradual move towards centralisation of power in the hands of European sovereigns and ultimately the nation-state. A nation-state requires the symbolism of a national community, and in many cases it seemed natural to turn to language, one of the more obvious forms of pre-existing community bonds. Language could be used as a unifying link, an obvious claim by which a population could be said to share a common will and a common destiny.

This view of the nation-state as symbolised by a common national language, together with the increasing role of the state as a major purveyor of services and employment opportunities and the potent principle of equality and human rights, are the sources of the "nationalism" problem from the mid-nineteenth century to this day. On the one hand, authoritarian, intolerant governments — or even governments which assume that individuals should not be using "inferior" languages — have had a tendency to try to stamp out anything that may be in opposition to their ideal symbolism of a unifying, pure national language. On the other hand, some governments have taken another approach, that the state does not need to force a single exclusive language on all individuals in all areas, and that it may be more divisive to try to stamp out all other languages than to accommodate some degree of language diversity.

In contemporary times, the trend in many states, and at the international level, towards the protection of individuals from the excesses of state authorities by the use of human rights has meant the recognition of a number of rights that pertain to or affect language. This means that the twentieth century has become a battlefield between two conflicting forces: the tendency towards the ever increasing centralisation of the nation-state and the convenience of a single common language seen as a unifying symbol, which is usually the language of the majority, and the recognition that there are legitimate limits to the authority of the state on how it can treat its population. The latter is especially true when it involves individuals who differ from the majority in matters that are fundamental to human nature such as race, religion, and of course language.

---

[98] The relevant provisions of all of these instruments are reprinted in the Appendix.

3. Freedom of Expression[1]

> Freedom of expression constitutes one of the essential foundations of society, one of the basic conditions for its progress and for the development of every man... Such are the demands of...pluralism, tolerance and broadmindedness without which there is no "democratic society". This means, amongst other things, that every "formality", "condition", "restriction" or "penalty" imposed in this sphere must be proportionate to the legitimate aim pursued.[2]

It was suggested in the preceding chapter that a number of fundamental human rights aimed at protecting individuals from abuses or unacceptable impositions by the state pertain to or affect language. Arguably a cornerstone amongst these rights is the freedom of expression. This chapter considers the actual content of the freedom of expression in state practice and international law and demonstrates how it was not until very recently that the actual relevance of this freedom in relation to private language matters began to be perceived. This chapter also explains why it is that freedom of expression can be a relevant human right in a number of areas.

3.1   PRELIMINARY REMARKS

During the drafting of the **Universal Declaration of Human Rights**[3] some contended that the rights of members of linguistic and other minorities were fully protected by Article 2, which guarantees the rights and freedoms set forth therein without distinction of any kind including language, and by the provisions on freedom of thought, conscience and religion, on freedom of the press and expression, on freedom of assembly, on the right to education, and on the right to participate in the cultural life of the community. Indeed, to this day many seem to take for granted that implicitly language is a component of freedom of expression,[4] and that "freedom of expression, in particular, are intimately linked to freedom of access to language".[5]

---

[1] An earlier version of this chapter appeared in de Varennes, Fernand (1994), "Language and Freedom of Expression in International Law", in *Human Rights Quarterly*, Vol. 16, N° 1, 163-186.

[2] **Handyside Case**, (1976) 24 European Court of Human Rights, Series A, at p. 23.

[3] UN GAOR, third session, third comm., first meeting, 716, at p. 731; see also Articles 18, 19, 20, 26 and 27 of the **Universal Declaration of Human Rights**.

[4] See de Witte, Bruno (1988), "Droits fondamentaux et protection de la diversité linguistique", in P. Pupier and J. Woehrling (eds.), *Language and Law: Proceedings of the First Conference of the International Institute of Comparative Linguistic Law*, Wilson & Lafleur, Montréal, at p. 91; Tabory, Mala (1980), "Language Rights as Human Rights", in *Israel Yearbook of Human Rights*, Vol. 10, 167-223, at p. 167; Woehrling, José (1987), "La réglementation linguistique de l'affichage public et la liberté d'expression, P.G. Québec c. Chaussure Brown's Inc.", in *McGill Law Journal*, Vol. 32, 878-894, at p. 885; Milian i Massana, Antoni (1992), "Droits linguistiques et droits fondamentaux en Espagne", in *Revue générale du droit*, Vol. 23, 561-581, at p. 576.

[5] McDougal, M.S., Lasswell, H.D., and Chen, Lung-chu (1980), *Human Rights and World Public Order*, Yale University Press, New Haven, USA, at p. 726.

Therefore, some have contended that Article 19 dealing with freedom of expression protects the rights of individuals speaking languages different from that of the majority. Whether language is an integral part of freedom of expression does not appear to have been specifically considered in the *travaux préparatoires*.[6]

Legal commentators generally have not addressed this matter, and publications dealing with freedom of expression are largely silent on this point. However, no one appears to have suggested that language is not a constituent of freedom of expression.

Traditionally, freedom of expression was deemed to guarantee effective political and social debate essential for the proper operation of any democratic system.[7] More recently, it has been considered individualistic in orientation, allowing persons to freely communicate amongst themselves in order to impart and receive information. Thus freedom of expression seems to extend well beyond the purely political realm, encompassing matters such as science, literature, theatre, arts, and commercial activities.[8]

3.2 STATE APPROACHES TO LANGUAGE AND FREEDOM OF EXPRESSION

El lenguaje es, por decirlo así, la manifestacion externa del espiritu de los pueblos. La lengua de éstos es su espiritu y su espiritu es su lengua. No puede espresarse nunca con suficiente fuerza la identidad de los dos.[9]

At the national level, there does seem to be a trend towards recognition that language is an integral part of freedom of expression, although many national courts have not dealt specifically with the matter. In Switzerland, for example, the *Tribunal fédéral* has indicated that language is

---

[6] See UN Documents E/CN.4/AC.1/3/Add.1, at pp. 126-129, 130-148; E/CN.4/21, at pp. 48 and 67; E/CN.4/SR.62, at pp. 14-16, and Verdoodt, Albert (1963), *Naissance et signification de la Déclaration universelle des droits de l'homme*, Nauwelaerts, Louvain-Paris, at pp. 183-191 for an excellent summary of the *travaux préparatoires* and freedom of expression. As for the *travaux préparatoires* surrounding the **International Covenant on Civil and Political Rights**, see Bossuyt, Marc J. (1987), *Guide to the Travaux Préparatoires of the International Covenant on Civil and Political Right*, Martinus Nijhoff, den Haag, Netherlands, at pp. 373-402.

[7] Mill, John Stuart (1946), *On Liberty and Considerations of Representative Government*, Blackwell, London, at p. 14:

> If all mankind minus one were of one opinion, and only one person were of the contrary opinion, mankind would be no more justified in silencing that one person, than he, if he had the power, would be justified in silencing mankind.

[8] Scanlon, T. (1978-79), "Freedom of Expression and Categories of Expression", in *University of Pittsburgh Law Review*, 519-543, at p. 519; see also **Markt Intern v. Germany**, 12 European Human Rights Report 161 (1989).

[9] Wilhelm von Humboldt, *Einleitung über die Verschiedenheit des menschlichen Sprachbaues und irhe Einfluss auf die geistige Entwicklegung des Menschengeschlechts*, 1836, Spanish translation in Igartua Salaverria, Juan (1989-90), "Nación, Cultura, Lengua", in *Revista de la Facultad de Derecho de la Universidad Complutense* 451.

a necessary condition to the exercise of all the fundamental rights connected with freedom of expression in written or verbal form.[10]

The Supreme Court of Canada arrived at a similar conclusion in some well-reasoned judgements which constitute perhaps the most extensive examination by a national court of the interrelationship between language and freedom of expression. In **Ford v. Québec**,[11] the Supreme Court considered the constitutionality of Article 58 of the Québec **Charte de la langue française** which, in most cases, made French the exclusive language of outdoor commercial signs. Its comments on this point are enlightening:

> Language is so intimately related to the form and content of expression that there cannot be true freedom of expression by means of language if one is prohibited from using the language of one's choice. Language is not merely a means or medium of expression; it colours the content and meaning of expression.[12]

The Supreme Court arrived at a similar conclusion in **Devine v. Québec**,[13] a case dealing with the constitutionality of Articles 52 and 57 of the **Charte de la langue française** which required the use of French jointly with any other language on certain commercial and financial documents. It cautioned, however, that freedom of expression in using one's language does not include the right to use exclusively one's language of choice.

More recently, the Supreme Court reiterated the interrelationship between language and freedom of expression:

> [T]he choice of the language through which one communicates is central to one's freedom of expression. The choice of language is more than a utilitarian decision; language is, indeed, an expression of one's culture and often of one's sense of dignity and self-worth. Language is, shortly put, both content and form.[14]

Interestingly, in **Ford v. Québec**, the Supreme Court considered a number of decisions of the European Commission on Human Rights, examined below, on the issue of language and freedom of expression. The Supreme Court made a definite distinction between freedom of expression as

---

[10] **Association de l'école française und Mitbeteiligte v. Regierungsrat und Verwaltungsgericht des Kantons Zürich**, (1965) Arrêts du Tribunal fédéral 91 I 480 (Switzerland), at p. 486:
> *Wie die personliche Freiheit, so ist auch die Sprachenfreiheit, das heißt die Befugnis zum Gebrauche der Muttersprache, eine wesentliche, ja bis zu einem gewissen Grade notwendige Voraussetzung für die Ausubung anderer Freiheitsrechte; im Falle der Sprachenfreiheit ist dabei an alle jene Grundrechte zu denken, welche die Freiheit der Ausserung durch das gesprochene oder geschriebene Wort gewahrleisten, wie die Meinungsausserungsfreiheit...*

[11] [1988] 2 S.C.R. 712 (Canada).

[12] These same provisions were to be raised at the United Nations Human Rights Committee which sided with Canada's highest court, as is shown in Section 3.3.3 dealing with the **Ballantyne, Davidson and McIntyre v. Canada** decision.

[13] [1988] 2 S.C.R. 790 (Canada).

[14] **Reference Re Criminal Code (Manitoba)**, [1990] 1 S.C.R. 1123 (Canada), at p. 1181.

a private activity, and the use of one's language of choice in any direct relation with any branch of government.

Although constitutional provisions in Italy, Belgium and Austria do not explicitly recognise that freedom of expression includes the freedom to use one's chosen language, some commentators feel that the two cannot be disassociated.[15]

The United States, which has only recently become a party to the **International Covenant on Civil and Political Rights**, has made some valuable contributions to the development of freedom of expression, generally known as freedom of speech under the **First Amendment** of the US Constitution.[16] The precise relationship between freedom of speech and language under the **First Amendment** has not specifically been examined, but one author has concluded from US Supreme Court decisions, such as **Red Lion Broadcasting Co. v. F.C.C.**,[17] that free speech includes the right to broadcast in foreign languages:

> Obviously, when broadcasting is only in English, the exclusively foreign-language-speaking listener has no suitable access to the ideas, experiences, views and voices which the Court finds to be his or her right... People who do understand English and therefore have access to English language broadcasting may still have a First Amendment right to a diversified programming schedule that would include foreign language broadcasting...[18]

Another early US Supreme Court decision arrives at a similar result; however, the reasoning appears to suggest that the issue may also involve discriminatory action by the government. In the Philippines during the 1920s, the US administration adopted legislation making it an offence to keep account books in any language other than English, Spanish, or a local dialect. As the legislation was interpreted as absolutely prohibiting Chinese merchants from keeping accounts in their own language, the Supreme Court declared:

> In view of the history of the Islands and of the conditions there prevailing, we think the Law to be invalid, because it deprives Chinese persons — situated as they are, with their extensive and important business long established — of their liberty and property without due process of Law, and denies them equal protection of the laws... We are clearly of the opinion that it is not within the police power...because it would be oppressive and arbitrary, to prohibit all Chinese merchants from maintaining a set of books in the Chinese language,

---

[15] de Witte, *supra*, note 4, at p. 92, and Milian i Massana, *supra*, note 4 at p. 576.

[16] The **First Amendment** to the United States **Constitution** provides that: "Congress shall make no law...abridging the freedom of speech, or of the press..."

[17] 395 U.S. 367 (1969) (United States).

[18] Piatt, Bill (1990), *¿Only English? Law and Language Policy in the United States*, University of New Mexico Press, Albuquerque, USA, at pp. 121 and 122. See also **Yu Cong Eng v. Trinidad**, 271 U.S. 500 (1926), an early United States Supreme Court decision on commercial activities which, although based upon an interpretation of what is known as due process and equal protection rights under the **Fourteenth Amendment** of the US **Constitution**, involves the issue of liberty in respect to commercial activities similar to that in the Canadian case of **Devine v. Québec** and might today be considered as involving freedom of commercial expression.

and in the Chinese characters, and thus prevent them from keeping advised of the status of their business and directing its conduct.[19]

Thus, in the US, imposing by law the exclusive use of a language in private affairs, in addition to being a violation of freedom of expression, can also constitute discriminatory legislation if deemed to be unreasonable or unwarranted. This was echoed by the Supreme Court of Canada more than half a century later in the **Devine v. Québec** case mentioned above.

There are finally a series of Swiss decisions where commercial expression, guaranteed by Article 31 of the **Federal Constitution**, is dealt with in a manner similar to that of freedom of expression in the private context. In **Zahringer v. Il decreto legislativo ticinese 28 settembre 1931 circa le insegne e le scritte destinate al pubblico**,[20] **Bar Amici**[21] and **Zürich Versicherungen**,[22] it appears to be acknowledged that language freedom (*Sprachenfreiheit*) in commercial activities cannot easily be cast aside, despite the valid constitutional interest of preserving the linguistic integrity and *visage* of cantons. The courts nevertheless recognised the validity of legislation requiring the use of the official language in addition to, but not excluding, an individual's language of choice. The *Tribunal fédéral* in **Zahringer** was however unwilling to accept the decree of 26 September 1931 requirement that the Italian text on all commercial signs be at least twice the size of any other language used.[23]

Despite the definite tendency to associate language and freedom of expression in national jurisdictions, until recently it was far from clear at the international level how language relates to the freedom of expression.

---

[19] **Yu Cong Eng v. Trinidad**, ibid.; see also Adams, Charles F. (1973), "Citado a Comparecer: Language Barriers and Due Process — Is Mailed Notice in English Constitutionally Sufficient?", in *California Law Review*, Vol. 61, 1395-1421, at p. 1420.

[20] Milian i Massana, *supra*, note 4, at p. 579.

[21] Arrêts du Tribunal fédéral 116 Ia 345 (Switzerland). The *Tribunal fédéral* concluded that the public interest in protecting the linguistic character of the Commune of Disentis overrides freedom in commercial activities, and that the government was thus entitled to prohibit the use of outdoor signs with no Romansch text.

[22] Decision of the *Tribunal fédéral* of 12 October 1992. An insurance company had to use the words *Turitg segiradas* or *segiradas turitgesas* in its commercial signs in the Commune of Disentis. See Steiert, Thierry (1993), *La Suisse et la Charte européenne des langues régionales ou minoritaires* (unpublished), EURORegion National Report, Fribourg, Switzerland, at p. 34.

[23] This point, on whether a restriction on the exclusive use of a particular language is a violation of freedom of expression, was indirectly mentioned by the United Nations Human Rights Committee in **Ballantyne, Davidson and McIntyre v. Canada**, Communications Nos. 359/1989 and 385/1989, 31 March 1993, discussed in Section 3.3.3. The Human Rights Committee seemed to imply that to require the use of an additional language would not constitute a violation.

3.3   INTERNATIONAL LAW, LANGUAGE AND FREEDOM OF EXPRESSION

3.3.1   *International Covenant on Civil and Political Rights*[24]

At the international level, it was obvious that freedom of expression included freedom with respect to the content of opinions expressed but there remained some ambiguity on the position occupied by language as the means of expressing opinions. It is likely, in view of the above-mentioned national authorities, that language is a constituent of freedom of expression in so far as it is a necessary component of the expression of opinions. Indeed, a simple reading of Article 19 would seem to support such an interpretation, since the freedom of expression "shall include...the freedom to...receive and impart information and ideas of all kinds...either orally, in writing or in print..." It would be absurd to pretend that everyone has the freedom to receive and impart information and ideas of all kinds, but only if they do so in a language hardly anyone in the jurisdiction understands, such as Sanskrit.

Until the United Nations Human Rights Committee (UNHRC) addressed the issue in 1993, the exact content of freedom of expression as well as the status of language in respect to freedom of expression were unclear despite various decisions emanating from the Human Rights Committee and the European Commission on Human Rights.

The UNHRC first had in 1990 the opportunity to consider the relationship between language and freedom of expression in **Dominique Guesdon v. France.**[25] Guesdon submitted that Breton was his first language and that French courts had violated his freedom of expression, amongst other rights, when they rejected his request that he and witnesses on his behalf testify in Breton and his demand that they be heard through the assistance of an interpreter.

The Committee rejected Guesdon's contention that he had been found guilty without having been heard because Guesdon was bilingual and chose not to speak in French, and was thus the "author" of his own misfortune. Furthermore, the Committee considered the freedom of expression argument inadmissible:

> As to the author's claim that he had been denied his freedom of expression, the Committee observed that the fact of not having been able to speak the language of his choice before

---

[24] Article 19 of the **International Covenant on Civil and Political Rights**, 999 United Nations Treaty Series 171, provides that:
   1. Everyone shall have the right to hold opinions without interference.
   2. Everyone shall have the right to freedom of expression; this right shall include freedom to seek, receive and impart information and ideas of all kinds, regardless of frontiers, either orally, in writing or in print, in the form of art, or through any other media of his choice.
   3. The exercise of the rights provided for in paragraph 2 of this Article carries with it special duties and responsibilities. It may therefore be subject to certain restrictions, but these shall only be such as are provided by law and necessary:
      (a) For respect of the rights or reputations of others;
      (b) For the protection of national security or of public order (*ordre public*), or of public health or morals.

[25] UN GAOR, Vol. II, forty-fifth session, at p. 61, UN Document A/45/40 (1990).

the French courts raised no issues under article 19, paragraph 2. The Committee therefore found that this aspect of the communication was inadmissible...[26]

In other similar communications (the "Breton cases"), the UNHRC preferred to declare the arguments based upon freedom of expression inadmissible. In **T.K. v. France,**[27] the author submitted that the *Tribunal administratif* of Rennes had refused to consider a case that he had submitted in the Breton language, and that subsequent letters of complaint in Breton had gone unanswered. The author contended that freedom of expression could not be limited to freedom to express oneself in French.

The Committee declared the communication inadmissible until such time as the author had exhausted all domestic remedies, even if he must do so in French, despite his allegation that it is precisely this requirement that violated his freedom of expression:

> The Committee observes that the matter of the exclusive use of French to institute proceedings in courts is the issue to be examined at first instance by the French judicial organs and that, under the applicable laws, this can be done only by using French. In view of the fact that the author has demonstrated his proficiency in French, the Committee finds that it would not be unreasonable for him to submit his claim in French to the French courts. Further, no irreparable harm would be done to the author's substantive case by using the French language to pursue his remedy.[28]

The UNHRC adopted a similar approach in **M.K. v. France,**[29] wherein it was submitted that the *Tribunal administratif* of Rennes had refused to consider a complaint directed against French tax authorities for having declined to write the author's address in Breton. The Committee again refused to study the substantive issue until such time as all domestic remedies had been exhausted, in French.

More recently, in **Yves Cadoret and Hervé Le Bihan v. France,**[30] the UNHRC had the opportunity to deal with the interrelationship between language and freedom of expression substantively. The authors had appeared before the *Tribunal correctionnel* of Rennes on charges of having vandalised three road signs. Although Breton was their first language, they had not been allowed to express themselves in Breton before the tribunal, nor had three witnesses they had called on their behalf been allowed to testify in Breton. They had consequently been found guilty and sentenced.

In their communications, they contended that the refusal of the courts to allow them to present their defence in Breton was a clear and serious restriction of their freedom of expression, contrary to Article 19(2) because it signified that they would only be allowed to air their views in French when in court. On this point, the state party submitted that because the authors were bilingual, they could express themselves in French in court; therefore, there was no restriction to their freedom of expression.

---

[26] Ibid., at paragraph 7.2.

[27] UN GAOR, Vol. II, forty-fifth session, Appendix X at p. 118, UN Document A/45/40 (1990).

[28] Ibid., at paragraph 8.4.

[29] *Supra*, note 27, at p. 127.

[30] Communications Nos. 221/1987 and 333/1988, 11 April 1991.

Once again, the Committee remained unconvinced by the authors' arguments:

> As to the authors' claim that they had been denied their freedom of expression, the Committee observed that the fact of not having been able to speak the language of their choice before the French courts raised no issues under article 19, paragraph 2. The Committee therefore found that this aspect of the communications was inadmissible...[31]

The Committee's view of the matter seems rather harsh, because in effect the state was requiring an individual, against his will, to speak a language that was not his primary tongue in court proceedings. In other words, the authors had to make what they considered to be an insidious choice: either submit to the use of a language not their own or be denied access to the courts, and even perhaps be found guilty of an offence without the opportunity of testifying. It is arguably a much more complex issue than simply one of having the freedom to use any language of choice.

The uncertainty remaining subsequent to these decisions as to the relationship between language and freedom of expression pursuant to Article 19 of the **International Covenant on Civil and Political Rights**, would have to wait another two years before the UNHRC definitely considered the issue head on in the Québec commercial signs language communications.[32]

3.3.2   *European Convention for the Protection of Human Rights and Fundamental Freedoms*

The situation in the European context was also nebulous because no case directly addressed the position of language in relation to the freedom of expression. In **Inhabitants of Leeuw-St. Pierre v. Belgium**,[33] the European Commission on Human Rights was asked to examine the matter of a group of Belgian citizens who had unsuccessfully requested administrative documents from their municipality in French. They claimed that the municipality's refusal to provide such documents in French violated their freedom of expression under Article 10. The Commission declared that the application was inadmissible *ratione materiae* because the **Convention** does not expressly guarantee "linguistic freedom" as it relates to the right to use one's language of choice in relations with municipal authorities.

This last point is particularly important. The Commission appears to acknowledge that there may be a clear distinction between the right to freedom of expression in one's language outside governmental activity on the one hand, and a right to have administrative formalities completed in one's language, on the other:

> These considerations are obviously applicable without restriction to the applicants' grievances regarding the use of languages in administration. It is clear that one has to distort the usual meaning of the passages [Articles 9 and 10 of the Convention] if one is to transform the right to express one's thought freely in the language of one's choice into a

---

[31] Ibid., at paragraph 5.2.

[32] *Supra*, note 23.

[33] (1965), 8 Yearbook of the European Convention on Human Rights 338.

right to complete, and insist on the completion of, all administrative formalities in that language.[34]

The Commission felt the applicants' argument would only be valid in so far as it could be based upon explicit provisions such as those in Articles 5(2) and 6(3) of the **Convention**.[35] To admit that it might have some foundation in Articles 9 and 10 would be tantamount to attributing to those two provisions such a wide scope that the specific guarantees given in Articles 5 and 6 would be superfluous.[36]

The European Commission on Human Rights proceeded to reject another application involving language and freedom of expression in **X v. Ireland**.[37] The applicant was a civil servant entitled to a children's allowance for each of his four children, provided he filled out a prescribed form. The form was entirely in Irish, which he, like the majority of Irish citizens, could apparently neither read nor write. He refused to comply with what he described as an "imposition" and a "language dictatorship", despite a warning that he would lose the allowance if he did not comply. When he insisted in obtaining a form printed in English, he lost the allowance. The applicant maintained that the requirement to use Irish exclusively in these forms constituted a violation of his freedom of expression guaranteed under Article 10.

The Commission's response was rather abrupt: it indicated that the requirement to complete the form in the Irish language did not in any way interfere with the applicant's freedom of expression, and that the application was inadmissible.

Not everyone agreed with the Commission's reasoning. One author complained that the situation in **X v. Ireland** did interfere with the applicant's freedom of expression under Article 10 because:

> ...printing a form necessary to receive money one is entitled to in a language spoken by only two percent of the population, regardless of the good motive behind it, is an interference in the freedom by which one can impart information.[38]

The same author believed that the Commission's refusal to consider the question seriously was due to the fact that the applicant could easily have had the form translated, and that the whole matter was trivial. However, the author in question failed to distinguish between purely private

---

[34] Ibid.

[35] These two provisions precisely spell out a right to certain information or assistance in one's primary language. Article 5(2) deals with the right to information in a language one understands for the basis of one's arrest, whereas 6(3) provides for the right to the free assistance of an interpreter when one does not understand the language used in court.

[36] *Supra*, note 33, at p. 348.

[37] (1970), 13 Yearbook of the European Convention on Human Rights 792.

[38] Morrison, Clovis C. (1981), *The Dynamics of Development in the European Human Rights Convention System*, Martinus Nijhoff, den Haag, Netherlands, at p. 101.

activities which impart information (i.e. newspapers, speeches at conferences, in private settings, etc.) and activities involving communication with the state in its public function capacity.[39]

Although not precisely involving the issue of freedom of expression and language, the European Commission in **Charlent v. Belgium** indirectly acknowledged that in private affairs freedom of expression included the freedom to use the language of one's choice:

> Whereas freedom of religion is not in question; whereas this is also true of the freedoms of thought, conscience and expression of the Applicants themselves, since nothing prevents them from expressing their thought freely in the language of their choice.[40]

Finally, in **Fryske Nasjonale Partij v. Netherlands**,[41] the applicants submitted that they had been prevented from standing as candidates in elections of the *Eerste Kamer der Staten-Generaal*[42] because they had submitted their registration for election in Frisian[43] and not in Dutch. They asserted, *inter alia*, that this infringed their freedom of expression guaranteed under Article 10 of the **Convention**. The European Commission on Human Rights once again indicated that freedom of expression and language preference may, in certain situations, be relevant when it stated that the "applicants...failed to demonstrate that they were prevented from using the Frisian language for other purposes".[44] Once again this part of the application was rejected *rationae materiae* as being incompatible with the provisions of the **Convention**.

Thus, the European Commission decided the matter consistently with its earlier cases by pointing out that freedom of expression does not guarantee the right to use the language of one's choice in administrative affairs.

3.3.3 *Clarification of Relationship*

On 31 March 1993, the United Nations Human Rights Committee handed down a decision that clarified, apparently once and for all, its position on the relationship between language and freedom of expression. At issue were provisions of the Québec **Charte de la langue française**, which, in most situations, made French the exclusive language of outdoor commercial signs. In

---

[39] The author's reaction to the Irish situation does warrant a comment, even if one accepts the premise that such a situation does not involve the issue of freedom of expression. Many would agree that to only provide government services, or funds as in **X v. Ireland**, to those who use a language understood by a tiny percentage of a state's population seems at the very least unfair and difficult to justify. What the Irish situation reflects is not an issue of the right to express oneself without government interference but the exact reverse: one is demanding that the government offer a public service, and more precisely a public service in one's language of choice. As will be seen in the chapter dealing with discrimination, the issue should have been raised as being unreasonable and a violation of the right to non-discrimination rather than under the freedom of expression.

[40] (1963) 6 Yearbook of the European Convention on Human Rights 445, at pp. 454-456.

[41] (1986) 45 Decisions and Reports 240 (European Commission of Human Rights), at p. 243.

[42] The "First Chamber of the States General" essentially functions as a senate.

[43] Frisian is a Germanic language spoken in the province of Friesland (*Fryslân*) in the Netherlands, as well as in Schleswig-Holstein and Niedersachsen in Germany.

[44] *Supra*, note 41, at p. 243.

Ballantyne, Davidson and McIntyre v. Canada,[45] the authors were English-speaking residents of the Province of Québec who claimed that the prohibition against using any language other than French on outdoor commercial signs or in a firm's name infringed upon their freedom of expression, guaranteed by Article 19 of the **International Covenant on Civil and Political Rights.**

The government of Québec argued that freedom of expression protected by Article 19 does not include commercial publicity, but is limited to matters involving political, cultural and artistic expression. It also maintained that even if commercial publicity were encompassed in freedom of expression, it did not include an individual's absolute right to choose the language of commercial signs. Finally, the government argued that even if the freedom of expression included freedom in the choice of language in commercial activities, the prohibition contained in the **Charte de la langue française** was reasonable given the importance of protecting the French language and culture in Québec.

The Committee rejected Québec's attempts to restrict the authors' freedom of expression. The Committee stated that Article 19(2) of the **Covenant** applies not only to ideas and subjective opinions which can be transmitted to others,[46] but also to any news or information, any expression, any commercial publicity or signs, and to any work of art. In other words, the Committee squarely rejected any attempt at limiting freedom of expression to a narrow field of activity such as political, cultural or artistic expression. The Committee also rejected the argument that commercial expression was somehow less worthy of protection under the **Covenant**, and that in such cases governments should have wider discretion in deciding what restrictions were appropriate or necessary in their country.

The government of Québec also contended that its provisions were necessary and reasonable in order to protect the French language in the province. In response, the Committee pointed out that Article 19 of the **Covenant** only permits restrictions on freedom of expression which are provided by law and necessary either to respect the reputations of others, or to protect national security, public order, health or morals. Although clearly "provided by law", the language restrictions relating to outdoor commercial signs in Québec were unnecessary, according to the Committee, because they protected neither the rights of other individuals, nor the public order, health or morals. Furthermore, even if the restrictions were valid based upon Article 19(2)(a) or (b), the government would have had to establish that they were justified. The government of Québec had made no attempt to do so as regards the provisions of the **Charte de la langue française**, beyond claiming that they were simply reasonable.

Although it was not strictly required in order to support its decision, the Committee acknowledged that the government could validly seek to protect the French language in Québec. It recognised that whilst a state may choose one or more official languages, it may not simply ban the use of non-official languages, at least as it relates to non-governmental services or activities. In essence, the Committee recognised that in an entirely non-governmental realm, any

---

[45] *Supra*, note 23.

[46] The Human Rights Committee added that the ideas and subjective opinions that Article 19(2) protects must not contravene the provisions of Article 20 of the **Covenant** which permit restrictions on the right to freedom of expression when it advocates violence, hatred or war. Article 20 states: "1. Any propaganda for war shall be prohibited by law. 2. Any advocacy of national, racial or religious hatred that constitutes incitement to discrimination, hostility or violence shall be prohibited by law."

attempt at restricting an individual's language choice clearly violates that individual's freedom of expression.

Following this decision, the Québec government amended its legislation, thus permitting the use of French and any other language(s) on commercial signs in so far as the French text is predominant.

3.4   ANALYSIS AND COMMENTS ON FREEDOM OF EXPRESSION AND LANGUAGE

A number of national jurisdictions clearly distinguish between the public use of language and private use as it relates to freedom of expression. Matters relating to the public use of language escape what is defined in these jurisdictions as freedom of expression, because such use involves a government's obligation to provide administrative, judicial or other government services — services which are usually provided in the state-sanctioned language. The prevalent understanding of "freedom" is that of non-intervention by the state in private or non-governmental affairs.

The example of a trial illustrates the distinction between the public and private use of language. In some of the cases discussed above, it was contended that to prohibit an accused from using his primary language, when he could understand the official language of the courts, violated his freedom of expression. However, a trial is not a private affair: it is a public function carried out by a segment of the state apparatus.[47] In other words, it is a state activity.[48] An individual cannot assert that the state has no power to intervene in his or her private choice of language of expression, because a trial is not a private forum for an individual to express her or his point of view. Rather, it is a public activity conducted under the auspices of the state for the public good.

The private use of a language is conceptually quite different from public use, where a state's intervention is solicited or mandatory, because the former encompasses the freedom to express oneself in any language in all non-official activities, such as between private individuals, in newspapers, theatres, and particularly during political meetings and conferences, wherein the objective sought is non-intervention of the state. As pointed out by Professor José Woehrling:

> *Dans ce vaste domaine de l'usage privé, l'individu doit être libre d'employer la langue de son choix : cette liberté linguistique découle logiquement et implicitement de la liberté d'expression et il n'est donc pas nécessaire de la garantir expressément dans une disposition constitutionnelle particulière. En d'autres termes, le libre choix de la langue dans l'usage privé constitue une dimension nécessaire de la liberté d'expression, une condition essentielle de la réalisation de celle-ci.*[49]

---

[47] A trial is a public function whether its nature is civil or criminal.

[48] When one is accused in a criminal trial or called to testify before a court, one would be hard put to claim that this activity is within the private domain.

[49] Woehrling, *supra*, note 4, at pp. 883 and 884. Similar comments are made in Milian i Massana, *supra*, note 4, at p. 576:

> *Cependant, cette liberté de la langue qui découle implicitement de la liberté d'expression ne peut être invoquée que dans le cadre des relations de nature privée. Dans les relations publiques, et plus concrètement pour ce qui est de l'emploi officiel, la liberté de choix de la*

Put differently, an individual has the freedom to impart information to others, and even to his government, in any language, but the state does not have a corresponding obligation to receive such information nor to respond to the individual's exercise of his freedom.

In examining the decisions of both the UNHRC and the European Commission regarding freedom of expression and language prior to 1993, one realises that all dealt with public or state activities. In other words, all of the cases involved individuals claiming that the state was positively obliged to acquiesce to their linguistic preference in state activities. In **Inhabitants of Leeuw-St. Pierre** and in **X. v. Ireland**, the right to receive administrative documents in a particular language was in issue. Then in the "Breton cases", **Dominique Guesdon v. France, T.K. v. France, M.K. v. France**, and **Yves Cadoret and Hervé Le Bihan v. France**, in issue was the right to use Breton in judicial or administrative proceedings. All of the above situations clearly go beyond the request that a state institution not interfere in private affairs and activities, which are more properly covered by the concept of a freedom.

Unfortunately, neither the European Commission nor the UNHRC clearly stated that this was the reason why on so many occasions they chose to treat the submissions on freedom of expression as inadmissible. Although the European Commission at times implied that language is a component of freedom of expression when private matters are in issue,[50] the Commission never stated that explicitly, and until recently an uncomfortable degree of uncertainty remained. Indeed, it may have been simpler, and would have been as logical and consistent with national attitudes and the opinion of many legal writers, to conclude that freedom of expression does not impose a positive linguistic obligation on states, but rather protects a right to non-interference of the state in private matters.

The severity of the consequences of maintaining that language is not an integral part of freedom of expression can be illustrated. A state could, for example, ban the publication of newspapers printed in a particular language or make it a criminal offence to address a conference in a particular language, as is the case in Algeria.[51] If freedom of expression included only freedom as to content, and not as to language as the medium,[52] then the state could require that opinions or content be expressed in the "legal" language or languages of the state.

---

langue pour les diverses communications est restreinte, précisément par les dispositions — normalement contenues dans la Constitution — qui déterminent la ou les langues qui sont reconnues en tant que langues officielles. Comme nous le savons, ces langues sont en principe (sous réserve d'autres dispositions concernant des secteurs particuliers) les seuls moyens de communication que l'on considère valables et efficaces dans les rapports de nature officielle.

[50] See, i.e., **Charlent v. Belgium**, *supra*, note 40, and **Inhabitants of Leeuw-St. Pierre v. Belgium**, *supra*, note 33.

[51] See the **Loi du 16 janvier 1991 portant généralisation de l'utilisation de la langue arabe** which imposes severe restrictions in the public and even private use of any language other than Arabic in Bendjedid, Chadli (1992), "Algérie — Généralisation de l'utilisation de la langue arabe", in *Revue de droit international et de droit comparé*, N° 1, 70-76, at p. 70.

[52] Some would argue that language is in itself part of the message or opinion.

Some would point out that Article 27 of the **International Covenant on Civil and Political Rights**[53] already provides for the use of a minority language between persons of that language group so that one need not include language as a necessary element of freedom of expression. This argument contains a number of weaknesses. It could be valid in certain cases, such as that of an individual belonging to a linguistic minority addressing members of his group, but would be of little assistance in the case of an individual attempting to address, in a prohibited language, a group of persons who are not members of the linguistic minority. This last example is not far-fetched. The President of the People's Labour Party and member of the Turkish Human Rights Association, Mr Aydin, was put on trial prior to his assassination at the State Security Court in Ankara for giving a speech in Kurdish at the annual meeting of the Human Rights Association in October 1990, a "crime" for which he served two months imprisonment.[54]

The extent to which Article 27 would protect against national legislation forbidding licences, as a general rule of policy, to radio stations whose programmes are in a minority vernacular is also questionable.[55] Finally, Article 27 contains a number of restrictions; for example, it pertains only to "linguistic minorities" existing in a given state. This restriction causes a number of misgivings because some states contend that no such minorities exist in their jurisdictions.[56] Moreover, Article 27 does not protect against the linguistic majority's language being severely restricted by the state. This problem was raised in **Ballantyne, Davidson and McIntyre v. Canada**; because English-speaking individuals are a majority in Canada, they could not claim their Article 27 rights were violated because they were not a "linguistic minority" in Canada, even if they were such a minority in one of the federal units of the state, the Province of Québec. Article 27 would appear to be of no use to local or regional minorities unless they are also a minority at the national level.

It would be preposterous to assert that an individual involved in a private activity, yet forbidden by the state to use his own language, is not a victim of an infringement upon his

---

[53] Article 27 reads as follows: "In those states in which ethnic, religious or linguistic minorities exist, persons belonging to such minorities shall not be denied the right, in community with the other members of their group, to enjoy their own culture, to profess and practice their own religion, or to use their own language."

[54] For an overview of various Turkish measures that may be breaches of Article 27, see Skutnabb-Kangas, Tove and Bucak, Sertaç (1994) "Killing a Mother Tongue — How the Kurds are Deprived of Linguistic Human Rights", in T. Skutnabb-Kangas and R. Phillipson (eds.), *Linguistic Human Rights: Overcoming Linguistic Discrimination*, Mouton de Gruyter, Berlin, pp. 347-370. The same situation may also constitute an offence in Algeria under Articles 18 and 31 of the **Loi du 16 janvier 1991 portant généralisation de l'utilisation de la langue arabe.**

[55] This last point involves a very complex and largely unexplored subject. Licensing restrictions can involve questions relating to the freedom of expression, to the non-discrimination principle, and to Article 27 of the **International Covenant on Civil and Political Rights**; all these are further discussed in Chapter 6. Only a few, rather unsatisfying, US cases have some relevance to this issue. For a description of these, see Piatt, *supra*, note 18, at pp. 120-123. See also **Report of the Waitangi Tribunal on Claims concerning the Allocation of Radio Frequencies**, Wai 26 & Wai 150, 1990 (New Zealand).

[56] The United Nations Human Rights Committee has indicated that it would not simply accept a state's contention that no minorities exist in its territory, and that it would apply objective criteria in determining such an issue.

freedom of expression. By definition, the government would be attempting to impose its preference as to the medium of transmission of information and ideas on a private activity. For these reasons, it is more consistent with traditional definitions of freedom of expression, and with the conclusions of national jurisdictions as well as the UNHRC's 1993 decision on this issue, to include language as an integral and necessary constituent of the freedom of expression.

Before 1993, all of the cases considered by the Human Rights Committee and the European Commission on Human Rights involved individuals called to testify before a tribunal, or individuals seeking a service from a state institution and compelled to address that state institution, against their will, in a language other than their primary one. Many may consider, as did the author commenting on the **X v. Ireland** case, that this amounts to a violation of one's freedom of expression. In reality, what these predicaments involve is the state apparatus seeking evidence or information or being probed to provide a service: in other words, they involve a state function. Clearly they do not involve an individual seeking to express his opinion or point of view in the private domain. If freedom of expression is mainly concerned with ensuring that the people are free to express themselves in private matters such as culture, politics, arts, and business, necessary for venting the populations' ideas and frustrations in order to maintain a healthy society, it does not follow that the state is obliged in all of its information gathering and official operations to give way to the people's linguistic preferences. The state machinery is still perfectly entitled to operate exclusively in the language of its choice in its activities, and is perfectly within its competence to require individuals to submit to this choice if they are able to do so, because individuals are still free to express themselves in any manner outside of the state's governmental activities.

In some situations, the state's discretion in matters relating to the imposition of its own language preference on individuals in the public sphere may be limited; however, this limitation will emanate from other obligations imposed upon a state, such as those related to the right to equality, and not from freedom of expression. As will be seen in the next chapter, non-discrimination on the ground of language may limit a state's discretion in its language preferences.

As shown in **Ballantyne, Davidson and McIntyre v. Canada**, the argument that language does not really affect the substantive right to freedom of expression, as long as one has an accessible language in which to express one's opinion, would appear fallacious. Although the UNHRC did not elaborate on the issue, it did indicate that freedom of expression extends to any possible medium of expression. Because the expression of opinions, information and ideas can be conveyed orally, in writing, or in print, one cannot suppose that the state may limit the speaker's choice of medium, other than by the limits provided in Article 19(3) of the **International Covenant on Civil and Political Rights** and in Article 10(2) of the **European Convention**.

Article 13(1) of the **American Convention on Human Rights** is quite categorical in this regard, in that it guarantees:

> ...freedom to seek, receive, and impart information and ideas of all kinds...either orally, in writing, in print, in the form of art, or through any other medium of one's choice.[57]

Logically, if one can freely express an opinion or idea through a particular style of art, a non-verbal medium, one can also express an opinion or idea through another particular medium, a

---

[57] (1969), Organisation of American States, Treaty Series, No. 36, at p. 1.

specific language. To maintain that allowing an individual to express himself in only the English language, for example, has no effect on his freedom of expression is like saying an artist may paint anything as long as the style utilised is abstract, and that such a restriction in no way infringes on the artist's freedom of expression. In both cases, the government intervenes in the private arena and tries to restrict the way in which one chooses to express one's opinions. Any limit to freedom of expression must be based upon the recognised restrictions under the various provisions of international treaties.

An argument not raised in **Ballantyne, Davidson and McIntyre v. Canada** is that the state does not violate freedom of expression unless an individual is completely unable to use or comprehend the state sanctioned language of expression. Once again this approach is seriously flawed. It seeks to create a restriction neither recognised nor even implicit in the rights provided for by Article 10 of the European **Convention** and by Article 19 of the **International Covenant on Civil and Political Rights**. It undermines the concept of universality of human rights and freedoms and presents a *de facto* state intervention in a private activity, one of the most sacred and cherished freedoms of a democratic society: the right to freely express one's opinions and ideas without government interference, other than that which is strictly necessary. Nothing in the European **Convention** nor the **International Covenant** would support the creation of a new limitation on freedom of expression by governments not provided for in these instruments.

The approach suggested here is consistent with the views expressed in a report by Raimo Pekkanen, judge of the European Court on Human Rights, and Hans Danelius, member of the European Commission on Human Rights, examining Estonian language legislation and its possible problems in relation to international human rights standards.[58] Estonia adopted on 18 January 1989 the **Language Law of the Estonian Soviet Socialist Republic** which attempts to promote the use of the Estonian language. However, as the authors of the report note, certain provisions of the law may contravene freedom of expression:

> While the question of what language shall be used before and by the courts and the administrative authorities may well be regulated by law, the legislator ought to be more cautious in imposing language requirements in private relationships, including private business. It may be assumed that the private persons or institutions concerned are best suited to decide themselves in what language they should conduct their mutual communications and the legislator should not, as a rule, interfere with their freedom in this regard...
>
> As regards journalists, the situation is particularly sensitive, because it touches upon the freedom of expression. The freedom of the press should in principle include freedom to choose the language in which a newspaper or journal is to be published, and journalists should not be hampered by any specific language requirements. In reality, a journalist's choice of language will depend on the group of readers to whom he wishes to address himself...
>
> The provision of Article 24 of the Language Law, according to which priority shall be given to Estonian language publishing, may also create some problems in relation to the principles of freedom of expression which, according to international standards, are to be applied in a non-discriminatory manner. However, much depends on the way Article 24 is interpreted and applied. If it merely means that literature in Estonian is encouraged and supported financially, there would seem to be no difficulty, but if those who express

---

[58] Human Rights in the Republic of Estonia, Raimo Pekkanen and Hans Danelius, Special Rapporteurs (1991), in *Human Rights Law Journal*, Vol. 13, N° 5-6, 236-256, at p. 241.

themselves in other languages are encountering difficulties in having their works printed and published, their right to freedom of expression may be at issue...

Article 33 of the Language Law requires that "the texts of signs, posters, notices and advertisements displayed in public shall be in the Estonian language" but adds that "translations shall be added in consideration of the needs of the local population". These provisions do not seem to create any problems as far as announcements by the public authorities are concerned. However, where private groups or individuals wish to convey messages by displaying them in public, the language requirement in Article 33 might be difficult to reconcile with the principles of freedom of expression. Indeed, the freedom of expression as protected under international conventions, including the European Convention on Human Rights, would not seem to admit any such restrictions except where it could be justified by strong public interests.[59]

3.5 CURRENT NATIONAL RESTRICTIONS ON THE PRIVATE USE OF LANGUAGE

The idea that freedom of expression requires not official recognition or other measures by the state to promote a particular language, but rather a policy of linguistic non-intervention in private affairs, would seem to have gained respectability and growing acceptance both internationally and in national legislation. However, there continues to be many examples worldwide where state restrictions on the private use of language would appear to violate freedom of expression. Just a few years ago, the Bulgarian Communist Government banned the use of the Turkish language in public.[60] The situation in Turkey, referred to earlier, would seem to have improved slightly since the interdiction to speak Kurdish in private or in the street, with ensuing heavy prison sentences, has been lifted. However, there appears to be some confusion as to the precise effect of the **Turkish Anti-Terrorist Act No. 3713** of 12 April 1991. Some maintain that the Act continues to prohibit use of Kurdish in public areas, which would constitute a violation of freedom of expression.[61] As was pointed out in a report to the Council of Europe,[62] there are also other restrictions prohibiting Kurdish in public meetings, public buildings, radio and television, etc. which may also constitue infringements upon freedom of expression.

---

[59] Ibid.

[60] *The Protection of Ethnic and Linguistic Minorities in Europe* (1993), John Packer and Kristian Myntti (eds.), Institute for Human Rights, Åbo Akademi University, Åbo, Finland, at p. 71:
> The policy (which the authorities insisted was "voluntarily" complied with by the Turks) dictated that all Turkish names had to be changed, and the use of the Turkish language in public was to be banned. Those who refused were denied their salaries, travel within the country, and administrative and judicial services... According to a popular joke, the Turkish language became the most expensive language in the world, because calling someone by a Turkish name cost a fine of 5 leva (the daily salary), and a short dialogue cost 50 leva.

[61] *Linguistic Rights of Minorities* (1994), Frank Horn (ed.), Northern Institute for Environmental and Minority Law, University of Lapland, Rovaniemi, Finland, at p. 231.

[62] See "The Situation of Human Rights in Turkey" (1992), in *Human Rights Law Journal,* Vol. 13, N° 11-12, 464-480.

Another problematic situation involves Article 128 of the **Prison Act** of Japan which provides that "no foreign language can be used during family visits unless permitted by the Prison Chief". The **Act** also provides in Article 131 that correspondence to an inmate, written in a foreign language, can be withheld by the Prison Chief, or the latter can order the inmate concerned to provide a Japanese translation, at his expense. East and Central Europe offers other possible violations, such as the ban in Transylvania by the ultra-nationalist Romanian authorities in Cluj of Hungarian-language signs and the severe restrictions on Hungarian gatherings,[63] although these appear to have been lifted.

In Algeria, the prohibition on writing Arabic in anything other then Arabic script (Article 2) or on showing movies in any language other than the country's official language (Article 17), the banning of any commercial or other signs in any language other than Arabic, except in designated tourist areas (Articles 19 and 20), as well as the general prohibition on the use of non-Arabic languages at conferences or other public fora (Articles 9 and 18), contained in the **Loi du 16 janvier 1991 portant généralisation de l'utilisation de la langue arabe** are also in conflict with current international and national understanding on the nature and effect of freedom of expression.

In February 1994, in order to protect the French language, France passed legislation which provided for restrictions on the use of "foreign" languages, even in private affairs. On 29 July 1994, the French *Conseil constitutionnel* handed down an opinion which clearly vindicates the reasoning of the United Nations Human Rights Committee: any attempt by the state to regulate private use of language is an unacceptable violation of freedom of expression.

A fair number of governments have in the past adopted legislation which restricts signs or advertisements to one or two approved languages in public, without distinguishing whether this restriction is limited to state agents and institutions, or whether it is also addressed to private individuals. In addition to Estonia's Article 33 mentioned above,[64] Kazakhstan,[65] Turkey,[66]

---

[63] Daily Telegraph, London, England, 10 February 1993, at p. 12.

[64] In December 1993, a draft language law was submitted to the Estonian Parliament (*Riigikogu*) which does not address many of the human rights concerns referred to earlier. The proposed Article 26 in particular appears to clearly violate freedom of expression:

> The text of any signs, references, announcements, notices and advertisements in public places shall be in Estonian, except in cases prescribed in Articles 11 and 16 of the present Law and unless otherwise provided by foreign agreements.
>
> Rules of the present Article do not apply to the missions of foreign countries.

The only exceptions relate to cultural minority organisations and appear to be a concession of the rights of these groups under Article 27 of the **International Covenant on Civil and Political Rights**, and the use of minority languages in certain local municipal institutions. Thus private individuals would appear to be still prohibited from using any language other than Estonian if the new law is passed.

[65] Article 29 of the 1989 **Kazakhstan Languages Act**, in *Recueil des législations linguistiques dans le monde — Tome V : L'Algérie, l'Autriche, la Chine, le Danemark, la Finlande, la Hongrie, l'île de Malte, le Maroc, la Norvège, la Nouvelle-Zélande, les Pays-Bas, le Royaume-Uni, la Tunisie, la Turquie, l'ex-URSS* (1994), Jacques Leclerc and Jacques Maurais (eds.), International Centre for Research on Language Planning, Québec, at p. 166.

[66] Articles 1 to 3 of **Act 2932 of 19 October 1983 on Publications in Languages other than Turkish**, in *Recueil des législations linguistiques dans le monde*, ibid., at pp. 138-139.

Indonesia,[67] Colombia,[68] and Mexico,[69] to name but a few, have such restrictions still in force, and it is doubtful these would survive after close scrutiny under the right to freedom of expression as now understood under international law.

3.6 OFFICIAL LANGUAGE REQUIREMENTS AND INDIVIDUAL FREEDOM OF EXPRESSION

Despite the above, it must be emphasised that freedom of expression does not appear to exclude some degree of state intervention in private language affairs. A state may claim with some justification that it is in its interest to attempt to unite its citizens and to encourage communication through the bond of a common, unifying, language. But what must always be kept in mind is that a common language does not mean an exclusive language, especially in private affairs. The United Nations Human Rights Committee clearly pointed out in **Ballantyne, Davidson and McIntyre v. Canada** that a government may require that the official or favoured language of the state be used in conjunction with an individual's language of preference[70] without this constituting an interference with freedom of expression, although there is still a debate on whether there can be state restrictions as to the relative importance attributed to the official language.[71]

---

[67] Apparently, Indonesia only permits advertising which uses the Latin alphabet, which results in a violation of the freedom of expression of private parties to use other scripts such as Chinese characters. For a discussion on the relationship between language and script, see Section 4.6.

[68] Articles 1 and 2, **Act No. 14 of 5 March 1979**, in *Recueil des législations linguistiques dans le monde — Tome VI : La Colombie, les États-Unis, le Mexique, Porto Rico et les traités internationaux* (1994), Jacques Leclerc and Jacques Maurais (eds.), International Centre for Research on Language Planning, Québec, at p. 4.

[69] Articles 3, 7 and 8, **Federal District Regulation of 1988 on Signs**, in *Recueil des législations linguistiques dans le monde*, ibid.

[70] The individual's freedom of expression is maintained since he is still entitled to use his language of choice, although he is given the additional burden of using two languages instead of one. It should be pointed out that there are probably limits to this type of requirement. If it becomes onerous or otherwise unjust, it could constitute a form of discrimination if it affects adversely only some segments of a state's population or is too impractical.

[71] In **Zahringer**, *supra*, note 20, the *Tribunal fédéral* found excessive a decree requiring the Italian text on all commercial signs to be twice the size of any other language used, although it could be claimed its decision actually is one based on the disproportionate and discriminatory requirements of the regulation. In much the same way in **Asian American Business Group v. City of Ponoma**, 716 F.Supp. 1328 (1989) (United States), a 1988 ordnance prohibited advertising in "foreign alphabetical characters" that occupied more than half of the space on signs for advertising copy. In effect, this restricted the use of foreign script, more specifically Chinese characters. The court decision is somewhat convoluted, but rests mainly on two grounds: that the ordnance amounted to a violation of freedom of expression, and that it constituted a violation of the **Fourteenth Amendment** because it affected a fundamental right (non-commercial speech) and failed to meet the standard of strict scrutiny by serving a compelling government interest. In other words, it was an infringement of the right to

Although such a requirement would likely impose a greater burden on individuals who intend to use another language in addition to the one mandated by the state, there is probably no denial of the freedom to use one's intended language, since one is not prohibited from speaking or writing in that language. The use of a second language is validated by "public interest" considerations, and may perhaps even go so far as to require that this additional language be given greater prominence. This is the approach taken by Québec after the **Ballantyne, Davidson and McIntyre v. Canada** decision, and is favoured in a number of countries.[72]

It would be possible to argue that the aforesaid requirement does not make sense in the case of a private newspaper published in a minority language. Could a state demand of a newspaper that it contain an official translation of its entire content? The answer to this hypothetical query is probably no,[73] but not because of a violation of freedom of expression, unless the requirements were so oppressive as to actually make it impossible to publish the newspaper using both languages. Indeed, beyond the situation where language requirements would in effect constitute an actual barrier, and thus a complete prohibition, of freedom of expression, requiring an official translation of a minority language newspaper could possibly also involve an issue of discrimination.

Any requirement which obliges an individual to use an official language in addition to his own language of preference creates an additional burden. Those who, for whatever reason, choose to use the official language exclusively are favoured in that they have no need to translate, to hire someone to respond to the state's additional language policy, nor to produce their promotional and advertisement materials in two languages. Persons who decide to exercise their freedom of expression using a different language will probably find themselves in a relatively more burdensome position. Whilst a state may require the concurrent use of an official language, this creates a distinction based on language, between individuals whose primary language of choice is different from the state-sanctioned language, and others for whom the official language is the preferred language in any event. This distinction, as will be seen in the next chapter, can in some cases constitute an unreasonable or unjustifiable burden. That being the case, there exists unacceptable discrimination, and it is in this way that the described government behaviour would probably constitute a violation of human rights.

---

equality as well as of freedom of expression.

[72] A 1993 Moscow decree allows bilingual outdoor signs as long as the non-Russian words are no larger than 10 centimetres high. The law is enforced by a team of 20 inspectors, who have the power to fine companies 2,000 to 20,000 roubles for signs not in Cyrillic script. Article 18 of a 6 May 1940 Italian regulation, apparently still in force, requires the prominent use of the Italian language on commercial signs; see also Article 1 of the Municipality of Tunis decree of 6 August 1957, in *Recueil des législations linguistiques dans le monde, supra,* note 65, at p. 136.

[73] This is also the conclusion of Professor Milian i Massana, *supra,* note 4, at p. 579, in his comments on the courts' approach to the problem in Canada and Switzerland. He indicates that democratic, multilingual states may legitimately require the use of an official language even in private activities such as commercial signs, as long as other languages are also permitted.

3.7 SUMMARY

Despite freedom of expression's position of prominence in societies based on respect of human rights and the obvious close ties between the language one uses and the expression of one's opinions, there was until recently little direct consideration of whether language was a component of freedom of expression. Although a number of decisions and authors in a fairly wide ranging number of states and in international law appeared to support such a conclusion, it was not altogether clear how or in which areas it was relevant.

One of the difficulties until recently seemed to have been the failure in many cases to distinguish between freedom of expression as a right to be free from state intervention in matters which are private by nature, and the situations involving state services or relations with individuals. It was not until the Supreme Court of Canada at the end of the 1980s and the United Nations Human Rights Committee in 1993 finally considered this issue directly that one can identify a clear delimitation and understanding of the interaction of freedom of expression and language in the former and its exclusion in the latter.

It has now become clear that freedom of expression carries with it a duty for states not to intervene in the use of language in private matters. The only situation where there may be some degree of state involvement is where the state may require of individuals that an official or national language be used in conjunction with an individual's language of choice. This would appear not to constitute a breach of freedom of expression because individuals are still free to use their preferred language, although the requirement could amount to a violation of freedom of expression as understood in international law if it created such a burden as to constitute an actual impediment to the exercise of one's freedom of choice.

The situation involving individuals interacting with public authorities in official or service areas (public education, public health care, social services, court and administrative services) is not one where freedom of expression is relevant, since it affects what can be termed public or official matters. In a typical case, an individual is not seeking the non-intervention of the state in private language affairs if s/he is claiming the right to have government documents or services in a particular language. On the contrary, one is demanding state involvement and its active participation by providing these resources and services in a specified language.

Although freedom of expression may be to all extents and purposes useless when it comes to the above type of activities in the public affairs domain, it does not mean state authorities have *carte blanche* in what they can require from individuals and the type of linguistic demands or burdens they can impose, since the right to non-discrimination has a major impact in this area.

4. Equality and the Prohibition of Discrimination Based Upon Language

Current human rights standards clearly establish that freedom of expression offers to individuals a measure of protection from undesirable state interference in private matters. However, it has no application when it comes to state language requirements or preferences in traditionally recognised areas of state activities — or public matters — such as the judiciary, public education, administrative services, etc. Although not as clearly demonstrated as with freedom of expression, the prohibition of discrimination is another fundamental human right that does play a critical role in language choices in public matters. In this chapter, an attempt is made to show why the application of non-discrimination on the basis of language is a more complex process than freedom of expression: since it is less "absolute" by nature than the latter, a judge must look at the individual and state interests and burdens in assessing whether a particular language policy or preference by a state or its agents are unreasonable. If it is, only then can it be described as discriminatory. Whilst some would argue this makes for a right which is difficult to apply, it would appear to be the only practical way to adapt to the multitude of situations and factors that can face governments and the language used by the inhabitants of such diverse states such as Nigeria, Canada, India or Paraguay.

4.1   PRELIMINARY REMARKS

Does not the sun shine equally for the whole world? Do we not all equally breathe the air? Do you not feel shame at authorising only three languages and condemning other people to blindness and deafness? Tell me, do you think that God is helpless and cannot bestow equality, or that he is envious and will not give it?

Saint Constantine[1]

Whilst freedom of expression necessarily implies non-interference of the state in certain private activities, non-discrimination is different because it involves many legitimate ties and exchanges between individuals and the state in the public domain. A government, for example, is much more than the exercise of political power; it is also, if not foremost in modern society, a purveyor of "services" and "benefits" which can run the gamut of human activity: education, health care, telecommunications, social services, police, courts, etc.

One of the most frequent misconceptions involving non-discrimination is the belief that a state measure imposing a single language for all signifies that everyone is treated the same and that therefore there is no active differentiation being made between individuals. Since everyone can attend the same school classes, or receive the same administrative forms and services, everyone is treated equally within the meaning of the principle of non-discrimination.

Increasingly, this point of view is being proven incorrect because of a fundamental error in the manner in which state action is being presented. The first step to undertake when assessing whether state action is discriminatory is to determine whether public authorities have adopted a line of conduct by which a fundamental personal characteristic is being used in order to determine access to or the level of enjoyment of a public service, benefit, or advantage. In other

---

[1] Quoted in *Readings in the Sociology of Language* (1968), Joshua A. Fishman (ed.), Mouton and Co. N.V. Publishers, den Haag, Netherlands, at p. 589.

words, is the state using a criteria based on language (or religion, race, etc.) in determining who has access to and how much they can benefit from government activities and resources such as public employment opportunities, public schooling, etc.?

By adopting a one-language-for-all policy, a state is using a linguistic criteria in determining who will have access to public schooling or public employment opportunities. Even more importantly, it is also creating a distinction, based upon language, on the degree to which individuals will be able to enjoy and benefit from these activities or services: anyone who is not a native speaker of the state favoured language will be more or less seriously disadvantaged, depending upon the type of service or activity involved, his level of fluency, and the language proficiency required by the state.

This error appears to be mostly conceptual because in practice many scholars and courts, through a variety of approaches, including the concepts of "real equality", "pluralistic equality" or the Aristotelian formula of "treating different things differently", arrive at a result which recognises that individuals are not substantively being treated equally in the case of a "one official language" policy.[2] Nevertheless, there is undeniably some confusion in explanation and terminology, which results from the failure to recognise that equality and non-discrimination must first be viewed in connection to whether a state is using religion, language, ethnic origin, etc. as a criteria in determining who will benefit from its largesse. Any language criteria employed constitutes a distinction, based upon language, which has the potential of being discriminatory if it is unreasonable.

It is widely accepted that not all distinctions are necessarily discriminatory: equality and the right to non-discrimination require that individuals be protected against unreasonable or unacceptable differential treatment. How a court of law is to decide whether a particular distinction is acceptable or not is a difficult task, as it involves a balancing act between the interests and priorities of the government — normally mirroring those of the majority group controlling the state machinery — and the interests and rights of individuals affected. The nature

---

[2] de Witte, Bruno (1985), "Linguistic Equality: A Study in Comparative Constitutional Law", in *Revista de Llengua i Dret*, Vol. 3, 43-126, at p. 44:

> In fact, the deceptively simple rule of equal treatment has undergone, in legal writing and constitutional case law, an important complexification and even transformation. The prohibition of unlawful differentiations remains an important aspect of it; but it is also increasingly recognised that "real" equality, in certain circumstances, *allows* for differentiation, or even requires some distinctive treatment. Indeed, the definition of equality to which most writers, but also most constitutional courts nowadays adhere is the classical Aristotelian definition of justice: "treating like things alike and different things differently". In linguistic as in other matters, the role of the equality principle is therefore ambiguous: sometimes, linguistic differences between persons may not be taken into account, while in other circumstances, the establishment of a differential treatment, the taking of special measures, is mandatory. Such differential treatment can, in its turn, take two different forms. On the one hand, measures of pluralist equality grant to members of linguistic minorities the same advantages which the majority already has on the basis of the generally applicable rules: the right to have their children educated in their language, the right to use their language at court or with the administrative authorities, etc. Measures of affirmative equality on the other hand, give some additional benefits to members of linguistic minorities, to compensate for their handicap of being a minority.

and number of factors to be considered in determining whether a state has acted in a discriminatory manner in language matters, as in others, are almost as varied as they are complex, but an attempt shall be made later to outline the most prominent ones.

Another issue which must be kept in mind is the distinction between direct or indirect discrimination.[3] A law prohibiting any person of Chinese origin from becoming a police officer is direct racial discrimination: such individuals are denied access to a position because of their race. But if a seemingly non-racial criterion such as literacy in the state's official language or requirement as to height is employed, it could still prove to be racial discrimination indirectly if one is able to demonstrate, for example, that a Chinese person will likely be unable to qualify for a position, where individuals belonging to his race are likely to be shorter in height or likely not to have the same level of proficiency as the majority in the official language. One of the clearest examples of indirect discrimination, or discrimination in fact, is to be found in a "classic", the **German Settlers Advisory Opinion**, of the Permanent Court of International Justice.[4]

Prior to the First World War, German settlers had acquired certain property rights on the land they occupied in what was later to become part of Poland. After the war, the Polish government adopted legislation which on its face appeared neutral as regards "race" and language, as it applied to all Polish nationals, without distinction. Its effect however was to eliminate property ownership by many German settlers, although it did in a few cases apply to non-German Polish nationals who had acquired property from the original German settlers. This made no difference, according to the Permanent Court of International Justice, because "there must be equality in fact as well as ostensible legal equality in the sense of the absence of discrimination in the words of the law". As a result, although "the law does not expressly declare that the persons who are to be ousted from the lands are persons of the German race, the inference that they are so is to be drawn even from the terms of the law".[5] In other words, government legislation which is on its face absolutely neutral in terms of race (or other criterion such as language) can in fact have a discriminatory impact because of the particular context, if it disproportionably affects certain racial (or linguistic) groups of individuals. Although the Polish legislation did not specifically mention the race of those aimed at therein, indirectly it was obvious that such legislation would have much more considerable impact upon German-speaking settlers than on other nationals.

4.2   DISCRIMINATION AND LANGUAGE IN STATE PRACTICE

Despite the fact that many states have developed their own particular interpretation of what constitutes discrimination, there remain many commonalities in respect to basic elements. In addition, the current evolution of our understanding of human rights, as well as the growing influence of international actors such as the United Nations Human Rights Committee and the

---

[3] Some confusion exists because of terminology: instead of direct or indirect discrimination, some jurisdictions refer to discrimination in law or in fact.

[4] **Advisory Opinion on the Question Concerning Lease Concessions to German Nationals who have become Polish Subjects**, (1922-1925) Permanent Court of International Justice, Series B, No. 6, 6.

[5] Ibid., at pp. 23-24.

European Court on Human Rights, have led to a cross-fertilisation of approaches and a growing consensus on the main elements.

A number of authors, especially in Europe, argue that the principle of non-discrimination must be applied in the following fashion: individuals whose primary language differs from that of the majority should be treated differently in order to be treated equally, according to the Aristotelian formula of treating equally what is equal and treating differently what is unequal.[6] Another approach apparently favoured in some states[7] is to focus upon the consequences, in acknowledging that what is superficially equal treatment may in fact lead to a very unequal result due to factors such as the race, the language or the religion of people affected. In other words, because people differ in a number of ways, a law which imposes the same requirements upon everyone may have very unequal consequences. Finally, there may be a third approach pointing that equality must not be considered in isolation but rather must be understood in conjunction with the principle of non-discrimination on the ground of a fundamental human characteristic such as language.

Whichever approach is taken, there are still some points in common: language considerations can be valid, but the actions and choices of a state in such matters are not unlimited and may be sufficiently unjustifiable or unreasonable as to be considered discriminatory.

In Spain, the Constitutional Tribunal considered language distinctions in a series of cases which provide some guidance on what constitutes discrimination. That state prohibits any discrimination in Article 14 of its **Constitution**,[8] and the presence of large groups of Catalan and

---

[6] See de Witte, Bruno (1988), "Droits fondamentaux et protection de la diversité linguistique", in P. Pupier and J. Woehrling (eds.), *Language and Law: Proceedings of the First Conference of the International Institute of Comparative Linguistic Law*, Wilson & Lafleur, Montréal, at p. 97. For one commentator, Professor Danièle Lochak, France's *Conseil constitutionnel* still has not directly addressed this issue. In that state, it could still be that a law of general application, applying to everyone, would not be discriminatory. She emphasises in Lochak, Danièle (1987), "Réflexions sur la notion de discrimination", in *Droit Social*, No. 11, 778-790, at p. 784 that: *"...la position adoptée par le Conseil constitutionnel pourrait céder devant le caractère choquant et manifestement discriminatoire de l'application d'une règle uniforme à des situations différentes."* Another author appears to be willing to acknowledge some flexibility in the application of the principle of non-discrimination in French law. See Farago, Bela (1993), "La démocratie et le problème des minorités nationales", in *Le débat*, No. 76, 6-24, at p. 20:

> *Or l'interprétation jurisprudentielle de ce principe admet la « discrimination positive » impliquant que les personnes se trouvant dans des situations différentes soient traitées différemment. Ainsi, par exemple, le droit à l'instruction (art. 2 du protocole no 1) pourrait impliquer, en vertu de l'article 14, que les États concernés par la présence de minorités nationales reconnues soient obligés d'assurer aux personnes appartenant à ces minorités une instruction dans leur langue maternelle.*

[7] See amongst others **Mandla v. Dowell Lee**, [1983] 2 A.C. 548 (United Kingdom); **Goldman v. Weinberger** 475 U.S. 503 (1983) (United States); **Gerhardy v. Brown** (1985) A.L.J.R. 311 (Australia); and **Andrews v. Law Society of British Columbia**, [1989] 1 S.C.R. 143 (Canada).

[8] Although language is not one of the explicitly listed prohibited grounds of discrimination in this provision, it nevertheless has been accepted that a difference based upon language can constitute a violation because of the open-ended nature of Article 14: any distinction which is discriminatory is a

Basque speakers on its territory, coupled with a fairly recent movement towards a decentralised form of government, have produced a number of legal challenges and debates involving language. For the most part, the principle of equality in *España* is associated to the traditional Aristotelian formula of treating differently those things which are different.[9] As a result, language distinctions are acceptable, as long as they are objectively reasonable. The test to apply in the determination of what is and what is not unreasonable is that of balancing the legitimate interests of the state and those of affected individuals. The process constitutes an effort to determine whether the government measure in issue is proportional in light of the objectives sought:

> *[L]e Tribunal constitutionnel estime qu'une inégalité de traitement contrevient à l'article 14 et constitue une discrimination lorsque l'inégalité ne peut être justifiée objectivement et raisonnablement; lorsqu'elle ne maintient pas une proportionnalité raisonnable entre les moyens employés et la finalité poursuivie; et enfin, lorsque les buts, même s'ils sont raisonnables, ne sont pas protégés par la Constitution.*[10]

According to Professor Milian i Massana, the Spanish Constitutional Court also requires that any language distinction by the state be associated to a constitutional objective, otherwise the measure, even if in fact quite reasonable, will be declared discriminatory and unreasonable.

It would be erroneous to assume that the approach in Spain has developed consistently and in the absence of controversy. For example, the Spanish Supreme Court's decisions initially resisted any approach which threatened the pre-eminence of the Castilian language; however, it appears that in more recent decisions the court acknowledges that it is legitimate to require knowledge of Euskara (Basque) or Catalan in the process of job selection and in attributing language bonuses.[11] More to the point, a link is established between a state imposed preference

---

violation of the **Constitution** unless it can be justified according to criteria identified by the courts. See also Decision STC of 21 December 1982, quoted in Milian i Massana, Antoni (1992), "Droits linguistiques et droits fondamentaux en Espagne", in *R^vue Générale du Droit*, Vol. 23, 561-581, at p. 568.

[9] Ibid., at p. 568:
> *Le fait que la Constitution proscrive la discrimination pour des raisons de langue ne signifie cependant pas que toute distinction fondée sur ce motif est interdite. Le principe d'égalité consacré à l'article 14 de la Constitution obéit à la conception aristotélicienne classique de la justice, selon laquelle l'égalité suppose un même traitement pour ce qui est semblable et un traitement différent pour ce qui est dissemblable. Ainsi, le principe d'égalité n'exige pas nécessairement un traitement uniforme et admet des traitements différenciés, dans le cadre de ce que l'on peut appeler l'égalité « pluraliste »* (pluralistic equality) *ou « affirmative »* (affirmative equality).

[10] Decision STC 22/1981, 2 July 1981, *supra*, note 8, at p. 568.

[11] Decisions 4645, STS 23 September 1986, and 8311, STS 20 November 1989, *supra*, note 8, at p. 570. For a convincing exploration of the failure of earlier Spanish decisions to properly analyse the issue of reasonable language differences by public authorities, see de Witte, *supra*, note 2, at pp. 77-79.

for a particular language or languages and non-discrimination: the preference is reviewable by the courts and will be maintained only if it is reasonable.[12]

In Austria, the Constitutional Court did not hesitate in striking down a law which was restricted to providing assistance to individuals having German as their primary language. It concluded that the linguistic differentiation in the **Law on the Assistance to Victims** (*Opferfuersorgegestz*) was arbitrary: objectively, there existed no valid reason to associate benefits to the language one speaks:

> *Eine Differenzierung der Anspruchsberechtigung im Rahmen des Opferfuersorgegestz nach der Sprachzugehoerigkeit oder der Herkunft aus dem deutschen Sprachgebiet und die Schlechterstellung der Sprache einer Minderheit ist niemals sachlich. Denn die Sprachzugehoerigkeit steht zu Aufgabe und Zweck der Opferfuersorge in keinem sachlichen Zusammenhang.*[13]

The United States of America provides some of the richest, and sometimes most frustrating, material on the nature and scope of the right to equality and non-discrimination. Although it has developed extensive legislation and guidelines detailing what is both a constitutional and legislative right in that state, the waters have on occasion been muddied by interpretations and limitations quite labyrinthine for the uninitiated. In addition to the **Fourteenth Amendment** of the **US Constitution**, that is the equal protection clause,[14] there are at the federal level two main pieces of legislation largely designed to implement and build upon the principles embodied in the **Fourteenth Amendment**: the **Civil Rights Act** of 1991 and the **Equal Employment Opportunities Act**.

One section of the **Civil Rights Act**, Title VII, prohibits certain discriminatory behaviour, but in two different manners, according to whether one claims to have been the victim of intentional discrimination, identified as disparate treatment by US courts, or whether one is the victim of non-intentional discrimination, called disparate impact. The first category, disparate treatment, implies a situation in which, for example, an employer intentionally treats an individual differently by reason of his race, colour, religion, sex or national origin. In the case of disparate

---

[12] *Supra*, note 8, at p. 571:

> *Devant se prononcer sur la constitutionnalité de l'un des articles de la loi fondamentale de normalisation de l'emploi de l'euskera, celui-ci a pu déclarer que « rien ne s'oppose à ce que les pouvoirs publics prescrivent, dans le cadre de leurs compétences respectives, la connaissance des deux langues pour accéder à certains postes de fonctionnaires, ou à ce que l'on considère comme un mérite particulier (comme cela est expressément stipulé) le niveau de connaissance de ces langues, étant entendu que le tout doit nécessairement se faire dans le respect des dispositions des articles 14 et 23 de la Constitution espagnole et sans que l'application du précepte légal en question ne constitue une discrimination ».*

[13] Judgment of 15 October 1960, in Sammlung, 1960/3822, 507 (Austria), quoted *supra*, note 2, at p. 77.

[14] "All persons born or naturalised in the United States...are citizens... No state shall make or enforce any law which shall abridge the privileges or immunities of citizens; nor shall any state deprive any person of life, liberty, or property, without due process of law; nor deny any person within its jurisdiction to equal protection of laws."

impact, the claim is that an allegedly neutral employment policy or practice disproportionably affects a protected group.

These categories raise a number of problems which have been recognised and criticised by commentators. What occurs when an employer has mixed motives for a particular practice? In order to demonstrate that there is disparate treatment, it must be established that the employer "intended" to discriminate; therefore, it becomes next to impossible to assess objectively what may be couched behind a large number of explanations and excuses.

Another section of the **Civil Rights Act**, Title VI, provides that:

> No person in the United States shall, on the ground of race, colour, or national origin, be excluded from participation in, be denied the benefits of, or be subjected to discrimination under any programs or activity receiving Federal financial assistance.

Although Title VI (and the **Fourteenth Amendment**) does not explicitly include or list differences based upon language, courts have on occasion accepted that differences of national origin can manifest themselves through language. Whether or not that was the intent at the time of the adoption of this legislation, it appears to prohibit, in at least some cases, an English-only policy where federal programmes or funding are involved.

A few examples may be useful in order to highlight the US approach. In the field of education, guidelines issued by the Department of Health, Education and Welfare (HEW) indicated:

> Where inability to speak and understand the English language excludes national origin minority group children from effective participation in the educational program offered by a school district, the district must take affirmative steps to rectify the language deficiency in order to open its instruction program to these students.[15]

These guidelines were drafted after the US Supreme Court concluded in **Lau v. Nichols**[16] that instruction in English only is detrimental to students having a limited knowledge of English and amounts to a denial of equal opportunity in education, since "English deficient" pupils find themselves so disadvantaged that the education they do receive is almost useless. However, these guidelines were subsequently withdrawn because of procedural irregularities.

In essence, equality demanded, at least in some cases, some concessions to language differences in the form of what has come to be called in the US "bilingual education", although such expression should not be confused with what is ordinarily understood by bilingual education in most other states.[17]

---

[15] Van Dyke, Vernon (1985), "Human Rights, Ethnicity, and Discrimination", in *Contributions in Ethnic Studies*, Greenwood Press, Westport, Connecticut, USA, pp. 3-77, at p. 43.

[16] 414 U.S. 563 (1974) (United States).

[17] Bilingual educational programmes in the US are mostly limited to a few years, the expectation being that by the end of those years the students will be in a position to continue their education in English. According to one author, *supra*, note 15, at p. 44:

> It is obviously not the thought that any constitutional right exists to bilingual and bicultural education, for a constitutional right would hold in all the states (not simply in those that enact the necessary legislation) and at every level of the educational system.

It should be emphasised that US courts have generally been unable to present a coherent response to claims of language discrimination. For example, in **Carmona v. Sheffield,**[18] the plaintiffs claimed that Spanish-speaking citizens were denied equal protection of the law because of a failure by the California Department of Human Resources Development to conduct its affairs and the state's programme of unemployment insurance benefits, including the printing of forms, the interviewing of applicants, etc., in Spanish in addition to English. The trial court was unwilling to even consider the validity of the plaintiffs' demands for the following reasons:

> [It] would require the state of California and presumably, all other states and the Federal Government to provide forms and to conduct its affairs and proceedings in whatever language is spoken and understood by any person or group affected thereby. The breadth and scope of such a contention is so staggering as virtually to constitute its own refutation. If adopted in as cosmopolitan a society as ours, enriched as it has been by the immigration of persons from many lands with their distinctive linguistic and cultural heritages, it would virtually cause the processes of government to grind to a halt. The conduct of official business, including the proceedings and enactments of Congress, the courts and administrative agencies, would become all but impossible... For historical reasons too well-known to require review herein, the United States is an English-speaking country.

The United States Court of Appeals, Ninth Circuit, confirmed this point of view on appeal, adding the following:

> Giving notice in English to these appellants is not a denial of equal protection. Even if we assume that this case involves some classification by the state, the choice of California to deal only in English has a reasonable basis.
> We believe that the additional burdens imposed on California's finite resources and California's interest in having to deal in only one language with all its citizens support the conclusion of reasonableness.[19]

A number of other US decisions generally follow the same reasoning, relying upon two or three motives: the United States is an English-speaking country, it is impossible to offer all services in all the languages spoken in the country, and it is reasonable to limit provision of or access to

---

Unfortunately, this author has adopted an all-or-nothing attitude with respect to the response which can be offered by law to remedy a discriminatory practice in language matters. Even if in some cases non-discrimination implies some concession in the language of instruction, it does not necessarily include, for example, instruction for everyone in any language at every level.

[18] 325 F.Supp. 1341 (1971) (United States).

[19] This decision has been criticised by scholars who have pointed out the Court of Appeals presentation of the options open to it are far too simplistic. See a discussion of the above quote, *supra*, note 2, at p. 110:

> A court need not grant a universal right to every person to use whichever language in all fields of public life, but can easily modulate its remedy in order to take account of numbers and available possibilities. It might well appear, then, that the bilingual staffing of a public service is not such a costly and complicated endeavour to preclude any judicial intervention.

most government services to English.[20] Recently, the Supreme Court employed a fourth, more unusual route: an employer may force employees, against their will, to speak English even when they are not working, since it is only an inconvenience which can in no way violate a person's rights.[21]

As for use of the **Fourteenth Amendment** of the **Constitution**, it has been invoked successfully in a limited number of cases,[22] either because language is not specifically referred to therein, or because of the difficulties government action based upon language has in qualifying for "strict scrutiny" by the courts, one of the three levels of control adopted by the US Supreme Court.

Depending upon a series of factors, a US court will adopt one of three levels of scrutiny when examining a claim of violation of the **Fourteenth Amendment**. The "three throngs", strict scrutiny, intermediate scrutiny and minimal scrutiny, carry with them a decreasing likelihood of success before US courts. Unless a case falls squarely into the strict scrutiny category, the chances of success are vastly diminished, and they are particularly weak in the case of limited scrutiny, where government is allowed a great deal of leeway in its affairs.

To be subjected to strict scrutiny control by the courts, a government action or legislation must involve either a "suspect category" such as race, religion or national or ethnic origin, or

---

[20] In **Guerrero v. Carleson**, 512 P.2d 833 (1973) (United States), Spanish-speaking citizens demanded that the State Department of Social Welfare and the County Department of Public Social Services not be allowed to terminate or reduce welfare benefits to recipients receiving aid for families with dependent children. The court rejected their claim that due process or equal protection required that notice of such measures to recipients, known by the state agencies to be only literate in Spanish, had to be in the language they understood:

> ...so also the rule sought by plaintiffs herein would reach far beyond the present facts. As plaintiffs candidly concede, a decision in their favour could not properly be limited to the AFDC program and the Spanish language, but would also apply (1) to Spanish-speaking recipients under any of the other half-dozen categorical assistance programs and (2) to any other language — Chinese or Japanese, Russian or Greek, Filipino or Samoan — in which a non-English-speaking recipient of such assistance was known to be literate, regardless of how small the language group might be. In addition it is difficult to see why such a rule would not also extend to any and all official communications to the public required to satisfy due process of law, whether it be summonses, citations, subpoenas, tax forms, delinquency or eviction or foreclosure notices, announcements of public hearings — or, contrary to our assertion in **Castro** ballots and election materials.

[21] **Garcia v. Spun Steak**, US Supreme Court, 22 June 1994. The Supreme Court actually refused to hear the appeal, thus indirectly approving the reasoning of the Ninth Circuit Court of Appeals on the issue. Old habits are hard to break in the United States. The Supreme Court seemed to be unaware that it was helping to perpetuate a tradition going back to the days of slavery, when Africans who were brought as slaves were forbidden to speak their native tongues to one another because of the fear of slaveholders that they would be plotting against them.

[22] In **Yu Cong Eng v. Trinidad**, 271 U.S. 500 (1926) (United States), at p. 528, the Supreme Court concluded that a Philippine statute which required merchants to keep their books in English, Spanish, or in a local dialect, thereby prohibiting Chinese merchants from utilising the only language they understood, was invalid "because it deprives Chinese persons...of their liberty and property without due process of law, and denies them the equal protection of the laws."

otherwise affect fundamental rights.[23] If it fits into one of these categories, courts will generally be very strict and will tend to recognise that the state has behaved in a discriminatory fashion unless the government has been able to demonstrate a highly convincing objective (overriding state interest) for such a violation, which could not be attained by using a less intrusive method. As language is not included as a suspect category — unless courts are willing to include it as an indirect indicator of ethnic or national origin which they do, inconsistently,[24] or unless it is associated to a fundamental right[25] — it may be difficult to claim discrimination on the grounds of language under the **Fourteenth Amendment**.

At the other end of the scale is minimal scrutiny, where evidence of a legitimate objective (legitimate state interest) rationally related to government action will normally be sufficient to convince a court that the difference in treatment is not discrimination.

The middle or intermediate level of scrutiny applies essentially in cases of sexual discrimination. Courts have to be convinced that the difference in treatment is substantially linked to an important governmental objective, or it will otherwise generally side with the individual alleging he or she is a victim of discrimination.

The existence of three levels of scrutiny results in a great deal of intellectual gymnastics in order to have a case fit squarely into the pigeon-holes of strict or intermediate scrutiny. It also calls for the need to develop a hierarchy of rights and freedoms which in many cases appears rather artificial and rigid when dealing with the control of government action.[26]

Although there is no doubt diversity in the wording used, and contradiction in the way courts have interpreted the actual meaning and impact of the principle of non-discrimination in the United States, there is nevertheless a fairly extensive number of governmental practices in many parts of that country which provide that where a large, geographically concentrated number of non-English primary speakers exists, public authorities, in order to act in a non-discriminatory manner, must provide at least some of their services in the language of these individuals.

Despite the fact that neither the **Constitution** nor US human rights legislation specifically identify language as a forbidden ground of distinction, this has not been an insurmountable obstacle for individuals who can claim that language discrimination indirectly affects them because of their race or national origin, grounds which are acknowledged in the US legal

---

[23] Rights recognised in the US **Constitution**, such as the right to vote, or the right to have access to courts, are deemed fundamental, but not the right to education.

[24] For example, the case of Spanish-speaking Hispanics, who at times are considered as a racial group.

[25] The right to vote being a fundamental right, it has been easier to obtain voting material in languages other than English. In **Puerto Rican Organization for Political Action v. Kusper**, 350 F.Supp. 606 (1972) (United States), the Chicago Board of Elections was ordered to provide voting instructions and ballots or ballot labels on voting machines in Spanish and English, because if they were "printed only in English, the ability of the citizen who understands only Spanish to vote effectively is seriously impaired."

[26] See Woehrling, José (1993), "L'article 1 de la Charte canadienne et la problématique des restrictions aux droits et libertés : l'état de la jurisprudence de la Cour suprême" in *Droits de la personne : l'émergence de droits nouveaux*, Éditions Yvon Blais, Cowansville, pp. 3-34, at p. 11.

order.[27] However, language as an indicator of race or national origin is, as will be seen, at best an indirect and imperfect match.

Across the Atlantic, in England and Wales, the **Race Relations Act** is the main piece of legislation prohibiting discrimination, and it only does so based upon a few recognised grounds which do not include language nor religion. Although the right to equality and the prohibition of discrimination is generally agreed to be aimed at the protection of or respect for an individual's rights, the English approach appears in some ways to be almost "collective". In **Mandla v. Dowell Lee**, a head teacher refused to admit a turban-wearing Sikh as a pupil of a private school on the basis of a "no headgear" rule. The Court of Appeal indicated:

> ...for a group to constitute an ethnic group in the sense of the Act of 1976, it must, in my opinion, regard itself, and be regarded by others, as a distinct community by virtue of certain characteristics. Some of these characteristics are essential; others are not essential but one or more of them will commonly be found and will help to distinguish the group from the surrounding community.[28]

The Court of Appeal acknowledged that a language common to a group, though not necessarily peculiar to it, could be one of the relevant characteristics of a distinct community.

The above explanation by the Court of Appeal were necessary because of the limits of English legislation. Although religious or language discrimination are not prohibited in the **Race Relations Act**, either one can be indirectly involved as proxies for either ethnic or racial groups, at least in situations where a particular ethnic or racial group are more likely to share a language or religion different from the majority. In England, as in the United States, governments have tended to be less than generous in respect to the grounds of discrimination covered by their non-discrimination legislation, making it a challenge for lawyers and victims to advance creative arguments to counter these lacunae and to convince a court of an indirect link between language and ethnic or national origin.

English case law does, however, acknowledge the possibility of such a link, and indeed recognises that the requirement of an ability to speak or write a particular language can impose a burden that may be unjustifiable. For example, even the requirement of the ability to speak English in England must be reasonably related to the tasks involved in a rational and balanced way, as such a requirement can have a disproportionate adverse impact on some, and not others, because of their personal characteristics.[29]

---

[27] Most Spanish-speaking US citizens can claim to be victims of racial discrimination, "Hispanics" being recognised by US courts as part of a racial category. But the absurdity of equating language with skin colour is fairly obvious. Some US institutions have had to distinguish, for example, between White Hispanics and Non-White Hispanics. Moreover, a Spaniard immigrant in the US would not fit the "Hispanic" racial category, and thus could not avail himself of the protection of the **Civil Rights Act**, whilst his neighbour from Puerto Rico could do so for the same type of language discrimination. Finally, it would be interesting to see how courts would react to John Murphy from El Paso whose father is Irish, and mother Hispanic, and whose primary language is Spanish.

[28] [1983] 2 A.C. 548 (United Kingdom).

[29] **Raval v. DHSS**, [1985] I.R.L.R. 370 (United Kingdom).

Despite this, there are a number of confusing English decisions dealing with the Welsh language. In **Jones v. Gwynedd County Council**,[30] the Council required a knowledge of Welsh as a condition of employment for work involving senior citizens. Although the Industrial Tribunal felt that the requirement was not justifiable because it was more an attempt to protect the Welsh language than a response to the interests of the seniors, in appeal it was concluded that the **Race Relations Act** could not assist the victims because they were ethnically Welsh and not English. It thus can be rather problematic in the United Kingdom to classify language into the applicable pigeon-holes of race or ethnic group.

In Japan, case law and the weight of commentators confirm that not every distinction is necessarily discriminatory and in violation of the right to equal protection under Article 14 of the **Constitution**, although there are no reported cases dealing precisely with language differences. In one matter, the Supreme Court of Japan[31] held that differential treatment based upon reasonable grounds does not violate equality as protected under the **Constitution** and that even distinctions affecting aliens are permissible if they are reasonable.

The **Constitution of Mauritius** offers some guidance on the application of non-discrimination by providing in Article 16 that discrimination means affording different treatment to different persons attributable wholly or mainly to their respective descriptions by race, caste, place of origin, political opinions, colour or creed. This implies that persons who are subjected to any disability or restriction because of one of these characteristics are potentially the victims of discrimination.

Canada, with its linguistic conflicts, offers some additional insight on what may be considered language discrimination although, with the exception of Québec and the territory of Yukon, discrimination on the explicit ground of language is generally not prohibited in the country. In this respect, one has to keep in mind that non-discrimination legislation is a fairly recent development in this Common Law country, and that traditional Common Law does not recognise any right to equality.

In **Ford v. Québec**[32] the Supreme Court of Canada had to determine whether Article 58 of the **Charte de la langue française**, making French the exclusive language for commercial signs, constituted an infringement of freedom of expression. It also considered whether the legislation amounted to discrimination on the ground of language, prohibited in Québec's non-discrimination legislation.

The majority of the court unambiguously stated that although the legislation applied to everyone, it would affect individuals differently based upon their language, as only French-speaking individuals would be entitled to use their primary language in commercial signs. Article 58 of the **Charte** thus created a distinction on the ground of language which in the Supreme Court's opinion was not justified.

Canada's highest court also was asked to review Articles 52 and 57 of the **Charte de la langue française** in a second illuminating case, **Devine v. Québec**.[33] Those provisions required that business documents and reports be maintained in French, in addition to any other language

---

[30] The Times, 25 July 1985, quoted in Beloff, Michael (1987), "Minority Languages and The Law", in *Current Legal Problems*, Vol. 40, 139-157, at p. 144.

[31] Judgement of 18 November 1964, Keishu, Vol. 18, No. 9 (Japan), at p. 579.

[32] (1988) 2 S.C.R. 712 (Canada).

[33] (1988) 2 S.C.R. 790 (Canada).

chosen by private parties. Although individuals were all subjected to the same legislation, the Supreme Court of Canada once again pointed out that different individuals would in fact be facing differential treatment on the ground of language, as those having French as their primary language would continue to use a single language in their affairs, whereas other individuals having another primary language would likely find themselves obliged to keep documents in two languages. However, because the latter were entitled to use their own language, in addition to French, the Supreme Court concluded that the measure, although constituting a minor violation of the right to non-discrimination, was not an unjustified, nor unreasonable, legislation:

> *En veillant à ce que les non-francophones puissent rédiger des formulaires de demandes d'emploi, des bons de commandes, des factures, des reçus et des quittances dans la langue de leur choix, de pair avec le français, l'article 57 interprété conjointement avec l'article 89, crée, tout au plus, une atteinte minimale aux droits à l'égalité. Bien que, comme l'appelante l'a soutenu, l'exigence de l'usage concurrent du français puisse créer un fardeau additionnel pour les marchands et les commerçants non francophones, il n'y a rien qui porte atteinte à leur capacité d'utiliser également une autre langue. Par conséquent, notre conclusion concernant l'application de l'article premier demeure même si, à première vue, la violation en cause de la Charte canadienne est une violation de l'article 15.*[34]

Though at times confusing and contradictory, these examples of various state approaches in applying the principle of non-discrimination do give a general sense of how language differences and non-discrimination can be approached. International instruments and decisions hold even greater consistency and pave the way for a comprehensive theoretical model of how equality and non-discrimination on the ground of language are to be understood and applied.

4.3   LANGUAGE DISCRIMINATION IN INTERNATIONAL LAW

Virtually every major international human rights instrument includes language as a ground upon which there may be no discrimination. Moreover, the interpretation of such instruments generally indicates a common understanding of the basic principles involved, although there remains a number of inconsistencies and differences on the exact nature and scope of non-discrimination in language matters. In order to better grasp these principles, it may be useful to step back into history and to view the background of today's international approach in regard to language discrimination.

4.3.1   *Pre-United Nations Period*

It is perhaps felt, in certain milieux, that the League of Nations era and the experiment with what are now known as "minorities treaties" have little to offer in light of contemporary concern with individual human rights such as freedom of expression and non-discrimination. This, however, ignores the true nature of these treaties, which were very much concerned with providing a

---

[34] Ibid., at p. 820.

mechanism for the protection of individual human rights, especially the right to equality, in addition to including measures aimed specifically at "national minorities".[35]

The Permanent Court of International Justice quite rightly stated, in an often quoted decision, that in order to secure for linguistic minorities the possibility of living peacefully alongside the population speaking the majority language, two things are necessary:

> The first is to ensure that nationals belonging to...linguistic minorities shall be placed in every respect on a footing of perfect equality with the other nationals of the state. The second is to ensure for the minority elements suitable means for the preservation of their racial peculiarities, their traditions and their national characteristics.[36]

The court went on to state that these requirements were inseparable since "there would be no true equality between a majority and minority if the latter were deprived of its own institutions and were consequently compelled to renounce that which constitutes the very essence of its being as a minority."

The Permanent Court of International Justice also had much to say in respect to what constitutes equality in the **German Settlers Advisory Opinion**,[37] comments which are still relevant and considered today. The case involved German-speaking Poles[38] who settled on lands that later became part of Poland, under contracts made with the Prussian state.

Poland was bound by Article 8 of the **Polish Minorities Treaty**, which guaranteed to racial minorities the same treatment and security "in the law and in fact" as that given to other Polish nationals. According to the court, this provision was important because:

> The intention of this Treaty was no doubt to eliminate a dangerous source of oppression, recrimination and dispute, to prevent racial and religious hatreds from having free play and to protect the situations established upon its conclusion, by placing existing minorities under the impartial protection of the League of Nations... The main object of the Minorities Treaty is to assure respect for the rights of Minorities and to prevent discrimination against them by any act whatsoever of the Polish state.[39]

The legislation in issue was essentially aimed at cancelling the contracts by which German-speaking settlers had been able to acquire title to property in parts of Poland. The legislation did not actually explicitly provide that these people were considered for differential treatment, and in fact it was clear the law was on its face "neutral" as far as race, language or origin were

---

[35] The concept of national or long-established minority is further explored in Chapter 5.

[36] **Advisory Opinion on Minority Schools in Albania**, (1935) Permanent Court of International Justice, Series A/B, No. 64, 3, also known as the **Minority Schools in Albania** case.

[37] *Supra*, note 4.

[38] It is interesting to note how terminology can vary considerably: the Permanent Court of International Justice spoke of persons of the German race, whereas today one could find the use of any one of the following to describe the same people: German-speaking Poles, German ethnics, Poles of German national origin, etc.

[39] *Supra*, note 4, at p. 25.

concerned. Moreover, there existed cases of non-German-speaking Poles having acquired property from the original German settlers, who were also affected by the provisions under attack.

Here is how the court dealt with the distinction between equality in law and in fact and the relevance of each:

> The facts that no racial discrimination appears in the text of the law of 14 July 1920, and that in a few instances the law applies to non-German Polish nationals who took as purchasers from original holders of German race, make no substantial difference... There must be equality in fact as well as ostensible legal equality in the sense of the absence of discrimination in the words of the law... [A]lthough the law does not expressly declare that the persons who are to be ousted from the lands are persons of the German race, the inference that they are so is to be drawn even from the terms of the law.[40]

The court recognised that although the Polish legislation made no direct reference to the Germans-speaking Poles, it was quite obvious that its effects were aimed at them and that they would be affected by the legislation a great deal more than anyone else. As a result, not all Polish nationals could enjoy the same civil and political rights and the same treatment and security in law as well as in fact. The German settlers were subjected to discriminatory treatment concerning their civil rights, in violation of the principle of equality, as other citizens holding contracts of sale or lease would largely be unaffected by the legislation.

This case clearly demonstrates the concern that individuals be treated in a fair and reasonable manner — a non-discriminatory manner — and that a state should not penalise or disadvantage some unjustifiably because they have a personal trait that happens to be "frowned" upon by the government, be it race, colour, religion or language.[41] Modern international law is thus the direct inheritor of a legal tradition going back, at least, to the League of Nations period.

4.3.2   United Nations System

Although the principle of non-discrimination is found in a large number of instruments under the United Nations system, all of these tend to repeat the same formula and appear consistent with the approach presented in the **German Settlers Advisory Opinion**. Amongst these, Article 1 of the **International Convention on the Elimination of All Forms of Racial Discrimination** defines racial discrimination as follows:

> ...any distinction, exclusion, restriction or preference based on race, colour, descent, or national or ethnic origin which has the purpose or effect of nullifying or impairing the recognition, enjoyment or exercise, on an equal footing, of human rights and fundamental freedoms in the political, economic, social, cultural or any other field of public life.[42]

---

[40] *Supra*, note 4, at pp. 23-24.

[41] One should be aware of differences in meaning in the term "race" under the minorities treaties and the way the same word is used today. In the interwar period, race referred to what would now be called ethnic or national origin distinctions, which may also include distinctions such as religion or language.

[42] See Section 2.1.6 in the Appendix.

The United Nations Human Rights Committee (UNHRC) by and large adopted this definition in its *General Comment on Non-Discrimination*. After considering a number of other international instruments, it noted:

> While these conventions deal only with cases of discrimination on specific grounds, the Committee believes that the term "discrimination" as used in the Covenant should be understood to imply any distinction, exclusion, restriction or preference which is based on any ground such as... language... and which has the purpose or effect of nullifying or impairing the recognition, enjoyment or exercise by all persons, on an equal footing, of all rights and freedoms. The enjoyment of rights and freedoms on an equal footing, however, does not mean identical treatment in every instance.[43]

This definition of non-discrimination coincides with a trend apparent since the very earliest period in the evolution of human rights after the Second World War, and even predating it as was shown above. There appears to have been a consensus during the drafting of the **Universal Declaration of Human Rights** that equality does not mean treating everyone identically in every circumstance. Mrs. Roosevelt, as chairperson of the United Nations Commission on Human Rights at the time, pointed out that "equality did not mean identical treatment for men and women in all matters, for there were certain cases, as for example, the case of maternity benefits, where differential treatment was essential".[44]

One can safely assume that most international law commentators would probably agree with the following comment on non-discrimination:

> As far as [the prohibition of discrimination] is concerned, it should be observed that Article 14 [of the European Convention] — despite the French text "sans distinction aucune" — does not prohibit every difference in treatment. On the contrary, the obligation contained therein may even entail unequal treatment. For Article 14 is not only concerned with formal equality — equal treatment of equal cases — but also with substantive equality: unequal treatment of unequal cases in proportion to their inequality.[45]

The **South West Africa Case (Second Phase)**[46] confirms the necessity of an understanding of equality such that it cannot turn a blind eye to differences. Judge Tanaka's dissident opinion in particular provides insight on the reasons why:

> [The principle of equality before the law] does not exclude the different treatment of persons from the consideration of factual differences such as...language, etc. To treat

---

[43] *General Comment on Non-Discrimination* (1989), United Nations Publications, New York, at paragraphs 7 and 8.

[44] McKean, Warwick (1983), *Equality and Discrimination under International Law*, Clarendon Press, Oxford, United Kingdom, at p. 65.

[45] Van Dyk, P. and Van Hoof, G.J.H. (1990), *Theory and Practice of the European Convention of Human Rights*", Kluwer Law and Taxation Publishers, Deventer-Boston, at p. 539. See also the discussion in Van Dyke, *supra*, note 15, at pp. 4-6.

[46] [1966] International Court of Justice 284.

different matters equally in a mechanical way would be as unjust as to treat equal matters differently.[47]

Judge Tanaka also made reference to the issue of language of education and the principle of equality, as follows:

> [I]f there exists the necessity to treat one race differently from another, this necessity is not derived from the physical characteristics or other racial qualifications but other factors, namely religious, linguistic, educational, social, etc. which in themselves are not related to race or colour... For instance, if we consider education...we cannot deny the value of vernacular as the medium of instruction and the result thereof would be separate schooling as between children of diverse population groups... In this case separate education and schooling may be recognised as reasonable. This is justified by the nature of the matter in question.[48]

The key word here is reasonable. What Judge Tanaka and Mrs. Roosevelt have emphasised is that to impose any requirement involving language, sex, or any other personal characteristic is legitimate as long as it is reasonable in the effects or burden it imposes on an individual.

Decisions emanating from the Human Rights Committee are unfortunately not very informative, probably because the Committee has not yet closely considered the exact requirements of equality and non-discrimination based upon language. It did deal very briefly with the issue of language distinctions in law, in relation to Article 26 of the **International Covenant on Civil and Political Rights** (equality before the law and equal protection of the law) in the Breton cases of **Dominique Guesdon v. France**,[49] and **Yves Cadoret and Hervé Le Bihan v. France**[50] examined above in chapter 3 on freedom of expression.

The authors of those communications submitted that legislation in France making French the only language to be used before criminal courts constituted discrimination based upon language, as they were not permitted to use Breton, their primary language, before the courts. The Human Rights Committee failed to consider closely the nature of their legal argument, only responding in all cases with the same comments:

> French law does not, as such, give everyone a right to speak his own language in court. Those unable to speak or understand French are provided with the services of an interpreter. This service would have been available to the author had the facts required it; as they did not, he suffered no discrimination under Article 26 on the ground of his language.

These comments are, to say the least, puzzling. France adopted the position that since everyone was subjected to the same requirement, it was impossible to speak of discrimination. In other words, if legislation imposes the same requirement for all to use only the official language in order to have access to the courts, then there is no possibility of any discrimination.

---

[47] Ibid.

[48] Ibid.

[49] UN GAOR, forty-fifth session at p. 61, UN Document A/45/40 (1990).

[50] Communications Nos. 221/1987 and 333/1988, 11 April 1991.

The same thing occurred in the Québec commercial sign case of **Ballantyne, Davidson and McIntyre v. Canada.**[51] Having essentially settled the matter by relying upon an infringement of the authors' freedom of expression, the Human Rights Committee nevertheless added that in its view, since the law applied to all business people in the province, be they anglophones or francophones, there could be no discrimination.

The Committee's comments must be approached with a great deal of caution, firstly because the issue of discrimination was only mentioned briefly — almost as an afterthought — and secondly because it appears to contradict the Committee's own definition of discrimination in its *General Comment on Non-Discrimination* as will be shown below.

It is also interesting to point out that, in practice, the United Nations has recognised that equality and non-discrimination may warrant language concessions when faced with a sufficiently large number of individuals in a compact area, as it suggested for the partition of Palestine:

> Thus when it recommended the partition of Palestine it specified that "the state shall ensure adequate primary and secondary education for the Arab and Jewish minority, respectively, in its own language and its cultural traditions." Presumably the "adequate" education was to be equally adequate, in which case the General Assembly endorsed the principle of separate but equal treatment so far as language is concerned.[52]

4.3.3 *American Continent*

A more illuminating example on how to deal with the right to non-discrimination and language is to be found in the **Advisory Opinion of 19 January 1984**[53] on the proposed amendments to the naturalisation provisions of the **Constitution of Costa Rica** of the Inter-American Court of Human Rights (hereinafter the **"Costa Rican Naturalisation Case"**). One of the amendments was to require that an applicant had to be able to speak, write and read Spanish in order to acquire citizenship.

As to the general principles involved, the Inter-American Court stated the following:

> The notion of equality springs directly from the oneness of the human family and is linked to the essential dignity of the individual... It is impermissible to subject human beings to differences in treatment that are inconsistent with their unique and congenerous character. Precisely because equality and non-discrimination are inherent in the idea of the oneness in dignity and worth of all human beings, it follows that not all differences in legal

---

[51] Communications Nos. 359/1989 and 385/1989, 31 March 1993.

[52] Van Dyke, *supra*, note 15, at p. 19. According to the author, such an arrangement is an example of differential treatment that may be necessary in order to attain real equality, and this is reasonable because in order to treat people equally it is at times desirable and even necessary to treat them differently, depending upon the class to which they belong. With all due respect, there is a fundamental point overlooked by this suggestion. The Arab and Jewish students are not being treated differently as regards language of instruction — on the contrary, they are receiving the exact same treatment, i.e. education through the medium of their primary language. Differential treatment based upon language would have existed if education had been provided to all in a language that is the primary tongue of only a part of the student population.

[53] Case No. OC-4/84.

treatment are discriminatory as such, for not all differences in treatment are in themselves offensive to human dignity... There may well exist certain factual inequalities that might legitimately give rise to inequalities in legal treatment that do not violate principles of justice. They may in fact be instrumental in achieving justice or in protecting those who find themselves in a weak legal position. For example, it cannot be deemed discrimination on the grounds of age or social status for the law to impose limits on the legal capacity of minors or mentally incompetent persons who lack the capacity to protect their interests. Accordingly, no discrimination exists if the difference in treatment has a legitimate purpose and if it does not lead to situations which are contrary to justice, to reason or to the nature of things. It follows that there would be no discrimination in differences in treatment of individuals by a state when the classifications selected are based on substantial factual differences and there exists a reasonable relationship of proportionality between these differences and the aims of the legal rule under review. These aims may not be unjust or unreasonable, that is, they may not be arbitrary, capricious, despotic or in conflict with the essential oneness and dignity of humankind.[54]

The Inter-American Court then went on to acknowledge that it may not always be simple to determine when a difference of treatment can be considered discriminatory, but did point out that considerations of public welfare were relevant, to a greater or lesser degree, in setting the above standards. States obviously have a certain margin of appreciation in these matters.

Specifically on the issue of imposing a language requirement in order to be eligible for citizenship, the court had no difficulty accepting that it was not unreasonable nor unjustified to require proof of the ability to communicate in the language of the country (the official language and that of the majority). However, the court had some reservations on the literacy requirement: even if in the end the criterion was judged to be non-discriminatory, it was clear that it could in some situations constitute discrimination on the ground of language, as proscribed by Article 24 of the **American Convention on Human Rights** if it were:

> ... an unreasonable and disproportionate discrimination in accordance with the nature and purpose of the right to a nationality with its inclusion in the law of the Convention as a whole, and with the circumstances of the society in which it is designed to function.[55]

Acknowledging the desirability that all Costa Ricans know and be able to communicate in Spanish, as it is the official language of the country, one of the judges noted that such a context does not mean that a state can simply impose any language requirement, even its official language, in complete disregard of the other languages used by its nationals, especially when the official language is not the primary tongue of a large number of individuals and indigenous peoples:

> [E]quality and non-discrimination cannot function in a vacuum nor, therefore, without the specific conditions of the society in which the people live. In this regard, my concern comes from the fact that there are among the country's own native-born people persons and substantial communities that do not know the Spanish language or that do not know it well,

---

[54] Ibid., at paragraphs 55, 56 and 57.

[55] Ibid., at paragraph 22.

and that do not even speak that language as their native language: Indian communities that, although they are small and isolated, retain their ancestral languages and even resist learning or having to use the official language; and there is an important Costa Rican community of Jamaican origin that retains its language and many of whose members at least have problems in expressing themselves correctly in Spanish. Of course, the Costa Rican state, aware of the desirability and even the duty of preserving the native cultures and the rights of minorities in the country, is conducting programs of instruction and for promoting of the culture in the Indian languages and, recognising its cultural situation, has provided courts and public bureaus with official interpreters of those native or minority languages.[56]

In final assessment, the Inter-American Court was of the opinion that it was not unreasonable, disproportionate, nor arbitrary to require persons desiring to acquire Costa Rican nationality to know the official language well enough to read and write in Spanish and to communicate in it.

The Inter-American Court considered the issue of language discrimination much more closely than the United Nations Human Rights Committee and arrived at a diametrically opposed conclusion: whereas the Human Rights Committee appeared to suggest that no discrimination could result from a law or policy imposing upon everyone the same language requirements, the Inter-American Court had no hesitation in considering such an arrangement as differential treatment on the ground of language which could, in appropriate cases, constitute discrimination.

4.3.4 Europe

More valuable insight on what constitutes language discrimination is provided in the decisions emanating from Europe in interpreting Article 14 of the Council of Europe **Convention for the Protection of Human Rights and Fundamental Freedoms** and the legislation and directives of the European Union prohibiting discrimination amongst nationals of the member-states.

In **Groener v. Minister for Education**,[57] the European Court of Justice considered national regulations on employment in Ireland, requiring basic knowledge of the Irish language. Such knowledge was not related to the actual performance of Groener's duties as an art teacher. The court had to determine whether such a policy was discriminatory since it had the effect of excluding other European Union nationals, contrary to Article 3 of **Regulation 1612/68**.

The court's approach held a great deal of deference to the emotional and symbolic ties between the Irish language and much of Irish society. Although Article 3 of the European Union regulation only permitted "conditions relating to linguistic knowledge required by reason of the nature of the post to be filled", the court went out of its way in establishing another possible exception: there may be social and cultural considerations which are relevant in determining whether linguistic requirements are discriminatory or not. In the case of Irish, the requirement of some knowledge of that language by teachers, as part of a policy for its promotion, was justified according to the court, although the subject of the course taught by Groener was not linguistic and teaching at the vocational school was as a general rule in English:

> The EEC Treaty does not prohibit the adoption of a policy for the protection and promotion of a language of a member state which is both the national language and the first official

---

[56] Ibid., at paragraph 23.

[57] Case 379-87, [1990] 1 Common Market Law Review 401.

language.... The importance of education for the implementation of such a policy must be recognised. Teachers have an essential role to play, not only through the teaching which they provide but also by their participation in the daily life of the school and the privileged relationship which they have with their pupils. In those circumstances, it is not unreasonable to require them to have some knowledge of the first national language.

This case is especially relevant for its treatment of the relationship between a language requirement and non-discrimination: the court recognised that any language imposition outside Article 3(1) of **Regulation 1612/68** (linguistic knowledge related to job performance) must be applied without discrimination, meaning amongst other things, that the level of linguistic knowledge required must not be disproportionate to the object of the policy.

In **Ministère Public v. Mutsch**,[58] a Belgian statute gave Belgian citizens living in the German-speaking part of the country the right to use the German language in criminal appeal proceedings. As a citizen of Luxembourg living in that area, Mr. Mutsch did not have the same right. The European Court of Justice held that the use of one's own language in court is to be considered as a "social advantage" to which, according to the same regulation dealt with in **Groener, Regulation 1612/68**, all European Union workers are equally entitled to. The court also stated that the principle of equal treatment means that European Union workers and their families have to be able to avail themselves of the same linguistic rights as the state's own citizens. Since Mutsch, as an European Union worker, did not have the same rights as other citizens, he was subject in this case to unlawful discrimination.

One commentator has suggested that **Ministère Public v. Mutsch** be considered in the following manner:

> States may still decide whether or not to grant linguistic rights to their own minorities. But if they grant such rights, Community workers speaking that same language should also be entitled to those rights.[59]

The decision in **Ministère Public v. Mutsch** is mainly interesting because it recognises the use of one's primary language as a benefit — or conversely the denial of its use as a burden or disadvantage — which must be considered when determining whether or not government action or restrictions are discriminatory. Whilst **Ministère Public v. Mutsch** dealt very narrowly with the issue of differences of treatment as between citizens of the European Union, it does nevertheless suggest that the use of one language in a court of law, as in other government "services" such as state schooling, impacts differently upon those who have a different primary language. The consequence which follows on a larger scale is that, unless otherwise justifiable, any exclusive state requirement of choice of language signals a difference of treatment, thereby denying to some a benefit enjoyed by others, more precisely the use of one's primary language.

No public activity by its very nature is outside the scope of non-discrimination. In **Mathieu-Mohin and Clerfayt**,[60] the European Court on Human Rights reviewed the principles embodied

---

[58] Case 137-84, (1985) European Court Reports 2681.

[59] de Witte, Bruno (1991), "The Impact of European Community Rules on the Linguistic Policies of the Member States" in Florian Coulmas (ed.), *A Language Policy for the European Community: Prospects and Quandaries*, Mouton de Gruyter, Berlin, New York, pp. 163-177, at p. 170.

[60] (1987) European Convention on Human Rights, Series A, No. 113.

in Article 3 of the **First Protocol of the Convention for the Protection of Human Rights and Fundamental Freedoms**. The applicants had been elected respectively to the Belgian Senate and House of Representatives from the bilingual electoral district of Brussels, but also in an administrative district which came under the Dutch-language Council in respect to certain matters. They had to submit to a test of eligibility for the Council consisting in a parliamentary oath in Dutch. The applicants, being francophones, took their oath in French instead and were denied the right to sit on the Council, despite the fact their administrative district came under the Dutch-language Council in respect of important matters for their voters. This, they claimed, either violated Article 3, **First Protocol of the Convention**, or violated Article 3 when read in conjunction with Article 14 of the **Convention**.

Article 3 of the **First Protocol** provides that states undertake "to hold elections by secret ballot, under conditions which will ensure the free expression of the opinion of the people in the choice of legislature". It appears fairly obvious that this right does not in itself contain a linguistic component. The court indicated that, as for the alleged violation of Article 3 of the **First Protocol** taken alone, it is not an absolute right and contains implied limitations. According to the court, the French-speaking electors involved do enjoy the right to vote and the right to stand for election on the same legal footing as Dutch-speaking electors. They are not deprived of their Article 3 sufficiently in this case since the limitation is not disproportionate to the point of thwarting the "free expression of the opinion of the people in the choice of the legislature".[61]

The European Court then proceeded to the question of the alleged violation of Article 14 of the **Convention** taken together with Article 3 of the **First Protocol**. Here it did not adopt the position that since language was not a part of the substantive right under Article 3, the applicants could not avail themselves of the non-discrimination provision. On the contrary, the European Court came rather to the conclusion that Article 14 could be evoked, but that in the circumstances the measure adopted by the state was not unreasonable nor disproportionate:

> The aim is to defuse the language disputes in the country by establishing more stable and decentralised organisational structures... In any consideration of the electoral system in issue, its general context must not be forgotten. The system does not appear unreasonable if regard is had to the intentions it reflects and to the respondent state's margin of appreciation within the Belgian parliamentary system — a margin that is all the greater as the system is incomplete and provisional.[62]

Final confirmation of this thesis may also be found in one of the leading post-World War II cases on the question of non-discrimination, the **Belgian Linguistic Case**,[63] raised under the Council of Europe **Convention for the Protection of Human Rights and Fundamental Freedoms**.

Six applications were received from 327 French-speaking parents who claimed, on their own behalf and on behalf of some 800 school-aged children, that the Belgian government contravened Articles 8 (right to family life) and 14 (non-discrimination provision) of the European **Convention**, as well as Article 2 of the **First Protocol** of the **Convention** (right to education), by obliging all children to be educated exclusively in Dutch at local state schools.

---

[61] Ibid., at p. 25.

[62] Ibid., at p. 25.

[63] **Belgian Linguistic Case**, [1968] 1 Yearbook of the European Convention on Human Rights 832.

The Belgian government had initiated a policy of linguistic regionalism by dividing the country into four regions, the first three respectively assigned on the basis of prevailing French, German and Dutch language use. The Brussels area constituted a special fourth bilingual region.

In each of the three unilingual regions, education was exclusively provided in the language of the majority, but a census was to be taken every ten years to ascertain linguistic trends in the communities in order to evaluate any changes that may warrant some corrections. However, a 1961 law abolished the question on language in the census, with the result that the linguistic boundaries were, for all practical purposes, permanently fixed. Additional legislation in July 1963 abolished all transitional French classes which had been tolerated or promised in certain Flemish localities under the old legislation. Six communes on the periphery of Brussels were designated as a distinct administrative district, although technically they were primarily in the Dutch language part of Belgium. In these communes, French was allowed as the language for primary state education, subject to a few conditions. However, this right was not extended to French-speaking children whose parents lived outside the communes and wished to send their children to those schools, whilst Dutch schools in the same communes in principle could accept any child, regardless of the residence or language of his or her parents.

A number of issues were raised by the applicants living in the Dutch unilingual territory, but only on one account did the European Court on Human Rights come to the conclusion that there had been discrimination in violation of Article 14 of the **Convention** read in conjunction with Article 2 of the **First Protocol**. The court found that the Belgian **Act** of 1963 prevented certain children, solely on the basis of the residence of their parents, from having access to the French language schools in the six communes near Brussels.

Briefly, the court recognised that Article 2 of the **First Protocol** was of no assistance to the petitioners since the right to education does not in itself enshrine the right to the establishment or subsidisation of schools in which education is provided in one's preferred language. The court then proceeded to analyse whether Article 14, read in conjunction with Article 2, had been violated and concluded that there was no violation of the **Convention** — not because Article 2 and Article 14 together cannot support a right to the establishment or subsidisation of schools in which education is provided in a given language — but rather because the Belgian legislation was a justified and reasonable measure in light of the country's particular political and social position:

> The Court...does not consider that the measures adopted in this matter by the Belgian legislature are so disproportionate to the requirements of the public interest which is being pursued as to constitute a discrimination contrary to Article 14 of the Convention, read in conjunction with the first sentence of Article 2 of the Protocol...[64]

Despite some ambiguity as to the exact meaning of the court's comments, a close look at its conclusion lends support to the position that limiting state education to one language is a distinction under Article 14 that can, in some cases, be deemed discriminatory:

> Article 14 does not prohibit distinctions in treatment which are founded on an objective assessment of essentially different factual circumstances and which, being based on the

---

[64] Ibid., at p. 886.

public interest, strike a fair balance between the protection of the interests of the community and respect for the rights and freedoms safeguarded by the Convention.

In examining whether the legal provisions which have been attacked satisfy these criteria, the Court finds that their purpose is to achieve linguistic unity within the two large regions of Belgium in which a large majority of the population speaks only one of the two national languages. This legislation makes scarcely viable schools in which teaching is conducted solely in the national language that is not that of the majority of the inhabitants of the region. In other words, it tends to prevent, in the Dutch-unilingual region, the establishment or maintenance of schools which teach only in French. Such a measure cannot be considered arbitrary. To begin with, it is based on the objective element which the region constitutes. Furthermore it is based on a public interest, namely to ensure that all schools dependent on the state and existing in a unilingual region conduct their teaching in the language which is essentially that of the region.[65]

These comments are consistent with the view that to impose a single language of instruction constitutes a difference of treatment for those who have a different primary language, and may in some situations be discriminatory. According to the court:

> ... the legislation has instituted an educational system which, in the Dutch unilingual region, exclusively encourages teaching in Dutch, in the same way as it establishes the linguistic homogeneity of education in the French unilingual region. These differences in treatment of the two national languages in the two unilingual regions are, however compatible [with Articles 2 and 14].[66]

Presumably, the exclusion of French from state schools in the Dutch region, although a difference of treatment based upon language within the meaning of Article 14, was not discriminatory in the Belgian context because it was reasonable and justified by the general linguistic scheme adopted in the country. In other words, it was not unreasonable for Belgium given the context of having divided the country into distinct, mostly unilingual regions. The difference of treatment imposed upon individuals with a primary language not used or recognised in a particular linguistic region constituted for that state a balanced and acceptable behaviour, given the purpose of achieving social and political peace in the country.[67]

4.4 DEFINING A STANDARD FOR THE APPLICATION OF NON-DISCRIMINATION ON THE GROUND OF LANGUAGE

It thus appears as a fairly consistent theme in international law and state practice that the exclusive use of a single language constitutes differential treatment which may in some cases be

---

[65] Ibid., at pp. 884-886.

[66] Ibid., at p. 884.

[67] Although the European Court's reasoning is impeccable, one could question whether other aspects of the linguistic scheme in Belgium are altogether justifiable.

discriminatory. Indeed, even the minorities treaties of the inter-war period acknowledged that in places where the inhabitants speaking a different language formed a considerable proportion of the population, they should at least have access to state services such as primary public education in their own language.[68] Since language is an aspect of the "services" rendered by the state in education, to only grant the advantage of instruction, or any other type of government service, in the primary language of some inhabitants of the country (generally the majority) places others at a disadvantage.

Obviously, there is no unanimity in respect to the substance of non-discrimination on the ground of language, and contradictions in international precedents and national practice are unavoidable. In the Breton cases, France held the position that a general law, applicable to everyone, requiring the exclusive use of French within the activities of public authorities meant that everyone was being treated equally, and the United Nations Human Rights Committee appeared to support this suggestion. For its part, the Supreme Court of the United States appears to be of the opinion that any requirement of the exclusive use of a language is a mere inconvenience when individuals are bilingual.

The Inter-American Court of Human Rights, the European Court of Justice, the European Court on Human Rights, and a number of states including Canada, have opted for a diametrically different understanding of what constitutes discrimination based on language. For them, any language requirement or preference by a state creates a distinction which advantages some individuals and disadvantages others, and may as a result be discriminatory. If such an approach is correct, one ends up with a formidable legal principle which is relevant to every facet of state activity and action, be it related to the judiciary, public service employment, educational policy and even naturalisation legislation. How precisely the principle of non-discrimination on the ground of language must be understood and applied therefore becomes a highly sensitive, but critical, exercise.

It is therefore essential to attempt to provide a comprehensive view of what constitutes language discrimination, based upon generally accepted principles of international law and state practice.

The most widely approved, and perhaps most well developed, definition of discrimination is the one used in many United Nations instruments and adopted by the Human Rights Committee in its *General Comment on Non-Discrimination*.[69] In this document, discrimination is identified as implying any distinction, exclusion, restriction or preference which is based on any ground such as language and which has the purpose or effect of nullifying or impairing the recognition, enjoyment or exercise by all persons, on an equal footing, of all rights and freedoms. This definition provides an appropriate theoretical framework from which to proceed, in order to attempt to identify some kind of coherent standard from the various approaches in existence.

---

[68] See Article 9 of the **Polish Minorities Treaty**, reprinted in Thornberry, Patrick (1991), *International Law and the Rights of Minorities*, Clarendon Press, Oxford, United Kingdom, at p. 399.

[69] *Supra*, note 43.

4.4.1   *Denial or Exclusion on the Ground of Language*

Denial or exclusion on the ground of language is probably the least problematic aspect of non-discrimination based upon language. Quite often, a government will limit access to certain services or benefits to those who use a certain language, or it may decree that employment opportunities in its workforce are predicated on a sufficient knowledge of a particular language. Anyone who cannot comply with such language requirements will be denied the benefit, service, or opportunity. As in **Lau v. Nichols,**[70] education in English only, for a child having no knowledge of the language, corresponds to a complete denial of the right to education. As in **Viola v. Canada,**[71] a language requirement for a public employment position denies, to those who do not know the language, any opportunity of obtaining such position. These cases illustrate that language is necessarily involved in any government activity and that those who cannot adequately use the state sanctioned language will be denied or excluded because of language.

Conversely, if an individual has some knowledge of the language required by a state, it cannot be claimed that there is an actual denial or exclusion unless his or her level of proficiency is so low as to effectively constitute a complete barrier and to preclude any real possibility of enjoying the benefit or service provided. This was the situation in **Lau v. Nichols** where the US Supreme Court indicated that public authorities were in effect excluding students from any meaningful education if account was not taken of their lack of knowledge of the English language.

4.4.2   *Language Distinction, Restriction or Preference*

The traditional Aristotelian formulation of equality is to treat equally what is equal and treat differently what is different. This leads some to conclude that as far as the language of predilection of a state and public authorities is concerned, individuals whose language differs should be treated differently in order for them to be treated equally. Most national and international provisions on equality have refined this traditional concept: equality combined with non-discrimination on the ground of fundamental personal characteristics imply that the state should not consider individual attributes or characteristics (such as colour of skin, religion or personal beliefs, sex, language, etc...) when it allocates its resources, provides services, or excludes or burdens individuals, unless it is necessary and reasonable to take into account these factors.

In the case of the colour of one's skin, it is very simple for a government to disregard this consideration and thus act in a completely fair and neutral way, since rarely would skin pigmentation be a valid consideration for access to the state's largesse.[72] The right to equality thus requires non-discriminatory treatment to be equated to disregard of a non-relevant personal trait. There should normally be no difficulty in completely setting aside any preference for people of a particular colour, thus ensuring there is no distinction amongst individuals because of colour of skin.

---

[70] *Supra*, note 16.

[71] [1991] 1 F.C. 373 (Canada).

[72] With the possible exception of special programmes aimed at redressing past injustices.

How to deal with a person's religion is more complicated. One's religion is also a personal trait, but is not immutable. It is, in theory, a fairly painless process for someone to freely change faith. A state, and in particular one claiming to be secular, can generally avoid any religious preference or consideration since most governmental activities and actions tend to be clearly outside of the religious realm.[73]

Whilst a state can completely disregard differences in colour of skin, and can in most cases ignore differences in religion, language[74] provides with an even greater level of challenge and difficulty to the state, because it cannot be language "neutral" when it interacts with its inhabitants or in its day to day operations. The state machinery must function in a language, or at most in a few languages, for most of its communication, work and service activities, making it impossible not to make any distinctions as to language. Therefore, a government is obliged to favour a particular language or a limited number of languages. This creates a distinction: by limiting itself to a single language, the state is involved in a difference or distinction of treatment. Government employment opportunities will be open to every individual, but only if they have sufficient knowledge of the official language. Since the state (instead of being neutral as it normally is when facing differences of colour of skin or religion) is actively favouring one specific language, it is actively involved in differential treatment between individuals on the basis of language.

The error made by France, sometimes by the United States and by the United Nations Human Rights Committee, is to limit themselves to the first element of the equation on equality and non-discrimination: equality means that everyone should be submitted to the same general legal requirements. That may be correct in first analysis. However, the prohibition of discrimination on grounds such as language involves a second element to the equation: legislation

---

[73] There are however limits. It is almost impossible for a state to simply ignore all religious favouritism. For example, many secular Western countries have legal provisions requiring commercial activities to cease on Sundays, considered by most Christians as a holy day of rest. Similar legal measures generally do not exist in these countries for the Sabbath or any other day of rest recognised in other religions. Although such legislation is general, affecting all individuals, it does not constitute identical treatment for everyone because it is not neutral: in respect to religion, it reflects a religious bias. Individuals who are of one of the Christian faiths are favoured and find themselves less affected or inconvenienced than individuals with religious practices of a different nature. This is therefore a situation of differential of treatment based upon religion, as the state has not refrained from favouring individuals because of their religion. However, such legislation may still not be discriminatory if it is deemed to be a reasonable preference or arrangement.

[74] Differential treatment because of accent should also be included when considering discrimination on the ground of language, since accent identifies an individual as having a "foreign" or simply different language as his primary tongue; see Perea, Juan F. (1994), "Ethnicity and Prejudice: Re-evaluating National Origin Discrimination under Title VII", in *William and Mary Law Review*, Vol. 35, 805-870, at p. 836:

> Persons who speak English with a "foreign-sounding" accent regularly are assumed to be "less intelligent" than persons who speak English with a more socially accepted accent. Similarly, the perceived intelligibility of different languages is influenced by bias against particular ethnic groups. The primary languages of subordinate groups, those perceived as lacking in prestige and power, are deemed more difficult to understand by the majority culture than the English language, which is deemed easy to understand.

affecting everyone should not create distinctions involving language, religion, etc, unless it is reasonable and necessary.

To assert that everyone is treated equally, without any distinction, when French and English are respectively the exclusive languages of government in France and the United States, fails to take into account that some individuals can be denied employment opportunities, for example, or at the very least will suffer an additional burden or disadvantage, because they are not treated the same as those who have French or English as their primary language, in regard to access to the benefits and services of the state in their own language. The imposition of a single language for use by government does not constitute equality of treatment for all, since some do not speak it or have a more limited knowledge of the language. Equality of treatment and non-discrimination require that in their relations with the state apparatus, individuals should not be affected or disadvantaged because of some fundamental human characteristic; as soon as any condition or consideration of personal characteristics such as sex, age, colour of skin, religion, language, etc. are involved, all individuals are not treated without distinction since the state has decided to consider one or more of these factors in the allocation of resources, access to services and employment opportunities, etc.

This point must be emphasised because of commentators and jurists who appear to be under the impression, as has been noted on a number of occasions, that the requirement of the same language for all is equal treatment. Thus, one of the world's leading legal experts on language legislation, Professor Bruno de Witte, has stated:

Yet in one basic respect linguistic minorities want to be treated differently: they want to be able to use, in dealing with the authorities, a language which is different from that of the majority. Equality is therefore an ambiguous concept; it can be invoked for claiming a treatment which is at the same time identical in substance but differentiated in (linguistic) form.[75]

---

[75] de Witte, Bruno (1992), "Conclusion: A Legal Perspective", in Sergij Vilfan (ed.), *Comparative Studies on Governments and Non-Dominant Ethnic Groups in Europe 1850-1940*, New York University Press, New York, pp. 303-314, at p. 303. Professor de Witte also stated on another occasion, *supra*, note 6, at p. 96, that:

> [L]a plupart des prestations administratives impliquent l'usage d'une ou de plusieurs langues déterminées. Ainsi, si la langue ne constitue jamais la totalité d'un service donné, elle constitue néanmoins une dimension nécessaire de chaque communication qui s'établit entre l'État et ses citoyens. Elle constitue, par rapport à la substance du service, un avantage annexe qui permet à ce service d'être reçu correctement par l'usager.
> Il est donc clair que l'utilisation de la langue constitue un avantage social et affecte la qualité du service rendu. Si le service est rendu dans une seule langue, tous les usagers sont traités de manière égale; en réalité, les usagers qui parlent une langue différente ne reçoivent pas un service également valable pour eux, alors qu'ils ont contribué à financer le service selon les mêmes critères.
> Il est clair...qu'un seul utilisateur ne pourra pas exiger l'adjonction d'une langue officielle supplémentaire, mais qu'un groupe comprenant près de la moitié de la population pourra légitimement le demander. Le principe juridique d'égalité servira à déterminer où se situe le point d'équilibre...

Although probably shared by many, his comments, the position of France, the US, and the Human Rights Committee proceed from the same essential but erroneous premise: in respect to the language favoured by public authorities, there is similar or equal treatment of everyone where everyone is subjected to the same language. In its simplest formulation, this is erroneous because equality means treating everyone the same regardless of age or colour of skin, or sex, or language, etc. As soon as authorities raise a condition of language, colour, sex, or age, then it creates a distinction, which may in some cases represent an unjustified disadvantage or burden.

A perhaps crude example can be given by comparing language and religious requirements. If a state were to impose by law as a condition of employment that employees be good Catholics or Muslims, it could hardly be claimed that the law treats everyone equally: although anyone could in theory convert to these faiths, and conversion is generally an easier process than acquisition of a new language, not everyone is a Catholic or Muslim. Instead of being "religious neutral", thus ensuring that everyone is treated equally without distinction as to religion, the state would have instituted a clear difference of treatment amongst individuals because of religion: only Catholics or Muslims need apply.

By substituting the words "good Catholics or Muslims" with "a good knowledge of French or English", it becomes apparent that far from signalling a "language neutral" criterion, the "one language for all" policy in effect creates a difference of treatment amongst individuals for whom these languages are primary, and those for whom they are not. The pitfall to avoid is the belief that "in substance" equality of treatment and non-discrimination in language matters implies the same language for everyone. In reality, equality must be without any distinction, and this in turn requires a state to completely set aside any language criterion or preference. If it cannot do so, it creates a distinction which will be disadvantageous for certain individuals. By choosing an official or exclusive language, a government is automatically creating a distinction on the ground of language in its allocation of resources, services and benefits, simultaneously creating various levels of difficulty for individuals having a different primary language.[76]

In the Breton cases concerning court and administrative proceedings, and in the **Ballantyne, Davidson and McIntyre v. Canada** decision involving commercial signs, the Human Rights Committee faced situations where as a practical matter, the parties were able, in one way or another, to respect the French-only legal policy of the French and Québec governments; notwithstanding this point, the Committee seems to have neglected to consider its own definition of non-discrimination, as it did not ask itself if the imposition of a single language was a restriction against the use of all other languages or a preference for the use of French. Either one is potentially discriminatory according to the Committee's own definition. Thus, the Committee's remarks that the French and Québec legislation could not be discriminatory, as it constituted

---

[76] Ibid., at p. 304. Professor de Witte did go on to recognise this aspect of the problems caused by any language preference by a state:

> In the context of public administration, those who have full command of the language will receive a service which is also more valuable in substance to them than to citizens who do not master the language, and this despite the fact that all citizens have contributed by their taxes to the functioning of the public service without distinction as to the language they speak. In other words, the public authorities, by using a single language in a plurilingual situation do not provide an equal treatment to all but operate what could be called a "cultural redistribution" in favour of those persons who speak the official language.

general legislation applicable to all, is quite simply inconsistent with its own stated views on how to interpret the principle of non-discrimination. The legislation clearly created a language preference, and restricted the use of all other languages.

Thus the United Nations Human Rights Committee and others have on occasion neglected to adequately consider what constitutes a language distinction, restriction or preference. To claim that a law applies to everyone in the same way implies that there truly is no consideration or requirement involving language (or race or religion, etc.). Whilst governments may have no choice but to "prefer" some language and restrict the use of others in its official activities and services, it is misleading to claim that it does so without distinction, restriction or preference, as the state clearly is not behaving in a "language neutral" fashion. In reality, an English- or Spanish-only policy adopted by public authorities is similar to a Whites-only policy: individuals are subject to state favouritism of a particular language or colour, although obviously in the case of language, the distinction, restriction or preference can be deemed reasonable in appropriate circumstances.

Some would claim, as has been done in the US, that the appropriate approach suggested here would place an impossible burden on governments, making it necessary to submit to the linguistic demands of every individual in the state. This fails to take into account another element in the determination of discriminatory practices, that is whether or not the distinction at issue based upon language, is reasonable.

4.4.3 *Discriminatory Purpose or Effect*

Most countries and players at the international level appear to acknowledge that discrimination does not require proof that a government intended to act in a discriminatory fashion. The wording used in the United Nations system is unambiguous: the reasons for adopting a particular piece of legislation or for following a certain course of action is by no means indispensable. Discriminatory effect is in itself sufficient to meet the requirements of the principle of equality and non-discrimination.

The reasons for this are in fact quite simple and straightforward. It would in all likelihood be extremely difficult and onerous to impose upon individuals the burden of proving to a court that a government had a particular purpose in choosing a certain line of conduct, unless the measure was so unreasonable that no other possible explanation could be retained. Indeed, legislation can often have a number of purposes, so that it becomes next to impossible for an individual to mount an effective challenge of a discriminatory state practice in the face of such obstacles. Even something as abhorrent as slavery, by using the so-called purpose test, could be explained away as an essentially economic measure and not one intending to be discriminatory.[77]

The only notable exception in this regard is the approach taken by courts in the United States. Courts have held that in the case of "disparate treatment" by employers subject to Title VII of the **Civil Rights Act**, victims must prove that the employer intentionally treated an

---

[77] Although the example is obviously an exaggeration, slavery has apparently been "theoretically" shown to be an effective economic model. Of course, the economic argument would have little attraction to individuals having to forego their human rights because of the economic advantages, for slaveholders, of such a policy.

individual differently by reason of race, colour, religion, sex or national origin.[78] Even the equality provision of the US **Constitution**, the **Fourteenth Amendment** requires some proof of discriminatory intent:

> Litigants have had virtually no success in bringing language claims under the fourteenth amendment... Two significant and probably overwhelming hurdles must be crossed before plaintiffs could successfully litigate under the Fourteenth Amendment: (1) level of scrutiny and 2) discriminatory intent... The second hurdle that language litigants must overcome in order to successfully bring a constitutional claim pursuant to the Fourteenth Amendment is discriminatory intent. In order to demonstrate intent, plaintiff's must show that "the decision maker...selected or reaffirmed a particular course of action at least in part 'because of' not merely 'in spite of' its adverse effects..." In effect, the requirement of discriminatory intent coupled with the difficulty in establishing a suspect class, have effectively undermined the use of the Fourteenth Amendment as a vehicle for language disputes.[79]

By adopting such a restrictive approach, it is extremely doubtful whether the practice of the United States in non-discrimination policies is consistent with international standards.

4.4.4   *Unfavourable Consequences of Preferential Treatment*

The language I have learnt these forty years,
My native English, now must forgo;
And now my tongue's use is to me no more
Than an unstringed viol or harp;
Or like a cunning instrument cas'd up
Or, being open, put into his hands

---

[78] A victim could also claim that an employer has adopted a policy that has a discriminatory effect, the so-called "disparate impact" cases, but he must then demonstrate that a "neutral" employment policy or practice has disproportionably affected a protected group. The problem with this two thronged approach is its rigidity: you either fall neatly into one of the two, or you cannot avail yourself of the protection of the **Civil Rights Act**. Language distinctions have on occasion been excluded because they are sometimes not deemed to be neutral, therefore a victim cannot use the disparate impact test and must prove an employer's discriminatory intent. Despite changes in the **Civil Rights Act of 1991** (Public Law No. 102-166, 105 Stat. 1071 (1991)) to ensure that courts not use the requirement of intentional discrimination in a way which would exclude most claimants seeking redress in lawsuits under Title VII, the Supreme Court in **St. Mary's Honor Center v. Hicks**, 113 S.Ct. 2742 (1993) (United States), by a vote of five to four concluded that it was insufficient for a plaintiff to demonstrate that an employer's stated reasons were pretexts. The majority held instead that a plaintiff must also prove that the employer's practice was additionally motivated by an intention to discriminate.

[79] Walker, Roger (1991), "Federal Bilingual, Bicultural Education: The Failure of Entitlement", in *University of Missouri - Kansas City Law Review*, Vol. 59, 769-800, at pp. 789-793. See also a similar conclusion in de Witte, *supra*, note 2, at p. 76: "[T]he insistence, in recent Supreme Court decisions, on the necessity to prove a discriminatory purpose of the legislator makes such indirect discriminations very difficult to challenge."

That knows no touch to tune or harmony.
Within my mouth you have engaol'd my tongue,
Doubly portcullis'd with my teeth and lips;
And dull, unfeeling, barren ignorance
Is made my gaoler to attend on me,
I am too old to fawn upon a nurse,
Too far in years to be a pupil now.
What is thy sentence, then, but speechless death,
Which robs my tongue from breathing native breath?

Shakespeare, Richard II, 1.3

Even if a state behaves in a discriminatory manner, shows a definite preference for a specific language, or even attempts to restrict access to services based upon language differences, an individual must also demonstrate that he or she was somehow disadvantaged or denied something which others are entitled to. He has to be the victim of a measure or practice which "nullifies or impairs the recognition, enjoyment or exercise by all persons, on an equal footing, of all rights and freedoms".[80]

There are many ways in which an individual can be unfavourably affected. To prohibit someone from having access to state-funded education because his primary language is not the country's official language clearly "nullifies" that individual's right to education, as does a practice where education in only one language acts as an absolute barrier to a child who has no understanding of the language used.

Moreover, instead of constituting an absolute denial of a right enjoyed by others, language requirements may impair, to varying degrees, an individual's exercise or enjoyment of a right available to others. Until fairly recently, Blacks in the United States had difficulty exercising the right to vote because of the application of English literacy tests. Whilst a few Blacks did have the right to vote in former Rhodesia, the state's education and property requirements effectively excluded the vast majority of the country's population from so doing. Thus, a state can impair an individual's enjoyment of rights or freedoms available to others simply by creating linguistic obstacles or burdens which will exclude or disadvantage some people.[81] Everyone is not treated

---

[80] See the *General Comment on Non-Discrimination, supra*, note 43, at paragraph 10. A distinction between provisions restricting the application of non-discrimination to rights and freedoms recognised in a constitution or treaty, as in the case of the European **Convention for the Protection of Human Rights and Fundamental Freedoms**, and those which prohibit discrimination in law or in fact in any field regulated and protected by public authorities, such as Article 26 of the **International Covenant on Civil and Political Rights** should be noted. In the latter situation, states must ensure that all of their legislation (even their constitution), its application, and the practices and actions of public authorities and their agents conform with the obligations related to the right to non-discrimination.

[81] *Supra*, note 15, at p. 39:

What the literacy and language test did was to give exclusive control over government to the English-speaking, permitting them to use government for their own advantage and for the disadvantage of others. It deprived others of an opportunity to hold government accountable. It left government without any compelling reason to tend to the interests of those who did not

on an equal footing in regard to language when everyone does not have the same primary language.

Both nullification and impairment, as generally understood, due to state preferences of one or a few languages in allocating resources or providing any other type of right or privilege, involve for some a disadvantage or denial of something which others are entitled to.

This has been recognised by many commentators who have pointed out that by excluding the use of most other languages, a linguistic majority can control a government and enjoy the privileges, jobs and services provided by the state in their own language, using the taxes paid by individuals speaking other languages as well as their "share" of the state's financial resources in a manner which benefits the majority community to which they belong.[82] Individuals for whom the official or state-favoured language is not the primary vernacular will find themselves at a disadvantage in terms of access to jobs and services,[83] education,[84] or in private business activities.[85]

The decisions of the Human Rights Committee in the Breton and **Ballantyne, Davidson and McIntyre v. Canada** cases provide a concrete illustration of what constitutes nullification or impairment of the recognition, enjoyment or exercise on an equal footing of all rights and freedoms. The respective French and Québec legislation required the exclusive use of the French language — no other languages were permitted as the language of tribunals or of outdoor commercial signs. Individuals had to submit to the restriction and were therefore prohibited from testifying or having exterior commercial signs in their own language. Whilst everyone was subjected to the same requirements, not everyone was treated on an equal footing because some were permitted to use their primary language, and others were not. Some individuals in France having to testify in court had the advantage of so doing in their primary language, French, but others were denied the same advantage or benefit to use their primary language: they are therefore disadvantaged or imposed an additional burden.

By imposing a language requirement, the state shows a definite preference towards some individuals on the basis of language. Since individuals do not necessarily share the same

---

know English, even if they were citizens. It opened the way to favouritism for one group and neglect and oppression for the rest.

[82] Skutnabb-Kangas, Tove (1981), *Bilingualism or Not: The Education of Minorities*, Clevedon, Avon, United Kingdom, at p. 305: "By comparison with majorities, minorities in most countries are oppressed both economically and politically (even if there are exceptions). They have the use of a smaller proportion of the country's resources than the majority."

[83] Meillet, A. (1928), *Les langues dans l'Europe Nouvelle*, Payot, Paris, at p. 104:
Pour autant que les citoyens ont affaire aux fonctionnaires publics, ils doivent employer le français, et, s'ils ne savent pas le bien comprendre et l'employer d'une manière juste, ils sont en état d'infériorité. Qui veut devenir fonctionnaire doit posséder le français commun, passablement pour être fonctionnaire inférieur, tout à fait pour briguer une situation plus élevée.

[84] Ammoun, Charles D. (1957), *Study of Discrimination in Education*, United Nations Publications, New York, at p. 108.

[85] Perea, Juan F. (1990), "English-Only Rules and the Right to Speak One's Primary Language in the Workplace", in *Journal of Law Reform*, Vol. 23, 265-318, at pp. 290-291.

language, some are favoured and others are not. In other words, the imposition of a single language for use in state activities and services is by no means a neutral act, since:

(1) The state's chosen language becomes a condition for the full access to a number of services, resources and privileges, such as education or public employment: those who cannot use it fluently, or who refuse to use the official/preferred language, will simply not be permitted to receive the same benefits and services conferred by the state on an equal footing.

(2) Those for whom the chosen state speech is not the primary language are thus treated differently from those for whom it is: the latter have the advantage or benefit of receiving the state's largesse in their primary tongue, whereas the former do not and find themselves in a more or less disadvantaged position, depending on their fluency, as compared to the second group.[86] Whether it is for employment in state institutions (which necessarily require a more or less higher level of fluency of the language privileged by the state) or the need to translate or obtain assistance because of a weak understanding of the language, a person faced with not being able to use his primary language assumes a heavier burden.[87]

This implies that a state's choice of language for services, employment and contacts with its inhabitants necessarily favours individuals who are already completely fluent in the chosen language, usually those for whom it is the mother tongue.[88] As Professor Yash Ghai remarked

---

[86] See for example the conclusion on the effects of language and education in *The Use of Vernacular Languages in Education* (1953), UNESCO, Paris:

> It is axiomatic that the best medium for teaching a child is his mother tongue. Psychologically, it is the system of meaningful signs that in his mind works automatically for expression and understanding. Sociologically, it is a means of identification among the members of the community to which he belongs. Educationally, he learns more quickly through it than through an unfamiliar linguistic medium.

For an excellent commentary on the extent to which teaching in one's primary language is an advantage, see Hastings, William K. (1988), *The Right to an Education in Maori: The Case from International Law*, Victoria University Press, Wellington, New Zealand, at pp. 5-11.

[87] From the above, it is already possible to tentatively outline a number of common elements of the concept of discrimination in international and national law, which shall be more fully explored below: (1) legislation or government policy which has the effect of favouring one or more language(s) for the state apparatus, its agencies or activities creates a distinction, based upon language and (2) in some cases this may be deemed discriminatory. The distinction may put certain individuals in a position of disadvantage since they cannot enjoy the same rights or benefits on an equal footing with those for whom the official or preferred language(s) is their primary language.

[88] Unless an individual comes from a truly bilingual family where two languages are consistently and equally used during childhood, the vast majority of people have one language with which they are more comfortable and with which they identify more closely. In most but not necessarily all cases, one's primary language is also the mother tongue. The level of proficiency is therefore normally higher in an individual's primary language, even though he or she may also have various degrees of fluency in other languages.

whilst explaining the origins of the conflict in Sri Lanka involving the Sinhala majority and the Tamil-speaking minority:

> The Sri Lankan language policy has been the subject of bitter controversy and one of the major reasons for the steady deterioration of ethnic harmony. At and after independence the language of administration was English (though the use of Sinhala and Tamil was also permitted). This was seen as conferring an advantage on the Tamils, who for various historical reasons had been more responsive to opportunities for modern education. It was also considered that the continued use of English was incompatible with the cultivation of the Sinhala ideology of the state and privileging the position of that community. At first (1956) Sinhala was made the sole official language. This provoked a great deal of resentment from the Tamils, particularly as having limited access to good land, they had looked to the civil service for employment, and their chances of promotion and recruitment were worsened by the new language requirement.[89]

Any state language preference invariably favours some and disadvantages others. It must again be emphasised that this is an unavoidable situation, since no state has the resources to provide all of its services in every language spoken within its jurisdiction. However, the linguistic policy actually adopted in a given state must be reasonable. The brief comments of the United States Supreme Court in **Garcia v. Spun Steak** are erroneous in contending that to not allow bilingual people to speak their primary language is only an "inconvenience", and cannot involve any type of discrimination. This example signals that the United States' equality legislation, or at least the interpretation of such legislation by some of its courts, does not respect international standards, nor does it conform with the approaches taken in **Groener v. Minister for Education** and **Ministère Public v. Mutsch**, nor again does it conform with other national approaches, not to

---

[89] See Ghai, Yash (1993), *Legal Responses to Ethnicity in South and South East Asia*, paper delivered at Conference "Ethnicity, Identity and Nationalism in South Africa: Comparative Perspectives", 20-24 April 1993, Rhodes University, Grahamstown, South Africa, at p. 19 (unpublished) for detailed statistics and excellent comments on the dramatic impact of the language preference of the state on the employment opportunities for the Tamil population. For an explanation of the background to the disintegration of Yugoslavia and the economic and political factors surrounding the refusal of Serbian authorities to respect the language rights enshrined in the country's constitution, see Tollefson, James W. (1991), *Planning Language, Planning Inequality*, Longman Inc., New York, at pp. 193-198.

mention sociological,[90] educational,[91] and psychological studies concerning the importance of language for individuals and communities alike.[92]

An English-only policy is a preference based upon language, which favours those who have English as a primary language.[93] Others are denied the same privilege or advantage of using their primary language. Such a policy may nonetheless be reasonable in some cases and thus be non-discriminatory, but the US trend to simply qualify a preference received by some as inconsequential is ill-founded given the prominence of language in personal, family and community life. The growing consensus at the national and international level is that any language preference constitutes differential treatment, which favours individuals having the "preferred" language as their primary tongue, and disadvantages those who do not.

4.5   REASONABILITY OF STATE LANGUAGE PREFERENCE(S)

Evidently, the above must not be understood to mean that all state language policies, because they unavoidably favour a language or a few languages, are therefore automatically

---

[90] Fishman, Joshua A. (1972), *The Sociology of Language*, Newbury House Publishers, Rawley, Massachusetts, at p. 4:

> [L]anguage is not merely a means of interpersonal communication and influence. It is not merely a carrier of content, whether latent or manifest. Language itself is content, a reference to loyalties and animosities, an indicator of social statuses and personal relationships, a marker of situations and topics as well as of the societal goals and the large-scale value-laden arenas of interaction that typify every speech community.

[91] See *The Use of the Vernacular in Education*, *supra*, note 86.

[92] The Supreme Court appears to have inadvertently committed a *faux pas* when it further agreed that someone who cannot speak English should always be entitled to use his or her language, and that any prohibition of his or her language preference would constitute discrimination. The Supreme Court seems to have ignored that this would encourage individuals speaking a minority language, and wishing to retain any right to use their primary language, to never learn the official or preferred language of government. Instead of favouring integration of minorities into the wider society, which has always been the objective of the famous "melting pot" approach of the US, the Supreme Court seems to have accidentally taken the contrary route. However, the door has been left open to a change of direction since the Supreme Court refused to hear the actual arguments in the **Garcia v. Spun Steak** case.

[93] It must be kept in mind that any measure aimed at favouring one language, or restricting the use of another, is potentially discriminatory. In a rather bizarre decision, the court in **Dimaranan v. Pomona Valley Hospital Medical Center**, 775 F.Supp. 338 (1991) (United States), concluded that a rule prohibiting the use of Tagalog (the primary language of Filipino nurses on staff at the hospital) was not an "English-only" rule and therefore not a discriminatory language restriction, as Hispanic nurses could still speak Spanish, etc. The logic behind this reasoning is rather weak, to say the least. If applied to racial distinctions, such reasoning would mean that a restaurant would not be acting in a discriminatory manner if it refused entry to Black customers, as long as other racial groups, such as Chinese, were allowed in with Whites!

discriminatory,[94] since international and national practices all appear to take into account a another element in the determination of what constitutes discrimination. Even when a government has adopted a course of action in language, which is unfavourable to individuals having a different primary tongue, the state policy may be reasonable[95] in light of its interests and particular demographical, historical and cultural context, as well as the burden and nature of the violation of an individual's rights and freedoms. What is reasonable in the particular context of one state may be completely unacceptable in another.[96]

How a court is to proceed when evaluating whether a law, affecting the language of state action and services, is discriminatory can be highly complex, but a fair balance must be struck between the general interests of the nation and the protection and respect of the rights of individuals who primarily use a different language. A number of factors can tentatively be identified from the decisions set forth above along with various international provisions going all the way back to the minorities treaties of the League of Nations era.

4.5.1   *National Unity*

Often perceived as a vital issue in a number of states is the policy of an official or single language as a means of ensuring that all citizens are united through a common language and thus able to participate fully in the national community and fully enjoy all of its benefits. This attitude has been dominant in many "immigrant" societies such as those states in North and South America which have an avowedly "assimilationist" policy, as well as in states which have more recently acquired independence and are attempting to create a new unifying national spirit to transcend tribal or ethnic divisions. Promotion of a single (usually the majority) language as the national language is not an uncommon, nor illegitimate, policy. In some cases, it may even be

---

[94] See *The Main Types and Causes of Discrimination, Memorandum submitted by the Secretary General* (1949), United Nations Publications, New York, at pp. 26-27:

   87. The word "discrimination" is used here in its pejorative sense, i.e., it is used to refer not to all differentiations, but only to distinctions which have been established to the detriment of individuals belonging to a particular group. The Sub-Commission on Prevention of Discrimination and Protection of Minorities has recognised this meaning of the word.

   88. Thus, discrimination might be defined as a detrimental distinction based on grounds which may not be attributed to the individual and which have no justified consequences in social, political or legal relations (colour, race, sex, etc.), or on grounds of membership in social categories (cultural, language, religious, political or other opinion, national circle, social origin, social class, property, birth or other status).

[95] The exact term may vary from one jurisdiction to another, but the basic principle remains the same. Whether speaking of "justifiable", "rationally related", or "necessary", it would seem that there must be a fair balance between the needs and interests of the state, and the interests, rights and freedoms of an individual.

[96] de Varennes, Fernand (1992), "Langue et discrimination au Canada", in *Canadian Journal of Law and Jurisprudence*, Vol. V, No. 2, 321-355, at pp. 321-355.

particularly understandable given the historical background of a number of countries, as in the case of the Baltic and other states of the former Soviet Union.[97]

What is perhaps not always appreciated is that the legitimate objective of having a state *lingua franca* does not mean that all language differences need to be eradicated. In the same fashion that it is unacceptable to oblige everyone to be of the same religion, and impossible for everyone to be of the same skin colour, modern democracies are increasingly tending to recognise that human differences such as language are not objectionable *per se*. In fact, the desire to adopt the use of an exclusive official language has rather sinister antecedents:

> The ideology of nationalism and the widespread ideas about the struggle for existence between superior and inferior races thus provided legitimacy for ousting "foreign" languages and cultures and absorbing the weak and so-called "primitive races". The aim was to make way for homogeneous national states. In Spain and the kingdom of Italy the unification process was combined with administrative centralism and the idea that the state should necessarily be based upon a linguistic and cultural monolithism. For Mussolini the denationalization of minorities was to promote an Italian "reconquest" of lost territories and "grandeur". Italianisation of schools and other cultural institutions was an aim based on a strong ideological foundation and an extremist vision of national greatness. In Franco's regime the concept of the Spanish language as the imperial language played a major role. Very few Spanish politicians challenged the policy of monolingualism in schools and acculturation of the various regions.[98]

Any policy favouring a single language to the exclusion of all others can be extremely risky if adopted in a context where a substantial number of individuals speaking a minority language do not know the official language, because it is then a factor promoting division rather than unification. Instead of integration, an ill-advised and inappropriate state language policy may have the opposite effect and cause a *levée de bouclier*. Whilst a state may quite legitimately impose a duty upon all of its nationals to learn the official language of government, as a means of avoiding the creation of ethnic ghettos as well as to create a common national unifying bond, this should not exclude the possibility of providing for other languages to be used by public authorities where it is reasonable to do so, especially where a large number of people are concentrated in the same region and share the same language.[99] A national language which

---

[97] Human Rights in the Republic of Estonia, Raimo Pekkanen and Hans Danelius, Special Rapporteurs (1991), in *Human Rights Law Journal*, Vol. 13, No. 5-6, 236-256, at p. 240.

[98] *Schooling, Educational Policy and Ethnic Identity* (1991), Janusz Tomiak (ed.), New York University Press, New York, at p. 39.

[99] As in the case of the Spanish **Constitution**, Article 3:
  3.1 *El castellano es la lengua española oficial del Estado. Todos los Españoles tienen el deber de conocerla y el derecho a usarla.*
  3.2 *Las demas lenguas españolas seran también oficiales en las respectivas Comunidades Autonomas de acuerdo con sus Estatutos.*

unifies does not have to be an exclusive language, even for official state activities and actions.[100]

Certainly, the argument for a common language would appear valid in order not to confine individuals to linguistic ghettos, thus limiting their access to the higher echelons of activities in the greater national community, but even this point should not be overemphasised: one of the most stable democracies in the Western World, Switzerland, has no need of a single common national language because of its highly decentralised form of cantonal governments which ensures, to a large degree, that access to resources, services and job opportunities would tend to be concentrated at the cantonal level and reflect one of the three main (official) languages used in the country.

Put differently, it is not always necessary nor even desirable to neglect the use of other languages in state activities and actions in the name of "nation building". A flexible policy, providing for the use of a non-official or regional language, whilst ensuring that the official language is also available for use, would be an appropriate response to a legitimate national interest in many situations, depending upon the other factors listed below. Such an approach would be more respectful of the principle of non-discrimination, for example, where large groups of individuals using a different primary language exist. Moreover, it has effectively been validated in a number of countries, including parts of the United States.[101]

To require from nationals of a state some knowledge of a common language, whilst constituting an additional burden for those individuals having a different primary language, would then appear to be a reasonable measure in many countries, as long as it does not entirely exclude the use of other languages.

---

[100] *Supra*, note 94, at p. 240:

> However, any such policy must be coupled with efforts to ensure that members of linguistic minorities are not at a substantial disadvantage in their dealings with the authorities. In particular, their right to access to the courts must not be made illusory by language requirements and they must also be able to make an effective use of their right to submit requests, petitions and appeals to the administrative authorities. In so far as they cannot use their own language before the courts and authorities, the assistance of interpreters or translators may be required.

[101] Garcia, Franco (1974), "Language Barriers to Voting: Literacy Tests and the Bilingual Ballot", in *Columbia Human Rights Law Review*, Vol. 6, 83-106, at p. 99:

> Although the state interest in encouraging the use of English and maintaining a single language system may be substantial, it is doubtful whether these goals may properly be achieved through denial of the ballot. In **Meyer v. Nebraska**, 262 U.S. 390 (1923), the Court emphasised that the lack of knowledge of English cannot be used as an excuse to deny citizens their fundamental rights [at p. 401]: "Certain fundamental rights [are guaranteed] to all those who speak other languages as well as to those born with English on the tongue. Perhaps it would be advantageous if all had ready understanding of our ordinary speech, but this cannot be coerced by methods which conflict with the Constitution — a desirable end cannot be promoted by prohibited means."

4.5.2   *Demographic Importance and Population Concentration*

A consistent consideration in many countries[102] and international instruments[103] when dealing with whether a difference of treatment on the ground of language is discriminatory is the number of individuals whose primary language is not the state-sanctioned idiom. Although the terminology varies, for example "substantial numbers", "according to the situation of each language", "appropriate measures", and "where possible", the basic principle remains the same: when a relatively large number of individuals use a particular language in a given state, it would appear unreasonable not to provide some level of state services and activities in their language. To some extent, this can be tied in to financial constraints (dealt with below) as has been acknowledged by the drafters of the **Convention-cadre sur la protection des minorités nationales:**

Conscients des difficultés inhérentes à la reconnaissance du droit, pour les minorités, d'utiliser leur propre langue dans leurs relations avec l'administration, les auteurs du projet de convention n'ont pas voulu énoncer un droit absolu, mais l'ont tempéré par la formule « dans la mesure du possible ». Cette condition signifie qu'un tel droit ne sera pas reconnu si par exemple les moyens financiers de l'État concerné sont insuffisants.[104]

---

[102] The United States' Food and Nutrition Service of the Department of Agriculture requires state agencies which administer Food Stamp programmes to provide bilingual staff and translated written materials in areas where there are a substantial number of low-income, non-English-speaking households. In general, a "substantial number" is defined as five percent of the low-income households in the area. A number of welfare agencies provide bilingual workers and translated materials to clients under a mandate by the Office of Civil Rights which has taken the position that failure to provide bilingual services results in unequal access to benefits and is unreasonable when there exists a sufficiently important concentration of individuals sharing a common, non-English language, thus constituting discrimination on the basis of national origin in violation of Title VI of the **Civil Rights Act.** California has adopted the same approach, by means of legislative measures recognising that individuals are entitled to forms and information related to public benefits in Spanish or in any other language spoken by a substantial number of the target population, and certain state agencies must provide bilingual staff if non-English-speakers exceed five percent of the clientele.
Notwithstanding claims that English and French have equal rights and privileges, Canadian practice in reality reflects much the same approach as the above examples in the United States, since most federal government activities and services are only offered in both official languages where there are sufficiently large concentrations of individuals speaking each official language.

[103] See amongst others the **Central European Initiative Instrument for the Protection of Minority Rights** (Articles 17 and 22), the **Document of the Copenhagen Meeting of the Conference on the Human Dimension** (Paragraph 34), the **European Charter for Regional or Minority Languages** (Articles 8-11), the **Draft of an International Convention on the Protection of National or Ethnic Groups or Minorities** (Articles 20 and 24), and the **Declaration on the Rights of Persons Belonging to National or Ethnic, Religious and Linguistic Minorities** (Article 4), all reprinted in the Appendix.

[104] Malinverni, Giorgio (1991), "Le projet de Convention pour la protection des minorités élaboré par la Commission européenne pour la démocratie par le droit", in *Revue universelle des droits de l'homme*, Vol. 3, No. 5, 157-165, at p. 161.

The number of speakers of a minority language is a factor which had already been recognised in the days of the minorities treaties, in relation to the equality principle in state education. For example, in the case of Poland, the treaty referred to towns and districts where there are "a considerable proportion of Polish nationals of other than Polish speech" in relation to the right to state schooling at the primary level.

Certainly if forty percent of a state's population uses as their primary vernacular a non-official language, state services such as public schools should be available to them, in their language, at all levels. The same should probably be true if they constitute thirty, twenty-five, or perhaps even twenty percent of the total national population. Below this percentage, it is more difficult to make a general statement on what is reasonable in a particular state, but it would generally appear to be unjustified to limit state activities to a language that is not the primary tongue of very large numbers of people.

Conversely, this implies that whilst some individuals will always be disadvantaged by the state when it favours one or a few language(s) to the exclusion of all others, no state is capable of using and providing all of its services and activities in every language spoken by individuals living on its territory. Even the most unilingual state in the world probably has speakers of a dozen or more languages in its territory, although ninety-nine percent of these may be composed of no more than a handful of individuals. It thus becomes a question of balance — of how many people are negatively impacted by the language preference of the government.

To give an example already seen in the United Nations system with the Breton cases, it is probably safe to conclude that generally legislation in France making French the language of public authorities and activities is not discriminatory because, realistically, Breton is only spoken by a relatively small number of people in the country, less than 300,000 people in the whole of France.[105] It would be difficult to attack French legislation in a case where the Breton language is not a highly significant demographical language. However, certain legislative measures could be adopted to offer a degree of government services, in a more limited manner, in some parts of Brittany. In other words, where speakers of Breton are numerous and concentrated, complete disregard of the primary language of these inhabitants, and the subsequent disadvantages and burdens they suffer because of this differential treatment, may be unreasonable and unjustified for certain administrative, educational or judicial state functions.

Tied in with the issue of relative number of individuals is geographic concentration, especially when one deals with progressively lower percentages of individuals. If, for example, only eight percent of the population in a country speaks a non-official language but they are concentrated in a small portion of the state — where they may even represent the majority — it becomes rather unreasonable not to permit some degree of use of their language in state services and activities. The high level of cantonal autonomy chosen by Switzerland has in large part allowed the use of this approach, for example, by providing access to public services and job opportunities to individuals who speak Italian even if they represent a rather small percentage (three percent) of the total population.

---

[105] *Mini-Guide to the Lesser Used Languages of the European Community* (1993), European Bureau for Lesser Used Languages, Dublin, at p. 9. Even this number is probably too high because the criterion to be used in determining whether there has been unfavourable differential treatment on the ground of language should be one's primary language and not mother tongue or ability to understand the language.

At even lower levels of relative numbers, the issue becomes difficult to evaluate. If percentage-wise, the number of individuals is fairly small, they can still be quite heavily concentrated in certain districts. Two examples of this type of situation are the Welsh-speakers in England and Breton-speakers in France. To determine whether or not a state is discriminating by practising an unfavourable language preference would require the consideration of all the other relevant factors, in order to arrive at a proper balancing of state interests versus the rights and interests of affected individuals.

Territorial concentration of individuals speaking a different language is a valid factor to take into account also in that greater concentration implies a higher number of individuals with little or no knowledge of the official or state-preferred language. Indeed, sufficiently concentrated linguistic groups tend to be self-replicating, self-sufficient communities where the language favoured by the state has minimal relevance:

> Sheer numbers have led to an infrastructure within the Spanish-speaking community which protects but also isolates the Spanish-speaker from the English-speaking community. In San Antonio, sixty-two percent of those low-income Mexican-Americans living in census tracts with more than 400 Spanish-speaking people could speak little or no English. A similar survey in census tracts in Los Angeles with high concentrations of low-income Mexican-Americans revealed that fifty-one percent of the residents could not speak any English. Another study of Puerto Ricans in New York found more than seventeen percent of the children and presumably almost twice that number of adults spoke little or no English. A study of Spanish-speaking people in the south west revealed that they averaged little more than eight years of education. When students left school, nearly three-fourths of them were below grade level. Inadequately equipped by education and disabled by language from taking jobs outside of the Spanish-speaking community, they lost much of the English which they had learned, and became further isolated.[106]

Whenever a linguistic minority is numerous and compact, it is more likely that many of its members are not fluent in the majority or official language. This by no means implies an unwillingness to learn the majority or official language, but rather reflects a natural consequence of their situation: in most aspects of their daily lives, these people will be in contact with other members of their community; as a result, they will have relatively few occasions or little need to use the official language. Therefore, despite a willingness to learn the official or state-favoured language, a particularly large linguistic community will react in a negative way to a monolingual government policy because some of its members are at a disadvantage as they have had little opportunity or need to use the official language.

4.5.3 *Differential Treatment between Citizens and Non-Citizens*

Non-discrimination does not signify that a state must in the allocation of its resources treat everyone in the same way in every situation. For example, it does not appear unreasonable for a state to privilege its own citizens and permanent residents over tourists or short-term residents

---

[106] Safford, Joan Bainbridge (1977), "No Comprendo: The Non-English-speaking Defendant and the Criminal Process", in *Journal of Criminal Law and Criminology*, Vol. 68, 15-30, at p. 17.

when determining who will have access to certain services. This does not suggest that non-citizens can be denied fundamental human rights or essential services in general. Depending on the nature of the service or benefit, a state may be entitled to favour its own citizens before others. In language matters, this means that a state can validly maintain that it need not offer exactly the same benefit to non-citizens and that it is reasonable to respond primarily to the linguistic composition of those members of its population that are citizens or permanent residents.

It must be emphasised that this factor has to be balanced with all the other considerations such as disadvantage to the individual, type and level of the service, financial resources of the state, etc. in order to determine in the end whether the state linguistic arrangement is reasonable.

4.5.4   *Individual Preference*

Even if a large number of individuals have a different primary language, a state could validly claim that it would not be discriminatory to refrain from offering services or activities in their language if these people freely choose not to use their language in their contacts and relations with public authorities. There is no denying that for a number of individuals the official language, or the language of the majority, will have a high level of attraction and they may wish to use it exclusively in many activities, even if it is not their primary vernacular.

Despite this, great care should be taken when considering this factor as it is fairly easy for a state to discourage individuals, directly or indirectly, from making a free choice. For example, in the Province of Nova Scotia, Canada, a group of French-speaking parents fought for years in order to obtain a primary school where education would primarily be offered in their language, despite the fact that this right is in theory guaranteed to them by the **Constitution**. Even when the parents succeeded in court, the local public school authorities selected an older school that no one else was utilising, quite a distance from where most of the children resided. As a result, faced with sending their children far away to an inadequate structure, many parents felt it was not worth upholding their preference, in view of how the authorities had presented their options.

Another trap which should be avoided in this regard is a claim that no actual request or demand has been made that public authorities use or offer their services in a minority language. If there are no established mechanisms to evaluate such a demand, individuals in a minority context would not be encouraged to come forward with their demands, particularly when they know full well that the state has no intention nor interest in responding to their preference.

Individual preference implies finally that state services and activities not be restricted to native speakers of the minority language as there may be recent immigrants or others who would prefer integrating into the local community where they live, even if the language of the community is not the official nor preferred language of the state.

4.5.5   *Practical Considerations, and Financial and Professional Resources*

Whilst "language is an automatic signalling system, second only to race in identifying targets for possible privilege or discrimination",[107] it must be admitted that a state has no choice, in practical terms, but to limit the language(s) used in governmental activity and public services.

---

[107] Deutsch, K. A. (1975), "The Political Significance of Linguistic Conflicts", in Savard & Vigneault (eds.), *Les États multilingues*, Presses de l'Université Laval, Québec, at p. 7.

A major factor which may weigh against a declaration that a law or state practice favouring one or a few languages is discriminatory can be lack of resources, either human, financial or material. Particularly in the case of languages not spoken by large populations, it would be too onerous to translate official documents, have employees available in sufficient numbers in every department, etc. In cases where numbers are small it may quite simply be financially impractical to provide every type of service in the minority language. For practical reasons, it can therefore be acceptable differential treatment on the ground of language to limit the number of languages to be used by the state.[108]

In the case of state education, there is also the situation where a language may be ill-equipped to face the exigencies of a modern school curriculum. A language may not yet have been reduced to writing or may not have developed a vocabulary adapted to the needs of a classroom. These difficulties would of course have to be surmounted if teaching in such language is to be possible. A state may therefore validly claim that it is reasonable not to provide for public education (or other types of services, especially those requiring written documents) in such a language if it is not feasible to access the required material and terminology. The relevance of this last point should not be exaggerated, however, as any language can be reduced to written form and can develop the appropriate vocabulary, given sufficient resources.[109]

4.5.6 *Legal or Traditional Concessions*

It could be argued that due consideration must be given to the case of individuals belonging to groups which have historically been granted special privileges or legal recognition in respect to the use of their language by public authorities. Any move by a state to set aside these concessions would appear more difficult to defend, and more intolerable to the groups and individuals concerned.

Indigenous peoples, in particular, may have a strong argument that they should receive state services such as education in their primary language, beyond what a strictly "numerical" criterion

---

[108] Even the financial consequences should not be exaggerated. In most public programmes, personnel costs are the main item of expenditure. This means that establishing a bilingual service instead of a unilingual one may involve displacing some people with bilingual individuals but it would normally require few additional personnel.

[109] Although some languages may be technically under-developed in terms of vocabulary or due to the absence of a written form, nothing in the structure of any language would preclude it from being adapted to become a vehicle of modern civilisation. See *The Use of Vernacular Languages in Education, supra*, note 86, and Ajulo, S.B. (1985), "Law, Language and International Organisations in Africa: The Case of ECOWAS", in *Journal of African Law*, Vol. 29, No. 1, 1-24, at pp. 12-13:

Alexandre, a French linguist and Africanist, in his paper entitled *Linguistic Problems of Contemporary Africa*, observed: "It should be wrong to say that African languages are a barrier to the teaching of science and technical subjects. The syntactical structure of those known to me would not provide any major obstacle to the pursuit of logical reasoning." Further, he admitted that the vocabulary of the African languages lack, for the moment, technical terminology. However, he contended that that should not constitute an insurmountable problem, "since, in fact the international technical terminology is based on an artificial assembly of Greek and Latin roots."

would perhaps normally warrant. In the case of indigenous peoples, the state may have a greater duty to respect their wishes in view of the nature of the relationship between the two, and of the duties and obligations involved. In other words, the threshold that must be reached in order for a state to demonstrate that legislation creating differential treatment on the ground of language is reasonable may be higher in the case of individuals using an indigenous language. This point of view is strongly reflected in treaties, declarations and practices currently emanating in international milieux[110] and countries.[111]

Other individuals who have historically been allowed to enjoy a recognised right or privilege to state services and activities in their primary language could also argue that the state has a heavier burden in demonstrating that its measures are not discriminatory. This factor has long been recognised, having being mentioned in the 1957 UN *Study of Discrimination in Education* by Special Rapporteur Ammoun, who admitted that the prohibition of teaching in a language can constitute a "formidable instrument of oppression and discrimination, especially when the schools possessed by the group are closed... against the will of the members of the distinct group".[112]

Finally, it would be in a state's own interest to consider the potentially destabilising effect of a challenge to already established language practices. A linguistic community with any numerical strength is unlikely to accept lightly any curtailment of previously enjoyed rights or privileges in relation to its language. A similar reaction could ensue in the case of measures affecting local or regional autonomy matters, since such institutional arrangements are likely to carry with them a corresponding degree of language autonomy for territorially based minorities. For example, one of the incidents leading up to the Croatian-Serbian conflict was the Croatian government's decision in the spring of 1990 to alter the **Constitution** so as to strip Croatian Serbs of autonomy. Krajina's local authorities were allegedly to be purged of Serbs, and signs in the Cyrillic script were to be replaced with the Latin-character versions used by Croats. Similarly, Slovakia's removal of the bilingual (Slovakian-Hungarian) designation by public authorities of towns and villages on traffic signs was perceived as a step backward which, when combined with other factors, led to a serious escalation of tensions.

4.5.7   *Compensatory Factors*

In some states, a government may be tempted to enforce laws and regulations aimed at correcting what are perceived to be unjust or oppressive language practices in the past. Many aspects of Latvian and Estonian legislation not only have the effect of making Latvian and Estonian the privileged languages to be used by public authorities; they are also to receive privileged

---

[110] Articles 14 and 15 of the UN's draft **Declaration on the Rights of Indigenous Peoples**, reprinted in Section 1.1.2 of the Appendix, do not appear to require any significant number of speakers of an indigenous language for individuals to be entitled to state supported activities such as education in their language.

[111] See in particular the evolution of indigenous linguistic policies in New Zealand, Australia, Finland, Norway, Mexico, Nicaragua, and the United States discussed in Chapter 7 on indigenous peoples.

[112] *Supra*, note 84.

assistance in order to redress the effect of pro-Russian policies during the period of Soviet domination.

A somewhat similar point of view has been raised in Spain, as the following extract shows:

> [T]he peripheral languages, which were not recognised at all and even actively persecuted under the Franco regime, have been elevated to the status of fully official language of their Community... While Castilian has always and without interruption been the language of the administration and of the educational system, Catalan, Basque and Galician must start from scratch: a specialised administrative language must be created, civil servants, educators and journalists must be trained in the language, text books and teaching aids must be printed, etc. In other words...the purpose is not to exercise a revenge for past injuries, but to eliminate the effects of this injustice for the future. Several Statutes of Autonomy accompany the provision of the formal equal status of Castilian and their respective regional language with a further provision authorising the Autonomous Community's political organs to enhance the status of the minority language, so that it can effectively overcome its legacy of oppression.[113]

Legal measures aimed at redressing the legacy of past state practices by stimulating the use of the now favoured language can take various forms: greater subsidies for preparing educational material in the preferred language, or financial assistance for book publishing, cinema or other cultural activities.[114]

It is submitted that government attempts to correct past objectionable state legislation and practices, particularly those which amounted to violations of human rights such as freedom of expression or the right to equality, are legitimate considerations which ought to be assessed in conjunction with other factors in determining the reasonableness of a present-day language preference.

Similarly, it is not objectionable *per se* for a state to assist more generously those individuals who may prefer using a language spoken by a small group or favour the development and use of a language which had not until recently developed a written form or scientific vocabulary.

4.5.8 *Level and Type of State Services or Benefits*

The appropriate level of language use by public authorities will vary according to a linguistic minority's demographic status and other factors already mentioned, but it should be remembered that there is no fixed level of services or model because of the many variables. Whether it be by the use of the words "reasonable", "possible", "justifiable", "according to the status of the language", etc., almost every relevant international instrument or national law adheres to a

---

[113] *Supra*, note 2, at p. 113.

[114] See Article 23(1) of the **Catalan Normalisation Act**, quoted in de Witte, *supra*, note 2, at p. 114:
La Generalitat debe estimular y fomentar con medidas adecuadas el teatro y la producción de cine en catalán, el doblaje y la substitución en catalán de películas no catalánas, los espectáculos y cualquier otra manifestación cultural pùblica en lengua catalán.

flexible, albeit vague formula in order to allow the adoption of steps and measures which reflect the specific situation in a given state and the number and needs of affected individuals.

It is for this reason the **European Charter for Regional or Minority Languages** presents a "sliding-scale" model: the bottom end of the scale suggesting the minimum right which members of a smaller, though sufficiently numerous, linguistic minority can expect, whereas the higher end of the scale includes much more generous rights, in recognition of the much larger number of individuals involved. A state would normally be unjustified in not granting more services in a given language as the number of beneficiaries increases.

Article 8 of the **Charter** demonstrates how the sliding-scale approach affects the type and level of language use in the area of state education:

1. With regard to education, the parties undertake, within the territory in which such languages are used, according to the situation of each of these languages, and without prejudice to the teaching of the official language(s) of the state, to:

a.　I. make available preschool education in the relevant regional or minority languages; or

II. make available a substantial part of preschool education in the relevant regional or minority languages; or

III. apply one of the measures provided for under (I) and (II) above at least to those pupils whose families so request and whose number is considered sufficient; or

IV. if the public authorities have no direct competence in the field of preschool education, favour and/or encourage the application of the measures referred to under (I) to (III) above;

b.　I. make available primary education in the relevant regional or minority languages; or

II. make available a substantial part of primary education in the relevant regional or minority languages; or

III. provide, within primary education, for the teaching of the relevant regional or minority languages as an integral part of the curriculum; or

IV. apply one of the measures provided for under (I) to (III) above at least to those pupils whose families so request and whose numbers is considered sufficient;

c.　I. make available secondary education in the relevant regional or minority languages; or

II. make available a substantial part of secondary education in the relevant regional or minority languages; or

III. provide, within secondary education, for the teaching of the relevant regional or minority languages as an integral part of the curriculum; or

IV. apply one of the measures provided for under (I) to (III) above at least to those pupils who, or where appropriate whose families, so wish in a number considered sufficient;...[115]

---

[115] The full text of this provision is reprinted in Section 2.2.6 of the Appendix.

At the bottom end of the scale, a state could limit itself to teaching the language of a national minority at preschool. If the number of pupils whose families so request is considered sufficient, a state should provide more generous rights and go up the scale to a substantial part of their education in the language of the minority. If the numbers of pupils are even higher, the state should proceed to a complete preschool programme in the language of the minority, and so on with all of the higher levels of education, always the more generous where the number of pupils is sufficiently large. The same approach would apply in general to the use of languages by public officials in other areas, including administrative and judicial affairs.

4.5.9   Social, Cultural and Religious Considerations

In **Groener v. Minister for Education**,[116] the European Court of Justice took into account the emotional and symbolic ties between the Irish language and Irish society generally in determining whether the state's policy constituted reasonable differential treatment. The requirement of some knowledge of Irish by teachers, as part of a state policy for its promotion, was justified according to the court even though the subject of the course taught by Groener was not linguistic and that teaching at the vocational school is normally in English. Although the example of the Irish language may at first glance appear unique, it is far from so being. In the case of indigenous peoples on the American Continent and Australasia, there is often a strong desire to regain what is perceived to be an integral part of their heritage, even though many, if not a majority, of these indigenous peoples no longer use their ancestral language as a primary vernacular. Recent national and international trends seem to confirm the high value of language maintenance for those concerned.

Thus, a state is entitled to consider the role a language plays as part of the social or cultural composition of individuals and community alike. Even if the imposition of language requirements such as in **Groener v. Minister for Education** was not directly connected with the job at hand, the central position of Irish in the national psyche led to the conclusion that the differential treatment on the ground of language was not unreasonable.

Similarly, it would appear to be quite appropriate to consider religious factors when determining whether state language distinctions or preferences are justified. Whether it is Hebrew in Israel or Arabic in many Muslim countries, language can be much more than a means of communication. To illustrate the type of prominence language may have for religious reasons, sociologist Joshua Fishman quoted the following observations concerning Arabic:

> The Qur'an is accepted as the highest linguistic achievement of the Arabic language in every possible respect; nobody can possibly vie with it; everybody should try humbly to emulate it. Nothing should be written which does not comply with the linguistic, idiomatic, literacy, and rhetorical conditions obtaining in the Qur'an. It would be considered almost treasonable if an Arab were to misspell a word or break one of the intricate numerous rules of Arabic grammar, especially if he were expected to have known the right form.[117]

---

[116] *Supra*, note 57.

[117] Fishman, Joshua (1972), *Language and Nationalism*, Newbury House Publishers, Rawley, Massachusetts, at p. 141.

Language can thus have religious or social significance that should not simply be ignored, although it must be kept in mind that this does not permit a state to adopt legislation which would infringe freedom of expression, not reflect the presence of a large number of speakers of another language, or disregard other human rights.

4.5.10 *Legitimacy of Goal or Objective*

Whether in the **Belgian Linguistic Case**,[118] the Inter-American Court of Human Rights' opinion in the **Costa Rican Naturalisation Case**,[119] or other international and national decisions involving discrimination, a frequent factor considered when evaluating the reasonability of differential treatment on the ground of language is the purpose of legislation or practice in issue. For example, the objective of ensuring social and political peace in Belgium through the division of the country along linguistic lines was deemed legitimate, in the **Belgian Linguistic Case**, just as in Switzerland, the need to maintain the linguistic homogeneity of cantons is considered as a legitimate, even vital, objective.[120]

In **Ballantyne, Davidson and McIntyre v. Canada**, the Québec commercial sign case, the Human Rights Committee even went so far as to acknowledge that the government could validly seek to protect the French language in Québec but that such a legitimate objective could not be invoked in order to ban the use of non-official languages in private affairs, although these comments were not specifically made in the context of the application of the principle of non-discrimination.

If legislation favouring certain individuals through a policy of adopting the exclusive or privileged use of one or a few languages is for illegitimate reasons, it would in almost all cases be deemed unjustifiable. For example, English literacy requirements for voting as practised at one time in the United States and former Rhodesia were clearly aimed at excluding Blacks or

---

[118] *Supra*, note 63, at pp. 884-885:
   Article 14 does not prohibit distinctions in treatment which are founded on an objective assessment of essentially different factual circumstances and which, being based on the public interest, strike a fair balance between the protection of the interests of the community and respect for the rights and freedoms safeguarded by the Convention. In examining whether the legal provisions which have been attacked satisfy these criteria, the Court finds that their purpose is to achieve linguistic unity within the two large regions of Belgium in which a large majority of the population speaks only one of the two national languages.

[119] *Supra*, note 53, at paragraphs 55, 56 and 57:
   Accordingly, no discrimination exists if the difference in treatment has a legitimate purpose and if it does not lead to situations which are contrary to justice, to reason or to the nature of things. It follows that there would be no discrimination in differences in treatment of individuals by a state when the classifications selected are based on substantial factual differences and not be arbitrary, capricious, despotic or in conflict with the essential oneness and dignity of humankind.

[120] In **Association de l'École française und Mitbeteiligte v. Regierungsrat und Verwaltungsgericht des Kantons Zürich** (1965) Arrêts du Tribunal fédéral 91 I 480 (Switzerland), a decision of 31 March 1965, the court ruled that regulations of the canton of Zürich requiring members of the French-speaking minority to send their children to German-language schools were justified by the need to preserve the linguistic homogeneity of the canton.

Spanish-speaking citizens from exercising their right to vote. Such differential treatment on the ground of language for a wholly illegitimate goal should rarely, if ever, be validated as a reasonable language distinction. It would most likely be considered totally unacceptable in almost every case to prohibit the use of non-official languages because some individuals are intolerant of others, just as adopting legislation segregating individuals, because some dislike others due to the colour of their skin, can never constitute a legitimate goal:

> Just as the Constitution forbids banishing blacks to the back of the bus so as not to arouse the racial animosity of the preferred white passengers, it also forbids ordering Spanish-speaking patrons to the "back booth or out" to avoid antagonizing English-speaking beer drinkers... The lame justification that a discriminatory policy helps preserve the peace is as unacceptable in bar rooms as it was in buses. Catering to prejudice out of fear of provoking greater prejudice only perpetuates racism. Courts faithful to the Fourteenth Amendment will not permit, either by camouflage or cavalier treatment, equal protection so to be profaned.[121]

4.5.11 *Proportionality between Aims and Means*

All of the above factors must be balanced in a final assessment of whether the end result is reasonable.[122] In its *General Comment on Non-Discrimination*, the United Nations Human Rights Committee suggested that not every differentiation of treatment would be discrimination, if the criteria for differentiation are reasonable and objective and if the aim is to achieve a purpose which is legitimate under the **Covenant**.[123]

In **Groener v. Minister for Education**, the European Court of Justice recognised that any requirement of linguistic knowledge outside Article 3(1) of **Regulation 1612/68** must not be disproportionate to the object of the policy. In the **Belgian Linguistic Case**, the European Court on Human Rights clearly stated that Article 14 does not prohibit every distinction in treatment. What was required was an objective assessment of the facts and, whilst considering the public interest involved, striking a fair balance between the protection of the interests of the community and the respect for the rights and freedoms safeguarded by the **Convention**.[124]

---

[121] **Hernandez v. Erlenbusch**, 368 F.Supp. 752 (1973) (United States).

[122] Despite differences in terminology (some courts speak of "rational", or "non-arbitrary", or "proportional"), the standards used by courts in many countries are for the most part similar: in the end there must be a balancing act in order to determine whether or not a state's differential treatment based on characteristics such as language, race or religion is acceptable. Semantically, there are certainly distinctions to be made between a test requiring "non-arbitrary" state behaviour and "proportional" conduct, the former seemingly indicating that courts should show a greater degree of restraint in assessing whether or not the behaviour of public authorities is discriminatory. In other words, legislation prescribing differential treatment can be disproportionate but it is not irrational. By and large, most states and the interpretation favoured by most international bodies lean towards determining the reasonability of state actions *via* their "proportionality".

[123] *General Comment on Non-Discrimination*, *supra*, note 43, at paragraph 13.

[124] *Supra*, note 63, at p. 884.

Some courts in the United States appear to have adopted a similar formula:

[D]ifferentiation as to race, language, or religion is discriminatory when it is unreasonable, arbitrary, unfair, capricious, or invidious; and, conversely, differentiation that occurs for a legitimate purpose and is rationally related to the purpose and necessary to its achievement is non-discriminatory.[125]

The same approach has essentially been employed in many jurisdictions including Canada,[126] Spain,[127], Belgium,[128] and even the United Nations:

That the right to equal treatment as to language has to be balanced off against other compelling interests is a principle that all accept. That is, they find a balancing test reasonable and justifiable. Everyone accepts the rule that for a right to be implemented there must be a relationship of proportionality between the benefits and the costs.[129]

The basic principle, as stated above, is that the requirement of use or knowledge of a certain language is a legitimate criterion which may be used by a state in determining who will have access to and receive the most benefit — or the least disadvantage — but only when the specific

---

[125] *Supra*, note 15, at p. 6.

[126] *Supra*, note 26, at pp. 13-14:

Dans l'affaire Oakes...le juge en chef Dickson a énoncé de la façon suivante le critère des moyens, ou "critère de proportionnalité": "À mon avis, un critère de proportionnalité comporte trois éléments importants. Premièrement, les mesures adoptées doivent être soigneusement conçues pour atteindre l'objectif en question. Elles ne doivent être ni arbitraires, ni inéquitables, ni fondées sur des considérations irrationnelles. Bref, elles doivent avoir un lien rationnel avec l'objectif en question. Deuxièmement, même à supposer qu'il y ait un tel lien rationnel, le moyen choisi doit être de nature à porter "le moins possible" atteinte au droit ou à la liberté en question... Troisièmement, il doit y avoir proportionnalité entre les effets des mesures restreignant un droit ou une liberté garantis par la Charte et l'objectif reconnu comme "suffisament important"."

[127] Decision of the Constitutional Tribunal of 2 July 1981, Boletin de Jurisprudencia Constitucional, 1981, No. 4, 243 (Spain), at p. 250:

[L]a igualdad es sólo violada si la desigualdad está desprovista de una justificación objetiva y razonable y la existencia de dicha justificación debe apreciarse en relacion a la finalidad y efectos de la medida considerada, debiendo darse una relación razonable de proporcionalidad entre los medios empleados y la finalidad perseguida.

[128] Council of State decision of 1 February 1973, Pasicrisie 1974, IV, 109 (Belgium), quoted in de Witte, *supra*, note 2, at p. 69.

[129] *Supra*, note 15, at pp. 16-17.

context or object of regulation makes the language criterion a balanced and reasonable requirement.[130]

4.6   DISCRIMINATION AND LANGUAGE FORMS AND SCRIPTS

4.6.1   *Disadvantages Due to Script Differences*

Script differences may render a language unintelligible for individuals only familiar with one script, even if phonetically the languages are identical. A person who has learned Serbo-Croatian in its Cyrillic script will normally be unable to comply, or at least be at a disadvantage, if required to read and write the same language with the Latin alphabet. In other words, script preferences imply the same type of differential treatment, at least as it relates to written usage of language, as would any other type of language distinction. People who have to satisfy job requirements demanding a strong ability to write a language in a script with which they are unfamiliar or less proficient, be it Arabic, Greek, Chinese, or Gurmukhi, are as much at a disadvantage as if they were being requested to have knowledge of a foreign language, even though phonetically there may be relatively insignificant variations. As with any other type of differential treatment on the ground of language, it then becomes a question of determining whether the state preference for one of the language's scripts is reasonable given the demographic reality of the state population, etc.

Tension related to script differences has appeared in a number of countries in Eastern and Central Europe, as well as in Asia. One example is the Croatian-Serbian conflict which was fanned when it was reported that the Croatian government had decided in 1990 to replace signs in the Cyrillic script with the Latin-character version in Krajina. Another conflict in Moldova[131] arose because individuals felt that the use of the Cyrillic script as medium of instruction for the Moldovan language in state schools is differential treatment and that it is to their disadvantage, as they claim to be more familiar with the Latin script.

Although recognition of script differences is to be found in a number of state constitutions (India, Kampuchea, Pakistan, Slovenia, Vietnam, amongst others), there has been scant legal discussion or consideration of this issue. The Supreme Court of India has on at least one occasion indirectly conceded the existence of a link between language and script, although great care should be taken in assessing Indian case law and its relevance in establishing a relationship between non-discrimination based upon language and script preference by the state, as a number

---

[130] In some cases, the use of language criteria and the differential treatment of individuals based upon language is obviously rational when it comes to selecting the personnel of a public authority or administrative service which is obliged to use this language. The same remains true for jobs in the private sector where a certain linguistic skill forms an inherent part of the job description and is rationally related to the tasks to be accomplished.

[131] On 2 September 1991, six days after Moldova declared its independence, the Second Extraordinary Session of the People's Deputies of the Dniestr Area declared a separate republic. Although many factors were obviously involved in the events leading up to the declaration, there is no doubt that the reaction to the Moldovan language policy which promoted the Latin alphabet over the Cyrillic and required Romanian in all schools played a role.

of constitutional provisions in that country also recognise a minority's right to conserve its distinct script.

In **D.A.V. College, Bhatinda v. State of Punjab,**[132] the D.A.V. College Trust Society, representing members of the Arya Samajis linguistic minority in Punjab, challenged the constitutional validity of Article 4(2) of the **Punjabi University Act, 1961** and subsequent regulations prescribing Gurmukhi script as the only medium of instruction and examination. They submitted that this amounted to a violation of Article 30(1) of the **Constitution**[133] since it affected their right to establish and administer their educational institutions in the language of their choice.

The Supreme Court concluded that whilst the state was entitled to choose Punjabi and the Gurmukhi script as the exclusive medium of instruction in the university, it could not compel affiliated colleges, established and administered by linguistic minorities, to teach in a particular language nor to give examinations in that language. Although Article 30(1) does not specifically refer to script differences, the Supreme Court did not hesitate to associate script as an element of language choice.

One Asian author has made the following observations on script differences:

> "Language" cannot, therefore, be interpreted in a solely linguistic sense to exclude such aspects as script, which may serve as symbols of group identity and form a heritage rooted in culture or religion. The use of Arabic script by Urdu-speaking Muslims of India and Pakistan is especially illustrative, as script makes a significant difference as a medium of communication in a world of literacy. The imposition of one form of script on a society that has used a different type for ages could be a form of domination encompassing language both as merely a means of communication and as the medium of a particular tradition or religion. When language has social, cultural, and political attributes apart from the mere communication value, it can ease any scheme of domination. For example, to require a group that has for centuries used one script to use another in all official matters could mean the exclusion of its members from public service, even if the official language is intelligible to its members. Similarly, the exclusive promotion of one language could mean the growth of a generation of the speakers of the other language who are denied linguistic access to their religion or culture when they are transmitted through a particular script. Arguably, in this sense each of the language variants should be considered autonomous to constitute "language" in minority protection.[134]

4.6.2   *Ideographic Script and Phonetically Distinct Languages*

Another problem sometimes overlooked when referring to language differences is that of ideographic scripts, which present a situation quite distinct from that of phonetically-based

---

[132] (1971) 2 S.C.R. 261 (India).

[133] Article 30(1) of the **Constitution of India** states: "All minorities, whether based on religion or language, shall have the right to establish and administer educational institutions of their choice."

[134] Ramga, Philip Vuciri (1992), "The Bases of Minority Identity", in *Human Rights Quarterly*, Vol. 14, 409-428, at pp. 427-428.

alphabets. For example, Chinese ideograms remain essentially the same whether used in Beijing, Xian, or Shanghai.[135] However, oral speech based on these ideograms is a completely different matter. These are phonetically-distinct languages which, despite using the same alphabet, are mutually unintelligible. When spoken, Cantonese or Mandarin are as "foreign" to each other as Spanish is to Ukrainian, although in the ideographic script there are essentially no differences.[136]

Whether it be for employment advancement within public authorities or entrance exams to universities, any state preference for one of the spoken forms of Chinese to the exclusion of others will disadvantage speakers of the other oral forms of the language. This type of differential treatment should be considered as a distinction on the ground of language, albeit only when involving verbal requirements. Thus, the approach in the case of phonetically-distinct languages sharing an identical ideographic script is no different from the above model proposed for evaluating whether the state's differential treatment is discrimination on the ground of language: is the differential treatment when the state favours one spoken form reasonable, given the objectives and interests of the state, the legitimacy of the goals sought in relation to the disadvantage or burden imposed on individuals, their numbers, the proportionality of the measure and its effects, etc.?

4.7 THIRD WORLD STATES, DISCRIMINATION, AND WORLD (EUROPEAN) LANGUAGES

Siempre la lengua fue compañera del imperio.[137]

4.7.1 General Observations

Discrimination will occur when differential treatment on the ground of language is unfavourable for some individuals or creates a preference for others, but an unusual problem exists when almost all inhabitants of a state find themselves disadvantaged by the language selected for use by public authorities. Can this be discrimination if everyone is denied equally the use of their primary language by the state machinery?

---

[135] Nevertheless, there are important differences between the ideographic script used in the People's Republic of China and the script used by Chinese in other countries such as Taiwan and Singapore.

[136] *Supra*, note 134, at pp. 426-427:

> [The] common name "Chinese" represents related languages such as Cantonese, Hakka, and Mandarin, which are as different from each other as the romance languages of French, Spanish, and Portuguese; the sole reason for such reference is common script. The fact of common script does not warrant the designation of any two languages as one, while common speech patterns do. The legal issue then is whether language should be determined with reference to speech or script or both.

[137] de Nebrija, Antonio (1492), "Gramàtica castellana", quoted in *Les langues autochtones du Québec* (1992), Jacques Maurais (ed.), Les Publications du Québec, Québec.

108 *Language and Non-Discrimination*

In order to understand how such a consideration may validly be raised, the context in which it occurs must be explained. A number of countries, all former colonies of European nations, face unique problems and solutions which are quite different from the rest of the world. Many have chosen as the main language for use by public authorities the tongue of their former colonial masters, despite the fact that it is usually not the primary speech of the vast majority of their nationals. This policy rests on two basic considerations, one being a valid point when applied in a reasonable and balanced manner, whilst the other remains, to say the least, suspect.

4.7.2 *Preference for a "Neutral" Lingua Franca*

Because newly-independent states, particularly in Africa, were artificial political constructs with little relation to the actual composition or political aspirations of their inhabitants, many governments found themselves facing deep-rooted tribal conflicts and divisions which could easily lead to wholesale instability unless state borders, as imperfect as they were, were unhesitatingly defended at all costs. Instead of being perceived as throwing the advantage decisively one way or another in the rivalries of the various domestic language communities, these states generally found it easier to simply maintain the primacy of a tribally "neutral" European language, most often French or English:

> The aim of introducing English is to introduce an official language that will steer the people away from lingo-tribal affiliations and differences and create conditions conductive to national unity in the realm of language.[138]

This aim of national unity through a common language is not objectionable as such, and the highly complex linguistic and ethnic mosaics in many former colonies would appear to support the argument that in a number of states such a policy is not intrinsically unreasonable given the problems facing these nations, even though a majority of individuals would have been better served in areas such as education and job opportunities if their primary language were in official use by public authorities.[139] The state interests in such an approach are strong. As political scientist Jean Laponce has pointed out, use of a international *lingua franca* like English and French avoids the domination of one linguistic group (Tagalog in the Philippines, Hindi in India, Chinese in Singapore) on individuals belonging to long established language communities which are numerically or politically weaker.[140] Other advantages in adopting a language of wider communication (i.e. an international European language) can be briefly summarised as follows:

1. Educational material, television and radio programmes, are more readily available.

---

[138] Alexander, Neville (1989), *Language Policy and National Unity in South Africa/Azania*, Buchu Books, Cape Town, at p. 44.

[139] In reality, many developing countries which have adopted English or French as an official language also use indigenous languages in state-funded educational institutions, at least at the primary level, as well as in regions where speakers of indigenous languages are particularly numerous and concentrated.

[140] Laponce, Jean A. (1987), *Languages and Their Territories*, University of Toronto Press, Toronto, at p. 190.

2. Its vocabulary is already developed to fulfil the exigencies of a modern society.

3. Knowledge of such a language will give all inhabitants of a developing country the ability to access international information and interact with individuals worldwide.

4. It can easily serve as a "link language" between the linguistic communities of a state, since it is "neutral" as far as advancing the interests of a particular ethno-linguistic group.

Unfortunately, it is far from clear whether the above advantages can truly be found by adopting the quasi-exclusive use of an international, European language. For one thing, the use of English or French in these countries may be "ethnically" neutral; however, it favours a very small minority of people, whilst further disadvantaging the majority of inhabitants:

We have to understand that unless the vast majority of the South African population are organically motivated to learn and use English for the conduct of their affairs, English will become or remain, as in so many African and Asian countries, the language of the privileged neo-colonialist middle class. In India, according to the UNIN Study on Namibia: "... English, the language of colonial dominance, was allowed to continue as the link language. But this was fraught with dangerous socio-economic consequences. It perpetuated a small English-knowing elite, largely urban, who clamoured for a policy of keeping education, as one commentator put is, in a linguistic polythene bag". In sharp contrast, 80 % of the population living in rural areas continued to be a disadvantaged group further hampered by their ignorance of English..."[141]

Moreover, only a fraction of the population realistically needs to communicate with the "rest" of the world, so that the need for an international language as the main medium of public and educational authorities will only be felt by this elite.

The continued domination of a colonial language also strikes some emotional cords, although the following comments probably reflect the realisation that it is somewhat illogical for public authorities to use a little known language when people in large areas share an indigenous vernacular:

I wonder why we should continue to make English the mode of expression in our courts... I wonder how Nigeria can claim to have shed all vestiges of colonialism when her citizens have to state their grievances in a foreign language...which has no equivalent for most of them... It is my humble and respectful submission that Nigerian courts should endeavour to encourage the conduct of proceedings in all courts in the language of the area of the court. This has to begin sometime.[142]

---

[141] *Supra*, note 138, at p. 60; see also *Planning Language, Planning Inequality, supra*, note 89, at p. 5: "The disadvantage of the SWAPO policy is that only those few Namibians who speak English will be able to serve in the government and other official positions. As a result, English-speakers will have significant advantages in education and employment."

[142] Adeyemi, O. A. (1972), "A Day in the Criminal Court", in T.O. Elias (ed.), *The Nigerian Magistrate and the Offender*, Ethiope, Benin City, Nigeria, at pp. 26-27.

By using a language not widely spoken by the inhabitants of a country, a state may also be concentrating its scarce resources in assisting a minute elite, since it is unlikely that most developing countries in such a situation are able to obtain a sufficient supply of qualified teachers to teach English or French properly in every region. As a result, well-off urban elites will continue to profit by the maintenance of English and French as official languages, ensuring privileged access to job opportunities within the state bureaucracy and legal and political machinery — a main source of employment in many developing countries — since they can keep their children in schools for a longer period of time and provide them with additional tutoring or overseas training. As observed one commentator in Nigeria:

> We would like to begin with the reservation that fewer Nigerians now master the basic language skills in English than in any one of Hausa, Igbo, and Yoruba. Now, consider that, since the economic debacle which has beset the nation since the second half of the 1970s has put an end to the universal primary education scheme, an increasing proportion of Nigeria's school age children no longer enrol for formal education, the only medium for the acquisition of English. Add to that the galloping rate of school drop-outs and the rate of reversion to illiteracy among both the drop-outs and those who complete the primary education... As argued above, the three major indigenous languages of Nigeria count over 70 % of Nigeria's population among their speakers. Ignoring for the moment multilingualism involving indigenous languages only, it is clear that the first twelve Nigerian languages from the point of view of their mother-tongue speakers would account for at least 90 % of the country's population. This means that any Government with serious considerations for participatory governance would reach a larger number of Nigeria's citizenry at any one time through any one of the three majority indigenous languages, namely Hausa, Igbo and Yoruba than it would through the English language. The same government will touch at least 70 % of all Nigerians if it chooses to operate through Hausa, Igbo and Yoruba combined; 80 % through these three and Fulani; and at least 90 % through the first twelve most widely spoken indigenous languages. First, as it stands, the Constitution guarantees fundamental rights to the individual, but takes away these same fundamental rights from the vast majority of the Nigerian by imposing incapacities on those who have no practical skills or any skill whatsoever in English. Thus, unless a Nigerian has practical skills in the English language, certified by a secondary school leaving examination as shall be approved from time to time by government, he or she must remain only a manipulable elector at best. He may not seek any elective office even at the local government level and may not be assigned executive responsibility in the public service at any level. Furthermore, he has no access to be informed about the laws which order and circumscribe his very existence except when he runs foul of them.[143]

Far from constituting an effective tool to assist the social and economic well-being of a country's population, the use of European languages, because of the lack of resources for formal education in some states, contributes to the exclusion of vast sections of the population in direct

---

[143] Oyelaran, Olasope O.(1991), "Language in Nigeria Towards the Year 2000", in J.-J. Symoens and J. Vanderlinden (eds.), *Symposium : Les langues en Afrique à l'horizon 2000*, Institut Africain and Académie Royale des Sciences d'Outre-Mer, Bruxelles, pp. 109-139, at pp. 135-137.

participation in the higher echelons of government, and in having access and benefiting from many if not most state services.

As for a perceived lack of sophistication and technical vocabulary of languages in developing countries, it is not a water-tight argument. Just as technical subjects can be taught in Catalan, Mandarin, and Hindi, and scientific research is done in these and many other "smaller" languages, there is no absolute barrier in this respect for non-international, non-European languages.

Whilst a policy of favouring a European language in developing countries would appear to constitute differential treatment which tends to advantage tiny urban elites,[144] or a small percentage of the population as in the case of South Africa, it remains that such differential treatment is not automatically unreasonable even though it will disadvantage large segments of the state's population. Developing countries present a particularly delicate balancing act, but the basic applicable principles in determining whether unjustified discrimination on the ground of language is in issue remain the same.

An interesting case of the use of a *lingua franca* is presented by Indonesia. The state's only official language, Bahasa Indonesia, is for all intent and purposes no one's mother tongue, since it is in reality a simplified language borrowing heavily from Malay. Unlike English in South Africa, Bahasa Indonesia is not the language of a former colonial power, nor is it the native tongue of a privileged racial or ethnic segment of the population. It is, practically speaking, the second language for most inhabitants of Indonesia, probably the closest thing to an actual "neutral" *lingua franca* in the world.

Because of the great language diversity on its territory and in order to avoid being accused of favouring the domination of one linguistic group, such as the Javanese, who represent about half of the population, the government has gone out of its way to promote as much as possible the exclusive use of Bahasa Indonesia. In fact, the language has been central in the state's efforts to unify the whole population of the country.

Since Bahasa Indonesia is not native to any major group, it could be claimed the state's policy tends to be unfavourable to everyone in about the same proportion. In this way, the legislation *in se* could be said to be non-discriminatory, although great care should be taken in

---

[144] Huta-Mukana, Mutombo (1991), "Les langues au Zaïre à l'horizon 2000", in J.-J. Symoens and J. Vanderlinden (eds.), *Symposium : Les langues en Afrique à l'horizon 2000*, Institut Africain and Académie Royale des Sciences d'Outre-Mer, Bruxelles, pp. 84-107, at p. 104:

> *Le français zaïrois est langue d'unité et de cohésion, et encore, de la minorité intellectuelle et/ou semi-intellectuelle qui ne représente, comme il a été dit plus haut, que plus ou moins 2,77 % de la population. C'est donc une langue de division entre ces intellectuels et le reste de la population. Le français demeurerait comme langue d'ouverture sur l'espace francophone, car l'ouverture du Zaïre sur l'extérieur tout court pourrait et devrait même se faire par le biais d'une ou de plus d'une langue autochtone, africaine. C'est à ce prix que s'acquerra la vraie forme d'indépendance totale. Ce que nous disons du français vaut aussi de toute autre langue étrangère, en l'occurence l'anglais qui est dispensé dans le système éducationnel au Zaïre. Tout en acceptant volontiers la pratique des langues étrangères, nous ne pouvons prôner leur substitution aux langues locales. C'est dire que ces dernières devront occuper la première place dans cette situation de coexistence avec les langues étrangères, et notamment le français, tant dans le système éducatif, politique, administratif, juridique que dans les médias en général.*

this respect: in reality, non-urban dwellers and individuals unable to attain higher levels of education will tend to have a less developed knowledge of Bahasa Indonesia, so that in their case, strict enforcement of Bahasa Indonesia-only rules could be claimed to be disproportionate requirements in areas with a high level of non-speakers or poor speakers of the official language.

Moreover, the government's policy may be overzealous as in some areas there appears to be interference with freedom of expression (advertisements are at times required to be exclusively in Bahasa Indonesia) and interference with the use of a minority's language (popular publications and all films, even for private viewing, are required to be in Bahasa Indonesia).

4.7.3   *Economic Success and State Preferences for World Languages*

Another factor raised in some non-Western countries in support of a policy favouring a so-called world language is that a state is vindicated in adopting such differential treatment based upon language, because it will assist the country in its efforts towards economic development, a consideration again mostly prominent in African states.

The legal weight to attribute to this factor when determining the reasonability of differential treatment based upon language should be minimal. It in fact appears to be unfounded. The poorest countries in Africa are for the most part those which have chosen French or English as an official language, whilst the vast majority of the new Asian economic success stories have opted for an indigenous language as the official idiom. In other words, there simply is no correlation between official language use and economic well-being. It would probably be surprising for the South Koreans or Japanese to be told that their language is an obstacle to economic development, which must be cast aside in favour of adopting English or French as an official language. According to one author:

> Many of the virtues and promises associated with advocacy for English have involved a large measure of (self)-deception. English has not guaranteed "access to modern technology" and "prosperity for all"...in any former colony. The language serves rather as a boundary-marker between the haves and have-nots internally, and the link externally to market forces that keep former colonies in a position of dependence. Western commercial interests may be very keen to achieve the same in post-communist countries.[145]

Countries like South Africa, where English is often presented as a panacea for the economic and social success of the Black population, should perhaps take heed of the US experience:

> Though it has long been one of our most publicised national goals, fluency in English alone does not produce success, even for majority-language speakers of Anglo-Saxon ancestry. The language situation is even more frustrating for minority-language speakers. For them, language — the most visible sign of their ethnicity — is often used as an excuse to hide deeper levels of discrimination. As Joshua Fishman has put it, as bluntly as the idiom of

---

[145] Phillipson, Robert and Skutnabb-Kangas, Tove (1994), "English, Panacea or Pandemic?", in *Sociolinguistica*, Vol. 8, 73-87, at p. 80.

the social scientist will allow, "Mastery of English is almost as inoperative with respect to Hispanic social mobility as it is with respect to Black social mobility."[146]

4.8   ETHNICITY OR RACE AS PROXIES FOR LANGUAGE DISCRIMINATION

4.8.1   *Under-Inclusiveness of Non-Discrimination Legislation*

Some states, especially many which have a Common Law tradition, do not recognise language as a prohibited ground of discrimination. This has resulted in efforts in such states to include language implicitly, under another prohibited ground of discrimination such as race, and national or ethnic origin. The results in such states have been at best mixed, and are often illogical.

Because differences in language and even accent are employed so frequently as a means of denying access to a wide range of services, benefits and preferences on an equal basis, lawyers and courts are sometimes tempted to circumvent the absence of language as a prohibited ground of discrimination by linking it to another personal characteristic: a proxy for language discrimination. The problem with such an approach is fairly obvious: since language is not identical to race, national or ethnic origin, some individuals will "fall in between the cracks" and not be able to avail themselves of the right to non-discrimination. John MacDonald, a French-speaking Canadian of mainly Scottish and Irish ancestry, would be unable to claim discrimination if he were refused employment because someone dislikes his accent or the fact he is "one of them", a francophone, even though he is eminently qualified for the position. Juanita Wong, who grew up in Amarillo, Texas, and whose primary language is Spanish similarly does not qualify within the appropriate pigeon-hole of language as an ethnic or racial marker, and thus would be excluded from any of the remedies provided by non-discrimination legislation. These examples are by no means exhaustive of the types of problem legislative under-inclusiveness will cause when language is not an explicitly prohibited ground of discrimination.

4.8.2   *State Responses to the Non-Inclusion of Language*

Although language can be used as an indirect marker for race or other types of characteristics such as national origin, ancestry or ethnicity, there is obviously an imperfect match and some individuals will occasionally "escape" protection. Whilst the need has been argued eloquently in the United States for a generous attitude,[147] which includes language as an element of ethnic

---

[146] Baron, Dennis E. (1990), *The English-Only Question: An Official Language for Americans?*, Yale University Press, New Haven, USA, at pp. 193-194.

[147] *Supra*, note 85, at p. 274:

> Primary language should be protected as an aspect of "national origin" for several reasons. First, the courts and the EEOC have interpreted the phrase "national origin" broadly and have extended the protection of Title VII to bar discrimination against persons with characteristics closely correlated with national origin. Second, the sociology of linguistics establishes the importance of primary language as a fundamental aspect of ethnicity and national origin. Third, although primary language is not immutable in the same sense as protected characteristics like race or sex, primary language is what this writer will term "practically immutable," and thus

or national origin discrimination so that an individual may be protected in any situation where he or she is the victim of discrimination because of ancestry, physical, cultural, or linguistic characteristics, it must be frankly admitted that a person's primary language and ethnic or national origin are simply not the same, even though they can sometimes be closely linked.[148]

Moreover, even though the Equal Employment Opportunities Commission in the United States has adopted a definition reflecting a flexible approach in linking language to either national origin or ethnic group,[149] the problem remains essentially unaffected as this definition is not binding upon courts and has frequently been simply ignored by judges, including the United States Supreme Court.[150]

Under-inclusiveness is also a problem in the case of the **Fourteenth Amendment** of the US **Constitution** since, unless language differences can be included under a "suspect class" or associated to a fundamental right, courts will not apply the strict scrutiny test, making it unlikely that language differences created by the government can be deemed to be a violation:

> Suspect classification under traditional indicia contains an element of political disparity. In
> **Rodriguez**, the Supreme Court defined a suspect class as a group "saddled with such

---

entitled to statutory protection.

[148] Piatt, Bill (1986), "Toward Domestic Recognition of a Human Right to Language", in *Houston Law Review*, Vol. 23, 885-901, at p. 901:
> [T]his writer would abandon the concept which forces protection of language rights into the "national origin" pigeonhole. The real interest we seek to protect when we afford some language protection appear to be the individual's rights to: 1) view the world through his or her own language and culture, and 2) not be shut off from the exercise of some fundamental legal right or the satisfaction of some basic human need because of a language barrier. Many of those individuals whose language rights we would protect are native-born United States citizens. Using a "national origin" fiction is thus analytically unsound, and may perpetuate the fear of some monolingual persons that the use of a language other than English is "foreign". Also, this writer would urge abandonment of limiting language protection under the theory that because language is "mutable", the right to its exercise should inherently be limited, at least as regards bilinguals. The exercise of the choice of a "world view" through the eyes of a religion is protected, although clearly such a choice is mutable.

[149] Keotahian, Avak (1985-86), "National Origin Discrimination in Employment: Do Plaintiffs Ever Win?", in *Employee Relations Law Journal*, Vol. 25. 481-513, at p. 470:
> The Commission defines national origin discrimination broadly as including, but not limited to, the denial of equal employment opportunity because of an individual's, or his or her ancestor's, place or origin; or because an individual has the physical, cultural or linguistic characteristics of a national origin group.

[150] The Equal Employment Opportunity Commission (EEOC) guidelines recognise that an individual's mother tongue or primary language is an important characteristic of national origin. Although Title VII does not explicitly authorise the EEOC to issue guidelines, the US Supreme Court has confirmed the EEOC's authority to do so. EEOC guidelines were generally entitled to a large degree of deference as long as they were not inconsistent with Congressional intent, at least until the US Supreme Court in June 1994 completely disregarded the guidelines in the **Garcia v. Spun Steak** case without any other explanation.

disabilities, or subjected to such a history of purposeful unequal treatment, or relegated to such a position of political powerlessness as to command extraordinary protection from the majoritarian political process." Federal courts, however, have specifically rejected "suspect class" classifications based solely on an individual's inability to speak English. The Second Circuit in **Soberal-Perez v. Heckler**, for example, ruled that suspect class status must be made on the basis of race or national origin. "Language, by itself, does not identify members of a suspect class." Similarly, the Ninth Circuit in **Olagues v. Russoniello** refused to grant Chinese-speaking and Spanish-speaking immigrants suspect class status purely on the basis of language.[151]

Whilst there is a great deal of validity to the claim that language is a central element in many cultures, and can in this way be the most vital link to national origin or ethnicity, the court in **Garcia v. Gloor Lumber**[152] did not err when it adopted the position that national origin and the language one chooses to speak are not identical. They are not the same, since not every individual of Chinese origin speaks a Chinese language, nor do all people of Hispanic origin still speak Spanish. Professor Juan Perea is correct in affirming that "[p]rimary language, like accent, is closely correlated...with national origin", but wrong when he asserts that it is inextricably linked with it.[153] What must be acknowledged is that language is different from national origin (or ethnicity, or ancestry), although it can in many cases be used as indirect evidence of discrimination on the ground of national origin because of the intimate relationship which often exists between the two.

Like racial minorities, linguistic minorities have frequently suffered throughout history unfavourable treatment, discrimination, and economic and social disadvantage, but US courts have in general rejected claims of violations of the **Fourteenth Amendment** unless the facts reveal a very close relationship between language and national origin or unless rights considered fundamental are involved.[154]

---

[151] *Supra*, note 79, at pp. 790-791; see also **Frontera v. Sindell**, 522 F.2d 1215 (1975) (United States).

[152] 618 F.2d 264 (1980) (United States).

[153] Perea, *supra*, note 85, at p. 276. Professor Perea subsequently revises his position and confirms that it may be more appropriate to address directly the under-inclusiveness of US legislation. Perea, *supra*, note 74, at pp. 830-831:

> What the agency is actually protecting, however, is not national origin but rather the traits of ethnicity. Its broad conception of "national origin" discrimination reads much like the broad understanding of ethnicity: "the physical, cultural or linguistic characteristics of national origin group." The problem with the EEOC's interpretation is the same as the problem with broad judicial interpretations of the statute: the statutory language and legislative history simply do not support it. Given the current Supreme Court's penchant for strict construction of civil rights statutes, these judicial and agency attempts to broaden the scope of Title VII will likely prove futile when the Court decides to review them. The only safe course, therefore, is to amend the statute in a manner that would support the efforts of the EEOC and some courts to expand Title VII to bar discrimination on the basis of ethnic traits.

[154] "Language Rights and the Legal Status of English-Only Laws in the Public and Private Sector" (1992), in *North Carolina Central Law Journal*, Vol. 20, 65-91, at p. 74.

Finally, failure to include language as an explicitly prohibited ground of discrimination may result in courts simply refusing to consider the arguments of alleged victims of discrimination. In **Garcia v. Spun Steak**, the US Supreme Court seems to have approved the refusal of the Ninth Circuit Court of Appeals to hear the arguments of the complainants to the effect that their employer was adopting an unfavourable, differential treatment policy by only allowing them to privately speak to one another in English during work hours. The Court of Appeals indicated that it would not even examine what constituted the most important point raised by the Spanish-speaking workers; that is, if some employees have the privilege of conversing with others on the job in their primary language in non-work related contexts, they should not be denied the same privilege:

> When the privilege is defined at its narrowest (as merely the ability to speak on the job), we cannot conclude that those employees fluent in both English and Spanish are adversely impacted by the policy. Because they are able to speak English, bilingual employees can engage in conversation on the job... The bilingual employee can readily comply with the English-only rule and still enjoy the privilege of speaking on the job.[155]

Since language was not an explicitly prohibited ground of discrimination, in **Garcia v. Spun Steak** the Ninth Circuit Court of Appeals and the Supreme Court simply chose to disregard the issue of law as to whether denial of the privilege of Spanish-speaking workers to speak their mother tongue with other Spanish-speaking workers, in a non-work related context, was reasonable. Instead, the judges in fact avoided to deal with the actual claim: why only a few employees were allowed the privilege of speaking their own language.

4.8.3   *Is Under-Inclusiveness Discriminatory?*

The difficulties these examples present could for the most part be eliminated by correcting their actual cause: the under-inclusiveness of national legislation which fails to recognise language as a prohibited ground of discrimination. Furthermore, it is doubtful that the non-inclusion of such a fundamental human characteristic meets international human rights standards. A state not including in its legislation non-discrimination on the ground of sex or race would be hard pressed to claim that it is not violating the **Universal Declaration of Human Rights**, the **International Covenant on Civil and Political Rights** and the multitude of other international instruments which for the most part are consistent in respect to the minimal grounds which must be included in non-discrimination legislation. Language, along with race, religion, and sex, is one of the mainstays of equality provisions.

That the under-inclusiveness of non-discrimination legislation could be a violation of international standards appears to be supported by the Human Rights Committee, which has on occasion questioned such a practice when considering state reports:

> *Le Comité des droits de l'homme des Nations unies a d'ailleurs fait référence à l'absence de certains motifs dans les textes législatifs canadiens, notamment que ses lois...ne*

---

[155] 998 F.2d 1480 (1993) (United States), at p. 1487.

contiennent pas une liste de motifs de discrimination prohibés qui soit aussi vaste que celle contenue à l'article 26 du Pacte international relatif aux droits civils et politiques.[156]

Moreover, some courts have acknowledged that the omission of certain grounds of discrimination can in itself be discriminatory, since some individuals will have available to them the protection of non-discrimination legislation but others will not.[157] In other words, the exclusion of any major ground of discrimination such as language will have the effect that not everyone has the benefit of the complaint and enforcement procedures and the equal protection of the law. Unless a state can show that language is included under another ground and that no individual will "fall in between the cracks", under-inclusiveness in a state's explicitly prohibited grounds of discrimination should in every case be deemed unreasonable and therefore discriminatory unless a state can guarantee that through other mechanisms the right to equality and non-discrimination of every individual will be respected. Amongst those sharing this point of view are Professor de Witte:

> American court decisions, in particular, have not been wary of ordering the extension of under-inclusive legislative classifications, even if this entailed increased governmental spending, and even beyond what was authorised by the budget. The dominant attitude in legal writing seems to be that "the courts act legitimately...when they employ common sense and sound judgment to preserve a law by moderate extension where tearing it down would be far more destructive of the legislature's will". In Italy too, there have been examples of the Constitutional Court pronouncing a so-called *accoglimento additivo*, i.e. ordering the extension of an existing measure to persons originally not covered by it.[158]

4.9   LANGUAGE RIGHTS, SPECIAL RIGHTS, OR AFFIRMATIVE ACTION?

This examination of what may constitute discriminatory behaviour by a state, when it prefers a language or imposes language requirements, points to one principal conclusion: equality and non-discrimination have the effect of requiring the use of the primary language(s) of inhabitants of a state by public authorities when a sufficiently large number of people speak a non-official or non-majority language. This means that the respect of the language preferences of individuals, where appropriate and reasonable, flows from a fundamental human right and is not some special concession or privileged treatment. Simply put, it is the right to be treated equally without discrimination, to which everyone is entitled.

---

[156] *Supra*, note 96, at p. 326.

[157] See for example **Re Blainey and Ontario Hockey Association et al.** (1986), 54 Ontario Reports (2d) 513 (Canada); the judgement of the Constitutional Court of 11 July 1975, in Foro Italiano, 1975, I 1882 (Italy); **Shapiro v. Thompson**, 394 U.S. 618 (1969) (United States); and **Weinberger v. Wiesenfeld**, 420 U.S. 636 (1975) (United States). The Italian and US decisions are quoted in de Witte, *supra*, note 2, at p. 62.

[158] *Supra*, note 2, at p. 62.

However, a large number of legal commentators seem to disagree with such a conclusion, or at least tend to confuse different issues and terminology whenever addressing the place of language in human rights. In one United Nations document on the protection of minority rights, the author states:

> Special rights for minority groups can be defined as the requirement to ensure suitable means, including differential treatment, for the preservation of minority characteristics and traditions which distinguish them from the majority of the population. Among these means are the implementation of special measures or positive action involving the rendering of concrete services, such as schools providing education in the minority language...
> Looking at minority rights from the perspective of "affirmative action" (i.e. positive state action aimed at protecting the minority or at promoting the enjoyment of their rights), it is conceivable that members of the majority could complain to the Committee that they are being discriminated vis-à-vis the minority members, e.g. concerning subsidies for cultural centres, financial aid for textbooks, etc. It is interesting to note that thus far no such case has been submitted to the Committee. Although it is impossible to predict exactly how the Human Rights Committee would decide a concrete case, its established jurisprudence would give reason to believe that a violation of Article 26 of the Covenant would not be found, provided that the distinctions in question are based on reasonable and objective criteria. In this context it is worth noting that social legislation, by its very nature, is intended to achieve social justice by making certain distinctions. A scheme of progressive taxation, for instance, makes distinctions (in a sense, discriminates) in favour of the poor at the expense of the wealthier. Such a scheme would not be deemed to be in breach of Article 26, since it would be based on a reasonable objective, not incompatible with the Covenant. Similarly, affirmative action aimed at ensuring the possibility of minorities to maintain their identity and traditions and to enjoy their culture would not constitute prohibited discrimination in the sense of Article 26 of the Covenant. In this sense, it would also be conceivable that a member of a minority could submit a case demanding affirmative action, if such action is necessary for him or her to exercise Covenant rights on a basis of equality with members of the majority.[159]

The author is clearly mistaken in apparently implying that Article 26 (non-discrimination) might be invoked in order to favour differences of treatment as between majorities and minorities: the provision is concerned with individual rights and is not dependent in any way on a majority-minority type of relationship. The principle weakness with such commentary is the failure to recognise that language is foremost an individual trait, as important in some cases as one's religion, and that the real victim of language preference by a state is the individual not having the primary language so preferred by the state. The state has chosen a course of action which creates a distinction favouring some, to the exclusion or detriment of others.

---

[159] Alfredssen, Gudmundur and de Zayas, Alfred (1993), "Minority Rights: Protection by the United Nations", in *Human Rights Law Journal*, Vol. 14, 1-8, at pp. 6-7; see also Albanese, Ferdinando (1991), "Ethnic and Linguistic Minorities in Europe", in *Yearbook of European Law*, Vol. 11, 313-337, at p. 321.

The commentary also contains statements to the effect that state-funded education in any language other than that of the majority is a special or positive measure which goes beyond what is required by the right to equality. This is also an error. What non-discrimination requires from a government is not special privileges for some because they are members of a minority group. Non-discrimination calls instead for the following: if the state provides to some of its inhabitants a service or benefit, such as education in their primary language, then it must do so in a non-discriminatory way. It is not, strictly speaking, a "special right": the state or government has no obligation to do anything, but if it chooses to provide any benefit or service, it must do so without discrimination. Of course, this does not imply, as noted on a number of occasions, that everyone has the right to instruction in his or her primary language, since a state may always be justified in limiting the number of languages in which it can respond, as long as it is reasonable to do so.

Perhaps part of the confusion exists because in some cases non-discrimination will have the added bonus of protecting linguistic minorities. If there are sufficiently large and concentrated numbers of people to warrant state-funded schools using their primary language as medium of instruction, this will quite obviously be of significant benefit to the community as a whole in its attempts to preserve its language and culture. But of course, this side-effect of non-discrimination is not available to all, since if the number of individuals is insufficient, non-discrimination will not require a state to provide schooling facilities in a language used only by a handful.

This potential dual impact of non-discrimination is in fact mentioned in an early United Nations study:

1. Prevention of discrimination is the prevention of any action which denies to individuals or groups of people equality of treatment which they may wish.

2. Protection of minorities is the protection of non-dominant groups which, while wishing in general for equality of treatment with the majority, wish for a measure of differential treatment in order to preserve basic characteristics which they possess and which distinguish them from the majority of the population. The protection applies equally to individuals belonging to such groups and wishing the same protection. It follows that differential treatment of such groups or of individuals belonging to such groups is justified when it is exercised in the interest of their contentment and the welfare of the community as a whole. The characteristics meriting such protection are race, religion and language. In order to qualify for protection a minority must owe undivided allegiance to the Government of the state in which it lives. Its members must also be nationals of that state...

7. The protection of minorities, on the other hand, although similarly inspired by the principle of equality of treatment of all peoples, requires positive action : concrete service is rendered to the minority group, such as the establishment of schools in which education is given in the native tongue of the members of the group. Such measures are of course also inspired by the principle of equality: for example, if a child receives its education in a language which is not its mother tongue, this might imply that the child is not treated on an equal basis with those children who do receive their education in their mother tongue. The protection of minorities therefore requires positive action to safeguard the rights of the

minority group, provided of course that the people concerned (or their parents in case of children) wish to maintain their differences of language and culture.[160]

Because of the awkward phrasing employed, distinguished commentators have concluded that equality and non-discrimination mandate "a negative, prohibitory mode through the suppression of manifestations of unequal treatment" whereas special protective measures for minorities required "positive measures" such as the establishment of public schools using the language of a minority.[161] These views depend upon a narrow interpretation of non-discrimination which now seems to have been largely discarded. Although there are certainly measures in international law specially designed for the protection of minorities, such as Article 27 of the **International Covenant on Civil and Political Rights**, the obligation to set up public schools using a non-official language as the medium of instruction, when a state has a sufficiently large number of speakers of such language, is not such a measure. In such a situation, it would be unreasonable, and therefore discriminatory, for a state to deny such individuals a benefit or advantage enjoyed by some others.

The error made by some scholars is to fail to consider closely what constitutes discrimination. As demonstrated earlier, use of a single language in public schools can constitute an inequality, as not everyone receives the same treatment: some receive instruction in their primary language, others do not. There is therefore differential treatment on the ground of language. Since a state is prohibited from behaving in such a way when it amounts to discriminatory preferential treatment, the negative prohibition mandates either a complete cessation of the unequal treatment by closing all public schools, or by not perpetuating the discriminatory and unreasonable treatment and having an appropriate degree of public schooling in another language of instruction.

"Special rights" are therefore clearly not the same as services provided in the language of a large number of individuals — who may happen to be members of a minority — because of the application of the right of non-discrimination where it is reasonable due to the number of speakers of the language, their concentration, etc.:

> The concept of special assistance or status should, therefore, refer only to measures made for minorities without the provision of corresponding measures for majorities. The only justification for doing so would be to restore equality where, in the past, there had been inequality, or where structural factors make equality difficult to preserve. The United Nations Human Rights Committee, in its General Comment 18(37), states that the principle of equality sometimes requires states to take affirmative action in order to diminish or eliminate conditions which cause or help to perpetuate discrimination. Where the general conditions of some groups prevent or impair their enjoyment of human rights, the Committee points out that specific action should be taken even if it might amount to

---

[160] *Supra*, note 94, at p. 2.

[161] See in particular Thornberry, Patrick (1991), *International Law and the Rights of Minorities*, Clarendon Press, Oxford, United Kingdom, at pp. 126-127.

preferential treatment. "[A]s long as such action is needed to correct discrimination in fact, it is a case of legitimate differentiation under the Covenant."[162]

4.10   STATE LANGUAGE PREFERENCE(S) AND POLITICAL AND ECONOMIC CONSIDERATIONS

[T]he importance of language as an element in nationality is difficult to over-estimate. Language is the key to all intellectual and a great part of spiritual life. A common language alone makes possible free and familiar intercourse between two human beings and creates of itself a bond between them. More than this: each language, with its choice of words, its turn of phrase, its every idiom and peculiarity, is a sort of philosophy which expresses the past history, the character, the psychological identity of those accustomed to use it. It is an instrument which, moulded by past generations, itself modifies the future. It is difficult for a foreigner to adopt the language of a people, without in some ways also adopting their habit of mind, and a child sucks in a sense of nationality with the very rhymes which it learns in the nursery. It is small wonder that many nation have practically identified their nationality with their language, regarding as lost to them those who have ceased to speak it.[163]

The above examination of differential treatment based upon language, and how to determine whether such treatment is discriminatory in light of the "reasonability" test, provide the legal considerations for a balanced and objective assessment of the linguistic policy and practices of a state, but it is only one element of a complex equation. Language preferences also have substantial political and economic ramifications. Although beyond the scope of this study, these aspects will be mentioned briefly, in order to shed some light upon the whole picture.

4.10.1   *A Question of Power*

By making language a predominant factor in access to employment and education opportunities, so that native speakers of the official or preferred tongue are more likely to reach the higher echelons of the state machinery, a government directly affects the political power structures of the state:

Outside education, national languages serve a similar purpose by rationing access to political institutions of power. The adoption of a national language depoliticises one variety, which is declared to be the symbol of all people (the nation). Resistance to the national language is therefore seen as opposition to national unity. Voting, service on local boards and committees, and other forms of political participation may be limited to individuals speaking

---

[162] Eide, Asbjørn (1991), "Minority Situations: In Search of Peaceful and Constructive Solutions", in *Notre Dame Law Review*, Vol. 66, 1311-1346, at pp. 1341-1342.

[163] Macartney, C.A. (1968), *National States and National Minorities*, Russell and Russell, New York, at pp. 7-8.

the national language. In such circumstances, it may seem absurd to have a leader who does not speak the national language. Yet this means that only speakers of the national language can become leaders or otherwise participate in official political activities. In this way, national languages, which restrict access to decision making in the name of nationhood, are inherently ideological.[164]

Whilst there is nothing intrinsically wrong if a state chooses to require everyone to learn a single dominant language, the error is to make it the exclusive language for government and state education when a substantial proportion of the population uses a different language. Having reached a *masse critique*, these communities tend to be concentrated territorially and to use their language as the ordinary medium for family and community activities. In such a context, a nationally dominant language will normally play a secondary role in most aspects of daily life, so that many, if not most, individuals in such communities will never reach the level of fluency of native speakers in the national language. Even if members of linguistic minorities (or of the non-official language) learn the dominant language, they will still suffer economic, political and social inequality because the state's language policy is not a balanced response to the demographic and socio-cultural reality of the country.

State language preferences, and especially measures aimed at the prohibition of use of other languages can, moreover, be perceived as an attempt to emphasise one group's dominance over another. Whilst many measures in this area may be fairly reasonable and thus acceptable to most, as for example not offering government services in a language only spoken by a few hundred individuals, other measures, especially where it affects people in their private affairs, will almost always be deemed unnecessary and a blatant attempt at suppressing the presence or manifestation of the "other" group.[165]

---

[164] *Planning Language, Planning Inequality, supra,* note 89, at p. 9.

[165] Religion and language are two human characteristics that can become highly politicised issues. See on this point Horowitz, Donald L. (1985), *Ethnic Groups in Conflict,* University of California Press, Cambridge, United Kingdom, at p. 222:

> Language is therefore a potent symbolic issue because it accomplishes a double linkage. It links political claims to ownership with psychological demands for the affirmation of group worth, and it ties this aggregate matter of group status to outright careerism, thereby binding elite material interests to mass concerns. Needless to say, language is not the only issue that can do this. Official religion served the same function in Burma. At first, the "special position of Buddhism" was "recognised", but in 1961 this equivocal phrasing was repealed by a State Religion Act that made Buddhism the official religion. The Act required the Public Service Commission, in recruiting candidates for government employment, to accord the same weight to a knowledge of Pali, the liturgical language, as to other subjects, a provision which reflected the careerist motivations of some proponents. But the main support for the state religion movement came from the countryside, a fact which cannot be explained without reference to the significance of the state religion as a symbol of Burman hegemony. This is precisely the way it was interpreted by minorities, especially the Kachins and Chins. Religion, then, can sometimes link elite and mass concerns. But clearly it is more plausible to think that fluency in the working language of a bureaucracy will become an issue more often than will facility in scripture.

By limiting its operations to the use of only one or a few languages, a state may unwillingly, or quite consciously, be signalling the dominance of those for whom the official or state-favoured language is the mother tongue. Their language is dominant, all others are not. They are therefore privileged in that they do not have to worry about learning another language, be it to have access to government employment or to public services. They are free to use their language at home, in business, in schools, in their community, and with the public authorities without considering whether it is a handicap not to be fluent in another language. Other people do not have the same privilege or right. Particularly in African states, a tiny English-speaking or French-speaking elite often controls state policy-making organs with a language policy which serves their interests whilst the masses remain largely excluded.[166]

Generally speaking, the dynamics of ethnic tension involving language, leading in some cases to political conflicts, occur not where language compromises are made or language rights are recognised, but where they have been avoided, suppressed or ignored.[167] This may surprise some who claim that language diversity in a state is risky, undesirable and should be discouraged (one could just as easily claim that religious diversity is risky, undesirable and should be discouraged). In support of such arguments, many will cite as examples the linguistic conflicts in Canada and Belgium: undeniable evidence, according to them, of the potential instability of all multilingual states.

In fact, these examples prove quite the contrary: in both cases, the political instability arose from a longstanding denial of rights relating to the use of the language of large segments of the population rather than any inherent undesirable quality of a state with a diverse linguistic mosaic. Both Canada and Belgium are cases of states which, until the last moment, consistently refused to recognise in fact and in law that a large portion of their populations did not speak the language privileged by the national government, or simply chose to ignore the demographic reality of their country, even in the case of Belgium where Dutch-speaking people are the majority.[168]

Finally, it remains highly questionable whether the refusal to recognise a democratically elected representative, because that person does not have a sufficient knowledge of the official language of the state, could ever be deemed to be a proportional response to a state's vital interests. In a number of Commonwealth countries, it is prohibited to be elected and sit as a member of the National Assembly unless one can demonstrate sufficient proficiency in the

---

[166] *Planning Language, Planning Inequality, supra,* note 89, at p. 201.

[167] Baron, *supra,* note 146, at p. 180. See also the point of view that non-discrimination when properly understood and applied may alleviate some of the causes of conflict, *supra,* note 162, at p. 1334:

> The principle of non-discrimination, if properly applied to situations involving minorities, can go a long way to preventing conflicts. Very often, the intensity of religious, national or ethnic conflicts can be traced to the lack of respect for individual human rights. This has long been a primary concern for the Sub-Commission, as evidenced by its numerous former studies. Time and again it has been emphasised that non-discrimination is vital to ensure complete impartiality in the administration of justice, particularly in regard to the conduct of law enforcement officials and security forces.

[168] de Varennes, Fernand (1995), *Language Conflicts in Eastern European and Central Asian States: Preliminary Report on Early Warning and Resolution Mechanisms,* Foundation on Inter-Ethnic Relations, den Haag, Netherlands, at pp. 6-7.

English language, as require, for example, Article 33 of the **Constitution of Mauritius**, and Article 38 of the **Antigua and Barbuda Constitution**.[169] Such measures appear to be aimed at excluding from political power whole segments of the population, hardly a fitting measure in any democracy.

4.10.2 *Language and Economic Opportunities*

[L]anguage is central to the whole communication network of any political system. Public authorities, particularly in a modernizing situation, are inevitably and increasingly drawn into language questions through the spread of citizen participation in politics, the provision of more administrative services, and perhaps most of all through the development of state-supported education. This means that one of the most successful methods for pacifying religious differences at an earlier date, namely, the withdrawal of the state from the arena of conflict, or de-politicization, is not available for most linguistic conflicts, and other methods of conflict resolution must be found. One can have separation of church and state, but in advanced societies separation of language and state is simply not possible. A major consequence of this central role of language in the communication network is that it is closely linked with most of the professional and bureaucratic employment opportunities, with the result that conflicts over language frequently involve high personal stakes in terms of career prospects for the groups concerned, and most of all for their most articulate and well-educated elites. Language conflicts therefore concern not simply languages as such, but tangible economic benefits as well.[170]

As political scientist Kenneth McRae succinctly demonstrates, language choices by a state are not only politically charged, they also have dramatic economic consequences for individuals.

Particularly in countries where some are unable to spend many years in the formal education system because of financial difficulties, as is often the case in developing countries, a policy favouring a language that is not the primary language of a large segment of the population will eventually lead to building unsurmountable barriers between the people and public authorities in terms of language. Many individuals will not be able to afford schooling, will have to work at a very young age, or will have to attend substandard programmes (as in the case of many rural African communities where French or English are taught by minimally fluent teachers).[171] This

---

[169] See Sections 3.83 and 3.5 in the Appendix.

[170] McRae, Kenneth D. (1986), *Conflict and Compromise in Multilingual Societies: Belgium*, Wilfrid Laurier University Press, Waterloo, Canada, at pp. 3-4.

[171] *Language and Society in Africa* (1992), Robert K. Herbert (ed.), Witwatersrand University Press, Witwatersrand, South Africa, at p. 127:

There seems to be a problem with the statement that an alien language such as English in Namibia can contribute to forming a national identity. The obvious problem with such a policy has been experienced in many African countries: only a small percentage of the population learn the language sufficiently well to be able to converse in it... English can only serve as a national communication vehicle if it is spread efficiently. We know the official language has not been spread very widely in many African countries and there are clear indications that this will be

results in their inability to learn French or English well enough to access many if not most of the state machinery jobs or to fully benefit from state services mainly dispensed through the use of a former colonial language:

> Those who support English are those who speak it, thereby, claiming for themselves significant advantages in competition for education, employment, and political power. Thus, though the rhetoric may vary, the effort to sustain a privileged position for English has a similar motivation in the United States, Britain, and the Philippines, namely, the advantages that one gains when one's language is used for official purposes.[172]

Others have also pointed out that denying instruction in the mother tongue, at least in the first years of formal education, unfavourably affects the competitive chances of the speakers of the non-favoured languages. One of the major end results of state language preferences can thus be associated with favouring the economic interests of one group of individuals, native-speakers of the dominant or official language, to the detriment of those who have not succeeded in securing some type of use of their own language by local or regional public authorities, with its consequent effects on employment opportunities.[173]

4.11   SUMMARY

Despite sometimes confusing or even contradicting views on the actual content and effect of the right to equality and the prohibition of discrimination, there appears to be in many states and at the international level a sufficient common understanding of this right to suggest how it may have a significant impact in language matters.

At its most essential level, non-discrimination constitutes a limit on the conduct of the state and its agents. Whenever the state acts, offers services, intervenes or imposes conditions or requirements on individuals in order to exercise rights or receive benefits, it must do so without taking into consideration the personal characteristics of the individuals involved. Everyone should be subjected to the same laws in the same way. This is the right to equality. Obviously, there comes a point where some types of distinction may be appropriate. Although everyone may be

---

no easier in Namibia than in any other country... English is spoken as a mother tongue by a very small section — perhaps 5 percent — of the Namibian population. However, since so few Namibians know it, the selection of English could cause serious problems in social, political, educational and economic terms. This statement is underlined by the experience in some Ovamba schools where, for the last five years, English has been used as the language of instruction. Since the teachers hardly know any English and the pupils do not have any opportunity for using it outside the classroom, many pupils have not learned very much English.

[172] *Planning Language, Planning Inequality, supra*, note 89, at p. 152.

[173] Deutsch, Karl (1979), *Tides Among Nations*, Free Press, New York, at p. 51: .
Modern economic competition, with its heavy premium on social contacts and linguistic skills in many middle-class occupations, automatically imposes heavy barriers on all those who do not share the language, experience, and culture pattern of the locally dominant group...

required to submit to the same law, legislation can for example impose certain conditions or requirements. The right to vote is limited to individuals who have reached at least 18 years of age. There is therefore a distinction as to age since only those who have reached the appropriate age have the right or privilege to vote, but non-discrimination does not exclude every type of distinction which involves a fundamental human characteristic. To argue otherwise would simply make the prohibition of discrimination unworkable.

The most prevalent understanding of the operation of non-discrimination, as contained in the United Nations Human Rights Committee's *General Comment on Non-Discrimination*, takes into account the need to balance a state's legitimate interests and goals in prescribing certain preferences or making distinctions that involve fundamental human characteristics with the disadvantage, denial or burden this imposes on individuals, or the advantages, benefits and privileges such conduct entitles some individuals and not others. Everything comes down to whether or not in the end one can describe the measure or conduct as being "reasonable" or "fair", or more graphically whether the scale can be said to tip more on the side of the state — in which case it can be said the state conduct is not discriminatory — or whether it tips more on the side of the individual(s) affected — in which case it would constitute a breach of the right.

Beyond theoretical musings, a very real difficulty in a number of states, and sometimes at the international level, has been not what the right involves in a general sense, but how it translates into practice in language matters.

On the one hand, it is clear that as with other fundamental human characteristics such as religion and race, the prohibition of discrimination on the ground of language is not an absolute. A state is never obligated to conduct all of its activities in every language which is spoken by the inhabitants in its territory. Non-discrimination does not prohibit every distinction involving a language, only those that are "unreasonable" when one considers all relevant factors: those that relate to the state's interests and goals, and those that relate to the individual's interests, rights and how s/he is affected.

On the other hand, a government cannot simply assume that it has *carte blanche* as to the language it adopts for the conduct of the affairs of the state and the way it interacts with its population. By the simple act of using one language exclusively in public schools, state services, administrative activities, or even prescribing the language in which court trials are conducted, a state is making a distinction based on language. It is showing a preference for this single, official or national language which will benefit some individuals for whom it is a primary language, to the detriment or disadvantage of others who either have no or lower proficiency in it or are denied the benefit or privilege of using their own primary language.

The selection of a language for the conduct of a state's affairs has very real advantages for some and disadvantages for others. Any individual who is not fluent in the language preferred by the state will have fewer employment opportunities in many areas, especially the public service which is increasingly seen as a major employer in modern states. Studies in the field of state education are almost universal in showing that instruction in the mother tongue is a more effective means of ensuring a high level of academic success and retention than is education in a "foreign" language. The ability to benefit from government services or programmes may be hampered by not being able to understand completely the language used by the state, or it may be more expensive or onerous to have to comply with the use of a language which is not one's own. Finally, in judicial matters an individual would be at a disadvantage if he or she is forced to testify in a language in which he or she may be more uncomfortable, leading to evidence which may not faithfully represent what he or she was trying to convey.

Even though these disadvantages are real, the proper application of non-discrimination does not guarantee that every individual's language of preference can or should be used by state authorities. What is required instead is a balancing act, an attempt to reach a reasonable outcome in light of legitimate state interests and goals, and the effect the state distinction between languages has on the individual and the advantage or benefit which others are receiving and he or she is not.

Without submitting an exhaustive list, it is possible to suggest a number of relevant considerations when attempting to determine whether a particular language distinction by a state's machinery or agents is discriminatory: the number of individuals who are denied a benefit or advantage enjoyed by others who may use their primary or preferred language; the territorial concentration of the individuals that find themselves disadvantaged or denied the same benefit; whether they are citizens, permanent residents or aliens; individual preferences; the degree of disadvantage or the burden a state's preference for a particular language causes to those who have a different primary language; the desirability of a common national language in a state; available resources and practicality; the state's goal(s) in favouring one language over others; whether a particular language has developed a written form; the social, cultural or religious importance of a language; the type of service or state conduct involved; the desirability of not discarding too quickly legal or traditional linguistic concessions; and even the desire to correct past oppressive state practices. All these factors and other relevant considerations must then enter into a balancing formula to determine whether the state's language distinction is a proportional or reasonable measure. In other words, is the state's preference in language matters appropriate when considering the aims sought, the means employed and the effect on individuals who are denied a benefit or suffer a disadvantage?

In practice, this would generally mean that non-discrimination can only be invoked successfully where there is a sufficiently large or concentrated number of individuals affected in relation to the type of state service or activity. If a state has decreed Language A as the only language to be used in state schools as medium of instruction, this would be advantageous to its inhabitants for whom Language A is their primary speech. If half the population has Language B as their primary language, they are at a disadvantage and do not enjoy the same benefit as speakers of Language A, namely the use of their primary language as medium of instruction.

Script differences should also be considered as an integral part of language distinctions, since individuals can be burdened or disadvantaged by a state's use of a script which affects their verbal or reading abilities. Employment and economic opportunities, enjoyment or access to state services or programmes can all be involved because of script differences.

Finally, the situation in a number of African and Asian states can be viewed as rather unique in some respects. In these states a number of governments have opted for a "neutral" language, in the sense of a language which is not the primary language of any substantial number of individuals. Since the vast majority of individuals are in essence affected in the same way by having an European language used by state authorities, it cannot be claimed anyone has a benefit or advantage that is denied to others. Therefore, the language preference of these states cannot be described as discriminatory since it must be shown that a state distinguishes on the basis of language, that it has adopted a line of conduct that favours some individuals and not others because they have different languages. It can be claimed that the requirement of establishing some type of unfavourable treatment of some individuals because of their language cannot be made out if no one is in fact advantaged by such a language practice.

One danger with this last approach which should not be overlooked is that certain elites may actually be privileged by such a policy, especially in terms of economic, political and educational opportunities, since they may have adopted the "neutral" European language as their primary tongue or have more resources at their disposal to ensure their greater fluency in the language.

5. Linguistic Minorities and the Use of their Language

Freedom of expression and non-discrimination offer to individuals a form of basic protection against the sometimes unreasonable or burdensome demands and impositions of the state in language matters, but they are both strictly speaking individual rights, unconcerned with the fate of linguistic minorities as a collectivity or community. Whilst it is true that both can have important consequences in ensuring the continued existence of linguistic communities, they are not a panacea for every woe, and especially would appear insufficient to guarantee that a minority will not be swamped by the power or influence of a linguistic majority. The application of the right of non-discrimination, for example, requires amongst others things an assessment of whether there is a sufficient number of speakers of a language in order to impose any duties on a state. This would suggest that, for smaller minorities, the limited number of individuals who share the same language makes non-discrimination of little or no relevance. Yet, because of the importance of language for many minorities, and the sincere desire amongst individuals and communities to maintain and use that which is central to their social and cultural identity, it has long been recognised in international law and in a growing number of states that these minorities should also have the right to freely use their language with other members of their community. This chapter considers how and why this right offers another fundamental guarantee with substantial impact in certain situations. Whilst this right may have a significant role to play in ensuring the survival of minorities as communities, it is still not a solution to all of their demands as will be shown.

5.1   PRELIMINARY REMARKS

One constant to be found throughout much of modern history, with some notable exceptions,[1] is the general recognition that minorities should be permitted to maintain activities and characteristics peculiar to their group. The first systematic formulation dates back to the minorities treaties of the interwar period, but the basic principle survived the demise of that system through provisions such as Article 27 of the **International Covenant on Civil and Political Rights** (hereinafter the **"Covenant"**). Many international instruments, as well as many states in their national legislation, recognise that members of linguistic and religious minorities

---

[1] Whilst countries such as France, Greece and Turkey have tended to adopt policies aimed at creating a centralised state united through national symbols such as the French, Greek and Turkish languages, in principle these countries have not denied the existence of basic freedoms or rights for linguistic and religious minorities. Their approach has been rather to adopt the position that some of these minorities do not exist on their territory. For example, France has chosen to interpret "minority" in its political sense: since the **Constitution** recognises everyone as equal, there can be no minority. Unfortunately, France's position is indefensible, as will be shown later, since "minority" under Article 27 does not imply any political or legal categorisation, but is rather a numerical description. This has also been confirmed by the United Nations Human Rights Committee's *General Comment No. 23(50)*, 6 April 1994, UN Document CCPR/C/21/Rev.1/Add.5, at paragraph 4.

are entitled to rights not necessarily explicitly guaranteed to members of the majority,[2] namely the right to use their language and practice their religion with other members of their group. Whilst this formulation appears straightforward enough, there remains in practice many problems related to the identity of the individuals who may claim these benefits, as well as uncertainty as to its exact content.

5.2   PRECURSORS OF THE CONTEMPORARY RIGHTS OF MINORITIES

Whether it is within the *Du Si* system in China, the *dhimma* in Muslim countries, or the League of Nations supervised minorities treaties system in the first half of this century, states which have not been determined to exterminate or forcibly remove entire populations from their territory — populations with members different from the majority or controlling population, generally in terms of race, religion or language — have tended for practical reasons to allow such populations a measure of autonomy in their internal relations.[3] At least until fairly recently, this was not due to any modern type of commitment to human rights, but rather to a sense of what was practical or desirable: it is usually simpler and easier to maintain control over such populations when a degree of freedom or autonomy in those aspects of their lives deemed most vital is allowed.

This sense of what is practical has also permeated Western human rights philosophy from the very beginning of this century.

5.2.1   *The Minorities Treaties*

The minorities treaties under the League of Nations contained various provisions aimed at ensuring the protection of a number of minorities,[4] but also contained specific provisions prohibiting discrimination. In fact, to call them "minorities treaties" is something of a misnomer: human rights treaties would be more appropriate since many provisions were not minority-specific but were for the benefit of all individuals.[5] For example, the **Polish Minorities Treaty**

---

[2] Possibly for a perceived lack of necessity, since the potential today for breach of linguistic and religious rights and freedoms of individuals belonging to the majority is, as a matter of fact, less evident.

3 Notable recent exceptions consist of Nazi Germany's attempts to exterminate Jews and the ethnic cleansing tragedy in Bosnia.

[4] The system was put into place in order to address dramatic territorial changes following the First World War and the resulting creation of large minorities in some countries.

[5] This is even acknowledged by the Permanent Court of International Justice in the **Advisory Opinion on Certain Questions, Arising Out of the Application of Article 4 of the Polish Minorities Treaty,** also known as the **Polish Nationality Case,** (1923) Permanent Court of International Justice, Series B, No. 7, at pp. 14-15:

> It is to be observed that these two clauses which serve as a basis for the provisions embodied in the Minorities Treaty do not speak restrictively of Polish nationals, that is to say of persons who in their capacity as Polish nationals constitute minorities within the whole body of nationals of the country; these clauses considerably extend the conceptions of minority and population, since they allude on the one hand to the inhabitants of the territory over which Poland has assumed sovereignty and on the other hand to inhabitants who differ from the majority of the

which served as a model for the other treaties of the period contains ten articles recognising some type of right or legal protection. Three articles acknowledge Poland's obligation to grant automatic citizenship to members of certain minorities; two guarantee rights and freedoms to all inhabitants, regardless of their citizenship; three limit the benefit of rights to Polish nationals (citizens) and two give Jewish communities control of and financial assistance for their own schools, but none of the above require proof of citizenship for all members of the communities to exercise their rights.[6]

The requirement of citizenship should be understood in the context that most individuals born or residing in Poland at the time had an almost automatic right to Polish nationality. This meant that the distinction between citizens and non-citizens became largely superfluous. Unfortunately, this point has been ignored by commentators interpreting Article 27 of the **Covenant** and other minority provisions by reference to the decisions and treaties of the League of Nations era, with particularly negative results in countries grappling with the difficult legacy of Soviet population strategies.[7]

The objectives of the minorities treaties were enumerated by the Permanent Court of International Justice in one decision as follows:

The idea underlying the treaties for the protection of minorities, is to secure for certain elements incorporated in a state, the population of which differs form them in race, language or religion, the possibility of living peacefully alongside that population and co-operating amicably with it, while at the same time preserving the characteristics which distinguish them from the majority, and satisfying the ensuing special needs.
In order to attain this object, two things were regarded as particularly necessary, and have formed the subject of provisions in these treaties.
The first is to ensure that nationals belonging to racial, religious or linguistic minorities shall be placed in every respect on a footing of perfect equality with the other nationals of the state.
The second is to ensure for the minority element suitable means for the preservation of their racial peculiarities, their traditions and their national characteristics.
These two requirements are indeed closely interlocked, for there would be no true equality between a majority and a minority if the latter were deprived of its own institutions, and

---

population in race, language or religion. The expression "population" seems thus to include all inhabitants of Polish origin in the territory incorporated in Poland. Again, the term "minority" seems to include inhabitants who differ from the population in race, language or religion, that is to say, amongst others, inhabitants of this territory of non-Polish origin, whether they are Polish nationals or not. This conclusion is confirmed by the terms of Article 2 of the Minorities Treaty, according to which the Polish Government undertakes to assure full and complete protection of life and liberty to all inhabitants without distinction of birth, nationality, language, race or religion, and declares that all inhabitants of Poland shall enjoy certain rights which are therein enumerated.

[6] The treaty is reprinted in its entirety in Thornberry, Patrick (1991), *International Law and the Rights of Minorities*, Clarendon Press, Oxford, United Kingdom, at pp. 399-403.

[7] Discrimination on the ground of language and naturalisation policies will be considered in detail in Section 6.4.

were consequently compelled to renounce that which constitutes the very essence of its being as a minority.[8]

One of the key issues under the treaties was who could claim membership in a minority, an issue vigorously debated still today as it relates to Article 27 of the **Covenant** and other similar provisions. The Permanent Court of International Justice's opted for a liberal approach in the **Polish Nationality Case**. By taking into account the background to the creation of the treaty and the interest in avoiding possible conflict and tension because of resentment by large groups of individuals finding themselves in states where the majority spoke a different language or practised a different religion, the court concluded that any inhabitant who differed from the majority of the population in race, language or religion should be entitled to claim membership in the religious, racial or linguistic minority group sharing the same.[9] As a result any individual in Poland who spoke German as a primary language, for example, regardless of his ethnic or national origin, could rightly demand recognition as a member of the German linguistic community.

Furthermore, the status of minority was recognised as purely demographic in nature and not related to political or economic considerations. A minority is constituted if it is not a majority in a given state, that is if it constitutes less than 50 percent of the population of the country. There is therefore no need for official state recognition of a minority situation, since it is a matter of fact and not a matter of political or legal recognition.[10]

Individual freedom of choice as to membership in a minority seemed to permeate the treaties. In the **Rights of Minorities in Upper Silesia (Minority Schools)** case, the court ruled that an individual could freely declare whether or not his child belonged to a racial, linguistic or religious minority, therefore entitling the latter to go to a minority school, although such declarations did not eliminate the need for some requirement of factual backup:

> [The] declarations must set out what their author regards as the true position in regard to the point in question and that the right freely to declare what is the language of a pupil or child, though comprising, when necessary, the exercise of some discretion in the appreciation of circumstances, does not constitute an unrestricted right to choose the language in which instruction is to be imparted or the corresponding school.[11]

In addition to imposing on states certain positive obligations, such as providing public schools having a minority language as the medium of instruction in cases where a considerable proportion of the population in towns and districts spoke a non-official or non-majority language, the treaties usually included the right for linguistic minorities to freely use their language in private institutions and schools. The drafters of Article 27 of the **Covenant** and subsequent international

---

[8] **Advisory Opinion on Minority Schools in Albania**, (1935) Permanent Court of International Justice, Series A/B, No. 64, 3, at p. 17.

[9] **Polish Nationality Case**, *supra*, note 5, at pp. 13-16.

[10] See **Interpretation of the Convention Between Greece and Bulgaria Respecting Reciprocal Emigration**, (1930) Permanent Court of International Justice, Series B, No. 17, at pp. 14-16, also known as the **Greco-Bulgarian Communities Case**.

[11] **Rights of Minorities in Upper Silesia (Minority Schools)**, (1928) Permanent Court of International Justice, Series A, No. 12, at p. 46.

instruments were in all likelihood inspired by this latter provision in their efforts to provide specific guarantees for minorities.

The need for such a provision in the minorities treaties was explained in the **Minority Schools in Albania** case.[12] The Permanent Court of International Justice examined the validity of an Albanian law aimed at abolishing all private schools in the country. This, according to the Greek government, was contrary to the **Albanian Minorities Treaty** which safeguarded in Article 5 the right of minorities to establish and maintain their own schools. The Albanian government argued that the law treated both the Albanian majority and the Greek-speaking minority in exactly the same way, since no private Albanian-language schools would be allowed to operate, and that Article 5 only guaranteed that both should "enjoy the same treatment and the same security, both in law and in fact".

Essentially, the Permanent Court of International Justice concluded that pursuant to Article 5, Greek-speaking Albanians enjoyed special rights not available to other Albanians, and in particular the right to their own private schools where the language of instruction would be Greek. This was required in order to ensure "suitable means for the preservation of their racial peculiarities, their traditions and their national characteristics." In other words, members of minority groups should be permitted some rights or freedoms not necessarily enjoyed by the majority, because their position as a minority renders them particularly vulnerable to the whims and domination of the majority.

For example, although public schools using Greek as the medium of instruction could exist and did in fact exist in Albania, because they were public schools they were subject to direct and extensive control by the Albanian government and, for the most part, non-Greek-speaking officials, leaving Greek-speakers with little influence on the quality and content of Greek-language instruction. In acknowledgment of these and other difficulties facing linguistic minorities in the context of public schooling, the court appears to have adopted the position that members of a minority should always be entitled to their "own" institutions, signifying institutions set up and controlled by the members of the minority community themselves, despite the fact that such a right may be denied to members of the majority.

5.2.2 Early United Nations Efforts

A similar approach was taken by the United Nations immediately following World War II and prior to the development of the two human rights covenants. In its 1947 partition plan for Palestine,[13] one of the main elements envisioned was to guarantee to members of the Jewish and Arab minorities of each of the new states the right to open and operate their own private educational institutions.

Nevertheless, during the drafting of the **United Nations Charter** there was deep-rooted ambivalence and conflicts between states as to whether or not a minorities provision should be included. Whilst the experience of racist policies aimed at genocide of a religious minority in Nazi Germany called for the recognition that states could not simply have *carte blanche* on how it treated minority citizens and aliens, countries such as the United States and Latin American states were reluctant to adopt any measures that would inhibit the assimilation of newcomers. This is why the **Charter** is restricted to the principle of non-discrimination, and lacks

---

[12] *Supra*, note 8, at p. 4.

[13] General Assembly Resolution 181(2), UN GAOR Second Session, 131, UN Document A/519 (1947).

consideration of whether or not individuals belonging to minorities should also be free to operate private educational institutions or to otherwise be free to use their language (or practice their religion) in a private context.

Efforts to include some special consideration for the protection of minorities were also unsuccessful when time came for the adoption of the **Universal Declaration of Human Rights**, but this was a brief *partie remise* as a more extensive treatment of the issue was already being initiated:

> The [United Nations Sub-Commission on the Prevention of Discrimination and the Protection of Minorities'] efforts to include an article on minorities in the Universal Declaration of Human Rights were unavailing in the face of rejection by the Commission on Human Rights. Following this, the General Assembly requested the Commission and Sub-Commission to make a thorough study of the problem of minorities. The Sub-Commission prepared a draft resolution for the Commission recommending that Member Governments provide minority groups with educational and judicial institutions using the groups' languages. It also proposed that a provision on minority rights be inserted into the UN Covenant on Civil and Political Rights — a successful proposal.[14]

As regards the **Universal Declaration,** a number of draft provisions guaranteeing public funds for schools and cultural institutions of linguistic minorities and the use of their language before public authorities (in the case of a minority constituting a substantial portion of a state's population) were prepared; however, they were unable to garner sufficient backing in the General Assembly, the contention mainly being (1) that minorities should not be protected but rather obliged to assimilate with the majority; (2) and that states were reluctant to being obliged to provide special concessions to groups which might imply financial and institutional obligations.[15] The failure to include a minorities provision in the **Universal Declaration** should not be considered a complete rejection of the need to respond generously to the presence of linguistic, racial and religious minorities in a state, as the General Assembly did in fact adopt a distinct resolution on minorities[16] and referred the whole matter for study. In other words, it sought to defuse the debate and arrive at a proposal which might be more acceptable to a majority of states. If anything, the debate proved that minority issues could not simply be ignored in dealing with human rights principles.

5.2.3   *Article 27 of the Covenant and Consensus on Non-Interference*

As mentioned, drafts of a minority provision submitted by members of the UN Sub-Commission on the Prevention of Discrimination and the Protection of Minorities were set aside, probably because they obliged states to provide for and support financially the use of minority languages in courts and in public educational institutions. The beginning of a consensus was to emerge once the wording of the minorities provision in the draft **International Covenant on Civil and Political Rights** began to reflect the recognition that states should refrain from intervening with

---

[14] See Thornberry, *supra,* note 6, at p. 129. Professor Thornberry's work also has a good description of the debates and internal workings of the United Nations regarding minority rights.

[15] Ibid., at pp. 136-137.

[16] General Assembly Resolution 217c(III), 10 December 1948.

minorities in the practice of their religion and the use of their language, and that this did not entail a minority right to assistance from the state. From an initial proposal that "...linguistic minorities shall not be denied the right to...use their own language",[17] the provision began to take the form in force today. As explained by Professor Thornberry:

> The Sub-Commission preferred that "persons belonging to minorities" should replace "minorities" because minorities were not subjects of law and "persons belonging to minorities" could easily be defined in legal terms. On the other hand, it was decided to include "in community with the other members of their group" after "shall not be denied" in order to recognise group identity in some form.[18]

The text of what was to become Article 27 remained the object of various amendment proposals. Chile proposed the addition of the following text "In those states in which ethnic, religious or linguistic minorities exist", which may seem rather superfluous: if there were no such minorities in a state, Article 27 would be irrelevant. However, the Chilean proposal must be read in light of the fact that some states feared that the provision might encourage segments of their inhabitants to isolate themselves from the rest of the population.[19]

Finally, something which was not included in the final version of Article 27 should be mentioned. A number of states wished to limit as much as possible the categories of individuals who could claim protection under Article 27. Those favouring rapid assimilation of minorities considered that only long-established and clearly defined "national minorities" should be protected, whilst others advocated the protection of anyone associated with an ethnic, religious or linguistic community. Article 27 as finally adopted has no restriction as to a specific group of linguistic, religious or ethnic minorities. On the contrary, the wording of the provision and its history support the conclusion that any individual who is truly a member of such a community may seek the protection of Article 27.

In essence, the consensus reached reflected the refusal by most states to accept proposals which would have obliged them to concede to every minority on its territory, regardless of its numbers,[20] the right to obtain public financial assistance to establish institutions, amongst other things. Since this was clearly unacceptable to most governments, the final provision merely reflects a commitment to refrain from interfering with individuals involved in language use,

---

[17] UN Document E/CN.4/Sub.2/112.

[18] *Supra*, note 6, at p. 149.

[19] Unfortunately, this last modification has provided a convenient escape route for states which, for whatever reason, prefer to disregard their guarantees. A state is free to deny the existence of a minority on its territory in an attempt to escape obligations associated to the protection of minorities guaranteed in Article 27. For example, a fascist regime such as that in Nazi Germany could deny the existence of a Jewish minority, or a state could deny the presence of indigenous peoples on its territory, etc. In order not to be restrained by a state's contention that it has no minorities, the Human Rights Committee has indicated that the existence of a minority is a factual determination and not one based upon a political declaration or legal determination.

[20] None of the initial proposals appeared to provide that the rights involved could be associated to any restriction. In theory therefore, the right to receive a response from public authorities in one's language of choice would have had to be respected even if a linguistic minority only represented a few hundred, or dozen, individuals in a state.

religious practices and cultural expression of a minority community. Both the background leading up to the adoption of the provision and its wording confirm that Article 27 is a non-interference clause for ethnic, religious or linguistic minorities:

> In those states in which ethnic, religious or linguistic minorities exist, persons belonging to such minorities shall not be denied the right, in community with the other members of their group, to enjoy their own culture, to profess and practise their own religion, or to use their own language.

Despite what should have been the obvious *raison d' être* and its scope of application, subsequent doctrine has to a large extent muddied the waters. The interpretation of Article 27 by many have created a great deal of confusion, although to its credit the UN Human Rights Committee has for the most part steered away from some of the mistaken views expressed by some scholars on this provision.

5.3   THE SCOPE AND MEANING OF MINORITIES UNDER ARTICLE 27

5.3.1   *Debate over Definitions*

The addition of the words "[i]n those states in which ethnic, religious or linguistic minorities exist" in Article 27 of the **International Covenant on Civil and Political Rights** has led to some debate as to what constitutes a minority. Some countries have persistently stated that the guarantee of equal rights for all in their state renders the notion of minority, in its politico-legal sense, inapplicable to them. For example, during the drafting of Article 27, the representative of Brazil expressed the view, apparently shared by many Latin American states, that any minority classification was inapplicable in their context for the following reasons:

> [The] mere coexistence of different groups in a territory under the jurisdiction of a single state did not make them minorities in the legal sense. A minority resulted from conflicts of some length between nations, or from the transfer of a territory from the jurisdiction of one state to that of another.[21]

Latin American states in general thus considered that immigrants and indigenous peoples could not be considered minorities.

In order to clarify the scope of Article 27, the Sub-Commission on the Prevention of Discrimination and the Protection of Minorities appointed Professor Francesco Capotorti to carry out a study which remains today an impressive document — going far beyond the narrow wording of Article 27 — examining the status and treatment of minorities throughout the world and exploring topics such as discrimination on the grounds of language and freedom of expression for minorities. The report also contains a widely circulated definition of minority:

> A group numerically inferior to the rest of the population of a state, in a non-dominant position, whose members — being nationals of the state — possess ethnic, religious or

---

[21] GAOR, sixteenth session, third committee, paragraphs 8-12, quoted in Thornberry, *supra*, note 6, at p. 154.

linguistic characteristics differing from those of the rest of the population and show, if only implicitly, a sense of solidarity, directed towards preserving their culture, traditions, religion or language.[22]

Unfortunately, many commentators have simply adopted this definition without considering whether or not it conforms with the intent and wording of Article 27. In fact, the definition adopts certain concepts which were categorically rejected when the provision was adopted, and has accentuated confusion amongst commentators. On the one hand, doctrine has chosen to consider "minority" as a politico-legal status, resulting in the exclusion of certain categories of individuals from the scope of Article 27 (non-citizens, dominant minorities, new or emerging minorities).[23] On the other hand, a number of scholars have pointed out that neither the *travaux préparatoires*, nor the actual wording of the provision supports such a conclusion.[24]

5.3.2   Objective or Subjective Minority?

The debate may be explained in part by the failure to distinguish between minority as a purely numerical criterion, and minority as the expression of political power and attitude. The definitions proposed by Capotorti and Deschênes[25] attempted to combine elements of both, but in so doing may have inadvertently led to a definition which is too restrictive, too difficult to apply, and essentially inconsistent with the plain wording of Article 27.

Professor Thornberry, who also chose to consider "minority" as a politico-legal status, attempted to support his albeit less than enthusiastic conclusion that non-citizens were excluded

---

[22] *Study on the Rights of Persons belonging to Ethnic, Religious and Linguistic Minorities, Francesco Capotorti, Special Rapporteur* (1979), United Nations Publications, New York, at paragraph 568. A subsequent definition was presented to the Sub-Commission by Judge Jules Deschênes, but adds little to the one advanced by Capotorti. If anything, it is even more restrictive as it implies that a minority group can only claim the protection of Article 27 if it collectively has the aim of achieving "equality with the majority in fact and in law", see *Peoples and Minorities in International Law* (1993), Catherine Brölmann, René Lefeber, and Marjoleine Zieck (eds.), Martinus Nijhoff, Dordrecht, Netherlands, at pp. 160-161. Capotorti's definition turned out to be controversial in the Sub-Commission, some challenging the limitation to citizens, others pointing out that the concept of "non-dominant" combined with "numerical minority" created problems in the case of a group being a numerical majority in the state but non-dominant, or in the case of a group being regionally dominant while numerically a minority in the state as a whole.

[23] Amongst the scholars that appear to lean in this direction are Thornberry, *supra*, note 6, at pp. 171-172; Capotorti and Deschênes, ibid., in their definition of minorities under Article 27; and Modeen, T. (1969), *The International Protection of National Minorities in Europe*, Åbo Akademi, Åbo, Finland, at p. 108.

[24] See in particular Wolfrum, Rüdiger (1993), "The Emergence of New Minorities as a Result of Migration", in Catherine Brölmann, René Lefeber, and Marjoleine Zieck (eds.), *Peoples and Minorities in International Law*, Martinus Nijhoff, Dordrecht, Netherlands, 153-166, at pp. 163-166; and Tomuschat, Christian (1983), "Protection of Minorities under Article 27 of the International Covenant on Civil and Political Rights", in *Völkerrecht als Rechtsordnung Internationale Gerichtsarbeit Menschenrechte*, Springer, Berlin, pp. 949-979, at p. 954.

[25] As to the definition proposed by Deschênes see, *supra*, note 22.

from the protection of Article 27 by reference to a few inconclusive comments from the *travaux préparatoires*, where some state representatives seemed to take it for granted that only citizens could be the object of protection under Article 27:

> The view of Iraq...was that the obligations of a state within its own territory could only be towards its own citizens. It was in that sense that she understood the word persons in the Article... The Representative of Pakistan...considered that members of minorities were as much loyal citizens as members of the majority of the community. The need for minority members to be loyal citizens was stressed by other delegations. Thus, the rarely explicit view emerging from the *travaux* is that foreigners are not minorities, or not minorities for the purposes of Article 27.[26]

With due respect to Professor Thornberry's impressive research, his conclusion is based, for the most part, on the premise that Special Rapporteur Capotorti was correct in proposing that non-citizens be excluded. However, Professor Thornberry and others who have adopted the same reasoning were led into error because they never questioned how and why the Special Rapporteur proposed such a definition, in apparent contradiction to the provision's wording, which does not explicitly exclude non-citizens.

Moreover, a number of scholars appear to ignore that during the drafting of Article 27, the majority of state representatives generally did not demonstrate any support for the vague comments of a few countries such as Iraq and Pakistan. Furthermore, a majority of representatives subsequently rejected a limited application of Article 27 rather convincingly. One proposal by Uruguay would have altogether excluded minority groups formed by immigrants.[27] A small number of states would have preferred inserting the words "national minorities" in order to emphasise the need for a group to be long-established in a state. Neither prevailed in the end, which lends stronger credence to the conclusion that minorities under Article 27 cannot be read as being limited to nationals.[28]

In addition to limiting minorities to nationals of a state, Capotorti's definition would appear to limit the guarantees of Article 27 only to ethnic, religious or linguistic minorities which are in a non-dominant position. Once again, justification for such a restricted interpretation cannot clearly be found in the wording of Article 27. Although it is a truism that a minority in a dominating position may well not need the protection provided by this provision, since after all they have the benefit of controlling public authorities, it does not thereby follow that such minorities are excluded from its scope.[29]

---

[26] *Supra*, note 6, at p. 172.

[27] See Wolfrum, *supra*, note 24, at p. 162.

[28] Unequivocally, Article 27 is aimed at ensuring the protection of all ethnic, religious or linguistic minorities, and is not limited to ethnic, religious or linguistic minorities which are also national minorities, in the sense of long-established groups of citizens. Capotorti failed to distinguish between the two, and his error would appear to have been repeated by others subsequently. For a more detailed consideration of this point, see Sections 5.8.1 and 5.8.2, *infra*.

[29] In fact, it can be argued that a minority in a position of domination in all likelihood owes its control to violation of other rights and freedoms, as was the case with the former racist regime in South Africa. In such cases, the solution is not to restrict the scope of Article 27 but to correct the unacceptable infringement of other rights. Moreover, in the case of apartheid, Article 27 would have

As for the explanation for Capotorti's perhaps surprising restriction of minority protection under Article 27 to citizens belonging to non-dominant minorities, such a restriction can be found in the minorities treaties of the League of Nations era and in a few other documents, including a definition proposed at one point by the Sub-Commission on the Prevention of Discrimination and the Protection of Minorities. However, this is unconvincing because many of the various documents referred to by Capotorti do not attempt to limit the definition of minorities as suggested.[30] In the end, Capotorti appears to have attempted to create a *pot-pourri* containing many of the various suggestions of objective and subjective elements advanced by state representatives, including for example the requirement that a group, in order to be considered a minority under Article 27, must "show, if only implicitly, a sense of solidarity, directed towards preserving their culture, traditions, religion or language."

In essence, Capotorti defined the notion of minority as a sociological and political condition in addition to a numerical one. Whilst there were certainly comments during the drafting of Article 27 consistent with the adoption of these criteria, the *travaux préparatoires* unambiguously show that there was no prevailing consensus with respect to adding any sociological or political aspects to the concept of minority as Capotorti chose to do.[31] Capotorti's final comments on why the application of the provision should be limited to nationals, for example, is particularly weak:

> The case of foreigners is different, however, from that of persons who possess the nationality of the country in which they live. As long as a person retains his status as a foreigner, he has the right to benefit from the protection granted by customary international law to persons who are in countries other than their own, as well as from any other special rights which may be conferred upon him by treaties or other special agreements. Article 27 of the Covenant should thus be interpreted as relating solely to nationals of the state.[32]

---

been useless to the controlling White minority since their control of the state machinery in South Africa would have guaranteed rights and privileges far exceeding anything Article 27 entitles members of a minority. The debate on the fight against intolerable violations of human rights through discriminatory practices belongs in another, proper forum.

[30] See Capotorti, *supra*, note 22, at paragraphs 2, 54, and footnote 15.

[31] Thornberry, although siding in the end with Capotorti, admits as much when he analyses the *travaux préparatoires*, *supra*, note 6, at pp. 169-171.

[32] Capotorti, *supra*, note 22, at paragraph 57. See also Alfredsson, Gudmundur (1990), *Report on Equality and Non-Discrimination: Minority Rights*, Council of Europe, Strasbourg, at p. 14:
> Immigrants from many different ethnic, cultural and linguistic origins voluntarily moving to and settling in one country, including migrant workers who chose not to return, are another category of people who may not require minority protection. They may be compelled by economic and other conditions, but they are nevertheless exercising a "free" choice and should accept the drawbacks and not only the benefits of that selection. This view coincides with a requirement often suggested, namely that a minority be well-established over a period of time before they are accorded special minority rights.

Alfredsson's explanation lacks strength in that an immigrant should not be required to forsake his language or religion by being in another state, nor does international law support such a draconian view. A Muslim *Gastarbeiter* in Germany is absolutely not required, nor has he "freely" accepted, to become a Christian, any more than he is obliged to accept exclusive use of the German language in

Customary international law is of little or no assistance if an immigrant is prohibited from using his language with other members of his community. Moreover, whilst non-citizens have a different status than nationals of a state, Capotorti fails to explain why this has any relevance to language use or religious practices.[33]

The truth of the matter is that the Special Rapporteur may well have left himself little choice but to restrict the definition of a minority, because the interpretation of Article 27 he advanced created obligations on states to provide a number of services and financial assistance to minorities.[34] The ensuing reluctance of some states to accept the application of Article 27 on their territory rests on the erroneous view of the possible demands it makes on states. This point will be discussed shortly.

The final nail to the coffin in respect to a restrictive view of what constitutes a minority is to be found in a series of decisions of the United Nations Human Rights Committee and its interpretation of Article 27, followed by two General Comments that dispel any lingering doubt as to the definition of a minority.

5.3.3 *Confirmation of Minority as a Strictly Numerical Status*

The above stack of cards advanced by some commentators as to the interpretation of Article 27 has fallen under a series of decisions and of the United Nations Human Rights Committee (UNHRC) and in two general comments. Almost every aspect of Capotorti's widely circulated definition has been set aside, although this has been largely unnoticed. Despite some grumbling and strong dissent by some Committee members, the UNHRC has clearly opted for a strictly numerical categorisation, consistently disregarding the social and political aspects of the definition

---

private and community activities with others sharing his native language.

[33] *Modern Law of Self-Determination* (1993), Christian Tomuschat (ed.), Martinus Nijhoff, Dordrecht, Netherlands, at p. 159:

> As to the limitation of citizens, the different kinds of non-citizens described above indicate that a much more precise analysis has to be carried out. A general exclusion of non-citizens from minority protection is not acceptable. There is, for instance, no inherent reason why settled groups of non-nationals should not have the right of to practice their religion (e.g. Orthodox Russian-speaking groups in Protestant Estonia) or use their own language between themselves. The limitation, by Capotorti, to nationals appears to be based on the assumption that customary law regarding aliens, or special treaties, will provide the necessary protection; it may, however, require further evidence to prove that this is always true.

[34] Having essentially accepted Capotorti's point of view that Article 27 requires positive steps on the part of states to provide the necessary resources in order for minorities to protect their essential characteristics, Thornberry found himself in the same trap as he himself acknowledges, *supra*, note 6, at p. 171:

> Many states are unwilling to accept voluntary immigrants taking the state's nationality as being "minorities"; *a fortiori* they are even less well disposed to accept the notion that foreigners are recipients of "minority rights". When coupled with the possible demands upon the state which may be made in consequence of an invocation of Article 27, the etymological approach reduces to absurdity. States can hardly be expected to promote foreign culture at their own expense; this obligation, if one exists in any legal sphere, would naturally devolve upon the home state of the group.

of a minority. In other words, it has now become clear that the existence of a minority lies in the strictly objective criterion of whether or not an ethnic, religious or linguistic group represents less than 50 percent of the state's population.

It must be remembered that during the drafting of Article 27, a small number of state representatives would have excluded indigenous peoples, dominant minorities, non-citizens, and "new" nationals from the definition of "minority", although they failed to garner a majority in order to do so. All of these states relied upon a number of explanations which all point to two main concerns: (1) the potential demands upon states by minorities, or (2) minorities as a social or political category.

As regards indigenous peoples as minorities, Deschênes preferred to steer away from the debate by stating that it is a "non-problem",[35] although Thornberry himself recognised that most indigenous peoples can be considered minorities, in strictly numerical terms.[36] It should be noted that indigenous peoples themselves generally react negatively to any attempt to categorise them as minorities; however, this is due to their perception of a minority as a political category, which is anathema to them since they claim to have retained their political sovereignty, a fact increasingly acknowledged in international law as will be discussed below.

In **Lovelace v. Canada**,[37] the UNHRC began to set the record straight by adopting a logical no-nonsense approach: Mrs. Lovelace was an indigenous person, a member of an ethnic and linguistic community called Maliseets which are numerically a minority in Canada, *ergo*, Mrs. Lovelace was a member of a minority.

The details of this matter are straightforward. Although Mrs. Lovelace was born a Maliseet and so registered by Canadian authorities, she lost her rights and status as an Indian in accordance with Article 12(1)(b) of the **Indian Act** after having married a non-Indian. In pointing out that an Indian man who marries a non-Indian woman does not lose his Indian status, Mrs. Lovelace claimed that the **Act** was discriminatory on the grounds of sex and contrary to Articles 2(1), 3, 23(1) and (4), 26 and 27 of the **International Covenant on Civil and Political Rights**.

In its decision, the Human Rights Committee decided to concentrate on the loss of the cultural benefits of living in an Indian community, the inability to use her language with other members of her community, and the loss of identity.

The Human Rights Committee then proceeded on the basis of the natural meaning of the words used in Article 27. It did not attempt to distinguish different social or political categories in order to determine whether Maliseets are a minority. It addressed the issue of whether or not Maliseets can be considered an ethnic or linguistic minority, and concluded that they are, being ethnically and linguistically different from the majority, and being numerically less than 50 percent of the population in Canada. Following this determination, the Human Rights Committee addressed the issue of whether or not Mrs. Lovelace was in fact a member of the Maliseet minority, and concluded in the affirmative.

Following these preliminary considerations, the Human Rights Committee concluded:

> [I]n the opinion of the Committee the right of Sandra Lovelace to access to her native culture and language "in community with the other members" of her group, has in fact been,

---

[35] Capotorti avoided stating clearly in his report whether indigenous peoples can be minorities under Article 27, although he does refer to indigenous groups on a few occasions.

[36] *Supra*, note 6, at p. 331.

[37] Communication 24/1977, UN Document A/36/40.

and continues to be interfered with, because there is no place outside the Tobique Reserve where such a community exists.[38] On the other hand, not every interference can be regarded as a denial of rights within the meaning of Article 27. Restrictions on the right to residence, by way of national legislation, cannot be ruled out under Article 27 of the Covenant.[39]

In **Kitok v. Sweden**[40] and **Ominayak v. Canada**,[41] the UNHRC similarly decided that indigenous peoples can be minorities pursuant to Article 27, and did not even consider the contrary option as a serious issue.

In **Ballantyne, Davidson and McIntyre v. Canada**,[42] a majority of members of the Human Rights Committee also discounted the requirement that a minority be in a non-dominant position as advanced by Capotorti and other scholars subsequently, in determining whether a group constitutes a minority under Article 27. The Human Rights Committee rejected claims based on Article 27 for the reason that "English-speaking citizens of Canada cannot be considered a linguistic minority", although in a separate opinion, four members of the Committee expressed concern over the majority opinion. In essence, the majority held that a language minority should be judged purely in terms of overall numbers in a state:

> As to Article 27, the Committee observes that this provision refers to minorities in states; this refers, as do all references to the "state" or to "states" in the provisions of the Covenant, to ratifying states. Further, Article 50 of the Covenant provides that its provisions extend to all parts of federal states without any limitations or exceptions. Accordingly, the minorities referred to in Article 27 are minorities within such a state, and not minorities within any province. A group may constitute a majority in a province but still be a minority in a state and thus be entitled to the benefits of Article 27. English-speaking citizens of Canada cannot be considered a linguistic minority.[43]

As for the authors of the separate opinion, they stressed that greater consideration should be given to potential difficulties, especially in a federal state where individuals may be subjected to legislation that is outside the reach of the federal (national) government:

> My difficulty with the decision is that it interprets the term "minorities" in Article 27 solely on the basis of the number of members of the group in question in the state party. The reasoning is that because English-speaking Canadians are not a numerical minority in Canada they cannot be a minority for the purposes of Article 27.
> I do not agree, however, that persons are necessarily excluded from the protection of Article 27 where their group is an ethnic, linguistic or cultural minority in an autonomous province

---

[38] This aspect of the Committee's decision is factually incorrect. There are other Maliseet communities near the Tobique Reserve.

[39] **Lovelace v. Canada**, *supra*, note 37, at paragraph 15.

[40] Communication 197/1985, UN Document A/43/40.

[41] Communication 167/1984, UN Document A/42/40.

[42] Communications Nos. 359/1989 and 385/1989, 31 March 1993.

[43] Ibid, at paragraph 11.2.

of a state, but it is not clearly a numerical minority in the state itself, taken as a whole entity... The history of the protection of minorities in international law shows that the question of definition has been difficult and controversial and that many different criteria have been proposed. For example, it has been argued that factors other than strictly numerical ones need to be taken into account. Alternatively, Article 50, which envisages the application of the Covenant to "parts of federal states" could affect the interpretation of Article 27.

To take a narrow view of the meaning of minorities in Article 27 could have the result that a state party would have no obligation under the Covenant to ensure that a minority in an autonomous province had the protection of Article 27 where it was not clear that the group in question was a minority in the state considered as a whole entity. These questions do not need to be finally resolved in the present matter and are better deferred until the proper context arises.[44]

In this decision, there was no debate as to whether English-speaking individuals should also be excluded because they are in a dominant position in Canada, which would have been a natural point to consider if dominance had any relevance. The majority of members of the Committee stuck to objective, numerical criteria.

The UNHRC cast aside any lingering doubt on whether non-citizens as a group are excluded from the definition of a minority under Article 27, as proposed by Capotorti and others, by unequivocally stating in its *General Comment on the position of aliens under the International Covenant on Civil and Political Rights*[45] that aliens who can demonstrate membership in a numerically inferior ethnic, religious or linguistic community shall not de denied the rights provided in Article 27. This is consistent with the general background to, and the wording of Article 27, as explains one leading scholar:

The United Nations General Assembly, when drafting and adopting Article 27 of the Political Covenant, already opted for a broader definition. The Third Committee did not accept a proposed Indian amendment aimed at replacing the word "persons" with "citizens". Both the *travaux préparatoires* and a systematic interpretation of the Political Covenant,

---

[44] Individual opinion by Mrs. Elizabeth Evatt, co-signed by Nisuke Ando, Marco Tulio Bruni Celli and Vojin Dimitrijevic. Whilst they have raised valid concerns, one has to remember on the one hand that the majority's conclusion is consistent with the plain meaning and *raison d'être* of Article 27: the only concession most states were willing to make at the time of drafting was to recognise that in a country, minorities can be subjected to serious mistreatment or disadvantages by being subjected to the whims of a majority, and that they should at least be free to conduct without interference those activities that are most intimately tied with their distinctive community. On the other hand, it could be validly maintained that the drafters of Article 27 simply overlooked that in a federal state, even a national majority may find itself subjected to serious mistreatment if it is a numerical minority in one of the federal units and outside the reach of federal (national) protection. The *travaux préparatoires* are silent on this issue.

[45] *General Comment 15(27)*, UN Document A/41/40, at p. 118.

which uses the term "citizens" only in Article 25, clearly indicate that Article 27 also applies to aliens.[46]

To ensure no one misunderstands what should have been fairly clear from the very beginning, the United Nations Human Rights Committee finally adopted in 1994 *General Comment No. 23(50)* on Article 27 which spells out the exact meaning of a minority under the **International Covenant on Civil and Political Rights**:

> The terms used in Article 27 indicate that the persons designed to be protected are those who belong to a group and who share in common a culture, a religion and/or a language. Those terms also indicate that the individuals designed to be protected need not be citizens of the state party... A state party may not, therefore, restrict the rights under Article 27 to its citizens alone.
>
> Article 27 confers rights on persons belonging to minorities which "exist" in a state party. Given the nature and scope of the rights envisaged under that article, it is not relevant to determine the degree of permanence that the term "exist" connotes. Those rights simply are that individuals belonging to those minorities should not be denied the right, in community with members of their group, to enjoy their own culture, to practice their religion and speak their language. Just as they need not be nationals or citizens, they need not be permanent residents. Thus, migrant workers or even visitors in a state party constituting such minorities are entitled not to be denied the exercise of those rights... The existence of an ethnic, religious or linguistic minority in a given state party does not depend upon a decision by that state party but requires to be established by objective criteria.[47]

This would appear to close the book on how to address the definition of minority under Article 27, at least by signalling that in essence subjective criteria have no relevance, despite some lingering resistance.[48] Minority is an objective, numerical status based upon ties with a language,

---

[46] Nowak, Manfred, "The Evolution of Minority Rights in International Law", in Catherine Brölmann, René Lefeber and Marjoleine Zieck (eds.), *Peoples and Minorities in International Law*, Martinus Nijhoff, Dordrecht, pp. 103-118, at p. 116. See also Bossuyt, Marc (1990), "The United Nations and the Definition of Minorities", in *Plural Societies Research Papers*, Vol. XXI, 129-136, at p. 131:

> If Article 27 contains mainly a negative obligation in the sense that governments are obligated to refrain from interfering with the culture, religion and language of minority groups, a definition becomes almost superfluous. It is also because Article 27 contains essentially only negative obligations that Article 27 may also be applied to aliens and to immigrants...

[47] 6 April 1994, Document CCPR/C/21/Rev.1/Add.5, at paragraphs 5.1 and 5.2.

[48] No doubt because of the mistaken premise that the definitions put forward by Capotorti and Deschênes conformed with the *raison d'être* and wording of Article 27, a number of subsequent instruments and national legislation were adopted limiting the exercise of certain rights to citizens (i.e. Article 1 of the **European Charter for Regional or Minority Languages**). The drafters of these instruments were also probably uncomfortable with the idea of having to recognise a state's obligation to provide assistance and services to non-citizens, especially in language matters. However, their discomfort is based upon the erroneous approach adopted by Capotorti and Thornberry to the effect that Article 27 mandates such obligations. It does not. Not all instruments followed this route, as evidenced by the 1992 UN **Declaration on the Rights of Persons Belonging to National or Ethnic,**

religion or ethnic group, and not any complicated formula excluding some groups because of subjective concepts, such as sociological or political condition, nor any other complicated formula involving dominance, need to show a sense of solidarity, length of residency in a state, nationality, etc.

From the above, a proper definition of minority for the purposes of Article 27 would be a group of individuals sharing common ethnic, religious or linguistic characteristics, and which are numerically inferior to the rest of the population of a state. As Capotorti correctly pointed out, this definition, because it is objective, renders unnecessary any requirement of recognition of minorities in the legal systems of states.[49]

5.4   INDIVIDUALS CAPABLE OF CLAIMING MINORITY MEMBERSHIP

5.4.1   *"Belonging to a Minority": An Objective Criterion*

Although the Human Rights Committee did not dwell in its *General Comment No. 23(50)* on which individuals are to be protected under Article 27, it did suggest that not everyone can claim to be entitled to the rights guaranteed to ethnic, religious or linguistic minorities, since "the terms used...indicate that the persons designed to be protected are those who belong to a group and who share in common a culture, a religion and/or a language."[50] Some real and tangible tie must exist between an individual and one of these categories. In other words, a person must demonstrate that he or she "belongs" to an ethnic, religious or linguistic group. Once again, the UNHRC appears to have opted for a no-nonsense, objective approach. In **Lovelace v. Canada**, the Human Rights Committee stated:

> The rights under Article 27 of the Covenant have to be secured to "persons belonging" to the minority. At present Sandra Lovelace does not qualify as an Indian under Canadian legislation. However, the Indian Act deals primarily with a number of privileges which, as stated above, do not as such come within the scope of the Covenant. Protection under the Indian Act and protection under Article 27 of the Covenant therefore have to be distinguished. Persons who are born and brought up on a reserve, who keep ties with their community and wish to maintain these ties must normally be considered as belonging to that minority within the meaning of the Covenant. Since Sandra Lovelace is ethnically a Maliseet Indian and has only been absent from her home reserve for a few years during the

---

Religious and Linguistic Minorities, which is not limited to citizens. The confusion created by attempting to incorporate subjective criteria in determining what constitutes a minority is obvious in *Report on the Rights of Minorities* (1990), Council of Europe Parliamentary Assembly Document 6294, Strasbourg, at p. 8.

[49] See Capotorti, *supra*, note 22, at p. 97:
> If the existence of a minority group within a state is objectively demonstrated, non-recognition of the minority does not dispense the state from the duty to comply with the principles in Article 27...

[50] *Supra*, note 47, at paragraph 5.1.

existence of her marriage, she is, in the opinion of the Committee, entitled to be regarded as "belonging" to this minority and to claim the benefits of Article 27 of the Covenant.[51]

The issue was also raised in **Kitok v. Sweden** in a more direct manner. The author, Ivan Kitok, was denied the right to become a member of a pastoral village and to exercise reindeer breeding, a traditional economic activity for Sami people, because of a Swedish law prohibiting such an activity by persons previously engaged in any other profession for more than three years. The measure was adopted not against the wishes of the Sami people, but as a means of protecting their culture:

> The *ratio legis* for this legislation is to improve the living conditions for the Sami who have reindeer husbandry as their primary income, and to make the existence of reindeer husbandry safe for the future... Reindeer husbandry was considered necessary to protect and preserve the whole culture of the Sami.[52]

Because of the cultural significance of reindeer breeding in Sami culture, the Human Rights Committee was willing to recognise that such economic activity falls under the right to enjoy Sami culture as guaranteed by Article 27; however, it also reached the conclusion that the Swedish legislation did not contravene Mr. Kitok's rights.

Kitok was denied membership in a Sami pastoral village not because he was not a member of the Sami ethnic minority, but rather because he was not entitled to pursue reindeer breeding.[53] As explained by the Human Rights Committee, it could not be denied that Ivan Kitok was objectively a member of an ethnic minority:

> It can...be seen that the Act provides certain criteria for participation in the life of an ethnic minority whereby a person who is ethnically a Sami can be held not to be a Sami for the purposes of the Act. The Committee has been concerned that the ignoring of objective ethnic criteria in determining membership of a minority, and the application to Mr Kitok of the designated rule, may have been disproportionate to the legitimate ends sought by the legislation. It was further noted that Mr Kitok has always retained some links with the Sami community.[54]

These comments from the Human Rights Committee are somewhat confusing since Mr. Kitok was not in truth being denied membership as a member of the Sami people. Most Sami in Sweden and other Nordic countries are not involved in reindeer husbandry, so that although an important symbolic and cultural activity for the community, any inability to participate in reindeer breeding or to live in one of the pastoral Sami villages does not affect one's membership in the greater Sami community that functions, for the most part, outside of these activities. Whereas in **Lovelace v. Canada**, the effect of the **Indian Act** was that Mrs. Lovelace could no longer be

---

[51] *Supra*, note 37, at paragraph 14.

[52] *Supra*, note 40, at paragraph 4.2.

[53] Some scholars have claimed Kitok was being denied membership in the Sami community. See Thornberry, *supra*, note 6, at pp. 211-212.

[54] *Supra*, note 40, at paragraph 9.7.

considered an Indian and live amongst her people, in **Kitok v. Sweden**, Kitok did not lose his status nor membership in the Sami people, though he was not permitted to live in a certain village dedicated to a type of activity from which he was excluded — like most Sami people.

Despite some misgivings, the Human Rights Committee finally concluded that since the measure appeared in any event to be justified, it did not constitute a violation of Article 27.[55] The possibility of interfering in certain minority activities under Article 27 at first appears surprising since nothing in the wording of the provision suggests that such an interference is permitted, but as will be shown below the Human Rights Committee's conclusion is well-founded, although its explanations could have been more detailed and straightforward.

5.4.2   *Need to Establish an Objective Link with a Linguistic Minority*

The reliance upon objective criteria of membership in both **Lovelace v. Canada** and **Kitok v. Sweden** implies, in the case of linguistic minorities, the need for an individual to demonstrate he or she is a member of such a minority. For example, more would be required than a mere declaration that one is a member of the French-speaking minority in Canada; one would probably also have to show at the very least that French is one's mother tongue or primary language.

By analogy, in **Kitok v. Sweden**, the author had always maintained "some link" with his ethnic group; in **Lovelace v. Canada**, the author could still speak Maliseet and attached value to the cultural practices of her people, even though she had not lived in her community for a number of years:

> [P]ersons who are born and brought up on a reserve, who have kept ties with their community and wish to maintain those ties must normally be considered as belonging to that minority.[56]

From these comments, it is clear that the establishment of the necessary ties between an individual and a minority community is not particularly onerous, although the ties still must be shown to exist objectively.

The Human Rights Committee's decision in **Lovelace v. Canada** does not appear to address what would specifically constitute satisfactory ties between an individual and a minority. Although the Maliseet people are identified throughout its decision as an ethnic minority, the Committee's decision relies heavily on the restriction imposed on Mrs. Lovelace in use of the

---

[55] This decision has been criticised by some scholars, notably Thornberry, *supra*, note 6, at p. 213. The unspoken difficulty facing the UNHRC was how to deal with legislation which is in fact favourable to the continued existence of a minority and supported by it. The **Kitok v. Sweden** case was in reality a confrontation between the author and the Sami community. The latter had been able to obtain legislation from the government with some measure of order and control over reindeer husbandry in order to ensure that the activity could be economically maintained for future generations. Article 27 is formulated as a right of non-interference from state authorities in certain activities involving minority groups, but cannot guarantee that a community will respect an individual's choice. A religious minority may, for example, choose to reject from their community certain individuals, and may even call upon a state to help implement its rejection. In such circumstances, it is not so much a case of the state intervening against a minority than one of the minority itself choosing a course of action which it deems necessary for its survival or well-being. See on this point Nowak, *supra*, note 46, at p. 109.

[56] *Supra*, note 37, at paragraph 16.

Maliseet language with other members of her group, without addressing language as a "tie" to a linguistic community.

Ethnicity, ancestry, ethnic origin or national origin all tend to correspond roughly to the same general concept: people tied together by common origins. Language can of course figure prominently as a marker of a group's common origin, but it is not an exact match: many people who are ethnically Chinese living in Canada, the United States or Thailand have in large numbers adopted the principal languages used in these countries and no longer speak Mandarin, Cantonese or Hakka with any fluency.[57] Membership in an ethnic community does not automatically mean that an individual has any real and objective tie with the language normally associated with his ethnic group, and thus such an individual could not claim a violation under Article 27 as a member of a linguistic minority.

In the breakaway region of Transdniestr, in Moldova, many individuals who are ethnically Ukrainians are now native speakers of Russian with little or no knowledge of Ukrainian, the language automatically associated with their ethnic group. Although an ethnic minority in Transdniestr, these individuals are linguistically Russian-speakers and a majority. Most indigenous peoples in Canada, with the exception of the Innu, are not members of a linguistic minority, because most of them speak almost exclusively English,[58] although they are obviously members of an ethnic minority. In Québec, many people who are ethnically Irish are now francophones. This means that though no one will dispute their identification with a particular ethnic group, "their" language is not consistent with such ethnic identification.

Moreover, it should not be forgotten that more than one ethnic group can be united together in a single linguistic community. The Spanish-speaking minority in the United States, for example, is composed of European Spaniards, immigrants and migrants, refugees from Latin America, and "Americans" whose ancestors have lived in the country for hundreds of years. Because ethnic communities do not correspond exactly with linguistic communities (although there will in some cases be extensive overlapping) great care must be shown in determining who can claim membership in the latter.

As concerns the association to a linguistic minority, a person would naturally "belong" if he speaks the same language. But this still lacks precision. Many individuals can speak more than one language, yet it would seem preposterous that an individual could claim membership in more than one linguistic minority.

Amongst the useful sources of guidance are the minorities treaties of the League of Nations era, which recognised the importance of individual freedom of choice as to membership in a minority. In the **Rights of Minorities in Upper Silesia (Minority Schools)** case,[59] the Permanent Court of International Justice ruled that an individual could freely declare whether or not his child belonged to a linguistic minority "according to his conscience and on his personal responsibility", but hastened to add that such declarations did have to be supported by some factual backup.

---

[57] Although one can speak of people of Chinese ancestry, there is no single Chinese language, but a number of different speeches sharing almost identical ideograms.

[58] de Varennes, Fernand (1994), "L'article 35 de la Loi constitutionnelle de 1982 et la protection des droits linguistiques des peuples autochtones", in *National Journal of Constitutional Law*, Vol. 4, N° 3, 265-303, at pp. 277-278.

[59] *Supra*, note 11.

In more recent international instruments and national legislation, the trend has been to recognise an individual's freedom to declare whether or not he belongs to a minority, since it is unavoidable that some may prefer participation in the majority cultural, religious or linguistic community and no longer identify with their minority background community in some respects. However, given the Human Rights Committee's reliance upon the necessity of objective ties, and on similar requirements going back to the minorities treaties, it would seem consistent with both the intent and the wording of Article 27 for an individual to be required to demonstrate objectively his/her ties to a linguistic minority and its language. This author would propose that it implies that: (1) the minority language is his/her mother tongue; (2) the minority language is a major component of his/her personal or family life; (3) the minority language is an important medium used for community ties, or (4) through any of these or other factors he/she identifies closely with the minority language and uses it.

The need for such a wide approach can be explained in the diversity of situations which can arise when dealing with individuals belonging to a linguistic minority, as opposed to an ethnic community. For example, a native speaker of Arabic emigrating to a country such as Canada may prefer in some cases to participate in the activities and life of the French-speaking minority because it is a language with which he is familiar, having studied it in school, or simply because the part of the country in which he lives is principally French-speaking. Although ethnically he is an Arab and Arabic is his mother tongue, he has chosen freely to "belong" to a community constituting a linguistic minority and has established ties consistent with such participation: his children may go to French language schools, French may be commonly used in the home, the family may attend community activities or associate with people using the language of Molière, etc.

Thus, determining that an individual belongs to a linguistic minority is not an issue of establishing some type of legal or political category, excluding for example people who are of different ethnic background or who are not native-born speakers of a minority language: it is purely a factual, objective determination based upon some concrete tie between an individual and a linguistic community. Knowledge of the official or majority language in a state, a common occurrence in respect to many members of linguistic minorities, should not in itself affect the legitimacy of a claim of belonging to a minority as the phrasing of Article 27 does not restrict its application to individuals with exclusive ties to a minority community. In the end at essence is whether an individual maintains some objective connection with a minority community through the use of its language.

5.4.3   *Requirements for Individual Membership*

Some of the Human Rights Committee's comments do raise another problem. In **Lovelace v. Canada**, the UNHRC recognised that Mrs. Lovelace's origins were Maliseet and went on to emphasise that she had also maintained her ties with the Tobique (Maliseet) community despite a hiatus of a few years. The Committee's reliance on such maintenance of ties with a minority might for some be interpreted to mean that some kind of continuous interaction must exist between a minority and an individual for that person to "belong" to that particular group.

Such a conclusion should be avoided. Whilst the maintenance of ties may be useful in order to objectively demonstrate whether an individual can be considered a member of an ethnic, linguistic, or religious minority, it is not determinative.

5.5   DEFINING THE RIGHTS TO USE A MINORITY LANGUAGE

5.5.1   *The Scope of Rights under Article 27*

One of the most controversial aspects of Article 27 is also probably the most important: its exact impact. What does the phrase "shall not be denied the right, in community with the other members of their group, to enjoy their own culture, to profess and practise their own religion, or to use their own language" actually guarantee?

There are essentially two distinct, diametrically opposed schools of thought as to the extent of the guarantees offered by Article 27. On the one hand, scholars such as Capotorti and Thornberry have concluded that the provision necessarily obligates states to provide what is sometimes called "positive action" for linguistic and other protected minorities: states must provide the means to ensure the actual survival and maintenance of their characteristics through appropriate financial assistance and a legal framework for institutions and activities vital to the minorities' interests. On the other hand, many others reject this interpretation, pointing out that the wording of Article 27 and its genesis are consistent with a much more restricted goal: non-interference of the state in private community activities tied in with language, religious or cultural usage. It is the latter point of view which now appears to have largely prevailed, at least within the United Nations system.

5.5.2   *The Origins of the Debate*

Although comments made by state representatives during the drafting of Article 27 offer mixed signals as to the scope of the rights being considered, it is safe to state that they generally confirm the view that "shall not be denied the right" is essentially a right of non-intervention for ethnic, religious or linguistic minorities. In his extensive review of the *travaux préparatoires*, Thornberry concedes that this is a legitimate conclusion, although he later sides with Professor Capotorti in rejecting the approach obviously chosen by the drafters of Article 27:

> The feeling among the majority of delegates to the Third Committee was that the draft Article provided represented a minimum rather than a maximum of rights for minorities, a situation which a number of states apparently found acceptable.
> [T]he only new duty represented by Article 27 was that of tolerance. It was widely assumed that the text submitted by the Sub-Commission would not place states and Governments under the obligation, for example, of providing special schools for persons belonging to linguistic minorities.[60]

Having rejected a Soviet proposal to include what would be considered as positive obligations to provide resources in order for minority communities to conduct their own cultural, religious or linguistic activities they deemed important, the goal and intent in adopting Article 27 was much more modest: to ensure a minimum level of rights, not necessarily available to other individuals, which would not restrict the ability of minorities to freely use their own language, practice their religion, or enjoy their own culture, whilst not imposing any obligations upon the states to intervene actively in assisting the minorities in their private affairs.

---

[60] *Supra*, note 6, at p. 179.

This was subsequently confirmed by the UN Sub-Commission on the Prevention of Discrimination and the Protection of Minorities where it was stated that Article 27 reflected the prevailing attitude of the international community: states were required to permit individuals who belonged to minorities to use their own language, practice their religion, and enjoy their culture, but this did not imply that they had the right to demand the adoption of positive measures or assistance from the state.[61]

The contemporary debate over the scope of rights guaranteed under Article 27 emanates principally from Capotorti's influential study. Whilst acknowledging the above events, Capotorti candidly admits he is setting aside what the drafters obviously meant, to adopt what he believed should preferably be in place:

> Nevertheless, there is the reason to question whether the implementation of article 27 of the Covenant does not, in fact, call for active intervention by the state. At the cultural level in particular, it is generally agreed that, because of the enormous human and financial resources which would be needed for a full cultural development, the right granted to members of minority groups to enjoy their own culture would lose much of its meaning if no assistance from the Governments concerned was forthcoming. Neither the non-prohibition of the exercise of such a right by persons belonging to minority groups nor the constitutional guarantees of freedom of expression and association are sufficient for the effective implementation of the right of members of minority groups to preserve and develop their own culture.[62]

In other words, Capotorti was ready to cast aside the clearly expressed intention of the drafters of an international treaty, not because of any dispute as to its wording or meaning, but because he believed more is required for the effective protection and development of minorities. Whereas the purpose of Article 27 as expressed by the drafters had been to protect minorities by prohibiting states from interfering in the affairs of minority communities in respect to their language, religion or culture, Capotorti substituted his own: the objective of Article 27 should be to guarantee the preservation and development of the language, religion and culture of minorities, including if necessary the active and sustained intervention of the state. As for the objective sought by the drafters of Article 27, it appears to have been one of *laisser vivre*, of allowing members of these minorities the right to maintain their language or religion freely without any assistance from the state, but also without any hindrance or oppression that has been the all too frequent burden of minorities throughout human history.

Unfortunately, many commentators have simply taken for granted that Capotorti's position either represented the actual meaning and scope of Article 27, or that it was essential to so interpret it, as they assumed no other rights offered sufficient guarantees to ensure the adequate protection of minorities. Those who have rallied to Capotorti's cause have done so for essentially the same reasons:

> *Cette interprétation dynamique, que les organes des Nations unies qui s'occupent des droits de l'homme font de l'article 27, suggère que celui-ci impose aux États une obligation de résultat accompagnée du moyen à utiliser pour y parvenir. Pour que soit atteint le résultat*

---

[61] UN Document E/CN.4/Sub.2/286, at paragraphs 155-157.

[62] See Capotorti, *supra*, note 22, at paragraph 213.

poursuivi (préservation de la culture, utilisation de la langue, pratique de la religion), une attitude passive des États ne suffit pas, leur intervention active et soutenue est indispensable, notamment par l'octroi des subventions publiques.[63]

Opponents of this point of view were quick to point out the inherent weakness of Capotorti's suggestions in this respect. Starkly put, neither the expressed *raison d'être*, as shown earlier, nor the phrasing of Article 27 support Capotorti's conclusion:

> Since Article 27 of the Political Covenant is phrased with the typically negative formulation that members of minorities "shall not be denied" certain rights, positive state obligations to affirmative action — i.e. by recognising minority languages before public authorities, by establishing reserves or by providing financial support for minority schools or cultural associations — cannot be inferred from this provision.[64]

5.5.3   Mistaken Premises

To be fair, Capotorti's approach was not entirely wishful thinking. His submissions on the necessity to secure some measure of state involvement in order to ensure the continued use of languages or continuing cultural practices were in fact quite valid. Yet, because of the limited scope of his mandate from the Sub-Commission on the Prevention of Discrimination and the Protection of Minorities, Capotorti could not explore how fundamental human rights such as freedom of expression and non-discrimination on the ground of language could assist linguistic and other minorities. Thus, he was precluded from conducting an in-depth analysis of such issues and proceeded in his work on the basis of two mistaken premises: that other rights guaranteed in the **Covenant** such as non-discrimination and freedom of expression are of little or no assistance to members of minorities, and that Article 27 has to involve positive action on the part of states if it is to ensure the protection of minorities. Capotorti may well have agreed with French Revolutionary Lacordaire that in the absence of concrete legal measures imposed by the state, *Entre le fort et le faible, la loi affranchit et la liberté opprime.*

Since freedom of expression and non-discrimination were, strictly speaking, outside Capotorti's mandate, he had no opportunity to conduct an extensive review of what constitutes discrimination and its considerable potential in state language policies, among other areas affecting minorities, nor was he able to appreciate that freedom of expression could have extensive consequences for minorities in language affairs.

As to his belief that Article 27 would be an empty shell if it were limited to a mere right of non-interference in a minority's use of its language, etc., Capotorti omitted to consider well known matters conclusively proving the contrary, such as the case of the **Minority Schools in Albania**.

---

[63] Bokatola, Isse Omanga (1992), *L'Organisation des Nations unies et la protection des minorités*, Établissements Émile Bruylant, Bruxelles, at pp. 212-213; see also Thornberry, *supra*, note 6, at p. 180.

[64] Nowak, *supra*, note 46, at p. 109; Wolfrum, *supra*, note 24, at p. 164; Dinstein, Yoram (1993), "The Degree of Self-Rule of Minorities in Unitarian and Federal States", in Catherine Brölmann, René Lefeber and Marjoleine Zieck (eds.), *Peoples and Minorities in International Law*, pp. 221-235, at pp. 228-230; Bossuyt, *supra*, note 46, at p. 131.

Under the minorities treaties, including that concerning Albania, two basic types of protection were guaranteed to minorities. When their numbers were sufficiently important, they were entitled to what Capotorti calls positive action and support from the state such as public education in the language of the minority. The second type of basic entitlement had no relationship with the numerical strength of minorities: they were freely entitled to establish and operate their own institutions appropriate to their needs, but the state was under no legal obligation to provide assistance for their maintenance.[65]

In the **Minority Schools in Albania** case, the Greek minority claimed that an amendment to the Albanian **Constitution**, abolishing all private schools, violated its rights under the latter type of provision in the **Albanian Minorities Treaty**, whilst Albania, on the other hand, argued that the amendment was not in breach of the rights of the Greek minority since it applied equally to the Albanian majority.[66]

The Permanent Court of International Justice felt it was necessary and appropriate to interpret the treaty provision as an attempt to ensure for minorities "suitable means for the preservation of their... peculiarities" and therefore concluded:

[Private educational institutions] are indispensable to enable the minority to enjoy the same treatment as the majority, not only in law but also in fact. The abolition of these institutions, which alone can satisfy the special requirements of the minority groups, and their replacement by government institutions, would destroy this equality of treatment, for its effects would be to deprive the minority of the institutions appropriate to its needs, whereas the majority would continue to have them supplied in the institutions created by the state.[67]

Although couched in terms of equality, these comments are not, strictly speaking, the application of a non-discrimination policy. Indeed, in **Minority Schools in Albania**, the Permanent Court of International Justice recognised that non-discrimination and the equal right to establish institutions in the minorities treaty provision, though closely related, are nevertheless distinct: whilst non-discrimination ensures that nationals belonging to racial, religious or linguistic minorities shall be placed in every respect on a footing of perfect equality with the other nationals of the state, the second category is to ensure for members of a minority suitable means for the preservation of their peculiarities, their traditions and their national characteristics. The two categories of rights are necessary in order to ensure social and political peace, by securing for linguistic, religious and racial minorities "the possibility of living peacefully alongside that [majority] population and co-operating amicably with it, whilst at the same time preserving the characteristics which distinguish them from the majority, and satisfying the ensuing special needs."[68]

---

[65] See for example Article 8 of the **Polish Minorities Treaty** in Thornberry, *supra*, note 6, at p. 401.

[66] The minorities treaty provision essentially provided that nationals belonging to racial, religious or linguistic minorities shall enjoy the same treatment and security in law and in fact as other nationals, and in particular that they shall have an equal right to establish, manage and control at their own expense, charitable, religious and social institutions, schools and other educational establishments, with the right to use their own language and to exercise their religion freely therein.

[67] *Supra*, note 8, at pp. 19-20.

[68] Ibid., at p. 17.

Thus, whilst the majority is not entitled to private schools under the second type of minorities treaty provision, linguistic minorities are so entitled as a minimum guarantee against the tyranny of the majority, a special consideration due to the potential for disadvantageous or oppressive and unfavourable measures being exercised by the state or imposed by the behaviour of the majority. Similarly, pursuant to Article 27, because ethnic, religious or linguistic minorities are so susceptible to the whims of the majority, they are entitled to special protection as a kind of guarantee for their cultural, religious or linguistic survival.

This is an example demonstrating how Capotorti may have been wrong in believing that Article 27 would be of little or no assistance if interpreted as a right of non-interference. The freedom to conduct private community educational activities for minorities, without any hindrance from the state, goes a long way towards attaining a minority's desire of being able to preserve its peculiarities (be they linguistic, religious, etc.). That this is the proper interpretation of Article 27 appears to be shared by a growing number of scholars and commentators:

> The obligations imposed upon the state by Article 27 were initially the subject of some uncertainty. It is now established that Article 27 only requires the state to desist from interfering with minorities wishing to practice their own culture. The state is not legally obliged to actively support minority cultures.[69]

It has finally been pointed out that Capotorti's approach would impose demands which would be impossible to fulfil upon state signatories of the **Covenant**:

> *En fait, pareille interprétation mettrait à la charge des États signataires des obligations financières que même les plus riches d'entre eux auraient de la difficulté à assumer, si l'on songe au multilinguisme croissant qui existe aujourd'hui dans la plupart des pays du monde à la suite des migrations économiques et de la multiplication des réfugiés.*[70]

5.5.4   *Article 27 as Right to Positive Protection and not Action*

Although the Human Rights Committee has never had to explicitly address the actual extent of the rights guaranteed in Article 27, its decisions in respect to Article 27 all confirm indirectly the non-interference nature of the provision as a minimal measure of protection of minorities, and all essentially contradict Capotorti's position.

In three decisions in which the Committee agreed to consider Article 27 submissions,[71] **Kitok v. Sweden, Lovelace v. Canada** and **Ominayak v. Canada**,[72] it concluded that by their

---

[69] Anghie, Antony (1992) "Human Rights and Cultural Identity: New Hope for Ethnic Peace?", in *Harvard International Law Journal*, Vol. 33, N° 2, 341-352, at p. 344; see also Dinstein, *supra*, note 64, at pp. 229-230; Tabory, Mala (1980), "Language Rights as Human Rights", in *Israel Yearbook on Human Rights*, Vol. 10, 167-223, at p. 182; and Modeen, *supra*, note 23, at p. 108.

[70] Woehrling, José (1992), "Les droits des minorités : La question linguistique et l'éventuelle accession du Québec à la souveraineté", in *Revista de Llengua i Dret*, Vol. 18, 95-153, at p. 143.

[71] In the Breton cases, the Committee did not proceed with the Article 27 aspect of the claims because of its decision that France had entered a reservation as to the application of this provision under Article 40 of the **Covenant**.

[72] Communication 167/1984, UN Document A/42/40.

legislation or actions, governments were interfering in the cultural life or language use of indigenous peoples constituting linguistic or ethnic minorities. All three matters confirm the "negative" nature of Article 27, namely that the state ought not to interfere with the enjoyment by members of a minority of certain private community activities. In **Kitok v. Sweden**, reindeer herding and the decision regarding who could reside within a minority community both came within the purview of Article 27 not as rights granted by the Swedish state but because they were examples of state intervention in a minority member's cultural life. In **Lovelace v. Canada**, the Canadian government was similarly involved in restricting a person from contacts and ties with her community. And in **Ominayak v. Canada**, government legislation and policies interfered with traditional community economic and social activities so intimately tied to culture that they amounted to a denial of the right to enjoy one's culture.

Admittedly, this does not necessarily exclude the possibility that Article 27 simultaneously guarantees non-intervention as well as active participation and support on the part of the state in appropriate cases, were it not for one almost unnoticed portion of the **Lovelace v. Canada** decision.

Mrs. Lovelace's claim included the submission that she had lost access to federal government programmes for indigenous peoples in terms of education, housing and social assistance because the **Indian Act** no longer recognised her as an Indian. These rights and privileges recognised by Canadian law are of the type constituting "positive and concrete assistance" for ethnic, religious or linguistic minorities. If the above-mentioned benefits were in any way connected, as suggested by Capotorti, to the right of a minority member not to be denied the enjoyment of his or her culture or the use of his or her own language in community with other members of the minority community, it would naturally follow that the Human Rights Committee would have responded to this line of reasoning.

The Committee did the exact opposite, in stating that the **Indian Act** deals primarily with a number of privileges which are outside the scope of the **Covenant**. In other words, even educational benefits provided by the state for an ethnic and linguistic minority are not within the scope of the rights guaranteed by Article 27, since the provision is basically one of non-interference by the state and not one requiring its active support for minorities.

This clearly contradicts the approach proposed by Capotorti and Thornberry, amongst others, and lends final confirmation to the contemporary point of view which is prevalent. Moreover, it is consistent with the intended meaning of the drafters and the adopted phrasing of the provision.

However, it must be said that the Human Rights Committee's recent *General Comment No. 23(50)* sheds very little light on this issue. At one point, it seems to confirm that the rights Article 27 confers on persons belonging to minorities is essentially one of non-intervention of the state:

> Those rights simply are that individuals belonging to those minorities should not be denied the right, in community with members of their group, to enjoy their own culture, to practice their religion and speak their language.[73]

The above does not seem to suggest that the rights conferred by Article 27 require a state to provide any type of concessions in terms of language such as public schooling or the right to use or speak the language of choice in court proceedings. The Committee then comments that Article

---

[73] *Supra*, note 47, at paragraph 5.2.

27 has an important role to play to protect minorities:

> Although Article 27 is expressed in negative terms, that article, nevertheless, does recognize the existence of a "right" and requires that it shall not be denied. Consequently, a state party is under an obligation to ensure that the existence and the exercise of this right are protected against their denial or violation. Positive measures of protection are, therefore, required not only against the acts of the state party itself, whether through its legislative, judicial or administrative authorities, but also against the acts of other persons within the state party.[74]

By emphasising that the protection conferred by Article 27 is against acts of the state or outside sources, these comments tend to confirm the view that this provision is essentially a shield against any measure that could interfere or pose a threat to an individual's right in community with members of his minority group to speak his language. But at the same time, it could certainly be argued that the use of the terms "positive measures" could also imply direct support from the state such as public education in a minority language, or even financial assistance for private minority schools, especially since the Human Rights Committee acknowledges in its *General Comment* that "Article 27 relates to rights whose protection imposes specific obligations on state parties" and that the "protection of these rights is directed to ensure the survival and continued development of the...identity of the minorities concerned".

In fact, the above reference to "positive measures" and "specific obligations" means that a state must always take appropriate steps to protect a minority's right to use its language, etc. when the state's actions or some other outside intervention poses a threat. Once again, this is exactly the scenario in all of the cases considered by the Human Rights Committee until now: in **Kitok v. Sweden, Lovelace v. Canada** and **Ominayak v. Canada**, it concluded that by their legislation or actions, governments did not protect the cultural life or language use of indigenous peoples constituting linguistic or ethnic minorities. **Ominayak v. Canada** is also an example of why the Human Rights Committee mentions the obligation of a state to protect minorities from the acts of non-state parties. In that case, government legislation and policies permitted activities by large companies that would have interfered with traditional indigenous cultural and economic activities. In other words, government legislation and policies permitted interference from the outside that constituted a violation of Article 27, since they affected a minority's right to be protected in its use of language, practice of religion or enjoyment of culture.

Finally, the Human Rights Committee suggested that it was quite appropriate for a state to adopt measures that go beyond protection and which actually assist a minority's ability to maintain its language, and that if a state adopts such special measures it should not necessarily be deemed to be unacceptable discrimination:

> Although the rights protected under Article 27 are individual rights, they depend in turn on the ability of the minority group to maintain its culture, language or religion. Accordingly, positive measures by states may also be necessary to protect the identity of a minority and the rights of its members to enjoy and develop their culture and language and to practice their religion, in community with the other members of their group. In this connection, it has to be observed that such positive measures must respect the provisions of Article 2(1) and 26 of the Covenant both as regards the treatment between different minorities and the treatment between persons belonging to them and the remaining population. However, as

---

[74] Ibid., at paragraph 6.1.

long as those measures are aimed at correcting conditions which prevent or impair the enjoyment of the rights guaranteed under Article 27, they may constitute a legitimate differentiation under the Covenant, provided that they are based on reasonable and objective criteria.[75]

In essence, the Human Rights Committee appears to be signalling that it will be quite receptive to any measure by a state that favours the maintenance of a minority's language, religion or culture, as long as it is reasonable in accordance with the principle of non-discrimination contained in Articles 2(1) and 26 of the **Covenant**, as has likewise been suggested previously in **Kitok v. Sweden**.

5.6 THE EXTENT OF PROTECTION FOR THE USE OF A MINORITY LANGUAGE

It is one thing to agree that linguistic minorities are free to use their language, but the question then becomes free to do what exactly. Surprisingly little has been written on the extent of the right of non-interference, although the following do point out the most relevant areas of the possible application of Article 27.

5.6.1 *Use of Language in Education*

Until fairly recently in human history, education was an informal activity conducted within the family, by religious congregations or spiritual guides, or through exposure of young individuals to the tasks and demands of daily life which would fall upon them as adults. Language acquisition also was part and parcel of this continual process of integration into the society formed by various communities.

The advent of the nation-state, coupled with the development of writing and then printing as well as of modern economies requiring a flexible and highly mobile labour force, meant that informal education had to be replaced, at least in most countries and communities, by state efforts to mould the citizens and workers of the future according to its needs. In most countries as of the second half of the nineteenth century, governments began to install mandatory public education systems and often chose to close private schools and instruction. In other words, the state removed from most families and communities the option of complete control over the education of their members and replaced it with its own model.

Whilst there may arguably be nothing intrinsically wrong with this, it has created for linguistic minorities a particularly onerous burden. For one thing, to remove children from the home for long periods of time and teach them in a language with which they are less familiar is more likely to disadvantage them in their academic performance and adaptation, which can in some cases be discriminatory. For linguistic minorities, state education also represents a more subtle menace: for much of their formative years, their youth would not or hardly be exposed to their language and, even in the case of public schooling in the minority language, their children would nonetheless still be under the tutelage of the interests, views, and more or less tolerant benevolence of the linguistic majority.

---

[75] Ibid., at paragraph 6.2.

These factors seem to confirm that not permitting a linguistic minority to carry on its own educational activities in its language has great potential for destabilisation. In any event, as the Permanent Court of International Justice suggested in the **Minority Schools in Albania** case, the right of minorities to operate private schools is more consistent with the principle of assisting minorities who may suffer some disadvantage because of their status. This is also reflected in many bilateral treaties between states[76] as well as in other international instruments.[77]

Article 27 thus appears to be part of a long-established and continuous legal continuum that the right for linguistic minorities to use their language amongst themselves must necessarily include the right to establish, manage and operate their own educational institutions where their language is used as the medium of instruction to the extent deemed to be appropriate by the minority itself.[78]

---

[76] Among the relevant provisions of treaties reprinted in the Appendix are **Article 8 of the Agreement between the Czech Republic and the Slovak Republic on Cooperation and Good Neighbourly Relations, Article 1 of the Agreement between the Ministry of National Education of the Republic of Poland and the Ministry of Culture and Education of the Republic of Lithuania Regarding the Educational System and University Education**, Article 4 of the **Germany-Russian Federation Protocol of Collaboration on the Gradual Restoration of Citizenship to Russian Germans**, Article 8 of the **Treaty Concerning the Protection of Minorities in Greece**, Article 6 of the **Treaty on Friendship and Cooperation between the Lithuanian Republic and Ukraine**, Article 67 of the **Treaty of Peace with Austria**, Article 40 of the **Treaty of Peace with Turkey**, and Article 14 of the **Treaty between the Republic of Lithuania and the Republic of Poland on Friendly Relations and Good Neighbourly Cooperation**.

[77] See for example Article 15 of the draft **Declaration on the Rights of Indigenous Peoples**, Article 16 of the **Central European Initiative for the Protection of Minority Rights** (limited to national minorities), Paragraph 32.2 of the **Document of the Copenhagen Meeting of the Conference on the Human Dimension** (national minorities), Article 11 of the **Parliamentary Recommendation 1134 (1990) on the Rights of Minorities** (Council of Europe), Article 5(1)(c) of the United Nations **Convention against Discrimination in Education**, Article 30 of the United Nations **Convention on the Rights of the Child**, Article 27(3) of the International Labour Organisation **Convention (No. 169) Concerning Indigenous and Tribal Peoples in Independent Countries**, and Article 13 of the **Convention-cadre sur la protection des minorités nationales**, all quoted in the Appendix.

[78] See Bossuyt, *supra*, note 46, at p. 132. Not every country is convinced of the validity of these principles. France denies the existence of minorities in its territory and has entered a reservation to this effect as regards the application of Article 27. As regards state legislation which appears to conform to Article 27, see Article 25 of the **Estonian Language Act** and Article 10 of the **Chinese Autonomy Law**, *Recueil des législations linguistiques dans le monde - Tome V : L'Algérie, l'Autriche, la Chine, le Danemark, la Finlande, la Hongrie, l'île de Malte, le Maroc, la Norvège, la Nouvelle-Zélande, les Pays-Bas, le Royaume-Uni, la Tunisie, la Turquie, l'ex-URSS* (1994), Jacques Leclerc and Jacques Maurais (eds.), International Centre for Research on Language Planning, Québec, at pp. 149 and 58. Article 10.3 of the 19 March 1991 **Latvian Act on Free Development and the Right to Cultural Autonomy of Nationalities and Ethnic Groups** provides the right of permanent residents to develop their own educational establishments by their own means.

5.6.2   *Other Institutions*

Another possible area of application of Article 27 concerns the right of linguistic minorities to use their language within various cultural, social or even political organisations. Whilst a state may permit the creation of minority organisations and thus not interfere with the right of association, members belonging to linguistic minorities may nonetheless be excluded from using their language as part of the activities of such organisations. For example, a draft language law of December 1993 recently considered by the Estonian Parliament includes a provision (Article 16) by which cultural institutions appear to be prohibited from using signs, announcements or notices in a minority language unless it is "necessary", with that determination apparently being in the hands of public authorities. Such a requirement does not conform to the letter nor to the spirit of Article 27, and other similar provisions, because it in effect denies to persons belonging to a linguistic minority the right to use, in community with the other members of their group, their own language when promoting or announcing publicly the activities of their institutions. Nowhere does Article 27 contain any allusion to such a restriction, which may moreover be a violation of freedom of expression. Turkey also has similar legislative prohibitions affecting the use of Kurdish by private institutions and organisations.[79] A more appropriate approach would be for a state to not legislate or otherwise not intrude upon the right of a private group or institution to use the language of its choice, in private and in public.

Furthermore, nothing in Article 27 would exclude, for example, political associations or pressure groups representing the interests of a particular linguistic minority from being allowed to use a minority language. For example, political associations may not be "persons" in the sense envisioned by the **International Covenant on Civil and Political Rights,** but it would likely be sufficient for the purposes of Article 27 and similar provisions to demonstrate that individual members of the political or pressure groups, who belong to linguistic minorities, were prohibited in using their language when attempting to communicate with other members of their group.[80]

5.6.3   *Names and Toponomy*

Another application of Article 27 which Capotorti and others failed to appreciate in discarding the interpretation of this provision as a non-intervention clause, relates to the issue of names.

A person's name, as pointed out by philosopher Charles Taylor, does not simply involve an administrative or bureaucratic task. It also signals that "we are made into beings that one addresses, and we are inducted into the community whose speaking continually remakes the

---

[79] On the other hand, Article 26 of the 1989 **Kazakhstan Languages Act** is a prime example of a flexible measure, recognising that linguistic minorities are free to use their language in public and in private whether for cultural, social or political purposes. See *Recueil des législations linguistiques,* ibid., at p. 165. A similar piece of legislation is the 19 March 1991 **Latvian Act on Free Development and the Right to Cultural Autonomy of Nationalities and Ethnic Groups** which guarantees to all permanent residents of Latvia freedom to decide their nationality, to observe their national traditions, to use their national symbols and celebrate their national festivals, to maintain relations with their compatriots abroad, to leave and return to Latvia, to set up their own national societies, associations and organisations.

[80] The July 1989 Algerian law on political parties prohibits the registration of groups "based exclusively on a particular religion, language, region, sex or race" and states that parties must use only the Arabic language in their public communiques.

language."[81] A name therefore is an important marker that a person belongs to a community, and any state restriction on the use of a person's name in a minority language would be particularly offensive for many, and a direct intervention in what is by its very nature an extremely private affair.

Unfortunately, such practices are not unheard of in Western and other countries, although democracies in general have tended to recognise that they are no longer an acceptable interference, if they ever were. In the case of Spain, the evolution towards a full-fledged democracy, committed to a greater respect for human rights, following the Franco regime also entailed abolishing legislation which at origin only permitted Castilian names. After allowing the use of names in any of the Spanish languages, Spain finally removed any limitation as to the language from which a name could be chosen:

> *En Espagne, la loi 17/1977 du 4 janvier 1977, portant sur la réforme de l'article 54 de la loi du registre civil, dispose que les Espagnols doivent inscrire leur nom « dans l'une des langues espagnoles », ce qui signifie que l'inscription du nom dans l'une des langues espagnoles autre que le castillan est permise. Cette loi, antérieure à la Constitution, mais promulguée pendant la période de transition de la dictature à la démocratie, a mis fin à la déplorable législation antérieure, typiquement fasciste, qui, depuis l'arrêté ministériel du 18 mars 1938, empêchait l'enregistrement des prénoms dans les langues espagnoles autres que le castillan.[82]*

These types of prohibitions are not limited to historical oddities. Slovakia modified on 3 May 1994 legislation which until then did not allow the country's linguistic minorities to use traditional, non-Slovakian forms of their first names and prohibited, for example, women from dropping the "-ova" ending from their surnames. In Argentina, members of the Welsh-speaking minority (as well as indigenous peoples) are apparently still not allowed to give their children names in Welsh (and indigenous languages), being obliged instead to choose from an official list of "Christian" names.[83] Iceland still requires all individuals to have an Icelandic name.[84] In Bulgaria, it was not until 10 November 1989 that members of the Turkish minority were permitted the possibility of restoring their names on 10 November 1989.[85] Only recently, with

---

[81] Taylor, Charles (1985), *Human Agency and Language — Philosophical Papers I*, Cambridge University Press, Cambridge, at p. 237.

[82] Milian i Massana, Antoni (1992), "Droits linguistiques et droits fondamentaux en Espagne", in *Revue Générale du Droit*, Vol. 23, 561-581, at p. 567. See also similar provisions aimed at forcing the exclusive use of Italian names during the fascist regime under Mussolini in Klein, G. (1986), *La politica linguistica del facismo*, Il Mulino, Bologna, at pp. 105-110.

[83] *World Directory Of Minorities* (1990), Minority Rights Group (ed.), Longman, Harlow, United Kingdom, at p. 63.

[84] See UN Document CCPR/C/46/Add.5.

[85] *The Protection of Ethnic and Linguistic Minorities in Europe* (1993), John Packer and Kristian Myntti (eds.), Institute for Human Rights, Åbo Akademi University, Åbo, Finland, at pp. 71-72:
> On 8 May 1984, the decision was taken to begin a campaign they called "Process of Renaissance". The policy (which the authorities insisted was "voluntarily" complied with by the Turks) dictated that all Turkish names had to be changed, and the use of the Turkish language

the return of democracy in Poland, where names had been "Polonised" under the unpublished **Prime Minister Act** of 1952, were members of certain linguistic minorities allowed to return to the original spelling of their first names and surnames consistent with their language.

Latvia provides perhaps the most recent and unfortunate example of a violation of Article 27, having recently adopted a language law which follows the same type of measures popular in oppressive regimes such as that of Franco's:

> Foreign given names and surnames shall be written and used in Latvian in conformity with rules of transforming given names and surnames of other languages into Latvian.[86]

The above restrictions would appear to be a prime example of the state stomping upon what is by its very nature an important minority use of language, and violate the spirit and explicit wording of Article 27.

However, an increasing number of treaties and international instruments inspired by Article 27 have recognised the legitimacy of this type of right relating to the use of a minority's language, including Article 7(2) of the **Convention-cadre sur la protection des minorités nationales**:

> *Les parties s' engagent à reconnaître à toute personne appartenant à une minorité nationale le droit d' utiliser son nom (son patronyme) et ses prénoms dans la langue minoritaire ainsi que le droit à leur reconnaissance officielle, selon les modalités prévues par leur système juridique.*[87]

---

in public was to be banned. Those who refused were denied their salaries, travel within the country, and administrative and judicial services. Uncooperative imams had their mosques denied official recognition. In some places, even traditional Turkish clothing was forbidden. Passports with Turkish names were all declared invalid.

[86] Article 18, **Language Law of the Republic of Latvia**, 31 March 1992. This may be contrasted with the Hungarian legislation, 1993 **Act No. LXXVII on the Rights of National and Ethnic Minorities** which provides in Article 12(1):

> *Toute personne appartenant à une minorité a le droit au libre choix de son prénom et de celui de son enfant, à l'inscription de son nom de famille et de son prénom au registre matrimonial ainsi qu'à leur utilisation dans les pièces officielles selon les règles de sa langue maternelle et ce dans les cadres et les limites de la réglementation en vigueur...*

[87] Among other treaties and instruments with similar provisions are Article 14 of the draft **Declaration on the Rights of Indigenous Peoples**, Article 11 of the **Central European Initiative Instrument for the Protection of Minority Rights**, Paragraph 6 of the **Resolution on the Languages and Cultures of Regional and Ethnic Minorities**, Article 10(5) of the **European Charter for Regional or Minority Languages**, Article 4 of the **Convention on Providing Special Rights for the Slovenian Minority Living in the Republic of Hungary and for the Hungarian Minority Living in the Republic of Slovenia**, Article 9 of the **Declaration on the Principles of Cooperation Between the Republic of Hungary and the Ukrainian Soviet Socialist Republic in Guaranteeing the Rights of National Minorities**, Article 10(1)(c) of the **Treaty of Peace with Italy**, Article 14(1) of the **Treaty Between the Republic of Lithuania and the Republic of Poland on Friendly Relations and Good Neighbourly Cooperation**, Article 15 of the **Treaty Between the Republic of Poland and the Republic of Belarus on Good Neighbourliness and Friendly Cooperation**, Article 15(2) of the

A word of caution should be raised as regards the above-mentioned **Convention-cadre** and other instruments such as the **European Charter for Minority or Regional Languages**. The rights enshrined therein are restrictive in the sense that such instruments are not, strictly speaking, aimed at minorities generally. They are limited — for political reasons — to guaranteeing certain rights to long-established groups of citizens living within state borders, sometimes referred to as "national minorities" or, in the case of Austria as *beheimatet*, minorities which are living and traditionally rooted in the country.

The exclusion of non-nationals or more recently established minorities from such provisions does not mean they can simply be forced to forsake their names and surnames. States which have ratified the **International Covenant on Civil and Political Rights**, and which have not entered into a reservation regarding the application of Article 27, would be expected to permit individuals the continued use of their names in the language of their community. For example, an Arabic-speaking worker in Latvia could not validly be forced to change his name to an appropriate Latvian language name under Article 27 of the **Covenant**, regardless of other treaties or instruments, even if he is not a member of a "national" minority.

Instead of naming a person, toponomy involves the naming of places, and may also be a source of conflict. Toponomy is dealt with somewhat differently than the former in that a distinction must constantly be respected between the private use of place-names in a minority language, and official toponomy in state areas and activities. Whilst the former, in conformity with Article 27, would prohibit the state from interfering in the individual use of toponomy in a minority language for non-state functions, this would have no relevance in respect to the state's use of place-names. It would be entitled to require the use of the place-names it has chosen in respect to official activities or areas.[88] But if a state tried to forbid individuals from using a place-name in their minority language on their own signs or posters, etc., this would likely entail a violation of Article 27.

5.6.4   The Issue of Script Prohibitions

Despite the paucity of discussion on the issue of script as it relates to Article 27, it would seem safe to say that any prohibition of the private use of a particular script by a linguistic minority is a denial of the right of individuals to use their language in community with other members of their group. As pointed out in the chapter on the prohibition of discrimination, script is intimately

---

Treaty Between the Republic of Poland and the Republic of Latvia on Friendship and Cooperation, Article 11 of the **Treaty Between the Republic of Poland and Ukraine on Good Neighbourliness, Friendly Relations and Cooperation**, and Article 20(3) of the **Vertrag zwischen der Bundesrepublik Deutschland und der Republik Polen über gute Nachbarschaft und freundschaftliche Zusammenarbeit**. All can be found in the Appendix.

[88] A state perhaps may not have total, unfettered discretion in such matters. There is at least an argument which can be made that where a linguistic minority is highly concentrated and long-established, it would be discriminatory to completely disregard the use, in conjunction with the place-name in the official language(s), of traditional and correct forms of place-names in minority languages because of the close identification to and historical significance of the land and communities minorities inhabit. Along these lines, an appropriate model would be the 10 May 1994 approval by the Slovak cabinet of an amendment to the law on the state's official language allowing towns and villages with a minority population reaching 20 percent or more to post bilingual signs.

related to the concept of language, so that a difference in script can render a language unintelligible or difficult to understand, just as would any other type of language differentiation.

Moreover, the recognition of the intimate link between language and script and of its importance for linguistic minorities exists in a number of constitutions, which acknowledge amongst other things the right of a minority to conserve its distinct script.[89] Very few states expressly prohibit the private use of distinct scripts, the most notable which do so being Indonesia, Turkey and Algeria.[90]

5.6.5   Media and Publications

Another possible situation in which Article 27 could be raised is where public authorities prohibit private media or publications in a minority language, notwithstanding that such a practice would likely also constitute a violation of the freedom of expression. Examples of this type of restriction are not as uncommon as one might believe. In 1985, a project related to a German language periodical was not approved by authorities in Poland, although this restriction has since been lifted. In Kirgizstan, official registration and thus the right to publish, has recently been denied to an Uzbek language Islamic journal. In early 1993, the mayor of Cluj, in Romania, banned certain Hungarian publications. A draft language law[91] considered in 1994 by the Estonian Parliament provides the legal basis for a government to control the language used in journalism, without distinguishing between private media and state agents or public media. This draft law opens the door to a possible restriction by Estonia of the language used by individuals "in community with other members" of linguistic minorities, especially the Russian-speaking minority, and could well constitute a violation of Article 27.[92]

Whilst the above more obviously signal a state's interference with the use of a minority language by individuals, a much more complicated problem occurs when one considers the issue of government control and allocation of radio and television frequencies. Basically, if a state is prohibited under Article 27 from interfering in the use of language by members of a linguistic minority, does this not imply that linguistic minorities have an unfettered freedom to use any frequency they please, without being subjected to the regulatory supervision of the state?

The answer to this question is likely not. It is essential to keep in mind the nature of Article 27 in order to appreciate the distinction between non-interference of the state and allocation of

---

[89] In **D.A.V. College, Bhatinda v. State of Punjab**, (1971) 2 S.C.R. 261 (India), the Supreme Court of India confirmed the nature of script as an element of language choice.

[90] For example, Article 2 of the **Loi du 16 janvier 1991 portant généralisation de l'utilisation de la langue arabe** states: "*Il est interdit de transcrire la langue arabe en caractères autres que les caractères arabes.*"

[91] Article 21 of the December 1993 draft language law of Estonia states: "In the fields of economy, including commerce, communication, dissemination of information, transport, medicine and social security, rules governing the use of language shall be prescribed by the Government of the Republic."

[92] Lithuanian legislation is also problematic because of a failure to distinguish between private media and media controlled by public authorities. The Lithuanian law of 1990 on the press and other mass media provides that information shall be in the Lithuanian language, except in cases of sufficient demand when it may also be distributed in other languages. Implicitly, such legislation allows public authorities to decide whether private newspapers and other media may appear in minority languages, in which case there would clearly be a violation of Article 27.

resources by the state. Pursuant to Article 27, a state should not be entitled to control in any way a linguistic minority's efforts to establish a private radio or television station using the minority language and aimed at a minority audience. This would appear to be a clear example of the use of language by members of a linguistic minority.

However, in order to be on the airwaves, members of a linguistic minority must also have access to broadcasting frequencies. In most states these frequencies are considered as public goods,[93] and countries which permit private broadcasting require that a licence to broadcast be obtained from an administrative authority. Thus, though it would appear that Article 27 guarantees to linguistic minorities the right to set up their own private media, it cannot be invoked in order to oblige a state to provide certain resources, such as airwave frequencies, which are public goods.

Nonetheless, the matter does not entirely end here because, as with any other state activity, public authorities are required to act in a non-discriminatory fashion,[94] and the refusal to grant broadcasting licences for private radio and television stations using a minority language could constitute discrimination on the basis of language. This issue is examined more closely in Chapter 6.

5.6.6   Use of a Minority Language at Home or in Public

In some cases a state or its agents will prohibit the use of a minority language in public places, whilst permitting or tolerating it in private settings. The Turkish **Anti-Terrorist Act No. 3713** of 12 April 1991 apparently still prohibits the use of the Kurdish language in public, although the private use in the home is no longer an offence.

Algerian legislation makes it an offence to hold public meetings or conferences in which any language other than Arabic is used, with the exception of international conferences using

---

[93] Barendt, Eric (1993), *Broadcasting Law — A Comparative Study*, Clarendon Press, Oxford, United Kingdom, at pp. 79-81. See also a recent Italian case confirming this interpretation, Decision 102/1990, (1990) Giur. cost. 610 (Italy).

[94] Piatt, Bill (1984), "Linguistic Diversity on the Airwaves: Spanish-Language Broadcasting and the FFC", in *La Raza Law Journal*, Vol. 1, N° 2, 101-119, at pp. 112-113:

1. Broadcasters have the obligation to meet the needs and interests of the minority groups in the communities in which they are licensed to serve. Where the minority community speaks only Spanish, failure of broadcasters to provide Spanish broadcasting constitutes a complete failure to serve that group.

2. Even if they also understand English, Hispanic-Americans may have an important interest in receiving Spanish broadcasting to maintain contact with and improve upon their Spanish-language ability. Failure of broadcasters to make Spanish-language broadcasting available to bilingual Hispanics creates an insensitive and hostile broadcast climate which has a particularly strong potential negative impact upon Hispanic children.

3. Non-Spanish-speaking individuals, Hispanics and non-Hispanics alike, may have an interest in acquiring language skills and greater cultural diversity by having access to Spanish-language broadcasting.

foreign languages.[95] However, the legislation goes so far as to ban any sign or poster in public view in a language other than Arabic, with the only exception being foreign languages in designated tourist areas.[96] As a result, the important Berber minority finds itself prohibited from using its language in the above described public situations, constituting a fairly obvious infringement of Article 27 — and probably of freedom of expression as well.

One problem which occurs in states having large populations of immigrants is the imposition upon pupils in state schools to speak only the official language of instruction whilst on school grounds. It may well be acceptable to require children to use the official or majority language when they are participating in activities associated with the school's public mandate;[97] however, does the same policy not constitute a violation of Article 27 if pupils are prohibited from speaking their language on school grounds in their leisure time? Although still under the care of public agents whilst playing in the school yard or being driven in a school bus, it is certainly debatable whether forbidding children from speaking amongst themselves in private, as they are entitled to do, is not an infringement of the right of individuals to use a minority language in community with other members of their group.

Similarly, any public institution which allows its employees some time to interact with others in private, during lunch or coffee breaks for example, would also likely violate Article 27 of the **Covenant** if such private activities were restricted to the majority language. Such a case occurred in a public hospital in Vancouver, Canada, where employees were forbidden from carrying on private conversations in Cantonese whilst on break from work.

No state currently prohibits the use of a minority by private individuals in their own home. However, there is one recent case in the United States where a judge has ordered a mother not to speak Spanish to her child at home in Amarillo, Texas. State District Judge Samuel Kiser equated the use of a minority language at home as a form of "child abuse":

> If she starts first grade with the other children and cannot even speak the language that the teachers and others speak, and she's a full-blooded American citizen, you're abusing that child... Now get this straight: you start speaking English to that child, because if she doesn't

---

[95] Article 9 of the **Loi du 16 janvier 1991 portant généralisation de l'utilisation de la langue arabe:**
Les sessions et séminaires nationaux ainsi que les stages professionnels et de formation et les manifestations publiques se déroulent en langue arabe. Il peut faire usage de langues étrangères, de façon exceptionnelle et parallèlement à la langue arabe, lors des conférences, rencontres et manifestations à caractère international.

[96] Article 19 of the **Loi du 16 janvier 1991 portant généralisation de l'utilisation de la langue arabe:**
La publicité sous quelque forme qu'elle soit, se fait en langue arabe. Il peut être fait à titre exceptionnel, le cas échéant, usage de langues étrangères parallèlement à la langue arabe, après autorisation des parties compétentes.

[97] State education being a "public service", the state is under no obligation to respect a student's language preference under Article 27, since the provision is one of non-intervention only. Students in class or other official activities are thus receiving a service from the state, and not using their language in community with other members of their linguistic minority. Of course, a linguistic minority may be entitled to instruction and use of its language in state-provided education, where appropriate under the application of the right to non-discrimination.

do good in school, then I can remove her because it's not in her best interest to be ignorant.[98]

Judge Kiser's reasoning is bizarre, to say the least. It never occurred to him that it may have been the state school system which is "abusive" by not taking into account the linguistic and educational needs of a very large segment of the population in Amarillo, Texas. For state authorities to force individuals to speak a "foreign" language in their own home is not only in breach of freedom of expression and non-discrimination, but also a violation of international obligations of the US under Article 27 of the **International Covenant on Civil land Political Rights**.

5.6.7   Use of Language with Members of Transborder Communities?

The phrasing of Article 27 does not seem to permit members of a linguistic minority the unfettered right to maintain contacts and use their language with individuals who do not reside within the borders of a state. Whilst an increasing number of treaties[99] have begun to include provisions guaranteeing a large degree of freedom in respect to contacts across state frontiers amongst persons belonging to a linguistic minority, Article 27 itself does not appear to so extend. As explained by one commentator, such an entitlement can be of great importance for minorities separated by a border in that it is a potential source of support and inspiration for its cultural and linguistic activities:

> *Il s'agit là d'un droit particulièrement important pour les minorités, si elles veulent promouvoir et renforcer leurs caractéristiques communes. Le droit consacré par cet écrit concerne tout d'abord les minorités dispersées sur le territoire d'un ou de plusieurs États. Il est en outre destiné à s'appliquer aux nombreuses minorités établies près des frontières et qui présentent les mêmes caractéristiques ethniques, religieuses ou linguistiques que la population des États voisins. Pour elles, le droit d'entretenir des contacts avec les populations limitrophes, y compris en se déplaçant dans ces États, revêt une importance particulière.[100]*

Perhaps by oversight, or possibly because it is a product of the Cold War era, the construction of Article 27 is more restrictive in scope, guaranteeing that individuals are not denied the right

---

[98] Reprinted from MacLean's Magazine, 11 September 1995, at p. 13.

[99] See Article 2(5) of the United Nations **Declaration on the Rights of Persons Belonging to National or Ethnic, Religious and Linguistic Minorities**, Article 23 of the **Central European Initiative Instrument for the Protection of Minorities**, Article 14 of the **European Charter for Regional or Minority Languages**, Article 17 of the **Convention-cadre sur la protection des minorités nationales**, Article 14 of the **Treaty Between the Republic of Lithuania and the Republic of Poland on Friendly Relations and Good Neighbourly Cooperation** and Article 15(2) of the **Treaty Between the Republic of Poland and the Republic of Latvia on Friendship and Cooperation**, reprinted in the Appendix.

[100] Malinverni, Giorgio (1991), "Le projet de Convention pour la protection des minorités élaboré par la Commission européenne pour la démocratie par le droit", in *Revue universelle des droits de l'Homme*, Vol. 3, N° 5, 157-165, at p. 161.

to use a minority language in community with "other members of their group", with "group" signifying a linguistic minority within the borders of a state. All other individuals outside the group, that is, those who do not belong to a linguistic minority in existence in a state, would thus appear to be excluded.

Unfortunately, neither the *travaux préparatoires* nor the research of scholars like Capotorti provide any assistance in shedding some light on this point.

5.7   LIMITATIONS TO THE RIGHTS

5.7.1   *Confusion Arising from Human Rights Committee Decisions*

The United Nations Human Rights Committee in two of its decisions involving Article 27 emphasised that not every interference by public authorities can be regarded as a denial of rights within the meaning of the provision. In **Lovelace v. Canada**, the Human Rights Committee admitted that the objectives of the Canadian legislation were in place to preserve the identity of the Maliseets from being overwhelmed by individuals not belonging to their ethnic and linguistic group. The reasoning of the Human Rights Committee begins to get murky when it is affirmed that any legal restriction affecting the right of a person belonging to an indigenous minority to reside on a reserve, must have both a reasonable and objective justification and be consistent with the other provisions of the **Covenant**, read as a whole; in particular, any state interference must be made in light of the general content of principles embodied in the **International Covenant on Civil and Political Rights**, including Articles 12, 17 and 23 in so far as they may be relevant, and particularly the provisions against discrimination, such as Articles 2, 3 and 26. The Human Rights Committee concluded that the government restriction was unjustifiable:

> The case of Sandra Lovelace should be considered in the light of the fact that her marriage to a non-Indian has broken up. It is natural that in such a situation she wishes to return to the environment in which she was born, particularly as after the dissolution of her marriage her main cultural attachment again was to the Maliseet band. Whatever may be the merits of the Indian Act in other respects, it does not seem to the Committee that to deny Sandra Lovelace the right to reside on the reserve is reasonable, or necessary to preserve the identity of the tribe. The Committee therefore concludes that to prevent her recognition as belonging to the band is an unjustifiable denial of her rights under Article 27 of the Covenant, read in the context of the other provisions referred to.[101]

In **Kitok v. Sweden**, the Human Rights Committee reiterated its view concerning the consideration of other provisions of the **Covenant** and the need for some sort of balancing of interests between an individual's desire to participate in activities related to the culture of his or her ethnic group and the interests of the minority community as a whole. As in **Lovelace v. Canada**, the measures adopted by Sweden were designed to protect Sami culture from being overrun in traditional areas such as reindeer breeding. In this case, however, the Human Rights Committee decided that there was no violation of Article 27:

> [In] this problem, in which there is an apparent conflict between the legislation, which seems to protect the rights of the minority as a whole, and its application to a single

---

[101] *Supra*, note 37, at paragraph 17.

member of that minority, the Committee has been guided by the *ratio decidendi* in the **Lovelace** case...namely, that a restriction upon the right of an individual member of a minority must be shown to have a reasonable and objective justification and to be necessary for the continued viability and welfare of the minority as a whole...[102]

The main difficulty with such reasoning is that it seems to imply that "the right not to be denied" guaranteed under Article 27 is qualified: a state may interfere and restrict a minority member's right to practice his or her religion, use his or her language or enjoy his or her culture if it has a reasonable and objective justification and if it is necessary for the continued viability and welfare of the minority as a whole. In other words, reasonable restrictions are permissible when they are in place for the minority's own protection.

The Committee's reasoning has been criticised on occasion as being too favourable towards states.[103] It's approach is also tenuous as nothing in the *travaux préparatoires*, or in the phrasing of Article 27, indicates that such a restriction was ever contemplated. That the Human Rights Committee was strained in its approach is apparent moreover in its recognition that it could not and did not rely exclusively on Article 27, but rather that it read the provision in the context of the principles embodied in other provisions of the **Covenant** such as non-discrimination. In any case, the Committee's reasoning in **Kitok v. Sweden** and **Lovelace v. Canada** can be understood in two distinct manners: (1) the right of non-interference under Article 27 is not absolute, or (2) the Human Rights Committee's comments actually relate not to Article 27, but to other provisions. The latter appears to be more logical and consistent with the background and wording of Article 27.

5.7.2 Conflict between Protection of Minorities and Individual Rights and Interests

In order to better apprehend the reasoning in both **Kitok v. Sweden** and **Lovelace v. Canada**, it is essential to understand the factual background of the two cases, such background not being clearly evident in the decisions released by the Human Rights Committee. The respective legislation restricting the rights of the two persons involved were not simply interferences by the states in the individual right of such persons to enjoy their culture or use their language with other members of their communities; the legislation constituted in reality measures to ensure the protection of culture and way of life under attack by the overwhelming attraction or presence of the majority society. In both cases, the measures were adopted with the approval of the leaders of the minorities involved.

Moreover, in both **Kitok v. Sweden** and **Lovelace v. Canada**, an important segment of the respective minority communities were either severely divided or strongly opposed to modifying the legislation. In fact, in the case of Mrs. Lovelace, her presence on the Tobique Reserve led to violent incidents, not because public authorities attempted to evict her from the reserve, but because some Maliseets were ready to take the law into their own hands in order to avoid an influx of people and children imbued with Western values and culture, which would further endanger the "weaker" culture's desperate attempts to save what it could of its values and traditions.

---

[102] *Supra*, note 40, at paragraph 9.8.

[103] *Supra*, note 6, at p. 213.

The dilemma posed by the fact that the legislative measures were aimed at the protection of the minorities involved and had the support of a substantial segment of these groups, put the Human Rights Committee in a rather uncomfortable position. It could see the value of not closing the door completely on other measures which might in the future be adopted to assist threatened minorities, but at the same time it had difficulty reconciling the wording of Article 27 with what, in practice, constituted a denial of the right of certain individuals to participate in some aspects of the life of their community.

Such a dilemma may occur in many other cases, which also provide an idea of the scope of the difficulties at issue. For example, a state may adopt legislation which recognises the authority of a linguistic minority to select the children entitled to attend its private schools. In order to protect the culture of the linguistic minority's main ethnic group, the people exercising such authority may prefer to exclude children who are the product of mixed marriages, or children of recent immigrants. Linguistically speaking, such children are members of the same minority, yet they are excluded from using their language in community with other members of their linguistic group. The Human Rights Committee seems to have sensed such potential difficulties in attempting to provide a flexible approach in the case of state actions which are adopted for the good of a minority but which nonetheless have the effect of excluding some individuals from minority activities.

If a state is precluded from interfering in the use of a minority's language, what happens when a minority, as a community, convinces the state to help it exclude some of its own members from certain activities for the collective good? In essence, the Human Rights Committee recognised that whilst an individual under Article 27 has the right to use his language, enjoy his culture, or practice his religion in community with other members of his group, free from state interference, the group itself is under no obligation to accept such individual. At the same time, if a measure was adopted for the protection of a minority and approved by the latter as such, it still had to be non-discriminatory, i.e. have a reasonable and objective justification and be necessary for the continued viability and welfare of a minority.

5.7.3   Consistency with other Provisions

The truth of the matter is that the Human Rights Committee was emphasising that Article 27 could not simply be applied in a vacuum. Whilst a policy of non-interference by a state is appropriate for ethnic, religious or linguistic minorities, this in no way gives governments a *carte blanche* when acting with the blessing and in the name of protection of a minority. In other words, protection of a minority does not detract from a state's commitment towards other human rights guaranteed under the **Covenant**. If a state adopts protective measures in compliance with the "positive duty" under Article 27, these measures must still be consistent with other human rights.

When read in this light, the reasoning in **Lovelace v. Canada** and **Kitok v. Sweden** makes sense, since it is not only Article 27 which is at issue, but additionally whether the government measures are consistent with Article 26, the non-discrimination clause.

Indirectly, the Human Rights Committee indicates that is what it is doing in applying Article 26 by adopting the terminology appropriate when balancing the interests of the state (taking the form of the protection of a minority) with the interests of the individuals (Lovelace and Kitok) in order to determine whether the law has a reasonable and objective justification and is necessary. In other words, it is not Article 27 itself that is qualified, but any legislation or state action that affects other rights protected under the **Covenant**, even if they are in place to protect a minority's rights under Article 27. Final confirmation of this interpretation seems to exist in the Human Rights Committee recent *General Comment No. 23(50)* where it simply states that "none of the rights protected under Article 27 of the **Covenant** may be legitimately exercised in a manner or to an extent inconsistent with the other provisions of the **Covenant**."[104]

5.8   OTHER INSTRUMENTS AND CONTROVERSY OVER THE PROTECTION OF MINORITIES

5.8.1   *The Distinction between Minorities and National Minorities*

Article 27 represents an important marker in a continuum throughout much of history: it is appropriate and even mandatory to recognise the fundamental nature of language, religion and culture for minorities. It also signals a significant, yet almost unnoticed shift from previous practices: instead of applying mainly to well-established groups composed of citizens of a state, Article 27 is truly universal as it applies to everyone in a state belonging to an ethnic, religious or linguistic minority.

A number of scholars, including Capotorti and Thornberry, failed to appreciate that Article 27 was not simply a reproduction of the minorities treaties provisions of the League of Nations era, but that it sought to correct one of their major flaws by providing protection not to a few privileged ethnic, religious or linguistic minority groups (national minorities), but to all individuals who might be the object of repression because of their minority membership and desire to celebrate with their own people the beauty and joy of their religion, language or culture.

This distinction between two different type of minorities — national minorities being a smaller category than minorities generally — must not be ignored because it is not uncommon for a state to provide to communities which have formed a constant feature of the country's character a greater degree of autonomy or entitlement to certain rights and privileges. In some cases, it is recognised that certain communities are intimately linked to the history or culture of a society, and thus deserving of special consideration. Some languages become important historical, cultural or religious symbols for a nation, even though they have been largely abandoned in daily life (Sanskrit in India) or they are spoken as a primary language by only a small proportion of the state population (Irish in Ireland).

In practice, states have shown a greater sensibility towards "indigenous" minorities than towards more recent arrivals. For example, the Government of Germany acknowledges that its Danish minority forms a national minority which possesses an historical area of settlement, just as the Sorbian minority has a hereditary area of settlement in Saxony and Brandenburg. According to the Federal Government, national minorities are ethnic groups whose members are German nationals living in well-defined areas of settlement for a long period of time.[105]

Hungary has also chosen to grant far-ranging and generous rights to various minorities in its 1993 **Act No. LXXVII on the Rights of National and Ethnic Minorities**. Despite its title, the act restricts its generous provisions to national minorities,[106] i.e. citizens who belong to

---

[104] *Supra*, note 47, at paragraph 8.

[105] Minister of Foreign Affairs, BTag-Ds. 12/585, 15 May 1991.

[106] Article 61(1) of the **Act** identifies the ethnic and linguistic minorities which fulfil these requirements:

communities which have existed in Hungary for a long period of time (at least 100 years) and demonstrate a spirit of solidarity in preserving their culture, language or religion. Although this appears to have been inspired by the Capotorti definition of a minority, it must be emphasised that the former made a mistake, and that a minority under Article 27 is not identical to what was considered a national minority during the League of Nations period and in most other national and international instruments.

More recent international instruments confirm a trend towards more generous, flexible treatment of national minorities, some of which are wider in scope than Article 27, and others which are quite similar. The OSCE **Document of the Copenhagen Meeting on the Human Dimension** contains a number of specific rights of persons belonging to national minorities. For example, Article 32 of the document is certainly inspired by the **Covenant:**

> Persons belonging to national minorities have the right freely to express, preserve and develop their ethnic, cultural, linguistic or religious identity and to maintain and develop their culture in all its aspects, free of any attempts at assimilation against their will. In particular, they have the right:
> - to use freely their mother tongue in private as well as in public;
> - to establish and maintain their own educational, cultural and religious institutions, organisations or associations, which can seek voluntary financial and other contributions as well as public assistance, in conformity with national legislation;
> - to profess and practise their religion, including the acquisition, possession and use of religious materials, and to conduct religious educational activities in their mother tongue;...
>
> Persons belonging to national minorities can exercise and enjoy their rights individually as well as in community with other members of their group. No disadvantage may arise for a person belonging to a national minority on account of the exercise or non-exercise of any such rights.

In other ways, the above document clearly goes beyond Article 27, containing provisions prohibiting discrimination, guaranteeing freedom of expression, etc, specifically as it relates to national minorities.

Instruments such as the **European Charter for Regional or Minority Languages** (Article 1), the **Convention-cadre sur la protection des minorités nationales** (Article 1), and the **Central European Initiative Instrument for the Protection of Minority Rights** (Article 1), do not purport to address the rights of every ethnic, religious or linguistic minority. These are more limited in scope because they are restricted to national minorities, whilst United Nations instruments such as the **International Covenant on Civil and Political Rights** and the UN **Declaration on the Rights of Persons Belonging to National or Ethnic, Religious and Linguistic Minorities** are not limited to national minorities, but address themselves to minorities in general.

Sont considérés, en vertu de la présente loi, comme autochtones en Hongrie : les groupes allemands, arméniens, bulgares, croates, grecs, polonais, roumains, ruthéniens, serbes, slovaques, slovènes, tziganes et ukrainiens.

5.8.2   *Fundamental Guarantees under Article 27 for Non-National Minorities*

It is not illegitimate *per se* for a state to provide some type of preference or additional rights and privileges for national minorities, but it is essential to keep in mind that non-national minorities are still entitled to the fundamental protection guaranteed by Article 27 of the **International Covenant on Civil and Political Rights**, even if they are excluded from a state's legislation related to national minorities.

The error which must be avoided at all cost is to equate the measures aimed at national minorities as representing faithfully the extent of a state's obligations under Article 27. As shown previously, the drafters of this provision clearly rejected attempts to limit Article 27 to the protection of "older" minorities, thus distancing themselves from the approach of the League of Nations era. Furthermore, it appears to have been their intention to truly make the provision "universal". They carefully chose the phrasing in order to make it clear that all persons within a state belonging to an ethnic, religious or linguistic minority are the subjects of Article 27, not just citizens of the state belonging to national minorities. Finally, the *raison d'être* of Article 27 was clearly to provide what was considered a minimum form of protection fundamental for minorities: the right to use their language, enjoy their culture, and practice their religion with other members of their group, no more, no less.

Recent instruments like the **European Charter for Regional or Minority Languages** and the **Convention-cadre sur la protection des minorités nationales** must be applauded for demonstrating how various rights such as freedom of expression and non-discrimination based upon language, along with the right of non-interference for minorities, can be crafted together to ensure appropriate and balanced responses to the legitimate needs and interests of minorities, but they only provide a framework for national minorities. They do not attempt to consider what would be an appropriate and balanced response to the legitimate needs and interests of non-national minorities.

Thus, Article 27 remains of prime importance since it is relevant to all individuals belonging to linguistic minorities, be they nationals or non-nationals.

5.9   SUMMARY

The right of individuals belonging to a linguistic minority to use their language with other members of their group has been part of international law since the time of the minorities treaties under League of Nations supervision. More recently, the right has re-appeared in a number of treaties, including Article 27 of the **International Covenant on Civil and Political Rights**.

What the right entails in practice, and who its beneficiaries are, has been the object of some debate, but it would appear fairly clear now that any individual who can claim membership of a linguistic minority is entitled to the protection offered by this right. Attempts to restrict the category of beneficiaries to citizens, well-established minority groups (or national minorities), non-dominant minorities, or even non-indigenous groups have all been proven to be wrong because they were founded on the mistaken belief that the state would have to provide resources to assist in the development of minorities, such as the creation of public schools using a minority language as medium of instruction, etc. A minority is to be understood as an objective, numerical minority in a state: less than 50 percent of its entire population.

As for the actual content of the right, it has a "wide" coverage, in the sense that it can affect any individual who is a member of a linguistic minority, but it is also "shallow", in the sense of only requiring from the state positive measures needed to ensure there is no interference in the use of a language by a minority community and its members. Instead of imposing the creation of state institutions and programmes specifically tailored for a minority's survival and development, a state must instead neither inhibit the private and community use of a language, nor permit others to do so. The latter facet of the right is perhaps an example of what may be described as "positive measures" from state authorities: they must not stand by and assist or permit other parties to intervene in the use of a minority's language by members of the group.

This right therefore offers an additional degree of protection in areas where the traditional human rights of freedom of expression and non-discrimination may not be available. The ability for a minority to create and operate private schools where the medium of instruction is their language is one such important area where, strictly speaking, neither freedom of expression nor non-discrimination would be of much assistance, especially if such private schools were forbidden generally. The right to operate private media, to establish organisations and institutions where members of the minority can use their language, to freely use names, surnames and topographical names in their language amongst themselves, all of these can be seen as being protected by the right of individuals to freely use their language with other members of their minority group, although in some of these activities freedom of expression or non-discrimination may also be relevant.

Finally, this guarantee for linguistic minorities should not be confused with the rights which many states additionally consider appropriate for long-established "national minorities". The latter are citizens of a state which can be considered as "minorities plus": their long-standing presence in a country make them a recognised constituent of the national culture and society, and they are deemed to be entitled to rights and privileges which other minorities may not be able to claim, such as the right to language promotion programmes using state resources, or even state schools using the minority language as language of instruction. Linguistic minorities *simpliciter* would not be entitled to the same state largesse, but would nevertheless still be eligible for the fundamental guarantees offered by human rights provisions such as Article 27 of the **International Covenant on Civil and Political Rights.**

6. State Language Preferences, Practices or Restrictions and Human Rights

In the previous chapters, it has been demonstrated that language preferences or restrictions by a state may breach fundamental human rights such as freedom of expression, non-discrimination, and the right of members of linguistic minorities to freely use their language in community with other members of their group. In practice, specific situations may involve a combination of these rights, as in the case where public authorities adopt measures which restrict an individual's use of his or her minority language with other members of his group and, at the same time, conflict with that person's freedom of expression. Despite some overlapping, the various human rights do provide a degree of protection in respect to language matters in distinct areas of activities. How these human rights may interact in various domains will be examined in this chapter.

6.1 THE LANGUAGE OF ADMINISTRATIVE AUTHORITIES AND PUBLIC SERVICES

[T]he effort by one language group to seek hegemony may contain within it the seeds of a cycle of resistance and repression. Hegemonic policies make compromises increasingly difficult and polarisation increasingly extreme. The resulting struggle is not "ethnic conflict" grounded in linguistic or cultural differences, but rather a conflict over power and policy resulting from the effort of one group to establish hegemony over others.[1]

6.1.1 Is Official Language Use Exclusive?

In most states, the existence of a declaration in respect to an official language or languages does not signify that public authorities are prohibited from utilising other languages when appropriate. In fact, equating the adoption of a single official language with the exclusion of all other languages in every type of situation is inconsistent with generally recognised human rights such as the right to an interpreter in legal proceedings, amongst others.

Official language status does signal that the use of such language in a state is provided by law; however, the exact scope of a right to use an official language can always be subjected to various limitations and considerations. Under the Canadian **Constitution**, the recognition of two official languages pursuant to Article 16 did not *in se* guarantee a right to any type of service in either official languages. Such an interpretation was handed down in a rather surprising decision of the Supreme Court of Canada.[2] Official language status, in the highest law of the land, was merely a "political" declaration which had to be further developed in other constitutional or legal provisions. Contrary to popular belief, even when the use of the English and French languages in Canada is guaranteed by a statute (and not by the **Constitution**), it is still generally limited to certain categories of public services emanating from the federal government in a few parts of the country, mostly in the provinces of Ontario, Québec and New Brunswick. At the level of the

---

[1] Tollefson, James W. (1991), *Planning Language, Planning Inequality*, Longman Inc., New York, at pp. 197-198.

[2] **Société des Acadiens du Nouveau-Brunswick v. Association of Parents for Fairness in Education**, (1986) 1 S.C.R. 549 (Canada).

provincial governments, some services may also be provided in both languages in the latter three provinces. Only a few specific federal services are, in theory, available in both languages in the whole of the country.[3]

The new South African **Constitution**, which recognises eleven official languages[4] — from isiZulu, which is the primary language of almost 30 percent of the country's population, to Tshivenda, which is the primary language of less than 2 percent of the population — is misleading, because official status does not actually imply guaranteed access to administrative or public services in all of these languages. In fact, the **Constitution** itself prepares the ground for dilution of the impact of official status, as "the use of official languages for the purposes of the functioning of government" must take into account issues of usage, practicality and expense.[5] In the case of Tshivenda, this will probably mean that it will be considered too expensive for most uses, so that official status will basically be an empty promise for speakers of Tshivenda. To borrow, and adapt to the context, a famous quote from British writer George Orwell, all languages are equal, but some languages are more equal than others.

In some cases, a state may attempt to combine the recognition of an official language, which in itself is quite legitimate, with a prohibition of the use of any other language in all contacts between public authorities and the population. This can in some cases amount to a violation of human rights.

A fear has been acknowledged, for example, in the United States that any declaration of English as the official language will lead to repressive or discriminatory measures. Following the adoption of a series of laws in Arizona, Colorado, Florida and North Carolina recognising English as the only official language, there were several instances of unfortunate events triggered by public authorities, and even by private citizens.[6] Non-English-speaking prisoners in Arizona were denied parole, public school-bus drivers in Colorado reprimanded children for speaking Spanish on the bus, driver's licence examinations in languages other than English were initially abolished,[7] and even the scientific (Latin) names of animals in public zoos were at one point considered to constitute a violation of English-only legislation.

The above examples suggest a profound misunderstanding of what official language status entails. Whilst a state is free to designate whatever language it prefers as official, and thus recognise its legal obligation to respond in the official language (or languages) — subject to appropriate limitations — such a designation can never entitle public authorities to violate the fundamental human rights of individuals. Judicial interpretation, legal provisions or administrative

---

[3] Despite claims from Canadian authorities that official bilingualism in the country is based upon an approach diametrically different from the territorially-based language models of Belgium and Switzerland, this is not quite the case. Most of the public services in both languages are only guaranteed in regions where a sufficiently high percentage of the population uses the second official language, or if there is a sufficiently high demand for services in both official languages in a region.

[4] See Article 3(1) of the **Constitution of South Africa**, reprinted in the Appendix.

[5] Ibid., Article 3(8).

[6] One supermarket clerk was suspended for responding to a co-worker in Spanish because of the mistaken belief by their employer that the new legislation recognising English as the official language meant that every US resident should henceforth only speak English at all times.

[7] Language Rights and the Legal Status of English-Only Laws in the Public and Private Sector (1992), in *North Carolina Central Law Journal*, Vol. 20, 65-91, at p. 66.

practices which view official language status as a green light for any type of conduct favouring the official language(s) are inacceptable if the result is an infringement of human rights. Declaring English, French or Spanish as an exclusive official language cannot be used as an excuse to violate a person's freedom of expression, nor to permit discriminatory practices on the ground of language.

6.1.2   *Language Discrimination and Public Authorities*

Whenever the number of individuals speaking a minority or non-official language in a state is substantial, especially if they are mainly citizens, public authorities in regions where these individuals are mostly concentrated should be able to respond to their requests as well as offer public services in their primary language. Failure to do so could constitute a violation of the right to non-discrimination.[8] A state's preference in respect to a particular language disadvantages speakers of different languages, because the state thereby creates a linguistic criterion in terms of the level of enjoyment of services and opportunities for employment. In addition to the fewer opportunities for employment in the state bureaucracy, non-native speakers with a lower proficiency in the official or majority language as compared to native speakers may experience disadvantages in the area of public services such as delays in obtaining appointments and interviews with bilingual public servants, the cost of paying another person to act as an interpreter during interviews and to assist with the completion of forms and consequent delays, the inability or varying level of difficulty to accurately communicate information in order to be eligible for public benefits, decisions or privileges involving public authorities, the unintentional communication of incorrect information by untrained family members and friends acting as interpreters, the inability to accurately communicate medical information to public health authorities and employees, additional costs such as family members' travel expenses and absences from work in order to interpret.[9]

Particularly when speakers of a non-official language are numerous and reside in a compact region, it is likely that many have a limited proficiency in the majority or official language because in most aspects of their daily lives these people are in contact with other members of their community and have relatively few occasions or little need to use another language. A particularly large linguistic community is more likely to strongly reject a monolingual government policy if many of its members are disadvantaged.

Use of a single language by state officials in state functions and documentation also has a highly visible impact on employment opportunities with public authorities, as it signals to those who do not master the official language as well as a native speaker that they will find

---

[8] In **Groener v. Minister for Education**, Case 379-87, [1990] 1 Common Market Law Review 401, the European Court of Justice rejected the submissions of the French government that a state's linguistic policy is somehow beyond the scope of Community law. The court stated that a linguistic policy cannot encroach upon a fundamental freedom in a discriminatory fashion. In other words, any language preference or related criterion, and the manner in which it is applied, must be proportionate to the objective sought.

[9] *Québec-Communauté française de Belgique : autonomie et spécificité dans le cadre d'un système fédéral* (1991), Wilson & Lafleur, Montréal, at p. 146.

government jobs largely unaccessible.[10] This is increasingly coming to light as a major cause of tension in places such as Estonia, Kazakhstan, Macedonia and Kirgizstan. Many states of the former Soviet Union are emphasising the priority of the new official state language, and Russian-speaking inhabitants who were formerly in a position of domination, or at least of advantage, are increasingly facing a language barrier to which they are unaccustomed, because of language requirements in employment.

Recognition of the important economic opportunity aspect associated to the use of a single language can be found in the *1994 Human Development Report* of the United Nations Development Programme where the following warning is given: "In several nations, ethnic tensions are on the rise, often over limited access to opportunities — whether to social services from the state or to jobs from the market. Individual communities lose out, or believe [they] lose out, in the struggle for such opportunities".[11]

Whilst the percentage and geographical concentration of individuals using a primary language distinct from the official language or that of the majority is perhaps the single most important factor to consider when determining whether state language preferences and requirements are discriminatory, there is no simple model which would be appropriate for all situations in every state. There is nevertheless a basic principle which would seem sufficiently adaptable to be applied in most countries. It would appear that to arrive at a reasonable equilibrium, between the interests of the state and the rights, interests and obligations of affected individuals in matters relating to language use by public authorities, a "sliding-scale" approach would be appropriate in order to arrive at a linguistic policy which does not discriminate on the basis on language.

A sliding-scale model can provide a balanced and reasonable response to the presence of various numbers of speakers of non-official or minority languages, either at the national, regional or local level. When authorities at any one of these levels face a sufficiently high number of individuals whose primary language is not the official or preferred state language, it would be discriminatory not to provide a level of service appropriate to the relative number of individuals involved.

In the case of local districts and their administration, where the speakers of non-official or minority languages are concentrated, local authorities should provide for an increasing level of services in the non-official or minority languages as the number of speakers of those languages increase. Beginning at the lower end of the sliding-scale model and moving to a progressively

---

[10] Alexander, Neville (1989), "The Language Question", in *Critical Choice for South African Society*, Institute for the Study of Public Policy, Johannesburg, pp. 3-9, at pp. 6-7;

In South African society as constituted at present the official language policy sustains and reinforces inherited social inequalities and racial divisions. For instance, to obtain well-paid employment in virtually any sphere, the prospective employee must be fluent in English and/or Afrikaans... This means that for most black people, such employment is unattainable simply because their home language is neither English nor Afrikaans and, in most cases, their schooling does not help them to acquire the necessary proficiency. Conversely, the present policy favours those of the white, coloured and Indian population registration groups because their home language is either English or Afrikaans or, in many cases, both.

[11] Globe and Mail, Toronto, 3 July 1994, at p. A8.

higher end, this would imply, for example:

1. making available widely used official documents and forms for the population in the non-official or minority language or in bilingual versions;
2. the acceptance by authorities of oral or written applications in the non-official or minority language;
3. the acceptance by authorities of oral or written applications in the non-official or minority language, and response thereto in that language;
4. having a sufficient number of officers, who are in contact with the public, in place to respond to the use of the non-official or minority language;
5. being able to use the non-official or minority language as an internal and daily language of work within public authorities.

This is a very general scheme and does not take into account other factors identified as relevant in Chapter 4 (section 4.5) in determining the reasonability of state language preferences and the disadvantages that these create for individuals, but it does provide some general guidance as to the minimal requirements which public authorities must respect in application of the right to non-discrimination when there is a demographically significant number of individuals disadvantaged by a state's language preferences or requirements.

It should be pointed out that many recent treaties and international instruments actually embody the concept of a sliding-scale. The **Central European Initiative Instrument for the Protection of Minority Rights** (Article 13: "whenever in an area the number of persons...reaches...a significant level"),[12] the **Convention-cadre pour la protection des minorités nationales** (Article 10: "*Dans les aires géographiques d'implantation substantielle ou traditionnelle...lorsque ces personnes en font la demande et que celle-ci répond à un besoin réel*"),[13] and the **European Charter for Minority or Regional Languages** (Article 10: "within the administrative districts...in which the number of residents...justifies the measures specified below and according to the situation of each language"),[14] to name but a few, all embody the implicit recognition that the appropriate treatment of individuals by public authorities must take into account the reasonability of state actions in language matters, in order to fulfil the requirements of non-discrimination. As has already been mentioned, the **European Charter for Minority or Regional Languages** is more a political document than a rights treaty, as it leaves to each state the option to "opt-out" of most of the treaty provisions in a manner which may disregard the human rights of affected individuals, as if it were possible to set aside certain basic principles such as freedom of expression through such an instrument. This unfortunate flaw has thankfully not been repeated in the **Convention-cadre pour la protection des minorités nationales.**

6.1.3   *Numerical Threshold*

As primordial as the numerical threshold appears to be in determining an appropriate and reasonable linguistic policy which satisfies the requirements of non-discrimination, the previously mentioned instruments do not give very precise guidelines as to when a state is mandated to take measures in order to avoid imposing an unreasonable burden or disadvantage upon too many

---

[12] See Section 1.2.2 in the Appendix.

[13] See Section 2.2.4 in the Appendix.

[14] See Section 2.2.6 in the Appendix.

people. Of course, the reason for this is that each country's situation is so different, and the number of variables so numerous, that each government must have a margin of appreciation in order to adapt the most proper mechanism to the unique situation of the state and of its speakers of various languages. Nevertheless, it is possible to cite a few examples in order to give a sense of what appears to be proportionally sound.

In India, the basic numerical thresholds were adopted in 1956 in a memorandum negotiated between the federal government and individual states: whenever any language is spoken by 30 percent or more of the population in any state or district, the state or district is recognised as bilingual and the relevant minority language is placed on the same footing as the regional language for use by public authorities; whenever the linguistic minority constitutes 15 to 20 per cent of the population in an area, government notices, rules, laws, etc. are reproduced in the language of the minority in that particular area.[15]

Article 8 of the December 1993 draft **Language Law of Estonia** provides that in municipalities where at least one-half of the permanent residents belong to a national minority, every person has the right to receive a response from the state and the municipal institutions of the administrative district and their officials in the language of the national minority as well as in Estonian. It should be pointed out that this requirement that at least half of the population belong to a national minority appears somewhat steep, certainly when compared to the practices in many other countries.

Canada has adopted regulations[16] providing for a rather complicated sliding-scale approach which depends not only upon the total number and/or percentage of speakers of the two official languages, but also upon the type of service provided by public authorities. Other than in a few key areas, where minimal services are to be available in both French and English, most bilingual federal government services are only available when the population in a census subdivision includes at least 5 percent of speakers of the official language minority (or at least 5,000 individuals in major cities having a population of more than 100,000). In some of the lesser populated census subdivisions, a few services can be obtained in both languages, even if there are as few as 500 speakers of the official minority language.

Within the public administration of the Basque Autonomous Community in Spain, Euskara and Castilian are to be used by administrative units in areas where the percentage of Euskara-speakers reaches 20 percent of the population.

The Finnish approach towards the presence of Swedish-speakers is even more flexible:

> In a bilingual municipality (commune) citizens have the right to be administered in Finnish or Swedish by both local and state authorities. The authorities are required to publish documents and announcements that affect the general public in both languages. The internal administrative language of a municipality is the language of the majority. In principle, state authorities should communicate with the municipalities in the principal language of the municipality. A municipality is considered unilingual — Finnish or Swedish — when the entire population speaks the same language or when the number of inhabitants who speak

---

[15] Dhar, T.N. (1987), "Language Planning and Development: Problems of Legislation amidst Diversity", in Lorne Laforge (ed.), *Proceedings of the International Colloquium on Language Planning*, Les Presses de l'Université Laval, Québec, pp. 238-254, at p. 246.

[16] **Official Languages (Communications with and Services to the Public) Regulations**, SOR/92-48, 16 December 1991.

the minority language is less than eight percent. If the minority exceeds eight percent or numbers 3000 persons, the municipality is bilingual. A bilingual commune is not declared unilingual until the minority falls below six percent.[17]

Despite misgivings expressed by some political leaders and courts in the United States,[18] there does exist at the legislative level recognition of the need to provide public services in languages other than English when there exists a sufficiently large number of individuals who speak a particular minority language. Under US federal law, state agencies which administer "food stamp" programmes must have bilingual staff and translated written materials in areas where there are a substantial number of low-income, non-English-speaking families. Five percent of the low-income households in an area is deemed to constitute a substantial number. Thus, in California, for example, people applying for and receiving public benefits are entitled to receive application forms and information materials in Spanish.[19]

In the Slovak Republic, the **1990 Official Language Act** recognises that public authorities have the obligation to provide services and respond in a non-official language in any region where at least 20 percent of the population consists of a national minority:

> If the members of a national minority form in a city or village 20 percent of the population at least, they may in such cities and villages use their language in official contact. If in these cities or villages a citizen who is not a member of the national minority comes into official contact, the procedure is carried on in the official language. The employees of state authorities and local self-government bodies are not obliged to know and use the language of the national minority. Public documents and the official agenda are made up in the official language.[20]

Although it appears that no international instrument attempts to provide a precise demographical standard for assessing when exactly the use of a non-official or minority language by public authorities is an appropriate and reasonable response to the principle of non-discrimination, at

---

[17] *Minority Languages Today* (1981), Einar Haugen, J. Derrick McClure and Derick Thomson (eds.), Edinburgh University Press, Edinburgh, at p. 133.

[18] In **Guerrero v. Carleson**, 109 Cal.Rep. 201 (1973) (United States), Spanish-speaking welfare recipients with limited proficiency in English lost their benefits due to a failure to respond to the welfare department's notice of an impending change in their status. The notice had been sent in English despite the department's knowledge that the recipients did not speak that language. The majority of the court rejected the argument that the public authorities were under an obligation to provide the notice in Spanish, in part because it felt that this would impose an impossible burden upon the state, as there is no way to distinguish amongst language groups and types of notice that ought to be provided. Moreover, every official communication or public service would have to be offered in every language spoken in the United States. In a strong dissent, one judge pointed out that the majority's basic assumption was wrong, as in reality the need to use different languages could easily and reasonably be distinguished according to the relative importance of their use and concentration of speakers.

[19] See **California Government Code**, Articles 7292, 7295 *et seq.* (West 1980).

[20] Article 6(2), **Slovak National Council Act No. 428/1990**, 25 October 1990. The legislation mainly affects 500 communities where Hungarian is widely spoken.

least one non-governmental organisation has attempted to do so in a **Draft Protocol to the International Convention on the Protection of National or Ethnic Minorities or Groups, Applicable to the States Members of the Council of Europe:**

> The ethnic group's language shall be the official language if in an autonomous corporate entity within a commune (including parts of the commune or factions of a commune equipped with independent sub-organs of the commune) at least 20 percent, in administrative and judicial districts at least six percent, or in larger administrative entities at least five percent of the residing population use the language of the ethnic group.[21]

Whilst the above only provide a very general idea of the many types of possible arrangements which exist in relation to state language practices, it is evident that a number of states accept to a greater or lesser extent the desirability of adopting a balanced response to the demographical reality within their territory as a means of maintaining social peace. This, in turn, may be an acknowledgment that any state language preference will have a negative impact upon some segments of the population, and if the percentage of those affected is sufficiently high, some type of accommodation must be reached. In determining the proper policy, each public authority must attempt to strike a balance by taking into account, amongst other things, the nature of the service offered, the frequency of contacts with the public, the linguistic composition of the region to be served and the importance of the services involved and their effect upon individuals. In essence, it must adopt a non-discriminatory conduct in relation to its language use.

Certain states have chosen a path which is somewhat different from that described above by opting for various degrees of regional autonomy. When provinces, *oblasts*, cantons or states are granted an extensive array of legal, judicial and administrative powers and corresponding financial resources, it becomes possible for a linguistic minority to acquire control over many facets of the public authority and the corresponding control over public language use. The Swiss cantons, the Åland Islands in Finland, and the Belgian cultural communities are all examples of the so-called principle of linguistic territoriality or *Territorialitatsprinzip*. In the case of Switzerland, for example, this principle signifies that even the relatively small population of Italian-speakers are able to constitute a majority in the canton of Ticino and have an extensive array of public services in their language, in addition to a great deal of local political power.

6.1.4 *Court and Administrative Proceedings*

Even in circumstances where the number of speakers is so low as to make it non-discriminatory to operate exclusively in one language in court or before administrative tribunals,[22] there may be situations where a state must take other steps to compensate the highly prejudicial effects of the state's linguistic preference upon some individuals.[23] Even in the case of a person having

---

[21] Article 16, reprinted in Section 1.3.8 of the Appendix.

[22] In the **Brunner** case, Arrêts du Tribunal fédéral 106 Ia 299 (Switzerland), the Court felt that at approximately 25 percent of the population, the German-speaking community in one of the districts of Fribourg constituted a "borderline" case where judicial bilingualism ought to be considered.

[23] As already noted in Chapter 4, international courts have admitted explicitly or implicitly that the use of one's language in court is an advantage, and the inability to use it is consequently a disadvantage. See **Ministère Public v. Mutsch**, Case 137-84, (1985) European Court Reports 2681; de Witte, Bruno

little or no knowledge of the language used in court proceedings, it is obviously not unreasonable, for practical and financial reasons for a state not to conduct its court proceedings in a language which is not widely used or known in the state. At the same time, there is no denying that the burden or disadvantage for a person in such a situation is exceptionally high. As with any other balancing of interests between the individual and the state, in assessing what is reasonable, one must ask whether there may not be a less onerous measure capable of being adopted by the state which will lessen the individual's burden or disadvantage.[24]

Most international treaties dealing with civil and political rights,[25] as well as most states,[26]

(1991), "The Impact of European Community Rules on Linguistic Policies of the Member States", in Florian Coulmas (ed.), *A Language Policy for the European Community: Prospects and Quandaries*, Mouton de Gruyter, Berlin, New York, pp. 163-177, at pp. 170-171; and, Rannat, Mohammed Ahmed Abu (1972), *Study of Equality in the Administration of Justice*, United Nations Publications, New York, at paragraph 432:

> ...aliens and members of linguistic minorities within a given country, if they do not command a knowledge of the language of the court, suffer difficulties in judicial proceedings unless proper provisions are made on their behalf. As has been seen in paragraphs 411-418, such arrangements are made free of charge for accused persons in the great majority of countries, and are also made or may be made free of charge to parties in non-criminal proceedings in some countries. But official provision of interpretation in return for payment by the person aided goes some way towards reducing discrimination on linguistic grounds in judicial proceedings.

[24] Interpretation is not an ideal solution, as it only alleviates without eliminating some of the disadvantages of proceedings in an unfamiliar language. See Schulman, Michael B. (1993), "No Hablo Inglés: Court Interpretation as a Major Obstacle to Fairness for Non-English-Speaking Defendants", in *Vanderbilt Law Review*, Vol. 46, 176-196, at p. 178:

> When a defendant testifies in a criminal case his testimony is critically important to the jury's determination of his guilt or innocence. The first noticeable difficulty in the present system of court interpretation is that non-English-speaking defendants are not judged on their own words. The words attributed to the defendant are those of the interpreter. No matter how accurate the interpretation is, the words are not the defendant's, nor is the style, the syntax, or the emotion. Furthermore, some words are culturally specific and therefore, are incapable of being translated. Perfect interpretations do not exist, as no interpretation will convey precisely the same meaning as the original testimony. While juries should not attribute to the defendant the exact wording of the interpretation and the emotion expressed by the interpreter, they typically do just that. In addition, American juries often are biased against non-English-speaking defendants; therefore, these defendants are disadvantaged from the outset of the case. Given that juries often determine the defendant's guilt or innocence based on small nuances of language or slight variations in emotion, how can it be fair for the defendant to be judged on the words chosen and the emotion expressed by the interpreter?

[25] Article 14 of the **International Covenant on Civil and Political Rights**, Article 5 of the **European Convention for the Protection of Human Rights and Fundamental Freedoms**, and Article 8 of the **American Convention on Human Rights**, all reprinted in the Appendix.

[26] de Witte, Bruno (1985), "Linguistic Equality: A Study in Comparative Constitutional Law", in *Revista de Llengua i Dret*, Vol. 3, 43-126, at p. 105:

> [P]ractically all countries provide for the assistance of an interpreter to the persons who do not have a sufficient knowledge of the language used by the [criminal] court; such aid is usually

have provisions recognising that when an accused faces proceedings in a language which he does not understand, he shall have the right to the assistance of an interpreter, most often free of charge. If a person is being charged with a criminal offence, he must also be informed of the nature of the charge in a language which he understands. This international standard may be considered as just another example of the possible application of equality and non-discrimination on the ground of language: that a person be subjected to a trial or proceeding in an unknown language is unquestionably a "distinction, exclusion, restriction or preference which...has the purpose or effect of nullifying or impairing the recognition, enjoyment or exercise" of a trial or proceeding when compared to an individual who has the benefit of proceedings in his or her primary language, although in most states such an association is not acknowledged. In some states it is linked with the principle of a "fair trial", of "due process", or of "fundamental" or "natural justice", or even to the right to confront witnesses and to be present at trial.[27] Even in

---

provided without cost for the accused, except, in some cases, for a reimbursement which can be claimed if the person is found guilty. Yet, this guarantee is only indirectly linked to the general principle of equality, and more closely to the more specific constitutional principles of "fair trial", "equality of arms", or, in the United States, "due process". Furthermore, recent improvements in this sector have been influenced, in many European countries, not so much by their own constitutional provisions as by the fair trial guarantees of the European Human Rights Convention; indeed, this is one of the areas in which this Convention most clearly went beyond the existing "minimum standard" of its contracting states.

Amongst the legislative measures enshrining this right are Article 18(3) of the **1991 Languages Act of the Soviet Socialist Republic of Russia**, *Recueil des législations linguistiques dans le monde - Tome V: L'Algérie, l'Autriche, la Chine, le Danemark, la Finlande, la Hongrie, l'île de Malte, le Maroc, la Norvège, la Nouvelle-Zélande, les Pays-Bas, le Royaume-Uni, la Tunisie, la Turquie, l'ex-URSS* (1994), Jacques Leclerc and Jacques Maurais (eds.), International Centre for Research on Language Planning, Québec, at p. 213; Article 13 of the **1989 Languages Act of the SSR of Kazakhstan**, ibid., at p. 162; and Section 753 of the **Evidence Code, 1965 (California)**. Many constitutions actually include the right to an interpreter in criminal proceedings: Malta (Article 35(2)); Mauritius (Articles 5 and 10); Nigeria (Article 6); Papua New Guinea (Article 37); and generally see Rannat, *supra*, note 23, at paragraph 432. One notable exception can be found in Japan, where the **Court Procedures Act** provides that a charge must describe the names and address of a suspect, the charges against him and other necessary information. However, there is nothing in the Act relating to the translation of the writ. Therefore, an arrest can be made simply by presenting a writ in Japanese, even though the person arrested does not understand the nature or content of the charges against him. Another legislative measure of doubtful conformity is the Spanish **Organic Law 14/1983**, of 12 December 1983, which makes available the right to an interpreter, free of charge, in criminal proceedings only to non-citizens. A court decision has concluded, however, that the Act is only valid if it is also available to Spanish citizens: see Milian i Massana, Antoni (1992), "Droits linguistiques et droits fondamentaux en Espagne", in *Revue Générale du Droit*, Vol. 23, 561-581, at pp. 579-580.

[27] In **Commonwealth v. Garcia**, 379 Mass. 422 (1980) (United States), at pp. 437-438, the Supreme Judicial Court of Massachusetts held that a language barrier could, during a criminal trial, affect an individual's right to a fair trial by effectively denying him the right to be "present" at his trial (in the sense of understanding what is occurring) and the right to confront adverse witnesses. See also **The State (Buchan) v. Coyne** 70 ILTR 185 (1936) (Ireland) regarding the right to an interpreter as it relates to natural justice. Because there is no constitutional right to an interpreter in the US, courts have been at pains to ensure such a right indirectly, through the use of the Sixth and/or Fourteenth

states where the legal system has traditionally not recognised the principle of non-discrimination (particularly Common Law states, until recently), the right to an interpreter has consistently been widely acknowledged.

For example, US courts have found that the due process clause of the **Fourteenth Amendment** may require the appointment of an interpreter for a non-English-speaking accused. Over time, the due process clause has been the vehicle for multiple, and occasionally complex, judicial doctrines. In the setting of a criminal proceeding, the denial of due process has been defined as the failure to observe that fundamental fairness essential to the very concept of justice:

> In order to declare a denial of it we must find that the absence of that fairness fatally infected the trial; the acts complained of must be of such quality as necessarily prevents a fair trial.[28]

US courts have also combined the **Fourteenth Amendment** with other constitutional clauses in order to acknowledge the need for non-English-speaking defendants to be informed of their right to simultaneous interpretation of criminal proceedings, at the government's expense:

> Not only for the sake of effective cross-examination, however, but as a matter of simple humaneness, Negron deserved more than to sit in total incomprehension as the trial proceeded. Particularly inappropriate in this nation where many languages are spoken is a callousness to the crippling language handicap of a newcomer to its shores, whose life and freedom the state by its criminal processes chooses to put in jeopardy.[29]

Despite the diversity of approaches in different states, the basic principles at issue all appear to have the same concerns: (1) the prejudice caused to an individual having little or no proficiency in the language of proceedings and the grave potential consequences in respect to his interests and his freedom cannot be cast aside for the sake of the state's convenience or interests, and (2) as judicial systems strive for fairness and just results, the inherent risks in proceedings where a

---

Amendments. For an excellent summary of the various US constitutional provisions which are invoked in respect to the right to an interpreter, see Cronheim, Alan J. and Schwartz, Andrew H. (1976), "Non-English-speaking Persons in the Criminal Justice System: Current State of the Law", in *Cornell Law Review*, Vol. 61, 289-311, at pp. 289-297.

[28] **Lisenba v. California**, 314 U.S. 219 (1941) (United States), at p. 236.

[29] **United States ex rel. Negron v. New York**, 434 F.2d 386 (1970) (United States), at p. 389; see also **MacDonald v. City of Montreal**, (1986) 1 S.C.R. 460 (Canada), at p. 499, and **Ngatayt v. The Queen**, (1980) 147 C.L.R. 1 (Australia), at p. 20:

> [When the incapacity to understand the proceedings is due to an inability to understand the language in which the proceedings are conducted]...if an interpreter is available the capacity is removed. Similarly, in deciding whether an accused is capable of understanding the proceedings so as to be able to make a proper defence it is relevant that he is defended by counsel. If the accused is able to understand the evidence, and to instruct his counsel as to the facts of the case, no unfairness or injustice will generally be occasioned by the fact that the accused does not know, and cannot understand, the law. With the assistance of counsel he will usually be able to make a proper defence. That of course is the test which s. 631 provides: is the accused capable of understanding the proceedings at the trial, so as to be able to make a proper defence?

defendant is unable to understand or properly defend himself because of a language barrier or handicap must be avoided whenever possible.

For example, Article 14(3) of the **International Covenant on Civil and Political Rights** provides as follows:

> In the determination of any criminal charge against him, everyone shall be entitled to the following minimum guarantees, in full equality:
> (a) to be informed promptly and in detail in a language which he understands of the nature and cause of the charge against him;...
> (f) to have the free assistance of an interpreter if he cannot understand or speak the language used in court;

Because of the highly prejudicial consequences of a criminal offence and the importance of court proceedings involved, a state is never entitled to set aside such minimal guarantees, which are in no way related to the number of people speaking a particular non-official or minority language in a state. As the fairness and legitimacy of the legal system are at stake, as well as the defendant's interests, the state must adopt what is perceived to be a reasonable measure in the circumstances: at minimum, it must provide free interpretation of court proceedings, as well as inform any individual being charged of the nature and cause of his offence, in a language which he understands.

In **Isop v. Austria,**[30] an applicant sought the right to use Slovene in civil court proceedings by invoking Article 6 (right to a fair hearing) and Article 14 (non-discrimination on the basis of language or national association) of the **Convention for the Protection of Human Rights and Fundamental Freedoms.** The European Commission on Human Rights concluded that these provisions, used in conjunction, do not guarantee linguistic freedom of individuals in their relations with public authorities such as courts. Important points raised throughout this study on language and human rights can be seen to apply to the case: on the one hand, the relatively small number of speakers of Slovene in Austria did not make the exclusive use of German in the Austrian court system discriminatory,[31] and on the other hand, the applicant's own knowledge of the German language made the use of an interpreter unnecessary. There existed no unacceptably harsh burden related to lack of proficiency in the language of proceedings.

When a sufficiently high numerical threshold of speakers of a language has been reached, states should provide for an appropriate level of use of this language in its institutions. Even when such a threshold has not been reached, interpreters must be provided to inform individuals of charges laid against them and for criminal court proceedings. Non-discrimination still demands a concession on the language front because of the severe disadvantages caused by a state's

---

[30] Application 808/60, 5 Yearbook of the European Convention on Human Rights 108.

[31] It should be remarked that the European Commission did not deal specifically with this issue, and that in some parts of Austria there may be grounds for greater use of the Slovene language. This may have been acknowledged in Austrian legislation, adopted after the **Isop v. Austria** case, ibid., which permits a greater use of Slovene in court proceedings. See Article 14 of **Federal Act of 7 July 1976 on the Legal Position of Minorities in Austria**, *Recueil des législations linguistiques, supra,* note 26, at p. 27.

language preference in proceedings involving individuals with too little proficiency in the chosen language.[32]

Other international decisions confirm this view, and even offer tantalising hints regarding links between the right to an interpreter and equality. In **Dominique Guesdon v. France**,[33] the author of the complaint faced charges of having damaged public property by defacing road signs in French. He indicated that 12 witnesses appearing on his behalf and he himself wished to give testimony in Breton and requested that their testimony be heard through the assistance of an interpreter. His request was denied by the *Tribunal correctionnel*. As the court refused to hear him and his witnesses in their language, and as they were unwilling to express themselves in French, the author was given a four months' suspended sentence and ordered to pay a fine of 2,000 francs. Guesdon claimed that the French courts had violated, amongst other things, his rights to a fair hearing, his right to have witnesses heard on his behalf and his right to have the assistance of an interpreter.

The Human Rights Committee correctly noted that the notion of a fair trial, within the meaning of Article 14 of the **International Covenant on Civil and Political Rights**, does not have the effect of entitling an accused in criminal proceedings to express himself in his language of preference:

> The Committee observes, as it has done on a previous occasion, that Article 14 is concerned with procedural equality; it enshrines, *inter alia*, the principle of equality of arms in criminal proceedings. The provision for the use of one official court language by states parties to the Covenant does not, in the Committee's opinion, violate Article 14. Nor does the requirement of a fair hearing mandate states parties to make available to a citizen whose mother tongue differs from the official court language, the services of an interpreter, if this citizen is capable of expressing himself adequately in the official language. Only if the

---

[32] See for example Articles 1 and 2 of **Act No. 1 of 28 January 1993** (Puerto Rico) in *Recueil des législations linguistiques dans le monde - Tome VI: La Colombie, les États-Unis, le Mexique, Porto Rico et les traités internationaux* (1994), Jacques Leclerc and Jacques Maurais (eds.), International Centre for Research on Language Planning, Québec, at p. 148; and Article 14 of the **1989 Languages Act of the SSR of Kazakhstan**, ibid., at p. 162:

> *La procédure des tribunaux administratifs se déroule en kazakh ou en russe ou dans la langue de la population d'une localité donnée. L'assistance d'un interprète aux personnes qui ne possèdent pas la langue de la procédure est garantie.*

In both cases, two languages (English and Spanish; Kazakh and Russian) have attained a sufficient numerical threshold to warrant their use in court proceedings; for all other languages, individuals have the right to an interpreter when their fluency in the languages of proceedings is too low. The same type of arrangement can be found pursuant to Article 47 of the **Act on the Regional Autonomy of National Minorities of the Peoples Republic of China**, *Recueil des législations linguistiques, supra*, note 26, at p. 68, where, beyond the use of local languages in court proceedings, there is also an individual entitlement to an interpreter where one does not understand the language of proceedings.

[33] Communication No. 219/1986.

accused or the defence witnesses have difficulties in understanding, or in expressing themselves in the court language, must the services of an interpreter be made available.[34]

These comments signal quite clearly that the language of proceedings — when it is not an accused's primary tongue — causes an inequality. In the case of individuals having pronounced difficulty with the language, this may be so detrimental that a state must always rectify such inequality to some extent: whilst not requiring modification of the language of proceedings to that of the accused, it does at minimum render obligatory the free use of an interpreter.[35]

The European Court on Human Rights arrived at a similar conclusion in **Kamasinski v. Austria**.[36] A US citizen, Theodor Kamasinski, was imprisoned in Austria for fraud and misrepresentation. As he had very little knowledge of the German language, he was given the assistance of an interpreter, but was unhappy with the quality of the translation. Moreover, following his conviction he did not receive a translation of court documents which he intended to use on appeal. He alleged that these incidents violated his rights under Article 6(3)(e) of the **Convention for the Protection of Human Rights and Fundamental Freedoms**.

The European Court stated that the Article 6 guarantees should be interpreted generously:

The right to the free assistance of an interpreter applies not only to oral statements made at the trial hearing but also to documentary material and the pre-trial proceedings. Paragraph 3(e) signifies that a person "charged with a criminal offence" who cannot understand or speak the language used in court has the right to free assistance of an interpreter for the translation or interpretation of all those documents or statements in the proceedings

---

[34] Ibid., at paragraph 10.2. See also similar conclusions reached by the European Commission on Human Rights in **K. v. France**, (1984) 35 Decisions and Reports 203, and **Bideault v. France**, (1986) 48 Decisions and Reports 232.

[35] In another case, the Human Rights Committee declared a communication inadmissible because the author had refused to exhaust local remedies in the language of administrative proceedings, claiming that he should be entitled to proceed with the assistance of an interpreter. In **M.K. v. France**, Communication No. 222/1987, UN Document A/45/40, the *Tribunal administratif* of Rennes had refused to consider a complaint which the author had submitted in Breton after French tax authorities had refused to indicate his address in Breton. The *Tribunal* subsequently ruled that the document had to be submitted in French if it were to be considered by the court. The author contended that the right to the assistance of an interpreter pursuant to Article 14(3)(f) of the **International Covenant on Civil and Political Rights** was being continuously violated in France. The Human Rights Committee declared the communication inadmissible as the author had not exhausted all domestic remedies. It also noted that the author was not being criminally prosecuted — under Article 14, the right to an interpreter only applies in criminal proceedings — but rather was seeking to initiate proceedings before an administrative court in order to establish that he had been denied rights protected by the **Covenant**. The Human Rights Committee concluded that even if the matter of the exclusive use of French in court proceedings was the issue complained of by the author, and that it would be examined in first instance by French judicial organs using French, this was not an unreasonable route, as the author was proficient in French and no irreparable harm would be done to his substantive case by using the French language to pursue his remedy.

[36] Judgment of 19 December 1989, European Court of Human Rights.

instituted against him which is necessary for him to understand or to have rendered into the court's language in order to have the benefit of a fair trial.[37]

However, the court emphasised that the provision does not go so far as to require a written translation of all of the items of evidence and official documents in a procedure, but rather a translation such that the defendant has knowledge of the case against him and is able to defend himself. Moreover, "the obligation of the competent authorities is not limited to the appointment of an interpreter but, if they are put on notice in the particular circumstances, may also extend to a degree of subsequent control over the adequacy of the interpretation provided."[38] In essence, there would be a violation of Article 6 if a translation were inadequate or otherwise affected the defendant's ability to defend himself or his right to a fair trial.

Some commentators have noted that the underlying concern in **Kamasinski v. Austria** is to avoid an inequality resulting from the language preference of the state which is too disadvantageous for a defendant:

> *L'on retrouve donc ici, comme point de départ de la réflexion, le souci des pères de la Convention de remédier à l'inégalité entre accusés, en l'occurence celle qui existe entre l'accusé comprenant le juge et celui ne le comprenant pas. Toute la question consiste cependant à savoir jusqu'où le respect de la Convention et de sa ratio legis commande de faire régner ce type d'égalité.*[39]

Obviously, it is impossible to attain absolute equality between a defendant who understands the language of the court and one who does not, as this would be a particularly burdensome requirement: it would be an extremely long and costly process to translate every single document and to have on every occasion simultaneous translation. This is why the European Court held that the requirements of Article 6 only go so far as to ensure what is required for an accused's defence, in order for him to understand the nature of the charges being brought against him, and in order for him to be able to properly appreciate the evidence being presented and the testimony

---

[37] Ibid., at paragraph 74.

[38] Ibid.

[39] "Kamasinski c. l'Autriche — Article 6 de la Convention pris isolément ou combiné avec l'article 14" (1991), in *Revue trimestrielle des droits de l'Homme*, N° 6, 217-240, at p. 223. In another case, **Luedicke, Belkacem and Koç**, (1978) European Convention on Human Rights, Series A, No. 126, the applicants, who did not understand German, were brought to trial for criminal offences in Germany. The European Court on Human Rights commented that Article 6 was inspired by the need to treat more equally individuals who know the language of criminal court proceedings and those who do not, and to compensate for the disadvantage this causes to the latter. On the issue of the free assistance of interpreters, the German government argued that this right under Article 6(3) was only in respect to a person "charged with a criminal offence". After conviction, such a person was no longer charged with a criminal offence, and under German legislation became liable for costs. The European Court disagreed, holding that Article 6(3)(e) guarantees the right to free translation without having to repay costs, and that this extends to all documentation or statements necessary for the accused to understand in order to have a fair trial.

of witnesses during the proceedings, and finally in order for him to effectively present his own evidence and testimony.[40]

The appropriate degree of interpretation will vary according to the complexity and seriousness of the case:

> *Ce qui détermine l'ampleur de l'aide à laquelle l'accusé peut prétendre, c'est le besoin concret et précis auquel elle correspond, celui-ci ne pouvant être correctement évalué qu'en tenant compte des circonstances particulières — tant objectives que subjectives — de la procédure litigieuse, telles la nature et la complexité des chefs d'accusation, l'attitude des autorités, les aptitudes du prévenu. Pour juger de la pertinence de ces critères dans un cas donné, la Cour se réserve de tenir compte aussi du comportement, des déclarations et réactions, voir des silences de l'accusé, premier concerné par le procès.*[41]

The European Court also had the opportunity to address the extent of the right to be informed promptly of the nature and cause of a criminal accusation in **Brozicek v. Italy**.[42] The applicant was charged with the offences of resisting the police, assault and wounding. The notification of the accusation against Brozicek was in Italian, which he did not understand. He was tried, *in absentia*, and convicted. Brozicek invoked Article 6(1) (right to a fair hearing) and Article 6(3)(a) (right to be informed of the nature and cause of an accusation in a language understood) of the European **Convention for the Protection of Human Rights and Fundamental Freedoms**. The majority of judges of the European Court on Human Rights concluded, on both counts, that there had been a violation of the **Convention**. Specifically on the subject of Article 6(3)(a), the European Court stated that any document constituting an "accusation" within the meaning of Article 6 should be provided to the applicant in a language which he understands. Since the competent judicial authorities had been informed by Brozicek of his lack of knowledge of Italian, it was their duty to ensure the observance of the requirements of Article 6(3)(a) unless they could in fact establish that the applicant had sufficient knowledge of Italian to understand the purport of the communication.[43]

The notion that equality amongst individuals might require providing interpretation for those at a disadvantage because they do not understand the language of proceedings is only one theoretical explanation of this right and may not be the most prevalent at that. In most countries, it is probably safe to say that the main motivation for recognition of the right to an interpreter is not a concern for the inequities as between individuals, but rather a desire that safeguards be in place to secure the fairness of the trial in practice. The crucial matter is to ensure that all parties are heard in a fair manner and that justice be done in the end. In this sense, the main concern is to arrive at a just and fair outcome, and not to counter any detriment or undue burden placed upon individuals because of the state's language preference.[44]

---

[40] *Supra*, note 36, at paragraph 79.

[41] *Supra*, note 39, at p. 237.

[42] (1989) European Convention on Human Rights, Series A, No. 167.

[43] Ibid., at paragraphs 38-41.

[44] The number of horror stories tied to not being able to understand the language of proceedings, even in states which recognise the right to interpretation, abound. In **R. v. Iqbal Begum**, Court of Appeal (Criminal Division) 22 April 1985, Appeal No. 6187/8/84 (United Kingdom), a female defendant was

Although most international treaties limit the right to an interpreter to the more serious cases of criminal proceedings, many states have extended some aspects of the same principle to proceedings of administrative tribunals or to civil cases.[45] In Sweden, the *Förvaltningslagen* (Administrative Procedure Act) and the *Förvaltningsprocesslagen* (Code of Procedure for the Administrative Courts) both require the presence of an interpreter when an authority is dealing with someone who is not in command of the Swedish language. In these and in criminal and civil court proceedings, according to the Code of Procedure (*Rättegansbalken*), Sweden provides for the use of an interpreter free of charge. One can see in these provisions a balancing of interests which is appropriate when considering what a reasonable, non-discriminatory language requirement is, as the public authority is required to consider the character of the matter, the language in question and if the matter is of great importance to the party.

In general, there would appear to be a greater tendency in most states to recognise in quasi-judicial, civil or administrative proceedings, a right to an interpreter as the importance of the issues involved are greater and the seriousness of the consequences for the individual higher. In immigration proceedings, particularly those which may result in deportation or exclusion, many states acknowledge in essence the same type of right to an interpreter as in criminal proceedings.[46]

Although most provisions indicate that an individual is entitled to the free assistance of an interpreter when he or she does not understand the language of proceedings, there is little indication of what precisely is meant by "understanding". As has been remarked in discussing the various degrees of disadvantage linked to variable proficiency in a language, "understanding" a language is not simply a black or white matter. For example, in **In re Muraviov**,[47] the Court of Appeals for California reversed a criminal conviction because it found that the defendant had not knowingly waived his right to counsel. The trial court had asked Muraviov four simple questions which could all be answered by "yes" or "no". The trial judge concluded that his answers indicated that he understood English and therefore proceeded without an interpreter. It

---

sentenced to imprisonment for life following her plea of guilty to murder. After she had been in prison for some years, it was discovered that she had not understood nor had any input in the criminal proceedings despite having had the services of an interpreter and a lawyer. It transpired that the interpreter did not even speak the same language as the defendant, an unbelievable mistake for which the latter payed dearly.

[45] Rannat, *supra*, note 23, at paragraph 434:
In civil cases, in the great majority of countries studied, a litigant without knowledge of the language of the court is provided by the authorities with interpretation. The cost is often borne, however, either by the assisted party or by the unsuccessful party or by the party required by the court to meet the expense.

[46] See **Leiba v. Minister of Employment and Immigration**, [1972] S.C.R. 660 (Canada); **Weber v. Minister of Employment and Immigration**, [1977] 1 F.C. 750 (Canada); and **El Rescate Legal Services v. Executive Review**, 941 F.2d 950 (1991) (United States). For a comprehensive review of US decisions confirming that because of the serious penalties which can result, deportation or exclusion proceedings warrant a right to an interpreter where appropriate to guarantee an individual's ability to present his case, see Mallya, Lynne (1992), "Deportation and Due Process: Does the Immigration and Naturalisation Act or the Fifth Amendment Provide for Full Interpretation of Deportation and Exclusion Hearings?", in *Law and Inequality*, Vol. 11, 181-208, at pp. 181-208.

[47] 13 Cal.Rep. 466 (1961) (United States).

turned out that the defendant had so little knowledge of English that he was largely unsure of what was being asked. After conducting its own hearing on the accused's ability to speak English, the Court of Appeals held that:

> [I]t should be obvious that if petitioner was unable to understand or speak English, his monosyllabic "yes" and "no" answers had no meaning.

Similarly, in **Dominique Guesdon v. France,** the Human Rights Committee clearly indicated that the right to an interpreter is not limited to situations where an individual has absolutely no knowledge of the language of proceedings, but arises whenever an "accused or the defence witnesses have difficulties in understanding, or in expressing themselves in the court language".[48]

In order to avoid this type of problem, some states have adopted legislation to give some direction on when an individual should be guaranteed access to an interpreter. In the United States, the **Court Interpreters Act of 1978**[49] requires the services of an interpreter in any criminal or civil action initiated by the United States government in a US district court where a party or witness "speaks only or primarily a language other than the English language...so as to inhibit such party's comprehension of the proceedings or communication with counsel or the presiding judicial officer or so as to inhibit such witness' comprehension of questions and the presentation of such testimony."

In **United States v. Carrion,**[50] the First Circuit Court of Appeals recognised that protection of a defendant's constitutional rights to a fair trial and to confront witnesses means having recourse to an interpreter, even if the defendant has some ability to understand and communicate in English:

> The right to an interpreter rests most fundamentally...on the notion that no defendant should face the Kafkaesque spectre of an incomprehensible ritual which may terminate in punishment... Yet how high must the language barrier rise before a defendant has a right to an interpreter?... Because the determination is likely to hinge upon various factors... considerations of judicial economy would dictate that the trial court, coming into direct contact with the defendant, be granted wide discretion in determining whether an interpreter is necessary... But precisely because the trial court is entrusted with discretion, it should make unmistakably clear to the defendant who may have a language difficulty that he has the right to a court-appointed interpreter if the court determines one is needed, and, whenever put on notice that there may be some significant language difficulty, the court should make such a determination of need.[51]

---

[48] *Supra*, note 33.

[49] **Public Law 95-539**; 92 Stat. 2040, 28 U.S.C.A. 1827.

[50] 488 F.2d 12 (1973) (United States).

[51] Ibid., at pp. 14-15. See also Safford, Joan Bainbridge (1977), "No Comprendo: The Non-English-speaking Defendant and the Criminal Process", in *Journal of Criminal Law and Criminology*, Vol. 68, 15-30, at pp. 20-25.

Finally, the court in **State v. Vasquez** observed the following:

> Degrees of understanding may present themselves between that of complete comprehension of the language to that of minor matters. The question, not properly heard or understood, may bring forth an answer that might turn the scales from innocence to guilt or from guilt to innocence. Then, too, the answer given might be made in words not entirely familiar or understood by the defendant...[52]

Nor should concerns over the right to an interpreter be perceived as a uniquely Western phenomenon. In fact, they may be particularly acute in other countries:

> In matters of law it is of course of extreme importance that all concerned should understand the implications of the process, and the questions and statements made. Thus while witnesses or accused may understand questions in, say, Swahili or English, they may not feel able to reply well enough in those languages. Consequently, there is a great need for and use of interpretation throughout the system, and there may sometimes be doubts as to the accuracy of this (since professional interpreters are not employed), such that, for example, interventions from the bench may be required.[53]

As a final remark, it should be obvious that the right to an interpreter requires that an adequately competent interpreter be available for use. Moreover, interpreters having an interest in the proceedings must be avoided. Decisions such as **Brown v. State**,[54] where it is claimed that it is unnecessary to have an interpreter who is unbiased towards the defendant, are clearly inappropriate. A more consistent attitude in light of the need to have a fair trial and to compensate for the defendant's disadvantage caused by a state's linguistic preference in proceedings would seem to require a completely disinterested interpreter.[55]

6.2   EDUCATION

> Therefore it seems better to me, if it seems likewise to you, that we turn some books which are most needful for all persons into the tongue which we can all understand; and that you act...to the end that all the youth now in England of free men who have the wealth to be able to apply themselves to it, be set to learning so long as they are no use for anything

---

[52] 121 P.2d 903 (1942) (United States), at pp. 905-06.

[53] Maw, Joan (1991), "Multilingualism in Tanzania", in J.-J. Symoens and J. Vanderlinden (eds.), *Symposium: Les langues en Afrique à l'horizon 2000*, Institut Africain and Académie Royale des Sciences d'Outre-Mer, Bruxelles, pp. 165-179, at p. 171.

[54] 59 S.W. 1118 (1900) (United States).

[55] **Lujan v. United States**, 209 F.2d 190 (1953) (United States), at p. 194:
> While in the nature of things, a disinterested interpreter is essential to an impartial interpretation of a witness' testimony, at the same time the trial court is necessarily accorded a wide discretion in determining the fitness of the person called, and the exercise of that discretion will not be disturbed on review in the absence of some evidence from which prejudice can be inferred.

else, until the time when they can read English writing well: let those afterwards be instructed further in the Latin language.

Alfred the Great[56]

6.2.1 *Consequences in Selecting a Language as Medium of Instruction*

It is undoubtedly true that a mother tongue is not merely a linguistic system which can, with impunity, be replaced by another language. A child's mother tongue is the language which allows him to impose a structure on the universe. It is associated with his thought processes, his sense of identity and his solidarity with his family and environment. As he matures, his mother tongue may become a symbol of regional or national pride, a means of gaining access to knowledge and wisdom. And it will usually be associated with feelings of warmth, intimacy, spontaneity.[57]

Children are not simply linguistic blank slates when they enter a school. In probably the closest thing possible to world-wide unanimity,[58] it is recognised that instruction in the mother tongue is, at least at the initial levels of education, the most effective way to instruct pupils. In other words, to educate children in a language with which they are less familiar is unfavourable to them. Such disadvantage can, as has been shown in a number of occasions, be discriminatory when it affects a sufficiently large group of people.

Perhaps the most comprehensive study in this field is found in a UNESCO document which examines closely the numerous factors that make instruction in a child's primary language the most desirable approach, whenever possible:

In learning any foreign language a child may find difficulty in mastering the alien vocabulary and syntax sufficiently to express his ideas in it. Where the foreign language belongs to a wholly alien culture he is faced with the added and much greater difficulties: to interpret to himself the new ideas in terms of his own medium of thought — his mother tongue — and to express his own ideas and thoughts through the new modes of the alien tongue. Ideas which have been formulated in one language are so difficult to express through the modes of another, that a person habitually faced with this task can readily lose his facility to express himself. A child, faced with this task at a age when his powers of

---

[56] Innis, Harold A. (1986), *Empire and Communications*, Press Porcépic, Victoria, Canada, at p. 130.

[57] *Language Planning and Language Education* (1983), Chris Kennedy (ed.), Unwin Publishers, London, at p. 165.

[58] Of course, there are always some exceptions, not to say aberrations. A Hawaiian statute was adopted during the Second World War which prohibited teaching of any foreign languages to children who had not passed the first four grades, even in private after-school programmes. The statute was based on an educational theory that the study of foreign languages (including Latin and Greek) in early years caused serious emotional disturbances, conflicts and maladjustment. The court accepted in **Mo Hoch Ke Lock Po v. Steinback**, 74 F.Supp. 852 (1947) (United States) the premise that "below average" students (i.e. children exposed to a native language other than English at home) would be detrimentally affected by foreign language study at an early age.

self-expression even in his mother tongue are but incompletely developed, may possibly never achieve adequate self-expression.[59]

The UNESCO experts concluded that every effort should be made to provide education in the mother tongue as late as possible, since the mother tongue as their primary language is the one these children understand best. Finally, they are more likely to find lessons in most subjects easier if they are taught it in their language:

> To expect him to deal with new information or ideas presented to him in an unfamiliar language is to impose on him a double burden, and he will make slower progress. Moreover, the parents will be in a better position to understand the problems of the school and in some measure to help the school in the education of the child.[60]

The view on these conclusions is almost universal.[61] Deprivation of an education in one's mother tongue has been convincingly linked to poor educational results[62] and the creation of a sense of psychological inferiority,[63] and even as a major source of potential ethnic conflict.[64]

---

[59] *The Use of Vernacular Languages in Education* (1953), UNESCO, Paris, at p. 690.

[60] Ibid., at p. 691.

[61] See Weinstein, Brian (1987), "Language Planning and Interests", in Lorne Laforge (ed.), *Proceedings of the International Colloquium on Language Planning*, Les Presses de l'Université Laval, Québec, 34-57, at p. 40, for a contrary point of view. One country where disturbing beliefs were widespread, although more as a temporary aberration according to some scholars, is the United States. Baron, Dennis E. (1990), *The English-Only Question: An Official Language for American?*, Yale University Press, New Haven, USA, at pp. 174-175 explains:
> Moreover, [US] psychologists until recently believed that immigrant and other non-English-speakers were mentally inferior to homegrown, anglophone Americans, and that bilinguals — in particular, first-generation Americans speaking a native language and learning English as well — suffered intellectual handicaps from having to think in two languages.

[62] See Baron, ibid, at p. 163; *Language of Inequality* (1985), N. Wolfson and J. Manes (eds.), Mouton Publishers, Berlin, at p. 247; McDougal, Myres et al. (1976), "Freedom from Discrimination in Choice of Language and International Human Rights", in *Southern Illinois University Law Journal*, Vol. 1, 151-174, at p. 159; **South West Africa Case (Second Phase)**, [1966] International Court of Justice 284, where Judge Tanaka observed that "if we consider education...we cannot deny the value of vernacular as the medium of instruction..."; and, Annis, Melissa (1982), "Indian Education: Bilingual Education — A Legal Right for Native Americans", in *American Indian Law Review*, Vol. 10, 333-360, at p. 339.

[63] Rosenbaum, Stephen (1981), "Educating Children of Immigrant Workers: Language Policies in France and the USA", in *American Journal of Comparative Law*, Vol. 29, 429-465, at p. 455; **Education Code**, Annotated California Codes, 1977, Section 52161.

[64] See Deutsch, Karl A. (1975), "The Political Significance of Linguistic Conflicts", in Savard & Vigneault (eds.), *Les États multilingues*, Presses de l'Université Laval, Québec, at p. 14; and, Ammoun, Charles D. (1957), *Study of Discrimination in Education*, United Nations Publications, New York, at p. 90; Mentzell, Peter (1993), "The German Minority in Inter-War Yugoslavia", in *Nationalities Papers*, Vol. XXI, No. 2, 129-143, at p. 132; and *World Directory Of Minorities* (1990),

This is especially true when the number of speakers is so high in an area that children are continuously exposed to and usually use their home language. It then becomes difficult for a child to comprehend why his primary language suddenly is frowned upon or even forbidden when he enters a classroom, whilst outside the school grounds he is almost completely surrounded by his primary tongue.

A state's decision to adopt an exclusive language as medium of instruction virtually guarantees that children with limited or no proficiency in the chosen language will endure serious disadvantages and fall behind as they either struggle to keep up with what is said in a language which is less familiar or simply withdraw into a world of their own:

> *La psycho-pédagogie appliquée à l'éducation a en effet souligné l'importance de la langue maternelle pour le développement sensori-moteur, affectif et cognitif de l'enfant.*
>
> *Si l'enfant reste inséré dans son milieu, s'il est en symbiose avec son environnement, on lui assure les conditions optimales d'une assimilation naturelle des opérations cognitives, on permet l'éclosion, l'épanouissement harmonieux des facultés intellectuelles. La langue maternelle offre en effet la seule possibilité de verbalisation active, indispensable pour l'appréhension des opérateurs de base, et condition de toute construction abstraite, opératoire ou logique.*
>
> *Si, au contraire, on ne respecte pas le droit élémentaire de tout enfant de se développer dans la langue de sa mère, de sa famille, de son milieu, si l'on refuse d'admettre que l'enfant est heureux dans sa langue maternelle comme dans les bras de sa mère, si on le maintient dans un état chronique de frustration affective en le plaçant « dans l'impossibilité matérielle d'extérioriser ses sentiments et ses intérêts », on lui impose un choix douloureux entre deux mondes sans communication et on le condamne à n'être sa vie durant qu'un inadapté socio-culturel.*[65]

Especially when they tend not to reflect the actual language of the surrounding community, inappropriate language practices or restrictions by the state tend to be rejected and sometimes enforced through oppressive and even violent measures.[66]

Minority Rights Group (ed.), Longman, Harlow, United Kingdom, at p. 249:
> [In Mauritania], a resurgence of ethnic unrest began in early 1979, again centring on the Arabization issue... The immediate issue was the poor examination results of black students in their 1979 end of year exams: the introduction of Arabic into the curriculum in the 60's and the subsequent weighting of marks in favour of Arabic subjects were blamed. Black teachers and pupils demonstrated and the police intervened. Senegal threw its weight behind demands for autonomy for Mauritania's blacks.

[65] Renard, R. (1991), "Éléments d'une problématique de l'aménagement linguistique en Afrique", in J.-J. Symoens and J. Vanderlinden (eds.), *Symposium : Les langues en Afrique à l'horizon 2000*, Institut Africain and Académie Royale des Sciences d'Outre-Mer, Bruxelles, pp. 43-49, at p. 45.

[66] Skutnabb-Kangas, Tove (1990), *Bilingualism or Not: The Education of Minorities*, Clevedon, Avon, United Kingdom, at p. 309:
> In the second place, minority children were often punished for speaking their own language, even outside the classroom. Many were made to go hungry, or physically punished in a variety of ways for speaking their own language. I have spoken to Torneå Valley Finns who were made to carry heavy logs on their shoulders or wear a stiff collar which prevented them from turning

Amongst the most dramatic consequences is the high level of pupils who tend to drop-out of school earlier because of burdensome and inappropriate educational language practices.[67] In countries such as Bolivia and Peru, it has been observed that the absence of any instruction in the language of children whose native language is not Spanish results in high illiteracy and drop-out rates. Even after a number of years of schooling, the type of bilingualism obtained is weak and fades once the student leaves the school and returns to a largely monolingual, non-Spanish-speaking community.[68]

The same phenomenon has been observed in different parts of the United States, and predicably becomes more marked as the size of the linguistic community increases, signalling a more frequent and comprehensive use of a minority language in various facets of every day life. In the case of the numerically important Spanish-speakers, the effects of English-only instruction are nothing short of shocking:

A 1967 study revealed that the longer a Puerto Rican child remained in New York schools, the more he fell behind his peers, and that nearly two-thirds of Puerto Rican eighth graders

---

their heads or looking down, all because they had spoken Finnish. I have Same friends who were beaten or kicked as children for answering questions in Same.... He describes how the children were lined up in the school playground when one of them had spoken a word or two in Finnish to have their ears boxed one by one. Many schools also organised the children to spy on one another, rewarding the child who reported another for speaking the forbidden language, often by giving her extra food. This whole system was such as to lead the children to believe not only that heir own language and culture were worthless, since they formed no part of the curriculum, but also that to speak the minority language (and to be part of the minority group) was a shameful thing that they had to get away from as soon as possible.

[67] As recognised in the following statute in the United States, **Education Code**, Annotated California Codes, 1977, Section 52161:

The Legislature finds that there are more than 288 000 school age children who are limited English proficient and who do not have the English language skills necessary to benefit from instruction only in English at a level substantially equivalent to pupils whose primary language is English. Their lack of English language communication skills presents an obstacle to such pupils' right to an equal educational opportunity which can be removed by instruction and training in the pupils' primary languages while such pupils are learning English. The Legislature recognises that the school dropout rate is excessive among pupils of limited English proficiency. This represents a tremendous loss in human resources and in potential personal income and tax revenues. Furthermore, high rates of joblessness among the dropouts contribute to the unemployment burden of the state.

[68] See also the conclusions of a Swedish educational report quoted in *Language Planning and Language Education, supra*, note 57, at p. 180:

Recent research has demonstrated, and strongly emphasised, the importance of the first (home) language for a child's emotional and intellectual development. If the home language is allowed to stagnate when a child begins school, and another language is introduced as the sole school language, there is a great risk of incomplete development of both languages. Experience has shown that the facility with which many immigrant pupils speak idiomatic Swedish can represent a superficial knowledge of the language, a facade which hides great deficiencies of vocabulary, reading comprehension and concept formation, while the home language is also characterised by the same deficiencies.

were more than three years behind in reading development. The drop-out rate of Mexican-American children in New Mexico was dramatised by the fact that in the late sixties over one-third of all Spanish-speaking children in that state were in the first grade, and that fifty-five percent of those above the first grade were more than two years over age for their grade. In Texas during the same period, eighty percent of all Mexican-American children who entered the first grade were not promoted. In California in 1970, fifteen per cent of the school population was Hispanic, yet almost thirty percent of educable mentally retarded (EMR) classes consisted of Spanish-surnamed children. Significantly, intelligence tests to determine EMR placement were administered in English only.[69]

Especially in the context of a large area where the official or state preferred language is in little use, an exclusive language policy in education can be disastrous. When the United States invaded Puerto Rico on 25 July 1898, public authorities began to forbid the use of Spanish in classes, and teachers could not be certified if they did not pass English exams. After three decades of this policy, 80 percent of the students in Puerto Rico had failed both Spanish and English and had dropped out of school.[70] The same results of high drop-out and illiteracy rates appear where the language of a former colonial power is used in African countries, and with indigenous peoples of South America when the exclusive language of instruction is a language largely unknown or unused by the majority of inhabitants.[71]

Of course, the degree of disadvantage suffered by students will depend on their level of proficiency in the state-sanctioned medium of instruction, but in the case of children with absolutely no knowledge of the language of instruction it may be more appropriate to speak of a state preference that results in an actual discriminatory exclusion from education rather than simply a case of a disadvantageous policy on the basis of language.

The US Supreme Court recognised this in **Lau v. Nichols**[72] when it indicated that English language requirements were a violation of equality since they shut out students with no knowledge of the language. English-only education for these children meant no education:

Under these state-imposed standards there is no equality of treatment merely by providing students with the same facilities, textbooks, teachers, and curriculum; for students who do not understand English are effectively foreclosed from any meaningful education.

---

[69] McFadden, Bernard (1983), "Bilingual Education and The Law", in *Journal of Law and Education*, Vol. 12, 1-27, at p. 14.

[70] *Language of Inequality, supra,* note 62, at p. 43.

[71] Renaud, P. (1991), "Essai d'interprétation des pratiques linguistiques au Cameroun : Les données, les choix et leur signification", in J.-J. Symoens and J. Vanderlinden (eds.), *Symposium : Les langues en Afrique à l'horizon 2000*, Institut Africain and Académie Royale des Sciences d'Outre-Mer, Bruxelles, pp. 51-83, at p. 64. In Paraguay, educational policies used to require that all children be educated in Spanish. This was the only exposure to Spanish for children living in rural areas predominated by monolingual Guaraní-speakers. Under these conditions, the number of grades completed in school would directly reflect a child's ability to speak Spanish. Faced with the sense of frustration common to students educated in a non-native language, these children were practically forced to drop out of school; see on this point Rubin, J. (1968), *National Bilingualism in Paraguay*, Mouton, den Haag, Netherlands, at p. 77.

[72] 414 U.S. 563 (1974) (United States).

Basic English skills are at the very core of what these public schools teach. Imposition of a requirement that, before a child can effectively participate in the educational program, he must already have acquired those basic skills is to make a mockery of public education. We know that those who do not understand English are certain to find their classroom experiences wholly incomprehensible and in no way meaningful.[73]

Since it was obvious that the Chinese-speaking minority received fewer benefits than the English-speaking majority from a school system using a language they do not understand as the medium of instruction, the US Supreme Court agreed they were denied the opportunity to participate in the educational programme, in other words excluded, and that this constituted a form of discrimination.

6.2.2   *Public Education and State Language Preferences*

It cannot be denied that the business of government is easier in a monolingual than multilingual nation. However, it does not follow that legislation or school policy requiring the use of the official language at all times will give the same results as actual monolingualism. On the contrary, it is fairly likely that absolute insistence on the use of the national language by people of another mother tongue may have a negative effect, leading the local groups to withdraw in some measure from the national life. In any event, it seems clear that the national interests are best served by optimum advancement of education, and this in turn can be promoted by the use of the local language as a medium of instruction, at least at the beginning of the school programme.[74]

Since children will either be excluded or at least disadvantaged by a state's decision to impose a language of instruction that is not their primary tongue, there has to be a balancing of interests to determine whether the burden imposed on them because of their language is reasonable and non-discriminatory. As with other types of state intervention by public authorities, there is no simple model that can be advanced that would be appropriate for all situations. Yet the basic principle applied when dealing with the actions of the state and public authorities is also applicable to public educational activities, and this implies a reasonable equilibrium between the interests of the state and the rights, interests and duties of affected individuals. This would mandate a "sliding-scale" approach mentioned earlier in order to arrive at a non-discriminatory educational policy.

It should be pointed out that, in general, international instruments recognising a right to education have consistently excluded a parent's automatic right to choose the language in which

---

[73] Ibid., at p. 566.

[74] *Supra*, note 59, at p. 693.

his child would receive a state's educational services.[75] It appears clear that the right to education was never intended to include the right to education in one's own language.[76]

The European Court on Human Rights came to the same conclusion in a highly influential judgement where it addressed itself directly to the *travaux préparatoires* and the context of Article 2 of the **First Protocol** of the **Convention for the Protection of Human Rights and Fundamental Freedoms** dealing with the right to education:

> ...the first sentence of Article 2 does not specify the language in which education must be conducted in order that the right to education should be respected. It does not contain precise provisions similar to those which appear in Articles 5(2) and 6(3)(a) and (e). However, the right to education would be meaningless if it did not imply in favour of its beneficiaries, the right to be educated in the national language or in one of the national languages, as the case may be.[77]

Although Article 2 is, *a priori*, "language neutral", it must of necessity include the right to learn at least one national language. The court further adds, on dealing with the second sentence of this provision on the religious and philosophical preferences of parents:

> This provision does not require of states that they should, in the sphere of education or teaching, respect parents' linguistic preferences, but only their religious and philosophical convictions... Moreover the "preparatory work" confirms that the object of the second sentence of Article 2 was in no way to secure respect by the state of a right for parents to have education conducted in a language other than that of the country in question: indeed in June 1951 the Committee of Experts which had the task of drafting the Protocol set aside a proposal put forward in this sense. Several members of the Committee believed that it concerned an aspect of the problem of ethnic minorities and that it consequently fell outside the scope of the Convention.[78]

Nor does the non-discrimination provision in combination with the right to education guarantee an individual's unrestricted freedom of choice as to the language of instruction to be used in state-provided education:

> Article 14, even when read in conjunction with Article 2 of the Protocol, does not have the effect of guaranteeing to a child or to his parents the right to obtain instruction in a language of his choice. The object of these two Articles, read in conjunction, is more

---

[75] Article 13 of the **International Covenant on Economic, Social and Cultural Rights**; Article 2 of **Protocol No. 1 to the Convention for the Protection of Human Rights and Fundamental Freedoms**; Article 13 of the **Additional Protocol to the American Convention on Human Rights in the Area of Economic, Social and Cultural Rights**; Article 5(e)(v) of the **Racial Discrimination Convention**, Article 28(1) of the **Convention on the Rights of the Child.**

[76] See on this point Lebel, Michel (1974), "Le choix de la langue d'enseignement et le droit international", in *Revue Juridique Thémis*, Vol. 9, No. 2, 221-248, at pp. 231 and 232.

[77] **Belgian Linguistic Case**, [1968] 1 Yearbook of the European Convention on Human Rights 832, at p. 858.

[78] Ibid., at pp. 861 and 862.

limited: it is to ensure that the right to education shall be secured by each contracting party to everyone within its jurisdiction without discrimination on the ground, for instance, of language. This is the natural and ordinary meaning of Article 14 read in conjunction with Article 2. Furthermore, to interpret the two provisions as conferring on everyone within the jurisdiction of a state a right to obtain education in the language of his own choice would lead to absurd results, for it would be open to anyone to claim any language of instruction in any of the territories of the contracting parties... The Court notes that, where the contracting parties intended to confer upon everyone within their jurisdiction specific rights with respect to the use or understanding of a language, as in Article 5(2) and Article 6(3)(a)(e) of the Convention, they did so in clear terms. It must be concluded that if they had intended to create for everyone within their jurisdiction a specific right with respect to the language of instruction, they would have done so in express terms in Article 2 of the Protocol. For this reason also, the Court cannot attribute to Article 14, when read in conjunction with Article 2 of the Protocol, a meaning which would secure to everyone within the jurisdiction of a contracting party a right to education conducted in a language of his own choice.[79]

Thus, the court's heavy reliance in its comments on the unrealistic expectation that both provisions should guarantee to everyone the right to state education in any language is consistent with the point of view that it is not discriminatory *per se* to limit the number of languages used as medium of instruction in state schools. By referring to the need of a proportionality test involving questions of administrative and financial reasons, the means employed and the aim sought, the court is indicating that it would not be discriminatory not to provide state schooling for everyone in any language.

Courts in a large number of states have also held that there does not exist, as far as state-funded education is concerned, an unqualified right to obtain an education in one's preferred language.[80] Obviously, to conclude otherwise would require for a state to provide public education in every child's primary language, even if there are 100 or more languages spoken in the country. Recognition of such a right would clearly be too onerous and unrealistic.

---

[79] Ibid., at pp. 866-868.

[80] In Canada, see **Ottawa Separate Schools v. Mackell**, (1917) 32 D.L.R. 1 (Canada) and **Québec (A.G.) v. Blaikie**, (1981) 1 S.C.R. 312 (Canada); in the United States, see Schmid, Carol (1987), "Language and Education Rights in the United States and Canada", in *International and Comparative Law Quarterly*, Vol. 36, 903-908, at p. 903, and Piatt, Bill (1990), ¿*Only English? Law and Language Policy in the United States*, University of New Mexico Press, Albuquerque, USA, at pp. 41-52; in Spain, see Milian i Massana, Antoni (1989), "Legal Considerations on the Linguistic Rights Recognized in the Education System in Catalonia", in *Language and Law: Proceedings of the First Conference of the International Institute of Comparative Linguistic Law*, P. Pupier and J. Woehrling (eds.), Wilson & Lafleur, Montréal, at p. 439. Even in the former Soviet Union, there was not a right to education in any language, but a more limited right to education in a "national language" within the relevant autonomous republic or province. See on this point Hannum, Hurst (1990), *Autonomy, Sovereignty, and Self-Determination*, University of Pennsylvania Press, Philadelphia, at pp. 363-365, and Weiner, Richard (1989), "70 Languages Equal and Free? The Legal Status of Minority Languages in the Soviet Union", in *Arizona Journal of International and Comparative Law*, Vol. 6, 73-96, at p. 73.

However, a more practical arrangement in the field of education, taking into account the number of speakers of a language, has been recognised and in place in many countries throughout history. During the League of Nations era, the minorities treaties contained provisions specifically involving the use of a minority language as medium of instruction in the state school system when appropriate:

> Provisions will be made in the public educational system in towns and districts in which are resident a considerable proportion of Albanian nationals whose mother-tongue is not the official language, for adequate facilities for ensuring that in the primary schools instruction shall be given to the children of such nationals, through the medium of their own language, it being understood that this provision does not prevent teaching of the official language being made obligatory in the said schools.[81]

Another Permanent Court of International Justice decision even more clearly demonstrated the link between equality and public schooling in a minority's language when appropriate because of their numerical importance. It stated that Article 9 of the **Polish Minorities Treaty** which called for adequate public facilities for ensuring to the children of Polish nationals of other than Polish speech primary instruction through the medium of their own language, represented the right of "minorities the members of which are citizens of the state to enjoy...amongst other rights, equality of rights...in matters relating to primary instruction".[82]

As indicated earlier, the first draft of what was to become the **Universal Declaration of Human Rights** also established a link between discrimination and the lack of public schooling and other government services in a minority's language when appropriate due mainly to the numbers of individuals involved:

> In the initial draft outline of the International Bill of Human Rights prepared by the Secretariat, it was proposed that "no one should suffer any discrimination whatsoever because of race, sex, language, or religion or political creed. There should be full equality before the law in the enjoyment of rights enunciated in the bill of rights." Moreover, states possessing "substantial numbers of persons differing in race, language, or religion from the majority of the population, should give such persons the right to establish and maintain out of an equitable proportion of public funds, schools, cultural and religious institutions, and they should be entitled to use their own language before the courts and other authorities and organs of state and in the press and in public assembly."[83]

To this day, perhaps unconsciously, many if not most states have policies that reflect more or less faithfully what is but a manifestation of the prohibition of discrimination in state-provided education. In Canada, the **Constitution** enshrines the right of members of the two linguistic groups representing about 90 percent of the country's population the right to education in the

---

[81] **Advisory Opinion on Minority Schools in Albania**, (1935) Permanent Court of International Justice, Series A/B, No. 64, 3, at p. 21, also known as the **Minority Schools in Albania** case.

[82] **Treatment of Polish Nationals in Danzig** (1932), Permanent Court of International Justice, Series A/B, No. 44, 1, at p. 9.

[83] McKean, Warwick (1983), *Equality and Discrimination under International Law*, Clarendon Press, Oxford, United Kingdom, at p. 63.

mother tongue, "where numbers warrant".[84] In Austria, the most numerous and concentrated minorities are the Slovenians, Hungarians and Croatians.[85] Depending on the percentage of each minority in a given territory, they are entitled to a greater proportion of public education in their language in conformity with the sliding-scale model.[86]

India's **Constitution** similarly contains a provision which directs every state, and every local authority within a state, to endeavour to provide "adequate" public facilities for instruction in the mother-tongue at the primary stage of education to the children of linguistic minorities,[87] adequacy resting mainly on the numerical importance of a minority. This is in addition to the division of India's states along essentially linguistic lines. These political divisions ensure that the larger linguistic communities have control over public schools and other institutions of learning, and thus ultimately they are in a position to ensure that most inhabitants can have their primary language used as medium of instruction in state schools. In the same way Switzerland's regime of cantonal autonomy ensures that most members of the country's four main linguistic groups have control over the public schools and educational activities in their cantons with corresponding use of their language as medium of instruction. This arrangement on a territorial basis is due to an assessment of the country's public interest against an individual's interest in instruction in her or his own language. In other words, the language of instruction is territorially determined and relatively few exceptions are permitted because the whole scheme is deemed necessary and reasonable in the Swiss context since it adequately ensures most speakers of the main languages in the country have access to state schooling in their language.[88]

---

[84] Article 23 of the **Canadian Charter of Rights and Freedoms**, in Section 3.23 of the Appendix. It should be emphasised that this provision contains a number of suspect qualifications on the exercise of the right. While the Supreme Court of Canada has recognised the validity of the sliding-scale approach in the field of education in **Mahé v. Alberta**, [1990] 1 S.C.R. 342 (Canada), it has failed to appreciate that it is in fact essentially applying the principle of non-discrimination. Canadian legal scholars and legislation have generally failed to realise that language policies are not simply a matter of a state's political prerogative, but can be subject to restrictions due to individual rights such as equality and freedom of expression. It then comes as no surprise that Canada has been "reprimanded" twice by the United Nations Human Rights Committee for measures affecting language in **Lovelace v. Canada**, Communication 24/1977, UN Document A/36/40, and **Ballantyne, Davidson and McIntyre v. Canada**, Communications 359/1989 and 385/1989.

[85] These minorities are also "national minorities" since they are living and traditionally rooted in Austria (*beheimatet*).

[86] For example, in Burgenland a minority language has to be used as the medium of instruction in areas where more than 70 percent of the population belong to the relevant minority. In areas where this percentage lies between 30 and 70, both German and the relevant minority language have to be used, whereas in areas with a lower percentage of speakers the minority language may be taught as a school subject. See Öhlinger, Theo (1993), *Minority Languages in Austria in the Light of the European Charter for Regional or Minority Languages*, EURORegion National Report, Fribourg, Switzerland (unpublished), at pp. 5 and 7.

[87] Article 350A, **Constitution of India**, Section 3.53 of Appendix.

[88] French translation of judgement in German reprinted from Lebel, *supra*, note 76, at p. 246:
    La garantie de la survie des quatres langues nationales, contenue dans l'article 116, premier alinéa, de la Constitution fédérale, serait impensable sans la garantie de leur emploi dans leurs

The European Court on Human Rights also concluded, in the case of Belgium, that a territorial division of the country along mainly unilingual regions that ensured access to public schooling in their language to most members of the three main linguistic communities was not discriminatory even if this prevented the establishment or the subsidisation by the state of French language schools in the unilingual Dutch part of the country because, in the Belgian context, the nation-wide scheme was deemed a justified and proportional measure. In Nigeria, each state adopts its own policy on the language of instruction in state schools. This normally results in the adoption of the primary language of the principal ethnic group of the region as the language of instruction. In areas where there is a great diversity of languages used but no common major language, English is often used in conjunction with teaching in the vernacular. The trend in Nigeria would appear to provide state education in the primary language whenever possible.

The Chinese government has also opted for the sliding-scale approach under Article 37 of the **Act for the Implementation of Regional Autonomy for Ethnic Minorities**, once again depending on population numbers and territorial concentration:

1. The ethnic language is the major language from primary school to high school. Chinese is taught from the third or fifth grade of primary school until the end of high school. Students are required to study one or two years of Chinese (Mandarin) before entering college. A special ethnic-language program is offered at college, where only science and technology are taught in Chinese; for all other courses such as language, literature, history, law, and economics the language of instruction is the ethnic language. This type of bilingual education is used by the Uygur in Xinjiang Uygur Autonomous Region.
2. In primary school and middle school the ethnic language is the major language while Chinese is taught as a subject from the second or third grade of primary school to the end of middle school. High schools in some areas continue to use this method, but others will adopt Chinese as the major language. In college the ethnic language is used only in language, literature, and history departments, while the other subjects are taught in Chinese. This system is used by the Mongolians in pastoral areas in the Inner Mongolian Autonomous Region and the Koreans in Yanbian Prefecture in Jilin Province. The Zhuang people in Guangxi Zhuang Autonomous Region are also experimenting with this method. Some primary schools in compact communities of the Zhuang people in Guangxi use Zhuang as the major language from the first to the sixth grade. All textbooks are translated from the standard primary-school textbooks in Chinese. Chinese classes are offered from the third grade until graduation. Where there is preschool education, Chinese language teaching starts from the last term of the second grade...[89]

Although not all countries consistently follow in every respect a sliding-scale model or even pretend there may be some type of legal obligation to do so, there are sufficient commonalities

---

cadres linguistiques respectifs. Cette prescription garantit la composition linguistique traditionnelle du pays. Il incombe aux cantons de veiller, dans le cadre de leur juridiction, sur le maintien et l'homogénéité des régions linguistiques. Ces mesures...doivent servir à la réalisation du but d'intérêt public qu'est le maintien des régions linguistiques et, d'autre part, protéger la dignité et la liberté de l'individu.

[89] Yaown, Zhou (1992), "Bilingualism and Bilingual Education in China", in *International Journal of the Sociology of Language*, Vol. 97, 37-45, at pp. 40-41.

to suggest many states are implicitly following the same principles,[90] despite Turkey with its Kurdish-speaking citizens and the United States with its Spanish-speaking inhabitants being two prominent exceptions.[91]

In acknowledgment that some type of balance should be reached, more recent treaties and international instruments have begun to recognise a link in public education between overall numbers of individuals sharing a same language, and a state's corresponding obligation to provide schooling for them in their language when this is practical and reasonable, including the **Declaration on the Rights of Persons Belonging to National or Ethnic, Religious and Linguistic Minorities,**[92] the **Central European Initiative Instrument for the Protection of Minority Rights,**[93] the **Document of the Copenhagen Meeting of the Conference on the Human Dimension,**[94] and the **Convention-cadre pour la protection des minorités nationales.**[95]

---

[90] See for example Articles 18 and 19 of the **1989 Act on the Use of Languages in Moldova,** *Recueil des législations linguistiques, supra,* note 26, at p. 197; Article 19 of the **Estonian Language Act** of 1989, ibid., at p. 147; Article 18 of the **Act on Languages in the SSR of Kazakhstan, 1989,** ibid., at p. 163; and Article 2B of the **1988 Education Act** of Malta, ibid., at p. 108.

[91] The US situation after **Lau v. Nichols,** *supra,* note 72, seemed promising for those arguing that state education limited to the national language may be discriminatory in certain cases, but this opening appears to have been largely closed by some decisions requiring a showing of intent to discriminate: see "Official English: Federal Limits on Efforts to Curtail Bilingual Services in the States" (1987), in *Harvard Law Review,* Vol. 100, 1345-1362, at pp. 1356 and 1357. A discriminatory effect for non-English-speaking students would in all likelihood in itself be insufficient in the US context, although it should be remembered US practice is inconsistent with international human rights standards in this regard.

[92] Article 4(3) indicates that where possible, persons belonging to minorities are entitled to appropriate state measures so that they may learn their mother tongue or be taught in their language. This provision is surprisingly timid in its wording since, regardless of a minority's numerical importance, a state could possibly claim that it is conforming to the **Declaration** by simply permitting teaching of the language, and not its use as medium of instruction. Another, perhaps more consistent interpretation would be that the use of terms such as "appropriate measures" in the provision signals the need to assess each case according to criteria such as the minority's relative size. Most other instruments spell out more precisely the need to take into account the demographic realities of the populations involved when determining the appropriate state measures in education.

[93] Article 17, reprinted in the Appendix, Section 1.2.2.

[94] Paragraph 34. The wording is quite similar to the UN **Declaration on the Rights of Persons Belonging to National or Ethnic, Religious and Linguistic Minorities** and should probably be interpreted in the same way.

[95] Article 14(2) provides:
> *Dans les aires géographiques d'implantation substantielle ou traditionnelle des personnes appartenant à des minorités nationales, s'il existe une demande suffisante, les parties s'efforcent d'assurer, dans la mesure du possible et dans le cadre de leur système éducatif, que les personnes appartenant à ces minorités aient la possibilité d'apprendre la langue minoritaire ou de recevoir un enseignement dans cette langue.*

Article 8 of the **European Charter for Regional or Minority Languages**[96] also reflects the sliding-scale formula that must be considered in public education in order to conform to the right of non-discrimination on the ground of language: the bottom end of the scale represents the minimal entitlement which members of a smaller, though sufficiently numerous, linguistic minority could expect, whereas at the higher end of the scale are to be found much more generous rights, in recognition of the much larger number of individuals involved. A state would normally be unjustified in not granting more generous rights as to the language of education as the number of beneficiaries gradually increases.

At the bottom end of the scale, a state could limit itself to teaching the language of a national minority at preschool, or if the number of pupils whose families so request is considered sufficient, go up the scale to a substantial part of the education; if the numbers are even higher, up to a complete preschool programme in the language of the minority, and so on with the higher levels of education, always the more generous where the number of pupils is sufficiently large and concentrated. States should seek a level of use of a minority language which best fits their demographic reality since Article 8 is applicable "according to the situation of each language". This would imply that the larger the number of speakers of a regional or minority language and the more linguistically homogeneous the population in a region, the "stronger" the option which should be adopted. When speaking of the sufficiency of numbers in a territory, the geographical location, the availability of transportation and the age of the children are examples of various factors that might be considered. Rigid approaches in the determination of the sufficiency are to be avoided.

Beyond the purely demographic factor, there may be valid reasons to be more flexible and generous towards a particular minority, such as for example the proximity of a kin-state and the political tensions in the region. Furthermore, some states have adopted a policy that tends to be fairly generous towards long established linguistic minorities in their territories. Certainly in the case of indigenous peoples, international law and the practice of many countries would tend to confirm this, as will be shown in the next chapter.

There can also be valid reasons not to provide for extensive use of a language as medium of instruction at higher levels of instruction despite the relative high number of its users. Some languages may lack a sufficiently developed vocabulary for the needs of the modern school curriculum. In such a situation, the most effective course would seem to be the following:

[A] second language will have to be introduced at an early stage, and as soon as the pupils have learnt enough of it the second language can become the medium of instruction. The

---

[96] The **European Charter**'s main weakness is that states are generally free to pick and choose from a number of "options" for each language used by a national minority in its territory, although they are supposed to choose what is appropriate. While in theory this is sound since one cannot expect that identical government services will be made available to one group composed only of a few hundred speakers as well as to a second linguistic minority of more than a million people, in practice it gives every state the freedom to seek the minimum level of rights possible. In other words, it gives the impression that any concession in relation to language is a political decision outside of any possible violation of basic human rights. In conformity with the **European Charter,** a state could select extremely limited rights to public use of a language that may involve millions of speakers in its territory. It never seemed to occur to the drafters of the **European Charter,** or perhaps they had to cast aside any such considerations, that issues such as freedom of expression and non-discrimination could be raised. See Section 2.2.6 of the Appendix for the relevant provision.

transition to a second language should normally take place gradually and should be made as smooth and as psychologically harmless as possible. Thus, if the second language is completely different from the mother tongue it should be taught as a subject for some years, and until such a time as the child has an adequate working knowledge of it, before it is brought into use as a full teaching medium.[97]

Despite being a less generous arrangement in light of the relative numerical importance of the speakers of a language, such an option would appear to be a balanced and reasonable response in such a context, and thus not constitute a discriminatory educational policy.

Other valid considerations that may be used in assessing the reasonability of a state decision to offer lesser levels or lowering the degree of use of a particular language as medium of instruction are the shortage of educational materials in a language, the shortage of suitably trained teachers, the state's financial resources and economic conditions, the prevalence in a region of a widely known *lingua franca*, and popular opposition to the use of the mother tongue as medium of instruction by the speakers of the language themselves.[98]

Even when the numbers of speakers of a language are large enough to warrant complete instruction in public schools in their language, a state would still be under the obligation to provide some instruction of the official or majority language to ensure these individuals are not excluded from participating in the larger society, and to avoid creating inequality by prohibiting them from having access to the activities and benefits tied in to this knowledge. Furthermore, "denial of such access may generate a self-perpetuating caste-like society, with benefits for a chosen few".[99] In other words, the adoption of educational policies consistent with the prohibition of discrimination in language matters should not result in the isolation of minorities in linguistic ghettos that excludes them from other benefits. Acquisition of the official language can occur through teaching it as a second language, and need not detract from the right, in appropriate cases, to use the minority language as the ordinary language of instruction.

The question of "linguistic ghettos" has to some extent been considered in international law. As noted by the Special Rapporteur of the Sub-Commission on Prevention of Discrimination and Protection of Minorities, Charles D. Ammoun in his *Study of Discrimination in Education*:

> In the first place, compulsory teaching in a single language, and *a fortiori*, prohibition of the teaching of the language and cultural heritage of a distinct group, have in some cases constituted a formidable instrument of oppression and discrimination, especially where the schools possessed by the group are closed, or transferred to the dominant group against the will of the members of the distinct group... In the second place, and, it might be said, conversely, it is also discriminatory to prevent children belonging to a distinct group from learning the majority language, knowledge of which is necessary for access to higher education. Discrimination would also exist if the level of education in the schools of the distinct group was not equivalent to that in ordinary schools.[100]

---

[97] *The Use of Vernacular Languages in Education, supra,* note 59, at p. 693.

[98] For an examination of most of these factors, see ibid., at pp. 693-697.

[99] *Language of Inequality, supra,* note 62, at p. 159.

[100] *Supra,* note 64, at p. 90.

Most of the international instruments and treaties mentioned earlier[101] that contain provisions concerning the entitlement to education in a non-official or minority language, where warranted by the number of speakers, nevertheless add that acquisition of the majority or official language must also be possible as part of a state's non-discriminatory education policy.[102] Especially when a language has relatively few speakers, or when the formal education received by most children is only a few years, they should be taught quite early the rudiments of the national language. A leader of the Miskito people in Nicaragua commented that although public instruction in their indigenous language was considered an important gain, most students would leave schools after three or four years of education. He felt that since they were for the most part being educated only in Miskito, they would not be exposed to any Spanish and thus be isolated from the larger society and its benefits, or at least suffer from a low fluency in the majority language. The dilemma faced by his people and others is that exclusive instruction in a minority or non-official language can also be discriminatory since it can have the effect of preventing "children belonging to a distinct group from learning the majority language, knowledge of which is necessary for access to higher education" or other opportunities. In the case of the Miskitos, their small number and short attendance in the formal public school system suggest it would be appropriate to provide for some teaching of the Spanish language at the very first years of education.

One attitude that should be dispelled is that linguistically-based schools are a form of segregation. On the contrary, it is long recognised in international law that this point of view is wrong. For example, Article 2(b) of the UNESCO **Convention Against Discrimination in Education** provides that:

> The establishment or maintenance, for religious or linguistic reasons, of separate educational systems or institutions offering an education which is in keeping with the wishes of the pupils' parents or legal guardians, if participation in such systems or attendance at such institutions is optional and if the education provided conforms to such standards as may be laid down or approved by the competent authorities, in particular for education of the same level.[103]

Unfortunately, the drafting of the above provision leaves something to be desired since it is unclear whether it applies to private educational activities, public schools, or both.

In **South West Africa Cases (Second Phase)**, Judge Tanaka also indicated that the existence of separate public schools operating along linguistic lines was not objectionable at all, but rather would be required in some situations in order to truly conform with the requirements of equality:

> For instance, if we consider education...we cannot deny the value of vernacular as the medium of instruction and the result thereof would be separate schooling as between

---

[101] *Supra*, notes 92-96.

[102] Legislation such as Article 4 of the **Slovak National Council Act No. 428/1990** of 25 October 1990 which requires in the schooling and education system that all citizens master the Slovak language to the extent required for the official and everyday use is therefore not objectionable *in se*.

[103] (1960) United Nations Treaty Series, Vol. 165, at p. 93.

children of diverse population groups... In this case separate education and schooling may be recognised as reasonable. This is justified by the nature of the matter in question.[104]

The unease felt in certain milieux with language-based schools may be due to the false perception that language divisions match racial divisions, and that separate schools on the basis of language would result in *de facto* racial segregation. Experiences in South Africa and the United States tend to reinforce this perception.

Two observations should be made concerning these fears. First, whilst it is true that a language can often correspond to a greater or lesser extent to a particular racial or ethnic group, it is not an exact match. Spanish in the United States is not spoken by a single racial group, but is shared by some Blacks, people of indigenous descent, individuals of European ancestry, Puerto Ricans, and other "Latinos", etc. Afrikaans and English in South Africa are not exclusively spoken as a primary language by Whites, but are also the home languages of many Blacks, Asians, "Coloureds", etc. The obsession with race and colour in the United States and South Africa leads some to assume that only people of a certain shade would frequent public schools using a minority or non-official language. This fails to concede, to put it bluntly, that the world is not simply divided into black or white: there are large numbers of children of mixed linguistic or ethnic background that do not fit the mould of mother tongue being equivalent to racial or ethnic group. Furthermore, there are children who, although they may belong to the majority ethnic or linguistic group, may prefer to attend the school where the language of instruction is the language of the community in which they live, even if it is not their own native tongue, and vice versa.

This brings up a second vital point: even if a state recognises it is obligated to act in a non-discriminatory way and must therefore provide public education where a non-official or minority language is the main or exclusive medium of instruction, can it restrict admission to these or force individuals against their will to send their children to such schools?

The topic is an extremely sensitive matter and is characterised by an extreme variety of approaches. The simplest one is to use the so-called territorial approach: a state's territory is divided in its entirety along linguistic lines that correspond roughly with the geographic distribution of its main language populations. In its purest form, this is what exists in Belgium, Switzerland (in most cantons),[105] the Åland Islands of Finland, and in parts of Denmark (Greenland and the Faroe Islands).[106] There is no free choice for individuals: everyone attending

---

[104] *Supra*, note 62.

[105] *The Situation of Regional or Minority Languages in Europe* (1994), Council of Europe, Strasbourg, at p. 135:

> Because of our federal structure, in which the cantons have complete autonomy in the educational field (except as regards the federal polytechnics, vocational training, the recognition of secondary school-leaving certificates, and certain other aspects of education), there is a great diversity of approaches to language teaching in Switzerland. However, one universal rule has gained acceptance: in all cantons, the first foreign language taught to schoolchildren is always one of the national languages... As a rule, the language of education at all levels is determined by the principle of territoriality, which is applied very strictly, except in the canton of Graubünden and in some districts situated on a linguistic boundary.

[106] Hetmar, Tytte and Jørgensen, J. Normann (1993), "Multilingual Concepts in the Schools of Europe — Denmark", in *Sociolinguistica*, Vol. 7, 79-89, at p. 83.

public schools will receive instruction in the language of the territory, regardless of their own primary tongue.

As explained earlier in the **Belgian Linguistic Case**, such an arrangement is not objectionable *in se* if it reflects fairly faithfully the actual demographics of the country; even if it is unavoidable that some individuals will find themselves on the "wrong side" of the linguistic divide and will thus be disadvantaged because they are unable to attend public institutions using their language as medium of instruction, the overall scheme may still be sufficiently reasonable, given the factors involved, as to be non-discriminatory.[107] However, a language-based territorial policy in public education can still be discriminatory if it excludes sufficient numbers of speakers from the benefit of instruction in their primary language or is too inflexible to take into account some appropriate exceptions.

For most countries, territorial division along linguistic lines may be in general unsuitable because of the intermixing of various language communities, the non-existence of any clear territory where one group dominates, or simply a government's unwillingness to follow such a route for fear of encouraging a sense of political disunity between its inhabitants. The second major approach to non-discriminatory practices in public education involves an assessment of whether the number of speakers of any language is "sufficient", "substantial" or "warrants" use of their language as medium of instruction in a given area. In a way, this still implicates an issue of territory, but it is not exclusive in the same manner as are the Swiss and Belgian examples since public schools using any number of languages can co-exist in the same region. This is the method favoured in states such as India and its multitude of languages, Canada (French and English),[108] Hungary (Hungarian and a number of "national minority languages"),[109] New

---

[107] In addition, it would seem appropriate for a state to adopt a flexible attitude in "borderline" cases. For example, if individuals speaking language A find themselves in linguistic territory B, yet are only a few kilometres or even metres from linguistic territory A and a public school that uses their mother tongue as medium of instruction, it is debatable whether a state's refusal to permit them to send their children to such a school or ensure their transportation there is reasonable and non-discriminatory. Whilst countries such as Canada tend to make concessions in such a situation, others such as Switzerland and Belgium do not. See Lüdi, Georges (1993), "Conceptions plurilingues dans l'enseignement européen — Suisse", in *Sociolinguistica*, Vol. 7, 32-48, at pp. 34-35. See also the possibility of transportation or subsidised lodging as reasonable arrangements in LeBouthillier, Yves (1990), "L'affaire Mahé et les droits scolaires", in *Ottawa Law Review*, Vol. 22, No. 1, 77-137, at p. 131.

[108] Article 23(3) of the **Canadian Charter of Rights and Freedoms** reads:
The right of citizens of Canada under subsections (1) and (2) to have their children receive primary and secondary school instruction in the language of the English or French linguistic minority population of a province:
(a) applies wherever in the province the number of children of citizens who have such a right is sufficient to warrant the provision to them out of public funds of minority language instruction; and
(b) includes, where the number of those children so warrants, the right to have them receive that instruction in minority language educational facilities provided out of public funds.

[109] Article 43 of **Act No. LXXVII of 1993 on the Rights of National and Ethnic Minorities.**

Zealand (English and Māori), Finland (Swedish and Finnish), Poland (Polish and Lithuanian),[110] the United Kingdom (Welsh and English),[111] etc. Once again, such an approach is quite legitimate, as long as due consideration is given to all the relevant factors discussed earlier in section 4.5 and does not result in the unreasonable exclusion of too many individuals from the benefit of instruction in their primary language.

It should be pointed out that in some cases it would appear appropriate to offer partial instruction in the non-official or minority language when this is what is preferred by the concerned individuals themselves or when the number of speakers of a language is particularly small.[112]

An interesting situation presented itself in Catalonia, Spain, where the *Tribunal Supremo* had arrived at the conclusion that the establishment of bilingual public schools in the *Generalitat* was a violation of international and constitutional law because it prevented parents from having their children educated exclusively in Castilian. The *Tribunal Supremo* defended its conclusion partly on the basis that there exists in international law an unfettered right to education in one's language since, under Article 26(3) of the **Universal Declaration of Human Rights**, parents *"tendrán derecho preferente a escoger el tipo de educación que habrá de darse a sus hijos"*.[113] The court also invoked individual freedom, moral integrity, and human dignity amongst constitutional rights in support of its thesis that an absolute right to education in one's primary language exists, although it then backtracked somewhat in trying to make it appear that the unfettered right to complete public instruction in one's language should be limited to an official language:

> *Pues bien, ya hemos razonado anteriormente que de los artículos 1.1 y 9.2 de la Constitución (valor superior a la libertad), de sus artículos 10 y 15 (dignidad y libre desarrollo de la personalidad) y de los apartados 2 y 5 de su artículo 27 (la educación como pleno desarrollo de la personalidad humana y la participación efectiva de todos los sectores afectados en la programación general de la enseñanza), se deriva un auténtico*

---

[110] *The Protection of Ethnic and Linguistic Minorities in Europe* (1993), John Packer and Kristian Myntti (eds.), Institute for Human Rights, Åbo Akademi University, Åbo, Finland, at p. 110:
> There are about 20,000 Lithuanians in Poland, living predominantly in the north-eastern part of Suwalki province, specifically around Sejny. Quite numerous Lithuanian communities have also been recorded in Silesia (Wroclaw), Pomerania (Szeczcin, Slupsk) and in Gdańsk, Olsztyn and Bialystok... It is of particular note that Lithuanian language education in Suwalki province is very well organised in 11 primary schools and one secondary school. Unlike the cases of Ukrainian and Byelorussian language education, Lithuanian language education meets almost in full the needs of the community.

[111] Ibid., at p. 134. Great care should be used when speaking of Welsh language schools in the United Kingdom; in fact, these schools would be more adequately described as bilingual schools, Welsh generally not being the exclusive medium of instruction.

[112] See ibid., at p. 25, for the extent of the use of Sorbian in German public schools; ibid., at p. 117 for bilingual Slovene-Hungarian schools in Slovenia; and ibid., at p. 73, concerning Article 39 of the **Constitutional Law No. 4** of 26 February 1948 and the degree of use of the French language in Valle d'Aosta, Italy: "In all regionally administered schools, an equal number of hours per week will be allocated to the teaching of French and Italian. Certain subjects may be taught in French."

[113] Sentencia del Tribunal Supremo 303/93, Madrid (Spain), 15 February 1994, at p. 10.

derecho de los padres (y de los hijos) a elegir la lengua oficial en que estos han de ser enseñandos en cualquier etapa educativa.[114]

The *Tribunal Supremo* on this point is clearly wrong. International decisions and case law in many countries[115] consistently indicate that there is no such thing as an inherent freedom of choice in relation to the language of public services or state schools. In theory, the *Tribunal Supremo*'s reasoning could mean that a single individual would be entitled to all public schooling, or any public service, in his mother tongue, even if he is the only speaker of the language in Spain.

What the *Tribunal Supremo* failed to consider is whether it is a discriminatory policy to require all students be educated, regardless of their home language, in bilingual public schools where teaching is approximately half in Castilian and half in Catalan.

Since Catalan and Castilian are both official languages in the *Generalitat*, and since knowledge of Castilian and Catalan is helpful, even highly desirable for employment purposes within the Catalan public authorities and many other aspects of activities, it does not seem unreasonable, *prima facie*, to have a truly bilingual policy where both languages are used equally within public schools,[116] although admittedly Castilian-speakers may assume a heavier burden of disadvantage because more of them may be monolingual.[117] Bilingual schools may be less

---

[114] Ibid., at p. 16.

[115] See *supra*, notes 75-77, and de Zayas, Alfred-Maurice (1993), "The International Judicial Protection of Peoples and Minorities", in *Peoples and Minorities in International Law*, Catherine Brölmann, René Lefeber, and Marjoleine Zieck (eds.), Martinus Nijhoff, Dordrecht, Netherlands, pp. 253-287, at p. 276. It was recognised in another Spanish decision, Sentencia del Tribunal Superior 135/94, 24 February 1994, Barcelona (Spain):

Y esta decisión del Parlamento de Cataluña reflejada en la Ley de Normalización Lingüística se revela no arbitraria, ya que el legislador ha adoptado sus prescripciones educativas en su dimensión lingüística procurando las medidas adecuadas (enseñanza del castellano y del catalán y enseñanza en castellano y en catalán), y de modo equilibrado, para alcanzar el fin tutelado por la Constitución (conocimiento pleno y de modo progresivo de ambas lenguas al finalizar la enseñanza secundaria), no revistiendo justificación que este sistema atente a los derechos del niño, siguiendo de modo fiel la jurisprudencia del Tribunal Constitucional (Sentencia de 6 de noviembre de 1986) y del Tribunal Europeo de los Derechos Humanos (Sentencia de 23 de julio de 1968).

[116] It should be emphasised that in some countries claims of bilingual education or schools are misleading. A truly bilingual school exists when two languages are used as medium of instruction. In the US, it is sometimes stated that simply teaching a foreign language corresponds to bilingual education. It does not.

[117] A more convincing interpretation in line with international standards can be found in Sentencia del Tribunal Superior 135/94, 24 February 1994, Barcelona (Spain):

Esta posición de paridad que asume la lengua catalana con la lengua castellana en la enseñanza en la Comunidad Autónoma de Cataluña no es irrazonable, desde una visión abierta, dinamica y no petrificada del texto constitucional...porque seria precisamente contrario a la Constitución integrada en su lectura con el Estatuto de Autonomia de Cataluña, como norma perteneciente al bloque de constitucionalidad, una consideración degrada de la lengua catalana como lengua minoritaria o singular o como lengua extranjera, alejada de su afirmación como

of a burden for native Catalan-speakers because many of them already have some degree of bilingualism when they enter the school system.

The Spanish *Tribunal Constitucional* subsequently confirmed that there is no absolute freedom of choice in relation to the language of instruction in state schools.[118] It pointed out the legislation implementing a form of gradual bilingualism in Catalan state schools did not contravene the constitutional duty of all citizens to learn the national language since all Catalan students would still be learning Castilian.

The *Tribunal Constitucional* also made comments on the question of the disadvantage of not being educated through the medium of one's primary, or habitual, language as an issue involving the right to equality protected under Article 14 of the Spanish Constitution:

> *En particular y desde la perspectiva del art. 27 C.E., pero también desde la relativa al art. 14, resulta esencial que la incorporación a la enseñanza en una lengua que no sea la habitual se produzca bajo el presupuesto de que los ciudadanos hayan llegado a dominarla, cuando menos en la medida suficiento para que su rendimiento educativo no resulte apreciablemente inferior al que hubieran alcanzado de haber recibido la enseñanza en su lengua habitual.[119]*

Essentially, the *Tribunal Constitucional* felt overall that the Catalan educational regime of gradually merging Catalan- and Castilian-speakers into a common bilingual programme of instruction at the higher levels of state education was reasonable and not unduly burdensome to Castilian-speaking students:

> *La Ley catalana 7/1983...responde plenamente a estas exigencias por cuanto su art. 14.2 garantiza el derecho a iniciar la incorporación al sistema educativo en la lengua habitual;*

---

lengua oficial y propria, en el sentido de original, de pertenencia de Cataluña... Resulta, conforme con el Pacto Internacional de Derechos Economicos, Sociales y Culturales de 16 de deciembre de 1986 que consagra al derecho a la educación, que debe capacitar a todas las personas para participar efectivamente en una sociedad libre; y con el Convenio Europeo para la protección de los Derechos Humanos y Libertades Fundamentales de 4 de noviembre de 1950, que, en su artículo 2 del Protocolo adicional primero, reconoce que a nadie se puede negar el derecho a la instrucción, observando, en su artículo 14 la prohibición de discriminación en el goce de los derechos y libertados por razón de lengua, como ha entendido el Tribunal Europeo de Derechos Humanos al enseñar que no se vulnera el derecho a la igualdad por la impocisión de diferencias de trato si se basan en una apreciación objetiva de circunstancias de hecho esencialmente diferentes, y que el derecho a la educación no tiene por efecto garantizar a los hijos o a sus padres el derecho a una instrucción impartida en la lengua de su elección, cuando se observa que en aplicación equilibrada de la Ley de Normalización Lingüíltica que persigue no la incomprehensión e indiferencia de la lengua castellana y catalana en el sistema de enseñanza sino la comunicación y homogenidad lingüíltica de las dos lenguas oficiales de la Comunidad, de modo que todos los alumnos, cualquiera que sea su lengua habitual de origen, disfrutan en el mismo grado e intensidad del sistema educativo público.

[118] Sentencia del Tribunal Constitucional 710/94, 23 December 1994.

[119] Ibid., at paragraph 11.

a la vez que prescribe medidas para que la lengua catalana "sea utilizada progresivamente a medida que todos los alumnos la vayan dominando".

Por ello, al determinar la utilización de la lengua propia de la Comunidad como lengua docente, los poderes autonómicos deben ponderar adecuadamente la consecución de aquella finalidad atendiento tanto al proceso de formación de la personalidad de los estudiantes en los sucesivos niveles del sistema educativo como a la progresividad inherente a la aplicación de dicha medida.[120]

On another point, the reasoning of the *Tribunal Supremo* is stronger when it considered whether legislation apparently making Catalan the only mandatory language for use in administrative and outside contact by public school authorities was legitimate. The court held that this may constitute a discriminatory measure since it was bound to affect unfavourably a large number of Castilian speakers. The court assumed the Catalan legislation would have the effect of excluding the use of Castilian:

El precepto en cuestión no prescribe que los horarios, y los comunicados, y los rótulos de dependencias y los avisos en los tablones de anuncios, etc., se redacten en catalán y en castellano, sino que se den exclusivamente en catalán, aqui sin posibilidad de que los interesados pidan otra cosa, puesto que el precepto no lo prevé, y, en efecto, los números 2 y 5 del artículo 13 del Decreto 362/83 (a diferencia de lo que ocurre con las actuaciones administrativas "interesadas por el público", que pueden hacerse en castellano, si así se pide, según el No. 4 del artículo 13), no permiten que los interesados soliciten que se practiquen también en castellano.[121]

On this issue the *Tribunal Constitucional* disagreed with the *Tribunal Supremo*'s reading of the legislation. It pointed out that it was an error to conclude the relevant provision excluded the use of Castilian since it simply made Catalan the normal or privileged language of business by the school authorities.

The *Tribunal Constitucional* reasoned the legislative measures were not discriminatory since they were based on legitimate objectives and did not mandate the exclusive use of Catalan by school authorities when in contact with Castilian-speakers:

Aun teniendo la Ley aquí considerada como objetivo principal la normalización del uso de la lengua catalana en todos los ámbitos, no cabe olvidar que también está dirigida a "garantizar el uso normal y oficial del catalán y del castellano"...; y los particulares, como se acaba de indicar, pueden utilizar la lengua de su elección en sus relaciones con los Centros educativos. Por lo que no sabe entender que el precepto cuestionado sea contrario al derecho de igualdad sera efectiva... Pues basta observar que si el catalán cooficial en Cataluña y lengua usual en la sociedad catalana, difícilmente cabe imputar al Centro docente, en atención al uso normal y habitual del catalán, la creación de un entorno que no es distinto al de la propria sociedad a la que sirve.[122]

---

[120] Ibid., at paragraph 11.

[121] Ibid., at p. 19.

[122] Ibid., at paragraph 21.

There is a final issue that may also be the most complicated to address. When a state is required to offer public education in more than one language under the right of non-discrimination because of the large number of native speakers of more than one language, etc., who is entitled to attend these activities? Only people of a certain ethnic background, or only those for whom the language of instruction is the home language? Only citizens?

The issue becomes one of access, and some states have adopted convoluted criteria to determine if an individual may attend public schooling in certain languages. In Canada, for example, Article 23 of the **Canadian Charter of Rights and Freedoms**[123] only guarantees access to minority language public schools[124] to individuals who qualify. Although in some cases a more generous attitude prevails in some provinces of Canada, not everyone is permitted under the **Constitution** to receive instruction in the official language in a minority position (French outside Québec, English in Québec). Article 23 limits admission to schools of an official linguistic minority to two general categories (a) citizens for whom the official minority language is a mother tongue which they still understand; or (b) citizens (or their children) who have received their primary education in the official minority language in Canada.

There is thus no true individual freedom of choice in Canada's public schools under the **Constitution**: non-citizens who are entitled to public instruction under Canadian legislation are still denied access to certain schools because they are non-citizens. Furthermore, even citizens cannot freely decide which public school their children can attend. A Canadian citizen whose mother tongue is Arabic, living in a community where French is the main language could be prohibited by the government from sending his children to the local French language public school if he lives outside Québec. Even if French is the home language for this family, and even though his children may now be monolingual French and have received their education in French (outside Canada), Article 23 excludes them, unless the provincial government decides to open up the categories of individuals admissible to these schools.[125]

Generally speaking, there has never been, under international law or in most countries, such a thing as complete freedom of choice as to the medium of instruction in public schools, nor an unrestricted right of access to a particular type of public education.[126] With the above example of Article 23 of the **Canadian Charter of Rights and Freedoms**, what must be considered on the point of exclusion or denial of access to certain types of public schools is whether such restrictions are themselves reasonable and balanced, since it could be claimed that non-citizens and certain categories of citizens are being denied a benefit enjoyed by others. If overall the need to deny access to these particular public schools appears to be unnecessary given the competing

---

[123] See Section 3.25 of the Appendix.

[124] English is considered, for educational purposes in Canada, a minority language in Québec, whereas French is the minority language in all other parts of the country.

[125] The wording of Article 23 rests in part on the unwillingness of certain provincial governments, in particular Québec, to create a constitutional right for immigrants to be admitted to the public school of their choice. In Québec during the late 1970s and early 1980s, it was seen as essential for the survival of the French language and culture in the province that immigrants should be absorbed, through public schooling in the French language, into the majority linguistic community of the province.

[126] See **Belgian Linguistic Case**, *supra*, note 77.

interests involved and the possible effects on the concerned individuals, it would be a discriminatory practice that violates the right to equality.[127]

Finally, the qualifications under Article 23 do not involve possible discrimination on the ground of language, but rather discrimination based either on status (citizenship) or national origin. Whilst states undeniably have a large margin of operation in deciding what preferences and benefits it may accord to its nationals as compared to non-nationals, it still does not have unfettered discretion in these matters. The human rights of equality and non-discrimination are especially relevant in a case such as this.

At least one of the restrictions in Article 23 appears suspect. In a family which has had their children educated in another country it remains possible they will be unacceptable to public school authorities for admission to the public school that uses their preferred language, even if they are citizens, if their first (home) language learned and still understood is not French or English and because they were not initially educated in Canada. Whilst in general Article 23 appears valid under the enunciated principles of equality and non-discrimination, there is an argument that can be made that the above limitation is perhaps excessive.

A different but connected problem occurs when a state directs that individuals must attend a public school where the medium of instruction used is primarily or completely the mother tongue. As indicated earlier, there has never been in international law an unrestricted freedom of choice for parents or children as far as to access to a specific type of public instruction. Each educational policy has to be assessed as to its reasonability, given the context and measures involved.

At one level, a state policy that every child must be instructed in public schools in his primary language is hardly objectionable or discriminatory in itself,[128] since it recognises that one's primary language is the best medium of instruction, at least in the first years of schooling. To this must be added the condition that students must still be given the opportunity to acquire an adequate knowledge of the official or majority language. Yet, even this policy should reflect the actual demographic and linguistic reality of the country. If a minority language is used by a tiny number of people, and that furthermore it is practically non-existent as far as language of services and employment by public authorities, a complete instruction in one's primary language would be rather disadvantageous in the long term. The wishes of the parents in such a case should be influential in designing the appropriate degree of use in instruction of the mother tongue and of the official or majority language.

At another level in Third World countries, especially in Africa, many parents may resist such a policy of primary language instruction, even when their language is the vernacular of a very large number of people, because they see mother tongue education as detrimental to the

---

[127] The Canadian conditions should be contrasted with the practice in Sweden, where there is, in theory, a right under the 1977 **Home Language Reform Act** to instruction in the mother tongue for immigrant and indigenous minority pupils. See Tingbjörn, Gunnar (1993), "Multilingual Concepts in the Schools of Europe-Sweden", in *Sociolinguistica*, Vol. 7, 207-217, at p. 208. See also Article 48(1) of Hungarian **Act No. LXXVII of 1993 on the Rights of National and Ethnic Minorities** which recognises that individuals who do not belong to a linguistic minority may prefer, and be permitted, to have their children instructed in minority language public schools.

[128] Article 2(b) of the UNESCO **Convention Against Discrimination in Education** discussed earlier does suggest that attendance at separate schooling designed for linguistic reasons should always be optional. However, it is unclear if this provision of the **Convention** addresses itself to minority schools of a private nature or public schools.

economic or employment opportunities of their children. In South Africa for example, there is a feeling apparently shared by many parents that public instruction in English is essential for the future of their children.[129]

They are at the same time both right and wrong. They are right in the sense that many more opportunities may be available to those with a higher fluency in English and Afrikaans because governments have traditionally favoured the use of these two languages by public authorities, the judiciary, etc. to the detriment of people with greater fluency in other, more widely known, languages. Such a policy, as has been shown in section 4.7, has the consequence that many job opportunities with public authorities, a highly attractive source of employment in many developing countries, is directly proportional to one's proficiency in the official language: the higher profile and best paid positions normally would require greater linguistic abilities in the official language.

In another way they are wrong, because it is not the education policy that should be considered more closely, but rather the language preferences of the state in public services and employment. Native speakers of English and Afrikaans, or those wealthy enough to be able to ensure longer years of formal education for their children, private tutoring, or even overseas university education, will always be at an advantage unless government favouritism is shifted towards the main languages used by its inhabitants — which may eventually become possible in a democratic South Africa. Furthermore, most studies and experiences show that instruction in a language not in line with the languages used by most people in larger communities means lower degrees of literacy, poor knowledge of both primary and official or majority languages and academic results, etc. In other words, the problem experienced in South Africa and other countries is not so much the use of African languages as the main language of instruction in public schools, but government policies in other areas that do not reflect the actual linguistic demographics of the country and which are probably discriminatory. It would be a better strategy to attack the real obstacle to upward economic and social mobility and source of disadvantage, namely the prominence of languages that are native to a small privileged minority in these countries.[130]

---

[129] See the unpublished paper by de V. Cluver, A. D. (undated), *Language Planning Models for a Post-Apartheid South Africa*, Pretoria, South Africa.

[130] For a more detailed consideration of the special problems facing Third World countries, see Dua, Hans R. (1987), "Comments on Brian Weinstein's Paper: Language Planning and Interests", in Lorne Laforge (ed.), *Proceedings of the International Colloquium on Language Planning*, Les Presses de l'Université Laval, Québec, pp. 60-67, at p. 66, and *Language of Inequality, supra*, note 62, at pp. 245-251. A vivid example of the possible consequences of inappropriate state policies favouring a language not widely understood by students is given in *Language and Society in Africa* (1992), Robert K. Herbert (ed.), Witwatersrand University Press, Witwatersrand, South Africa, at p. 64:

> These campaigns, after almost ten years (1989), produced mixed results. They successfully popularised the idea of English as the Namibian national and official language. The introduction of English, however, as the sole medium of instruction by the Owambo administration, with the help of poorly qualified Asian expatriates, was a disaster. The failure rate in matric examinations increased by almost 50 percent. The boycott of lectures by students at the University of Namibia in order to enforce English as the sole medium of instruction ended in discredit. Lecturers who began to teach in English-only were in many cases asked by the students to revert to Afrikaans. Students, even those from Owamboland, could not follow the lectures well.

6.2.3   *Private Education Activities by Linguistic Minorities*

A man's proper vernacular is nearest unto him in as much as it is more closely united to him, for it is singly and alone in his mind before any other.

Dante[131]

Whilst a state only has an obligation to act in a non-discriminatory way in the provision of public schooling when there is a sufficiently large number of students that are affected by the language choices of the state, the situation of linguistic minorities and private education[132] presents a different approach altogether. As shown in the historical overview and in the discussion on Article 27 of the **International Covenant on Civil and Political Rights**, it now appears to be a generally accepted standard to allow members of a linguistic minority to freely carry on activities in their own language. There also appears to be a growing consensus that this includes the right to instruct privately their children in their language, free from state restrictions, save general educational standards and the government's legitimate interest in requiring from all citizens some knowledge of the majority or official language, but also without any obligation on the state to provide financial support. Whilst some experts feel that the freedom to conduct educational activities in a minority language is almost a trivial right if it is not backed by a state's financial resources,[133] it should be remembered that it was never the intent of the drafters of Article 27 to provide too many concessions to linguistic minorities. For better or for

---

[131] Quoted in *Empire and Communications, supra*, note 56, at p. 133.

[132] It is noteworthy that the Supreme Court of India had the opportunity to answer the question of what is a minority in **In re Kerala Education Bill**, (1959) S.C.R. 995 (India). The majority opined that it was easy to say that a linguistic minority meant a community which was numerically less than 50 percent. The important question was, 50 percent of what? It is possible that a minority may be concentrated in a part of a state, so that it is in majority there though it may be in minority in the context of the whole of the state population. In the context of an act of a state legislature the Supreme Court held that minority must be determined by reference to the entire state, and any minority which is numerically less than fifty percent of the entire state population would be regarded as a minority for the purposes of Article 30(1). This is the same objective approach as has been suggested as appropriate for interpreting Article 27 of the **International Covenant on Civil and Political Rights** and similar provisions throughout this study.

[133] As eloquently summarised in Héraud, Guy (1966), *Peuples et langues d'Europe*, Éditions Denoël, Paris, at p. 71:

« *Une langue qu'on n'enseigne pas est une langue qu'on tue* », constatait Camille Jullian. Or l'initiative privée ne peut remplacer l'État. Comment trouver, en effet, en toute région allogène, des gens assez avertis, courageux, dévoués, pour créer les associations scolaires nécessaires, assez persévérants pour les faire fonctionner de manière continue? Il faudrait encore assurer le financement de façon régulière et stable. Or, en l'absence de subsides publics, il ne saurait s'agir que de contributions volontaires des familles; voilà donc une catégorie de citoyens qui serait ainsi taxée deux fois : une fois pour procurer une école à leurs enfants, une seconde fois pour payer l'école des autres! Il faudrait enfin que toutes les familles envoient les enfants à l'école minoritaire. Comment remplir tant de conditions à la fois?

worse, Article 27 only affords a minimal guarantee of non-interference in certain areas, though in a number of countries even this small concession is difficult to accept in practice.

It must be emphasised that before the wholesale involvement of states in education which began in the second half of the nineteenth century in many countries, most educational activities were carried out by religious groups and private parties. This also meant that minorities with sufficient resources were able to ensure educational activities in their own language. State interference and ultimate control over education signalled for many the end of these activities and the replacement of private minority schools by public schools using, for the most part, the language of the majority.[134]

A key decision based on the minorities treaties during the League of Nations mandate explains why such schools are not only critical for the survival of linguistic minorities, but also essential if ethnic conflicts are to be avoided. In fact, such was the importance of such a right that the Permanent Court of International Justice went out of its way to recognise a linguistic minority's right to establish its own schools even if the minority treaty at issue did not actually guarantee it specifically.

As mentioned on previous occasions, the Permanent Court of International Justice in **Minority Schools in Albania**[135] examined the validity of an Albanian law aimed at abolishing all private schools in the country. This, according to the Greek government, was contrary to the **Albanian Minorities Treaty** which safeguarded in Article 5 the right of minorities to establish and maintain their own private schools. The Albanian government for its part argued that the law treated both the Albanian majority and the Greek-speaking minority in exactly the same way, since no private Albanian-language schools would be allowed to operate, and that Article 5 only

---

[134] Countries where freedom of individuals are highly valued or constitutionally protected offered a greater degree of protection, at least on occasion, for the private educational activities of minorities. Two US Supreme Court decisions confirm the tie between freedom and private schools and instruction in the language of a minority. In **Farrington v. Tokushige**, 273 U.S. 284 (1927) (United States), at p. 298. Hawaii's attempt to restrict private foreign-language schools was seen as going beyond mere regulation and as an attempt to eliminate them completely, thus affecting the parents' liberties:

> The School Act and the measures adopted there under go far beyond mere regulation of privately-supported schools... They give affirmative direction... Enforcement of the Act probably would destroy most, if not all, of them... The Japanese parent has the right to direct the education of his own child without unreasonable restriction; the Constitution protects him as well as those who speak another tongue.

In **Meyer v. Nebraska**, 262 U.S. 390 (1923) (United States), the Supreme Court also confirmed the tie between individual liberty as recognised in the Fourteenth Amendment and private teaching in a minority language. The court clearly stated that individuals are entitled to freely conduct private instruction not in English, at pp. 399-400:

> [The Fourteenth Amendment] denotes not merely freedom from bodily restraint but also the right of the individual to contract, to engage in any of the common occupations of life, to acquire useful knowledge, to marry, establish a home and bring up children, to worship God according to the dictates of his own conscience, and generally to enjoy those privileges long recognised at common law as essential to the orderly pursuit of happiness by free men.
>
> The established doctrine is that this liberty may not be interfered with, under the guise of protecting the public interest, by legislative action which is arbitrary or without reasonable relation to some purpose within the competency of the state to effect.

[135] *Supra*, note 81, at p. 4.

guaranteed that both should "enjoy the same treatment and the same security, both in law and in fact".

The Permanent Court of International Justice concluded that Greek-speaking Albanians enjoyed, thanks to Article 5, rights not available to other Albanians, and in particular the right to their own private schools where the language of instruction would be Greek.

Contemporary international law on this point is somewhat murky, at least at the initial stages of development after the Second World War. For example, the Sub-Commission on Prevention of Discrimination and Protection of Minorities presented to the Human Rights Commission a "minorities article" which at one point provided, amongst other things, that:

> In states inhabited by well defined ethnic, linguistic or religious groups which are clearly distinguished from the rest of the population and which want to be accorded differential treatment, persons belonging to such groups shall have the right as far as is compatible with public order and security to establish and maintain their schools... if they so choose.[136]

This and a number of subsequent drafts were not adopted because of a rejection of the principle of educational institutions established by and for linguistic minorities *in se*, but as a refusal to guarantee public funds for these institutions. States were reluctant to being forced to provide any rights to minorities as a group that might imply financial and institutional obligations.

Perhaps surprisingly, the UN **Declaration on the Rights of Persons Belonging to National or Ethnic, Religious and Linguistic Minorities** does not attempt to clarify this point, although taken as a whole there would appear to be little doubt that linguistic minorities are, at a minimum, entitled to establish and administer their own schools using their own language as the medium of instruction. Article 1(1) of the **Declaration** indicates states are required to "protect the existence and...linguistic identity of minorities...and shall encourage conditions for the promotion of that identity." Short of actually financially supporting a minority's schools, it would appear states would at the very least be obliged to not prohibit private educational activities in a minority's language. The widespread recognition in international law of a linguistic minority's right to create and operate its own educational activities and institutions, as reflected in previously mentioned bilateral treaties[137] and international instruments,[138] lends support to the

---

[136] UN Document E/CN.4/SR.52, 9.

[137] Among the relevant provisions of treaties reprinted in the Appendix are Article 8 of the **Agreement between the Czech Republic and the Slovak Republic on Cooperation and Good Neighbourly Relations**, Article 1 of the **Agreement between the Ministry of National Education of the Republic of Poland and the Ministry of Culture and Education of the Republic of Lithuania Regarding the Educational System and University Education**, Article 4 of the **Germany-Russian Federation Protocol of Collaboration on the Gradual Restoration of Citizenship to Russian Germans**, Article 8 of the **Treaty Concerning the Protection of Minorities in Greece**, Article 6 of the **Treaty on Friendship and Cooperation between the Lithuanian Republic and Ukraine**, Article 67 of the **Treaty of Peace with Austria**, Article 40 of the **Treaty of Peace with Turkey**, Article 14 of the **Treaty between the Republic of Lithuania and the Republic of Poland on Friendly Relations and Good Neighbourly Cooperation**, Article 8 of the **Treaty between the Republic of Poland and the Czech and Slovak Republic on Good Neighbourliness, Solidarity and Friendly Cooperation**, Article 15 of the **Treaty between the Republic of Poland and the Republic of Belarus on Good Neighbourliness and Friendly Cooperation**, Article 15 of the **Treaty between the Republic of Poland and the Republic of Latvia on Friendship and Cooperation**, and Article 11 of the **Treaty**

argument that this has now become a generally recognised international standard. For example, paragraph 32.2 of the OSCE **Document of the Copenhagen Meeting of the Conference on the Human Dimension**, although limited to national minorities, acknowledges explicitly their right:

> ...to establish and maintain their own educational...institutions, organisations or associations, which can seek voluntary financial and other contributions as well as public assistance, in conformity with national legislation;

Furthermore, this provision also clearly demonstrates that the right to create and operate minority schools does not include a state's obligation to provide financial resources for these activities, although a state is free to do so "in conformity with national legislation."

Even countries not generally regarded as having a great sensitivity to linguistic minorities have started to recognise and follow this trend. France has recently adopted legislation that not only acknowledges the German-speaking minority's right to create private schools, but goes even further than is probably required by Article 27 and provides for public financial assistance for these institutions in the regions of Alsace and Moselle, as has Estonia with its 1993 **Law on Cultural Autonomy for Ethnic Minorities.**[139] Minority schools in Australia also receive a subsidy of $30 (Australian) per pupil, provided they are open to students from any ethnic background, and operate on a non-profit basis.

Funding to private minority schools raises a number of additional issues where the right to equality and non-discrimination may also enter into play. Whilst Article 27 in itself does not mandate state financial support for such schools, the right of non-discrimination would require, if a state provides financial assistance to any private school, that it do so in a reasonable and balanced way. This means that in general private educational activities in a minority language should also be eligible to any type of financial assistance provided to others by the government. It should be remarked that non-discrimination does not correspond to identical treatment: a state may quite reasonably allocate a higher proportion of funds to private schools using a minority language of instruction in consideration of the higher costs of educational materials in a lesser used language, or as an acknowledgment that certain minorities were the object of past discrimination or repression which has made it necessary to offer some type of compensation or special entitlements.

---

between the Republic of Poland and Ukraine on Good Neighbourliness, Friendly Relations and Cooperation.

[138] See for example Article 14 of the draft **Declaration on the Rights of Indigenous Peoples**, Article 16 of the **Central European Initiative for the Protection of Minority Rights** (limited to national minorities), Paragraph 32.2 of the **Document of the Copenhagen Meeting of the Conference on the Human Dimension** (national minorities), Article 11 of **Parliamentary Recommendation 1134 (1990) on the Rights of Minorities** (Council of Europe), Article 5(1)(c) of the United Nations **Convention against Discrimination in Education**, Article 30 of the **United Nations Convention on the Rights of the Child**, Article 27(3) of the International Labour Organisation **Convention (No. 169) Concerning Indigenous and Tribal Peoples in Independent Countries**, and Article 13 of the **Convention-cadre pour la protection des minorités nationales**, all found in the Appendix.

[139] Article 8 of the **Loi relatif au statut et à la promotion de la langue en Alsace et en Moselle**, January 1993. This right has been confirmed in more recent French legislation, Article 11 of the **Loi 94-665 du 4 août relative à l'emploi de la langue française.**

Obviously, there are also some states which have adopted policies in complete disregard of these standards. Since 1967, it has been against the law in Tanzania for a citizen to attend any elementary school where the medium is not Swahili. Turkey does not tolerate any use of Kurdish as a language of instruction, either in private or public institutions. The Japanese government apparently also prohibits private schools which use the Korean language, though there is one exception: some local governments maintain a power to authorise the establishment of private schools and have allowed private schools for Korean-speakers. The difficulty with this option is that these schools are not treated as official schools by the Japanese government under the **Education Act**, and the education provided is therefore not accredited by the national education authorities. Finally, legislation in Algeria appears to exclude any use of the Berber language.[140]

Even countries not generally thought as having a negative attitude towards minorities have practices that may violate Article 27:

Swiss cantons have the right to pass laws either for unilingualism or for bilingualism, in all spheres under their jurisdiction, particularly in education, culture, work, and public administration. In Belgium (with the exception of Brussels) the two major linguistic communities each have their own particular territorial institutions which govern unilingualism in education, culture, and the workplace. Most Swiss and Belgians are thus deprived of the choice of language in which their children will be educated, since the local authorities determine in fact the language of education in private as well as public schools.[141]

In both Belgium and Switzerland,[142] the policy of territorial monolingualism, when applied to private minority educational activities, appears to be highly suspect. Although drafted in both cases as part of a nation-wide arrangement seen as essential to safeguard the political and social stability of the state, indiscriminate application of linguistic monolingualism to the private activities of minorities may have been an unnecessary overreaction. There are, at least in Switzerland, misgivings as to the actual need for such a restrictive approach in the case of linguistic minorities.[143]

---

[140] Article 15 of the **Loi du 16 janvier 1991 portant généralisation de l'utilisation de la langue arabe** stipulates that all educational activities must be in Arabic only, except when involving the teaching of foreign languages.

[141] Laponce, Jean A. (1987), *Languages and Their Territories*, University of Toronto Press, Toronto, at p. 162.

[142] See the discussion in Dessemontet, François (1984), *Le droit des langues en Suisse*, Éditeur officiel du Québec, Québec, at p. 125, on a decision of the *Tribunal administratif de Berne* of 10 November 1975 confirming the complete prohibition of private schooling in French in the Canton of Bern with a German-speaking majority.

[143] Steiert, Thierry (1993), *La Suisse et la Charte européenne des langues régionales ou minoritaires*, EURORegion National Report, Fribourg, Switzerland, at pp. 8-9:
Dans une décision concernant l'école française (une école privée) de la ville de Zurich, le Tribunal fédéral a statué que les cantons pouvaient se fonder sur l'article 116 de la Constitution pour déterminer la langue dans laquelle l'enseignement est donné, même dans les écoles privées, et qu'il leur était loisible de prescrire qu'après un certain délai, les élèves doivent être aptes à suivre les cours dans la langue nationale du canton et passer dans une école où

Two countries, Turkey and Greece, have in some respects gone beyond the requirements of Article 27 of the **International Covenant on Civil and Political Rights** and similar provisions in their treatment of linguistic minorities[144] because of obligations that have been recognised under the terms of treaties concluded in 1920.[145] The Greek Orthodox minority of Istanbul and the Muslim minority of Western Thrace are entitled "to establish, manage and control at their own expense, any charitable, religious and social institutions, any schools and other establishments for instruction and education with the right to use their own language and to exercise their own religion freely therein". The Turkish and Greek governments have in some regards gone beyond these provisions and provide the financial resources for the operation of private minority schools. For example, the Turkish-speaking minority in Greece runs its own schools (with about 11,000 pupils and 770 teachers) at the expense of the Greek state, although only half of the syllabus is taught in Turkish. The administration of minority schools can choose to use either the Arabic or Roman script.

However, it seems both countries have started to reduce the number of hours of instruction in the minority language and interfere in ways that are causing hardship to both the Turkish- and Greek-speaking minorities:

> In the vital field of education the Greek authorities have steadily increased teaching in Greek at the expense of Turkish. From the 1960's onwards religious teachers from the Arab world have progressively been reduced while the employment of teachers from Turkey to Turkish schools in Western Thrace has been stopped. Since 1968 only graduates from a special academy in Thessaloniki can be qualified to teach in Turkish schools... The situation has deteriorated with the authorities introducing an entrance exam for the two Turkish minority schools in Komotini and Xanthi — there are some 300 Turkish primary schools — and a directorate from the government in March 1981 stipulating that graduate examinations from Turkish secondary and high schools have to be in Greek. The implementation of this law in 1985 with in some cases merely a few months' notice was extremely hard on the students. The result of these measures has been a dramatic decline in secondary school students in Turkish schools from 227 in Xanthi and 305 in Komotini in 1983-84, to 85 and 42 respectively in 1986-87...[146]

---

l'enseignement est dispensé dans cette langue. Cette décision a soulevé une vague de contestations, car une application aussi stricte du principe de territorialité ne saurait se justifier que s'il s'agit de protéger une langue menacée, ce qui n'est certainement pas le cas de la langue allemande en ville de Zurich.

[144] It should be emphasised that both states, for political reasons, are particularly sensitive towards certain minorities. The Kurdish-speaking minority in Turkey has been subjected to repressive measures as to the use, in public and in private, of their language, whilst Greece to this day even denies the existence of an Albanian-speaking (Arvanite) minority in its territory.

[145] See Sections 2.3.19 and 2.3.33 of the Appendix for the relevant articles.

[146] *World Directory Of Minorities, supra,* note 64, at p. 129. Nor has Turkey been a model in its own treatment of the Greek-speaking minority's right to use their language in community with other members of their group, as shown by the following comments in the same report at pp. 192-193:

> In 1964 Greek Orthodox priests were forbidden to teach religion or conduct morning prayers in minority schools and Turks have since been appointed as teachers in all minority schools. Students were obliged to enrol in their nearest school rather than in a school of their choice and

Many aspects of these interventions appear objectionable since they actively discourage or restrict the minority's free use of their language in their own schools. The decision by Greek public authorities to decrease the use of the Turkish language as medium of instruction in private minority schools would appear to be a violation of Article 27 of the **Covenant,** as is probably the imposition by the same authorities of an entrance exam for the two Turkish minority schools. The use of Greek as the language of graduate examinations for students from private Turkish secondary and high schools is a more complex matter. On the one hand, Greek authorities could claim that the examination is not direct intervention with any individual's right to use his or her language in private minority schools. On the other hand, it could be maintained that the measure is actually an indirect interference, since its effect is to discourage members of a linguistic minority to exercise their legitimate and recognised right as understood in international law.

There is additionally the need to remember that other rights can sometimes be relevant in a minority's use of its language. Even if it cannot be established convincingly that the above language examination requirement is a violation of Article 27, the measure is probably discrimination on the ground of language. By adopting a policy of Greek-only graduate examinations, public authorities are imposing on Turkish-speaking students from private minority schools a highly unfavourable criterion. The burden imposed on these students is unlikely to be considered as a reasonable or balanced response to any vital state interest, and would therefore constitute an unacceptable language distinction unless the number of minority students affected is so low as to make the requirement a proportionate and reasonable measure.

The Greek situation also raises a number of important aspects that have not yet been clearly considered, namely the scope of a minority's right to establish and control the content and format of private educational activities in their language, as well as a state's own interests and obligations in these matters.

India is perhaps best able to provide some insight on these issues because of the many Indian court decisions and constitutional and legal provisions that reflect a vast experience in relation to the right of linguistic minorities to use their language in private educational activities. It also provides some guidance on how the right of non-discrimination can interact with this right.

An important aspect of the right of members of a linguistic minority to use their language in the private education field appears to be that educational activities must really be "their own", in other words that they have actual control over the creation and operation of these activities. The recognition of this aspect of a minority's right can be found in Article 30(1) of the **Constitution of India**[147] which guarantees to all religious or linguistic minorities "the right to establish and administer educational institutions of their choice." Furthermore, if public authorities do grant assistance to private educational institutions, Article 30(2) requires that the aid be provided without discrimination. In other words, whilst a linguistic minority is free to establish its own private educational institutions, this does not impose any positive obligation on a state to provide facilities or resources for private education in a minority language.[148]

The Indian Supreme Court indicated in **State of Bombay v. Bombay Education Society** that a linguistic minority's right to carry on its own educational activities is not limited to acquisition of the minority language. It necessarily includes imparting general education in the

---

the teaching of the Greek language has been severely reduced.

[147] Section 3.53 in the Appendix.

[148] *Minorities and the Law* (1972), Mohammed Imam (ed.), Indian Law Institute, New Delhi, at p. 45.

minority language:

> There is no limitation placed on the subjects to be taught in such educational institutions. As such minorities will ordinarily desire that their children should be brought up properly and efficiently and be eligible for higher university education and go out in the world fully equipped with such intellectual attainments as will make them fit for entering the public services, educational institutions of their choice will necessarily include institutions imparting general secular education also. In other words, the article leaves it to their choice to establish such educational institutions as will serve both purposes, namely the purpose of conserving their religion, language or culture, and also the purpose of giving a thorough good general education to their children.[149]

But a state's obligation not to interfere with a linguistic minority's right to open, operate and manage its own educational activities does not mean that the state cannot adopt appropriate regulations and standards. It has been deemed appropriate for the government in India to impose conditions on minority institutions in return for state recognition. The standards of education in private schools are not a part of management, nor are they directly at issue in choosing the language to be used as medium of instruction. This signifies that state recognition of the education received by children in a private minority school can validly be contingent on satisfying appropriate standards as to the quality and content of instruction:

> The right of a minority to "administer" obviously cannot include the right to "mal-administer". A minority cannot ask for an educational institution run by it in unhealthy surroundings, or without any competent and qualified teachers, or which does not maintain any fair standard of teaching. The right of the state to impose reasonable regulations as a condition for aid or recognition does not authorise it to take away minority's right to administer educational institutions of their choice. Regulations which may be imposed lawfully as a condition of receiving grant or recognition must be directed to making the institution effective as an educational institution, while retaining its character as a minority institution. Regulations may be imposed in the true interests of efficiency of instruction, discipline, health, sanitation, morality, public order and the like.[150]

The UNESCO **Convention Against Discrimination in Education** also recognises that a state may require from private minority institutions that their standard of education not be lower than the general standard laid down or approved by the competent authorities.[151]

Another interesting problem tackled by Indian courts has been the question of admission policies adopted by linguistic minorities in the management of their own educational activities. Article 30(1) of the **Constitution** (and presumably similar provisions such as Article 27 of the **Covenant**) only guarantees access to these educational activities or institutions to members of a linguistic minority. Unless a person is a member of such a minority, he or she is not free to participate in them.

---

[149] (1954) A.I.R. 560 (India), at p. 569.

[150] *Supra*, note 148, at p. 16.

[151] See Article 5(1)(c)(ii) in Section 2.1.1 of Appendix.

However, members of a linguistic minority may decide that it is desirable to open the doors of their educational institutions to other individuals, whilst a government may object to such an arrangement.[152] In **State of Bombay v. Bombay Education Society**, state authorities had issued an order prohibiting the admission of children whose mother tongue was not English in English-language minority schools in order to encourage the use of Hindi as the language of instruction. The order had the effect that many Anglo-Indian schools in Bombay saw their number of students fall drastically. In its decision, the Supreme Court concluded that non-English-speaking students were not entitled to admittance to minority schools because they were not members of the minority. Nevertheless, they still had the benefit of constitutional provisions guaranteeing to everyone the right to non-discrimination. The Supreme Court thus felt that the state order was an unreasonable restriction which amounted to unwarranted discrimination, contrary to the **Constitution of India**.[153] **In re Kerala Education Bill**,[154] the Supreme Court also held that the admission of a non-member in a minority institution does not take away its minority character.

Finally, a state may legitimately require that all children in private minority educational activities also learn the majority or official language without this being perceived as an interference with the minority's right, as long as the minority can continue to use its language as medium of instruction to the extent it feels is appropriate. In fact, it could even be claimed that it is essential for linguistic minorities to teach the majority or official language whilst retaining the minority language as medium of instruction in order to avoid the creation of linguistic ghettos that would result in the possible exclusion of members of these minorities from participation in the wider society. This is acknowledged in instruments such as the UNESCO **Convention Against Discrimination in Education** where it is stated that linguistic educational activities must not prevent "members of these minorities from understanding the culture and language of the community as a whole and from participating in its activities..."[155]

6.3   MEDIA

6.3.1   *Preliminary Remarks*

Many international instruments confirm that media (television, radio, publications) and language concerns should be divided into two broad categories: state-controlled media and privately-run

---

[152] It should be pointed out that the final decision on admission policies should rest on members of the concerned minority. However, because governments do recognise these schools or provide aid to them, there is probably a state obligation to ensure that non-discriminatory admission practices are in place in these institutions.

[153] *Supra*, note 148, at pp. 85-86.

[154] (1959) S.C.R. 995 (India).

[155] Article 5(1)(c)(i) can be found in the Appendix. The UNESCO **Convention** has been described as out of date because of its timidity and numerous qualifications in addressing the educational rights of linguistic minorities. On this point see Hastings, William K. (1988), *The Right to an Education in Maori: The Case from International Law*, Victoria University Press, Wellington, New Zealand, at p. 21.

operations.[156] The latter would normally require non-intervention by the state in decisions concerning language use or preference. Thus a law which would prohibit private newspapers from appearing in a given language would clearly be a violation of freedom of expression and possibly Article 27 of the **International Covenant on Civil and Political Rights** and other similar provisions. It would also be a rather obvious source of tension between the state — generally representing the interests of the majority population — and linguistic minorities.

The line between private and public media can sometimes be blurred, especially in countries with little tradition of a free press. Furthermore, there may be indirect ways for a state to control the media, such as when a state restricts access to paper supply, which indirectly could prohibit the publication of newspapers in a minority or non-official language. There could also be state involvement and control through the refusal of a transmission permit for privately-operated radio or television stations attempting to broadcast in a minority or non-official language.

As for the situations where states exercise direct or indirect control of certain media, it can become a source of conflict since excluded linguistic communities may be antagonised if there is an absence or claimed deficiency as to the use of their language in broadcasting or written print by the state.[157] As has been demonstrated on a number of occasions, state activities in the realm of the public media, and the language choices the state necessarily has to make in this area, raises the matter of allocation of public resources and of employment opportunities for all of its inhabitants. A one language policy within the state media disadvantages members of a non-majority or non-official language groups in career options, which in newer or Third World states with weak economies is no minor concern.

6.3.2   *Private Media and State Language Restrictions*

Even democracies traditionally respectful of human rights have periodically behaved in intolerant, even xenophobic ways to the presence of speakers of other languages in their midst, and most states have almost invariably at one point or another violated the freedom of expression of individuals in the process. For example, in Australia until 1956 there were regulations preventing private radio stations from transmitting in "foreign languages" for more than 2.5 percent of their total broadcasting time, and requiring that all messages in languages other than English be

---

[156] See for example Article 18 of the **Central European Initiative Instrument for the Protection of Minorities**, Article 11 of the **Convention on the Fundamental Rights of Ethnic Groups in Europe**, Article 17 of the **Convention on the Rights of the Child**, and Article 11 of the **European Charter for Regional or Minority Languages**.

[157] For example, Albanian-speakers in Macedonia raise the one-hour daily television broadcast allocated in their language as proof of their unjust treatment at the hands of the government.

translated.[158] The use of Kurdish on the airwaves is still prohibited in Turkey,[159] as are private broadcasts in Berber in Algeria.[160]

As a general proposition, states should not attempt to limit in any way the private use of language in the media. For private newspapers, this implies no legislation or other measures restricting the use of any language, nor any indirect attempt to restrict freedom of expression through, for example, control of newsprint availability.[161] Any attempt to interrupt direct reception of radio and television broadcasts from neighbouring countries because of the language of these transmissions could also be a violation of freedom of expression. As for private radio or television stations broadcasting in part or completely in a minority or non-official language, a state does not have an obligation, at least under international law, to provide them funding or a broadcasting permit.

---

[158] The word "foreign" has often been used in countries like Australia, the United States and Canada in the sense of "non-English", thus including the languages of indigenous peoples and other groups (French and Spanish) which have as great a claim as English, or better in the case of indigenous languages, to being "native". In the US, private media in these languages have been attacked or closed down by governments during periods of intolerance despite US claims of respect of the freedom of the press. See Perea, Juan F. (1992), "Demography and Distrust: An Essay on American Languages, Cultural Pluralism, and Official English", *Minnesota Law Review*, Vol. 77, 269-373, at p. 330. Even in the country of *égalité, fraternité, liberté*, it was only in October 1984 that the French government repealed a 1945 law regulating the language of publication of the press in Alsace. The original provision provided that no more than 75 percent of all articles in the media on sport or addressed to youth could be in a language other than French (i.e. German in this case).

[159] The Globe and Mail, Toronto, 19 August 1994, and paragraph 13(iii) of the **Resolution 985 (1992) on the Situation of Human Rights in Turkey**, reprinted in "The Situation of Human Rights in Turkey" (1992), in *Human Rights Law Journal*, Vol. 13, N° 11-12, 464-480.

[160] Other concerns have been expressed on the effect of the **Estonian Language Law** on journalists working for private media in "Human Rights in the Republic of Estonia, Raimo Pakkanen and Hans Danelius, Special Rapporteurs" (1991), in *Human Rights Law Journal*, Vol. 13, No. 5-6, 236-256, at p. 241.

[161] The only limitations that should be permissible are those generally recognised in application of the freedom of expression. See on this point Article 11(2) of the **European Charter for Regional or Minority Languages**:

> The parties undertake to guarantee freedom of direct reception of radio and television broadcasts from neighbouring countries in a language used in identical or similar to a regional or minority language, and not to oppose the retransmissions of radio and television broadcasts from neighbouring countries in such a language. They further undertake to ensure that no restrictions will be placed on the freedom of expression and free circulation of information in the written press in a language used in identical or similar form to a regional or minority language. The exercise of the above mentioned freedoms, since it carries with it duties and responsibilities, may be subject to such formalities, conditions, restrictions or penalties as are prescribed by law and are necessary in a democratic society, in the interest of national security, territorial integrity or public safety, for the prevention of disorder of crime, for the protection of health or morals, for the protection of reputation or rights of others, for preventing disclosure of information received in confidence, or for maintaining the authority and impartiality of the judiciary.

There are three matters that require closer scrutiny when speaking of language use and the private media. Although not directly an issue of freedom of expression, the distribution of radio and television frequencies by the state, decisions affecting the programming content and its language linked to broadcasting licensing, and the allocation of financial assistance to private media may raise issues involving non-discrimination.

On the one hand, many states now permit private radio and television broadcasting.[162] The European Court on Human Rights has also confirmed on a number of occasions that broadcasting, like the press, is covered by Article 10 of the European human rights convention guaranteeing freedom of expression.[163] Yet on the other hand, broadcasting frequencies are generally considered to be public goods, and their regulation for the public good by the state is therefore considered as appropriate and not to constitute a violation of freedom of expression.[164]

Difficulties occur when the state, through its regulatory agent, decides who will be permitted to have access to these "public" airwaves. The right of non-intervention guaranteed to linguistic minorities by Article 27 of the **International Covenant on Civil and Political Rights** and similar provisions are of no assistance in such a situation since airwave frequencies are not part of the private realm. In other words, states are probably not obliged to grant a private broadcasting frequency every time it is demanded by a linguistic minority under international legal standards such as Article 27. Whilst this may appear initially to be a Catch-22 situation, it is not in practice. The solution has been indirectly identified by the European Court on Human Rights in the recent case of **Informationverein Lentia and Others v. Austria**,[165] where it indicated that in exercising its general regulatory powers when allocating airwave frequencies, a state must observe its obligations under international legal instruments, which include Article 27 or similar provisions. Thus, this means that a state must consider a linguistic minority's right to communicate with its members in its language, *via* the airwaves. It could be argued however that in cases where there is already in the same area a large number of private radio or television stations (for the size of the concerned group) broadcasting in the language of the minority, sufficient weight is given to the non-intervention guaranteed under Article 27, and the public

---

[162] Barendt, Eric (1993), *Broadcasting Law — A Comparative Study*, Clarendon Press, Oxford, United Kingdom, at p. 54.

[163] **Groppera v. Switzerland** (1990) 12 European Human Rights Reports 321 and **Autronic v. Switzerland** (1990) 12 European Human Rights Reports 485. The European Court of Human Rights had earlier ruled that newspapers enjoyed the protection of Article 10 in **Sunday Times v. UK** (1979) 2 European Human Rights Reports 245.

[164] *Supra*, note 162, at pp. 77-79. See the conclusion along similar lines of the Italian Constitutional Court in Decision 102/1990 [1990] Giur. cost. 610 (Italy). See also Trudel, Pierre and Abran, France (1991), *Droit de la radio et de la télévision*, Éditions Thémis, Montréal, at pp. 135-136:

> *Les textes internationaux proclamant la liberté d'expression reconnaissent la possibilité d'un traitement différent pour les médias électroniques et le droit des États à assujettir l'accès à l'usage des fréquences de radiodiffusion à un régime d'autorisation préalable. Ainsi, l'article 10 de la Convention européenne des droits énonce que l'affirmation de la liberté d'expression n'empêche pas les États de soumettre les entreprises de radiodiffusion à un régime d'autorisation... L'on a généralement considéré que les activités de radiodiffusion supposent, à la différence des médias écrits, l'usage d'une ressource jugée rare, les fréquences radioélectriques, qui sont réputées faire partie du domaine public.*

[165] Case 36/1992/381/455-459.

regulatory agency would be entitled to deny licences for additional frequencies in such a situation.

In **Informationverein Lentia and Others v. Austria**, the European Court on Human Rights explained that the nature of broadcasting required that the state conduct regulatory decisions concerning the utilisation of broadcast power and frequencies. It also gave some important guidelines on how the state, in determining licensing requirements, should evaluate private broadcasting applications:

> As the Court has already held, the purpose of that provision is to make it clear that states are permitted to regulate by a licensing system the way in which broadcasting is organised in their territories, particularly in its technical aspects... Technical aspects are undeniably important, but the grant or refusal of a licence may also be made conditional on other considerations, including such matters as the nature and objectives of a proposed station, its potential audience at national, regional or local level, the rights and needs of a specific audience and the obligations deriving from international legal instruments.[166]

Criteria such as the rights and the needs of audiences at various levels and international law obligations, including those of linguistic minorities, would thus appear to be key factors to consider.

As with any other type of activity by public authorities, state allocation of airwave frequencies to radio or television stations that use exclusively a majority or official language will tend to be more favourable towards individuals with greater fluency in this language, and correspond more closely to their linguistic needs. In a country where public authorities favour exclusively the majority or official language, it means that the linguistic and cultural needs of speakers of non-official or minority language are qualitatively and quantitatively disregarded. Such a policy could be discriminatory, and probably a violation of Article 27 of the **International Covenant on Civil and Political Rights,** if linguistic minorities found themselves completely excluded from operating private stations in their language.

Especially when the number of speakers of a language is fairly large in an area, to refuse a private radio or television licence for broadcasting services in their language would appear unreasonable, since it denies them a benefit or advantage that is available to others, namely the benefit of radio or television programmes in their own language. At the very least such a refusal disregards their needs and preferences. Once again, the many factors such as geographic distribution and concentration of the speakers and others must be examined in order to determine whether a public authority's refusal to grant a licence is discriminatory or not. Another relevant consideration in this area would be the number of other private stations broadcasting stations in the same coverage area, and whether these sufficiently respond to the needs and preferences of the population.

One problem in licensing decisions experienced in the United States is the determination of the needs and interests of affected individuals. In determining these needs and interests the US regulatory agency, the Federal Communications Commission (FCC), has sometimes tended to consider exclusively the linguistic needs of individuals who had absolutely no knowledge of

---

[166] Ibid., at paragraph 32.

English.[167] This means that when large numbers of individuals are bilingual, even if their primary language is not English, the FCC has often adopted the position that it is not necessary to licence private radio or television stations broadcasting in their language,[168] although where there is a sufficiently large ethnic population, the FCC sometimes presumes that non-English programming is desirable without inquiring as to the percentage of people who do not speak English on the assumption that a large number of them probably do not.

It would appear the Federal Communications Commission's general policy is potentially discriminatory if one considers the standard of non-discrimination at the international level. As defined by most international instruments and the UN Human Rights Committee in its *General Comment on Non-Discrimination*, discrimination does not only occur when an individual is "excluded" by the language preference(s) of the state, but can also be said to exist whenever he or she is disadvantaged or subjected to unfavourable treatment if the state's conduct is deemed unreasonable. Even if an individual understands English, he or she is still not receiving the same privilege or service as a native speaker of English when private broadcasting is not provided in his or her primary language. He or she is denied the same advantage enjoyed by others, because of a public authority's predilection for the majority language.[169] Furthermore, the state would

---

[167] There appears to be a great deal of confusion on how to address the language needs of the US population in private broadcasting. Relevant decisions include **Tampa Times Co. v. FCC**, 230 F.2d 224 (1956) (United States), **In re Great Lakes Television, Inc.**, 25 F.C.C. 470 (1958) (United States), and **In re La Fiesta Broadcasting Co.**, 6 F.C.C. 2d 65 (1966) (United States). All are closely considered in Piatt, Bill (1984) "Linguistic Diversity on the Airwaves: Spanish-Language Broadcasting and the FCC", in *La Raza Law Journal*, Vol. 1, No. 2, 101-119, at pp. 103-115. The same author summarises the US situation in the following words, ibid., at p. 104:

> [FCC] cases contain varying discussions and analyses of the "need" for such broadcasting, its "suitability", the "obligation" to provide it, and the level of "control" that should be exercised over it. Some cases place importance on the number of ethnic persons in the broadcast audience who speak only the foreign language. Others ignore the "linguistic exclusivity" requirement. Later cases confuse minority ownership of broadcast facilities with the language issue. The result is an absence of an adequate standard for measuring the parameters of the foreign-language broadcasting requirement.

[168] See **Tucson Radio, Inc. v. FCC**, 35 F.C.C. 2d 584 (1972) (United States):

> Broadcast stations are trustees of the public airwaves and must design their programming to meet the needs and interests of their communities. If a substantial segment of the community thinks and speaks in the Spanish language only, and cannot understand the English language, the broadcast stations in that area must be responsive to this fact. Accordingly, if a petitioner can show i) that a substantial segment of the community speaks exclusively a language other than English; ii) that a need exists for aural broadcast service in that language; iii) that none of the existing stations would serve this need; and iv) that the prospects for obtaining such service by resort to existing Commission remedies are poor, the Commission would then entertain a petition for waiver of its primary service rule.

Whilst there are undoubtedly many private Spanish language radio and television stations in the United States, in practice, the demographic and economic clout of this linguistic group has made it impossible to ignore their broadcasting needs in many, but not all, parts of the country.

[169] For an excellent exploration and analysis of the issue of language and broadcasting policies in the US, see Piatt, *supra*, note 167, at pp. 112-115.

in effect be ignoring the cultural and linguistic needs and preferences of individuals for whom English is not a mother tongue.

An approach more closely consistent with the prohibition of discrimination would be more like the following suggestion:

> The FCC could require that the ascertainment surveys be expanded to include a determination of whether Spanish-language broadcasting is desired by the public in the area the broadcaster is to serve, and if so, what percentage of the broadcaster's programming the public would like to see presented in Spanish. The FCC would then require, as a condition of licensing, that the broadcaster provide a portion of its programming in Spanish equal to the survey results. The survey would be redone every three years in conjunction with licence renewal and the figure for Spanish-speaking broadcasting would be adjusted accordingly. Broadcasting content would still be left to the broadcaster's discretion subject to existing requirements that broadcasting be in the public interest. The only change would be in the language in which a portion of the programming would be presented.[170]

The policies favoured in a number of other countries and at the international level would appear to be generally closer to a non-discriminatory approach than US attitude in broadcasting licensing and linguistic content. Article 11 of the **European Charter for Regional or Minority Languages** provides that when the number of speakers of a minority or regional language reaches a certain level ("according to the situation of each language"), public authorities should adopt measures aimed at ensuring that they are properly served in their language by private media when these authorities are active in this field (through licensing, programme content requirements, etc.). In other words, as the number of speakers of a language increases in a region, the media, and especially the broadcasting media, should respond to the proportionate needs and interests of this population. Public authorities must to the extent of their involvement in the field of private media adopt a policy that reflects these needs and interests with appropriate measures:

b) I. to encourage and/or facilitate the creation of at least one radio station in the regional or minority languages, or
II. to encourage and/or facilitate the broadcasting of radio programmes in the regional or minority languages on a regular basis;

c) I. to encourage and/or facilitate the creation of at least one television channel in the regional or minority languages, or
II. to encourage and/or facilitate the broadcasting of television programmes in the regional or minority languages on a regular basis;

d) to encourage and/or facilitate the production and distribution of audio and audio-visual works in regional or minority languages;

e) I. to encourage and/or facilitate the creation and/or maintenance of at least one newspaper in the regional or minority languages; or
II. to encourage and/or facilitate the publication of newspaper articles in the regional or minority languages on a regular basis;[171]

---

[170] Ibid., at p. 115.

[171] Article 11(1) of the **European Charter for Regional or Minority Languages.**

Another example of a response consistent with the prohibition of discrimination can be found in Canadian broadcasting, where the need to address the specific cultural and linguistic needs of audiences has been recognised, and includes, in the case of indigenous peoples, the obligation "to play a distinct role in fostering the development of aboriginal cultures and/or, possibly, the preservation of ancestral languages."[172] Moreover, the Canadian Radio-Television and Telecommunications Commission (CRTC) adopted in July 1985 a comprehensive policy paper on cultural and linguistic plurality in broadcasting in Canada.[173] Whilst solemnly affirming the high value placed on linguistic diversity and how each language is as important as any other, it also recognises that, practically speaking, every demand for a private broadcasting permit cannot be granted:

> *Le Conseil considère qu' en raison des limitations du spectre des fréquences, il ne peut accorder de licence pour un service en une seule langue à chacun des groupes ethniques d'un marché donné. Il encourage donc la collaboration entre détenteurs de licence de manière à ce que ces derniers fournissent des services élargis aux groupes ethniques qui résident dans la zone de desserte de leur entreprise, tout en tenant compte des besoins variés de leurs collectivités... De plus, lorsque la population ethnique d'une région augmente et qu' elle requiert des services élargis de radiodiffusion, le CRTC admet la possibilité de modifier une licence de radiodiffusion en vue de permettre à l' exploitant de diffuser un pourcentage plus élevé d' émissions à caractère ethnique, voir même devenir une station à caractère ethnique...*[174]

What the CRTC is admitting is that, in addition to responding to the linguistic needs and preferences of all Canadians, a major factor in determining the language to be used in broadcasting will be the relative demographic importance of the speakers of a language. In other words, the Canadian approach is a reflection of the principle of non-discrimination on the ground of language in the field of broadcast licensing and linguistic content.

The appropriateness of responding to the linguistic interests and needs of all inhabitants when allocating broadcasting licences and determining the language(s) of private media is further confirmed in a number of court decisions in different countries. Article 20 of the Spanish **Constitution** recognises multilingualism in Spain and states that it will guarantee access to the state media of important social and political groups, with due respect to the existing social and linguistic pluralism. In **Minister for Posts and Telegraph v. Cáit Bean Ui Chadhain**, the Irish Supreme Court held:

> In performing its functions the [Broadcasting] Authority shall in its programming — (a) be responsive to the interests and concerns of the whole community, be mindful of the need for understanding and peace within the whole island of Ireland, ensure that the programmes reflect the varied elements which make up the culture of the people of the whole island of

---

[172] **Native Broadcasting Policy**, 20 September 1990, Canadian Radio-Television and Telecommunications Commission, Ottawa.

[173] **Public Notice 85-139**, 4 July 1985, Canadian Radio-Television and Telecommunications Commission, Ottawa.

[174] Ibid., quoted in *Droit de la radio et de la télévision, supra,* note 164, at pp. 928-929.

Ireland and have special regard for the elements which distinguish that culture and in particular for the Irish language.[175]

The above also suggest that in addition to distributing broadcasting licences, a public authority can impose linguistic content conditions when it decides a private broadcaster will be granted a broadcasting licence. Once again, such a requirement will have to be a reasonable and proportional response to the needs, rights and interests of individuals concerned and the state's own interests since it involves the right to use a public good (frequencies). Failure to reach a proper balance could be discriminatory, especially when speakers of a non-official or non-majority language are numerous in a region or locality or incompletely served in their language by existing private broadcasters.[176] International courts have also recognised in this regard that television (and by extension, radio) signals constitute a type of service.[177] Thus, it appears acknowledged, at least at the European Union level, that whilst a state is entitled to fix quotas as to the linguistic content of these broadcasts, it must still do so in a non-discriminatory way.[178]

The third matter to consider arises when a state intervenes with the private media by providing some type of assistance to private newspapers, radio or television stations, either because they are in the official or majority language, or on the contrary because they are in other languages. Examples of the former can be found in Catalonia and the Netherlands, where governments actively provide grants in support of private initiatives that respectively promote the

---

[175] 16 July 1982, quoted in O Màille, Tomas (1990), *The Status of the Irish Language — A Legal Perspective*, Bord na Gaeilge, Dublin, at p. 12.

[176] Some concern exists that linguistic requirements by public authorities can have restrictive effects on trade between countries. The answer to this is essentially the same one proposed throughout much of this study: while any linguistic preference by a state does in fact create a distinction based upon language and will unavoidably favour some to the detriment of others, it has to be determined whether the language favouritism is a balanced and reasonable response after assessing the various interests involved. In short, such a distinction is not necessarily discriminatory, but could be if it is not reasonable. See generally de Witte, Bruno (1991), "The Impact of European Community Rules on Linguistic Policies of the Member States" in Florian Coulmas (ed.), *A Language Policy for the European Community: Prospects and Quandaries*, Mouton de Gruyter, Berlin, New York, pp. 163-177, at p. 167:

> Can Member States justifiably impose requirements as to the linguistic origin of programmes, or as to the language in which the programmes should be transmitted? What is certainly not allowed is a discriminatory treatment; in a fairly recent case of the **Bond van Nederlandse Adverteerders v. The Netherlands**, a Dutch regulation which prohibited advertisements on foreign channels using the Dutch language were found to be incompatible with the EEC Treaty. The reverse of this, namely the imposition on national broadcasters of a duty to use the national language or (more commonly) to broadcast a certain amount of programmes produced in that language, has also restrictive effects on the trade in broadcasting services. But this restriction was, after some discussion, accepted in the recently adopted EEC Directive on transfrontier television.

[177] **Sacchi Case**, [1974] European Court Reports 409, at p. 427.

[178] Salvatore, Vincenzo (1992), "Quotas on TV Programmes and EEC Law", in *Common Market Law Review*, Vol. 29, No. 5, 967-990, at pp. 968-971, 981-984, and 986.

use of Catalan in all types of media activities or Dutch in publishing. Clearly, as has been previously shown, measures that promote and encourage the use of the official or majority language are not objectionable *in se*. Amongst various factors in support of such a policy can be the desire of national unity through the bond of a common, though not necessarily exclusive, language. Here again, what must always be kept in mind is that this type of practice is obviously more favourable to those who enjoy a greater benefit from such efforts, namely people for whom the official or majority language is their primary language. However, the exclusion of some media from this type of financial assistance because they function in other languages would only be discriminatory if the measures are deemed unreasonable given the various rights, goals and interests involved. In the case of the promotion of the Catalan language through private media, the *Generalitat* may be able to argue that its "normalisation" efforts are reasonable in light of the harsh consequences of previous restrictions and history of repressive linguistic restrictions of the Franco regime and Spanish governments, and that Castilian-language private media are already sufficiently vibrant, and Castilian-speakers sufficiently well-served in their language, that similar assistance is unnecessary.

In some cases, a state may provide financial assistance to private media using a non-official or minority language that is unavailable to the media operating in the official or majority language. In Canada, the federal government provided, until recently under the Natives Communications Programme, financial assistance to fifteen private aboriginal language newspapers across the country. It still provides funds under the Northern Native Broadcast Access Programme to television and radio broadcasting in indigenous languages, many of them by private, non-profit, entities. In Hungary, newspapers publishing in the languages of national minorities are guaranteed a financial contribution under the state budget.[179] Under **Act No. 416** of 5 August 1981 on the regulations governing publishing houses and measures to promote publishing in Italy, daily newspapers published entirely in French, Ladin, Slovene or German in the autonomous regions of Valle d'Aosta, Friuli-Venezia Giulia and Trentino-Alto Adige, have also received increased grants from the state.[180]

Once again, these policies are not objectionable in themselves, because non-discrimination does not require identical treatment in every situation. If such a policy does not unduly favour the speakers of a language, then it may be a reasonable arrangement given the interests and goals being addressed. Even if the private media operating in the majority or official language are excluded from these "special assistance programmes", it could be claimed validly that a particular scheme is a proportional response to the needs and preferences of some individuals not being properly served by other media in their language, due to their small number, geographic dispersion, or as a result of past state practices aimed at discouraging the use of their language. Such a state initiative to remedy the imbalance would thus possibly be held reasonable and non-discriminatory.

6.3.3   State Media and Language Discrimination

As with any other type of state service, benefit or activity, the involvement of the state in public media must conform to the requirements of non-discrimination on the ground of language. Once

---

[179] *The Situation of Regional or Minority Languages in Europe* (1994), Council of Europe, Strasbourg, at p. 46.

[180] Ibid., at p. 71.

more, this means that state authorities must adopt a sliding-scale model: if the state controls, operates or finances any media, it should do so in a non-discriminatory fashion and reflect in the time and resources allocated the linguistic composition of its population. Furthermore, it should not be forgotten that the linguistic policies of public authorities will affect considerably the employment opportunities in the state media of non-native speakers of the official or majority language preferred.

When considering what would be an appropriate and reasonable linguistic balance, one would have to consider once again the myriad of factors identified earlier such as the numerical importance of the speakers of the language, their location and geographic concentration, etc. Starting at the lower end of the scale, state practices should generally reflect the actual number of speakers of a non-official or minority language in the following way:

(1) the regular broadcasting of radio programme(s) in the minority or non-official language (these could take diverse forms, from one hour or less a week to many hours every day, according once again to a minority's growing strength);

(2) the regular broadcasting of television programme(s) in the minority or non-official language (at increasing levels);

(3) the creation of one or more radio stations operating in the minority or non-official language;

(4) the creation of one or more television channel(s) in the minority or non-official language;

If the state is actively involved in newspaper publication, it should likewise devote a fair proportion of resources and/or space for the use of minority languages when parts of its population involve sufficiently large linguistic minorities.[181]

In practice, many states already respect the overall scheme of a balanced and reasonable response to the presence of large numbers of individuals with a different primary language than the official or majority tongue. They recognise more or less explicitly that the needs of these individuals would not be satisfied by the exclusive use in the public media of the official/majority language and that these individuals would not be receiving the same benefit if their language was not being used.

Switzerland offers an interesting model in this field. The objective of language policy in public broadcasting has been to serve the population of each linguistic area in its own language to an appropriate degree. This means that most individuals speaking one of the main languages in use in the country (German, French, and Italian, as well as Romansch to a lesser extent) will have access to public television or radio in their language. The Swiss have additionally considered that the public broadcasting programming budgets should be divided amongst the three public broadcasting services (German, French, Italian) according to a fixed formula that favours the smaller linguistic populations. Although more generous to the Italian and French populations, the ratio being 42:34:24 for the German, French, and Italian regional television (in radio, the budgetary ratio is 45:33:22), the more favourable treatment of these individuals is

---

[181] See also Article 11(1)(a) of the **European Charter for Regional or Minority Languages**, and Barendt, *supra*, note 162, at p. 54:

> The idea that public service broadcasting should reflect that country's culture to itself is acceptable. This broad policy constitutes a justification for the requirements that a certain proportion of programmes should be made in the country's language, a common rule in France.

probably not discriminatory, since it can be argued that Swiss citizens, regardless of their language, should have access as far as possible to equivalent public broadcasting services in all three main, territorially-based, languages.[182]

Public media in Australia,[183] Hungary,[184] Italy (especially German, French, Ladin and Slovene),[185] Great Britain,[186] and a multitude of other states similarly include minority or non-official language broadcasting to a degree that more or less adequately reflects the demographic weight, needs and interests of their respective linguistic populations.

6.4   OF CITIZENS AND OTHERS

6.4.1   *Preliminary Remarks*

Settlers are arriving here from different regions and provinces. They are attracted by the splendour of your court. Those countries which have only one language and one custom are weak and fragile. This is what I order you to do, my son: Take care of your foreigners,

---

[182] See also Steiert, *supra*, note 143, at p. 31, and *The Situation of Regional or Minority Languages in Europe*, *supra*, note 179, at pp. 135-136:

> Article 2 of the Federal Broadcasting Act stipulates that radio and television should, broadly speaking, "help listeners and viewers to form their opinions freely, provide them with varied and accurate information, see to their general education and their entertainment, and extend their civic knowledge". They should also "make the public aware of the country's diversity and its population, promote Swiss artistic creation and make it easier for listeners and viewers to participate in cultural life by conveying knowledge and ideas". This extract setting out the aims of the Act, formulated in general terms, covers all aspects of language promotion (duties of information, education, variety, cultural promotion and stimulation of the public). In a wider framework, one can say that yet another of the Act's provisions is concerned with language promotion: "The various regions of the country must be adequately served by radio and television"... The Federal Broadcasting Act (Article 26 et seq.) also stipulates clearly that the Swiss Broadcasting Company (SSR) is primarily responsible for attaining the general aims and carrying out the functions assigned to it — in the interests of linguistic diversity and national understanding. With regard to languages, an important provision requires the SSR to broadcast specific radio programmes in each region in which a national language is spoken (Article 27, paragraph 1).

[183] Zolf, Dorothy (1989), "Comparisons of Multicultural Broadcasting in Canada and Four Other Countries", in *Canadian Ethnic Studies*, Vol. XXI, No. 2, 13-26, at pp. 18-20.

[184] See *The Situation of Regional or Minority Languages in Europe*, *supra*, note 179, at p. 46, and Article 18 of the **Act No. LXXVII of 1993 on the Rights of National and Ethnic Minorities**.

[185] *The Situation of Regional or Minority Languages in Europe*, ibid., at p. 71.

[186] Ibid., at pp. 141-142.

esteem and support them. They should favour your country to others. Keep in mind, everybody has been born as a free human being. Do not keep anyone as a bond.

Saint Stephan[187]

One matter of intense debate, especially in newly independent states formerly part of the Soviet Union, is who will be granted citizenship. Part the legacy of the Soviet period has been the presence of a high percentage of Russian-speakers now inhabiting some of these states. A number of them have imposed language requirements to qualify for citizenship, a practice which is relatively common.[188]

Citizenship matters tend to raise highly sensitive issues. In the United States, courts have even arrived at the conclusion that citizenship decisions are completely outside the powers of the judiciary but that reasoning appears erroneous. The crux of the problem in the US and in some other states may be one of perception: it is sometimes believed that because citizenship goes to the very political core of a state, it should somehow be outside the scope of judicial review and left to the discretion of the political leadership. Yet, although not a "right" in the technical sense, the citizenship process still involves government action and legislation. Furthermore, individuals who gain citizenship obtain a "benefit", "franchise" or "privilege" from the state that is being denied to others because of governmental linguistic policies and preferences. In this sense the citizenship process involves an activity by public authorities within the purview of the principles of equality and non-discrimination, as is any other type of state action, though the margin of manoeuvre for a government in this area would probably be greater than in others.

The mistake committed in the US and repeated by some scholars is to assume that the non-existence of a "right to citizenship" means that human rights are of no relevance to naturalisation except to avoid situations of statelessness.[189] In reality, as with any other state activity, once a government decides to "act" it must do so in a non-discriminatory way. In other words, once a government decides to grant citizenship to individuals, it must abide by human rights principles:

---

[187] *Scriptores rerum Hungaricum Temore ducum regumque stripis Arpadianae gestarum*, translation quoted in Von Komlossy, Joseph (1994), *Regionalism in the Carpathian Basin — Is it a Vision or a Reality?*, paper presented at the Conference of Europe of Regions "Regionalism and the Europe of the Future", 19-22 August 1994, Copenhagen, Denmark, at p. 1.

[188] de Witte, *supra*, note 26, at pp. 86-87:

> A similar link between language skills and the granting of a certain franchise or benefit is made in some countries, who make the knowledge of the national language a prerequisite for naturalisation. Such conditions exist in many Third World, but also in some Western countries. In the United States, section 304 of the Nationality Act holds that: "No person...shall be naturalised as a citizen of the United States upon his own petition who cannot demonstrate: (1) an understanding of the English language, including an ability to read, write and speak words in ordinary usage in the English language..." Article 69 of the **Code de la Nationalité française** also holds that "no one can be naturalised if he does not justify his assimilation to the French community, notably by a sufficient knowledge, depending on his condition, of the French language."

[189] See Türk, Danilo (1993), "Some Elements for Consideration on Policies concerning National Minorities", in *Report on an Expert Consultation in Connection with the Activities of the CSCE High Commissioner on National Minorities*, Foundation on Inter-Ethnic Relation, den Haag, Netherlands.

a "White-only" citizenship policy would clearly be in breach of the prohibition of discrimination. Though citizenship is clearly a prerogative of the state in the sense that the state is not obligated to grant it to anyone, once it has initiated a naturalisation process it must respect the human right to equality and non-discrimination in its policies.

This point has been a major source of confusion, particularly in Baltic states, and the issues it raises are likely to be unsettled for a number of years. Two Council of Europe experts in 1991 had this to say concerning Estonia's then proposed citizenship legislation and its language requirements:

> As regards the human rights aspect of this problem, it should first be noted that neither the European Convention on Human Rights nor any other international human rights convention recognises the right to a certain citizenship as a human right. Consequently, it must in principle be left to each state to determine the conditions for acquiring its citizenship... However, if substantial parts of the population of a country are denied the right to become citizens, and thereby are also denied for instance the right to vote in parliamentary elections, this could affect the character of the democratic system in that country. As regards the European Convention on Human Rights, the question could be raised whether in such a situation the elections to the legislature would sufficiently ensure the free expression of the opinion of the people, as required by Article 3 of the First Protocol to the Convention.[190]

These comments are unfortunate because they seem to imply that governments have no legal obligation to apply principles of non-discrimination in matters relating to citizenship. Somehow, the experts appear to ignore how many states have interpreted their human rights obligations involving naturalisation policies, and especially seem to be unaware of an important international decision dealing precisely with language and citizenship that clearly contradicts their conclusion.

6.4.2   *Discrimination and Citizenship*

> America is a political union — not a cultural, linguistic, religious, or racial union.... Of course, we as individuals would urge all to learn English for that is the language used by most Americans as well as the language of the marketplace. But, we should no more demand English language skills for citizenship than we should demand uniformity of religion. That a person wants to become a citizen and will make a good citizen is more than enough.[191]

This quote perhaps illustrates a recurrent difficulty in a number of states worldwide: whilst most recognise that it is a desirable characteristic for all citizens to share a common language — though some like Switzerland have done very well without one — the requirement that all citizens be fluent in the official or majority language may sometimes be raised because of the narrow and mistaken view that the state is some kind of religious, racial or linguistic union.

---

[190] *Supra*, note 160, at paragraphs 35 and 36.

[191] Honourable Cruz Reynoso, quoted in Ong Hing, Bill (1993), "Beyond the Rhetoric of Assimilation and Cultural Pluralism: Addressing the Tension of Separatism and Conflict in an Immigration-Driven Multiracial Society", in *California Law Review*, Vol. 81, 863-925, at p. 864.

By denying them citizenship, some states have been able to deny to large segments of their inhabitants many rights and privileges.[192] But instead of criticising the fact that some other political or social rights are being denied to large groups of non-citizens, the Council of Europe experts quoted earlier should have looked at the root cause of the problem, namely the criteria being used to determine who receives citizenship in the first place. To treat citizens and non-citizens differently is not in itself inherently objectionable, although once again there are limits to the extent a state can disadvantage individuals because of their political status which derive from the prohibition of discrimination.

One United Nations document confirms that a state is not free to discriminate as it pleases when deciding who can become a citizen, indicating that the following situations constitute unacceptable inequality:

(a) Establishment or enforcement of specific legal barriers or restrictions implying the denial to individuals of a particular social group of the right to a nationality, or of the right to change their nationality;
(b) Any arbitrary administrative act or omission denying or restricting the rights mentioned in the preceding paragraph to individuals belonging to a particular social group.[193]

Contrary to the assertions of some experts, the determination of citizenship is subject to the prohibition of discrimination. Any restriction or requirement adopted by public authorities must be examined in order to establish whether it is a reasonable and proportional measure in light of the numerous factors and interests involved. As the UN Human Rights Committee suggested in its *General Comment on Non-Discrimination*, "any distinction, exclusion, restriction or preference" which is based on language and "has the purpose or effect of nullifying or impairing the recognition, enjoyment or exercise by all persons, on an equal footing", of the privilege, right, benefit or franchise that citizenship represents, must be carefully assessed as to whether it is reasonable and therefore non-discriminatory. In other words, the requirement of a degree of fluency in an official or majority language constitutes a distinction or preference that will have the effect of not allowing all people to enjoy, on an equal footing, the benefits or acquisition of citizenship. Since not everyone speaks the official or majority language fluently, in the same way as not everyone shares the same religion or is of the same colour, some people are not being treated on an equal footing when the law favours a specific race, religion or language. Any "White-only", "Christian-only", or "English-only" state policy, be it in public education, employment practices or naturalisation decisions, must be assessed as to its reasonability and proportionality in the balancing act of individual and societal rights, obligations and interests.

---

[192] See Mullerson, Rein (1993), "Minorities in Eastern Europe and the Former USSR: Problems, Tendencies and Protection", in *Modern Law Review*, Vol. 56, 793-811, at p. 808; Article 1 of the Federal Government of Austria Decree of 31 May 1977, in *Recueil des législations linguistiques dans le monde, supra*, note 26, at p. 35: "*Seuls les citoyens de nationalité autrichienne pourront se réclamer du droit d'utiliser la langue slovène en tant que langue officielle au même titre que la langue allemande*"; and Article 1 of **Act No. LXXVII of 1993 on the Rights of National and Ethnic Minorities of Hungary**.

[193] *The Main Types and Causes of Discrimination, Memorandum submitted by the Secretary General* (1949), United Nations Publications, New York, at pp. 35-36.

A highly significant decision in this regard is the Inter-American Court of Human Rights' **Advisory Opinion of 19 January 1984 (Costa Rican Naturalisation Case)**[194] which was considered earlier in Chapter 4. One of the amendments examined by the court required that an applicant had the ability to speak, write and read Spanish in order to acquire citizenship.

The Inter-American Court began by holding that nationality is an inherent right of all human beings, and that despite the fact that the conferral and regulation of nationality are matters for each state to decide, contemporary developments in international law now impose certain limits on the broad powers enjoyed by the states in that area:

> [The] manner in which states regulate matters bearing on nationality cannot today be deemed within their sole jurisdiction; those powers of the state are also circumscribed by their obligations to ensure the full protection of human rights.[195]

The Inter-American Court, whilst admitting that states have a wide margin of appreciation in determining the naturalisation policy appropriate for their specific cultural, social and political context,[196] proceeded to indicate that the imposition of a language requirement was a difference of treatment of individuals that could in some circumstances be considered discriminatory. The majority of judges did not feel that the Spanish language requirements in the proposed amendment were too unreasonable, in the context of that country, and concluded that they fell within the state's margin of appreciation:

> Consistent with its clearly restrictive approach, the proposed amendment also provides for new conditions which must be complied with by those applying for naturalisation. Draft Article 15 requires, among other things, proof of the ability to "speak, write and read" the Spanish language; it also prescribes a "comprehensive examination on the history of the country and its values". These conditions can be deemed, *prima facie*, to fall within the margin of appreciation reserved to the state as far as concerns the enactment and assessment of the requirements designed to ensure the existence of real and effective links upon which to base the acquisition of the new nationality. So viewed, it cannot be said to be unreasonable and unjustified to require proof of the ability to communicate in the language

---

[194] Case No. OC-4/84.

[195] Ibid., at paragraph 32.

[196] Ibid., at paragraph 36:

> Since it is the state that offers the possibility of acquiring its nationality to persons who were originally aliens, it is natural that the conditions and procedures for its acquisition should be governed primarily by the domestic law of the state. As long as such rules do not conflict with superior norms, it is the state conferring nationality which is best able to judge what conditions to impose to ensure that an effective link exists between the applicant for naturalisation and the systems of values and interests of the society with which he seeks to fully associate himself. That state is also able to decide whether these conditions have been complied with. Within these same limits, it is equally logical that the perceived needs of each state should determine the decision whether to facilitate naturalisation to a greater or less degree; and since a state's perceived needs do not remain static, it is quite natural that the conditions for naturalisation might be liberalised or restricted with the changed circumstances.

of the country or, although this is less clear, to require the applicant to "speak, write and read" the language.[197]

The majority thus felt that the requirement included in the draft amendment did not constitute discrimination for reasons of language because it was not unreasonable and disproportionate. One judge dissented to some extent in the final result, though for the most part he shared the majority's basic approach to the issue of citizenship and non-discrimination. His analysis provides further guidance on the various factors to consider when attempting to draw a fair balance between state interests and the individual right of non-discrimination.

Acknowledging the desirability that all Costa Ricans know and be able to communicate in Spanish, he noted that this did not mean that a state could simply use a language in complete disregard of other languages used by a large number of individuals in the country:

> [E]quality and non-discrimination cannot function in a vacuum nor, therefore, without the specific conditions of the society in which the people live. In this regard, my concern comes from the fact that there are among the country's own native-born people persons and substantial communities that do not know the Spanish language or that do not know it well, and that do not even speak that language as their native language: Indian communities that, although they are small and isolated, retain their ancestral languages and even resist learning or having to use the official language; and there is an important Costa Rican community of Jamaican origin that retains its language and many of whose members at least have problems in expressing themselves correctly in Spanish. Of course, the Costa Rican state, aware of the desirability and even the duty of preserving the native cultures and the rights of minorities in the country, is conducting programs of instruction and for promoting of the culture in the Indian languages and, recognising its cultural situation, has provided courts and public bureaus with official interpreters of those native or minority languages.[198]

These comments suggest that a reasonable and non-discriminatory naturalisation policy must reflect in a balanced way the population of a state: it cannot simply operate in a vacuum in complete disregard of the languages in actual use in the country. A direct corollary of this is that the presence of substantial speakers of a minority or non-official language must be acknowledged, especially if many of them are not fluent in the official/majority language.

The general reasoning in this case implies that it could very well be discriminatory to impose a language requirement in order to be entitled to citizenship, if for example a substantial percentage of the state's own inhabitants do not speak the required language. This would seem to indicate that to demand knowledge of the official or majority language for the acquisition of citizenship could well be discriminatory if 50, 40 or even 30 percent of a state's inhabitants primarily use another language.

Confirmation of the soundness of this view can be found in the practices of many states with substantial speakers of other languages. In Canada, knowledge of French or English is usually deemed necessary for naturalisation, even though French is the primary language of only 25 percent of the country's population.[199] In Switzerland, knowledge of Italian can be sufficient,

---

[197] Ibid., at paragraph 63.

[198] Ibid., at paragraph 23.

[199] Article 5(1)(c) of the **Citizenship Act.**

even if the number of citizens who speak Italian is around three percent. And even more flexible is Great Britain, where the **British Nationality Act**[200] acknowledges that citizenship can be acquired by those with a knowledge of either English, Gaelic or Welsh, a clear indication of the historical and traditional role of these linguistic minorities in British society as Gaelic is the primary language of probably less than one percent of the population.

As for judicial attitude in the United States, it is of little assistance in clarifying these issues for two main reasons: (1) the absence of language as a prohibited ground of discrimination in US law and the requirement of proof of discriminatory intent in many situations; (2) the refusal of some courts to examine whether government naturalisation policies are consistent with human rights standards.

US immigration and naturalisation laws contain a requirement of literacy in English for naturalised citizenship,[201] and a literacy requirement for admission to the United States.[202] The background of these provisions also reveal an unfortunate and dark side to US linguistic policies in the field of citizenship:

> Scholars began to conclude that supposed biological and cultural inferiorities, including linguistic differences, would preclude representatives of various nationalities or religious groups from ever being able to become what was called 100 percent Americans. These new immigrants were characterised, for example, by Edward Ross, a prominent academician and nativist, as "beaten men from beaten races representing the worst failures in the struggle for existence". The Yiddish, Italian, Serbo-Croatian and other tongues they brought with them confirmed their inability to assimilate in the eyes of nativists.[203]

US courts, including the US Supreme Court, have on occasion turned a blind eye to the human rights arguments, even when federal legislation was clearly motivated by racist concerns, as with a law that excluded Chinese immigrants from entering the country:

> If therefore, the government of the United States, through its legislative department considers the presence of foreigners of a different race in this country, who will not assimilate with us, to be dangerous to its peace and security, their exclusion is not to be stayed...[204]

Surprisingly, even contemporary US decisions reflect an unwillingness of judges to question whether government actions are subject to human rights considerations when involving citizenship matters. There are cases that take the view that citizenship is a privilege granted only when governmental interests are met, and that the government is free to attach any precondition

---

[200] Article 1, **British Nationality Act**, 1981, *Recueil des législations linguistiques, supra*, note 26, at pp. 133-132.

[201] See 8 U.S.C. 1423 (1988).

[202] See 8 U.S.C. 1182(25) (1988).

[203] Piatt, *supra*, note 80, at p. 12.

[204] **Chae Chan Ping v. United States**, 130 U.S. 581 (1889) (United States), at p. 606, quoted in Piatt, ibid., at p. 13.

it deems appropriate,[205] or that it may withhold naturalisation upon any ground or without any reason.[206] In theory, even a "White-only" immigration policy would not be objectionable in the US unless courts adopt a different approach closer to international standards.

Nevertheless, there are perhaps indications of a growing realisation that the current US approach to citizenship matters should be reconsidered. For example, it has been observed that English language requirements are not a neutral requirement and that they will particularly disadvantage certain individuals to an extent that could be discriminatory:

> The requirement favours permanent resident aliens from national origins and ethnic groups that speak the English language. It is assumed than the immigrant from England or Scotland finds this requirement less burdensome than the immigrant from Eastern Europe, Japan, or Mexico. True enough, the requirement nonetheless applies to the Scot and Englishman, but the advantage of being able to speak the language is itself significant. This disproportionate impact feature is in line with what is argued here to be a stigmatizing intent and impact in the law. This view is developed further in subsequent discussion.[207]

The above quoted scholar further suggests that in the case of Spanish-speaking individuals, an English literacy requirement in particular is an unreasonable demand:

> The assumption is that in enacting the English literacy requirement of the naturalisation process, Congress intended to disadvantage persons of non-English speaking national origins or ethnic groups and that this fixes a "badge of opprobrium on citizens of the same ancestry." For example, in the view of this writer an obstacle to citizenship that affects resident aliens of Mexican ancestry because of their mother tongue is necessarily a reflection on the value the government places on Chicano citizens with the identical mother tongue. The English literacy requirement is an embodiment of a governmental attitude that Chicano citizens, because Spanish is their primary language, are less worthy citizens than those whose native tongue is English.[208]

The weakness in the traditional US position, in light of the reasoning adopted by the Inter-American Court of Human Rights in the **Costa Rican Naturalisation Case**, is that it is probably not objectionable *in se* for a state to impose a language requirement which reflects the actual composition of its inhabitants. In the United States, where the vast majority of people either have English as a primary language or at least know the language, the English language requirement would seem to be similar to the Costa Rican context, and it would seem difficult to argue that the US policy is so unreasonable as to be discriminatory, especially since a government's margin of appreciation in naturalisation matters is probably very wide.

There is however one deficiency in the US regulations that is possibly unreasonable and therefore discriminatory. As indicated in the **Costa Rican Naturalisation Case**, naturalisation

---

[205] **In re Thanner**, 253 F.Supp. 283 (1966) (United States), at pp. 285-86.

[206] See **In re Quintana**, 203 F.Supp. 376 (1962) (United States), at p. 378.

[207] Gonzalez Cedillo, Ricardo (1983), "A Constitutional Analysis of the English Literacy Requirement of the Naturalization Act", in *St. Mary's Law Journal*, Vol. 14, 899-936, at pp. 919-920.

[208] Ibid., at p. 922.

policies must not be adopted in a vacuum: they must reflect the true conditions of the society in which people live. In the United States, Spanish is the most widely used language in the country after English. It is long-established in the country, predating even English, and its use in the media, government and communities is substantial. Arguably, one could contend that US legislation is inadequate by not considering the fact that millions of its own citizens speak mainly Spanish and not English. A more balanced response for US naturalisation policy would thus appear to require either Spanish or English fluency, just as have done many countries mentioned earlier with substantial populations of non-official or non-majority language speakers.

6.4.3   *Naturalisation as a Corrective Process?*

An extremely sensitive situation involving language and citizenship considerations has arisen in a number of countries formerly part of the Soviet Union. Especially in the Baltic states of Latvia, Lithuania, and Estonia, governments have had to decide how to deal with the demographic changes brought about during the Soviet era and how to redress the consequences of Soviet migration and linguistic policies when looking at their naturalisation policies. In the process, some states appear to have gone to extremes that may prove to be a source of tension and continuing conflict, partly because they are contentious in light of human rights standards.

In many of the newly independent states of the former Soviet Union, large numbers of Russian- and Ukrainian-speakers were ordered to move to the Baltic, Siberian and Central Asian regions of the empire in order to build and operate industries, or were stationed there as soldiers. Furthermore, it was undoubtedly a strategy of Josef Stalin to dilute the ethnic composition of parts of the Soviet Union and to punish some groups — such as the Chechens — by forcibly removing them from what had been their traditional homelands.

As a consequence of these policies, large numbers of Russian-speaking individuals were born and now live in countries where they are now seen as "occupiers" or "foreigners" because they are not descendants of the original inhabitants of the state, although most of them were given no choice during the Soviet era.

Essentially, two types of naturalisation approaches were followed: the "zero option" which permitted all individuals normally resident in the new country the option to acquire citizenship (Lithuania, Moldova, Kazakhstan); and the "indigenous option" which granted quasi-automatic citizenship to the original inhabitants of the country before Soviet rule (Estonia, Latvia[209]) and their descendants, whilst subjecting anyone else to a series of linguistic and residency requirements. It is also the latter approach that has proved to be particularly offensive for some and a source of friction between Russia and a few of her neighbours. States which have chosen the zero option appear to have largely avoided these problems.

On the one hand, it is maintained on occasion that the measures adopted by authorities having chosen the "indigenous option" are necessary:

Since the national identity of Estonians is intimately linked to their language, which is not spoken anywhere else in the world, it is important and legitimate for Estonians to give a

---

[209] Latvia has also set quotas on the number of new citizens to be accepted each year.

high priority to the active use of the Estonian language in all spheres of activity in Estonia.[210]

According to this point of view, steps must be taken to correct the legacy of the Soviet era and to preserve and strengthen Latvian and Estonian identity, especially its linguistic aspect. Therefore, individuals seeking citizenship must show an interest in becoming integrated into Latvian or Estonian society by acquiring a basic knowledge of the language of the original majority. For example, Article 2 of the 10 February 1993 **Law on Estonian Language Requirements for Applicants for Citizenship** adopted by the *Riigikogu* (the Estonian Parliament) stipulates that applicants for citizenship must: (a) have a listening comprehension of general information and official statements; (b) be able to hold a conversation; (c) be able to read and comprehend texts written in everyday language; (d) be able to compose standard applications in writing, be able to fill out applications and other forms, and be able to compose a curriculum vitae. Article 3 excludes certain categories of people from completing an examination on their level of language fluency.

On the other hand, it is questionable whether some aspects of these language requirements are appropriate given the demographic realities of Latvia and Estonia. As objectionable as may have been Soviet practices, most of the Russian-, Ukrainian- or Belarussian- speakers now living in Estonia and Latvia were mere pawns in the process, and most of them were born there or have no families, jobs or homes elsewhere. It also appears that the linguistic requirements for citizenship will exclude the majority of the population of non-Estonian or non-Latvian origin from becoming citizens in the near future since it would likely be a matter of years until most of the population of non-Estonian or non-Latvian origin would reach the required level of proficiency, even after intensive language training.

Indeed, it is rather naive to believe that it is a simple matter to acquire any type of proficiency in a few years when many Russian-speakers in these countries live in communities where there is very little opportunity to practice extensively the Estonian or Latvian language on a regular and consistent basis. In Latvia, the proportion of native speakers of the language has gone from about 75 percent in 1935 to just under 52 percent in 1989. This means that speakers of Russian as a primary language are probably close to half of the total population of the country. Much of the north-east of Estonia is largely Russian-speaking, and few of them presently qualify for citizenship.[211] In these two countries, the reality is that it is highly unlikely for a non-native speaker of Latvian or Estonian to acquire more than a minimal knowledge of either language within a few short years unless he or she has the time and resources to dedicate himself or herself intensively to the task. This is however unlikely scenario for a labourer or factory worker living in predominantly Russian-speaking regions.[212]

---

[210] *Situation of Human Rights in Estonia and Latvia — Report of the Secretary General* (1993), United Nations Publications, New York, at p. 10.

[211] Ibid., at p. 10: "In Narva only approximately 7,000 of the 85,000 population are Estonian citizens; in Sillamäe only 600 of the 21,000 population are Estonian citizens."

[212] There is a growing realisation of the unrealistic expectations. See ibid., at p. 10:

Although four years have elapsed since the adoption of the language law, only a relatively small percentage of ethnic Russians, Belarussians and Ukrainians living in Estonia have learned the Estonian language during this period. It appears that the former Estonian SSR did not adequately implement the law and that conditions for effective bilingualism were not created. In this

Thus, despite the pronouncements of some legal scholars, it is incorrect to maintain that each state is completely free to determine the conditions for acquiring citizenship.[213] The Inter-American Court of Human Rights was unambiguous in holding that the naturalisation process was still subject to basic human rights such as non-discrimination on the ground of language, and that due regard had to be given to the situation existing in every state in deciding whether linguistic citizenship requirements are reasonable.

In the case of the language requirements in Estonia and Latvia, it is probably not unreasonable or disproportionate to recognise automatically Latvian or Estonian citizenship for those who possessed it prior to Soviet annexation in 1940 and their descendants, even if they do not have to demonstrate proficiency in Estonian or Latvian. It has been shown in section 4.5 that a state preference or distinction that favours some individuals and not others can still be deemed reasonable in light of the need of a *lingua franca*, to compensate for or correct past injustices, or in recognition of the cultural or historical importance of a language.

However, there is room for misgivings about the provisions which require sufficient knowledge of the Latvian or Estonian language. The exclusive preference given to Latvian and Estonian seems a perhaps disproportionate and unreasonable means in an attempt to rectify past Soviet practices, bearing in mind the number of permanent residents who are not of Estonian or Latvian "ethnic origin" but who were born in Estonia or Latvia. The consequences of the denial of citizenship appears particularly onerous because it affects very large groups of individuals who really have no other home.

Furthermore, it is a mistake to disregard the historical reality of the position of the Russian language in both countries. Before the Soviet invasion, Russian-speakers constituted about eight percent of the total population of Latvia, and 10.5 percent in Estonia. Whether one looks at the situation in 1940, or at the situation as it is today, the Estonian- and Latvian-only language requirements appear disproportionate since they do not take into account "the specific conditions of the society in which the people live" or the presence "among the country's own native-born people persons and substantial communities that do not know the...language or that do not know it well" as was suggested necessary in order to avoid a discriminatory naturalisation policy in the **Costa Rican Naturalisation Case.**

There is finally some historical support for the argument that Estonian and Latvian naturalisation processes are too rigid. In one case, the Permanent Court of International Justice observed that the acquisition of citizenship was of supreme importance under the system of human rights guarantees affecting minorities:

In Article 3, which supplements Article 91 of the Peace Treaty of Versailles, it declares in the first place to be Polish nationals, subject to a right of individual option, all German nationals habitually resident in the territories incorporated in Poland... In the second place, under Article 4, it grants the same nationality to persons born in the above-mentioned territories, that is to say, originating from these territories, provided they are born of parents habitually resident there, and that they do not renounce, within a period of two years, the nationality which they have acquired. In laying down the condition with regard to the

_____

connection the Mission also observes that some Russian-speaking local authorities apparently did not take the necessary steps to give priority to the learning of the Estonian language in their communities in preparation for Estonian citizenship.

[213] *Supra*, note 160, at p. 239.

residence of the parents the authors of the Treaty desired to reduce as far as possible the element of chance. A birth occurring in a family established in the territory, on the regular and permanent footing presupposed by habitual residence, would not be an accidental circumstance taking place during a temporary sojourn or visit. The establishment of his parents in the territory on this basis creates between the child and his place of birth a moral link which justifies the grant to him of the nationality of this country; it strengthens and supplements the material bond already created by the fact of his birth.[214]

In a situation where individuals have established some type of permanence in a country that subsequently underwent territorial changes (or arguably a change of status), it was deemed reasonable to accommodate their presence instead of penalising them because they were not of the right language (or religion). Individuals who habitually reside in a country thus probably demonstrate the type of bond that may be sufficient to warrant the acquisition of citizenship. At the very least, this suggests that in some regards the linguistic requirements for naturalisation in countries such as the US, Estonia and Latvia may be too restrictive and in breach of the prohibition of discrimination.[215]

6.5   SUMMARY

Freedom of expression, non-discrimination, and the right of members of a linguistic minority to use their language with other members of their group are clear human rights which a state must respect in its actions and in providing services and benefits. State conduct is thus subjected to certain fundamental limits deemed essential in terms of respect for all human beings as well as to maintain social peace and order.

In practice, these three rights may interact, mingle and complement each other in a number of areas. As far as general use of a single official or majority language by public authorities is concerned, the prohibition against discrimination prohibits invocation of an "official language" policy by a state as a shield against the need to respond to any language demands from its population. Official language should never be seen as permitting exclusive use of a language in complete disregard for fundamental human rights.

As far as the human right which has the greatest impact when a state is involved in offering services or any type of advantage or benefit to individuals, it appears the prohibition of discrimination is of major significance. When considering what constitutes a non-discriminatory language preference by state authorities, a "sliding-scale model" offers a practical formula which is able to take into account important factors such as the number of speakers of a language, their territorial concentration, the level of public services being sought, the disadvantages, burdens or benefits a state's linguistic practice imposes on individuals, and even a state's human and material resources. In essence, it means that the level of services provided by public authorities

---

[214] **Advisory Opinion on Certain Questions, Arising Out of the Application of Article 4 of the Polish Minorities Treaty (Polish Nationality Case),** (1923) Permanent Court of International Justice, Series B, No. 7, at p. 18.

[215] The United Nations Human Rights Committee recently indicated that the naturalisation criteria in Latvia excluding large numbers of non-Latvian speakers from citizenship could be considered discriminatory. See UN Doc. CCPR/C/79/Add.53 of 26 July 1995.

in a given language must, by and large, reflect the relative numerical strength of the population in a municipality, district, region or province which uses this language.

Since judicial proceedings are conducted as part of a state's structure, they can also be described as a state "service" or activity. But in addition to going through the same balancing process of the sliding-scale model when considering whether a state's linguistic preferences are consistent with the prohibition of discrimination, there are situations where a state is obliged to make some type of concession in language matters even if only one individual is adversely affected by the language of proceedings chosen by a state. Because of the very serious consequences of criminal proceedings, it is universally recognised that an accused who does not understand the language of proceedings must have the right to the free assistance of an interpreter. In this and in a few other examples of a state's obligations in judicial matters, even if it only involves a single individual, it can be said that the disadvantage suffered by one person with no or little knowledge of the language of court proceedings is so serious that a state can never derogate from the obligation to provide some compensation for the inequality suffered, through means of an appropriate degree of interpretation services.

Where a state provides public education, the prohibition of discrimination also imposes generally a duty to offer instruction in the languages spoken by its population to a level that roughly corresponds to the number of speakers of a language. This is the so-called sliding-scale model. Once again, this approach is linked to the advantages derived from being able to use one's primary language. Children are clearly disadvantaged, or do not receive the same benefit, if some are not educated in the language with which they are most comfortable. It then becomes a matter of determining if a state's conduct is a reasonable measure when considering the degree of disadvantage, the goals of the state's policy, the number of individuals adversely affected, etc.

Because of the need to balance the various rights and interests involved, and because of the ultimate aim of attaining factual as well as legal equality, the prohibition of discrimination in public education can never be invoked in an attempt to deprive children the benefits of learning the official or majority language of the state in which they live. This means that even though the prohibition of discrimination may call for the use of a non-official or minority language as the exclusive or quasi-exclusive medium of instruction in appropriate circumstances, it cannot be used to support an educational policy which would isolate these individuals in "linguistic ghettos" and exclude them completely from other benefits that may only be available in the official or majority language. In other words, all individuals should at least have the opportunity to learn the official or majority language, even if the medium of instruction used in public schools is different.

Private schools which use a minority language as the medium of instruction are an example of the combined effects of non-discrimination and the right of members of a minority to use their language with other members of their group. The latter right means that a state must allow these schools to open and operate freely, although public authorities are entitled to impose requirements as to appropriate academic standards and may also require that all students attain a reasonable level of proficiency in the official or majority language. This last aspect again reflects the application of non-discrimination in order to avoid the creation of linguistic ghettos to the ultimate disadvantage of pupils in private minority language schools.

States are not obligated to provide financial or other resources to private schools. If they do, private schools using a minority language as medium of instruction should also be entitled to these benefits in conformity with the prohibition of discrimination. Because non-discrimination should not be confused with identical treatment, a state may legitimately find it desirable to provide greater resources to minority schools in recognition of the higher costs, the more numerous difficulties in operating such establishments, or the need to compensate for previous disadvantageous state practices and policies towards the minority.

The public/private divide is also relevant when dealing with the issue of the language of the media. In the case of public media, such as state owned or operated television, radio or publications, the prohibition of discrimination in language matters requires that the level and type of these benefits or services be generally available in direct proportion to the number and concentration of speakers of a specific language.

As for private operations, freedom of expression would demand that state authorities not interfere in the language of the media. Some additional requirement such as a degree of bilingualism could be imposed on private media, as long as it does not constitute an obstacle to the free use of language as a constituent of freedom of expression, and as long as it does not impose a discriminatory requirement by imposing unacceptable burdens or disadvantages to which others are not subjected. If a state provides some form of assistance to private media, it follows that private media operating in a minority language should also be eligible for these resources in a non-discriminatory way, although the prohibition of discrimination allows for a flexible formula permitting states to tailor such assistance in ways that suit its social and factual background.

In the case of linguistic minorities, the entitlement of members to use their language with other members of their group would appear to signify that they should always have the right to private media, although this does not impose on a state the obligation to provide the resources to make this possible. One exception to this principle exists in the allocation of telecommunications frequencies for radio or television. Since such frequencies are generally considered to be public resources, the balancing of a linguistic minority's right for its members to freely use their language amongst themselves and a state's control of the only means to apply this in the field of private radio or television would seem to be particularly troublesome. However, the allocation of public radio or television frequencies raises the issue of non-discrimination. It therefore imposes a duty on a state to ensure that linguistic minorities have access to an appropriate number and type of frequencies, but not an unfettered number since frequencies constitute a public good to which minorities cannot claim unrestrained ownership.

Finally, no area of state activity falls naturally outside the protection of human rights. This becomes particularly important when dealing with naturalisation matters which until recently were mistakenly thought to be immune from the scope of the prohibition of discrimination. On the contrary, naturalisation is clearly subject to fundamental human rights such as non-discrimination on the ground of language. Any decision as to citizenship and naturalisation must reflect a proportionate and reasonable outcome in light of a state's interests and goals, the linguistic composition of its population, and the interests, rights and impact on the individual(s) affected.

7. Indigenous Peoples and Language[1]

> Language is a gift from the Creator. Embodied in aboriginal language is our unique relationship to the Creator, our attitudes, beliefs, values, and the fundamental notion of what is truth.[2]

Rights such as freedom of expression, non-discrimination and the right of members of linguistic minorities to use their language with other members of their group supply a tapestry of what appears to be a generally accepted fundamental degree of protection for individuals in a large number of areas, but they are all essentially individual rights. The object of these rights is not to protect or ensure the development of the language of any group per se, although they may indirectly have this effect, especially in dealing with larger linguistic communities.

There do however appear to be certain communities that may be able to claim additional rights beyond what these individual rights normally provide. This chapter will examine the case of indigenous peoples, who are increasingly perceived in international and national law as being entitled to "special considerations" that include the possibility of various degrees of political autonomy and other measures in order to protect and even revitalise their cultures, communities and languages.

7.1   PRELIMINARY REMARKS

As with other individuals, members of indigenous peoples[3] may claim that they are treated in

---

[1] An earlier version of this chapter has appeared in the Murdoch University School of Law Electronic Law Journal, April 1995, as an article entitled "Indigenous Peoples and Language".

[2] *The Aboriginal Language Policy Study — Phase II: Implementation Mechanism* (1988), National Indian Brotherhood, Ottawa, at p. 91.

[3] It should be remarked that in international law, most of the rights ascribed to "indigenous peoples" are also ascribed to "tribal peoples", but that both groups lack a clear definition. In fact, many scholars are at pains to truly distinguish "indigenous" peoples from long-established minorities such as the Basques, Berbers or Karens. In Alfredsson, Gudmundur (1990), *Report on Equality and Non-Discrimination: Minority Rights*, Council of Europe, Strasbourg, at p. 15, it is claimed that the "crucial factor in the definition of indigenous peoples is their original inhabitation of the land on which, unlike the minorities, they have lived from time immemorial". However, if this were true, the Basques would constitute an indigenous people. More realistically, one scholar has admitted that it is difficult to find a valid explanation to exclude some groups whilst admitting others. See Hannum, Hurst (1988), "New Developments in Indigenous Rights", in *Virginia Journal of International Law*, Vol. 28, 649-678, at p. 664:

> Some governments, such as India and Bangladesh, wanted to limit the definition to those peoples in the Western Hemisphere and Australasia. Ultimately, the Working Group opted for a "flexible" approach to avoid formal adoption of a definition. Nonetheless, the governments of China, the USSR, India, and Bangladesh continued to equate indigenousness and colonisation, thereby denying that there are any "indigenous" peoples within their territories. Despite efforts to suggest that only those peoples invaded by European colonial powers or their descendants are "indigenous", it seems clear that Asian hill tribes such as the Karen and Hmong, and Arab

a disadvantageous manner if public authorities and the resources of the state are not responsive to their demands for equal treatment and non-discrimination in respect to language. Whether or not the state's behaviour should be deemed discriminatory will depend upon factors such as demographic considerations, whether the indigenous language exists in written form, the financial resources of the government, the type and level of services demanded in the indigenous language, etc.

Furthermore, if an indigenous people is numerically less than 50 percent of a state's total population, it objectively is a numerical minority and is thus entitled to the rights guaranteed to minorities under Article 27 of the **International Covenant on Civil and Political Rights**,[4] including the right to establish and operate its own schools, using its language as medium of instruction, free from government intervention, or assistance. This has been confirmed in cases which have gone before the United Nations Human Rights Committee, such as **Lovelace v. Canada**,[5] **Ominayak v. Canada**,[6] and **Kitok v. Sweden**.[7] It has also been confirmed by the Inter-American Commission on Human Rights in the Miskito case.[8] The Commission considered the Miskitos of Nicaragua as a minority community, despite its best efforts to avoid using the term "minority".[9] Finally, if the freedom of expression of any indigenous person were restricted, this would also constitute a breach of widely accepted human rights standards.

Moreover, it appears increasingly accepted that indigenous peoples are entitled to preferential treatment in linguistic affairs, relative to that afforded to other individuals. This is due not to their position as a minority, which they may not necessarily constitute in some states, but to the acknowledgment in international law, as well as in some national jurisdictions, that they occupy a unique political and legal niche, with corresponding "privileges" not necessarily available to others.

---

and African nomadic tribes, who pursue traditional life-styles, should also be included in a commonsense understanding of "indigenous." Less certain would be the inclusion of Central Asian peoples such as the Armenians, Baluchis, Tatars, and Kurds, or survivors of overland invasions by peoples of similar ethnicity, such as occurred in Africa and much of Asia.
See also generally *Study of the Problem of Discrimination Against Indigenous Populations, José R. Martinez Cobo, Special Rapporteur* (1987), United Nations Publications, New York.

[4] (1966) United Nations Treaty Series, Vol. 999.

[5] Communication 24/1977, UN Document A/36/40.

[6] Communication 167/1984, UN Document A/42/40.

[7] Communication 197/1985, UN Document A/43/40.

[8] **Report of the Commission on the Situation of Human Rights of a Segment of the Nicaraguan Population of Miskito Origin and Resolution on the Friendly Settlement Procedure Regarding the Human Rights Situation of a Segment of the Nicaraguan Population of Miskito Origin,** OEA/Ser.L/V/II.62, Document 26, 1984.

[9] Indigenous peoples often resent being identified as a minority because most of their demands are not based on their status as a numerical minority, but as a political entity whose sovereignty they maintain has never been completely surrendered. Therefore, they feel that to present their demands couched in terms of a minority issue risks weakening the political nature of their status and claims.

7.2   HISTORICAL OVERVIEW

7.2.1 *The Languages of Indigenous Peoples in International Law*

The recognition that indigenous peoples ought to be treated differently is not a new phenomenon. At the close of the nineteenth century there were already international conferences dealing with Africa and its native tribes (in Berlin in 1884-85 and in Brussels 1889-90). The **Covenant of the League of Nations**[10] contained a provision which in essence recognised that states had a fiduciary-type responsibility to assist "peoples not yet able to stand by themselves under the strenuous conditions of the modern world": therein "well-being and development" was seen as a "sacred trust of civilisation". States were also obliged to "undertake to secure just treatment of the native inhabitants of territories under their control".[11]

However, prior to and immediately following the Second World War, most international instruments remained silent on the issue of any special status or rights pertaining to indigenous peoples. The only real exceptions were the instruments of the International Labour Organisation (ILO), which began its work on the treatment of indigenous peoples in the 1920s. Beginning in 1926 with a committee of experts on native labour, the ILO then constituted a series of treaties involving some issues relevant to indigenous peoples, including **Convention (No. 29) on Forced Labour; Convention (No. 50) on Recruitment of Indigenous Workers; Convention (No. 64) on Contracts of Employment (Indigenous Workers)**, and **Convention (No. 65) on Penal Sanctions (Indigenous Works)**.[12]

It was not until some years after the Second World War that international interest in the rights of indigenous peoples increased dramatically, culminating in a study in 1953 which would ultimately pave the way for the first comprehensive international treaty to recognise the need for some concessions in respect to the use of indigenous languages.

The languages used by members of indigenous peoples appeared as a legal concern for the first time in 1957 in the ILO **Convention (No. 107) Concerning the Protection and Integration of Indigenous and Other Tribal and Semi-Tribal Populations in Independent Countries**.[13] The prevailing tone of the treaty is clearly assimilationist, as it deals mostly with methods by which to permit the use of indigenous languages as a temporary measure prior to the adoption by indigenous peoples of "modern" languages and the cultures of dominant Western-based populations. For example, Article 23 of the **Convention** provides that a state's educational programmes should be adapted to the stage that the indigenous populations have reached in their social, economic and cultural integration into the national community.

As one author has pointed out:

> The degree of logical coherence between a commitment to preserve a language, and one to secure its gradual elimination from use is not great. The commitment to preserve is, to be

---

[10] (1934) 7 Hudson, World Court Reports 10.

[11] See Articles 22 and 23 quoted in an excellent paper by Lerner, Nathan (1992), "The 1989 ILO Convention on Indigenous Populations: New Standards?", in Yoram Dinstein and Mala Tabory (eds.), *The Protection of Minorities and Human Rights*, Martinus Nijhoff, Dordrecht, Netherlands, at p. 214.

[12] Ibid.

[13] See Section 2.1.10 in the Appendix.

sure, only to preserve as far as possible so that the balance is tipped in favour of elimination.[14]

Even if it is recognised in the **Convention** that indigenous children should be taught to read and write in their mother tongue or in the main vernacular language of the community, it is only a temporary measure until the transition from the mother tongue to the national or official languages of the country takes place in a "progressive" way. Some thirty years later, the **Convention** appears to be out of date and far removed from the prevailing views of indigenous peoples and, perhaps, many state governments.

At the United Nations, two more recent initiatives demonstrate a growing awareness of and interest in the special needs and position of indigenous peoples. In 1971, the UN Sub-Commission on the Prevention of Discrimination and the Protection of Minorities appointed Mexican Ambassador José R. Martinez Cobo to undertake a study on the problem of discrimination against indigenous populations. As shall be seen below, the influential report of the Special Rapporteur contains an in-depth analysis of many issues beyond that of discrimination. Moreover, a Working Group of the UN Sub-Commission was formed in May 1982 to review developments relating to indigenous peoples and to submit conclusions and recommendations as to appropriate measures to promote respect for their human rights and fundamental freedoms. The Working Group's efforts led to a draft **Declaration on the Rights of Indigenous Peoples** in August 1994 which was forwarded to the UN Commission on Human Rights. In 1995, the UN Commission decided to set up a special working group for a further review of the draft declaration.[15]

Following the United Nations initiatives, and in reaction to increasing criticism directed towards the **1957 ILO Convention**, the International Labour Organisation convened in 1986 a meeting of experts, which eventually led to the adoption in 1989 of the **ILO Convention (No. 169) Concerning Indigenous and Tribal Peoples in Independent Countries** (the "**1989 ILO Convention**").[16]

The trend towards guaranteeing state support for greater use of indigenous languages becomes apparent in this instrument. Gone is the urgency to integrate completely indigenous peoples at the expense of their own language and culture. The word "integration" is eliminated from the preamble and replaced with an expressed need to adopt "new international standards...with a view to removing integrationist orientation of the earlier standards". The preamble goes on to recognise the aspirations of indigenous peoples to exercise control over their own institutions, ways of life and economic development, which includes the maintenance and development of their identities, languages and religions.

---

[14] Thornberry, Patrick (1991), *International Law and the Rights of Minorities*, Clarendon Press, Oxford, United Kingdom, at p. 362.

[15] The most recent draft is UN Doc. E/CN.4/Sub.2/1994/56 reprinted in Section 1.1.2 of the Appendix. Some states have raised a number of concerns on the content of the draft, with Malaysia, Bangladesh and Indonesia amongst others claiming that they would be favourably inclined towards adopting the draft declaration if it was clear that there are no indigenous peoples on their territories. The actual adoption of the draft may still be a matter of several years because of these controversies.

[16] See Section 2.1.11 in the Appendix.

The **1989 ILO Convention** then goes on to identify how states must respect the language rights of indigenous peoples. Generally, Article 2 provides that governments have the responsibility to develop (with the participation of the peoples concerned) action to protect their rights, and stresses the need for respect for their social and cultural identity, their customs and traditions and their institutions, including obviously their linguistic component.

Perhaps the most revealing provision is Article 28, which provides that:

1. Children belonging to the peoples concerned shall, wherever practicable, be taught to read and write in their own indigenous language or in the language most commonly used by the group to which they belong. When this is not practicable, the competent authorities shall undertake consultations with these peoples with a view to the adoption of measures to achieve this objective.
2. Adequate measures shall be taken to ensure that these peoples have the opportunity to attain fluency in the national language or in one of the official languages of the country.
3. Measures shall be taken to preserve and promote the development and practice of the indigenous languages of the peoples concerned.

From complete integration to practical accommodation in language matters, the trend at the international level is quite clear. Although indigenous peoples are still required to learn the official or majority language of the state in which they live, they are no longer to be forced into abandoning their own language and culture. On the contrary, states would appear to have under the treaty the obligation to provide resources so that indigenous children can learn their ancestral language whenever it is practical. In fact, if the most recent international initiative on indigenous peoples (the UN draft **Declaration on the Rights of Indigenous Peoples**) is any indication, the obligations of states towards such peoples may be even greater than those towards individuals under traditional human rights, even extending to a government responsibility to support and provide resources for the revitalisation of indigenous languages.

7.2.2 *The Languages of Indigenous Peoples and State Practices*

As explained in the historical introduction of this study, reactions and attitudes of various colonisers and governments towards the presence of indigenous peoples varied with time as did the relative strength and political power of such peoples. In some cases, the use of indigenous languages was approved of and even encouraged in order to ensure the conversion of non-Christian communities. In other cases, it was easier for missionaries to learn widespread indigenous languages in order to attain the objective sought. Indigenous languages in Latin America thus moved from an initial position of favour, in order to facilitate conversion efforts and the administration of territories, to an increasingly repressive situation which came about as the position of indigenous peoples weakened:

After the 1812 War with the United States, British colonisers no longer required aboriginal peoples as allies — or for that matter, as explorers or traders. Their value rapidly diminished, with the result that aboriginal tribes became stigmatised as obstacles to the progressive settlement of Canadian society. Moreover, by refusing to relinquish their identity and assimilate into "higher levels" of "civilisation", aboriginal peoples were dismissed as an inferior and unequal species whose rights could be trampled on with impunity... A policy of assimilation evolved as part of this project to subdue and subordinate aboriginal peoples. From the early nineteenth century on, elimination of the "Indian problem" was one of the colony's — later the Dominion's — foremost concerns. Authorities rejected extermination as a solution, but focused instead on a planned process of cultural change known as assimilation. Through assimilation, the dominant sector sought to undermine the cultural distinctiveness of aboriginal tribal society; to subject the indigenes to the rules, values and sanctions of Euro-Canadian society; and to absorb the de-cultured minority into the mainstream through a process of "anglo-conformity". The means to achieve this outward compliance with Euro-Canadian society lay in the hands of missionaries, teachers, and law-makers.[17]

In the US, teachers speaking only English were employed and instructed to assimilate indigenous children into the majority-controlled society. These children were punished — they were beaten or had their mouths washed out with soap — if they lapsed into their native language: "at the boarding schools many of them were forced to attend by a government which at times withheld food from parents who wanted to keep their children at home."[18]

Similar methods were widely used in countries all over the world in an effort to mould individuals belonging to non-dominant groups, specifically minorities and indigenous peoples. This occurred particularly after the seventeenth century as states intervened more and more directly into what had previously been community-oriented activities, including education:

> In 1812 the government junta advised schoolteachers that Spanish was the language of the classroom and to banish Guaraní from school usage. "In school the use of Guaraní in class hours was prohibited. To enforce this rule, teachers distributed to monitors bronze rings which were given to anyone found conversing in Guaraní... [On] Saturday, return of the

---

[17] Quoted in de Varennes, Fernand (1994), "L'article 35 de la Loi constitutionnelle de 1982 et la protection des droits linguistiques des peuples autochtones", in *National Journal of Constitutional Law*, Vol. 4, N° 3, 265-303, at p. 274.

[18] Baron, Dennis E. (1990), *The English-Only Question: An Official Language for Americans?*, Yale University Press, New Haven, USA, at p. 165; see also *Language of Inequality* (1985), N. Wolfson and J. Manes (eds.), Mouton Publishers, Berlin, at p. 174; and Piatt, Bill (1990), *¿Only English? Law and Language Policy in the United States*, University of New Mexico Press, Albuquerque, USA, at pp. 4-5:

> Policies of European colonists and succeeding American administrations, some of which can only be considered genocidal, often resulted in the extermination of the native peoples and languages. We are all too familiar with the long saga of oppression and brutalization resulting in the herding of native Americans onto isolated reservations. This herding, and the subsequent attempts to force native children into an English-speaking educational system and environment, sought to achieve the so-called civilisation of these peoples including the replacement of their native tongues with English. In the case of the conquistadors and their accompanying religious figures, the civilising language was Spanish.

rings was requested and each one caught with a ring was punished with four or five lashes".[19]

The Sami people in Scandinavia were submitted to many of the same techniques. For example, from the second part of the nineteenth century, Norwegian authorities carried out a policy of assimilation in education as part of the Norwegian nation-building process in which the idea of "one nation - one language" played a prominent role. This was followed by other measures involving state language preferences, which were to have a highly destructive impact on Sami society:

> In 1902, a law was passed to the effect that state-owned land in Finnmark could be sold or hired only to Norwegian citizens who were able to speak, read and write the Norwegian language and who used this language in everyday life. This regulation was primarily directed against Finnish immigrants, but its impact on the Sami population was at least as severe.[20]

Before European settlement of Australia, there were approximately 250 Aboriginal and Torres Strait Islander languages in the continent. Approximately one third of these continue to be spoken by some people, however, many are spoken only by a handful of older individuals. Their disappearance has nothing to do with their inability to adapt to the context of a technologically driven society, but much to do with repressive, even genocidal, actions by public authorities or members of the dominant majority:

> Every turn in policy of government and the practice of the non-[Aboriginal and Torres Strait Islander] community was postulated on the inferiority of the Aboriginal people; the original expropriation of their land was based on the idea that the land was not occupied and the people uncivilised; the protection policy was based on the view that Aboriginal people could not achieve a place in the non-[Aboriginal and Torres Strait Islander] society and that they must be protected against themselves while the race died out; the assimilationist policy assumed that their culture and way of life is without value and that we confer a favour on them by assimilating them into our ways; even to the point of taking their children and removing them from family.[21]

Such a scenario, recurrently experienced by indigenous peoples worldwide, must be understood in terms of economic and political power in addition to the legal manifestations of such power: the invading population group would take control of the land from indigenous peoples in order to exploit local resources and to establish effective political power over the territory. With consolidation of power and control over recently acquired territories, the conquering authorities

---

[19] Rubin, J.(1968), *National Bilingualism in Paraguay*, Mouton, den Haag, Netherlands, at p. 480.

[20] Vikør, Lars S. (1993), *The Nordic Languages: Their Status and Interrelations*, Novus Press, Oslo, at p. 90.

[21] Quoted in *Language and Culture: A Matter of Survival* (1992), Australian Government Publishing Service, Canberra, at p. 17.

found it expedient at times to impose their way of life upon indigenous populations, whose traditions they often considered primitive, in order to support the legitimacy of their own claims of ownership and dominion.[22]

Thus, many of the policies affecting indigenous peoples were based upon the assumption that indigenous populations, cultures and languages would eventually disappear naturally or by absorption into other segments of the population and the emerging national culture of the new state:

> It was expected that the indigenous languages would disappear...in the face of the dynamism, the equality and the attraction of the official languages — international languages which were assumed to have real or imaginary advantages of all kinds, and were considered particularly suited to science, technology, art and civilisation. For that reason, no stress was laid on state plans to teach the indigenous languages or use them as languages of instruction for some of the initial phases of education. That was assumed to be contrary to the best interests of those societies and involved danger for national unity, since it was feared that it would lead inevitably to linguistic insularity and excessive social and political fragmentation.[23]

By the beginning of the second half of this century, however, national attitudes had begun to undergo a marked shift contemporaneously to changing international attitudes and standards on the issue of the appropriate legal and institutional response to the presence of indigenous peoples and their languages. Mexico was the scene of serious discussions during the 1950s suggesting that it was inappropriate to teach in Spanish in an environment where the mother tongue was an indigenous language. By the middle 1960s, the principle of early literacy in the native language plus the teaching of Spanish as a second language became the official policy of the Mexican

---

[22] Torres, Raidza (1991), "The Rights of Indigenous Populations: The Emerging International Norm", in *Yale Journal of International Law*, Vol. 16, 127-175, at p. 133.

[23] *Study of the Problem of Discrimination Against Indigenous Populations*, supra, note 3, at p. 11. See also *Derecho Indigena y Derechos Humanos en América Latina* (1988), Rodolfo Stavenhagen (ed.), Instituto Interamericano de Derechos Humanos and El Colegio de México, México, at pp. 346-347:

> *Hasta qué punto una política educativa respetuosa de las culturas indígenas y que tienda a potencializar su desarollo dinámico, es compatible con la idea motriz de unidad y desarollo nacional que es la ideología dominante en los países latinoamericanos, constituye uno de los debates más agudos de las sociedades nacionales lationamericanas actualmente. ¿ Hasta qué punto los derechos sociales y culturales de los pueblos consagrados en los pactos y otros instrumentos internacionales pueden aplicarse a los grupos indígenas del continente en cuanto se refiere al derecho a recibir educación en su propia lengua y a la protección y respeto de su cultura por el resto de la sociedad nacional ? La respuesta a esta pregunta, alrededor de la cual aún no existe consenso, tiene implicaciones para las legislaciones de nuestros países. En un mondo cada vez más integrado y dominado en escala universal por las tendencias homogeneizadoras de los medios de comunicación de masas, los derechos culturales de los pueblos y de las colectividades aparecen cada vez con mayor insistencia como uno de los derechos humanos básicos o una de las libertades fundamentales de esta época.*

government. In the 1970s, a growing demand appeared for the whole educational programme in the larger indigenous communities to be truly bilingual and bicultural:

> This means that, for the first time in the educational history of Mexico, the Indian languages and cultures are being given due recognition in school programmes. It is hoped that all subjects during the whole of the primary school cycle will be taught in the mother tongue, in those areas where this is spoken by a local majority; that Spanish will be introduced from the beginning as a second language and that the Indian students will become fully bilingual; that in all relevant subjects the local culture will be prominently dealt with (for example, local and regional history, geography, customs, traditions, ethnobiology, etc.). At the same time, at the national level, the curriculum should be organised in such a fashion that schoolchildren all over the country will become aware of the pluricultural makeup of their nation, and respect for and knowledge of the minority cultures should become a part of the national curriculum. Of course, the full hispanicization of all minority ethnic groups is still the stated objective, but no longer to the exclusion of the minority cultures as such.[24]

Indigenous peoples seem to have been making impressive gains in many countries, especially in public education. In Norway, Sami was again allowed as a language of instruction in primary schools in 1959. In 1969, Norwegian legislation formalised the right of children of Sami-speaking parents in Sami districts to be instructed in the language of the indigenous community. Finally, by 1990, the Norwegian **Primary School Act** read as follows:

> 1. Children in Sami districts have the right to be taught Sami and to be instructed through the medium of Sami. From the seventh year on the pupils themselves decide on this matter. Children taught in or through the medium of Sami are exempted from instruction in one of the two Norwegian language varieties in the eighth and ninth year.
> 2. On advice from the local school board the municipality board may decide that Sami-speaking children shall be instructed in Sami all nine years and that Norwegian-speaking children shall learn Sami as a subject.
> 3. Instruction in or through the medium of Sami may also be given to children with a Sami background outside the Sami districts. If there are at least three Sami-speaking pupils at a school, they may demand instruction in Sami.[25]

In the 1980s, all three Scandinavian countries had begun to elaborate legal guarantees in respect to the right to use the Sami language. Norway, with the largest population of Sami, adopted the first Sami language law in 1990, followed by Finland in 1991 with its **Law on the Use of the Sami Language Before the Authorities**. Sweden's attitude has been much more reserved than its neighbours on this issue, although it does have in place a few regulations on the use of Sami. All three states have directly elected Sami "Parliaments" which came into being in Finland in

---

[24] Stavenhagen, Rodolfo (1990), "Linguistic Minorities and Language Policy in Latin America: The Case of Mexico", in Florian Coulmas (ed.), *Linguistic Minorities and Literacy: Language Policy Issues in Developing Countries*, Mouton Publishers, Berlin, pp. 56-62, at pp. 60-61.

[25] *Supra*, note 20, at p. 91.

1973, in Norway in 1987, and in Sweden in 1993. Although these are strictly consultative bodies, the fact that they are elected does give them considerable weight with the legislators when faced with issues of importance to the Sami.

In the last twenty-five years, Latin American countries have also begun to move in a similar direction as regards the right to use indigenous languages. In March 1975, Peru enacted **Decree No. 21** recognising Quechua as an official language of the Republic because, as set out in the Preamble, large sections of the indigenous population "have no direct access to knowledge of the laws". The decree also provides that where the parties only speak Quechua, legal proceedings shall be conducted in that language, and that the Ministry of Education shall provide "all necessary support for institutions engaged in...the teaching and promotion of the language in question ». The teaching of Quechua is declared to be compulsory at "all levels of education in the Republic". In Bolivia, the **Supreme Decree No. 23036 of 28 January 1992** contains provision for the implementation of the *Programa de Educación Intercultural Bilingue* in the Guaraní, Aymara and Quechua communities.[26] In Mexico, the **Executive Decree of 27 January 1992** amends Article 4 of the **Constitution** by including a provision which protects the development of indigenous languages, culture, uses, customs, resources and social organisations. In Paraguay, **Law 28 of 10 September 1992** renders mandatory the teaching of both national languages (Spanish and Guaraní) at the elementary, secondary and university levels.[27] Even France, in its overseas territory of New Caledonia, has acknowledged the need to respond to the special legal and political situation of indigenous peoples, as well as the need to adopt appropriate linguistic policies.[28] There are many more examples of this evolution in national legislation.[29]

---

[26] Gaceta oficial, 13 March 1992.

[27] Gaceta oficial de la República del Paraguay, 11 September 1992.

[28] Turcotte, D. (1982), *Composition ethnique et politique linguistique en Nouvelle-Calédonie: Adoption, implantation et diffusion du français comme langue officielle et véhiculaire unique*, International Centre for Research on Bilingualism, Québec, at pp. 22-23.

[29] See the status of the indigenous language in Greenland in *Linguistic Rights of Minorities* (1994), Frank Horn (ed.), Northern Institute for Environmental and Minority Law, University of Lapland, Rovaniemi, Finland, at pp. 79-80; Article 210 of the **Constitution of Brazil** which guarantees to indigenous communities the use of their languages in regular basic education; and Article 16 of the **Ley 23.302 sobre la Política Indígena y Apoyo a las Comunidades Aborígenes**, 8 November 1985, Boletín Oficial de la República Argentina, 12 November 1985:

> *La enseñanza que se imparta en las áreas de asentamiento de las comunidades indígenas asegurará los contenidos curriculares previstos en los planes comunes y, además, en el nivel primario se adoptará una modalidad de trabajo consistente en dividir el nivel en dos ciclos: en los tres primeros años, la enseñanza se impartirá con la lengua indígena materna correspondiente y se desarrollará como materia especial el idioma nacional; en los restantes años, la enseñanza será bilingüe. Se promoverá la formación y capacitación de docentes primarios bilingües, con especial énfasis en los aspectos antropológicos, lingüíticos y didácticos, como asimismo la preparación de textos y otros materiales, a través de la creación de centros y/o cursos especiales de nivel superior, destinados a estas actividaded.*
> *Los establecimientos primarios ubicados fuera de los lugares de asentamiento de las comunidades indígenas, donde asistan niños aborígenes (que sólo o predominantemente se*

A notable change of heart is also observable in the United States which, until perhaps some twenty years ago, had been intransigent towards indigenous peoples, their languages and their cultures:

> In 1978 the state legislature of Hawaii recognised Hawaiian as an official language; subsequently a language revitalisation program was established. Ten years later... a Hawaiian senator introduced a proposal in both houses of Congress which resulted in the adoption of the Native American Languages Act in October 1990. In October 1992, additional legislation was passed, setting up a grant program "to ensure the survival and continuing vitality of Native American languages"... The Native American Languages Act acknowledges that the "United States has the responsibility to act together with Native Americans to ensure the survival of these unique cultures and languages", and establishes a federal policy "to preserve, protect and promote the rights and freedom of Native Americans to use, practice and develop Native American languages" and to "encourage and support the use of Native American languages as a medium of instruction". The grant system supports community projects, teacher training, materials development, training for radio and television production, language documentation and equipment purchase.[30]

Although progress has also been made in Canada, most indigenous peoples do not actually have the right to demand the use of their language as medium of instruction in that country. The governments in the Province of Québec and the Northwest Territories (where a large percentage of the population is indigenous) have the most generous attitudes and legislation in place, but most governments in Canada generally do not allow the use of indigenous languages in state-supported schools as medium of instruction, nor even allow the instruction of indigenous languages except perhaps for one or two hours every week, despite important sums of money being allocated to indigenous peoples by governments for education.[31] In other areas, the

---

> *expresen en lengua indígena) podrán adoptar la modalidad de trabajo prevista en el presente artículo.*

[30] Fettes, Mark (1994), "The International Context of Aboriginal Linguistic Rights", in *Canadian Centre for Linguistic Rights Bulletin*, Vol. 1, N° 3, 6-11, at p. 10.

[31] *Les langues autochtones du Québec* (1992), Jacques Maurais (ed.), Les Publications du Québec, Québec, at pp. 158-159:

> *Dans plusieurs écoles administrées par des bandes ou par le gouvernement fédéral ou relevant de l'administration provinciale, on assiste alors à l'implantation progressive, sur le plan linguistique, de projets pilotes d'éducation bilingue qui comportent le plus souvent une éducation préscolaire en langue vernaculaire et, combinées à l'apprentissage de l'anglais ou du français, certaines périodes d'enseignement des langues autochtones ou en langue autochtone durant les cinq premières années du primaire. Bientôt, d'après des statistiques gouvernementales de 1980-1981, les programmes d'études de 65% des écoles fédérales, 19% des écoles provinciales et 34% des écoles administrées par les bandes en viennent à inclure les langues autochtones. Toutefois, l'élaboration d'un véritable programme scolaire autochtone, touchant à la fois le primaire et le secondaire, reste pour la majorité des bandes autochtones une perspective plus que lointaine.*

government of Canada has been more generous, as for example the funding of indigenous language broadcasting.[32]

Finally in New Zealand, numerous court decisions have confirmed that the Māori language is protected under the **Waitangi Treaty** as a *te reo Māori*, a valued Māori treasure.[33] Thus, partly in recognition of New Zealand's treaty obligations, Māori was made an official language in 1987 and legislation was adopted in order to fulfil the following obligations in respect to the language of the indigenous Māori:

1. Law and policies preventing the use of Māori in the courts are inconsistent with the principles of the treaty.
2. The education and broadcasting systems overemphasise English and thus fail to give adequate protection to Māori.
3. Māori should be recognised in the courts and in dealing with any department or local authority.[34]

Whilst there is undoubtedly a visible trend towards the recognition of the fundamental importance of language for indigenous peoples in many countries, not all states share the view that there is a need to accommodate the language preferences of indigenous peoples.

Apparently, governments in Malaysia, India, Burma, and Bangladesh have at times claimed that everyone is indigenous and that no one is entitled to any special or differential treatment. Moreover, a number of Asian governments have cited the need for a national language to promote national unity, and some have launched assimilation programmes reminiscent of the techniques used by European colonialists in America and Australia: children are removed from their families and sent to government boarding schools where instruction is in the official or majority language.[35] There may be even more sinister explanations for such practices:

But behind such legitimate concerns often lurks a poorly disguised contempt for cultures seen as backward. The Commission for a New Asia, which is a group of leading intellectuals from the region, recently expressed a commonly held official view: "In no

---

[32] Ibid., at p. 168.

[33] See for example **Attorney General v. New Zealand Māori Council** [1991], 2 N.Z.L.R. 129 (New Zealand), **Attorney General v. New Zealand Māori Council (No. 2)** [1991], 2 N.Z.L.R. 147 (New Zealand), **New Zealand Māori Council v. Attorney General** [1992], 2 N.Z.L.R. 576 (New Zealand).

[34] Although the New Zealand legislation refers to the equal legal status of English and Māori, this is absolutely not the true effect of the provisions currently in place: for example, the right to use Māori in court proceedings only allows for the assistance of an interpreter. Whereas an English-speaking defendant will always have the right and advantage to be judged in his own language, the same is never available to a Māori in his own language. To paraphrase George Orwell, some are more equal than others. For the situation in Australia, see *Language and Culture: A Matter of Survival, supra*, note 21, at pp. 51-89.

[35] See *The Ethnic Dimension in International Relations* (1993), Bernard Schechterman and Martin Slann (eds.), Praeger, Westport, Connecticut, at pp. 148-149, regarding similar incidents involving indigenous peoples in Brazil and Venezuela in the 1970s.

Asian society should we be prepared to perpetuate the existence of groups which will be fascinating human anachronisms worthy only for the study of 21st century anthropologists".[36]

In 1993, many indigenous inhabitants of Easter Island openly challenged the Chilean government, demanding control over their land and the use of their native language, Rapa Nui, as the main language in their schools. Even states with a longer established tradition of accommodation towards indigenous peoples have encountered problems in implementation. In Mexico, public school teachers are often unwilling or unprepared to present indigenous languages in a serious context within the classroom. Indigenous language materials, if they are available, are often translations of Spanish originals with no reference to the indigenous cultures. In a number of other states, the good will of public authorities is sometimes confronted with extreme scarcity of resources or cuts in public expenditures such as public education.

Even the armed uprising of indigenous peoples, including members of the Tzeltal, Tzotzil, Tojolabal and Chol, in Chiapas, Mexico, in January 1994 rested to some degree on the inability of the Mexican government to carry through with its constitutional and legal obligations in respect to the use of indigenous languages. Many public teachers in indigenous communities are unable to speak the local language, and school material and books are often only available in Spanish, in apparent violation of the constitution. During negotiations with the rebels, the government agreed to provide education in their native language and to revise school curriculums to include more indigenous history and culture.[37]

Despite these problems, there is no denying that national practices appear to lean towards granting indigenous peoples more generous concessions in language and culture than they would perhaps be entitled to if they were considered as simply another minority or individuals.

7.3   INDIGENOUS LANGUAGES AND HUMAN RIGHTS TODAY

7.3.1   *Evolving International Standards*

La langue yaquie est un don d'Itom Achai, le créateur de notre peuple et elle doit, par conséquent, être traitée avec respect. Notre ancienne langue est le fondement de notre héritage culturel et spirituel sans lequel nous ne pourrions exister de la façon prévue par notre Créateur. L'éducation est la transmission de la culture et des valeurs; par conséquent, nous déclarons que l'éducation yaquie sera le moyen de transmission de la langue et de l'héritage spirituel et culturel. Nous déclarons de plus que tous les aspects de l'enseignement devront refléter la beauté de notre langue yaquie, de notre culture et de nos valeurs. Ce sera la politique de la tribu yaquie Pascua qu'aucun membre de la tribu ne

---

[36] Globe and Mail, Toronto, 14 May 1994, at p. A10.

[37] In another, non-violent, confrontation, some 800 Achuar, Quicha, and Shuar marched from their villages to the capital city of Quito, Ecuador, in April 1992, galvanising several thousand more indigenous people to join them along the way. In response, Ecuador's president promised to accept a long-standing demand regarding the use of indigenous languages as medium of instruction.

devra être contraint par une autorité externe non yaquie à renier ou à avilir la langue yaquie... La langue yaquie est la langue officielle de la nation yaquie Pascua et peut être utilisée dans l'administration gouvernementale (pouvoirs législatif, exécutif et judiciaire), mais par respect pour les personnes parlant espagnol et anglais, l'espagnol et l'anglais peuvent être utilisés dans les affaires officielles du gouvernement...[38]

Indigenous peoples are recognised as having in international law a position which differs from individuals or minorities generally.[39] In addition to the rights to which they may be entitled as minorities, and in addition to the right to non-discrimination or freedom of expression, indigenous peoples appear to be entitled to other measures because of their unique political and legal status.

Although the main driving force behind early international instruments was the desire to assimilate indigenous peoples into the mainstream of society as quickly as possible, and at any cost, the trend today is markedly different: indigenous peoples, whilst still being called to participate in the larger society by learning a state's official or majority language, should be allowed to, and even assisted in, preserving their languages, customs, and culture. These new and evolving norms imply that a state may obligated to provide financial and institutional assistance in order to develop and promote indigenous languages. These norms would also seem to indicate that even in the case of a language used by a relatively small number of indigenous people, a state may be obligated to provide resources for its maintenance, if the indigenous people seek to enforce their right to the promotion and safeguard of their language.[40]

The fundamental difference between the international documents and norms relating to individual human rights in general and those dealing with indigenous peoples in particular appears to be the following: whereas a state has a positive obligation to provide for certain services such as state education in a minority or non-official language only when there is a sufficiently high number of speakers of such language, indigenous peoples would not seem to be subject to the same requirement in respect to relative numbers. Furthermore, the latter would appear to be entitled to an appropriate degree of political autonomy which would include the means and resources to protect and use their language in community and institutional settings.

Special Rapporteur José R. Martinez Cobo noted that in addition to the level of legal recognition for the use of an indigenous language appropriate to the number of speakers of the

---

[38] The Yaqui Nation of Arizona, *supra*, note 31, at p. 39.

[39] *Supra*, note 22, at p. 158:

> Because United Nations sub-committees establish working groups when they recognise that an issue is unique to a particular group or political situation, the establishment of the Working Group suggests that after 1982 the United Nations considered indigenous concerns to be substantially different from those faced by other minorities... A number of governments have also recognised the unique nature of indigenous problems. Many states, such as Nicaragua, are currently abandoning their integrationist policies and are discussing the creation of special aboriginal programmes to protect indigenous rights. Other countries, like Canada, while still not recognising all indigenous rights, are at least consulting with indigenous peoples and creating special indigenous programs. Such developments have led, albeit indirectly, to the crystallisation of an indigenous norm.

[40] See in particular Articles 14 and 15 of the draft **Declaration on the Rights of Indigenous Peoples**, in Section 1.1.2 of the Appendix.

language, consistent with the application of non-discrimination on the ground of language, "in no circumstances should it be less than that of an auxiliary language in public education and other specific functions that may be established."[41] In other words, regardless of its demographic importance, an indigenous language should always be entitled to some type of legal status.

In the area of public education, the Special Rapporteur pointed out that as a strict minimum, indigenous children should always be taught the language of their people, regardless of their numbers:

> The state must make an effort to provide, at the primary level sufficient facilities for the teaching of the mother tongue of indigenous children; in all circumstances it must teach them to read and write in their mother tongue and consolidate this knowledge before teaching them any other dialect or language as a second or acquired language.[42]

The **1989 ILO Convention** and the UN draft **Declaration on the Rights of Indigenous Peoples** incorporate, to a significant extent, the suggestions of the Special Rapporteur in this respect.

Even in its Preamble, the **1989 ILO Convention** refers to the appropriateness of removing the assimilationist character of earlier standards. Articles 2 and 6 provide for the duty of a state to cooperate with indigenous peoples in the full realisation of their social, economic and cultural rights, with respect to their social and cultural identity, their customs and traditions and their institutions. In addition to the need for cooperation, the **1989 ILO Convention** calls for the duty to "consult the peoples concerned, through appropriate procedures and in particular through their representative institutions, whenever consideration is being given to legislative or administrative measures which may affect them directly" as well as to "establish means for the full development of these peoples' own institutions and initiatives, and in appropriate cases provide the resources necessary for this purpose." Indigenous peoples have the right to retain their own customs and institutions, as long as they are compatible with fundamental human rights.

The **Convention** as a whole reflects an emphasis on indigenous peoples as political or cultural units which are entitled to the respect of the state, as well as the maintenance of, and even appropriate resources for, their institutions. Article 6 which refers to "representative institutions" appears to acknowledge that the political structures of indigenous peoples are to be recognised and consulted as part of a state's own legal and political order.[43]

---

[41] *Study of the Problem of Discrimination Against Indigenous Populations*, *supra*, note 3, at p. 18.

[42] Ibid., at p. 20.

[43] Many states acknowledge as part of their internal law that indigenous peoples have either retained some degree of inherent sovereignty that has not been extinguished by conquest or control by invading or newly arrived peoples, or have a continuing legal status that clearly sets them apart. In the United States, indigenous peoples are deemed to be "sovereign, domestic dependent nations" which have entered into a trust relationship with the government and which are considered as distinct political entities. Similarly in Canada, it appears increasingly that indigenous peoples have retained some degree of autonomy as political entities. The Samis of Scandinavia have made even more impressive gains during the last 10 years through the creation of Sami Parliaments, despite their current limited role as consultative bodies. The Mayas of Guatemala still maintain that they have a surviving political right of autonomy. A number of Latin American states, in particular Nicaragua and Colombia, have granted

On the linguistic front, Article 27 of the **1989 ILO Convention** begins with the principle that educational policies must reflect the special needs and incorporate the histories, knowledge, value systems and the further social, economic and cultural aspirations of indigenous peoples. Moreover, Article 27(3) provides that:

> In addition, governments shall recognise the right of these peoples to establish their own educational institutions and facilities, provided that such institutions meet minimum standards established by the competent authority in consultation with these peoples. Appropriate resources shall be provided for this purpose.

Whilst Article 27 of the **International Covenant on Civil and Political Rights** and Article 27(3) of the **1989 ILO Convention** are essentially identical in recognising the right to establish private educational institutions, they differ in one important aspect: in the latter, indigenous peoples are entitled to appropriate resources from the state to make this possible, something that the **Covenant** does not provide for.

The **1989 ILO Convention** also has a provision dealing with public schools and indigenous peoples. Article 28(1) provides that indigenous children "shall, wherever practicable, be taught to read and write in their own indigenous language or in the language most commonly used by the group to which they belong. When this is not practicable, the competent authorities shall undertake consultations with these peoples with a view to the adoption of measures to achieve this objective."

Whilst some of the provisions of the **1989 ILO Convention** are likely inspired by the prohibition of discriminatory practices, it is undeniable that others go beyond this norm: indigenous peoples deserve "special measures" because of their unique political position within a state, or perhaps because of their traditional political autonomy. Though there may be other explanations why indigenous peoples as a group should be treated differently from individuals generally, it remains fairly clear that regardless of their relative demographic importance, states should, whenever practical, protect and promote the development and use of indigenous languages and assist indigenous children in learning the language of their ancestors. The language

---

to indigenous communities extensive powers, at least partly in recognition of their unique political status. See amongst others Hannum, *supra*, note 3, at pp. 675-676; Torres, *supra*, note 22, at pp. 133-134; Melkevik, Bjarne (1992), "L'organisation de l'autonomie politique autochtone : L'exemple des Samés (Lapons) de Norvège", in *Manitoba Law Journal*, Vol. 21, No. 3, 406-425, at p. 406; Consejo de Organizaciones Mayas de Guatemala (1991), *Derechos Específicos del Pueblo Maya*, Editorial Cholsamaj, Guatemala, at p. 13; Cumming, Peter and Ginn, Diana (1986), "First Nations Self-Government in Canada", in *Nordic Journal of International Law*, Vol. 55, 86-116, at pp. 91-92; and the eloquent description of Thomas Berger, quoted in Macklem, Patrick (1993), "Distributing Sovereignty: Indian Nations and Equality of Peoples", in *Stanford Law Review*, Vol. 45, 1311-1367, at p. 1328:

> After the Europeans came and occupied the continent, driving the Natives into enclaves, even these enclaves came under attack, because they were limited to Native people. But they are political communities, founded on tradition and culture, not on race. These political communities are not vestigial: rather they are repositories of Native hopes and ideals of self-government.

rights of indigenous peoples are thus linked to their unique status as members of a political and social entity increasingly recognised in international law.

Notwithstanding the above, the **1989 ILO Convention** does raise some difficult issues. For example, whilst a state should provide public schooling where indigenous languages are taught wherever this is practical, it is not obvious what is meant by the use of the term "practical". A reasonable interpretation would be that even if the number of individuals seeking public education in an indigenous language is relatively small, this ought not to be a complete barrier: a state should at minimum respect these individuals' right to learn the language of their people wherever it is practical to do so. Of course, there are factors which may make it impossible, such as if a language only exists in verbal form. One could also conclude that financial considerations may be involved, particularly if the number of individuals is so small that it would clearly be outlandish to spend large sums of money to produce teaching material in a language used, for example, by a few dozen individuals in a state where resources for education are already hard-pressed. In a situation where it is not practical for the state itself to ensure that every indigenous child be taught to read and write in the language of his or her people, it should then explore with indigenous peoples other ways of complying with the requirements of the **1989 ILO Convention.**[44]

It should also be emphasised that Article 27(3) does not appear to guarantee entire instruction in indigenous languages, but only that children of indigenous peoples are to be taught to read and write the language of their people.

Indeed, the tone of the **1989 ILO Convention** is somewhat timid compared to the present wording in the provisions of the UN draft **Declaration on the Rights of Indigenous Peoples.** Recognising the right of indigenous peoples to self-determination in Article 3 (by virtue of which they may freely determine their political status and pursue their economic, social and cultural development), the **Declaration** then enumerates an impressive series of rights which extend beyond what has generally been considered mandatory for minority groups or individuals, including:

1. The right to autonomy and self-government (Article 3).
2. The right to maintain and strengthen their distinct political, economic, social and cultural characteristics, as well as their legal systems, whilst retaining their rights to participate fully, if they so choose, in the political, economic, social and cultural life of the state (Article 4).
3. The right to be protected from "cultural" genocide, including the prevention of and redress for any act which has the aim or effect of depriving them of their integrity as distinct societies, or of their cultural or ethnic characteristics or identities, or any form of forced assimilation or integration by imposition of other cultures or ways of life (Article 7).
4. The right to revitalise, use, develop and transmit to future generations their histories, languages, oral traditions, philosophies, writing systems and literatures, and to designate and retain their own names for communities, places and persons. Furthermore, states have the obligation to take effective measures to ensure this right is protected (Article 14).
5. The right of indigenous children to all levels and forms of education of the state. This is combined with the right of all indigenous peoples to establish and control their

---

[44] See also on this topic the recommendations in *Study of the Problem of Discrimination Against Indigenous Populations, supra,* note 3, at pp. 16-18.

educational systems and institutions providing education in their own languages, in a manner appropriate to their cultural methods of teaching and learning. Indigenous children living outside their communities still have the right to be provided access to education in their own culture and language. Furthermore, states must take effective measures to provide appropriate resources for these purposes (Article 15).

6. The right to autonomy or self-government, as a form of self-determination, in matters relating to their internal and local affairs, including culture, religion, education, information, media, health, housing, employment, social welfare, economic activities, land and resources management, environment and entry by non-members, as well as taxation powers for financing these autonomous functions (Article 31).

7. The collective right to determine their own citizenship in accordance with their customs and traditions, whilst maintaining the right to citizenship of the states in which they live, as well as the right to determine the structures and to select the membership of their institutions in accordance with their own procedures (Article 32).

8. The right to promote, develop and maintain their institutional structures and their distinctive juridical customs, traditions, procedures and practices, as long as they conform to internationally recognised human rights standards (Article 33).

In fact, the difference between the approach towards the rights of indigenous peoples in the UN draft **Declaration on the Rights of Indigenous Peoples**, as compared to the approach towards the rights of minorities generally in instruments such as the **International Covenant on Civil and Political Rights**, is nothing short of striking. The UN draft **Declaration** unequivocally suggests that indigenous peoples should occupy a privileged political and legal position: they should have the right to autonomous governing and legal structures and institutions, including some power of taxation and control over their resources. Linked to this right to autonomy would be an inherent right to use their indigenous languages within their structures and institutions.

Moreover, it would seem that the state could be obligated to assist indigenous peoples in "correcting" past injustices and practices which amount to "cultural" genocide. The weakness of some indigenous languages, particularly in North America and Australia, is due to assimilationist state policies, often enforced brutally or at least against the will of indigenous peoples, with ensuing consequences in terms of economic and educational advancement. According to Article 7, indigenous peoples would have the right to obtain redress from the principal offenders, namely public authorities. Although the provision appears to be mainly concerned with the prevention of and redress for current state practices that deprive indigenous peoples of their "integrity as distinct societies, or of their cultural or ethnic characteristics", it is certainly arguable that some measure of redress must be implemented since most of the original causes of the present disintegration of indigenous cultures and languages are attributable to state sponsored or condoned practices that were common until fairly recently.

In the field of education, the UN draft **Declaration** proposes to go even further than the **1989 ILO Convention**. Whilst in the latter, the extent of the right to instruction of indigenous languages appears to be limited to the acquisition of an ability to read and write one's own indigenous language, the right as proposed in Article 15 could extend to all levels and forms of public education in indigenous languages, in addition to the right to establish and control private indigenous educational systems and institutions supported by state resources. In other words, the UN draft **Declaration** suggests that indigenous peoples, regardless of the number of speakers of their languages, should be entitled to be educated through the medium of their language in public schools. The unqualified wording sets Article 15 apart from provisions relying on the principle of non-discrimination where a state is entitled to limit the number of languages which may be used as medium of instruction in public supported schools where it is reasonable and warranted because of the numbers of children involved. The UN draft **Declaration** is thus far more generous than those instruments setting down rights to which speakers of a minority or non-official language would normally be entitled in view of traditional individual human rights.

Although the principles of the draft **Declaration** if they are ever adopted will carry moral weight and represent a noble expression of the willingness to recognise the needs and aspirations of indigenous peoples in a generous and flexible way, it is difficult to envision how provisions such as Article 15 can survive in their present, unqualified, form. There are, for example, some indigenous peoples which now only number a few hundred speakers, and sometimes even fewer.[45] It would appear quite literally impossible for a state to guarantee access to education at all levels in an indigenous language used by only a handful of people. Conversely, this may also be the intent of the drafters of Article 15: the provision guarantees the right to public instruction in an indigenous language except where it is impossible to do so. Of course, indigenous peoples themselves can always decide on varying degrees of use of their language as medium of instruction.

Surprisingly, the UN draft **Declaration on the Rights of Indigenous Peoples** does not mention that indigenous peoples are entitled or obligated to learn the official or majority language of the state they inhabit, although in practice it is doubtful any indigenous community would wish to isolate itself completely from the rest of society. Moreover, since the wishes of indigenous peoples are paramount in these matters, a state could not oblige upon indigenous peoples an indigenous-language-only education policy which would segregate them from society at large.

Finally, the Organisation of American States is also considering a declaration which contains many similar features to the United Nations draft. It represents a further acknowledgment that in relation to indigenous peoples, a state must be highly responsive to their linguistic in recognition of the serious consequences of inappropriate or exclusive language preferences of the state apparatus. In the area of state education, Article VIII of the draft **Inter-American Declaration on the Rights of Indigenous Peoples**[46] confers on states the obligation to operate educational systems in the indigenous languages, whilst at the same time providing the necessary training and means for mastery of the official language. Furthermore, indigenous peoples would be entitled under Article IX to establish and operate their own private educational programmes and institutions, and states would be obligated to provide financial aid and any other type of assistance to implement this right.

As for the use of indigenous languages by state officials in general, Article VIII indicates that states must provide for some use of indigenous languages to an appropriate degree in most

---

[45] See the situation for many indigenous languages in Canada in de Varennes, *supra*, note 17, at pp. 278-279.

[46] Draft approved by the Inter-American Commission on Human Rights, OEA/SER/L/V/II.90, 21 September 1995. Reprinted in Section 1.2.13 inthe Appendix.

areas. Where indigenous languages are predominantly used in a region, they should additionally have the same status as the state's official language(s):

> The states shall take effective measures to enable indigenous peoples to understand administrative, legal and political rules and procedures and to be understood in relation to these matters. In areas where indigenous languages are predominant, states shall endeavour to establish the pertinent languages as official languages and to give them the same status that is given to non-indigenous official languages.

7.3.2 *Contemporary National Practices*

In societies with oral language traditions the languages provide an irreplaceable repository of experience, history, mythology, spiritual belief, law and socio-cultural organisation and values. This derives from the very nature of language itself, the major mediator between experiences and thought and culture. The Aboriginal interpretation of Australia — its landscape, environment and the experiences of its inhabitants — is among the most ancient of any in the world. Being unique to this continent these languages are an important and irreplaceable source of self-knowledge for Australia and of inestimable value to Aborigines and their prospects of cultural survival.[47]

Governments in recent years have also begun to recognise the unique political and legal position of indigenous peoples, along with related rights regarding the use, development and even revival of their languages. Many states, such as Nicaragua, have begun to abandon their integrationist policies and are discussing the creation of special programmes to protect indigenous languages.[48] The United States, Finland and New Zealand have adopted specific legislation guaranteeing such rights, whilst others like Canada appear to be edging towards the same direction.

For the Māoris in New Zealand, their language is guaranteed as a measure of protection in the **Waitangi Treaty**, signed between this indigenous people and the British Crown in the

---

[47] Lo Bianco, Joseph (1987), *National Policy on Languages*, Australian Government Publications Service, Canberra, at p. 10.

[48] Even in states claiming to recognise the right of indigenous peoples to be taught in their own language, there can be a number of shortcomings, such as the absence of schools in or near indigenous communities, the lack of qualified teachers with the necessary knowledge of the relevant indigenous language and culture, and the absence of educational material in indigenous languages. Moreover, in teaching the official language, insufficient care may be taken to prevent a pupil from being cut off from his mother tongue, and in many cases this continues to be a deliberate, if illegal or inappropriate, objective. See on this point *Study of the Problem of Discrimination Against Indigenous Populations, supra*, note 3, at p. 10, and *Des peuples enfin reconnus* (1994), Marie Léger (ed.), Éditions Écosociété, Montréal, at p. 178:

> *Malgré une disposition constitutionnelle le permettant, il n'y a pas d'éducation bilingue pour les enfants autochtones, le programme qui leur est destiné est le même que celui des autres élèves de la République et il se donne en espagnol. Toutefois, comme une proportion significative des enseignants est d'origine kuna, cela permet d'adapter, de facto, le contenu de certains cours.*

nineteenth century. The treaty provides that the Māori people's treasures (*taonga*) are to be protected by the Crown. New Zealand courts have decided that the existence of close ties between Māori culture and customs, and their native language, *te reo Māori*, signifies that language is one of the treasures which the state is required to protect,[49] and that this protection includes, at least, the right to acquisition of that language by the Māori people in state-funded schools.[50]

Something similar is occurring in Scandinavian countries. The Finnish Parliament, for example, has adopted a **Sami Language Act** which provides, amongst other things, for the legal right of the Sami to certain government and educational services in their ancestral language, even though there are fewer than 50,000 Sami in the entire state. The **Act** recognises in its preamble that the Sami have these rights because of their unique position in Finnish society.[51]

---

[49] See **New Zealand Maori Council** v. **Attorney General**, [1992] 2 N.Z.L.R. 576 (New Zealand), and the preamble of the **Maori Language Act, 1987**: "Whereas in the Treaty of Waitangi the Crown confirmed and guaranteed to the Māori people, among other things, all their taonga: And whereas the Māori language is one such *taonga*..."

[50] See generally Hastings, William K. (1988), *The Right to an Education in Maori: The Case From International Law*, Victoria University Press, Wellington, New Zealand, at pp. 22-26. It should not be assumed that the recognised obligations under the **Waitangi Treaty** constitute absolute protection of the rights of indigenous peoples to obtain services and benefits from public authorities in their own language. Courts in New Zealand have been unwilling to impose a precise line of conduct upon the government in observance of the provisions of the **Treaty** unless a practice or decision is shown to have been arrived at in an unreasonable fashion. In other words, courts are reluctant to explore too closely the linguistic obligations under the **Treaty** and prefer to leave the whole matter to the government itself. Thus, the Māori almost have to prove bad faith on the part of the government before being able to obtain any redress in court. See on this point the reasoning in **Attorney General v. New Zealand Maori Council** [1991], 2 N.Z.L.R. 129 (New Zealand), at p. 130:

> Broadcasting was a development of Western civilisation not foreseen by the makers of the Treaty. Naturally the Treaty does not specifically deal with it. Nevertheless the Treaty principles of partnership and protection of *taonga*, past neglect of them at times, and New Zealand's international obligations can be argued to combine to make it incumbent on the Crown to take reasonable steps to enable Māori language and culture to be promoted by broadcasting. But there is no need to express an opinion on that argument, because even on that approach I do not think that it could possibly be said that the precise path to be followed could only be defined by the Courts. The Waitangi Tribunal and Parliament have accepted that the Treaty guarantees protection for the Māori language as a *taonga*, but the Treaty certainly does not lay down what should be done for that purpose in allocating radio frequencies. It is a field in which, on any view, a range of options is open. If the Government, giving due weight to the Treaty principles, elects between the available options reasonably and in good faith, it seems to me that the Treaty is complied with.

[51] See **Act on the Use of the Sami Language before the Authorities**, 8 March 1991/516. The rights of the Samis to be taught their language in public schools and to use it before public authorities in Norway and Sweden are described in *The Situation of Regional or Minority Languages in Europe* (1994), Council of Europe, Strasbourg, at pp. 92-96 and 126-128, and Melkevik, Bjarne (1991), "Autochtones et droit : le nouveau droit norvégien des Samés (Lapons)", in *Les Cahiers de Droit*, Vol. 32, 33-57, at pp. 43-54.

It is in the Province of Québec and in the Northwest Territories[52] that indigenous peoples in Canada find the greatest level of protection and use of their languages by public authorities and in public education, sometimes by way of agreements with local or regional indigenous governmental authorities.[53] But in most Canadian provinces, indigenous peoples have little or no right to use their language with public authorities, and many indigenous children do not receive in public schools any real opportunity to acquire an ability to read and write their language.

The United States has followed suite to international trends by recently adopting the **Native American Languages Act.**[54] This appears to be a recognition of the special political status of indigenous peoples and corresponding linguistic obligations on the part of the federal government. US federal obligations, because of this special relationship, include the duty to work together with indigenous peoples to ensure the survival of their languages.[55]

The US policy to respect its obligations in this regard includes the following:

1. To preserve, protect and promote the rights and freedom of Native Americans to use, practice and develop Native American Languages.

---

[52] *Supra*, note 30, at p. 9.

[53] *Supra*, note 31, at pp. 161-162. See also Article 88 of the **Charte de la langue française**, 1993 Revised Statutes of Québec, Chapter C-11:

Notwithstanding sections 72 to 86, in the schools under the jurisdiction of the Cree School Board or the Kativik School board, according to the Cree, Inuit and Naskapi Public Education Act, the languages of instruction shall be Cree and Inuktitut, respectively, and the other languages of instruction in use in the Cree and Inuit communities in Québec on the date of the signing of the Agreement indicated in section 1 of the Act approving the Agreement concerning James Bay and Northern Québec (chapter C-67), namely, 11 November 1975. The Cree School Board and the Kativik School Board shall pursue as an objective the use of French as a language of French as a language of instruction so that pupils graduating from their schools will in future be capable of continuing their studies in a French school, college or university elsewhere in Québec, if they so desire. After consultation with the school committees, in the case of the Crees, and with the parents' committees, in the case of the Inuit, the commissioners shall determine the rate of instruction of French and English as languages of instruction.

[54] 30 October 1990, 104 STAT. 1153.

[55] Ibid., at Article 102:

(1) the status of the cultures and languages of Native Americans is unique and the United States has the responsibility to act together with Native Americans to ensure the survival of these unique cultures and languages;

(2) special status is accorded Native Americans in the United States, a status that recognises distinct cultural and political rights, including the right to continue separate identities;

(3) the traditional languages of Native Americans are an integral part of their cultures and identities and form the basic medium for the transmission, and thus survival, of Native American cultures, literatures, histories, religions, political institutions, and values;...

(8) acts of suppression and extermination directed against Native American languages and cultures are in conflict with the United States policy of self-determination for Native Americans;...

2. To recognise the right of Indian tribes and other Native American governing bodies to use the Native American languages as a medium of instruction in all schools funded by the Secretary of the Interior.

3. To fully recognise the inherent right of Indian tribes and other Native American governing bodies, states, territories, and possessions of the United States to take action on, and give official status to, their Native American languages for the purpose of conducting their own business.[56]

State-funded schools for indigenous peoples in the US can thus be obliged to use indigenous languages as medium of instruction when it is deemed desirable by indigenous peoples themselves.

The indigenous people in the Danish territory of Greenland have also made important gains, in line with international trends, in the use of their language:

> There was a growing realisation that genuine emancipation of the Greenlandic people and modernisation of their society was impossible without emancipating and modernising the indigenous language. When Home Rule came in 1979, it was agreed that Greenlandic should be the main language... Since then, marked progress has taken place. Greenlandic has become the medium of instruction in the schools, and, while Danish used to be taught from the first year onwards, it is now delayed until the third year. It is also generally acknowledged that even children of Danish parents living in Greenland should learn Greenlandic.[57]

In the French territory of New Caledonia, indigenous peoples have been granted some autonomy powers, including the right to teach their language and culture in public schools.[58] In Nicaragua, the **Atlantic Coast Autonomy Law** recognises the right of the Atlantic Coast communities to preserve their cultural identity, and their languages, as well as the right to use and enjoy the waters, forests and communal lands for their own benefit. For example, Article 12(5) provides that members of these indigenous communities are entitled to be educated in their own languages, through programmes which take into account their historical heritage, their traditions and the characteristics of their environment, all within the framework of the national education system.

The degree of consistency in state practice and in the demands emanating from indigenous peoples themselves point to a growing consensus that indigenous peoples are entitled to some type of political autonomy and to education in their native language. The following demands of the Mayas of Guatemala are surprisingly close to what appear to be the evolving consensus at the international level:

- *Oficializar los idiomas Mayas a nivel de cada comunidad lingüística.*

---

[56] Ibid., Article 104.

[57] *Supra*, note 20, at p. 110.

[58] Article 7, **Loi no 88-82 du 22 janvier 1988 portant statut du territoire de la Nouvelle-Calédonie**, Journal officiel de la République de France, 26 January 1988, at p. 1231.

- Hacer obligatorio el aprendizaje y uso los idiomas Mayas a los funcionarios de servicios públicos ubicados en regiones con población Maya. Los funcionarios públicos que no pertenecen a la comunidad lingüística en que prestan sus servicios, deben poseer el conocimiento y manejo corriente del idioma propio de dicha comunidad.
- Impartir justicia en el idioma Maya de acuerdo a la comunidad lingüística donde se procese al encausado.
- Utilizar la lengua Maya de cada comunidad lingüística como lengua docente en los programas de educación...
- Implementar programas de emergencia para contribuir al rescate de las comunidades lingüísticas en vías de extinción (Xinkas, Itzaes, Tekos, etc.)...
- Reestructurar el Ministerio de Educación para que presupuestaria, orgánica y estructuralmente desarrolle los subsistemas de educación del Pueblo Maya, Ladino, Xinka y al Garífuna. El Pueblo Maya debe disponer y decidir sobre sus propias escuelas en los diversos niveles de la enseñanza escolar, personal bilingüe y propio material didáctico.
- Sistematizar la enseñanza del las ciencias, la tecnología, las artes y la filosofía Maya, en sus distintos niveles. El alumno Maya debe conocer y aprender desde su propia cosmovisión ya que perfil y las directrices del Estado, reflejan otros valores y otra visión del mundo.
- El Estado debe reconocer el derecho del Pueblo Maya de disponer de sus propias escuelas para la formación de Maestros Bilingües para todos los niveles y especialidades de la labor escolar.[59]

Although it is certainly not possible to claim there is unanimity in state practices or views as to the rights of indigenous peoples, one can certainly suggest there is widespread acceptance that they are, as a group, entitled to measures that go beyond what individuals or members of linguistic minorities are able to demand in relation to the use, protection or status of their languages.

7.4   SUMMARY

Indigenous peoples have throughout history suffered extensively from various forms of oppression and even brutality from the invading and colonising powers. Attempts to eradicate what was, and in some parts of the world still is, considered to be inferior or undesirable communities and cultures led to measures aimed at the elimination of indigenous languages, or in the words of one US politician, to "kill the savage but save the man".

Instead of attempting to subjugate or eradicate these peoples, current international and national trends appear to acknowledge that the presence of indigenous peoples need not be considered a threat, but can actually be accommodated within the existing state.

A primary aspect of these new attitudes is the growing acceptance that indigenous peoples have, as collectivities, the right to internal self-determination, a right to some appropriate degree of political autonomy within an existing state which carries with it the resources to operate

---

[59] Consejo de Organizaciones Mayas de Guatemala, *supra*, note 43, at pp. 14-19.

various institutional structures using indigenous languages to the extent chosen by the concerned peoples themselves.

Whilst there is certainly no unanimity, both international and national law appear to be heading towards increased recognition of the special position which indigenous peoples occupy within a society's legal and political order. The latter are not simply another minority group, but would seem to deserve greater latitude, and also greater assistance, in the maintenance of their traditional customs, practices and languages than their demographic strength would normally warrant. This is particularly so when applying the right to non-discrimination or the right to use their languages with other members of their communities.

There is therefore a definite visible trend towards recognition of the unique relationship between a state and its indigenous peoples which would appear to require concrete government measures allowing the use of their languages, and even correcting the results of previous assimilationist practices through revitalisation measures. At the very least, it would appear that a state has the obligation to provide resources for the use of indigenous languages as a medium of instruction in education, to a degree which reflects the true desires of the peoples involved when it is practical or possible to do so. This obligation could also extend to granting some degree of autonomy which would include the use of indigenous languages in indigenous political, legal and social institutions.

8.0 Conclusion

This study began with a fairly simple question: why should human rights be used to protect language? Yet the question itself is based on the false assumption that individuals who claim the state should somehow acknowledge their linguistic preferences are seeking a type of special treatment in order to protect their language. To answer the question bluntly, human rights are not and have never been concerned with safeguarding languages. Their very *raison d'être* is the treatment of human beings at the hands of state authorities, of providing safeguards against certain types of conduct deemed unacceptable. However, it does not follow that traditional human rights have absolutely no relevance when speaking of language matters.

What this empirical study has attempted to determine is how certain well-established human rights can in practice have an impact when state authorities create burdens and benefits through their linguistic policies or restrict the private use of language. It would appear that rights such as freedom of expression, the right to non-discrimination on the ground of language, and the right of individuals belonging to linguistic minorities to use their language with other members of their group, when properly applied and understood, provide a flexible framework capable of responding to many of the more important demands of individuals, minorities or linguistic groups.

One recurrent theme in this study which should be emphasised is that it is not the existence of a minority or of a large group of individuals with certain characteristics which differ from those of the predominant majority in matters such as language which in itself leads inevitably to conflict, as the examples of Switzerland and Finland show. Generally, it is when individuals are subjected to discrimination, denied their freedom of expression or are otherwise unable to use their language, or when they cannot obtain their "just desserts" from public authorities to the degree appropriate to the strength of their relative number, that a "linguistic minority" or "ethnic" problem is created. Most often, it is the exclusion of all but one tongue and the resulting disadvantages, resentment and discord which create linguistic or ethnic friction.

Exclusive use of an official or majority language by public authorities has led to violence and conflict when undertaken irrespective of the disadvantage it creates for large segments of a state's inhabitants. The decision by India in 1967 to adopt only English and Hindi as official languages incited serious anti-English and anti-Hindi riots in various parts of the country. Sudan is another example of the serious economic and social consequences that can result from inappropriate state language preferences. The imposition of Arabic as an official language on the non-Arab southern region was one of the factors which ignited a civil war which continues to ravage the country. And finally, the bloody conflict in Sri Lanka largely found its original catalyst and was fanned because of the perceived unfair economic consequences of a Sinhala-only policy for Tamil-speakers.[1]

Although necessarily general in scope, this study has attempted to address in a concrete fashion the application of human rights standards in the more relevant areas such as education,

---

[1] In many of these conflicts, language is not the only factor leading to violence and unrest. Religion or race are also often at issue. Nonetheless, language carries with it a great deal of symbolic value, concrete economic effects, and is moreover a highly visible and emotional marker which cannot be generally avoided by states. This makes language an ideal catalyst for political and social mobilisation which leaders and elites have recognised throughout history. The best manner in which to avoid conflicts invoking language as a rallying point is to practice a reasonable and balanced policy for the use of the more widespread languages in a state.

both public and private, public authorities and services, the judiciary, the media, again both public and private, as well as the use of language preferences in highly sensitive areas such as citizenship. Special attention has been paid to the issue of the languages of indigenous peoples because of a growing consensus, both in international law and in many national jurisdictions, that such peoples occupy a unique legal status which results in rights and privileges differing slightly from those rights specifically bestowed upon members of linguistic minorities or to individuals generally such as non-discrimination and freedom of expression.

Amongst the main conclusions drawn from a thorough analysis of these rights is that freedom of expression must be understood to include language. This signifies that some of the more intrusive prohibitions by state authorities, such as the prohibition on using a non-official or non-majority language in private newspapers or in posters or in other forms of diffusion of information are without a doubt a violation of one of the most basic of human rights.

Another important observation is that non-discrimination on the ground of language may be the single most powerful right for individuals seeking more just and responsive conduct from public authorities in language matters. When properly understood and applied, non-discrimination offers a balanced mechanism which recognises that a state may have legitimate reasons for favouring one or a few select languages in carrying out its affairs. This includes such diverse factors as costs, desirability of a common language, available resources, etc. Non-discrimination is therefore a right which may take into consideration factors such as the objectives pursued by state authorities when they favour a particular language and its speakers, the degree of importance of the service or right involved, the number of individuals that are disadvantaged or inconvenienced by the state's policies, whether they are citizens, permanent residents or have a weaker attachment to the state, and even the geographic distribution of the affected individuals. Non-discrimination on the ground of language undoubtedly cannot respond to every demand in every circumstance, but it does offer a middle-of-the-road response that takes into consideration the interests of the state and of those individuals who have a language that differs from the official or majority language. No public authority or state institution can disregard the effect of its conduct on large numbers of speakers of other languages when providing benefits and services to the public. This implies that these benefits or services, in particular state provided or funded education, must be available in the language(s) of these individuals in a degree which is roughly proportionate to their overall numbers.

This study has also shown that many misconceptions over the proper interpretation of Article 27 of the **International Covenant on Civil and Political Rights** could have been avoided by reference to non-discrimination. Although the exact scope of Article 27 may still be subject to some debate, the United Nations Human Rights Committee has made it fairly clear that the provision does not oblige a state to provide public services in the language of a minority. What the provision does do, however, is prevent public authorities from intervening when members of a linguistic minority are using their language amongst themselves. It creates an obligation on a state to ensure minorities can freely use their language and in this respect may require "positive measures" in the form of legislation to protect minorities from outside interference, either by private parties or public officials. Thus this right permits linguistic minorities to carry on activities which can be deemed in some cases essential to their well-being as a community, such as private schools or community projects involving their language. In their desire to ensure the greatest protection possible for linguistic minorities and their language, some scholars tried to read into Article 27 a rather heavy state obligation to provide public education and other services in the language of all minorities. Whilst their intentions were undoubtedly noble, it drove some states to retract into restrictive measures vis-à-vis minorities — including denying their existence or only recognising "national" minorities — for fear of assuming an onerous economic and administrative burden. It was also unnecessary to a large extent since freedom of expression and non-discrimination already offer the means of responding to the need to protect individuals from oppressive or unreasonable state behaviour. Non-discrimination is especially useful in this regard since it provides a generally recognised, and therefore less threatening, right for states that has the added advantage of taking into account the national state interests as well as those of the individual.

Finally, it was essential to set the record straight on a number of other misconceptions. Language is not a uniquely Western concern nor one of recent interest in international and national law. Nor is it related to some type of "cultural" or "secondary" category of rights. It has always been present, albeit discreetly, as a part of the traditional human rights that are at the very core of modern democratic thought. The continuing evolution towards greater juridical recognition of the importance of human rights when considering a state's language preferences, as demonstrated by the multitude of treaties, declarations, and other international, regional, and national legislation or instruments, is nothing short of impressive as the Appendix to this study shows. In essence, these standards are a powerful acknowledgment that the "natural" predilection for those who control a state's machinery to impose their language preferences — and unavoidably, some disadvantage or burden — on the weaker segments of the population has to be tempered in appropriate cases.

It is worth emphasising that all of the above issues must also be understood in terms of the unique position of language as a source of ethnic conflict. On the one hand, language plays a central role in terms of economic opportunity and success. The prevailing or exclusive use of one language in a state will benefit individuals who have greater fluency in the official or majority language as far as access to the resources and opportunities made available by the state is concerned. The reason language is becoming more prominent as a human right concern must also be seen in relation to the changing role of the state in this century. The modern state has become a major purveyor of services and employment or economic opportunities in many countries. It has become highly invasive in many aspects of daily life and now provides a wide range of services to the public. Because the state has no option but to use one or more languages in its various activities, those who are primary speakers of the preferred language gain an enormous advantage over others. Thus, the language favoured by a state affects social and economic mobility.

On the other hand, language is also fundamental to all human societies because it is central to feelings of community, culture and history, of tradition and "belonging". We are, after all, "language animals". It figures prominently as the main link between an individual and his or her community. Furthermore, just as it is impossible — and undesirable — that we should all have the same religion or be of the same colour, not all individuals can have or should have the same primary language.

This has the potential of creating tension within a state, since language is capable of arousing strong emotions by being both intimately a community bond and an integral part of an individual's persona. In addition to their symbolic role in some communities, linguistic links are highly visible and can be co-opted for nationalist political goals as primary beacons of identity. Add to this the very real disadvantages or burdens that will ensue if a state disregards the needs or interests of a large number of its inhabitants who may have a non-official or non-majority primary language, and you have a recipe for conflict if due care is not taken to reach a "fair balance". Human rights such as freedom of expression, the right to non-discrimination on the ground of language, and the right of individuals belonging to linguistic minorities to use their language with other members of their group may all be able to play a part in reaching this desirable balance.

de Tocqueville was right in describing language as probably one of the strongest ties that can unite mankind. What should be added is that language also has the potential of being one of the most divisive if state authorities adopt measures that disregard fundamental human rights standards. More likely than not, such conduct would fan the flames of discontent to the point where language becomes a powerful rallying banner for tension and ultimately conflict.

APPENDIX

TREATIES, DECLARATIONS AND INTERNATIONAL DOCUMENTS

For practical reasons, only provisions dealing specifically with language are reprinted. As a result, many provisions doubtless relevant to language issues (freedom of expression, general prohibitions of discrimination, right to a fair trial) are omitted unless they include an express reference to language. A few exceptions are made in cases involving the rights of minorities or indigenous peoples.

1. International Declarations and other Non-Binding Instruments

1.1 UNITED NATIONS SYSTEM

1.1.1 *Declaration on the Rights of Persons Belonging to National or Ethnic, Religious and Linguistic Minorities*

General Assembly Resolution 47/135, adopted 18 December 1992.

Article 1
1. States shall protect the existence and the national or ethnic, cultural, religious and linguistic identity of minorities within their respective territories, and shall encourage conditions for the promotion of that identity...

Article 2
1. Persons belonging to national or ethnic, religious and linguistic minorities (hereinafter referred to as persons belonging to minorities) have the right to enjoy their own culture, to profess and practise their own religion, and to use their own language, in private and in public, freely and without interference or any form of discrimination.
2. Persons belonging to minorities have the right to participate effectively in cultural, religious, social, economic and public life.
3. Persons belonging to minorities have the right to participate effectively in decisions on the national, and where appropriate, regional level concerning the minority to which they belong or the regions in which they live, in a manner not incompatible with national legislation.
4. Persons belonging to minorities have the right to establish and maintain their own associations.
5. Persons belonging to minorities have the right to establish and maintain, without discrimination, free and peaceful contacts with other members of their group and with persons belonging to other minorities, as well as contacts with other members of their group and with persons belonging to other minorities, as well as contacts across frontiers with citizens of other states to whom they are related by national or ethnic, religious or linguistic ties.

Article 3
1. Persons belonging to minorities may exercise their rights, including those set forth in this Declaration, individually as well as in community with other members of their group, without any discrimination.
2. No disadvantage shall result for any person belonging to a minority as the consequence of the exercise or non-exercise of the rights set forth in this Declaration.

Article 4

1. States shall take measures where required to ensure that persons belonging to minorities may exercise fully and effectively all their human rights and fundamental freedoms without any discrimination and in full equality before the law.

2. States shall take measures to create favourable conditions to enable persons belonging to minorities to express their characteristics and to develop their culture, language, religion, traditions and customs, except where specific practises are in violation of national law and contrary to international standards.

3. States should take appropriate measures so that, wherever possible, persons belonging to minorities have adequate opportunities to learn their mother tongue or to have instruction in their mother tongue.

4. States should, where appropriate, take measures in the field of education, in order to encourage the knowledge of history, traditions, language and culture of the minorities existing within their territory. Persons belonging to minorities should have adequate opportunities to gain knowledge of the society as a whole.

1.1.2   *Draft Declaration on the Rights of Indigenous Peoples*

UN Doc. E/CN.4/Sub.2/1994/56.

Article 3

Indigenous peoples have the right of self-determination. By virtue of that right they freely determine their political status and freely pursue their economic, social and cultural development.

Article 4

Indigenous peoples have the right to maintain and strengthen their distinct political, economic, social and cultural characteristics, as well as their legal systems, while retaining their rights to participate fully, if they so choose, in the political, economic, social and cultural life of the state.

Article 7

Indigenous peoples have the collective and individual right not to be subjected to ethnocide and cultural genocide, including prevention of and redress for :

(a) Any action which has the aim or effect of depriving them of their integrity as distinct peoples, or of their cultural values or ethnic identities;...

(d) Any form of assimilation or integration by other cultures or ways of life imposed on them by legislative, administrative or other measures;

Article 14

Indigenous peoples have the right to revitalise, use, develop and transmit to future generations their histories, languages, oral traditions, philosophies, writing systems and literatures, and to designate and retain their own names for communities, places and persons. States shall take effective measures, whenever any right of indigenous peoples may be threatened, to ensure this right is protected and also to ensure that they can understand and be understood in political, legal and administrative proceedings, where necessary through the provision of interpretation or by other appropriate means.

Article 15

Indigenous children have the right to all levels and forms of education of the state. All indigenous peoples also have this right and the right to establish and control their educational systems and institutions providing education in their own languages, in a manner appropriate to their cultural methods of teaching and learning.

Indigenous children living outside their communities have the right to be provided access to education in their own culture and language.

States shall take effective measures to provide appropriate resources for these purposes.

Article 17

Indigenous peoples have the right to establish their own media in their own languages. They also have the right to equal access to all forms of non-indigenous media. States shall take effective measures to ensure that state-owned media duly reflect indigenous cultural diversity.

Article 19

Indigenous peoples have to right to participate fully, if they so choose, at all levels of decision-making in matters which may affect their rights, lives and destinies through representatives chosen by themselves in accordance with their own procedures, as well as to maintain and develop their own indigenous decision-making institutions.

Article 31

Indigenous peoples, as a specific form of exercising their right to self-determination, have the right to autonomy or self-government in matters relating to their internal and local affairs, including culture, religion, education, information, media, health, housing, employment, social welfare, economic activities, land and resources management, environment and entry by non-members, as well as ways and means for financing these autonomous functions.

Article 32

Indigenous peoples have the collective right to determine their own citizenship in accordance with their customs and traditions. Indigenous citizenship does not impair the right of indigenous individuals to obtain citizenship of the states in which they live.

Indigenous peoples have the right to determine the structures and to select the membership of their institutions in accordance with their own procedures.

Article 33

Indigenous peoples have the right to promote, develop and maintain their institutional structures and their distinctive juridical customs, traditions, procedures and practices, in accordance with internationally recognised human rights standards.

1.1.3 *United Nations Charter (1945), Declaration Regarding Non-Self-Governing Territories*

Article 1

The Purposes of the United Nations are...

3. To achieve international cooperation in solving international problems of an economic, social, cultural, or humanitarian character, and in promoting and encouraging respect as to race, sex, language, or religion.

Article 55

With a view to the creation of conditions of stability and well-being which are necessary for peaceful and friendly relations among nations based on respect for the principle of equal rights and self-determination of peoples, the United Nations shall promote...

(c) universal respect for, and observance of, human rights and fundamental freedoms for all without distinction as to race, sex, language, or religion.

1.1.4   *Universal Declaration of Human Rights*

General Assembly Resolution 217 A (III) of 10 December 1948.

Article 2

1. Everyone is entitled to all the rights and freedoms set forth in this Declaration, without distinction of any kind, such as race, colour, sex, language, religion, political or other opinion, national or social origin, property, birth or other status.

1.1.5   *Vienna Declaration and Programme of Action*

United Nations World Conference on Human Rights, 1-25 June 1993.

19. Considering the importance of the promotion and protection of the rights of persons belonging to minorities and the contribution of such promotion and protection to the political and social stability of the states in which such persons live, the World Conference on Human Rights reaffirms the obligation of states to ensure that persons belonging to minorities may exercise fully and effectively all human rights and fundamental freedoms without any discrimination and in full equality before the law in accordance with the Declaration on the Rights of Persons Belonging to National or Ethnic, Religious and Linguistic Minorities.

The persons belonging to minorities have the right to enjoy their own culture, to profess and practise their own religion and to use their own language in private and in public, freely and without interference or any form of discrimination.

25. The World Conference on Human Rights calls on the Commission on Human Rights to examine ways and means to promote and protect effectively the rights of persons belonging to minorities as set out in the Declaration on the Rights of Persons belonging to National or Ethnic, Religious and Linguistic Minorities. In this context, the World Conference on Human Rights calls upon the Centre for Human Rights to provide, at the request of Governments concerned and as part of its programme of advisory services and technical assistance, qualified expertise on minority issues and human rights, as well as on the prevention and resolution of disputes, to assist in existing or potential situations involving minorities.

26. The World Conference on Human Rights urges states and the international community to promote and protect the rights of persons belonging to national or ethnic, religious and linguistic minorities in accordance with the Declaration on the Rights of Persons belonging to National or Ethnic, Religious and Linguistic Minorities.

1.2   REGIONAL INSTRUMENTS

1.2.1   *American Declaration of the Rights and Duties of Man*

Organisation of American States, Bogota, 2 May 1948.

Article 2
    All persons are equal before the law and have the rights and duties established in this Declaration, without distinction as to race, sex, language, creed or any other factor.

1.2.2   *Central European Initiative Instrument for the Protection of Minority Rights*

Bratislava, 12 July 1994. Draft proposal for consideration by official representatives of 10 Central European states. Opened for signature as a non-binding instrument in November 1994.

Article 1
    States recognise the existence of national minorities as such, considering them integral parts of the society in which they live and guarantee the appropriate conditions for the promotion of their identity.
    For the purpose of this instrument the term "national minority" shall mean a group which is smaller in number than the rest of the population of a state, whose members, who are nationals of that state, have ethnic, religious or linguistic features different from those of the rest of the population, and are guided by the will to safeguard their culture, traditions, religion or language.

Article 7
    States guarantee the right of persons belonging to national minorities to express, preserve and develop their ethnic, cultural, linguistic or religious identity and to maintain and develop their culture in all its aspects.

Article 7 bis
    Without prejudice to democratic principles, states, taking measures in pursuance of their general integration policy, shall refrain from pursuing or encouraging policies aimed at the assimilation of persons belonging to national minorities against their will and shall protect these persons against any action aimed at their assimilation.

Article 10
    Any person belonging to a national minority shall have the right to use his/her language freely, in public as well as in private, verbally and in writing.

Article 11
    Any person belonging to a national minority shall have the right to use his/her surname and first names in his/her language and the right to official acceptance and registration of such surname and names.

Article 12
Any person belonging to a national minority, in exercising his/her religious freedom, shall have the right to use his/her own language in worship, teaching, religious practice or observance.

Article 13
Whenever in an area, the number of persons belonging to a national minority reaches, according to the latest census or other methods of ascertaining its accuracy, a significant level, these persons shall have the right, wherever possible, to use, in conformity with applicable national legislation, their own language in oral and written form, in their contacts with the public authorities of the said area. These authorities may answer, as far as possible, in the same language.

Article 14
In conformity with their national legislation states may allow, where necessary through bilateral agreements with other interested states, in particular with neighbouring states, the displaying of bilingual or plurilingual local names, street names and other topographical indications in areas where the number of persons belonging to a national minority reaches, according to the latest census or other methods of ascertaining its accuracy, a significant level. The display of signs, inscription or other similar information of private nature in the minority language should not be subject to specific restrictions, other than those generally applied in this field.

Article 16
States recognise the right of persons belonging to a national minority to establish and maintain their own preschools and educational establishments and possibly obtain their recognition in conformity with the relevant national legislation. Such establishments may seek public financing or other contributions.

Article 17
Notwithstanding the need to learn the official language of the state concerned, every person belonging to a national minority shall have the right to learn his/her own language and receive an education in his/her own language. The states shall endeavour to ensure the appropriate types and levels of public education in conformity with national legislation, whenever the number of persons belonging to a national minority, according to the latest census or other methods of ascertaining its accuracy, is at a significant level. In the context of the teaching of history and culture in such public educational establishments, adequate teaching of history and culture of the national minorities should be ensured.

Article 18
States guarantee the right of persons belonging to a national minority to avail themselves of the media in their own language, in conformity with relevant state regulations and with possible financial assistance. In case of television and radio in public ownership, the states will assure, whenever appropriate and possible, that persons belonging to national minorities have the right of free access to such media including the production of such programmes in their own language.

Article 21

In accordance with the policies of the states concerned, states will respect the right of persons belonging to national minorities to effective participation in public affairs, in particular in decisions affecting the areas where they live or in the matters affecting them. Therefore states note the efforts undertaken to protect and create conditions for the promotion of the ethnic, cultural, linguistic and religious identity of certain national minorities by adopting appropriate measures corresponding to the specific circumstances of such minorities as foreseen in the CSCE documents.

Article 22

Whenever the number of persons belonging to a national minority reaches, according to the latest census or other methods of ascertaining its accuracy, the majority of the population in an area, states will promote the knowledge of the minority language among officers of the local and decentralised state administrative offices. Efforts should be made to recruit, if possible, officers, who, in addition to the knowledge of the official language, have sufficient knowledge of the minority language.

Article 23

Every person belonging to a national minority, while duly respecting the territorial integrity of the state, shall have the right to have free and unimpeded contacts with the citizens of another country with whom this minority shares ethnic, religious or linguistic features or a cultural identity. States shall not unduly restrict the free exercise of those rights. Furthermore states will encourage transfrontier arrangements at national, regional and local levels.

1.2.3   *Charter of Paris for a New Europe*

Conference on Security and Cooperation in Europe (now the Organisation on Security and Cooperation in Europe), Paris, 21 November 1990.

We affirm that the ethnic, cultural, linguistic and religious identity of national minorities will be protected and that persons belonging to national minorities have the right freely to express, preserve and develop identity without any discrimination and in full equality before the law.

Human dimension

... Determined to foster the rich contribution of national minorities to the life of our societies, we undertake further to improve their situation. We reaffirm our deep conviction that friendly relations among our peoples, as well as peace, justice, stability and democracy, require that the ethnic, cultural, linguistic and religious identity of national minorities be protected and conditions for the promotion of that identity be created. We declare that questions related to national minorities can only be satisfactorily resolved in a democratic political framework. We further acknowledge that the rights of persons belonging to national minorities must be fully respected as part of universal human rights.

1.2.4   *Concluding Document of the Stockholm Conference on Confidence- and Security-Building Measures and Certain Aspects of Security and Disarmament in Europe*

Conference on Security and Co-operation in Europe (now the Organisation on Security and Cooperation in Europe), Stockholm, 19 September 1986.

Co-operation in the Field of Economics, of Science and Technology and of the Environment

... The participating states will ensure that migrant workers from other participating states, and their families, can freely enjoy and maintain their national culture and have access to the culture of the host country.

Aiming at ensuring effective equality of opportunity between the children of migrant workers and the children of their own nationals regarding access to all forms and levels of education, the participating states affirm their readiness to take measures needed for the better use and improvement of educational opportunities. Furthermore, they will encourage or facilitate, where reasonable demands exists, supplementary teaching in their mother tongue for the children of migrant workers.

Co-operation in Humanitarian and other Fields

... [The participating states] will deal favourably with applications for travel abroad without distinction of any kind, such as race, colour, sex, language, religion, political or other opinion, national or social origin, property, birth, age or other status. They will ensure that any refusal does not affect applications submitted by other persons.

... They will ensure in practice that persons belonging to national minorities or regional cultures on their territories can disseminate, have access to, and exchange information in their mother tongue.

... They will renew their efforts to give effect to the provisions of the Final Act and the Madrid Concluding Document relating to less widely spoken languages. They will also encourage initiatives aimed at increasing the number of translations of literature from and into these languages and improving their quality, in particular by the holding of workshops involving translators, authors and publishers, by the publication of dictionaries and, where appropriate, by the exchange of translators through scholarships.

They will ensure that persons belonging to national minorities or regional cultures on their territories can maintain and develop their own culture in all its aspects, including language, literature and religion; and that they can preserve their cultural and historical monuments and objects.

... They will ensure access by all to the various types and levels of education without discrimination as to race, colour, sex, language, religion, political or other opinion, national or social origin, property, birth or other status.

... They will ensure that persons belonging to national minorities or regional cultures on their territories can give and receive instruction on their own culture, including instruction through parental transmission of language, religion and cultural identity to their children.

1.2.5 *Concluding Document of the Vienna Meeting on the Follow-up to the Conference*

Conference on Security and Co-operation in Europe (now the Organisation on Security and Co-operation in Europe), Vienna, 15 January 1989.

11. [The participating states] confirm that they will respect human rights and fundamental freedoms, including the freedom of thought, conscience, religion or belief, for all without distinction as to race, sex, language or religion. They also confirm the universal significance of human rights and fundamental freedoms, respect for which is an essential factor for the peace, justice and security necessary to ensure the development of friendly relations and co-operation among themselves, as among all states.

13. In this context [the participating states] will...
>13.7 - ensure human rights and fundamental freedoms to everyone within their territory and subject to their jurisdiction, without distinction of any kind such as race, colour, sex, language, religion, political or other opinion, national or social origin, property, birth or other status;

16. In order to ensure the freedom of the individual to profess and practice religion or belief, the participating states will, *inter alia*, ...
>16.6 - respect the right of everyone to give and receive religious education in the language of his choice, whether individually or in association with others;...
>16.9 - respect the right of individual believers and communities of believers to acquire, possess, and use sacred books, religious publications in the language of their choice and other articles and materials related to the practise of religion or belief;

18. They will protect and create conditions for the promotion of the ethnic, cultural, linguistic and religious identity of national minorities on their territory. They will respect the free exercise of rights by persons belonging to such minorities and ensure their full equality with others.

1.2.6 *Directive du 26 janvier 1965 concernant le rapprochement des dispositions législatives, réglementaires et administratives, relatives aux spécialités pharmaceutiques*

European Union, Brussels, 26 January 1965. Directive 65/65/CEE. Reprinted from Labrie, Normand (1993), *La construction linguistique de la communauté européenne*, Honoré Champion, Paris, at p. 179.

Article 18
Les indications prévues à l'article 13 premier alinéa points 6, 7 et 8 doivent être rédigées sur l'emballage extérieur et sur le récipient des spécialités pharmaceutiques dans la ou les langues du pays de mise sur le marché.

1.2.7   *Directive du 18 juin 1974 relative au rapprochement des législations des États membres concernant les agents émulsifiants, stabilisants, épaississants et gélifiants pouvant être employés dans les denrées alimentaires*

European Union, Brussels, 18 June 1974. Directive 74/329/CEE. Reprinted from Labrie, Normand (1993), *La construction linguistique de la communauté européenne*, Honoré Champion, Paris, at pp. 177-178.

Article 8
4. Les États membres ne peuvent interdire l'introduction dans leur territoire et la mise dans le commerce des substances énumérées à l'annexe I pour la seule raison qu'ils considèrent l'étiquetage comme insuffisant, si les indications prévues au paragraphe 1 figurent sur les emballages ou récipients et si celles prévues au paragraphe 1 sous b) et c) sont rédigées dans au moins une langue officielle de la Communauté. Toutefois, chaque État membre destinataire peut exiger que ces dernières mentions soient rédigées dans sa ou ses langues officielles.

1.2.8   *Directive du 25 juillet 1977 visant à la scolarisation des enfants des travailleurs migrants*

European Union, Brussels, 25 July 1977. Directive 77/486/CEE. Reprinted from Labrie, Normand (1993), *La construction linguistique de la communauté européenne*, Honoré Champion, Paris, at pp. 376-378.

Article 2
Les États membres prennent, conformément à leurs situations nationales et à leurs systèmes juridiques, les mesures appropriées afin que soit offert sur leur territoire, en faveur des enfants visés à l'article 1, un enseignement d'accueil gratuit comportant notamment l'enseignement adapté aux besoins spécifiques de ces enfants, de la langue officielle ou de l'une des langues officielles de l'État d'accueil.
Les États membres prennent les mesures nécessaires pour la formation initiale et continue des enseignants qui assurent cet enseignement.

Article 3
Les États membres prennent, conformément à leurs situations nationales et à leurs systèmes juridiques, et en coopération avec les États d'origine, les mesures appropriées en vue de promouvoir, en coordination avec l'enseignement normal, un enseignement de la langue maternelle et de la culture du pays d'origine en faveur des enfants visés à l'article 1.

1.2.9 *Directive du 18 décembre 1978 relative au rapprochement des législations des États membres concernant l'étiquetage et la présentation des denrées alimentaires destinées au consommateur final ainsi que la publicité faite à leur égard*

European Union, Brussels, 18 December 1978. Directive 79/112/CEE. Reprinted from Labrie, Normand (1993), *La construction linguistique de la communauté européenne*, Honoré Champion, Paris, at p. 176.

Article 14
   Les États membres s'abstiennent de préciser au-delà de ce qui est prévu aux articles 3 à 11 les modalités selon lesquelles les mentions prévues à l'article 3 et à l'article 4 paragraphe 2 doivent être indiquées.
   Toutefois, les États membres veillent à interdire sur leur territoire le commerce de denrées alimentaires si les mentions prévues à l'article 3 et à l'article 4 paragraphe 2 ne figurent pas dans une langue facilement comprise par les acheteurs sauf si l'information de l'acheteur peut être assurée par d'autres mesures. Cette disposition ne fait pas obstacle à ce que lesdites mentions figurent en plusieurs langues.

1.2.10 *Directive du 24 septembre 1990 relative à l'étiquetage nutritionnel des denrées alimentaires*

European Union, Brussels, 24 September 1990. Directive 90/496/CEE. Reprinted from Labrie, Normand (1993), *La construction linguistique de la communauté européenne*, Honoré Champion, Paris, at p. 177.

Article 7
   2. Les États membres veillent à ce que les informations couvertes par la présente directive apparaissent dans une langue facilement comprise par les acheteurs, sauf si l'information de l'acheteur est assurée par d'autres mesures. Cette disposition ne fait pas obstacle à ce que lesdites informations figurent en plusieurs langues.

1.2.11 *Document of the Copenhagen Meeting of the Conference on the Human Dimension*

Conference on Security and Cooperation in Europe (now the Organisation on Security and Cooperation in Europe), Copenhagen, 29 June 1990. Reprinted in (1990) *International Legal Materials*, Vol. 29, at p. 1305.

   25. The participating states confirm that any derogations from obligations relating to human rights and fundamental freedoms during a state of public emergency must remain strictly within the limits provided for by international law, in particular the relevant international instruments by which they are bound, especially with respect to rights from which there can be no derogation. They also reaffirm that...
   25.4 - such measures will not discriminate solely on the grounds of race, colour, sex, language, religion, social origin or of belonging to a minority.

31. Persons belonging to national minorities have the right to exercise fully and effectively their human rights and fundamental freedoms without any discrimination and in full equality before the law.

The participating states will adopt, where necessary, special measures for the purpose of ensuring to persons belonging to national minorities full equality with the other citizens in the exercise of human rights and fundamental freedoms.

32. To belong to a national minority is a matter of a person's individual choice and no disadvantage may arise from the exercise of such choice.

Persons belonging to national minorities have the right freely to express, preserve and develop their ethnic, cultural, linguistic or religious identity and to maintain and develop their culture in all its aspects, free of any attempts at assimilation against their will. In particular, they have the right:

32.1 - to use freely their mother tongue in private as well as in public;

32.2 - to establish and maintain their own educational, cultural and religious institutions, organisations or associations, which can seek voluntary financial and other contributions as well as public assistance, in conformity with national legislation;

32.3 - to profess and practise their religion, including the acquisition, possession and use of religious materials, and to conduct religious educational activities in their mother tongue;...

32.5 - to disseminate, have access to and exchange information in their mother tongue;...

Persons belonging to national minorities can exercise and enjoy their rights individually as well as in community with other members of their group. No disadvantage may arise for a person belonging to a national minority on account of the exercise or non-exercise of any such rights.

33. The participating states will protect the ethnic, cultural, linguistic and religious identity of national minorities on their territory and create conditions for the promotion of that identity. They will take the necessary measures to that effect after due consultations, including contacts with organisations or associations of such minorities, in accordance with the decision-making procedures of each state.

Any such measures will be in conformity with the principles of equality and non-discrimination with respect to the other citizens of the participating state concerned.

34. The participating states will endeavour to ensure that persons belonging to national minorities, notwithstanding the need to learn the official language or languages of the state concerned, have adequate opportunities for instruction of their mother tongue or in their mother tongue, as well as, wherever possible and necessary, for its use before public authorities, in conformity with applicable national legislation.

In the context of the teaching of history and culture in educational establishments, they will also take account of the history and culture of national minorities.

35. The participating states will respect the right of persons belonging to national minorities to effective participation in public affairs, including participation in the affairs relating to the protection and promotion of the identity of such minorities.

The participating states note the efforts undertaken to protect and create conditions for the promotion of the ethnic, cultural, linguistic and religious identity of certain national minorities by establishing, as one of the possible means to achieve these aims, appropriate local or autonomous administrations corresponding to the specific historical and territorial circumstances of such minorities and in accordance with the policies of the state concerned.

36. The participating states recognise the particular importance of increasing constructive co-operation among themselves on questions relating to national minorities. Such co-operation seeks to promote mutual understanding and confidence, friendly and good-neighbourly relations, international peace, security and justice.

Every participating state will promote a climate of mutual respect, understanding, co-operation and solidarity among all persons living on its territory, without distinction as to ethnic or national origin or religion, and will encourage the solution of problems through dialogue based on the principles of the rule of law.

40. The participating states clearly and unequivocally condemn totalitarianism, racial and ethnic hatred, anti-semitism, xenophobia and discrimination against anyone as well as persecution on religious and ideological grounds. In this context, they also recognise the particular problems of Roma (gypsies).

They declare their firm intention to intensify the efforts to combat these phenomena in all their forms and therefore will:

40.1 - take effective measures, including the adoption, in conformity with their constitutional systems and their international obligations, of such laws as may be necessary, to provide protection against any acts that constitute incitement to violence against persons or groups based on national, racial, ethnic or religious discrimination, hostility or hatred, including anti-semitism;

40.2 - commit themselves to take appropriate and proportionate measures to protect persons or groups who may be subject to threats or acts of discrimination, hostility or violence as a result of their racial, ethnic, cultural, linguistic and religious identity, and to protect their property;

1.2.12 *Document of the Moscow Meeting of the Conference on the Human Dimension*

Conference on Security and Cooperation in Europe (now the Organisation on Security and Cooperation in Europe), Moscow, 3 October 1991. Reprinted from (1991) *International Legal Materials*, Vol. 30, at p. 1670.

23.1 The participating states will ensure that...

(ii) anyone who is arrested will be informed promptly in a language which he understands of the reason for his arrest, and will be informed of any charges against him;

28.7 The participating states will endeavour to refrain from making derogations from those obligations from which, according to international conventions to which they are parties, derogation is possible under a state of public emergency. Measures derogating from such obligations must be taken in strict conformity with the procedural requirements laid down in those instruments. Such measures will neither go further nor remain in force longer than strictly required by the exigencies of the situation; they are by nature exceptional and should be interpreted and applied with restraint. Such measures will not discriminate solely on the grounds of race, colour, sex, language, religion, social origin or of belonging to a minority.

38. The participating states recognise the need to ensure that the rights of migrant workers and their families lawfully residing in the participating states are respected and underline their right to express freely their ethnic, cultural, religious and linguistic characteristics. The exercise of such rights may be subject to such restrictions as are prescribed by law and are consistent with international standards.

38.4 They recommend that the CSCE in its future work on the human dimension consider appropriate means to hold focused discussions on all issues regarding migrant workers, including *inter alia*, familiarisation with the language and social life of the country concerned.

1.2.13 *Draft of the Inter-American Declaration on the Rights of Indigenous Peoples*

Draft approved by the Inter-American Commission on Human Rights, OEA/SER/L/V/II.90, 21 September 1995.

Article II
3. The states also recognise that the indigenous peoples are entitled to collective rights in so far as they are indispensable to the enjoyment of the individual rights of their members. Accordingly they recognise the right of the indigenous peoples to collective action, to their cultures, to profess and practice their religious beliefs and to use their languages.

Article V
The states shall not take any action which forces indigenous peoples to assimilate and shall not endorse any theory, or engage in any practice, that imports discrimination, destruction of a culture or the possibility of the extermination of any ethnic group.

Article VII
3. States shall recognise, and respect, indigenous life-styles, customs, traditions, forms of social organisation, use of dress, languages and dialects.

Article VIII
1. States recognise that indigenous languages, philosophy and outlook are a component of national and universal culture, and as such shall respect them and facilitate their dissemination.
2. The states shall take measures to see to it that broadcast radio and television programs are broadcast in the indigenous languages in the regions where there is a strong indigenous presence, and to support the creation of indigenous radio stations and other media.
3. The states shall take effective measures to enable indigenous peoples to understand administrative, legal and political rules and procedures and to be understood in relation to these matters. In areas where indigenous languages are predominant, states shall endeavour to establish the pertinent languages as official languages and to give them the same status that is given to non-indigenous official languages.
4. When indigenous peoples wish, educational systems shall be conducted in the indigenous languages and incorporate indigenous content, and that shall also provide the necessary training and means for complete mastery of the official language or languages.

Article IX
   1. Indigenous peoples shall be entitled a) to establish and set in motion their own educational programs, institutions and facilities, b) to prepare and implement their own educational plans, programs, curricula and materials, c) to train, educate and accredit their teachers and administrators. The states shall endeavour to ensure that such systems guarantee equal educational and teaching opportunities for the entire population and complementarity with national educational systems.
   2. States shall ensure that those educational systems are equal in all ways to that provided to the rest of the population.
   3. States shall provide financial aid and any other type of assistance needed for the implementation of the provisions of this Article.

1.2.14 *Helsinki Final Act*

Conference on Security and Co-operation in Europe (now the Organisation on Security and Co-operation in Europe), Helsinki, 1 August 1975.

VII. Respect for human rights and fundamental freedoms, including the freedom of thought, conscience, religion or belief
   The participating states will respect human rights and fundamental freedoms, including the freedom of thought, conscience, religion or belief, for all without distinction as to race, sex, language or religion.

1.2.15 *Helsinki Summit Decisions*

Conference on Security and Cooperation in Europe (now the Organisation on Security and Cooperation in Europe), Helsinki, 10 July 1992. Reprinted from (1992) *International Legal Materials*, Vol. 31, at p. 1385.

The participating states...

   24. Will intensify in this context their efforts to ensure the free exercise by persons belonging to national minorities, individually or in community with others, of their human rights and fundamental freedoms, including the right to participate fully, in accordance with the democratic decision-making procedures of each state, in the political, economic, social and cultural life of their countries including through democratic participation in decision-making and consultative bodies at the national, regional and local level, *inter alia*, through political parties and associations;

   25. Will continue through unilateral, bilateral and multilateral efforts to explore further avenues for more effective implementation of their relevant CSCE commitments, including those related to the protection and the creation of conditions for the promotion of the ethnic, cultural, linguistic and religious identity of national minorities;

   36. Restate that human rights and fundamental freedoms are universal, that they are also enjoyed by migrant workers wherever they live and stress the importance of implementing all

CSCE commitments on migrant workers and their families lawfully residing in all participating states;

37. Will encourage the creation of conditions to foster greater harmony in relations between migrant workers and the rest of the society of the participating state in which they lawfully reside. To this end, they will seek to offer, *inter alia*, measures to facilitate the familiarisation of migrant workers and their families with the languages and social life of the respective participating state in which they lawfully reside so as to enable them to participate in the life of the society of the host country;

1.2.16 *Recommendation 1134 (1990) on the Rights of Minorities*

Council of Europe, Strasbourg, 1 October 1990.

11. In respect of national minorities — that is to say, separate or distinct groups, well defined and established on the territory of a state, the members of which are nationals of that state and have certain religious, linguistic, cultural or other characteristics which distinguish them from the majority of the population — the following principles should apply...
ii. national minorities shall have the right to maintain and develop their culture;
iii. national minorities shall have the right to maintain their own educational, religious and cultural institutions. For this purpose, they shall also have the right to solicit voluntary financial and other contributions including public assistance;
iv. national minorities shall have the right to participate fully in decision-making about matters which affect the preservation and development of their identity and in the implementation of those decisions;...

12. Furthermore, in respect of linguistic minorities, the Assembly adopts the following two principles:
i. persons belonging to a linguistic minority shall have access to adequate types and levels of public education in their mother tongue;
ii. linguistic minorities shall have the right to obtain, provide, possess, reproduce, distribute and exchange information in their mother tongue regardless of frontiers.
13. As far as the European states are concerned they should...
ii. take all the necessary legislative, administrative, judicial and other measures to create favourable conditions to enable minorities to express their identity, to develop their education, culture, language, traditions and customs;...
iv. abstain from pursuing policies aimed at forced assimilation of national minorities, from taking administrative measures affecting the composition of the population in areas inhabited by national minorities, and from compelling such minorities to remain confined in geographical and cultural "ghettos";
v. fully implement the provision of Article 27 of the International Covenant on Civil and Political Rights which reads as follows: "In those states in which ethnic, religious or linguistic minorities exist, persons belonging to such minorities shall not be denied the right, in community with the other members of their group, to enjoy their own culture, to profess and practise their own religion, or to use their own language."

15. In addition, it draws attention to the obligations contained in the international instruments relating to national, ethnic, religious and linguistic minorities, by which the states participating in the CSCE process are bound.

1.2.17 *Recommendation 1177 (1992) concerning the Rights of Minorities*

Council of Europe, Strasbourg, 5 February 1992.

1. L'histoire a constitué le continent européen en une mosaïque de peuples différents par leur langue, leur culture, leurs traditions et coutumes, leur pratique religieuse.
2. Ces peuples se sont tellement brassés, imbriqués les uns dans les autres, qu'aucun découpage territorial ne peut les circonscrire totalement et exclusivement. Les frontières étatiques héritées des deux dernières guerres mondiales n'y sont pas parvenues. Celles de l'avenir, quelles quelles soient, n'y réussiraient pas non plus.
3. Il ne peut y avoir dans un État démocratique de citoyens de deuxième zone : la citoyenneté est égale pour tous. La première et ultime garantie de cette égalité de droits et de devoirs découle du respect rigoureux des droits de l'homme pour les États et de leur ratification de la Convention européenne des Droits de l'Homme.
4. A l'intérieur de cette citoyenneté commune, des citoyens qui partagent avec d'autres des caractéristiques spécifiques
- d'ordre culturel, linguistique ou religieux notamment - peuvent cependant désirer se voir reconnaître et garantir la possibilité de les exprimer.

1.2.18 *Recommendation 1201 (1993) on an Additional Protocol on the Rights of National Minorities to the European Convention on Human Rights*

Council of Europe, Strasbourg, 1 February 1993. Text of the proposal for an additional protocol to the Convention for the protection of Human Rights and Fundamental Freedoms, concerning persons belonging to national minorities.

Article 1
For the purpose of this Convention, the expression "national minority" refers to a group of persons in a state who:
(a) reside on the territory of that state and are citizens thereof;
(b) maintain longstanding, firm and lasting ties with that state;
(c) display distinctive ethnic, cultural, religious or linguistic characteristics;
(d) are sufficiently representative, although smaller in number than the rest of the population of that state or of a region of that state;
(e) are motivated by a concern to preserve together that which constitutes their common identity, including their culture, their traditions, their religion or their language.

Article 3
1. Every person belonging to a national minority shall have the right to express, preserve and develop in complete freedom his/her religious, ethnic, linguistic and/or cultural identity, without being subjected to any attempt at assimilation against his/her will.

Article 7

1. Every person belonging to a national minority shall have the right freely to use his/her mother tongue in private and in public, both orally and in writing. This right shall also apply to the use of his/her language in publications and in the audiovisual sector.

2. Every person belonging to a national minority shall have the right to use his/her surname and first names in his/her mother tongue and to official recognition of his/her surname and first names.

3. In the regions in which substantial numbers of a national minority are settled, the persons belonging to a national minority shall have the right to use their mother tongue in their contacts with the administrative authorities and in proceedings before the courts and legal authorities.

4. In the regions in which substantial numbers of a national minority are settled, the persons belonging to that minority shall have the right to display in their language local names, signs, inscriptions and other similar information visible to the public. This does not deprive the authorities of their right to display the above-mentioned information in the official language or languages of the state.

Article 8

1. Every person belonging to a national minority shall have the right to learn his/her mother tongue and to receive an education in his/her mother tongue at an appropriate number of schools and of state educational and training establishments, located in accordance with the geographical distribution of the minority.

2. The persons belonging to a national minority shall have the right to set up and manage their own schools and educational and training establishments within the framework of the legal system of the state.

Article 10

Every person belonging to a national minority, while duly respecting the territorial integrity of the state, shall have the right to have free and unimpeded contacts with the citizens of another country with whom this minority shares ethnic, religious or linguistic features or a cultural identity.

Article 11

In the regions where they are in a majority the persons belonging to a national minority shall have the right to have at their disposal appropriate local or autonomous authorities or to have a special status, matching the specific historical and territorial situation and in accordance with the domestic legislation of the state.

Article 12

2. Measures taken for the sole purpose of protecting ethnic groups, fostering their appropriate development and ensuring that they are granted equal rights and treatment with respect to the rest of the population in the administrative, political, economic, social and cultural fields and in other spheres shall not be considered as discrimination.

1.2.19 *Report of Experts on National Minorities*

Conference on Security and Cooperation in Europe (now the Organisation on Security and

Cooperation in Europe), Geneva, 19 July 1991. Reprinted from (1991) *Human Rights Law Journal*, Vol. 12, at pp. 332-334.

II.

The participating states stress the continued importance of a thorough review of implementation of their CSCE commitments relating to persons belonging to national minorities.

They emphasise that human rights and fundamental freedoms are the basis for the protection and promotion of rights of persons belonging to national minorities. They further recognise that questions relating to national minorities can only be satisfactorily resolved in a democratic political framework based on the rule of law, with a functioning independent judiciary. This framework guarantees full respect for human rights and fundamental freedoms, equal rights and status for all citizens, including persons belonging to national minorities, the free expression of all their legitimate interests and aspirations, political pluralism, social tolerance and the implementation of legal rules that place effective restraints on the abuse of governmental power.

Issues concerning national minorities, as well as compliance with international obligations and commitments concerning the rights of persons belonging to them, are matters of legitimate international concern and consequently do not constitute exclusively an internal affair of the respective state.

They note that not all ethnic, cultural, linguistic or religious differences necessarily lead to the creation of national minorities.

III.

They reconfirm that persons belonging to national minorities have the right freely to express, preserve and develop their ethnic, cultural, linguistic or religious identity and to maintain and develop their culture in all its aspects, free of any attempts at assimilation against their will.

IV.

The participating states reconfirm the importance of adopting, where necessary, special measures for the purpose of ensuring to persons belonging to national minorities full equality with the other citizens in the exercise and enjoyment of human rights and fundamental freedoms. They further recall the need to take the necessary measures to protect the ethnic, cultural, linguistic and religious identity of national minorities on their territory and create conditions for the promotion of that identity; any such measures will be in conformity with the principles of equality and non-discrimination with respect to the other citizens of the participating state concerned.

They recognise that such measures, which take into account, *inter alia*, historical and territorial circumstances of national minorities, are particularly important in areas where democratic institutions are being consolidated and national minorities issues are of special concern.

Aware of the diversity and varying constitutional systems among them, which make no single approach necessarily generally applicable, the participating states note with interest that positive results have been obtained by some of them in an appropriate democratic manner by, *inter alia*:
- advisory and decision-making bodies in which minorities are represented, in particular with regard to education, culture and religion;
- elected bodies and assemblies of national minority affairs;

- local and autonomous administration, as well as autonomy on a territorial basis, including the existence of consultative, legislative and executive bodies chosen through free and periodic elections;
- self-administration by a national minority of aspects concerning its identity in situations where autonomy on a territorial basis does not apply;
- decentralised or local forms of government;
- bilateral and multilateral agreements and other arrangements regarding national minorities;
- for persons belonging to national minorities, provision of adequate types and levels of education in their mother tongue with due regard to the number, geographic settlement patterns and cultural traditions of national minorities;
- funding the teaching of minority languages to the general public, as well as the inclusion of minority languages in teacher-training institutions, in particular in regions inhabited by persons belonging to national minorities;
- in cases where instruction in a particular subject is not provided in their territory in the minority language in all levels, taking the necessary measures to find means of recognising diplomas issued abroad for a course of study completed in that language;
- creation of government research agencies to review legislation and disseminate information related to equal rights and non-discrimination;
- provision of financial and technical assistance to persons belonging to national minorities who so wish to exercise their right to establish and maintain their own educational, cultural and religious institutions, organisations and associations;
- governmental assistance for addressing local difficulties relating to discriminatory practises (e.g. a citizens relations service);
- encouragement of grassroots community relations efforts between minority communities, between majority and minority communities, and between neighbouring communities sharing borders, aimed at helping to prevent local tensions from arising and address conflicts peacefully should they arise; and
- encouragement of the establishment of permanent mixed commissions, either inter-state or regional, to facilitate continuing dialogue between the border regions concerned.

The participating states are of the view that these or other approaches, individually or in combination, could be helpful in improving the situation of national minorities on their territories.

VII.

In access to the media, they will not discriminate against anyone based on ethnic, cultural, linguistic or religious grounds. They will make information available that will assist the electronic mass media in taking into account, in their programmes, the ethnic, cultural, linguistic and religious identity of national minorities.

1.2.20 *Resolution on Languages in the Community and the Situation of Catalan*

European Union, Strasbourg, 11 December 1990.

The European Parliament...

1. Stresses the importance of the use made of languages by the European Communities, which should endeavour to be seen by the peoples of Europe not as an extraneous foreign body but as an integral part of the daily life of the individual citizen;

2. Believes that Petitions Nos 113/88 by the Catalan Parliament and 161/88 by the Parliament of the Balearic Islands will express this need with regard to Catalan, an official language in the region of the peoples represented by the two Parliaments which submitted these petitions under the terms of their respective Statutes of Autonomy and those of the general provisions of Article 3 of the Spanish Constitution of 1978;

3. Notes that with regard to the objective of the petitions in question, the rules governing the languages of the institutions of the Community under the provisions of Article 217 of the EEC Treaty, Article 190 of the EUROATOM Treaty and Council Regulation No 1 of 15 April 1958 are determined by the Council acting unanimously and that for member states which have more than one official language, the language to be used must, at the request of such states, be determined by the general rules of their laws;

4. Calls on the Council, comprised of representatives of the member states, and the Commission to take whatever steps are necessary to achieve the following objectives:
- the publication in Catalan of the Community's treaties and basic texts;
- the use of Catalan for disseminating public information concerning the European institutions in all the media;
- the inclusion of Catalan in the programmes set up by the Commission for learning European languages;
- the use of Catalan by the Commission's offices in its written and oral dealings with the public in the Autonomous communities in question;

5. Welcomes the fact that under the Rules of Procedure of the Court of Justice, Catalan may already be used at the Court by witnesses and experts if they are unable adequately to express themselves in one of the procedural languages of the Court;

> 1.2.21 *Resolution on the Languages and Cultures of Regional and Ethnic Minorities (European Union)*

European Parliament, Strasbourg, 30 October 1987.

The European Parliament...

3. Points out once again the need for the member states to recognise their linguistic minorities in their laws and thus create the basic condition for the preservation and development of regional and minority cultures and languages;...

5. Recommends to the member states that they carry out educational measures including:
- arranging for pre-school to university education and continuing education to be officially conducted in the regional and minority languages in the language areas concerned on an equal footing with instruction in the national languages,
- officially recognising courses, classes and schools set up by associations which are authorised to teach, under the regulations in force in the country concerned, and which use a regional or minority language as the general teaching language,

- giving particular attention to the training of teaching staff in the regional or minority languages and making available the educational resources required to accomplish these measures,
- promoting information on educational opportunities in the regional and minority languages,

6. Recommends to the member states that they carry out administrative and legal measures including:
- providing a direct legal basis for the use of regional and minority languages, in the first instance in the local authorities of areas where a minority group does exist,
- reviewing national provisions and practices that discriminate against minority languages, as called for in Parliament's resolution of 16 January 1986 on the rise of fascism and racism in Europe,
- requiring decentralised central government services also to use national, regional and minority languages in the areas concerned,
- officially recognising surnames and place names expressed in a regional or minority language,
- accepting place names and indications on electoral lists in a regional or minority language;

7. Recommends to the member states that they take measures in respect of the mass media, including:
-granting and making possible access to local, regional and central public and commercial broadcasting systems in such a way as to guarantee the continuity and effectiveness of broadcasts in regional and minority languages,
- ensuring that minority groups obtain organisational and financial support for their programmes commensurate with that available to the majority,...
- putting the latest achievements in communications technology to the service of the regional and minority languages,
- taking account of the extra costs entailed by provision for special scripts, such as Cyrillic, Hebrew, Greek, etc.;

8. Recommends to the member states that they take measures in respect of the cultural infrastructure including:
- ensuring that representatives of groups that use regional or minority languages are able to participate directly in cultural facilities and activities,
- the creation of foundations and institutes for the study of regional and minority languages, one of whose tasks would be to set up the educational machinery for the introduction of regional and minority languages in schools and draw up a "general inventory" of the regional and minority language concerned,
- the development of dubbing and subtitling techniques to encourage audiovisual productions in the regional and minority languages,
- provision of the necessary material and financial support for the implementation of these measures;

9. Recommends to the member states that they take social and economic measures including:
- providing for the use of the regional and minority languages in public concerns (postal service, etc.),

- recognition of the use of the regional and minority languages in the payments sector (giro cheques and banking),
- providing for consumer information and product labelling in regional and minority languages,
- providing for the use of regional languages for road and other public signs in street names;

10. Recommends to the member states that they take measures in respect of the regional and minority languages that are used in several member states, particularly in frontier areas, including:
- providing for the appropriate cross-frontier cooperation machinery for cultural and linguistic policy,

12. Calls on the Commission to...
- take account of the languages and cultures of regional and ethnic minorities in the Community when working out the various areas of Community policy, particularly with regard to Community measures in the field of cultural and educational policy,...
- reserve the necessary broadcasting time for minority cultures in European television,
- give the necessary attention to linguistic minorities in the Community's information publications;

15. Stresses categorically that the recommendations contained in this resolution are not to be interpreted or implemented in such a way as to jeopardise the territorial integrity or public order of the member states;

16. Instructs its appropriate committee to draw up separate reports on the languages and cultures of non-permanent Community citizens. Community citizens living in another member state from that from which they come, migrants and overseas minorities and points out that each of these groups share many of the disadvantages of speakers of lesser used languages and that their specific problems deserve detailed and separate treatment;

1.2.22 *Résolution sur les minorités linguistiques et culturelles dans l'Union européenne (European Union)*

European Parliament, Strasbourg, 9 February 1994. Reprinted from *Contact Bulletin*, European Bureau for Lesser Used Languages, 1994, Volume 11, No 1, at pp. 3-5.

Le Parlement européen...

2. souligne une nouvelle fois la nécessité, pour les États membres, de reconnaître leurs minorités linguistiques et d'adopter les dispositions juridiques et administratives requises afin de mettre en place les conditions voulues pour préserver et développer ces langues;

3. est également d'avis que toutes les langues et cultures moins répandues devraient, en outre, bénéficier dans les États membres d'un statut légal approprié;

4. estime que ce statut devrait au moins supposer l'utilisation et le développement de ces langues et cultures au niveau de l'enseignement, de la justice, de l'administration publique, des médias, de la toponymie et des autres secteurs de la vie publique et culturelle sans porter

préjudice à l'utilisation des langues de grande diffusion lorsque cela facilite la communication à l'intérieur de chacun des États membres et l'Union dans son ensemble.

5. précise que le fait, pour une partie des ressortissants d'un État, de parler une langue et d'avoir une culture différentes de celle qui prédomine dans l'État ou dans une partie ou région de cet État ne doit donner lieu à aucune discrimination et, en particulier, à aucun type de marginalisation sociale qui puisse entraver l'accès à l'emploi ou le maintien dans un emploi;

6. soutient la Charte européenne des langues régionales ou minoritaires, à laquelle a été conférée la forme juridique d'une convention européenne, en tant qu'instrument à la fois efficace et souple de protection et de promotion des langues de moindre diffusion;

9. encourage vivement les États membres ainsi que les régions et les collectivités locales concernées à étudier la possibilité de conclure des accords visant à la création d'institutions linguistiques transfrontalières pour les langues et les cultures de moindre diffusion qui sont utilisées dans deux ou plusieurs États voisins ou simultanément dans plusieurs États membres;

10. invite la Commission à:
a) contribuer, dans le cadre de ses compétences, à l'application des initiatives prises par les États membres de ce domaine;
b) tenir compte des langues de moindre diffusion et des cultures qu'elles reflètent lorsqu'elle définit certaines politiques communautaires; prendre des dispositions pour répondre aux besoins des usagers des langues de moindre diffusion de la même manière qu'aux besoins des usagers des langues majoritaires, dans tous les programmes d'enseignement et les programmes culturels, dont « Jeunesse pour l'Europe », ERASMUS, TEMPUS, « Dimension européenne », « Platform Europe », MEDIA, ainsi que les programmes de traduction des oeuvres littéraires contemporaines;
c) encourager l'usage des langues de moindre diffusion dans la politique audiovisuelle de l'Union par exemple dans le contexte de la télévision haute-définition, ainsi qu'à aider les producteurs et les responsables de la diffusion dans des langues moins répandues à réaliser de nouveaux programmes en format 16:9;
d) faire en sorte que la technologie moderne des télécommunications numériques, qui permet de densifier les transmissions par câble, serve à diffuser un plus grand nombre de langues minoritaires;

11. invite le Conseil et la Commission à:
a) continuer à soutenir et à encourager les organisations européennes représentant les langues de moindre diffusion, en particulier le Bureau européen pour les langues moins répandues, et à leur accorder les ressources nécessaires;
b) faire en sorte que les programmes communautaires en faveur des langues de moindre diffusion et des cultures qu'elles reflètent disposent d'une dotation budgétaire appropriée, et proposer un programme d'action pluriannuel dans ce domaine;
c) tenir dûment compte de l'héritage linguistique et culturel des régions dans l'élaboration de la politique régionale et dans l'attribution des ressources du FEDER, en soutenant des projets de développement régional intégré comportant des mesures visant à soutenir les langues et les cultures régionales, ainsi que dans l'élaboration de la politique sociale et dans l'attribution des ressources du FSE;

d) tenir dûment compte des besoins des usagers de langues de moindre diffusion dans les pays d'Europe centrale et orientale dans l'élaboration des programmes communautaires pour la reconstruction économique et sociale, en particulier le programme PHARE;
e) encourager la traduction de livres et d'oeuvres littéraires ainsi que le sous-titrage de films entre langues minoritaires ou vers des langues de l'Union;
f) faire en sorte qu'en encourageant les langues minoritaires, l'Union européenne ne porte pas préjudice aux principales langues nationales concernées, et ce en s'assurant que l'enseignement scolaire des langues principales n'est pas affecté;

12. demande que les langues d'outremer parlées dans les territoires appartenant aux États membres bénéficient des mêmes droits et des mêmes dispositions que les langues continentales;

13. en ce qui concerne les langues autochtones non territoriales (comme le rom, le sinto et les langues des communautés juives), invite tous les organes compétents à appliquer *mutatis mutandis* les recommandations faites dans la présente résolution;

14. souligne que les recommandations de la présente résolution ne sont pas de nature à compromettre l'intégrité territoriale ou l'ordre public des États membres et, en outre, ne doivent pas être interprétées comme impliquant le droit de mener une activité ou d'entamer une action contraires aux objectifs de la Charte des Nations unies ou à toute autre obligation prévue par le droit international;

1.2.23 *Vienna Declaration on Human Rights*

Council of Europe Summit, Vienna, 9 October 1993.

In this political context thus outlined, we, Heads of State and Government of the member states of the Council of Europe, resolve...
- to enter into political and legal commitments relating to the protection of national minorities in Europe and to instruct the Committee of Ministers to elaborate appropriate international legal instruments (see decision in Appendix II),

Appendix II
We, Heads of State and Government of the member states of the Council of Europe, have agreed as follows, concerning the protection of national minorities:
... States should create the conditions necessary for persons belonging to national minorities to develop their culture, while preserving their religion, traditions and customs. These persons must be able to use their language both in private and in public and should be able to use it, under certain conditions, in their relations with the public authorities.

1.3   NON-GOVERNMENTAL DOCUMENTS

1.3.1   *Covenant of the Unrepresented Nations and Peoples Organisation*

Reprinted from *Peoples and Minorities in International Law* (1993), Catherine Brölmann, René Lefeber, and Marjoleine Zieck (eds.), Martinus Nijhoff, Dordrecht, Netherlands, at pp. 325-329.

Article 5

Participation is open to all nations and peoples who are inadequately represented at the United Nations and whose representative body, as defined in Article 6 of this title, fulfils all requirements set out in this title and declares...

(e) Respect for all peoples and population groups, including minority or majority populations within territories inhabited by the participant but belonging to different ethnic, religious or linguistic groups.

Article 6

For the purposes of this Covenant:

A nation or people shall mean a group of human beings which possess the will to be identified as a nation or people and to determine its common destiny as a nation or people, and is bound by a common heritage which can be historical, racial, ethnic, linguistic, cultural, religious or territorial.

A section of a people constituting a minority, living on a portion of its ancestral territory, incorporated into a state other than a state representing that people, is included in this Article's definition.

1.3.2 *Declaración Final del I Simpósio Internacional de Línguas Europeas e Lexislacións*

International Symposium of European Languages and Legislation, Santiago de Compostela, Spain, 18 October 1992.

1. - Que as lexislacións lingüísticas sexan destinadas a favorecer, sempre e antes de nada, os procesos de normalización de cada unha das linguas.

2. - Que, dado que moitas leis actuais parten de presupostos dificilmente respeitosos coas finalidades mencionadas, sexan reformadas aquelas disposicións legáis, tanto constitucionais como de outros níveis, que puideren frear ou limitar o desenvolvimento normal de todas as línguas.

3. - Que calquer lexislación lingüística garanta e potencie a oferta de uso de todas as línguas, tamén nos ámbitos formais, coa finalidade de criar necesidades de utilizá-las nas suas próprias áreas.

4. - Que nengunha fronteira, nen estatal nen administrativa no interior dos estados constituíntes, interfira no mantimento da unidade obxectiva das línguas e dos falantes.

5. - Que o princípio de territorialidade das línguas interveña para resolver os problemas actuais de superposición e de clasificación política e xurídica das línguas en dominantes e dominadas ou maioritárias o minoritárias en tanto que categoria.

6. - Que nunha Europa cada vez máis intercomunicada, a preséncia e actuación dos meios de comunicación social podan desenvolver-se para todas as línguas nun plano de igualdade.

7. - Que, vista a inadecuación entre a demanda social e a vitalidade das línguas fronte as políticas lingüísticas actuais, os poderes públicos representativos asuman máis responsabilidades na fidelidade que deben ás comunidades lingüísticas que administran.

8. - Que as convencións e tratados internacionais intereuropeus vaian interpretando-se ou perfeccionando-se, e que eventualmente sexan revisados no sentido de abriren camiños á igualdade lingüística efectiva de todos os citadáns e dos seus respectivos colectivos ou povos.

1.3.3   *Déclaration d'Athène sur les droits des minorités*

Assembly of the European Congress, Athens, 13 December 1992.

Article 1
a/ Tout groupe de citoyens numériquement inférieur au reste de la population, possédant des caractéristiques culturelles, religieuses ou linguistiques spécifiques, et dont les membres sont animés de la volonté de préserver leur culture, leurs traditions, leur religion ou leur langue, a droit à l'existence, à la préservation et au développement de son identité.

b/ Un tel groupe sera considéré comme une minorité au sens de la présente Déclaration et traité comme tel.

c/ De ce droit fondamental à l'existence découlent les droits propres aux minorités pour assurer dans l'État et dans la société non seulement leur préservation mais aussi leur développement.

Article 2
a/ La protection des droits des minorités est une composante des Droits de l'Homme, par nature, elle ne lui est donc pas contraire et, en pratique, elle ne peut lui être opposée.

b/ La protection internationale des droits des minorités constitue un facteur de coopération et de relations de bon voisinage.

Article 3
L'exercice de tous les Droits de l'Homme, tels qu'énoncés par la Déclaration universelle des Droits de l'Homme et garantis par de multiples instruments internationaux, tout particulièrement la Convention européenne de sauvegarde des Droits de l'Homme, doit être garanti par tout État à toute personne; cet exercice est le premier droit des individus appartenant à une minorité et le préalable à la reconnaissance aux minorités de droits propres à caractère individuel et collectif.

Article 4
a/ Aucun individu ne peut être privé de la pleine jouissance des Droits de l'Homme en raison de son appartenance ou son refus d'appartenance à une minorité. Appartenir à une minorité relève d'une décision individuelle et aucun désavantage ne peut résulter de ce choix.

b/ Les États prennent toutes les mesures propres à assurer aux personnes appartenant à des minorités l'exercice intégral et effectif de tous les droits de l'Homme et de toutes les libertés publiques, sans aucune discrimination et dans des conditions de pleine égalité devant la loi.

Article 5

Les personnes appartenant à des minorités ont le droit, en accord avec les principes d'une société démocratique, de participer pleinement à la vie publique de leur pays à tous les niveaux, notamment à la vie culturelle, religieuse, sociale, scientifique et économique sous tous ses aspects.

Article 6

a/ L'adoption de mesures spéciales en faveur des minorités ou des personnes appartenant à des minorités et destinées à promouvoir une pleine égalité entre elles et le reste de la population ou visant à tenir compte de leurs conditions spécifiques n'est pas considérée comme un acte de discrimination.

b/ Les considérations d'ordre économique ne peuvent être invoquées pour dénier aux minorités l'exercice de leurs droits.

Article 7

a/ Les minorités ont droit au respect, à la préservation et au développement de leur identité culturelle, religieuse ou linguistique.

b/ Les États favorisent l'instauration des conditions propres à promouvoir cette identité.

Article 8

a/ Les minorités ont le droit d'être protégées contre toute activité susceptible de menacer leur existence et leur identité.

b/ Les États prennent les mesures appropriées pour assurer le respect de ce droit.

Article 9

a/ Les minorités ont le droit de préserver leur identité et d'en développer les expressions sous toutes formes, à l'abri de toute mesure d'assimilation pratiquée contre leur volonté.

b/ Les États doivent promouvoir la connaissance de l'histoire, des traditions, de la langue et de la culture des minorités situées sur leur territoire.

Article 13

a/ Les personnes appartenant à des minorités linguistiques ont le droit de faire usage librement de leur langue, aussi bien en public qu'en privé.

b/ Les États prennent les mesures appropriées pour favoriser l'exercice de ce droit.

Article 14

Lorsqu'une minorité atteint un certain pourcentage substantiel de la population d'une région ou de la population totale, les personnes appartenant à cette minorité ont le droit de s'adresser dans leur propre langue aux autorités politiques, administratives ou judiciaires de cette région ou, le cas échéant, de l'État. Ces autorités sont tenues de respecter ce droit dans toute la mesure du possible.

Article 15

L'étude de la langue maternelle est un droit. L'enseignement dans les écoles publiques comporte, pour les élèves appartenant à une minorité, l'étude de leur langue maternelle. Dans la mesure du possible, l'enseignement de tout ou partie du programme est dispensé dans la langue maternelle des élèves appartenant à une minorité. Toutefois, si l'État n'est pas en mesure de pouvoir à un tel enseignement, il doit faciliter aux enfants qui le désirent la fréquentation d'écoles privées. Dans ce dernier cas, l'État a le droit d'imposer que la ou les langue(s) officielle(s) soi(ent) aussi enseignée(s) dans ces écoles.

Article 17

a/ Les personnes appartenant aux minorités ont le droit de participer de manière effective aux affaires publiques, en particulier aux décisions affectant leurs intérêts.

b/ Les États tiendront compte de l'existence des minorités dans le découpage du territoire national en subdivisions politiques et administratives, ainsi qu'en circonscriptions électorales; ils s'abstiennent de poursuivre ou d'encourager une politique ayant pour but de modifier les proportions de la population dans les régions habitées par des minorités.

Article 21

a/ Aucune disposition de la Déclaration ne peut être interprétée comme autorisant une quelconque activité contraire aux règles fondamentales du droit international, ainsi qu'aux principes des Nations unies y compris l'égalité souveraine, l'intégrité territoriale et l'indépendance politique des États mentionnés par la Déclaration des Nations unies sur les droits des personnes appartenant à des minorités nationales ou ethniques, religieuses et linguistiques.

1.3.4 *Declaration of Tlahuitoltepec on the Fundamental Rights of the Indigenous Nations, Nationalities and Peoples of Indo-Latin America*

Tlahuitoltepec, Mexico, 18 May 1994.

Article 1

We the representatives of the indigenous Indo-Latin American nations, nationalities and peoples unanimously agree that we have always been and will forever continue to be peoples with our own history, religion, culture, education, language and other fundamental characteristics of nations, nationalities and peoples.

Article 13

We the indigenous nations, nationalities and peoples understand our cultures to be any manifestation that expresses the comprehensive concept of our relationship with our Mother Earth and our relationships among ourselves, as human beings in a community. Out cultures include elements such as language, social, political and economic customs, the arts, sciences, medicine and religion.

1.3.5 *Déclaration universelle des droits collectifs des peuples*

General Assembly of Non-State Nations of Europe, Barcelona, 27 May 1990. Reprinted from *Recueil des législations linguistiques dans le monde — Tome VI* (1994), Jacques Leclerc & Jacques Maurais (eds.), International Centre for Research on Language Planning, Québec.

Article 9

Tout peuple a le droit d'exprimer et de développer sa culture, sa langue et ses règles d'organisation, et de se doter pour ce faire de ses propres structures politiques, d'enseignement, de communication et d'administration publique, sur son aire de souveraineté.

1.3.6   *Draft Convention on the Protection of Ethnic Groups in Europe*

Federal Union of European Nationalities, Gdansk, Poland, 12 May 1994.

Article 2

1. For the purposes of this Protocol the term "ethnic group" shall mean a community:
(a) compactly or dispersedly settled on the territory of a state party;
(b) which is smaller in number than the rest of the population of a state party;
(c) whose members, who are nationals of that state;
(d) which have ethnical, linguistic or cultural features different from those of the rest of the population,
(e) whose members are guided by the will to safeguard these features.
2. The term "ethnic group" shall apply neither to migrant workers and their families lawfully residing in the states parties, nor to other immigrants, groups of refugees or persons seeking asylum; their rights have been established or shall be established independently of the rights of ethnic groups.

Article 4

1. Persons belonging to ethnic groups shall have the right to the respect, evolution and development of their identity, i.e. they shall have the right freely to express, preserve and develop their ethnic, cultural and linguistic identity, and to maintain and develop their culture in all its aspects, free of any attempts at assimilation.

Article 5

1. Persons belonging to ethnic groups have the right to exercise fully and effectively their human rights and fundamental freedoms without any discrimination and in full equality before the law...
3. These equal opportunities shall be guaranteed through special protective measures; these measures shall be considered to be in conformity with the principles of equality and non-discrimination with respect to the other citizens and shall not be considered as acts of discrimination.
4. Such special protective measures for the establishment and maintenance of equal opportunities shall be adopted by the state parties with regard to the rights of in particular:
(a) Language;
(b) education;...
(g) political representation;
(h) autonomy;

Article 6

1. Persons belonging to ethnic groups shall have the right to use their mother tongue (ethnic group right) in private as well as in public, both orally and in writing.
2. Persons belonging to ethnic groups shall have this right also in contacts with the public administration, the judicial authorities and with all public institutions or institutions intended for public purposes regardless of their legal status; they shall be entitled to receive communications from these institutions in — or also in — their mother tongue (ethnic group language).

3. The exercise of this right shall be guaranteed in all administrative units of their settlement areas preferably directly, at least through translation.

4. Persons belonging to ethnic groups shall have in particular the right:

(a) when arrested, to be informed promptly in their mother tongue (ethnic group language) of the reasons of their arrest and of any charge against them;

(b) when charged with a criminal offence, to be informed in their mother tongue (ethnic group language) promptly and in detailed manner of the nature and cause of the accusation against them and to defend themselves in this language, if necessary with the free assistance of an interpreter.

5. In the settlement areas of persons belonging to ethnic groups they shall have the right to the use and equal status of their language in legislation, administration and judiciary, in particular within public collegial bodies and in communications such as official publications, general information, official signs as well as acts directed to the public sphere or intended for the public use.

6. Persons belonging to ethnic groups shall have the right to use their own surnames and firstnames in their mother tongue (ethnic group language) and to have them officially recognised. This right shall also include the re-establishment of personal names in the form of their own language free of charge.

7. In the settlement areas of persons belonging to ethnic groups they shall have the right to local names, signs, inscriptions and other similar public information in the mother tongue (ethnic group language). This does not deprive the authorities of their right to display the above-mentioned information in the official language or languages of the state; however, any arbitrary modification of traditional denominations in the mother tongue (ethnic group language) which hitherto have been used exclusively in original form in an ethnic group language shall be inadmissible.

Article 7

1. Persons belonging to ethnic groups shall have the right to learn their mother tongue (ethnic group language) and to be instructed in it within the whole system of education including, besides the compulsory schooling, e.g. also the kindergartens, preschool education, secondary education, technical and vocational education, vocational continuing education, university and adult education.

2. This right shall be guaranteed through an appropriate number of state schools and other educational establishments, located in accordance with the geographical distribution of the persons belonging to an ethnic group.

3. Whenever outside the settlement areas of persons belonging to ethnic groups the minimum number of pupils required to build a class is not achieved in schools reasonably near, the pupils in question shall be in any case entitled to learn their mother tongue (ethnic group language).

4. For sectors outside the existing compulsory school system such as kindergartens, preschool education, secondary education, technical and vocational education, vocational continuing education, university and adult education, appropriate institutions guaranteeing the instruction in the mother tongue (ethnic group language) shall be established and diplomas issued abroad for courses completed in the mother tongue (ethnic group language) or in the nearest related language shall be recognised. If such institutions should not be demanded by a sufficient number of persons belonging to ethnic groups, the diplomas issued abroad for courses completed in their language or in the nearest language shall be recognised.

5. Persons belonging to ethnic groups shall have the right to set up and manage their own schools, educational and training establishments within the framework of the legal education system.

6. To enjoy the right of education, persons belonging to ethnic groups shall at least be entitled at all levels and for all types of education, to a share in public grants proportionate to their share in the total population; this shall apply also for education abroad in the mother tongue (ethnic group language) or in the nearest related language.

7. Schooling of and in the mother tongue (ethnic group language) shall be in principle provided by teachers for whom the respective language is also their mother tongue. For educational systems based on joint teaching for persons belonging to ethnic groups and those of the majority population, special rules shall be provided taking into account in an appropriate manner the interests of persons belonging to ethnic groups.

8. In the case of minority schools the persons belonging to ethnic groups, within the framework of the general principles of national school legislation, shall have the right to:

(a) co-determination in the establishment of curricula, the appointment of teachers and the supervision of schools;

(b) adapt school subjects to their particular needs;

(c) instruction also of their own history and culture.

9. State parties shall be responsible for the financing of the educational system of persons belonging to ethnic groups. The state parties shall guarantee that pupils belonging to ethnic groups who wish to attend private schools, may do so. Such private schools shall be promoted or financed by the state party at least to the same extent as private schools in general are promoted or financed by that state.

10. The state parties shall guarantee that persons belonging to ethnic groups shall be taught the national language within the compulsory schooling system.

11. In areas in which ethnic groups are settled, persons belonging to the majority population shall be guaranteed to be taught the language of the ethnic group as well as their history and culture.

Article 10

1. Persons belonging to ethnic groups shall have the right to disseminate and exchange information through print and audio-visual media in their mother tongue (ethnic group language); they shall have likewise the right to have access to such information within and across national frontiers.

2. In particular, they shall have the right to equal access to the state's or to other public mass media, as well as the right to their own means of communication and adequate public subsidies for this purpose.

3. The right of information shall include the freedom to receive television and radio programmes broadcast from foreign countries in which the same mother tongue is spoken.

Article 11

4. In the settlement areas of persons belonging to ethnic groups, institutional multilingualism shall be compulsory in all public institutions or institutions intended for public purposes.

1.3.7   *Draft of an International Convention on the Protection of National or Ethnic Groups or Minorities*

Internationales Institut für Nationalitätenrecht und Regionalismus. Reprinted from Chaszar, Edward (1988), *The International Problem of National Minorities*, Indiana University of Pennsylvania, Indiana, at pp. 121-134.

Article 3
Every member of a national or ethnic group or minority has the right to use his own language or dialect in private, in all social, economic and similar relations, and in public, notwithstanding the legal position of his group or minority.

Article 7
The state must not undertake, support or favour a policy of artificial or enforced assimilation.

Article 10
Nobody may be denied the right to assimilate voluntarily with the majority of the population of the state of which he is a national.

Article 11
2. A national or ethnic group or minority in the sense of the present Convention exists if a number of nationals of the given state, being in numerically inferior, non-dominant position, and possessing ethnic or linguistic characteristics differing from the rest of the population, show, if only implicitly, a sense of solidarity with a view towards preserving their culture, traditions, or language, and possessing also an adequate representation, asks for legal recognition as a national or ethnic group or minority.

Article 13
1. The protection of a national or ethnic minority or group may be organised on a national or international level or on both levels. The kind, range and scope of the protection depends on the freely expressed will of the members of the minority group, on its demographic distribution as well as on international obligations of the given state.
2. The main kinds of protection on a national level are the following:
(a) the right of self-determination as expressed in the UN Declaration of Principles of International Law on Friendly Relations and Cooperation among states in accordance with the Charter of the UN (GA Res. 2625, XXV);
(b) cultural autonomy;
(c) linguistic autonomy;

Article 14
The modes of implementing the right of self-determination of a national or ethnic minority or group consist in the right to
(a) freely secede from the given state in order to establish a sovereign and independent state, or to associate with or integrate into an independent state, in the second alternative with the consent of the receiving state;

(b) free emergence into any other political status (for instance, territorial autonomy, self-government, personal autonomy or any other agreed arrangement within the framework of the state directly concerned) or

(c) freely form legislative and/or administrative regional or local autonomy within the framework of the state directly concerned.

Article 16

The types of self-determination mentioned in Article 14 (b) and (c) may also be granted if, in a given territory of the state, nationals reside possessing ethnic or linguistic characteristics differing from the rest of the population and showing if only implicitly, a sense of solidarity with a view towards preserving their culture, traditions, or language and also possessing an adequate representation, ask for such an arrangement.

Article 18

A national or ethnic minority or group has the right to use a specific wireless and television channel — channels to be accorded in concordance with relevant international agreements — and to transmit any program in its own language at adequate times.

Article 19

Cultural autonomy consists further in an educational system providing instruction on all educational levels in the language of the group. Every child belonging to the group has the right to this education, provided the persons responsible for his education are willing to make use of this right. The relevant curricula have to take into account the needs of the group as well as the principles enshrined in the state's Constitution. Diplomas and certificates issued by the educational institutions of the group shall have public recognition. The provisions of the UNESCO Convention against Discrimination in Education of 1960 shall be applied respectively.

Article 20

1. Linguistic autonomy consists in facilitating the use of the mother tongue before administrative and judicial authorities. If more than a certain percentage of the inhabitants of a certain judicial or administrative district — the percentage to be fixed by agreement between the competent state authorities and the representatives of the relevant minority or group — belong to one or more national or ethnic minority or group, their language has to be recognised as official languages. District may not be delimited in a way so as to prevent the realisation of this right. In cases of linguistic autonomy, topographic signs have to bear bi- or multilingual inscriptions.

2. This linguistic autonomy should particularly be observed with regard to the rights of personal liberty, of fair trial and in all matters of social welfare.

3. If necessary, state authorities shall consider the possibility of applying ethnic criteria with regard to the assignments of posts, especially in regions where the group language is recognised as the official language. In areas where the group resides, a percentage of the posts in the public service of the state, the provinces and communes — the percentage to be fixed by agreement between the competent state authorities and the representatives of the relevant minority or group — shall be made available to members of that minority or group.

Article 24

The state (in federal states their composite territorial units as well), the provinces and municipal bodies where national ethnic minorities or groups reside in considerable strength (the relevant percentage to be fixed by agreement between the competent state authorities and the representatives of the relevant minority or group), may create Councils in order to render if possible for the groups to formulate and articulate their interests and desires, in particular with regard to the provisions laid down in the present Convention.

1.3.8 Draft Protocol to the International Convention on the Protection of National or Ethnic Minorities or Groups, Applicable to the States Members of the Council of Europe

Internationales Institut für Nationalitätenrecht und Regionalismus. Reprinted from Chaszar, Edward (1988), *The International Problem of National Minorities*, Indiana University of Pennsylvania, Indiana, at pp. 135-143.

Article 11
The scope and extent of the competences to be attributed to organs of territorial autonomy shall be fixed by law in accordance with the legitimate representatives of the ethnic group. The autonomous organs shall be granted at least comprehensive competences of a cultural nature (cultural autonomy) as well as rights of decision in questions of basic social and economic policy.

Article 14
The scope and extent of competences which are attributed to the organs of an autonomous corporate entity shall be fixed by law and in accordance with the legitimate representatives of the ethnic group. The law must prescribe the internal structure of the entity and shall envisage the cultural development and the respect for linguistic rights of the ethnic group.

Article 15
In ethnic regions vested with territorial autonomy, the ethnic group's language is the official language of the administration — including mail service, railway service, public hospitals, supply institutions and public social assurances — and in courts of justice)in higher instances only if a party to a lawsuit has residence in the autonomous region; in case of juridical persons, if it has its seat in the autonomous region). The language used for internal purposes by the administration and the courts of justice shall be the language of the ethnic group in cases where the administrative organs and tribunals are competent for single communes or are established on the commune level (including organs of arbitration).

Article 16
The ethnic group's language shall be the official language if in an autonomous corporate entity within a commune (including parts of the commune or factions of a commune equipped with independent sub-organs of the commune) at least 20 %, in administrative and judicial districts at least 6 %, or in larger administrative entities at least 5 % of the residing population use the language of the ethnic group.

Article 17
In ethnic groups region vested with territorial autonomy, topographic inscriptions shall be in the language of the ethnic group. In territories vested with corporate autonomy, topographic inscriptions shall be bilingual but in any case equal to the official language with regard to type, size and arrangement of the written text. In both cases printed forms must also be available in

the language of the ethnic or linguistic minority. Topographic inscriptions include all sign boards, the inscriptions and designations of offices, schools, railway stations, post offices, police stations, public hospitals, social assurances and inscriptions in public maps. On traffic sign boards the names of domestic communes located in an other language area are to appear only in the language of the other area.

Article 18

The respective standard language is considered as "language of the ethnic group". The use of a dialect may be permitted orally in dealings with public offices, if all parties immediately concerned have a command of that dialect.

Article 19

Kindergartens and preschool institutions are to be established for all children of members of ethnic groups requiring a preschool education provided that a sufficient number of children have applied for it. A decision as to the existence of these conditions shall be made in a generous and accommodating manner. The language of instruction and care of the children shall be the language of the ethnic group; Article 18 applies.

Article 20

Ethnic groups are entitled to the establishment and maintenance of a sufficient number of elementary schools to be located in their area of settlement in compliance with compulsory education, and with the ethnic group's language as language of instruction. Linguistic minorities (groups of citizens, irrespective of any profession under Article 9, of a mother tongue other than that of the majority of the population of the state) have the same right for their hereditary linguistic regions. The official language is a compulsory subject of instruction for all elementary grades in so far as the autonomous authorities have so ordered. In elementary schools for linguistic minorities the official language is to be taught in any case.

Article 21

Should parents or other persons responsible for children or pupils at higher educational institutions (including professional and/or other institutions of higher learning) wish, or should the ethnic group or an autonomous inspectorate of education (in case such an inspectorate is established — Article 25) so demand, such schools are to be instituted; school curricula shall provide for the language of the ethnic group as subject of instruction where a sufficient number of pupils have applied for it. A decision as to the existence of these conditions shall be made in a generous and accommodating manner.

Article 22

Ethnic groups are entitled to the establishment of public universities or similar educational institutions whenever in the first semester a sufficient number of members of the ethnic group have applied for enrolment in each of the main curricula. A decision as to the existence of these conditions shall be made in a generous and accommodating manner.

Article 23

On all levels of elementary and higher schools of the ethnic group or a linguistic minority it must be provided that the culture, the history, the social and economic structure of the ethnic group or the linguistic minority be a subject of the school curricula; the lessons are to be held in the language of the respective minority or group.

Article 24

Ethnic groups are permitted autonomously to establish educational institutions and schools of the kind mentioned in Articles 19-22 in accordance to national legislation on education. In such cases the ethnic groups are responsible for the material and personnel expenditures of these institutions. If they are unable to meet the expenses, the state (or, if educational matters fall within the competence of parts of federal states, the relevant part of a federal state) is responsible for covering the costs.

Article 25

Particular inspectorates of education shall be established for educational institutions and schools of ethnic groups and linguistic minorities. The civil servants of those entities must command the language of the ethnic group or of the linguistic minority as well as the official language.

Article 28

If an ethnic group does not possess its own radio or television installations and cannot possess such installations due to a lack of financial means, the group has a right to adequate transmission time with the radio of public or publicly concessioned radio installations during suitable hours. A decision as to what has to be considered "adequate" and "suitable" shall be made in a generous and accommodating manner. Radio and television programmes intended for ethnic groups are to be prepared by members of the ethnic groups standing for the support of the preservation of the ethnic group. Ethnic groups may not be burdened with the costs of these programmes except for the usual broadcasting taxes. Should only private broadcasting corporations exist in the given state, that state (or part of a federal state) must provide the ethnic group with the means of arranging for programmes in their own language, composed by their own members in so far as they stand for the support of the preservation of the ethnic group. These provisions apply also to television services.

Article 29

Members of ethnic groups (linguistic minorities) have the right to use their Christian and family names in the wording and style corresponding to the tradition of the ethnic group (linguistic minority). Official registers and documents are to be kept in the above mentioned language and are to be altered accordingly if so demanded. Special taxes may not be imposed for this service.

Article 30

Access to all public offices and posts is to be granted to members of ethnic groups in the same manner as it is granted to members of the majority population. At all public offices whose competence comprises territories in which ethnic groups or parts of such groups in the sense of this Protocol reside, public servants must be appointed who belong to the relevant ethnic group and guarantee the support of the preservation of the ethnic group. The number of these public servants must correspond, within each type of service rank, to the percentage which is equal to that part of the ethnic group in relation to the whole population residing in this territory for which the relevant authority is competent. Public servants may only be entrusted with tasks which are of particular importance for the preservation and advancement of an ethnic group in case such public servants stand for the support of the preservation of the ethnic group.

1.3.9   *Kiruna Declaration on Human Rights*

World Council of Indigenous Peoples, Kiruna, Sweden, 27 September 1977.

Article 2
   We, therefore, wish to make clear those irrevocable and inborn rights which are due to us in our capacity as Aboriginals:
   1. Right to autonomy;
   2. Right to maintain our culture, language and traditions in freedom;...
   14. Right to an appropriate education in accordance with our culture and out traditions, without any foreign elements and within the framework of an educational system which recognises the values of our culture and acknowledges an official status to our language at all educational levels.

1.3.10   *Proposal for a European Convention for the Protection of Minorities*

European Commission for Democracy Through Law, 8 February 1991. Council of Europe Doc. CDL (91) (7) (1991).

Article 1
   1. The international protection of the rights of ethnic, linguistic and religious minorities, as well as the rights of individuals belonging to those minorities, as guaranteed by the present Convention, is a fundamental component of the international protection of Human Rights, and as such falls within the scope of international co-operation.
   2. It does not permit any activity which is contrary to the fundamental principles of international law and in particular of sovereignty, territorial integrity and political independence of states.
   3. It must be carried out in good faith, in a spirit of understanding, tolerance and good neighbourliness between states.

Article 2
   1. For the purpose of this Convention, the term "minority" shall mean a group which is smaller in number than the rest of the population of a state, whose members, who are nationals of that state, have ethnical, religious or linguistic features different from those of the rest of the population, and are guided by the will to safeguard their culture, traditions, religion or language.
   2. Any group coming within the terms of this definition shall be treated as an ethnic, religious or linguistic minority.
   3. To belong to a national minority shall be a matter of individual choice and no disadvantage may arise from the exercise of such choice.

Article 3
   1. Minorities shall have the right to be protected against any activity capable of threatening their existence.
   2. They shall have the right to the respect, safeguard and development of their ethnical, religious, or linguistic identity.

Article 4
1. Any person belonging to a minority shall have the right to enjoy the same rights as any other citizen, without distinction and on an equal footing.
2. The adoption of special measures in favour of minorities or of individuals belonging to minorities and aimed at promoting equality between them and the rest of the population or at taking due account of their specific conditions shall not be considered as an act of discrimination.

Article 6
1. Persons belonging to a minority shall have the right to freely preserve, express and develop their cultural identity in all its aspects, free of any attempts at assimilation against their will.
2. In particular, they shall have the right to express themselves, to receive and to issue information and ideas through means of communication of their own.

Article 7
Any person belonging to a linguistic minority shall have the right to use his language freely, in public as well as in private.

Article 8
Whenever a minority reaches a substantial percentage of the population of a region or of the total population, its members shall have the right, as far as possible, to speak and write in their own language to the political, administrative and judicial authorities of this region or, where appropriate, of the state. These authorities shall have a corresponding obligation.

Article 9
Whenever the conditions of Article 8 are fulfilled, in state schools, obligatory schooling shall include, for pupils belonging to the minority, study of their mother tongue. As far as possible, all or part of the schooling shall be given in the mother tongue of pupils belonging to the minority. However, should the state not be in a position to provide such schooling, it must permit children who so wish to attend private schools. In such a case, the state shall have the right to prescribe that the official language or languages also be taught in such schools.

Article 12
The rights set forth in Articles 5, 7 and 10 of this Convention shall be subject only to such limitations as are prescribed by law and are necessary in a democratic society in the interests of public safety, for the protection of public order, health or morals, or for the protection of the rights and freedoms of others.

Article 13
States shall refrain from pursuing or encouraging policies aimed at the assimilation of minorities or aimed at intentionally modifying the proportions of the population in the regions inhabited by minorities.

Article 16
States shall take the necessary measures with a view to ensuring that, in any region where those who do belong to a minority represent the majority of the population, those who do not belong to this minority shall not suffer from any discrimination.

1.3.11   *Universal Declaration of Linguistic Rights*

Tenth draft, International PEN Committee for Translation and Linguistic Rights and Centre Internacional Escarré per les Minories Etniques i les Nacions, October 1995, Barcelona, Spain.

Article 1

1. This Declaration considers as a language community any human society established historically in a particular territorial space, whether this territory be recognised or not, which identifies itself as a people and has developed a common language that is the normal means of communication between its members. The term "language specific to a territory" refers to the language of the community historically established in such a space.

2. The rights defined in this Declaration refer to the territorial space of each language community understood, not only as the geographical area where the community lives, but also as a social and functional space vital to the full development of the language.

3. For the purpose of this Declaration, groups belonging to a language community are also deemed to be in their own territory and to belong to a language community in the following circumstances:

(i) when they are separated from the main body of their community by political or administrative borders;

(ii) when they have been historically established in a small area surrounded by members of other language communities; or

(iii) when they are established in an area which they share with the members of other language communities with similar historical antecedents.

4. This Declaration considers that nomad language communities are in their own territory when they are within their historical areas of migration.

Article 2

This Declaration is based on the principle that the rights of all language communities are equal and independent of the concept of regional or minority languages. These terms are not used in this Declaration because, though in certain cases the rights of linguistic minorities can only be exercised if they are recognised as such, denominations such as regional or minority languages have frequently been used to restrict the rights of language communities.

Article 3

1. This Declaration excludes from the concept of language communities any group which has settled recently in the territorial space of another community but which does not possess equivalent historical antecedents. Examples of such groups are immigrants, refugees, deported persons and members of diasporas.

2. The individual language rights recognised in other declarations to the members of such groups must not imply any restriction to the rights of the host language community.

Article 4

This Declaration considers that a language cannot be considered as the language specific to a territory merely on the grounds that it is the official language of the state or has been traditionally used within the territory for administrative purposes or for certain cultural activities.

Article 5

1. The rights established in this Declaration for language communities and their members

in the context of their own territory do not imply any restriction to the individual linguistic rights established by other declarations, conventions or international covenants which have no territorial delimitation.

2. This Declaration considers that persons who settle in the territory of another language community have the right and the duty to maintain towards this community an attitude of *integration*. This term is understood to mean the resocialisation of such persons in the host society, in such a way that they retain their original cultural characteristics while sharing with the host society sufficient references, values and forms of behaviour to enable the society as a whole to operate without greater difficulties than those that are usual in monocultural societies. *Assimilation*, a term which is understood to mean acculturation in the host society, in such a way that the original cultural characteristics are replaced by the references, values and forms of behaviour of the host society, is acceptable only as a result of a free individual decision.

Article 6

Whenever various language communities and groups compete within a shared territory, the rights formulated in this Declaration must be exercised on a basis of mutual respect and in such a way that democracy may be guaranteed to the greatest possible extent.

In order to establish the appropriate articulation between the respective rights of such language communities and groups and the persons belonging to them, the quest for a satisfactory sociolinguistic balance must take into account factors such as their respective historical antecedents in the territory, their relative vitality, and their democratically expressed will.

Article 7

1. All languages are the expression of a collective identity and of a distinct way of perceiving and describing reality and must be able to enjoy the conditions required for their development in all functions.

2. Whereas language is a tool of communication used by individuals, it is collectively that it is constituted and made available to individuals within a community, for which it is an instrument of cohesion, identification and communication.

Article 8

This Declaration considers the language community and the individuals who compose it as subjects of linguistic rights.

Article 9

1. All language communities have the right to be guaranteed sufficient powers of self-organisation and management of their own resources to permit the use of their language in all functions.

2. All language communities have the right to dispose of whatever means are necessary to ensure the transmission and future development of their language.

Article 10

All language communities have the right to preserve their linguistic and writing system without induced or forced interference.

Article 11

All language communities have equal rights, regardless of their degree of political sovereignty, their social and economic situation, and the degree of codification attained by their language.

Article 12
All language communities have the right to dispose of whatever systems of translation into and from other languages are needed to guarantee the rights contained in this Declaration.

Article 13
1. Everyone has the right to carry out all activities in the public sphere in his/her language without any limitation, provided it is the language of the territory where s/he resides.
2. Everyone has the right to use his/her language in the personal and family sphere.

Article 14
1. Everyone has the right to know the language specific to the territory in which s/he lives and to use it in all spheres.
2. Everyone has the right to be polyglot and the right to know the language most conducive to his/her personal development or social mobility, without prejudice to the guarantees established for the public use of the language specific to the territory.

Article 15
The provisions of this Declaration cannot be interpreted or used to the detriment of any norm or practice which is more favourable to the internal or international status of a language or to its use within the territory to which it is specific.

Article 16
1. All language communities have the right to the official use of their language within their territory.
2. All language communities have the right for legal and administrative acts, public and private documents and records in public registers which are drawn up in the language of the territory to be valid and effective and no one can allege ignorance of this language.

Article 17
All language communities have the right to communicate in their own language with the central, territorial and supraterritorial and local services of the public authorities and of those administrative divisions which include the territory to which the language is specific.

Article 18
1. All language communities have the right to dispose in their language of all official documents pertaining to relations which affect the territory to which the language is specific, whether such documents be in printed, machine-readable or any other form.
2. The public authorities must make forms and standard administrative documents, whether in printed, machine-readable or any other form, available in all territorial languages and place them at the disposal of the public through the services pertaining to the territories to which each language is specific.

Article 19
1. All language communities have the right for laws and other legal provisions which concern them to be published in a language specific to the territory.

2. Public authorities who have more than one territorially historic language within their jurisdiction must publish all laws and other legal provisions of a general nature in each of these languages, whether or not their speakers understand other languages.

Article 20

1. Representative assemblies must have as their official language(s) the language(s) historically spoken in the territory they represent.

2. Supraterritorial representative assemblies, which cover a larger territory with more than one territorially historic language, must have all such languages as official languages.

Article 21

1. Everyone has the right to use the language historically spoken in a territory, both orally and in writing, in the Courts of Justice located within that territory. The Courts of Justice must use the language specific to the territory in their internal actions and, if on account of the legal system in force within the state, the proceedings continue elsewhere, the use of the original language must be maintained.

2. Notwithstanding the above, everyone has the right to be tried in a language which s/he understands and to obtain the services of an interpreter free of charge.

Article 22

All language communities have the right for records in public registers to be drawn up in the language specific to the territory.

Article 23

All language communities have the right for documents authenticated by notaries public or certified by other authorised public servants to be drawn up in the language specific to the territory where the notary or other authorised public servant performs his/her functions.

Article 24

1. Education must contribute to foster the capacity for linguistic and cultural self-expression of the language community of the territory where it is provided.

2. Education must contribute to the maintenance and development of the language spoken by the language community of the territory where it is provided.

3. Education must always be at the service of linguistic and cultural diversity and of harmonious relations between different language communities throughout the world.

Article 25

All language communities have the right to decide to what extent their language is to be present, as a vehicular language and as a subject of study, at all levels of education within their territory: preschool, primary, secondary, technical and vocational, university, and adult education.

Article 26

All language communities have the right to dispose of all the human and material resources necessary to achieve the desired presence of their language at all levels of education within their territory: properly trained teachers, appropriate teaching methods, finance, buildings and equipment, textbooks, traditional and innovative technology.

Article 27

All language communities have the right to receive an education which will enable them to acquire a full command of their own language, including the different abilities relating to all the usual spheres of use, as well as the most extensive possible command of any other language they may wish to know.

Article 28

All language communities have the right to receive an education which will enable them to acquire a sufficient knowledge and command of all languages related to their own cultural tradition, such as substituted, literary or sacred languages different from the language habitually used by the community.

Article 29

All language communities have the right to receive an education which will enable them to acquire a thorough knowledge of their cultural heritage (history, geography, literature, and other manifestations of their own culture), as well as the most extensive possible knowledge of any other culture their members may wish to know.

Article 30

The language and culture of all language communities must be the subject of study and research at university level.

Article 31

All language communities have the right to preserve and use their own system of proper names.

Article 32

1. All language communities have the right to use place names in the language specific to the territory, both orally and in writing, in the private, public and official spheres.

2. All language communities have the right to preserve autochthonous place names. Such place names cannot be arbitrarily abolished, distorted or adapted, nor can they be replaced if changes in the political situation, or changes of any other type, occur.

Article 33

All language communities have the right to refer to themselves by the name used in their own language. Any translation into another language must be as similar as possible to the name used by the community itself.

Article 34

Everyone has the right to the use of his/her own name in his/her own language in all spheres and the right to the most accurate possible phonetic transcription of his/her name in another alphabet when necessary.

Article 35

All language communities have the right to decide the extent to which their language is to be present in all the communications media in their territory, whether local and traditional media, those with a wider scope, or those using more advanced technology, regardless of the method of dissemination or transmission employed.

Article 36

All language communities have the right to dispose of all the human and material resources required in order to ensure the desired degree of presence of their language and the desired degree of cultural self-expression in the communications media in their territory: properly trained personnel, finance, buildings and equipment, traditional and innovative technology.

Article 37

All language communities have the right to receive, through the communications media, a thorough knowledge of their cultural heritage (history, geography, literature and other manifestations of their own culture), as well as the greatest possible amount of information about any other culture their members may wish to know.

Article 38

The languages and cultures of all language communities must receive equitable and non-discriminatory treatment in the communications media throughout the world.

Article 39

The groups described in Article 1, paragraphs 3 and 4, of this Declaration, have the right for their language to be present in the communications media of the territory where they are established. This right is to be exercised in harmony with the rights of the other language communities in the territory.

Article 40

1. All language communities have the right to use, maintain and foster their language in all forms of cultural expression.

2. All language communities must be able to exercise this right to the full without any community's space being subjected to hegemonic occupation by a foreign culture.

Article 41

All language communities have the right to full development within their own cultural sphere.

Article 42

All language communities have the right of access to the works produced in their language.

Article 43

All language communities have the right of access to intercultural programmes, by means of the dissemination of adequate information, and the right to receive support for activities such as teaching the language to foreigners, translation, dubbing, post-synchronisation and subtitling.

Article 44

All language communities have the right for the language specific to the territory to take precedence in cultural events and services (libraries, videotheques, cinemas, theatres, museums, archives, computer software production, folklore, cultural industries, and all other manifestations of cultural life).

Article 45

All language communities have the right to preserve their linguistic and cultural heritage, including its material manifestations, such as collections of documents, the artistic and architectural heritage, historic monuments and inscriptions in their own language.

Article 46

1. All language communities have the right to use their language in socioeconomic activities within their territory.

2. All language communities have the right to dispose in their own language of all the means necessary for the performance of their professional activities, such as documents and works of reference, instructions, forms and computer software.

3. The use of other languages in this sphere can only be required in so far as it is justified by the nature of the professional activity involved. In no case can a more recently arrived relegate or supersede the language specific to the territory.

Article 47

1. All language communities have the right to use their language with full legal validity in economic transactions of all types, such as the sale and purchase of goods and services, banking, insurance, job contracts and others.

2. No clause in such private acts can exclude or restrict the use of a language in the territory to which it is specific.

3. All language communities have the right to dispose, in their own language, of the documents required for the performance of the above-mentioned operations, such as forms, cheques, contracts, invoices, receipts, delivery notes, order forms, and others.

Article 48

All language communities have the right to use their language in all types of socioeconomic organisations such as labour and union organisations, and employers', professional, trade and craft associations.

Article 49

1. All language communities have the right for their language to occupy a clearly predominant place in advertising, signs, external signposting, and all other elements that make up the image of the country.

2. All language communities have the right to receive complete oral and written information in their own language on the products and services proposed by commercial establishments in the territory, such as instructions for use, labels, lists of ingredients, advertising, guarantees and others.

3. All public signs and announcements affecting the safety of the public must be expressed at least in the language specific to the territory, in conditions which are not inferior to those of any other language.

Article 50

1. Everyone has the right to use the language specific to the territory in his/her relations with firms, commercial establishments and private bodies and to be served or receive a reply in the same language.

2. Everyone has the right, as a client, customer, consumer or user, to receive oral and written information from establishments open to the public in the language specific to the territory.

Article 51
Everyone has the right to carry out his/her professional activities in the language specific to the territory unless the functions inherent to the job require the use of other languages, as in the case of language teachers, translators or tourist guides.

TRANSITORY PROVISIONS

First
The public authorities must take all appropriate steps to implement the rights proclaimed in this Declaration within their respective areas of jurisdiction.

Second
The public authorities must ensure that the authorities, organisations and persons concerned are informed of the rights and correlative duties arising from this Declaration.

FINAL DISPOSITIONS

First
This Declaration proposes the creation of a Council of Languages within the United Nations Organisation. It is the task of the General Assembly of the United Nations Organisation to set up this Council, define its functions and appoint its members, and to create the body in international law which is to protect language communities with regard to the implementation of the rights recognised in this Declaration.

Second
This Declaration recommends and promotes the creation of a World Commission on Linguistic Rights. This body is to be of a non-official and consultative nature and composed by representatives of Non-Governmental Organisations and organisations belonging to the field of linguistic law.

2.   **Treaties**

2.1   INTERNATIONAL AND UNITED NATIONS SYSTEM

2.1.1   *Convention Against Discrimination in Education*

Adopted 14 December 1960.

Article 1
1. For the purposes of this Convention, the term "discrimination" includes any distinction, exclusion, limitation or preference which, being based on race, colour, sex, language, religion, political or other opinion, national or social origin, economic condition or birth, has the purpose or effect of nullifying or impairing equality of treatment in education and in particular :
(a) Of depriving any person or group of persons of access to education of any type or at any level;
(b) Of limiting any person or group of persons to education of an inferior standard;

(c) Subject to the provisions of Article 2 of this Convention, of establishing or maintaining separate educational systems or institutions for persons or groups of persons; or

(d) Of inflicting on any person or group of persons conditions which are incompatible with the dignity of man.

Article 2

When permitted in a state, the following situations shall not be deemed to constitute discrimination, within the meaning of Article 1 of this Convention...

(b) The establishment or maintenance, for religion or linguistic reasons, of separate educational systems or institutions offering an education which is in keeping with the wishes of the pupil's parents or legal guardians, if participation in such systems or attendance at such institutions is optional and if the education provided conforms to such standards as may be laid down or approved by the competent authorities, in particular for education of the same level;

Article 5

1. The states parties to this Convention agree that...

(c) It is essential to recognise the right of members of national minorities to carry on their own educational activities, including the maintenance of schools and, depending on the educational policy of each state, the use or the teaching of their own language, provided however :

> i) That this right is not exercised in a manner which prevents the members of these minorities from understanding the culture and language of the community as a whole and from participating in its activities, or which prejudices national sovereignty;
>
> ii) That the standard of education is not lower that the general standard laid down or approved by the competent authorities; and
>
> iii) That attendance at such schools is optional.

2.1.2 *Convention Relative to the Protection of Civilian Persons in Time of War*

Geneva, 12 August 1949.

Article 50

The Occupying Power shall, with the cooperation of the national and local authorities, facilitate the proper working of all institutions devoted to the care and education of children...

Should the local institutions be inadequate for the purpose, the Occupying Power shall make arrangements for the maintenance and education, if possible by persons of their own nationality, language and religion, of children who are orphaned or separated from their parents as a result of the war and who cannot be adequately cared for by a near relative or friend.

Article 65

The penal provisions enacted by the Occupying Power shall not come into force before they have been published and brought to the knowledge of the inhabitants in their own language. The effect of these penal provisions shall not be retroactive.

Article 71

No sentence shall be pronounced by the competent courts of the Occupying Power except after a regular trial.

Accused persons who are prosecuted by the Occupying Power shall be promptly informed, in writing, in a language which they understand, of the particulars of the charges preferred against them, and shall be brought to trial as rapidly as possible.

Article 82

The Detaining Power shall, as far as possible, accommodate the internees according to their nationality, language and customs. Internees who are nationals of the same country shall not be separated merely because they have different languages.

Article 93

Internees shall enjoy complete latitude in the exercise of their religious duties, including attendance at the services of their faith, on condition that they comply with the disciplinary routine prescribed by the detaining authorities.

Ministers of religion who are interned shall be allowed to minister freely to the members of their community. For this purpose the Detaining Power shall ensure their equitable allocation amongst the various places of internment in which there are internees speaking the same language and belonging to the same religion.

2.1.3   *Convention on the Rights of the Child*

Adopted 20 November 1989.

Article 2

1. States parties shall respect and ensure the rights set forth in the present Convention to each child within their jurisdiction without discrimination of any kind, irrespective of the child's or his or her parents' or legal guardian's race, colour, sex, language, religion, political or other opinion, national, ethnic or social origin, property, disability, birth or other status.

2. States parties shall take all appropriate measures to ensure that the child is protected against all forms of discrimination or punishment on the basis of the status, activities, expressed opinions, or beliefs of the child's parents, legal guardians, or family members.

Article 17

States parties recognise the important function performed by the mass media and shall ensure that the child has access to information and material from a diversity of national and international sources, especially those aimed at the promotion of his or her social, spiritual and moral well-being and physical and mental health. To this end, states parties shall...

(d) encourage the mass media to have particular regard to the linguistic needs of the child who belongs to a minority group or who is indigenous;

Article 29

1. States parties agree that the education of the child shall be directed to...

(c) the development of respect for the child's parents, his or her own cultural identity, language and values, for the national values of the country in which the child is living, the country from which he or she may originate, and for civilisations different from his or her own;

Article 30

In those states in which ethnic, religious or linguistic minorities or persons of indigenous origin exist, a child belonging to such a minority or who is indigenous shall not be denied the right, in community with other members of his or her group, to enjoy his or her own culture, to profess and practise his or her own religion, or to use his or her own language.

Article 40

1. States parties recognise the right of every child alleged as, accused of, or recognised as having infringed the penal law to be treated in a manner consistent with the promotion of the child's sense of dignity and worth, which reinforces the child's respect for the human rights and fundamental freedoms of others and which takes into account the child's age and the desirability of promoting the child's reintegration and the child's assuming a constructive role in society.

2. To this end, and having regard to the relevant provisions of international instruments, states parties shall, in particular, ensure that...

(b) every child alleged as or accused of having infringed the penal law has at least the following guarantees...

(vi) to have the free assistance of an interpreter if the child cannot understand or speak the language used;

2.1.4 *Geneva Convention for the Amelioration of the Condition of Wounded, Sick and Shipwrecked Members of Armed Forces at Sea*

Geneva, 12 August 1949.

Article 31

As far as possible, the Parties to the conflict shall enter in the log of the hospital ship in a language he can understand, the orders they have given the captain of the vessel.

Article 42

Such personnel, in addition to wearing the identity disc mentioned in Article 19, shall also carry a special identity card bearing the distinctive emblem. This card shall be water-resistant and of such size that it can be carried in the pocket. It shall be worded in the national language, shall mention at least the surname and first names, the date of birth, the rank and the service number of the bearer, and shall state in what capacity he is entitled to the protection of the present convention.

2.1.5 *Geneva Convention Relative to the Treatment of Prisoners of War*

Geneva, 12 August 1949.

Article 17

Every prisoner of war, when questioned on the subject, is bound to give only his surname, first names and rank, date of birth, and army, regimental, personal or serial number, or failing this, equivalent information...

The questioning of prisoners of war shall be carried out in a language which they understand.

Article 22

The Detaining Power shall assemble prisoners of war in camps or camp compounds according to their nationality, language and customs, provided that such prisoners shall not be separated from prisoners of war belonging to the armed forces with which they were serving at the time of their capture, except with their consent.

Article 35

Chaplains who fall into the hands of the enemy Power and who remain or are retained with a view to assisting prisoners of war, shall be allowed to minister to them and to exercise freely their ministry amongst prisoners of war of the same religion, in accordance with their religious conscience. They shall be allocated among the various camps and labour detachments containing prisoners of war belonging to the same forces, speaking the same language or practising the same religion.

Article 41

In every camp the text of the present convention and its annexes and the contents of any special agreement provided for in Article 6, shall be posted, in the prisoners' own language, in places where all may read them. Copies shall be supplied, on request, to the prisoners who cannot have access to the copy which has been posted.

Regulations, orders, notices and publications of every kind relating to the conduct of prisoners of war shall be issued to them in a language which they understand. Such regulations, orders and publications shall be posted in the manner described above and copies shall be handed to the prisoners' representative. Every order and command addressed to prisoners of war individually must likewise be given in a language which they understand.

Article 44

Officers and prisoners of equivalent status shall be treated with the regard due to their rank and age.

In order to ensure service in officers' camps, other ranks of the same armed forces who, as far as possible, speak the same language, shall be assigned in sufficient numbers, account being taken of the rank of officers and prisoners of equivalent status.

Article 71

As a general rule, the correspondence of prisoners of war shall be written in their native language. The Parties to the conflict may allow correspondence in other languages.

Article 79

In all cases the prisoners' representative must have the same nationality, language and customs as the prisoners of war whom he represents. Thus, prisoners of war distributed in different sections of a camp, according to their nationality, language or customs, shall have for each section their own prisoners' representative, in accordance with the foregoing paragraphs.

Article 105
The prisoner of war shall be entitled to assistance by one of his prisoner comrades, to defence by a qualified advocate or counsel of his own choice, to the calling of witnesses and, if he deems necessary, to the services of a competent interpreter...

Particulars of the charge or charges on which the prisoner of war is to be arraigned, as well as the documents which are generally communicated to the accused by virtue of the laws in force in the armed forces of the Detaining Power, shall be communicated to the accused prisoner of war in a language which he understands, and in good time before the opening of the trial. The same communication in the same circumstances shall be made to the advocate or counsel conducting the defence on behalf of the prisoner of war.

Article 107
Any judgment and sentence pronounced upon a prisoner of war shall be immediately reported to the Protecting Power in the form of a summary communication, which shall also indicate whether he has the right of appeal with a view to the quashing of the sentence or the reopening of the trial. This communication shall likewise be sent to the prisoners' representative concerned. It shall also be sent to the accused prisoner of war in a language he understands, if the sentence was not pronounced in his presence. The Detaining Power shall also immediately communicate to the Protecting Power the decision of the prisoner of war to use or to waive his right of appeal.

> 2.1.6 *International Convention on the Elimination of All Forms of Racial Discrimination*

Adopted 21 December 1965.

Article 1
1. In this Convention, the term "racial discrimination" shall mean any distinction, exclusion, restriction or preference based on race, colour, descent, or national or ethnic origin which has the purpose or effect of nullifying or impairing the recognition, enjoyment or exercise, on an equal footing, of human rights and fundamental freedoms in the political, economic, social, cultural or any other field of public life.

2. This Convention shall not apply to distinctions, exclusions, restrictions or preferences made by a state party to this Convention between citizens and non-citizens.

3. Nothing in this Convention may be interpreted as affecting in any way the legal provisions of states parties concerning nationality, citizenship or naturalisation, provided that such provisions do not discriminate against any particular nationality.

4. Special measures taken for the sole purpose of securing adequate advancement of certain racial or ethnic groups or individuals requiring such protection as may be necessary in order to ensure such groups or individuals equal enjoyment or exercise of human rights and fundamental freedoms shall not be deemed racial discrimination, provided, however, that such measures do not, as a consequence, lead to the maintenance of separate rights for different racial groups and that they shall not be continued after the objectives for which they were taken have been achieved.

2.1.7 *International Convention on the Protection of the Rights of all Migrant Workers and Members of their Families*

Adopted 18 December 1990.

Article 1
1. The present Convention is applicable, except as otherwise provided hereafter, to all migrant workers and members of their families without distinction of any kind such as sex, race, colour, language, religion or conviction, political or other opinion, national, ethnic or social origin, nationality, age, economic position, property, marital status, birth or other status.

Article 7
States parties undertake, in accordance with the international instruments concerning human rights, to respect and to ensure to all migrant workers and members of their families within their territory or subject to their jurisdiction the rights provided for in the present Convention without distinction of any kind such as sex, race, colour, language, religion or conviction, political or other opinion, national, ethnic or social origin, nationality, age, economic position, property, marital status, birth or other status.

Article 16
5. Migrant workers and members of their families who are arrested shall be informed at the time of arrest as far as possible in a language they understand of the reasons for their arrest and they shall be promptly informed in a language they understand of any charges against them...

8. Migrant workers and members of their families who are deprived of their liberty by arrest or detention shall be entitled to take proceedings before a court, in order that the court may decide without delay on the lawfulness of their detention and order their release if the detention is not lawful. When they attend such proceedings, they shall have the assistance, if necessary without cost to them, of an interpreter, if they cannot understand or speak the language used.

Article 18
3. In the determination of any criminal charges against them, migrant workers and members of their families shall be entitled to the following minimum guarantees:
(a) To be informed promptly and in detail in a language they understand of the nature and cause of the charge against them;...
(f) To have the free assistance of an interpreter if they cannot understand or speak the language used in court;

Article 22
2. Migrant workers and members of their families may be expelled from the territory of a state party only in pursuance of a decision taken by the competent authority in accordance with law.

3. The decision shall be communicated to them in a language they understand.

Article 30
Each child of a migrant worker shall have the basic right to access to education on the basis of equality of treatment with nationals of the state concerned. Access to public pre-school educational institutions or schools shall not be refused or limited by reason of the irregular

situation with respect to stay or employment of either parent or by reason of the irregularity of the child's stay in the state of employment.

Article 33
1. Migrant workers and members of their families shall have the right to be informed by the state of origin, the state of employment or the state of transit as the case may be concerning:
(a) Their rights arising out of the present Convention;
(b) The conditions of their admission, their rights and obligations under the law and practise of the state concerned and such other matters as will enable them to comply with administrative or other formalities in that state.
2. States parties shall take all measures they deem appropriate to disseminate the said information or to ensure that it is provided by employers, trade unions or other appropriate bodies or institutions. As appropriate, they shall co-operate with other states concerned.
3. Such adequate information shall be provided upon request to migrant workers and members of their families, free of charge, and, as far as possible, in a language they are able to understand.

Article 45
2. States of employment shall pursue a policy, where appropriate in collaboration with the states of origin, aimed at facilitating the integration of children of migrant workers in the local school system, particularly in respect of teaching them the local language.
3. States of employment shall endeavour to facilitate for the children of migrant workers the teaching of their mother tongue and culture and, in this regard, states of origin shall collaborate whenever appropriate.
4. States of employment may provide special schemes of education in the mother tongue of children of migrant workers, if necessary in collaboration with the states of origin.

2.1.8   *International Covenant on Civil and Political Rights*

Adopted 16 December 1966.

Article 2
1. Each state party to the present Covenant undertakes to respect and to ensure to all individuals within its territory and subject to its jurisdiction the rights recognised in the present Covenant, without distinction of any kind, such as race, colour, sex, language, religion, political or other opinion, national or social origin, property, birth or other status.

Article 14
3. In the determination of any criminal charge against him, everyone shall be entitled to the following minimum guarantees, in full equality:
(a) to be informed promptly and in detail in a language which he understands of the nature and cause of the charge against him;...
(f) to have the free assistance of an interpreter if he cannot understand or speak the language used in court;

Article 24
1. Every child shall have, without any discrimination as to race, colour, sex, language,

religion, national or social origin, property or birth, the right to such measures of protection as are required by his status as a minor, on the part of his family, society and the state.

Article 26
All persons are equal before the law and are entitled without any discrimination to the equal protection of the law. In this respect, the law shall prohibit any discrimination and guarantee to all persons equal and effective protection against discrimination on any ground such as race, colour, sex, language, religion, political or other opinion, national or social origin, property, birth or other status.

Article 27
In those states in which ethnic, religious or linguistic minorities exist, persons belonging to such minorities shall not be denied the right, in community with the other members of their group, to enjoy their own culture, to profess and practise their own religion, or to use their own language.

2.1.9 *International Covenant on Economic, Social and Cultural Rights*

Adopted 16 December 1966.

Article 2
2. The states parties to the present Covenant undertake to guarantee that the rights enunciated in the present Covenant will be exercised without discrimination of any kind as to race, colour, sex, language, religion, political or other opinion, national or social origin, property, birth or other status.

2.1.10 *International Labour Organisation Convention (No. 107) Concerning the Protection and Integration of Indigenous and Other Tribal and Semi-Tribal Populations in Independent Countries*

Adopted 26 June 1957.

Article 23
1. Children belonging to the populations concerned shall be taught to read and write in their mother tongue or, where this is not practicable, in the language most commonly used by the group to which they belong.
2. Provision shall be made for a progressive transition from the mother tongue or the vernacular language to the national language or to one of the official languages of the country.
3. Appropriate measures shall, as far as possible, be taken to preserve the mother tongue or the vernacular language.

Article 26
1. Governments shall adopt measures, appropriate to the social and cultural characteristics of the populations concerned, to make known to them their rights and duties, especially in regard to labour and social welfare.

2. If necessary this shall be done by means of written translations and through the use of media of mass communication in the languages of these populations.

2.1.11 *International Labour Organisation Convention (No. 169) Concerning Indigenous and Tribal Peoples in Independent Countries*

Adopted 27 June 1989.

Article 2

1. Governments shall have the responsibility for developing, with the participation of the peoples concerned, coordinated and systematic action to protect the rights of these peoples and to guarantee respect for their integrity.

2. Such action shall include measures for :

a) Ensuring that members of these peoples benefit on an equal footing from the rights and opportunities which national laws and regulations grant to other members of the population;

b) Promoting the full realisation of the social, economic and cultural rights of these peoples with respect for their social and cultural identity, their customs and traditions and their institutions;

c) Assisting the members of the peoples concerned to eliminate socio-economic gaps that may exist between indigenous and other members of the national community, in a manner compatible with their aspirations and ways of life.

Article 6

1. In applying the provisions of this Convention, governments shall :

(a) Consult the peoples concerned, through appropriate procedures and in particular through their representative institutions, whenever consideration is being given to legislative or administrative measures which may affect them directly;

(b) Establish means by which these peoples can freely participate, to at least the same extent as other sectors of the population, at all levels of decision-making in elective institutions and administrative and other bodies responsible for policies and programmes which concern them;

(c) Establish means for the full development of these peoples' own institutions and initiatives, and in appropriate cases provide the resources necessary for this purpose.

Article 8

1. In applying national laws and regulations to the peoples concerned, due regard shall be had to their customs or customary laws.

2. These peoples shall have the right to retain their own customs and institutions, where these are not incompatible with fundamental rights defined by the national legal system and with internationally recognised human rights. Procedures shall be established, whenever necessary, to resolve conflicts which may arise in the application of this principle.

3. The application of paragraphs 1 and 2 of this Article shall not prevent members of these peoples from exercising the rights granted to all citizens and from assuming the corresponding duties.

Article 27

1. Education programmes and services for the peoples concerned shall be developed and

implemented in co-operation with them to address their special needs, and shall incorporate their histories, their knowledge and technologies, their value systems and their further social, economic and cultural aspirations.

2. The competent authority shall ensure the training of members of these peoples and their involvement in the formulation and implementation of education programmes, with a view to the progressive transfer of responsibility for the conduct of these programmes to these peoples as appropriate.

3. In addition, governments shall recognise the right of these peoples to establish their own educational institutions and facilities, provided that such institutions meet minimum standards established by the competent authority in consultation with these peoples. Appropriate resources shall be provided for this purpose.

Article 28
1. Children belonging to the peoples concerned shall, wherever practicable, be taught to read and write in their own indigenous language or in the language most commonly used by the group to which they belong. When this is not practicable, the competent authorities shall undertake consultations with these peoples with a view to the adoption of measures to achieve this objective.

2. Adequate measures shall be taken to ensure that these peoples have the opportunity to attain fluency in the national language or in one of the official languages of the country.

3. Measures shall be taken to preserve and promote the development and practise of the indigenous languages of the peoples concerned.

Article 30
1. Governments shall adopt measures appropriate to the traditions and cultures of the peoples concerned, to make known to them their rights and duties, especially in regard to labour, economic opportunities, education and health matters, social welfare and their rights deriving from this Convention.

2. If necessary, this shall be done by means of written translations and through the use of mass communications in the languages of these peoples.

2.1.11 *Protocol Additional to the Geneva Conventions of 12 August 1949, and Relating to the Protection of Victims of International Armed Conflicts*

United Nations Treaty Series, Volume 1125, 3.

Article 9
1. This part, the provisions of which are intended to ameliorate the condition of the wounded, sick and shipwrecked, shall apply to all those affected by a situation referred to in Article 1, without any adverse distinction founded on race, colour, sex, language, religion or belief, political or other opinion, national or social origin, wealth, birth or other status, or on any other similar criteria.

Article 75
1. In so far as they are affected by a situation referred to in Article 1 of this protocol, persons who are in the power of a party to the conflict and who do not benefit from more favourable treatment under the conventions or under this protocol shall be treated humanely in

all circumstances and shall enjoy, as a minimum, the protection provided by this article without any adverse distinction based upon race, colour, sex, language, religion or belief, political or other opinion, national or social origin, wealth, birth or other status, or on any other similar criteria. Each party shall respect the person, honour, convictions and religious practices of all such persons.

3. Any person arrested, detained or interned for actions related to the armed conflict shall be informed promptly, in a language he understands, of the reasons why these measures have been taken. Except in cases of arrest or detention for penal offences, such persons shall be released with the minimum delay possible and in any event as soon as the circumstances justifying the arrest, detention or internment have ceased to exist.

Article 78
3. With a view to facilitating the return to their families and country of children evacuated pursuant to this article, the authorities of the Party arranging for the evacuation and, as appropriate, the authorities of the receiving country shall establish for each child a card with photographs, which they shall send to the Central Tracing Agency of the International Committee of the Red Cross. Each card shall bear, whenever possible, and whenever it involves no risk of harm to the child, the following information:
(i) the child's native language, and any other languages he speaks;

2.2   REGIONAL TREATIES

2.2.1   *African Charter on Human and Peoples' Rights*

Organisation of African States, Nairobi, 27 June 1981.

Article 2
Every individual shall be entitled to the enjoyment of the rights and freedoms recognised and guaranteed in the present Charter without distinction of any kind such as race, ethnic group, colour, sex, language, religion, political or any other opinion, national and social origin, fortune, birth or other status.

Article 22
1. All peoples shall have the right to their economic, social and cultural development with due regard to their freedom and identity and in the equal enjoyment of the common heritage of mankind.

2.2.2   *Agreement Establishing the Commonwealth of Independent States*

Minsk, 8 December 1991. Reprinted from (1992) *International Legal Materials*, Vol. 31, at p. 138.

Article 3
The high contracting parties, desirous of facilitating the expression, preservation and development of the distinctive ethnic, cultural, linguistic and religious characteristics of the

national minorities resident in their territories and of the unique ethno-cultural regions that have come into being, will extend protection to them.

2.2.3 *American Convention on Human Rights*

Organisation of American States, San José, Costa Rica, 22 November 1969.

Article 1
1. The states parties to this Convention undertake to respect the rights and freedoms recognised herein and to ensure to all persons subject to their jurisdiction the free and full exercise of those rights and freedoms, without any discrimination for reasons of race, colour, sex, language, religion, political or other opinion, national or social origin, economic status, birth, or any other social condition.

Article 8
2. Every person accused of a serious crime has the right to be presumed innocent so long as his guilt has not been proven according to law. During the proceedings, every person is entitled, with full equality, to the following minimum guarantees:
(a) the right of the accused to be assisted without charge by a translator or interpreter, if he does not understand or does not speak the language of the tribunal or court;

2.2.4 *Convention-cadre pour la protection des minorités nationales (Europe)*

Council of Europe, opened for signature, 10 October 1994.

Article 5
1. Les parties s'engagent à promouvoir les conditions propres à permettre aux personnes appartenant à des minorités nationales de conserver et développer leur culture, ainsi que de préserver les éléments essentiels de leur identité que sont leur religion, leur langue, leurs traditions et leur patrimoine culturel.
2. Sans préjudice des mesures prises dans le cadre de leur politique générale d'intégration, les parties s'abstiennent de toute politique ou pratique tendant à une assimilation contre leur volonté des personnes appartenant à des minorités nationales et protègent ces personnes contre toute action destinée à une telle assimilation.

Article 6
1. Les parties veilleront à promouvoir l'esprit de tolérance et le dialogue interculturel, ainsi qu'à prendre des mesures efficaces pour favoriser le respect et la compréhension mutuels et la coopération entre toutes les personnes vivant sur leur territoire, quelle que soit leur identité ethnique, culturelle, linguistique ou religieuse, notamment dans les domaines de l'éducation, de la culture et des médias.

Article 9

1. Les parties s'engagent à reconnaître que le droit à la liberté d'expression de toute personne appartenant à une minorité nationale comprend la liberté d'opinion et la liberté de

recevoir ou de communiquer des informations ou des idées dans la langue minoritaire, sans ingérence d'autorités publiques et sans considération de frontières. Dans l'accès aux médias, les parties veilleront, dans le cadre de leur système législatif, à ce que les personnes appartenant à une minorité nationale ne soient pas discriminées.

2. Le premier paragraphe n'empêche pas les parties de soumettre à un régime d'autorisation, non discriminatoire et fondé sur des critères objectifs, les entreprises de radio sonore, télévision ou cinéma.

3. Les parties n'entraveront pas la création et l'utilisation de médias écrits par les personnes appartenant à des minorités nationales. Dans le cadre légal de la radio sonore et de la télévision, elles veilleront, dans la mesure du possible et compte tenu des dispositions du premier paragraphe, à accorder aux personnes appartenant à des minorités nationales la possibilité de créer et d'utiliser leurs propres médias.

4. Dans le cadre de leur système législatif, les parties adopteront des mesures adéquates pour faciliter l'accès des personnes appartenant à des minorités nationales aux médias, pour promouvoir la tolérance et permettre le pluralisme culturel.

Article 10

1. Les parties s'engagent à reconnaître à toute personne appartenant à une minorité nationale le droit d'utiliser librement et sans entrave sa langue minoritaire en privé comme en public, oralement ou par écrit.

2. Dans les aires géographiques d'implantation substantielle ou traditionnelle des personnes appartenant à des minorités nationales, lorsque ces personnes en font la demande et que celle-ci répond à un besoin réel, les parties s'efforceront d'assurer, dans la mesure du possible, des conditions qui permettent d'utiliser la langue minoritaire dans les rapports entre ces personnes et les autorités administratives.

3. Les parties s'engagent à garantir le droit de toute personne appartenant à une minorité nationale d'être informée, dans le plus court délai, et dans une langue qu'elle comprend, des raisons de son arrestation, de la nature et de la cause de l'accusation portée contre elle, ainsi que le droit de se défendre dans cette langue, si nécessaire avec l'assistance gratuite d'un interprète.

Article 11

1. Les parties s'engagent à reconnaître à toute personne appartenant à une minorité nationale le droit d'utiliser son nom (son patronyme) et ses prénoms dans la langue minoritaire ainsi que le droit à leur reconnaissance officielle, selon les modalités prévues par leur système juridique.

2. Les parties s'engagent à reconnaître à toute personne appartenant à une minorité nationale le droit de présenter dans sa langue minoritaire des enseignes, inscriptions et autres informations de caractère privé exposées à la vue du public.

3. Dans les régions traditionnellement habitées par un numbre substantiel de personnes appartenant à une minorité nationale, les parties, dans le cadre de leur système législatif, y compris, le cas échéant, d'accords avec d'autres états, s'efforceront, en tenant compte de leurs conditions spécifiques, de présenter les dénominations traditionnelles locales, les noms de rues et autres indications typographiques destinées au public, dans la langue minoritaire également, lorsqu'il y a une demande suffisante pour de telles indications.

Articles 12

1. Les parties prendront, si nécessaire, des mesures dans le domaine de l'éducation et de la recherche pour promouvoir la connaissance de la culture, de l'histoire, de la langue et de la religion de leurs minorités nationales aussi bien que de la majorité.

2. Dans ce contexte, les parties offriront notamment les possibilités de formation pour les enseignants et d'accès aux manuels scolaires, et faciliteront les contacts entre élèves et enseignants des communautés différentes.

3. Les parties s'engagent à promouvoir l'égalité des chances dans l'accès à l'éducation à tous les niveaux pour les personnes appartenant à des minorités nationales.

Article 13

1. Dans le cadre de leur système éducatif, les parties reconnaissent aux personnes appartenant à une minorité nationale le droit de créer et de gérer leurs propres établissements privés d'enseignement et de formation.

2. L'exercice de ce droit n'implique aucune obligation financière pour les parties.

Article 14

1. Les parties s'engagent à reconnaître à toute personne appartenant à une minorité nationale le droit d'apprendre sa langue minoritaire.

2. Dans les aires géographiques d'implantation substantielle ou traditionnelle des personnes appartenant à des minorités nationales, s'il existe une demande suffisante, les parties s'efforceront d'assurer, dans la mesure du possible et dans le cadre de leur système éducatif, que les personnes appartenant à ces minorités aient la possibilité d'apprendre la langue minoritaire ou de recevoir un enseignement dans cette langue.

3. Le paragraphe 2 du présent article sera mis en oeuvre sans préjudice de l'apprentissage de la langue officielle ou de l'enseignement dans cette langue.

Article 15

Les parties s'engagent à créer les conditions nécessaires à la participation effective des personnes appartenant à des minorités nationales à la vie culturelle, sociale et économique, ainsi qu'aux affaires publiques, en particulier celles les concernant.

Article 16

Les parties s'abstiennent de prendre des mesures qui, en modifiant les proportions de la population dans une aire géographique où résident des personnes appartenant à des minorités nationales, ont pour but de porter atteinte aux droits et libertés découlant des principes énoncés dans la présente convention-cadre.

Article 17

1. Les parties s'engagent à ne pas entraver le droit des personnes appartenant à des minorités nationales d'établir et de maintenir, librement ou pacifiquement, des contacts au-delà des frontières avec des personnes se trouvant régulièrement dans d'autres états, notamment celles avec lesquelles elles ont en commun une identité ethnique, culturelle, linguistique ou religieuse, ou un patrimoine culturel.

2.2.5 *Convention for the Protection of Human Rights and Fundamental Freedoms (Europe)*

Council of Europe, Rome, 4 November 1950.

Article 6

2. Everyone who is arrested shall be informed promptly, in a language which he understands, of the reasons for his arrest and of any charge against him...

3. Everyone charged with a criminal offence has the following minimum rights:

(a) to be informed promptly, in a language which he understands and in detail, of the nature and cause of the accusation against him;...

(e) to have the free assistance of an interpreter if he cannot understand or speak the language used in court.

Article 14

The enjoyment of the rights and freedoms set forth in this Convention shall be secured without discrimination on any ground such as sex, race, colour, language, religion, political or other opinion, national or social origin, association with a national minority, property, birth or other status.

2.2.6   *European Charter for Regional or Minority Languages*

Council of Europe, Strasbourg, 5 November 1992.

PART I

GENERAL PROVISIONS

Article 1

Definitions

For the purposes of this Charter:

a) the term "regional or minority languages" means languages that are:

I. traditionally used within a given territory of a state by nationals of that state who form a group numerically smaller than the rest of the state's population, and

II. different from the official language(s) of that state;

it does not include either dialects of the official language(s) of the state or the languages of migrants;

b) "territory in which the regional or minority language is used" means geographical area in which the said language is the mode of expression of a number of people justifying the adoption of the various protective and promotional measures provided for in this Charter;

c) "non-territorial languages" means languages used by nationals of the state which differ from the language or the languages used by the rest of the population of the state but that, although they are traditionally used within the territory of the state, cannot be identified with a particular area thereof.

Article 2
Undertakings

1. Each party undertakes to apply the provisions of Part II to all regional or minority languages spoken within its territory and complying with the definition in Article 1.

2. In respect of each languages specified at the time of ratification, acceptance or approval, in accordance with Article 3, each party undertakes to apply a minimum of thirty-five paragraphs

or sub-paragraphs chosen from among the provisions of Part III of the Charter, including at least three chosen from each of the Article 8 and 12 and one from each of the Articles 9, 10, 11 and 13.

Article 3
Practical Arrangements
1. Each contracting state shall specify in its instrument of ratification, acceptance or approval, each regional or minority language, or official language which is less widely used on the whole part of its territory, to which the paragraphs chosen in accordance with Article 2, paragraph 2, shall apply.
2. Any party may, at any subsequent time, notify the Secretary General that it accepts the obligations arising out of the provisions of any other paragraph of the Charter not already specified in its instrument of ratification, acceptance or approval, or that it will apply paragraph 1 of the present article to other regional or minority languages, or to other official languages which are less widely used on the whole or part of its territory.
3. The undertakings referred to in the foregoing paragraph shall be deemed to form an integral part of the ratification, acceptance or approval and will have the same effect as from their date of notification.

Article 4
Existing Regimes of Protection
1. Nothing in this Charter shall be construed as limiting or derogating from any of the rights guaranteed by the European Convention on Human Rights.
2. The provisions of this Charter shall not affect any more favourable provisions concerning the status of regional or minority languages or the legal regime of persons belonging to minorities which may exist in a party or are provided for by relevant bilateral or multilateral agreements.

Article 5
Existing Obligations
Nothing in this Charter may be interpreted as implying any right to engage in any activity or perform any action in contravention of the purposes of the Charter of the United Nations or other obligations under international law, including the principle of the sovereignty and territorial integrity of states.

Article 6
Information
The parties undertake to see to it that the authorities, organisations and persons concerned are informed of the rights and duties established by this Charter.

Article 7
Objectives and principles
1. In respect of regional or minority languages, within the territories in which such languages are used and according to the situation of each language, the parties shall base their policies, legislation and practise on the following objectives and principles:
a) the recognition of the regional or minority languages as an expression of cultural wealth;
b) the respect of the geographical area of each regional or minority language in order to ensure that existing or new administrative divisions do not constitute an obstacle to the promotion of the regional or minority language in question;

c) the need for resolute action to promote regional or minority languages in order to safeguard them;

d) the facilitation and/or encouragement of the use of regional or minority languages, in speech and writing, in public and private life;

e) the maintenance and development of links, in the fields covered by this Charter, between groups using a regional or minority language and other groups in the state employing a language used in identical or similar form, as well as the establishment of cultural relations with other groups in the state using different languages;

f) the provision of appropriate forms and means for the teaching and study of regional or minority languages at all appropriate stages;

g) the provisions of facilities enabling non-speakers of a regional or minority living in the area where it is used to learn it if they so desire;

h) the promotion of study and research on regional or minority languages at universities or equivalent institutions;

i) the promotion of different types of transnational exchanges, in the fields covered by this Charter, for regional or minority languages used in identical or similar form in two or more states.

2. The parties undertake to eliminate, if they have not yet done so, any unjustified distinction, exclusion, restriction or preference relating to the use of a regional or minority language and intended to discourage or endanger the maintenance or development of a regional or minority language. The adoption of special measures in favour of regional or minority languages aimed at promoting equality between the users of these languages and the rest of the population or which take due account of their specific conditions is not considered to be an act of discrimination against the users of more widely-used languages.

3. The parties undertake to promote, by appropriate measures, mutual understanding between all the linguistic groups of the country and in particular the inclusion of respect, understanding and tolerance in relation to regional or minority languages among the objectives of education and training provided within their countries and encouragement of the mass media to pursue the same objective.

4. In determining their policy with regard to regional or minority languages, the parties shall take into consideration the needs and wishes expressed by the groups which use such languages. They are encouraged to establish bodies, if necessary, for the purpose of advising the authorities on all matters pertaining to regional or minority languages.

5. The parties undertake to apply, *mutatis mutandis*, the principles listed in paragraphs 1 to 4 above to non-territorial languages. However, as far as these languages are concerned, the nature and scope of the measures to be taken to give effect to this Charter shall be determined in a flexible manner, bearing in mind the needs and wishes, and respecting the traditions and characteristics, of the groups which use the languages concerned.

Article 8
Education

1. With regard to education, the parties undertake, within the territory in which such languages are used, according to the situation of each of these languages, and without prejudice to the teaching of the official language(s) of the state, to:

a)   I. make available preschool education in the relevant regional or minority languages; or

II. make available a substantial part of preschool education in the relevant regional or minority languages; or

III. apply one of the measures provided for under (I) and (II) above at least to those pupils whose families so request and whose number is considered sufficient; or

IV. if the public authorities have no direct competence in the field of preschool education, favour and/or encourage the application of the measures referred to under (I) to (III) above;

b)   I. make available primary education in the relevant regional or minority languages; or

II. make available a substantial part of primary education in the relevant regional or minority languages; or

III. provide, within primary education, for the teaching of the relevant regional or minority languages as an integral part of the curriculum; or

IV. apply one of the measures provided for under (I) to (III) above at least to those pupils whose families so request and whose numbers is considered sufficient;

c)   I. make available secondary education in the relevant regional or minority languages; or

II. make available a substantial part of secondary education in the relevant regional or minority languages; or

III. provide, within secondary education, for the teaching of the relevant regional or minority languages as an integral part of the curriculum; or

IV. apply one of the measures provided for under (I) to (III) above at least to those pupils who, or where appropriate whose families, so wish in a number considered sufficient;

d)   I. make available technical and vocational education in the relevant or regional or minority languages; or

II. make available a substantial part of technical and vocational education in the relevant regional or minority languages; or

III. provide, within technical and vocational education, for the teaching of the relevant regional or minority languages as an integral part of the curriculum; or

IV. apply one of the measures provided for under (I) to (III) above at least to those pupils who, or where appropriate whose families, so wish in a number considered sufficient;

e)   I. make available university and other higher education in regional or minority languages; or

II. provide facilities for the study of these languages as university and higher education subjects; or

III. if, by reason of the role of the state in relation to higher education institutions, subparagraph i. and ii. cannot be applied, encourage and/or allow the provision of university and higher education in regional or minority languages or of facilities for the study of these languages as university and higher education subjects;

f)   I. arrange for the provision of adult and continuing education courses which are taught mainly or wholly in the regional or minority languages; or

II. offer such languages as subjects of adult and continuing education; or

III. if the public authorities have no direct competence in the field of adult education, favour and/or encourage the offering of such languages as subjects of adult and continuing education;

g)   make arrangements to ensure the teaching of the history and the culture which is reflected by the regional or minority language;

h) provide the basic and further training of the teachers required to implement those of paragraphs (a) to (g) accepted by the party;

i) set up a supervisory body or bodies responsible for monitoring the measures taken and the progress achieved in establishing or developing the teaching of regional or minority languages and for drawing up periodic reports of their findings, which will be made public.

j) with regard to education and in respect of territories other than those in which the regional or minority languages are traditionally used, the parties undertake, if the number of users of a regional or minority language justifies it, to allow, encourage or provide teaching in or of the regional or minority language at all the appropriate stages of education.

Article 9
Judicial authorities

1. The parties undertake, in respect of those judicial districts in which the number of residents using the regional or minority languages justifies the measures specified below, according to the situation of each of these languages and on condition that the use of the facilities afforded by the present paragraph is not considered by the judge to hamper the proper administration of justice:

a) in criminal proceedings:

I. to provide that the courts, at the request of one of the parties, shall conduct the proceedings in the regional or minority languages; and/or

II. to guarantee the accused the right to use his/her regional or minority language; and/or

III. to provide that requests and evidence, whether written or oral, shall not be considered inadmissible solely because they are formulated in a regional or minority language; and/or

IV. to produce, on request, documents connected with legal proceedings in the relevant regional or minority language, if necessary by the use of interpreters and translations involving no extra expense for the persons concerned;

b) in civil proceedings:

I. to provide that the courts, at the request of one of the parties, shall conduct the proceedings in the regional or minority languages; and/or

II. to allow, whenever a litigant has to appear in person before a court, that he or she may use his or her regional or minority language without thereby incurring additional expense; and/or

III. to allow documents and evidence to be produced in the regional or minority languages if necessary by the use of interpreters and translation;

c) in proceedings before the courts concerning administrative matters:

I. to provide that the courts, at the request of one of the parties, shall conduct the proceedings in the regional or minority languages; and/or

II. to allow, whenever a litigant has to appear in person before a court, that he or she may use his or her regional or minority language without thereby incurring additional expenses; and/or

III. to allow documents and evidence to be produced in the regional or minority languages if necessary by the use of interpreters and translations;

d) to take steps to ensure that the application of subparagraphs (i) and (iii) of paragraphs (b) and (c) above and any necessary use of interpreters and translations does not involve extra expense for the persons concerned.

2. The parties undertake:

a) not to deny the validity of legal documents drawn up within the state solely because they are drafted in a regional or minority language; or

b) not to deny the validity, as between the parties, of legal documents drawn up within the country solely because they are drafted in a regional or minority language, and to provide that they can be invoked against interested third parties who are not users of these languages on condition that the contents of the document are made known to them by the person(s) who invoke(s) it; or

c) not to deny the validity, as between the parties, of legal documents drawn up within the country solely because they are drafted in a regional or minority language.

3. The parties undertake to make available in the regional or minority languages the most important national statutory texts and those relating particularly to users of these languages, unless they are otherwise provided.

Article 10
Administrative authorities and public services

1. Within the administrative districts of the state in which the number of residents who are users of regional or minority languages justifies the measures specified below and according to the situation of each language, the parties undertake, as far as this is reasonably possible, to:

    a)   I. ensure that the administrative authorities use the regional or minority languages; or

            II. ensure that such of their officers as are in contact with the public use the regional or minority languages in their relations with persons applying to them in these languages; or

            III. ensure that users of regional or minority languages may submit oral or written applications and receive a reply in these languages; or

            IV. ensure that users of regional or minority languages may submit oral or written applications in these languages; or

            V. ensure that the users of regional or minority languages may validly submit a document in these language;

b) make available widely used administrative texts and forms for the population in the regional or minority languages or in bilingual versions;

c) allow the administrative authorities to draft documents in a regional or minority language.

2. In respect of the local and regional authorities on whose territory the number of users of regional or minority languages is such as to justify the measures specified below, the parties undertake to allow and/or encourage;

a) the use of regional or minority languages within the framework of the regional or local authority;

b) the possibility of users of regional or minority languages to submit oral written applications in these languages;

c) the publication by regional authorities of their official documents also in the relevant regional or minority languages;

d) the publication by local authorities of their official documents also in the relevant regional or minority languages;

e)the use by regional authorities of regional or minority languages in debates in their assemblies, without excluding, however, the use of the official language(s) of the state;

f) the use by local authorities of regional or minority languages in debates in their assemblies, without excluding, however, the use of the official language(s) of the state;

g) the use or adoption, if necessary in conjunction with the name in the official language(s), of traditional and correct forms of place-names in regional or minority languages.

3. With regard to public services provided by the administrative authorities or other persons acting on their authority, the parties undertake, within the territory in which regional or minority languages are used, in accordance with the situation of each language and as far as this is reasonably possible, to:

a) ensure that the regional or minority languages are used in the provision of the service; or

b)allow users of regional or minority languages to submit a request and receive a reply in these languages; or

c) allow users of regional or minority languages to submit a request in these languages.

4. With a view to putting into effect those provisions of paragraphs 1, 2 and 3 accepted by them, the parties undertake to take one more of the following measures:

a) translation or interpretation as may be required;

b) recruitment and, where necessary, training of the officials and other public service employees required;

c) compliance as far as possible with requests from public service employees having a knowledge of a regional or minority language to be appointed in the territory in which that language is used.

5. The parties undertake to allow the use or adoption of family names in the regional or minority languages at the request of those concerned.

Article 11
Media

1. The parties undertake, for the users of the regional or minority languages within the territories in which those languages are spoken, according to the situation of each language, to the extent that the public authorities, directly or indirectly, are competent, have power or play a role in this field, and respecting the principle of the independence and autonomy of the media:

a) to the extent that radio and television carry out a public service mission:

I. to ensure the creation of at least one radio station and one television channel in the regional or minority languages, or

II. to encourage and/or facilitate the creation of at least one radio station and one television channel in the regional or minority languages, or

III. to make adequate provision so that broadcasters offer programmes in the regional or minority languages;

b) I. to encourage and/or facilitate the creation of at least one radio station in the regional or minority languages, or

II. to encourage and/or facilitate the broadcasting of radio programmes in the regional or minority languages on a regular basis;

c) I. to encourage and/or facilitate the creation of at least one television channel in the regional or minority languages, or

II. to encourage and/or facilitate the broadcasting of television programmes in the regional or minority languages on a regular basis;

d) to encourage and/or facilitate the production and distribution of audio and audio-visual works in regional or minority languages;

e) I. to encourage and/or facilitate the creation and/or maintenance of at least one newspaper in the regional or minority languages; or

II. to encourage and/or facilitate the publication of newspaper articles in the regional or minority languages on a regular basis;

f)   I. to cover the additional costs of those media which use regional or minority languages, wherever the law provides for financial assistance in general for the media; or

II. to apply existing measures for financial assistance also to audio-visual productions in regional or minority languages;

g) to support the training of journalists and other staff for media using regional or minority languages.

2. The parties undertake to guarantee freedom of direct reception of radio and television broadcasts from neighbouring countries in a language used in identical or similar to a regional or minority language, and not to oppose the retransmission of radio and television broadcasts from neighbouring countries in such a language. They further undertake to ensure that no restrictions will be placed on the freedom of expression and free circulation of information in the written press in a language used in identical or similar form to a regional or minority language. The exercise of the above mentioned freedoms, since it carries with it duties and responsibilities, may be subject to such formalities, conditions, restrictions or penalties as are prescribed by law and are necessary in a democratic society, in the interest of national security, territorial integrity or public safety, for the prevention of disorder of crime, for the protection of health or morals, for the protection of reputation or rights of others, for preventing disclosure of information received in confidence, or for maintaining the authority and impartiality of the judiciary.

3. The parties undertake to ensure that the interests of the users of regional or minority languages are represented or taken into account within such bodies as may be established in accordance with the law with responsibility for guaranteeing the freedom and pluralism of the media.

Article 12
Cultural activities and facilities

1. With regard to cultural facilities and activities especially libraries, video libraries, cultural centres, museums, archives, academies, theatres and cinemas, as well as literary work and film production, vernacular forms of cultural expression, festivals and the culture industries, including *inter alia* the use of new technologies, the parties undertake, within the territory in which such languages are used and to the extent that the public authorities are competent, have power or play a role in this field, to:

a) encourage types of expression and initiative specific to regional or minority languages and foster the different means of access to works produced in these languages;

b) foster the different means of access in other languages to works produced in regional or minority languages by aiding and developing translation, dubbing, post-synchronisation and subtitling activities;

c) foster access in regional or minority languages to works produced in other languages by aiding and developing translation, dubbing, post-synchronisation and subtitling activities;

d) ensure that the bodies responsible for organising or supporting cultural activities of various kinds make appropriate allowance for incorporating the knowledge and use of regional or minority languages and cultures in the undertakings which they initiate or for which they provide backing;

e) promote measures to ensure that the bodies responsible for organising and supporting cultural activities have at their disposal staff who have a full command of the regional or minority language concerned, as well as of the language(s) of the rest of the population;

f) encourage direct participation by representatives of the users of a given regional or minority language in providing facilities and planning cultural activities;

g) encourage and/or facilitate the creation of a body or bodies responsible for collecting, keeping a copy of and presenting or publishing works produced in the regional or minority languages;

h) if necessary create and/or promote and finance translation and terminological research services, particularly with a view to maintaining and developing appropriate administrative, commercial, economic, social, technical or legal terminology in each regional or minority language.

2. In respect of territories other than those in which the regional or minority languages are traditionally used, the parties undertake, if the number of users of a regional or minority language justifies it, to allow, to encourage and/or provide appropriate cultural activities and facilities in accordance with the preceding paragraph.

3. The parties undertake to make appropriate provision, in pursuing their cultural policy abroad, for regional or minority languages and the cultures they reflect.

Article 13
Economic and social life

1. With regard to economic and social activities, the parties undertake, within the whole country, to:

a) eliminate from their legislation any provision prohibiting or limiting without justifiable reasons the use of regional or minority languages in documents relating to economic or social life, particularly contracts of employment, and in technical documents such as instructions for the use of products or installations;

b) prohibit the insertion in internal regulations of companies and private documents of any clauses excluding or restricting the use of regional or minority languages, at least between users of the same language;

c) oppose practises designed to discourage the use of regional or minority languages in connection with economic or social activities;

d) facilitate and/or encourage the use of regional or minority languages by means other than those specified in the above subparagraphs.

2. With regard to economic and social activities, the parties undertake, in so far as public authorities are competent, within the territory in which the regional or minority languages are used, and as far as this is reasonably possible, to:

a) include in their financial and banking regulations provisions which allow, by means of procedures compatible with commercial practise, the use of regional or minority languages in drawing up payment orders (cheques, drafts, etc.) or other financial documents, or, where appropriate, ensure the implementation of such provisions;

b) in the economic and social sectors directly under their control (public sector), organise activities to promote the use of regional or minority languages;

c) ensure that social care facilities such as hospitals, retirement homes and hostels offer the possibility of receiving and treating in their own language persons using a regional or minority language who are in need of care on grounds of ill health, old age or for other reasons;

d) ensure by appropriate means that safety instructions are also accessible in regional or minority languages;

e) arrange for information provided by the competent public authorities concerning the rights of consumers to be made available in regional or minority languages.

Article 14
Transfrontier exchanges
>The parties undertake:
>a) to apply existing bilateral and multilateral agreements which bind them with the states in which the same language is used in identical or similar form, or if necessary to seek to conclude such agreements, in such a way as to foster contacts between the users of the same language in the states concerned in the fields of culture, education, information, vocational training and permanent education;
>b) for the benefit of regional or minority languages, to facilitate and promote cooperation across borders, in particular between regional or local authorities in whose territory the same language is used in identical or similar form.

2.2.7 *European Convention on Offences Relating to Cultural Property*

23 June 1985 (not in force as of 1 January 1993).

Article 9
>1. Unless the Parties otherwise agree, letters rogatory shall be in the language of the requested Party, or in the official language of the Council of Europe that is indicated by the requested Party in a declaration addressed to the Secretary General of the Council of Europe, or where no such declaration has been made in either of the official languages of the Council of Europe.

2.2.8 *European Convention on Transfrontier Television*

Council of Europe, Strasbourg, 5 May 1989.

Article 10
>3. The parties undertake to look together for the most appropriate instruments and procedures to support, without discrimination between broadcasters, the activity and development of European production, particularly in countries with a low audiovisual production capacity or restricted language area.

2.2.9 *North American Free Trade Agreement*

December 1992.

Article 501
Certificate of Origin
>1. The parties shall establish by January 1, 1994 a Certificate of Origin for the purpose of certifying that a good being exported from the territory of a party into the territory of another party qualifies as an originating good, and may thereafter revise the Certificate by agreement.
>2. Each party may require that a Certificate of Origin for a good imported into its territory be completed in a language required under its law.

Article 911
Technical Cooperation
1. Each party shall, on request of another party:
(a) provide to that party technical advice, information and assistance on mutually agreed terms and conditions to enhance that party's standards-related measures, and related activities, processes and systems;
(b) provide to that party information on its technical cooperation programs regarding standards-related measures relating to specific areas of interest; and
(c) consult with that party during the development of, or prior to the adoption or change in the application of, any standards-related measure.
2. Each party shall encourage standardising bodies in its territory to cooperate with the standardising bodies in the territories of the other parties in their participation, as appropriate, in standardising activities, such as through membership in international standardising bodies.

Article 912
Limitations on the Provision of Information
Nothing in this Chapter shall be construed to require a party to:
(a) communicate, publish texts, or provide particulars or copies of documents other than in an official language of the party;

Annex 913.5.a-4
Subcommittee on Labelling of Textile and Apparel Goods
3. The Subcommittee shall develop and pursue a work program on the harmonisation of labelling requirements to facilitate trade in textile and apparel goods between the parties through the adoption of uniform labelling provisions. The work program should include the following matters:
(a) pictograms and symbols to replace, where possible, required written information, as well as other methods to reduce the need for labels on textile and apparel goods in multiple languages;

Article 501
Certificate of Origin
1. The parties shall establish by January 1, 1994 a Certificate of Origin for the purpose of certifying that a good being exported from the territory of a party into the territory of another party qualifies as an originating good, and may thereafter revise the Certificate by agreement.
2. Each party may require that a Certificate of Origin for a good imported into its territory be completed in a language required under its law.

Annex 1210.5
2. The parties shall encourage the relevant bodies in their respective territories to develop mutually acceptable standards and criteria for licensing and certification of professional service providers and to provide recommendations on mutual recognition to the Commission.
3. The standards and criteria referred to in paragraph 2 may be developed with regard to the following matters...
(g) local knowledge: requirements for knowledge of such matters as local laws, regulations, language, geography or climate;

Reservations and Exceptions to Investment, Cross-Border Trade in Services and Financial
Services Chapters

Annex I - Schedule of Mexico
 The use of the Spanish language is required for the broadcast, cable or multipoint
distribution system distribution of radio or television programming, except when the Secretaría
de Gobernación authorises the use of another language...
 The use of the Spanish language or Spanish subtitles is required for advertising broadcast
or otherwise distributed in the territory of Mexico.
 Advertising included in programs transmitted directly from outside the territory of Mexico
may not be distributed in those programs when they are retransmitted in the territory of
Mexico.

2.2.10 *Treaty on European Union*

European Union, Maastricht, 7 February 1992. Reprinted from (1992), *International Legal
Materials*, Vol. 31, p. 247.

Article 126
 1. The Community shall contribute to the development of quality education by encouraging
cooperation between member states and, if necessary, by supporting and supplementing their
action, while fully respecting the responsibility of the member states for the content of teaching
and the organisation of education systems and their cultural and linguistic diversity.
 2. Community action shall be aimed at...
 - developing the European dimension in education, particularly through the teaching and
dissemination of the languages of the member states;

Article 128
 1. The Community shall contribute to the flowering of the cultures of the member states,
while respecting their national and regional diversity and at the same time bringing the common
cultural heritage to the fore...
 4. The Community shall take cultural aspects into account in its action under other
provisions of this Treaty.

Appendix to the Treaty on European Union: Declaration on the Use of Languages in the Field
of the Common Foreign and Security Policy
 The Conference agrees that the use of the languages shall be in accordance with the rules
of the European Communities.
 For COREU communications, the current European Political Cooperation will serve as a
guide for the time being.
 All common foreign and security policy texts which are submitted to or adopted at meetings
of the European Council and of the Council as well as all texts which are to be published are
immediately and simultaneously translated into all the official Community languages.

2.3   BILATERAL AND MULTILATERAL INSTRUMENTS

2.3.1   *Agreement about the Basic Principles of Bilateral Relations, Friendship and Cooperation between the Russian Federation and the Uzbekistan Republic*

Unofficial translation from Russian provided by Normand Labrie.

Article 6
Negotiating parties will guarantee to persons residing in their territory, regardless of their nationality, gender, language, religion political or other beliefs, civil, political, social, economic and cultural rights and freedoms in accordance with generally recognised norms of international law...

Negotiating parties will conclude agreements concerning legal assistance in civil, marital and criminal procedures, consular agreements and other documents imperative for guaranteeing the rights of their citizens residing on the other parties' territories.

Article 7
Negotiating parties affirm that respect towards persons belonging to national (ethnic) minorities as part of generally recognised human rights, appear as principal factors of peace, equity, stability and democracy in Russian Federation and in the Republic of Uzbekistan.

Negotiating parties guarantee the rights of ethnic minorities to fully and effectively realise and utilise their human rights and basic freedoms without any discrimination and under the conditions of full equality concerning the law.

Negotiating parties guarantee the rights of persons belonging to national (ethnic) minorities, either individually or in cooperation with other persons belonging to national minorities, to freely express, maintain and develop their ethnic, cultural, linguistic or religious identity, create favourable conditions for encouragement of that identity and will not allow any attempts of forceful assimilation.

Negotiating parties respect the rights of persons belonging to national minorities to effectively participate in the national government.

Negotiating parties take the responsibility to take effective measures to prevent and interfere with any activities on its territories which appear to be violations against persons or groups on national, racial, ethnic or religious grounds, discrimination, hostility or hatred.

2.3.2   *Agreement on the Cooperation between the Ministry of National Education of the Republic of Poland and the Ministry of Education of the Republic of Belarus for the Years 1992-1993*

Warsaw, 5 March 1992. Unofficial translation from Polish provided by Normand Labrie.

Article 7
The states parties will ensure all necessary help to promote the knowledge of the native languages and to improve native language education at all levels (preschool, primary school, high school, college and university) among the Belarussian citizens of Polish nationality living in Belarus, and among Polish citizens of Belarussian nationality living in Poland.

In schools and universities that teach in the minority's language the parties will consider the need for improving qualifications in both native language teachers and subject area teachers.

2.3.3 *Agreement on the Cooperation between the Ministry of National Education of the Republic of Poland and the Ministry of Education of Ukraine for the Years 1993-1995*

Kiev, 12 January 1993. Unofficial translation from Polish provided by Normand Labrie.

Article 3
The states parties will be desirous of providing their citizens who are members of the Ukrainian minority in Poland and Polish minority in Ukraine, with the possibility to learn their national language at all levels of education (preschools, primary, high schools, and universities). They will also help each other to supply text books, literature for teachers and teaching equipment.

Article 12
Regarding the issue of the education of the citizens that are members of the Ukrainian minority in Poland and of the Polish minority in Ukraine, the states parties will cooperate with the social organisations representing these minorities and will consider their recommendations in the process of qualifying students for full-time studies, courses, practica, or other types of schooling.

2.3.4 *Agreement between the Czech Republic and the Slovak Republic on Cooperation and Good Neighbourly Relations*

23 November 1992.

Article 8
The states parties acknowledge that persons belonging to the Slovak national minority in the Czech Republic and persons belonging to the Czech national minority in the Slovak Republic have the right individually, as well as in community with other members of their group, to freely express, preserve and develop their ethnic, cultural, linguistic and religious identity, as well as to develop their culture in the way they desire without any attempts to assimilate them against their will...

The states parties declare that the persons referred to in this provision have in particular the right, individually or in community with other members of their group:
- to use freely their mother tongue privately or in public and, notwithstanding the need to know the official language of their respective state, the right to use their mother tongue in contacts with state authorities in conformity with national legislation;
- to have access, as well as to disseminate and exchange, information in their mother tongue; - to have adequate opportunity to learn their mother tongue;
- to establish and maintain their own economic, educational, cultural and religious institutions, organisations and associations.

2.3.5 *Agreement between Finland and Sweden Relating to Guarantees in the Law of 7 May 1920 on the Autonomy of the Åland Islands*

Reprinted from *Documents on Autonomy and Minority Rights* (1993), Hurst Hannum (ed.), Martinus Nijhoff, Dordrecht, Netherlands, at pp. 141-143.

3. The new guarantees to be inserted in the autonomy law should specially aim at the preservation of the Swedish language in the schools, at the maintenance of the landed property in the hands of the Islanders, at the restriction within reasonable limits of the exercise of the franchise by newcomers, and at ensuring the appointment of a Governor who will possess the confidence of the population...

At its meeting of June 27th, M. Hymans read the following text containing the agreement which the two parties had reached on the question of guarantees:

1. Finland, resolved to assure and to guarantee the population of the Åland Islands the preservation of their language, of their culture, and of their local Swedish traditions, undertakes to introduce shortly into the Law of Autonomy of the Åland Islands of May 7th, 1920, the following guarantees:

2. The Landsting and the Communes of the Åland Islands shall not, in any case, be obliged to support or to subsidise any other schools than those in which the language of instruction is Swedish. In the scholastic establishments of the state, instruction shall also be given in the Swedish language. The Finnish language may not be taught in the primary schools supported or subsidised by the state or by the commune without the consent of the interested commune.

3. When landed estate situated in the Åland Islands is sold to a person who is not legally domiciled in the Islands, any person legally domiciled in the Islands, or the Council of the province, or the commune in which the estate is situated, has the right to buy the estate at a price which, failing agreement, shall be fixed by the Court of First Instance (*Häradsratt*) having regard to current prices.

Detailed regulations will be drawn up in a special law concerning the act of purchase, and the priority to be observed between several offers.

This law may not be modified, interpreted, or repealed except under the same conditions as the Law of Autonomy.

4. Immigrants into the Åland Archipelago who enjoy rights of citizenship in Finland shall acquire the communal and provincial franchise in the Islands only after five years of legal domicile. Persons who have been five years legally domiciled in the Islands shall not be considered as immigrants.

2.3.6 *Agreement on the Foundations of Relations between the Republic of Finland and the Russian Federation*

Helsinki, 20 January 1992. Unofficial translation, Ministry for Foreign Affairs of Finland.

Article 10
The parties shall give their support to the preservation of the identity of Finns and Finno-

Uric peoples and nationalities in Russia and, correspondingly in Finland, the identity of persons originating in Russia. They shall protect each other's languages, cultures and historical monuments.

2.3.7 *Agreement between the Ministry of National Education of the Republic of Poland and the Ministry of Culture and Education of the Republic of Lithuania Regarding the Educational System and University Education*

Vilnius, 21 February 1992. Unofficial translation from Polish provided by Normand Labrie.

Article 1
The parties, according to their full powers and possibilities and acting according to the law of Poland and Lithuania, will expand cooperation in the field of education, including all forms and levels of education for children and youngsters, and improve the qualifications of teachers.

The parties, according to their powers and possibilities, will do their best to create opportunities for children of the Polish minority living in Lithuania and children of the Lithuanian minority living in Poland to learn their native language, culture and the history of the country they are now living in, and to become loyal citizens with full rights.

The parties will do their best to provide children of the Polish minority living in Lithuania and children of the Lithuanian minority living in Poland with education in their native language, and with the possibility of learning about their native culture, tradition, and history as well as learning the official language of the country, its culture and history, and to become its equal and loyal citizens.

The parties — according to their law — will give rights of issuance of diplomas to non-public schools at the primary and high school level at which Lithuanian language education is provided in Poland and Polish language education is provided in Lithuania. Documents of graduation issued by those schools will have the same power as documents issued by public schools, providing that the level of education in those non-public schools will fulfil the requirements of national standards for education.

2.3.8 *Agreement between the Republic of the Gambia and the Republic of Senegal concerning the Establishment of a Senegambia Confederation*

1981. Reprinted from Blaustein, Albert P. and Epstein, Dana Blaustein (1986), *Resolving Language Conflicts: A Study of the World's Constitutions*, U.S. English, Washington, D.C., at p. 67.

Section 4
The official languages of the Confederation shall be such African languages as are specified by the President and Vice-President of the Confederation; English and French.

2.3.9 *Agreement between the United Kingdom and Singapore*

March-April 1957, London.

The following provisions for the protection of Malay and minority interests in Singapore should be included in the Constitution:

(i) It shall be the responsibility of the Government of Singapore constantly to care for the interests of racial and religious minorities in Singapore. In particular, it shall be the deliberate and conscious policy of the Government of Singapore at all times to recognise the special position of the Malays, who are the indigenous people of the Island and are in most need of assistance, and accordingly, it shall be the responsibility of the Government of Singapore to protect, safeguard, support, foster and promote their political, educational, religious, economic, social and cultural interests and the Malay language.

2.3.10 *Convention on Providing Special Rights for the Slovenian Minority Living in the Republic of Hungary and for the Hungarian Minority Living in the Republic of Slovenia*

Ljubljana, 6 November 1992.

Article 1

The high contracting parties shall ensure that national minorities and individuals belonging to them have the possibility of preserving, developing, and expressing fully their cultural, linguistic, and religious Slovenian and Hungarian identities. To this end, they shall create in the fields of education, culture, mass communications, publishing and scientific research, as well as in the economic sphere and other areas activities to promote all facets of the minorities' development.

Article 2

The high contracting parties shall take the utmost care to promote the acquisition and study in the mother tongue of these minorities in pre-school, elementary, secondary and higher education institutions, as well as the acquisition of knowledge of the culture, history and present reality of the mother-nation and the national minority.

To this end, the high contracting parties shall seek to exchange experiences in the educational system of the national minorities, especially bilingual teaching, and the possible use of each others educational material.

In addition, they shall promote the exchange of teachers, students and educational training materials, as well as the organisation of courses and professional training. They will also allow the other high contracting party to grant state and foundation scholarships for all types of postgraduate education, especially education for teachers and theologists.

They shall encourage the study and acquisition of the language, culture and history of the national minorities and their mother-nation by individuals belonging to the majority nation.

Article 4

The high contracting parties shall ensure members of the national minorities may use freely their own language in private and public life, including the free use and registration of their original surnames and given names.

The high contracting parties undertake to ensure within the territory historically inhabited by their respective national minorities the equal use of both languages, especially in regard to toponomy and public signs, in the local administration, in oral and written communications, and before administrative, judicial, and other public institutions.

Article 5

The high contracting parties recognise these minorities have the right to receive and disseminate information through radio and television broadcasts in their mother tongue.

To this end, they shall ensure the national minorities can exercise and develop their own communication activities. They shall support the free flow of information in the languages of the national minorities, as well as support cooperation between the mass media of the minority and the majority.

Each of the high contracting parties shall provide for the transmission of radio and television broadcasts, as well as regular and suitable time for radio and television programs in the mother language of their respective minorities. They shall also permit reception of radio and television broadcasts from the other high contracting party in the minority's mother tongue.

2.3.11 *Declaration on the Principles of Cooperation between the Republic of Hungary and the Ukrainian Soviet Socialist Republic in Guaranteeing the Rights of National Minorities*

Budapest, 31 May 1991. Translation from the Hungarian Ministry of Foreign Affairs.

Article 3

The parties shall, in their efforts to promote democracy and a state ruled by law, take into account the legitimate interests of the national minorities in their respective policies and shall take the necessary political, legal and administrative measures to help create favourable conditions for the preservation and development by the national minorities of their ethnic, cultural, linguistic and religious identities. Such measures shall serve the interests of the whole society and shall not result in encroachments on the rights of other citizens.

Article 8

The parties shall take no administrative, economic or other measures designed to assimilate the minorities or change the composition of populations in territories inhabited by nationalities.

Article 9

The parties shall adopt such legal, administrative and other measures as may be necessary to ensure that the national minorities may freely exercise their right to use their mother tongue, both orally and in writing, in their individual lives and in community life, including the right to use their national names, forename as well as family name.

Exercise of this right shall not detract from the obligation to learn the official language or languages of the parties.

Article 10

The parties agree that they shall make it possible for the national minorities to learn their mother tongue and to study in their mother tongue at all levels of education. The practical problems this may entail will be resolved as necessary, and in accordance with the parties' current laws and capabilities, by a Mixed Commission to be set up under Article 16 of the present Declaration. The parties shall enable members of the national minority living in the territory of the other party to pursue studies at their own institutions of higher education, to participate in further training, and to exchange experts in the fields of education and culture. The parties shall endeavour to observe the principle of equivalence at all levels of education, and shall recognise the fact of their respective citizens' enrolment in, and studies at, educational institutions based in the territory of the other party.

Article 12
    The parties declare that believers belonging to national minorities shall have a right to exercise their religion and shall have the right to acquire, possess, produce and use devotional materials and engage in religious activities in their mother tongue, including training in the mother tongue.

Article 13
    The parties recognise the right of the national minorities to disseminate, exchange and receive information in their mother tongue without discrimination of any kind, and they shall take concrete measures to provide support for mass communication in the mother tongue.

2.3.12   *Germany-Russian Federation Protocol of Collaboration on the Gradual Restoration of Citizenship to Russian Germans*

21 February 1992. Reprinted from (1992) *International Legal Materials*, Vol. 31, at p. 1301.

Article 1
    1. The Government of the Russian Federation aims its intention to re-establish gradually the German Republic in those areas on the Volga traditionally occupied by the ancestors of the German people without in the process adversely affecting the interests of those people currently resident in those areas. Both parties shall pursue this intention to the best of their ability with the aim of ensuring that the national and cultural identity of the Russian Germans is maintained.

Article 2
    1. Both parties agree that the establishment of an autonomous regional authority will be of major importance for the economic, cultural and social development of the republic which is to be created, in which residents of both German and other nationalities will be able to find and maintain a home.

Article 4
    1. In order to provide support both for the German minority in Russia in their maintenance of their national identity and for the restoration of national citizenship to the Volga Germans, both parties shall promote the provision of unlimited opportunities to establish cultural, social, communal and educational organisations which will increase the feeling of solidarity amongst German people and provide favourable conditions in which German people and those of other nationalities can live together.

2.3.13   *Indo-Sri Lanka Agreement to Establish Peace and Normalcy in Sri Lanka*

29 July 1987.

    1.1 Desiring to preserve the unity, sovereignty and territorial integrity of Sri Lanka;

1.2 Acknowledging that Sri Lanka is a multiethnic and multilingual plural society consisting, *inter alia*, of Sinhalese, Tamils, Muslims (Moors), and Burghers;

1.3 Recognising that each ethnic group has a distinct cultural and linguistic identity which has to be carefully nurtured;

1.4 Also recognising that the Northern and Eastern Provinces have been areas of historical habitation of Sri Lankan Tamil-speaking peoples, who have at all times hitherto lived together in this territory with other ethnic groups;

1.5 Conscious of the necessity of strengthening the forces contributing to the unity, sovereignty and territorial integrity of Sri Lanka, and preserving its character as a multiethnic, multilingual and multi-religious plural society in which all citizens can live in equality, safety and harmony, and prosper and fulfil their aspirations;

2. Resolve that...

2.18 The official language of Sri Lanka shall be Sinhala. Tamil and English will also be official languages.

> 2.3.14 *Joint Declaration of the Government of the United Kingdom of Great Britain and Northern Ireland and the Government of the People's Republic of China on the Question of Hong Kong*

19 December 1984. Reprinted from *Documents on Autonomy and Minority Rights* (1993), Hurst Hannum (ed.), Martinus Nijhoff, Dordrecht, Netherlands, at pp. 219-272.

Article 9

In addition to the Chinese language, English may also be used as an official language by the executive authorities, legislature and judiciary of the Hong Kong Special Administrative Region.

Article 136

On the basis of the previous educational system, the Government of the Hong Kong Special Administrative Region shall, on its own, formulate policies on the development and improvement of education, including policies regarding the educational system and its administration, the language of instruction, the allocation of funds, the examination system, the system of academic awards and the recognition of educational qualifications.

Community organisations and individuals may, in accordance with law, run educational undertakings of various kinds in the Hong Kong Special Administrative Region.

> 2.3.15 *Mémorandum d'accord entre les gouvernements de l'Italie, du Royaume-Uni, des États-Unis d'Amérique et de la Yougoslavie*

London, 5 October 1954. Reprinted from Recueil des législations linguistiques dans le monde — Tome VI (1994), Jacques Leclerc & Jacques Maurais (eds.), International Centre for Research on Language Planning, Québec. Slovenia is now the successor state to Yugoslavia for the purposes of the linguistic minority provisions of this treaty. Under the Treaty of Osimo between Italy and Yugoslavia dated 10 November 1975, the contracting parties decided to terminate the protection provided in the memorandum under international law by making the linguistic minorities subject to new legislation in each country guaranteeing at least the same rights.

Article 2

Les membres du groupe ethnique yougoslave dans la zone administrée par l'Italie et les membres du groupe ethnique italien dans la zone administrée par la Yougoslavie jouiront des mêmes droits et du même traitement que les autres habitants des deux zones.
Cette égalité implique qu'ils jouiront...
e) de l'égalité de traitement en ce qui concerne l'utilisation des langues, dans les conditions indiquées à l'article 5 ci-après;

Article 4

Le caractère ethnique et le libre développement culturel du groupe ethnique yougoslave, dans la zone sous administration italienne, et ceux du groupe ethnique italien, dans la zone sous administration yougoslave, devront être préservés.
a) Les deux groupes auront le droit d'avoir leur propre presse rédigée dans leur langue maternelle;...
c) Les deux groupes devront avoir à leur disposition des jardins d'enfants et des écoles primaires, secondaires et professionnelles qui dispensent l'enseignement dans leur langue maternelle. Des écoles de cette nature fonctionneront dans toutes les localités de la zone sous administration italienne où se trouvent des enfants appartenant au groupe ethnique yougoslave et toutes les localités de la zone sous administration yougoslave où se trouvent des enfants appartenant au groupe ethnique italien. Le gouvernement italien et le gouvernement yougoslave s'engagent à maintenir en activité, au profit des groupes ethniques des zones relevant de leur administration, les écoles existantes qui sont rémunérées dans la liste annexée au présent statut; avant de procéder à la fermeture de l'une quelconque de ces écoles, ils devront prendre l'avis de la Commission mixte prévue dans l'article final du présent statut;
d) Ces écoles jouiront de l'égalité de traitement avec les autres écoles de même type dans les zones administrées par l'Italie et la Yougoslavie respectivement, en ce qui concerne la fourniture de manuels scolaires, de locaux et d'autres moyens matériels, le nombre et la situation du personnel enseignant et la reconnaissance des diplômes. Les autorités italiennes et yougoslaves s'efforceront de faire en sorte que l'enseignement dispensé dans ces écoles le soit par les maîtres dont la langue maternelle est la même que celle des élèves.
Les autorités italiennes et yougoslaves feront adopter dans le plus bref délai les mesures légales nécessaires pour que l'organisation permanente desdites écoles soit réglée conformément aux dispositions qui précèdent. Les membres du personnel enseignant de langue italienne qui, à la date où le présent mémorandum d'accord a été paraphé, enseignaient dans les établissements scolaires situés dans la zone administrée par la Yougoslavie, et les membres du personnel enseignant de langue slovène qui, à la même date, enseignaient dans les établissements scolaires situés dans la zone administrée par l'Italie ne seront pas révoqués de leurs fonctions pour la raison qu'ils ne possèdent pas le diplôme d'enseignement requis.

Article 5

Les membres du groupe ethnique yougoslave, dans la zone administrée par l'Italie, et les membres du groupe ethnique italien, dans la zone administrée par la Yougoslavie, pourront faire usage de leurs langues respectives dans leurs rapports tant privés qu'officiels avec les autorités administratives et judiciaires de deux zones. Ils auront le droit de recevoir des autorités une réponse dans la même langue, soit directement, soit par l'intermédiaire d'un interprète, dans le cas de réponses données verbalement; pour ce qui est de la correspondance, les autorités devront au moins fournir une traduction des réponses.

Les pièces de caractère officiel concernant les membres desdits groupes ethniques, y compris les décisions judiciaires, devront être accompagnées d'une traduction dans la langue appropriée. Il en sera de même des avis officiels, ainsi que des publications et des proclamations publiques.

Dans la zone sous administration italienne, les inscriptions figurant sur les bâtiments publics ainsi que les noms des localités et des rues seront rédigés dans la langue du groupe ethnique yougoslave aussi bien que dans celle de l'autorité administrante, dans les districts électoraux de la commune de Trieste et dans les autres communes où les membres de ce groupe ethnique constituent un élément appréciable (un quart au moins) de la population; dans les communes de la zone sous administration yougoslave où le groupe ethnique italien constitue un élément appréciable (un quart au moins) de la population, ces inscriptions et ces noms seront rédigés en italien aussi bien que dans la langue de l'autorité administrante.

2.3.16 *State Treaty for the Re-Establishment of an Independent and Democratic Austria*

Vienna, 15 May 1955.

Article 6

1. Austria shall take all measures necessary to secure to all persons under Austrian jurisdiction, without distinction as to race, sex, language or religion, the enjoyment of human rights and of the fundamental freedoms, including freedom of expression, of press and publication, of religious worship, of political opinion and of public meeting.

2. Austria further undertakes that the laws in force in Austria shall not, either in their content or in their application, discriminate or entail any discrimination between persons of Austrian nationality on the ground of their race, sex, language or religion, whether in reference to their persons, property, business, professional or financial interests, status, political or civil rights, or any other matter.

Article 7

1. Austrian nationals of the Slovene and Croat minorities in Carinthia, Burgenland and Styria shall enjoy the same rights on equal terms as all other Austrian nationals, including the right to their own organisations, meetings and press in their own language.

2. They are entitled to elementary instruction in the Slovene or Croat language and to a proportional number of their own secondary schools; in this connection school criteria shall be reviewed and a section of the Inspectorate of Education shall be established for Slovene and Croat schools.

3. In the administration and judicial districts of Carinthia, Burgenland and Styria, where there are Slovene, Croat or mixed populations, the Slovene or Croat language shall be accepted as an official language in addition to German. In such districts topographical terminology and inscriptions shall be in the Slovene or Croat language as well as in German.

4. Austrian nationals of the Slovene and Croat minorities in Carinthia, Burgenland and Styria shall participate in the cultural, administrative and judicial systems in these territories on equal terms with other Austrian nationals.

5. The activity of organisations whose aim is to deprive the Croat or Slovene population of their minority character or rights shall be prohibited.

Article 8
Austria shall have a democratic government based on elections by secret ballot and shall guarantee to all citizens free, equal and universal suffrage as well as the right to be elected to public office without discrimination as to race, sex, language, religion or political opinion.

> 2.3.17 *Statement on the Principles of Cooperation between the Republic of Hungary and the Russian Federation in the Field of Assurance of the Rights of National or Ethnic, Religious and Linguistic Minorities*

Budapest, 11 November 1992.

Article 4
The parties, starting from the fact that social peace and individual freedom, and the need for comprehensive assurance of these, are universal values, consider it their most important task to develop favourable conditions for the preservation and development of the ethnic, cultural, linguistic and religious identity of the minorities. These measures must serve the interests of the whole society and cannot lead to curtailment of the rights of other citizens.

Article 9
The parties consider unacceptable any administrative, economic or other measures directed at the forcible assimilation of the minorities or the alteration of the ethnic composition of districts within the territory occupied by the minorities.

Article 10
The parties consider it expedient to pass the legal, state-administrative and other measures required for the minorities to avail themselves freely, in writing and verbally, of their rights to use their native language in both personal and social life, including use of their national names and surnames.

The exercise of this right does not preclude the obligation to learn the state language or languages.

Article 12
The parties respect the right of religious believers belonging to the minorities to practise their religion, and within this to obtain, possess, produce and utilise the devotional materials in their native language required for pursuing this activity, including training conducted in the native language.

Article 13
The parties respect the right of the minorities to protect and represent their fundamental interests, and also to have free access to information in their native language, including the right to distribute and exchange such information, and according to the scope available to receive state assistance for the purpose.

2.3.18 *Traité sur les bases des relations entre la RSFS de Russie et la RSS d'Ukraine*

Kiev, 19 November 1990.

Article 3

Les Hautes Parties Contractantes, souhaitant contribuer à l'expression, au maintien et au développement de l'originalité ethnique, culturelle, linguistique et religieuse des minorités nationales peuplant leur territoire et représentant des régions ethno-culturelles uniques, assurent leur protection.

2.3.19 *Treaty Concerning the Protection of Minorities in Greece*

Sèvres, 10 August 1920.

Article 2

Greece undertakes to assure full and complete protection of life and liberty to all inhabitants of Greece without distinction of birth, nationality, language, race or religion.

Article 7

All Greek nationals shall be equal before the law and shall enjoy the same civil and political rights without distinction as to race, language or religion.

In particular, Greece undertakes to put into force within three years from the coming into force of the present Treaty an electoral system giving due consideration to the rights of racial minorities. This disposition is applicable only to the new territories acquired by Greece since August 1, 1914.

Differences of religion, creed or confession shall not prejudice any Greek national in matters relating to the enjoyment of civil or political rights, as, for instance, admission to public employments, functions and honours, or the exercise of professions and industries.

No restrictions shall be imposed on the free use by any Greek national of any language in private intercourse, in commerce, in religion, in the press or in publications of any kind, or at public meetings.

Notwithstanding any establishment by the Greek Government of an official language, adequate facilities shall be given to Greek nationals of non-Greek speech for the use of their language, either orally or in writing, before the courts.

Article 8

Greek nationals who belong to racial, religious or linguistic minorities shall enjoy the same treatment and security in law and in fact as the other Greek nationals. In particular they shall have an equal right to establish, manage and control, at their own expense, charitable, religious and social institutions, schools and other educational establishments, with the right to use their own language and to exercise their religion freely therein.

Article 9

Greece will provide in the public educational system in towns and districts in which a considerable proportion of Greek nationals of other than Greek speech are resident adequate facilities for ensuring that in the primary schools the instruction shall be given to the children of such Greek nationals through the medium of their own language. This provision shall not prevent the Greek Government from making the teaching of the Greek language obligatory in the said schools.

In towns and districts where there is a considerable proportion of Greek nationals belonging to racial, religious or linguistic minorities, these minorities shall be assured an equitable share in the enjoyment and application of the sums which may be provided out of public funds under the state, municipal or other budgets for educational, religious or charitable purposes.

The provisions of this Article apply only to the territories transferred to Greece since January 1, 1913.

Article 12

Greece agrees to accord to the communities of the Valachs of Pindus local autonomy, under the control of the Greek state, in regard to religious, charitable or scholastic matters.

> 2.3.20 *Treaty between the Federal Republic of Germany and the German Democratic Republic on the Establishment of German Unity*

Berlin, 31 August 1990.

Protocol 14 re Article 35

The Federal Republic of Germany and the German Democratic Republic declare in connection with Article 35 of the Treaty...

3. The Sorbian people and their organisations shall be free to cultivate and preserve the Sorbian language in public life.

> 2.3.21 *Treaty between the Federal Republic of Germany and Romania concerning Friendly Cooperation and Partnership in Europe*

Bucharest, 21 April 1992.

Article 15

2. Members of the German minority in Romania have the right individually, as well as with other members of their group, to freely express, preserve and develop their ethnic, cultural, linguistic and religious identity without any attempt to assimilate them against their will. They have the right before the law to exercise fully and effectively their human rights and fundamental freedoms without any discrimination whatsoever. Members of the German minority have the right to participate effectively in common affairs, including cooperation in matters concerning the protection and support of their identity.

Article 16

1. Romania will protect and support the identity of members of the German minority in Romania through concrete measures, especially conditions for the operation of German schools and German cultural institutions in areas where members of this group live. Romania will make possible and facilitate measures of the Federal Republic of Germany in support of the German minority in Romania.

2.3.22 *Treaty on the Foundations of Good Neighbourly Relations and Cooperation between the Republic of Hungary and Ukraine*

Kiev, 6 December 1991.

Article 17
    The contracting parties, in full harmony with the Charter of Paris on a new Europe and other relevant documents of the Conference on Security and Cooperation in Europe, express their conviction that friendly contacts between their peoples, as well as peace, fairness, stability and democracy require that the ethnic, cultural, linguistic and religious identities of national minorities are granted mutual defence, and all necessary terms are created to ensure that the parties shall take unilateral and joint steps to promote the implementation of such commitments in accordance with the document entitled "Declaration on the Principles of Co-operation between the Republic of Hungary and the Ukrainian Soviet Socialist Republic in Guaranteeing the Rights of National Minorities" and the attached protocol, signed on 31 May 1991. In their international contacts, the parties shall independently and jointly take steps in the interest of implementing the international documents relevant to national minorities.

2.3.23 *Treaty on the Foundations of Intergovernmental Relations between the Russian Soviet Federative Socialist Republic and the Lithuanian Republic*

29 July 1991.

Article 4
    The high contracting parties guarantee equal rights and freedoms to their citizens, irrespective of their nationality or any other distinctions.
    The Lithuanian Republic guarantees to persons of the Russian Soviet Federative Socialist Republic entitled to citizenship, who were living permanently on the territory of Lithuania before 3 November 1989 and still reside there, and who have a permanent place of work or other legal means of living in the Lithuanian Republic, the right to acquire citizenship of the Lithuanian Republic, in accordance with their own free will and according to the procedure set out in the legislation of the Lithuanian Republic. The Lithuanian Republic shall not apply to these persons residential qualifications, knowledge of the Lithuanian language or any pre-conditions for the acquisition of citizenship other than those which have been instituted with respect to all other persons.
    The Lithuanian Republic guarantees the right to acquire citizenship of the Lithuanian Republic to persons entitled to Russian Soviet Federative Socialist Republic citizenship who arrived in Lithuania in the period between 3 November 1989 and the day of the signing of the present Treaty, who are living permanently in the Lithuanian Republic and have a permanent place of work in the enterprises, organisations and institutions of the Lithuanian Republic or other means of living. The said persons have the right to acquire citizenship of the Lithuanian Republic on the basis of their own free will and according to the procedure set out in the laws of the Lithuanian Republic. No residential qualifications or requirements with respect to knowledge of the Lithuanian language shall be applied to these persons.

Article 5
    Each high contracting party shall define in its laws, in accordance with the generally

recognised principles and rules of international law, the rights and duties arising from the status of being a citizen of that party.

The high contracting parties guarantee to all persons indicated in Article 4 of the present Treaty, residing on their territory, irrespective of their nationality, civil and political, social, economic and cultural rights and basic human freedoms, in accordance with the generally recognised principles and rules of international law and the legislation of the country of residence, including the right of persons belonging to ethnic, religious or linguistic minorities, in community with the other members of their group or officially registered community, to enjoy their own culture, to profess and practise their own religion, and to use their own language.

2.3.24 *Treaty on Friendly Relations and Cooperation between the Republic of Croatia and the Republic of Hungary*

16 December 1992.

Article 17
2. Citizens of Croatian nationality in the Republic of Hungary, as well as the citizens of Hungarian nationality in the Republic of Croatia, have the right, individually or together with other members of their community, to freely express, preserve or develop their ethnic, cultural, language and religious identity; no one can force them into assimilation against their will. They have the right to freely use their mother tongue, privately or in public, to disseminate and exchange information in that language and have access to all such information. They have the right to use their human rights and fundamental freedoms before the law entirely and efficiently, in full equality and without any discrimination.

Article 19
The parties to this Treaty agree that printed materials in the language of the other state may be freely printed, distributed and read. Materials published in the other state may be freely imported and distributed, in accordance with Articles 19 and 20 of the International Covenant on Civil and Political Rights.

2.3.25 *Treaty on Friendship and Cooperation between the Lithuanian Republic and Ukraine*

To be signed in Vilnius in 1994.

Article 6
In matters concerning the protection of the rights of national minorities, the high contracting parties shall be guided by the international principles and standards laid down in the Universal Declaration of Human Rights, the international covenants on human rights, the relevant UN and CSCE documents, and also the European Convention on the Protection of the Rights and Basic Freedoms of Man and its protocols.

The high contracting parties guarantee to the Ukrainian national minority in the Lithuanian Republic and to the Lithuanian national minority in Ukraine the following rights: use of and tuition in the native language or study of the native language in state educational institutions, or via national cultural associations; development of national cultural traditions; profession of their own religion; satisfaction of demands for literature, art and news media; establishment of national cultural and educational institutions, and any other activity which does not contradict current legislation of the party concerned.

Persons belonging to the Ukrainian national minority in the Lithuanian Republic and persons belonging to the Lithuanian national minority in Ukraine have the right individually or in community with other members of their ethnic group, to freely express, maintain and develop their ethnic, cultural, linguistic and religious characteristics without any discrimination and on the basis of full equality before the law.

2.3.26 *Treaty on Friendship, Cooperation and Good Neighbourliness between the Republic of Bulgaria and Romania*

Sofia, 27 January 1992.

Article 10
... Each of the contracting parties shall establish conditions favouring the teaching of the language of the other party at schools, universities and other institutions, and for this purpose shall help the other party in organising these activities and in improving the qualification of the teachers.

2.3.27 *Treaty on Friendship, Good Neighbourliness and Cooperation between the Russian Federation and the Republic of Georgia*

Tbilisi, 3 February 1994.

Article 7
The high contracting parties will guarantee to their citizens equal rights and freedoms, irrespective of their nationality, sex, language, religion and political and other convictions.

Article 9
The high contracting parties confirm that respect for the rights of persons belonging to national minorities, as a part of universally recognised human rights, as well as the observation by them of their obligations to the state, equally with the remaining citizens of the given party, are important factors of peace, justice, stability and democracy in the Russian Federation and the Republic of Georgia.

The parties, in accordance with the universally recognised rules of international law and the obligations adopted within the framework of the CSCE, guarantee to persons belonging to national minorities full and effective enjoyment of human rights and fundamental freedoms without any form of discrimination and in conditions of total equality before, the law, and also the free expression, preservation and development of their ethnic, cultural, linguistic or religious distinctiveness. They will create conditions for promoting this distinctiveness.

2.3.28   *Treaty of Good Neighbourliness and Friendly Cooperation between the Czech and Slovak Federal Republic and the Federal Republic of Germany*

Prague, 27 February 1992.

Article 20

1. The contracting parties fulfil minimally the political commitments founded in the CSCE documents, particularly the Document of the Copenhagen Conference of June 29, 1990 on the Human Dimension of the CSCE, as commitments of a legal character.

2. Accordingly, members of the German minority in the Czech and Slovak Federal Republic, which means persons having Czechoslovak citizenship, who have a German background or identify themselves with the German language, culture, or traditions, have in particular the right, individually or in association with other members of their group, to free speech, preservation and development of their ethnic, cultural, linguistic, and religious identity free from any attempts to assimilate them against their will. They have a right to exercise their human rights and basic freedoms fully and effectively without any discrimination and in complete equality under law.

Article 21

1. Persons of Czech or Slovak descent in the Federal Republic of Germany have a right, individually or in association with other members of their group, to preserve and freely develop their ethnic, cultural, linguistic, and religious identity. They have a right to exercise their human rights and basic freedoms fully and effectively without any discrimination and in complete equality under the law.

Article 25

1. The contracting parties confirm their will to afford to all interested persons of the other party a broad access to German, Czech and Slovak language and culture and support respective state and private initiatives and institutions.

2. They will expend every effort to provide instruction in the other state's language at every level of school and in other educational institutions. They will also support initiatives toward the founding of schools with instruction in both languages. They will make every endeavour to widen opportunities at their universities for studies of the culture, literature and languages of the other state, i.e. for Czech, Slovak and German studies.

2.3.29   *Treaty of Good Neighbourliness and Friendly Cooperation between the Slovak Republic and the Republic of Hungary*

March 1995.

Article 14

The contracting parties shall foster the climate of tolerance and understanding among their citizens of different ethnic, religious, cultural and linguistic origin. In agreement with their international legal commitments, the contracting parties shall ensure equal and effective protection of the rights of any person irrespective of race, skin colour, sex, language, religion, political or other conviction, nationality or social origin.

Article 15
1. The contracting parties confirm that the protection of national minorities and of the rights and freedoms of persons belonging to those minorities forms an integral part of the international protection of human rights and, as such falls within the scope of international cooperation and, in this sense, it is therefore not an exclusively domestic affair of individual states but it is a subject of legitimate concern of the international community. The contracting parties recognise that their cooperation in this area contributes to the strengthening of good neighbourly relations, mutual understanding, friendship and confidence between their countries and, at the same time, to the strengthening of international security, stability and European integration.

2. As regards the protection of national minorities and the rights of persons belonging to those minorities, the contracting parties shall apply the following principles:

(c) persons belonging to national minorities shall have the right, individually or in community with other members of their group, to express, maintain and develop their ethnic, cultural, linguistic or religious identity and to maintain and develop their culture in all its aspects;

(d) reaffirming their general integration policy, the contracting parties shall refrain from policies and practices aimed at assimilation of persons belonging to national minorities against their will and shall protect these persons from any action aimed at such assimilation. The parties shall refrain from measures which alter the proportions of the population in areas inhabited by persons belonging to national minorities and are aimed at restricting the rights and freedoms of those persons that would be to the detriment of the national minorities;

(e) persons belonging to national minorities shall have the right, in conformity with the legislation and with the objective of cultivating, developing and conveying their identity, to establish and run their own organisations, associations, including political parties, as well as educational, cultural and religious institutions. Both governments shall create the legislative conditions to this effect;

(f) persons belonging to national minorities shall have the right to effective participation in the decisions at the national and, where appropriate, at the regional level and affecting the minorities or the regions inhabited by the minorities in the manner which is not incompatible with the domestic legislation;

(g) persons belonging to the Hungarian minority in the Slovak Republic and those belonging to the Slovak minority in the Republic of Hungary shall have the right to use, individually or in community with other members of their group, orally and in writing, their minority language both in private and in public. They shall also have the right, in conformity with the domestic legislation and with the international commitments undertaken by the two parties, to use their minority language in contacts with administrative authorities, including public administration, and in court proceedings, to display the names of municipalities in which they live, street names and names of other public areas, topographical indications, inscriptions and information in public areas in their minority language, to register and use their first names and surnames in this language, to have adequate opportunities in the framework of the state educational system and - without prejudice to the learning of the official language or the teaching in this language - for being taught the minority language or for receiving instruction in this language and the right of access to public mass media without discrimination and the right to their own media. The contracting parties, in conformity with their international undertakings, shall take all the necessary legal, administrative and other measures for the implementation of the aforementioned rights unless their respective legal systems already contain such provisions.

2.3.30   *Treaty on Good Neighbourly Relations, Friendship and Cooperation between Ukraine and the Republic of Moldova*

23 October 1992.

Article 7

The high contracting parties will guarantee the rights of persons belonging to national minorities according to the provisions of UN and CSCE instruments.

The high contracting parties recognise for persons belonging to national minorities and residing on the territory of the other party the right, individually and in community with others, to the free expression, preservation and development of their ethnic, cultural, linguistic and religious identity, as well as the right to be safe from any attempts of assimilation against their will.

Article 8

The high contracting parties support the development of the identity of national minorities by concrete measures such as providing favourable conditions for the activities of educational and cultural institutions, for radio and television programmes in the mother tongue of the minorities in parts of the country where they are concentrated, and will assist the other high contracting party in this area.

2.3.31   *Treaty of Peace with Austria*

Saint-Germain-en-Laye, 10 September 1919. It is doubtful this treaty is still in force, but the minority provisions have nevertheless been included since they are part of Austria's constitutional law.

Article 66

All Austrian nationals shall be equal before the law and shall enjoy the same civil and political rights without distinction as to race, language or religion...

No restriction shall be imposed on the free use by any Austrian national of any language in private intercourse, in commerce, in religion, in the press or in publications of any kind, or at public meetings.

Notwithstanding any establishment by the Austrian Government of an official language, adequate facilities shall be given to Austrian nationals of non-German speech for the use of their language, either orally or in writing, before the courts.

Article 67

Austrian nationals who belong to racial, religious or linguistic minorities shall enjoy the same treatment and security in law and in fact as the other Austrian nationals. In particular they shall have an equal right to establish, manage and control at their own expense charitable, religious and social institutions, schools and other educational establishments, with the right to use their own language and to exercise their religion freely therein.

Article 68

Austria will provide in the public educational system in towns and districts in which a considerable proportion of Austrian nationals of other than German speech are resident adequate facilities for ensuring that in the primary schools the instruction shall be given to the children of such Austrian nationals through the medium of their own language. This provision shall not prevent the Austrian Government from making the teaching of the German language obligatory in the said schools.

In towns and districts where there is a considerable proportion of Austrian nationals belonging to racial, religious or linguistic minorities, these minorities shall be assured an equitable share in the enjoyment and application of the sums which may be provided out of public funds under the state, municipal or other budgets for educational, religious or charitable purposes.

2.3.32 *Treaty of Peace with Italy*

Paris, 5 September 1946.

Article 10

1. German-speaking inhabitants of the Bolzano Province and of the neighbouring bilingual townships of the Trento Province will be assured complete equality of rights with the Italian-speaking inhabitants, within the framework of special provisions to safeguard the ethnical character and the cultural and economic development of the German-speaking element.

In accordance with legislation already enacted or awaiting enactment the said German-speaking citizens will be granted in particular:

(a) elementary and secondary teaching in the mother-tongue;

(b) parification of the German and Italian languages in public offices and official documents, as well as in bilingual topographic naming;

(c) the right to re-establish German family names which were italianised in recent years;

(d) equality of rights as regards the entering upon public offices, with a view to reaching a more appropriate proportion of employment between the two ethnical groups.

2. The populations of the above-mentioned zones will be granted the exercise of autonomous legislative and executive regional power. The frame within which the said provisions of autonomy will apply, will be drafted in consultation also with local representative German-speaking elements.

2.3.33 *Treaty of Peace with Turkey*

Lausanne, 24 July 1923.

Article 38

The Turkish Government undertakes to assure full and complete protection of life and liberty to all inhabitants of Turkey without distinction of birth, nationality, language, race or religion.

Article 39

Turkish nationals belonging to non-Moslem minorities will enjoy the same civil and political rights as Moslems.

All the inhabitants of Turkey, without distinction of religion, shall be equal before the law.

Differences of religion, creed or confession shall not prejudice any Turkish national in matters relating to the enjoyment of civil or political rights, as, for instance, admission to public employments, functions and honours, or the exercise of professions and industries.

No restrictions shall be imposed on the free use by any Turkish national of any language in private intercourse, in commerce, in religion, in the press or in publications of any kind, or at public meetings.

Notwithstanding the existence of the official language, adequate facilities shall be given to Turkish nationals of non-Turkish speech for the oral use of their own language before the Courts.

Article 40

Turkish nationals who belong to non-Moslem minorities shall enjoy the same treatment and security in law and in fact as the other Turkish nationals. In particular they shall have an equal right to establish, manage and control at their own expense, any charitable, religious and social institutions, any schools and other establishments for instruction and education, with the right to use their own language and to exercise their own religion freely therein.

Article 41

As regards public instruction, the Turkish Government will grant in towns and districts, where a considerable proportion of non-Moslem nationals are resident, adequate facilities for ensuring that in the primary schools the instruction shall be given to the children of such Turkish nationals through the medium of their own language. This provision will not prevent the Turkish Government from making the teaching of the Turkish language obligatory in the said schools.

In towns and districts where there is a considerable proportion of Turkish nationals belonging to non-Moslem minorities, these minorities shall be assured an equitable share in the enjoyment and application of the sums which may be provided out of public funds under the state, municipal or other budgets for educational, religious or charitable purposes.

The sums in question shall be paid to the qualified representatives of the establishments and institutions concerned.

2.3.34 *Treaty between the Republic of Lithuania and the Republic of Poland on Friendly Relations and Good-Neighbourly Cooperation*

26 April 1994.

Article 13

2. Members of the Polish minority in the Republic of Lithuania holding Lithuanian citizenship who are of Polish descent or who acknowledge Polish nationality, culture, tradition, or who recognise the Polish language as their mother tongue, and members belonging to the Lithuanian minority in the Republic of Poland holding Polish citizenship who are of Lithuanian descent or who acknowledge Lithuanian nationality, culture, tradition or who recognise the Lithuanian language as their mother tongue, have the right, individually or together with other members of their group, to freely express, maintain and develop their national, cultural, linguistic and religious identity without discrimination and in conditions of full equality under the law.

Article 14

1. The contracting parties declare that persons referred to in Article 13 paragraph 2 have in particular the right to:

- freely use the language of the national minority in private and in public;
- have access to information in their language, to disseminate and exchange [that information] and to have at their disposal their own mass media;
- learn the language of their national minority and be taught in that language;
- in accordance with domestic law, establish and maintain their own institutions, organisations and associations, in particular cultural, religious and educational, including schools of all levels, which may compete for voluntary financial or other help, from inside the country or abroad, as well as state aid, and also to take part in international non-governmental organisations;
- profess and practise their religion, including the acquisition, possession and use of religious material and the conduct of religious educational activity in the language of the national minority;
- establish and maintain undisturbed contacts with each other on the territory of their state, as well as contacts across the border with citizens of other states, with whom they share a common national origin;
- use names and surnames in the pronunciation and written form accepted in the language of the national minority. Detailed regulations pertaining to the spelling of first names and surnames will be defined in a separate agreement;

Article 15
The contracting parties will, on their territories, protect the national, cultural, linguistic and religious identity of persons referred to in Article 13, paragraph 2 and create conditions for its development.
The parties in particular:
- will consider admitting the use of the national minorities languages in their administrative offices, especially in those administrative-territorial units, in which the national minority makes up a substantial part of the population;...
- will assure adequate possibilities for teaching the language of the national minority and for learning it, in kindergartens, primary and secondary schools;...
- will refrain from any activity which might lead to assimilation of members of the national minority against their will and refrain, in accordance with international standards, from activities which would lead to demographic changes in the composition of the population in areas inhabited by national minorities.

2.3.35 *Treaty between the Republic of Poland and the Czech and Slovak Federal Republic on Good Neighbourliness, Solidarity and Friendly Cooperation*

6 October 1991.

Article 8
1. The contracting parties confirm that persons belonging to the Czech and Slovak national minority in the Republic of Poland and persons belonging to the Polish national minority in the Czech and Slovak Federal Republic have the right, individually or together with other members of their group, to freely express, maintain and develop their ethnic, cultural, linguistic and religious identity and to develop their culture in all directions without any attempts at assimilation against their will.

2. The contracting parties declare that persons referred to in paragraph 1 have in particular the right, individually or together with other members of their group, to:
- freely use their own mother tongue in private and in public, as well as to have access, disseminate and exchange information in their language;
- have adequate possibilities of teaching their mother tongue and of receiving education in their mother tongue;
- establish and maintain their own economic, educational, cultural and religious institutions, organisations and associations.

2.3.36 *Treaty between the Republic of Poland and the Republic of Belarus on Good Neighbourliness and Friendly Cooperation*

23 June 1992.

Article 14

1. The contracting parties confirm that persons belonging to the Polish minority in the Republic of Belarus as well as the Belarussian minority in the Republic of Poland have the right individually or together with other members of their group, to freely maintain, develop and express their ethnic, cultural, linguistic and religious identity without discrimination and in conditions of full equality under the law.

2. The contracting parties confirm that affiliation to a national minority is a matter of individual choice of a person and that no negative effects may result from this choice.

Article 15

The contracting parties guarantee that persons referred to in Article 14 have in particular the right, individually or together with other members of their group to:
- freely use their own mother tongue in private and in public, have access, disseminate and exchange information in that language;
- use their names and surnames in the form accepted in their mother tongue;
- establish and maintain their own educational, cultural and other institutions, organisations and associations, which may compete for voluntary financial or other help as well as state aid in accordance with domestic law, taking advantage of access to mass media and also to take part in the activities of international non-governmental organisations;
- profess and practise their religion, including the acquisition and use of religious material and the conduct of religious educational activity in the mother tongue;

Article 16

3. The contracting parties will try to secure for persons, mentioned in Article 14, adequate possibilities of teaching them their mother tongue or teaching in that language in educational institutions, and also, where possible and necessary, using their mother tongue in their dealings with public authorities. The teaching programmes of educational institutions, in which the above-mentioned persons take part, will take account, on a wider scale, of the history and culture of the national minorities.

2.3.37 *Treaty between the Republic of Poland and the Republic of Estonia on Friendly Cooperation and Baltic Good Neighbourliness*

2 July 1992.

Article 15
    3. The parties will help citizens of the Republic of Poland of Estonian descent and citizens of the Republic of Estonia of Polish descent to maintain and propagate their ethnic identity and their own culture.

2.3.38 *Treaty between the Republic of Poland and the Republic of Latvia on Friendship and Cooperation*

1 July 1992.

Article 15
    1. The contracting parties, in accordance with binding international standards relating to the protection of national minorities, recognise the rights of members of the Latvian minority in the Republic of Poland and the Polish minority in the Republic of Latvia, individually or together with other members of their minority, to maintain, express and develop their ethnic, cultural, linguistic and religious identity without discrimination and in conditions of full equality under the law.
    2. The contracting parties will undertake necessary actions with the aim of realising national minority rights, in particular the right to:
    - teach and learn their mother tongue, to freely use it, as well as the right to access, disseminate and exchange information in their language;
    - establish and maintain their own educational, cultural and religious institutions and associations, which may solicit voluntary financial and other contributions, as well as public aid in accordance with domestic law;
    - profess and practise their religion and carry out educational religious activity in the mother tongue;
    - use names and surnames in the pronunciation and written form accepted in the mother tongue;
    - establish and maintain undisturbed contacts with each other within the country of residence, as well as across the border;
    - possess their own press and publishing houses and have access to radio and television in their region.

2.3.39 *Treaty between the Republic of Poland and Romania on Friendly Relations and Cooperation*

25 January 1992.

Article 15
    1. Polish citizens of Romanian descent permanently resident in the Republic of Poland and Romanian citizens of Polish descent have the right, individually or together with other members

of their group, to freely express, maintain and develop their ethnic, cultural, linguistic and religious identity without discrimination and with the guarantee of full equality under the law.

2.3.40 *Treaty between the Republic of Poland and the Russian Federation on Friendly and Good Neighbourly Cooperation*

22 May 1992.

Article 16

3. The parties will help citizens of the Republic of Poland originating from Russia and citizens of the Russian Federation of Polish descent to maintain and propagate their ethnic identity, their own culture and the teaching of their mother tongue at pre-school and school levels.

2.3.41 *Treaty between the Republic of Poland and Ukraine on Good Neighbourliness, Friendly Relations and Cooperation*

18 May 1992.

Article 11

1. The parties, in accordance with generally binding international standards relating to the protection of national minorities, recognise the rights of members of the Polish minority in the Ukraine and the Ukrainian minority in the Republic of Poland, individually or together with other members of their group, to maintain, express and develop their ethnic, cultural, linguistic and religious identity without discrimination and in conditions of full equality under the law. The parties will undertake necessary action with the aim of realising this right, in particular the right to:

- teach and learn their mother tongue, to freely use their language, as well as the right to access, dissemination and exchange of information in this language,
- establish and maintain their own educational, cultural and religious institutions and associations,...
- use names and surnames in the form accepted in the mother tongue,

2.3.42 *Treaty between the Russian Federation and the Republic of Kazakhstan on Friendship, Cooperation and Mutual Assistance*

Moscow, 25 May 1992.

Article 14

The contracting parties will promote the development and guarantee the protection of the ethnic, cultural, linguistic and religious identity of national minorities on their territory and create conditions for the promotion of their identity.

Each party guarantees the right of persons belonging to national minorities, individually as well as in community with other members of their group, to express freely, preserve and develop their ethnic, cultural, linguistic or religious identity, as well as to maintain and develop their culture in all its aspects, without being subjected to any attempt at assimilation against their will.

The parties guarantee the right of persons belonging to national minorities to exercise fully and effectively their human rights and fundamental freedoms and to make use of them without any discrimination and in conditions of full equality before the law.

The parties guarantee the right of persons belonging to national minorities to participate effectively and adequately, according to their needs, in governmental affairs relating to the protection and promotion of their identities.

The parties will conclude an agreement on cooperation in guaranteeing the rights of persons belonging to ethnic, linguistic, cultural and religious minorities.

Article 15

The contracting parties will take effective measures, including the adoption of appropriate legislation, in order to prevent and stop any incitation to violence against each other, based on national, racial, ethnic or religious intolerance, hostility or hatred, as well as in order to protect persons or groups which could be the subject of threats or acts of violence, discrimination or hostility by reason of ethnic, linguistic, cultural and religious identity, and at protecting their property.

The parties will, if necessary, create a bilateral commission on human rights.

Article 27

The contracting parties will encourage in every possible way a comprehensive development of languages and cultures of all nations and nationalities living on their territories, as well as the teaching of national languages in preschool and educational institutions.

2.3.43 *Treaty between the Russian Federation and the Republic of Kirgizstan on Friendship, Cooperation and Mutual Assistance*

Moscow, 10 June 1992.

Article 9

The contracting parties guarantee to persons residing on their territories, irrespective of their nationality, sex, language, religion, political and other differences, generally recognised civil, political, social, economic and cultural rights and freedoms.

Article 11

The contracting parties commit themselves to carry out on their territories effective measures, including adoption of appropriate legislation, in order to prevent and stop any incitation to violence against persons or groups based on national, racial, ethnic or religious intolerance, hostility or hatred.

The contracting parties will undertake on their territories effective measures aimed at protecting persons or groups that are or can be subject to threats or acts of violence, discrimination or hostility based on their ethnic, linguistic, cultural or religious identity and at protecting their property.

The contracting parties will conclude an agreement on cooperation in guaranteeing the rights and legitimate interests of persons belonging to ethnic, linguistic, cultural and religious minorities.

Article 12

The contracting parties guarantee the protection of ethnic, cultural, linguistic or religious identity of national minorities on their territories and create conditions for an encouragement of their identity.

Each contracting party guarantees the rights of persons belonging to national minorities, individually as well as in community with other members belonging to the same minority, to freely express, preserve and develop their culture in all its aspects without being subjected to any attempt of assimilation against their will.

Article 21

The contracting parties encourage in every possible way cooperation and contacts in the fields of culture, art, education, tourism and sport, and support free exchange of information. The parties will conclude a separate agreement on this issue.

They encourage the teaching of languages of the people of Russia in the Republic of Kirgizstan and of the state language of Kirgizstan in the Russian Federation, including pre-school and educational institutions of the parties.

> 2.3.44   *Treaty between Ukraine and the Republic of Belarus*

29 December 1990.

Article 4

The parties promote the expression, safeguard and development of ethnic, cultural, linguistic or religious identity of national minorities settled on their territories and forming unique ethnic regions.

> 2.3.45   *Vertrag über gute Nachbarschaft, Partnerschaft und Zusammenarbeit zwischen der Bundesrepublik Deutschland und der Union der Sozialistischen Sowjetrepubliken*

9 November 1990.

Artikel 15

Die Bundesrepublik Deutschland und die Union der Sozialistischen Sowjetrepubliken werden im Bewußtsein der jahrhundertelangen gegenseitigen Bereicherung der Kulturen ihrer Völker und deren unverwechselbaren Beitrags zum gemeinsamen kulturellen Erbe Europas sowie der Bedeutung des kulturellen Austausches für die gegenseitige Verständigung der Völker ihre kulturelle Zusammenarbeit wesentlich ausbauen.

Beide Seiten werden das Abkommen über die Errichtung und die Tätigkeit von Kulturzentren mit Leben erfüllen und voll ausschöpfen.

Beide Seiten bekäftigen ihre Bereitschaft, allen interessierten Personen umfassenden Zugang zu Sprachen und Kultur der anderen Seite zu ermöglichen und fördern staatliche und private Initiativen.

Beide Seiten setzen sich nachdrücklich dafür ein, die Möglichkeiten auszubauen. in Schulen. Hochschulen und anderen Bildungseinrichtungen die Sprache des anderen Landes zu erlernen und dazu der juweils anderen Seite bei der Aus- und Fortbildung von Lehrkräften zu helfen sowie

Lehrmittel, einschließlich des Einsatzes von Fernsehen, Hörfunk, Audio-, Video- und Computertechnik zur Verfügung zu stellen. Sie werden Initiativen zur Errichtung zweisprachiger Schulen unterstützen.

Sowjetischen Bürgern deutscher Nationalität sowie aus der Union der Sozialistischen Sowjetrepublik stammenden und ständig in der Bundesrepublik Deutschland wohnenden Bürgern, die ihre Sprache, Kultur oder Tradition bewahren wollen, wird es ermöglicht, ihre nationale, sprachliche und kulturelle Identität zu entfalten. Dementsprechend ermöglichen und erleichtern sie im Rahmen der geltenden Gesetze der anderen Seite Förderungsmaßnahmen zugunsten dieser Personen oder ihrer Organisationen.

2.3.46 *Vertrag zwischen der Bundesrepublik Deutschland und der Republik Polen über gute Nachbarschaft und freundschaftliche Zusammenarbeit*

June 1991.

Artikel 20

1. Die Argehörigeb der deutschen Minderheit in der Republik Polen, das heißt Personen polnischer Staatsangehörigkeit, die deutscher Abstammung sind oder die sich zur deutschen Sprache, Kultur oder Tradition bekennen, sowie Personen deutscher Staatsangehörigkeit in der Bundesrepublik Deutschland, die polnischer Abstammung sind oder die sich zur polnischen Sprache, Kultur oder Tradition bekennen, haben das Recht, einzeln oder in Gemeinschaft mit anderen Mitgliedern ihrer Gruppe ihre ethnische, kulturelle, sprachliche und religiöse Identität frei zum Ausdruck zu bringen, zu bewahren und weiterzuentwickeln, frei von jeglichen Versuchen, gegen ihren Willen assimiliert zu werden. Sie haben das Recht, ihre Menschenrechte und Grundfreiheiten ohne jegliche Diskriminierung und in voller Gleichheit vor dem Gesetz voll und wirksam auszuüben.

2.3.47 *Vertrag zwischen der Bundesrepublik Deutschland und der Republik Ungarn über freundschaftliche Zusammenarbeit und Partnership in Europa*

Budapest, 6 February 1992.

Artikel 19

1. Die Vertragsparteien vereinbaren die rechtliche Verbindlichkeit des im Dokument des Kopenhagener Treffens über die menschliche Dimension des KSZE vom 29.Juni 1990 sowie in weiteren KSZE-Dokumenten niedergelegten Standards zum Schutze von nationalen Minderheiten.
2. Die Angehörigen der deutschen Minderheit in der Republik Ungarn haben demzufolge insbesondere das Recht, einzeln oder in Germeinschaft mit anderen Mitgliedern ihrer Gruppe ihre ethnische, kulturelle, sprachliche und religiöse Identität frei zum Ausdruck zu bringen, zu bewahren und weeiterzuentwickeln, frei von jeglichen Versuchen, gegen ihren Willen assimiliert zu werden. Sie haben das Recht, sich privat und in der Öffentlichkeit ihrer Muttersprache frei zu bedienen, in ihr Informationen zu verbreiten und auszutauschen und dazu Zugang zu haben. Sie haben das Recht, ihre Menschenrechte und Grundfreiheiten ohne jegliche Diskriminierung und in voller Gleichheit vor dem Gesetz voll und wirksam auszuüben.
3. Die Zugehörigkeit zur deutschen Minderheit in der Republik Ungarn ist persönliche Entscheidung jedes einzelnen, die für ihn keinen Nachteil mit sich bringen darf.

Artikel 22

1. Die Vertragsparteien bekräftigen ihre Bereitschaft, allen interessierten Personen breiten Zugang zu Sprache und Kultur des anderen Landes zu ermöglichen, und sie unterstützen entsprechende staatliche und private Initiativen und Institutionen.

2. Die Vertragsparteien befüworten die Verbreitung der klassischen sowie zeitgenössischen Literatur des anderen Landes in Originalsprache und Übersetzung.

3. Die Vertragsparteien setzen sich nachdrücklich dafür ein, die Möglichkeiten auszubauen, in Schulen, Hochschulen und anderen Bildungseinrichtungen die Sprache des anderen Landes zu erlernen. Sie werden Initiativen zur Gründung von Schulen mit Unterricht in beiden Sprachen unterstützen. Sie werden sich bemühen, die Möglichkeiten des Studiums der Germanistik und Hungaristik an den Hochschulen des anderen Landes auszuweiten.

4. Dei Vertragsparteien werden bei der Aus und Fortbildung von Lehrkräften sowie der Entwicklung und Bereitstellung von Lehrmaterial, einschließlich des Einsatzes von audio-visuellen Materialien und Computertechnik, zusammenarbeiten.

3. National Constitutional Provisions

As with the previous sections, only the provisions dealing specifically with language, or of particular interest, are reproduced here. Furthermore, following the disintegration of the Soviet Union, many new states have entered into the process of modifying their constitutions. This section therefore includes the most recent draft provisions available in English at the time of publication. Many of the provisions shown here were obtained through embassies, the American Bar Association's Central and East European Law Initiative or are from the following publications: Blaustein, Albert F. and Flanz, Gilbert H. (1988), *Constitutions of the Countries of the World*, Oceana Publications, Dobbs Ferry, New York; Blaustein, Albert P. and Epstein, Dana Blaustein (1986), *Resolving Language Conflicts: A Study of the World's Constitutions*, U.S. English, Washington, D.C.; *Langues et constitutions* (1993), François Gauthier et al. (eds.), Les Publications du Québec, Québec, and Turi, Giuseppe (1977), *Les dispositions juridico-constitutionnelles de 147 États en matière de politique linguistique*, International Centre for Research on Bilingualism, Québec. These two last books contain some national language legislation and other interesting information.

3.1   AFGHANISTAN

30 November 1987.

Article 28

All subjects of Afghanistan are equal in law. All subjects of Afghanistan, without consideration of racial, national or tribal links, language, sex, place of residence, religion, education, kinship, wealth and social position have equal rights and duties. The equality of rights of the subjects in every walk of life, economic, political and cultural, will be realised. Nobody shall use their democratic rights and freedoms against the interests of the Democratic Republic of Afghanistan and the rights of the other subjects.

Article 29.5
The state will adopt measures for the development and improvement of a national and progressive education; the elimination of illiteracy; education in one's mother tongue; the improvement and broadening of compulsory primary and secondary education and advanced, professional and technical compulsory education.

Article 40
The ratification of laws, decrees and all other ratification of the Revolutionary Council are implemented by a majority vote of the members. Laws and decrees are enforced after their publication in the official gazette, unless otherwise stated in the draft law. Laws and decrees of the Revolutionary Council will be published in Pashto and Dari and can be published in other languages of the people of Afghanistan.

Article 57
The consideration and solution of cases in the courts will be rendered in Pashto and Dari or in the language of the majority of the inhabitants of the locality. The two sides of a lawsuit, if they do not understand the language with which the trial is carried out, are entitled to familiarise themselves with the materials and documents of the case through an interpreter and are guaranteed the right to address the court in their mother tongue.

3.2   ALBANIA

Draft of 17 December 1993.

Article 13
The official language in the Republic of Albania is Albanian.

Article 25
During the criminal process, no one may be deprived of the right...
(c) to have the assistance, without charge, of a translator, when he does not speak or does not understand the Albanian language;

Article 40
All are equal before the law, without distinction of sex, race, religion, ethnicity, language, political belief or parentage.

Article 41
Persons who belong to national minorities have the right to exercise in full equality before the law, fundamental human rights and freedoms. They have the right freely to express, preserve and develop their ethnic, cultural, religious and linguistic identity and to teach and study in their mother tongue.
This right may not be interpreted to justify acts that foster ethnic division or strife.
No one may be impeded in declaring or forced to declare his nationality.

3.3 ALGERIA

February 1989.

Article 3
The national and official language is Arabic.

3.4 ANDORRA

1993.

Article 2
2. The official language of the state is Catalan.

3.5 ANTIGUA AND BARBUDA

1 November 1981.

Article 5
2. Any person who is arrested or detained shall be informed orally and in writing as soon as reasonable and practicable, in the language that he understands, of the reason for his arrest or detention.

Article 15
2. Every person who is charged with a criminal offence...
(b) shall be informed orally and in writing as soon as reasonably practicable, in language that he understands, of the nature of the offence with which he is charged;...
(f) shall be permitted to have without payment the assistance of an interpreter if he cannot understand the language used at the trial of the charge.

Article 29
Subject to the provisions of Section 30 of this Constitution any person who at the date of his appointment...
(c) is able to speak and, unless incapacitated by blindness or other physical cause, to read the English language with sufficient proficiency to enable him to take an active part in the proceedings of the Senate,
shall be qualified to be appointed as a Senator.

Article 38
Subject to the provisions of Section 39 of this Constitution, any person who at the date of his election...
(c) is able to speak and, unless incapacitated by blindness or other physical cause, to read the English language with sufficient proficiency to enable him to take an active part in the proceedings of the House,
shall be qualified to be elected as a member of the House.

3.6   ARGENTINA

22 August 1994.

Article 75
Corresponde al Congreso:
17. Reconover la preexistencia etnica y cultural de los pueblos indigenas argentinos.
Garantizar el respeto a su identidad y el derecho a una educacion bilungue e intercultural;...

3.7   AUSTRIA

1970.

Article 8
Without prejudice to the rights provided by federal law for linguistic minorities, German is the official language of the Republic.

3.8   BAHAMAS

10 July 1973.

Article 20
2. Every person who is charged with a criminal offence...
(f) shall be permitted to have without payment the assistance of an interpreter if he cannot understand the language used at the trial of the charge;

3.9   BAHRAIN

26 May 1973.

Article 18
All people shall be equal in human dignity, and citizens shall be equal in public rights and duties in the eye of the law, without discrimination because of race, origin, language, religion or belief.

3.10   BARBADOS

30 November 1966.

Article 13
2. Any person who is arrested or detained shall be informed as soon as reasonably practicable, in a language that he understands, of the reasons for his arrest or detention and shall be permitted, at his own expense, to retain and instruct without delay a legal adviser of his own choice, being a person entitled to practice in Barbados as a barrister or solicitor, and to hold

private communication with him; and in the case of a person who has not attained the age of sixteen years he shall also be afforded a reasonable opportunity for communication with his parent or guardian.

<u>Article 18</u>
2. Every person who is charged with a criminal offence...
(b) shall be informed as soon as reasonably practicable, in a language that he understands and in detail, of the nature of the offence charged;...
(f) shall be permitted to have without payment the assistance of an interpreter if he cannot understand the language used at the trial of the charge;

3.11   BELARUS

Adopted 1 March 1994.

<u>Article 17</u>
1. The official language of the Republic of Belarus shall be Belarusian.
2. The Republic of Belarus shall safeguard the right to use the Russian language freely as a language of inter-ethnic communication.

<u>Article 50</u>
1. Everyone shall have the right to preserve his ethnic affiliation, and equally, no one may be compelled to define or indicate his ethnic affiliation.
2. Insults to ethnic dignity shall be prosecuted by law.
3. Everyone shall have the right to use his native language and to choose the language of communication. In accordance with law, the state shall guarantee the freedom to choose the language of education and teaching.

3.12   BELGIUM

7 February 1831. Modified 8 August 1980 and 1 January 1989.

<u>Article 1</u>
... An act of Parliament may exempt certain territories, whose boundaries it shall determine, from being divided into provinces, place them directly under the executive authority and subject them to an individual status.
Such an act must be passed by a majority vote in each linguistic group of each of the Houses, on condition that the majority of the members of each group is present and that the total number of votes in favour in each of the two linguistic groups attains two thirds of the votes cast.

<u>Article 3b</u>
Belgium comprises four linguistic regions: the French language region, the Dutch language region, the bilingual region of Brussels-Capital, and the German language region.
Every commune in the Kingdom belongs to one of these linguistic regions.
The boundaries of the four regions may only be altered or amended by an act of Parliament passed on a majority vote in each linguistic group of each of the Houses, on condition that the

majority of the members of each group are present and that the total voters in favour within the two linguistic groups attain two thirds of the votes cast.

Article 3c

Belgium comprises three communities: the French Community, the Flemish Community, and the German-speaking Community.

Each community enjoys the powers invested in it by the Constitution or by such legislation as shall be enacted in terms thereof.

Article 23

The use of the languages spoken in Belgium is optional; it may only be regulated by law and only in the case of acts by public authorities and of legal matters.

Article 32b

For those cases prescribed in the Constitution, the elected members of each House are divided into a French language group and a Dutch language group in such manner as is laid down by law.

Article 38b

Except in the case of budgets and laws requiring a special majority, a reasoned motion signed by at least three quarters of the members of one of the linguistic groups and introduced after the report has been tabled and before the final voting in public session may declare that the provisions of a draft or proposed bill which it specifies are of such a nature as to have a serious effect on relations between the communities.

In such cases, parliamentary procedure is suspended and the motion is referred back to the Cabinet which, within a period of thirty days, gives its reasoned findings on the motion and invites the House to reach a decision either on those findings or on the draft or proposed bill in such form as it may have been amended.

This procedure may only be applied once by the members of a linguistic group in respect of one and the same draft or proposed bill.

Article 59b

1. There is a Council and an Executive for the French Community and a Council and an Executive for the Flemish Community whose composition and functioning are determined by law. Representatives of both Councils are elected.

With a view to the implementation of Article 107d, the Council of the French Community and the Council of the Flemish Community, together with their Executives, may exercise respectively in the Walloon region and the Flemish region powers under the terms and conditions laid down by law....

3. Furthermore, the Community Councils, each in its own sphere, shall determine by decree, to the exclusion of the Legislative, the use of languages for:

(1) administrative matters;

(2) the education provided in establishments which are set up, subsidised or recognised by the public authorities;

(3) industrial relations between employers and their staff together with such business instruments and documents as are laid down by the law and regulations.

4. Such decrees as are promulgated in pursuance of Section 2 shall have the force of law respectively in the French language region and in the Dutch language region and also in respect

of institutions established in the bilingual region of Brussels-Capital which, by virtue of their activities must be considered as belonging exclusively to one or other of the Communities.

Such decrees as are promulgated in pursuance of Section 3 shall have force of law respectively in the French language region and in the Dutch language region except as regards:

- such communes or groups of communes which are adjacent to another linguistic region where the law lays down or permits the use of a language other than that of the region in which they are located;

- departments whose activities extend beyond the linguistic region in which they are established;

- national and international institutions referred to in legislation whose activity is common to more than one community.

4b. Unless legislation to the contrary is adopted by the majority as provided in Section 1, last paragraph, such decrees as are promulgated in pursuance of Section 2b shall have the force of law respectively in the French language region and in the Dutch language region and also in respect of institutions established in the bilingual region of Brussels-Capital which, by virtue of their activities must be considered as belonging exclusively to one or other of the communities.

Legislation adopted by the majority as provided in Section 1, last paragraph will determine the authorities responsible in the bilingual region of Brussels-Capital for the exercise of powers not under community jurisdiction in relation to matters under paragraph 2b.

Article 59c

1. There is a council and an executive for the German language community whose composition and functioning are determined by law.... Its decrees shall have the force of law in the German language region...

3. Upon proposal from their respective executives, the Council of the German language community and the Council of the Walloon region may by decree jointly decide that the German language Council and Executive can exercise, in the German language region, the powers of the Walloon region.

Article 86b

With the possible exception of the Prime Minister, the Cabinet comprises an equal number of French-speaking and Dutch-speaking ministers.

Article 107d

Belgium comprises three regions: the Walloon region, the Flemish region and the Brussels region.

The law confers on the regional bodies which it sets up and which are composed of elected representatives the power to rule on such matters as it shall determine, to the exclusion of those referred to in articles 23 and 59b, within such jurisdiction and in accordance with such procedure as it shall determine.

Such law must be passed with a majority vote within each linguistic group of both Houses, providing the majority of the members of each group are present and on condition that the total votes in favour in the two linguistic groups attains two-thirds of the votes cast.

Article 108c

2. For those cases laid down in the Constitution and by legislation, the members of the urban area council are divided into a French language group and a Dutch language group in the manner prescribed by law.

The executive body is composed of an uneven number of members. With the exception of the Chairman, there are the same number of members in the French language group as in the Dutch language group.

3. Except in the case of budgets, a reasoned motion signed by at least three-quarters of the members of a linguistic group in the urban area council and tabled before the final voting in public sessions may declare that such provisions as it specifies in a draft or proposed regulation or decree by the urban area council are likely to do grave harm to relations between the communities...

This procedure may only be applied once by the members of a linguistic group in respect of one and the same draft or proposal.

4. In the urban area there is a French committee for culture and a Dutch committee for culture which are composed of an equal number of members elected respectively by the French language group and by the Dutch language group in the urban area council.

Each has the same powers in respect of its community as the other organising authorities:

(1) in pre-schooling, post-educational and cultural matters;

(2) in education.

Article 132

Until such time as the Catholic University of Louvain, including its ancillary branches of intermediate and technical education, is transferred outside the Dutch language region, the Council for the French community shall, notwithstanding article 59b, section 4, paragraph 1, have jurisdiction over this institution.

The linguistic system at present in force, both as regards education and administration matters, will continue to apply until such appointed time.

Article 140

The text of the Constitution is drawn up in French and in Dutch.

3.13   BELIZE

21 September 1981.

Article 5

2. Any person who is arrested or detained shall be entitled

(a) to be informed promptly, and in any case no later than forty-eight hours after such arrest or detention, in a language he understands, of the reasons for his arrest or detention;

Article 6

3. Every person who is charged with a criminal offence...

(f) shall be permitted to have without payment the assistance of an interpreter if he cannot understand the language used at the trial.

Article 19

1. When a person is detained by virtue of a law that authorises the taking during a period of public emergency of measures that are reasonably justifiable for the purpose of dealing with the situation that exists in Belize during that period, the following provisions shall apply, that is to say:

(a) he shall, with reasonable promptitude and in any case not more than seven days after the commencement of his detention, be informed in a language that he understands of the grounds upon which he is detained and furnished with a written statement in English specifying the particulars of those grounds;

3.14   BENIN

1981.

Article 3
... All nationalities shall be free to use their spoken and written language and to develop their own culture.

3.15   BOLIVIA

2 February 1967, as modified 1 April 1994..

Article 6
Todo ser humano tiene personalidad y capacidad juridica, con arreglo a les leyes. Goza de los derechos, libertades y garantias reconocidas por esta Constitucion, sin distincion de raza, sexo, idioma, religion, opinion politica o de otra indole, origen, condicion economica o social, u otra cualquiera.

Article 116
...La gratuidad, publicidad, celeridad y probidad son condiciones esenciales de la administracion de justicia. El Poder Judicial es responsable de proveer defensa legal gratuita a los indigentes, asi como traductor cuando su lengua materna no sea el castellano.

Article 171
Se garantizan respetan y protegen en el marco de la Ley los derechos sociales, economicos y culturales de los pueblos indigenas que habitan en el territorio nacional y especialmente los relativos a su identidad, valores, lenguas, costumbres e instituciones.

El Estado reconoce la personalidad juridica de las comunidades andinas y campesinas y de las asociaciones y sindicatos canpesinos, de acuerdo a la Ley.

Las autoridades naturales de las comunidades indigenas y campesinas podran ejercer funciones administrativas y jurisdiccionales, siempre que no sean contrarias a esta Constitucion y las leyes.

3.16   BOSNIA AND HERZEGOVINA

Proposed Constitution of the Federation, 18 March 1994.

Article 6
1. The official languages of the Federation shall be the Bosniac language and the Croatian language. The official script will be the Latin alphabet.

2. Other languages may be used as means of communication and instruction.

3. Additional languages may be designated as official by a majority vote of each House of the Legislature, including in the House of Peoples a majority of the Bosniac Delegates and a majority of the Croat Delegates.

II. HUMAN RIGHTS AND FUNDAMENTAL FREEDOMS

Article 2

The Federation shall ensure the application of the highest level of internationally recognised rights and freedoms provided in the instruments listed in the Annex. In particular:

(a) All persons within the territory of the Federation shall enjoy the rights...

(iv) To freedom from discrimination based on race, colour, sex, language, religion or creed, political or other opinions, and national or social origin;...

(xviii) To protection of minorities and vulnerable groups.

3.17   BOTSWANA

30 September 1966.

Article 5

2. Any person who is arrested or detained shall be informed as soon as reasonably practicable, in a language that he understands, of the reasons for his arrest or detention.

Article 10

2. Every person who is charged with a criminal offence...

(b) shall be informed as soon as reasonably practicable, in a language that he understands and in detail, of the nature of the offence charged;...

(f) shall be permitted to have without payment the assistance of an interpreter if he cannot understand the language used at the trial of the charge;

Article 62

Subject to the provisions of section 63 of this Constitution, a person shall be qualified to be elected as a member of the National Assembly if, and shall not be qualified to be so elected unless...

(d) he is able to speak, and unless incapacitated by blindness or other physical cause, to read English well enough to take an active part in the proceedings of the Assembly.

Article 80

4. Subject to the provisions of subsections 5 and 6 of this section a person shall be qualified to be elected as a Specially Elected Member of the House of Chiefs if, and shall not be qualified to be so elected unless...

(c) he is able to speak and, unless incapacitated by blindness or other physical cause, to read English well enough to take an active part in the proceedings of the House;

3.18   BRAZIL

5 October 1988.

Article 147
3. The following may not register as voters:
(a) Illiterate persons;
(b) Those who do not know how to express themselves in the national language;

Article 176
3. Legislation on education shall adopt the following principles and standards:
(1) Elementary education shall be given only in the national language;

Article 210
2. Regular basic education will be given in the Portuguese language; indigenous communities are also guaranteed the use of their mother tongue and of appropriate teaching techniques.

Article 231
The social organisation, customs, and languages, beliefs and traditions of the Indians are recognised, as well as their aboriginal rights to the lands they traditionally occupy, it being within the competence of the Union to demarcate them, protect and guarantee respect for all of their estate.

3.19   BRUNEI

29 September 1959.

Article 82
1. The official language of the state shall be the Malay language and shall be in such script as may by written law be provided.
2. Notwithstanding subsection 1, for a period of five years after the coming into operation of this section, and thereafter until otherwise by written law provided, the English language may be used for all official purposes.
3. The official language of the proceedings of the Privy Council, of the Council of Ministers and of the Legislative Council shall be Malay, provided that:
(a) with the leave of the person presiding, any Member may speak English; and
(b) whenever it shall be necessary for the better convenience of any Member of any Council as aforesaid who is not conversant with the Malay language to do so, such Member may, with the leave of the person presiding, employ an interpreter during the proceedings of such Council; and every interpreter so employed shall, before entering upon his duties for the first time, make and subscribe before the person presiding an oath or declaration in the form set out as Form VII in the Schedule.
4. An official version in the English language shall be provided of anything which, by this Constitution, or by any written law, or by the Standing Orders, is required to be printed or in writing, and such version shall, in addition to the official Malay version, be accepted as an authentic text.

5. Notwithstanding subsection 1, for a period of five years after the coming into operation of this section, and thereafter until otherwise by written law provided, the authoritative text of

(a) all bills to be introduced, or amendments thereto to be moved, in the Legislative Council; and

(b) all written laws and instruments, shall be printed in both the Malay and English languages; but in case of any doubt or conflict between the Malay and the English texts:

(i) subject to paragraph (ii), if such conflict or doubt arises in any bill, written law or instrument, other than this Constitution, the Succession and Regency Proclamation or the Nationality Legislation (S.121/61), the English language shall prevail; and

(ii) if such conflict or doubt arises in this Constitution, the Succession and Regency Proclamation or the Nationality Legislation but not any order made thereunder, the Malay text shall prevail.

3.20   BULGARIA

12 July 1991.

Article 3
Bulgarian is the official language of the Republic.

Article 36
1. Every citizen has the right and the obligation to study and use the Bulgarian language.
2. Citizens, for whom the Bulgarian language is not the mother tongue, will have the right to study and use their own language alongside the duty to study the Bulgarian language.
3. Cases where only the official language is to be used will be determined by law.

3.21   BURKINA FASO

27 November 1977.

Article 3
The official language is French.

Measures aimed at the promotion and official recognition of indigenous languages will be determined by law.

3.22   BURMA

3 January 1974.

Article 21
(b) The national races shall enjoy the freedom to profess their religion, use and develop their language, literature and culture, follow their cherished traditions and customs, provided that the enjoyment of any such freedom does not offend the laws or the public interest.

Article 102

The Burmese language shall be used in the administration of justice. Languages of the national races concerned may also be used, when necessary, and arrangements shall be made to make interpreters available.

Article 152

(b) Burmese is the common language. Languages of the other national races may also be taught.

Article 153

(b) Every citizen shall have the right to freely use one's language and literature, follow one's customs, culture and traditions and profess the religion of his choice. The exercise of this right shall not, however, be to the detriment of national solidarity and the socialist social order which are the basic requirements of the entire Union. Any particular action in this respect which might adversely affect the interests of one or several other national races shall be taken only after consulting with and obtaining the consent of those affected.

Article 197

Interpretation of the preamble, articles, clauses, words and expressions contained in this Constitution shall be based only on the Burmese text.

Article 198

Burmese shall be used as the official language for the purpose of uniformity and clarity in communications between the higher and lower level organs of the state and between such organs at the same level. If necessary the language of the national race concerned may be used.

3.23   BURUNDI

13 March 1992.

Article 8

The national language is Kirundi. The official languages are Kirundi and other languages determined by law.

3.24   CAMEROON

20 May 1972.

Article 1

... The official languages of the United Republic of Cameroon are French and English.

Article 29

The President of the Republic promulgates legislation adopted by the National Assembly within fifteen days of their transmission unless he requests a second reading or submits it to the Supreme Court for review...

Publication is in both official languages of the Republic.

Article 44

This Constitution will be registered and published in the State Official Gazette in French and English, the French text being authoritative. It will then become the Constitution of the United Republic of Cameroon.

3.25   CANADA

Constitution Act, 1867. Modified 17 April 1982. Official text.

Article 133

Either the English or the French language may be used by any person in the debates of the Houses of the Parliament of Canada and of the Houses of the Legislature of Quebec; and both those languages shall be used in the respective records and journals of those Houses; and either of those languages may be used by any person or in any pleading or process in or issuing under this Act, and in or from all or any of the courts of Quebec.

The Acts of Parliament of Canada and of the Legislature of Quebec shall be printed and published in both those languages.

Constitution Act, 1982 (Canadian Charter of Rights and Freedoms).

Article 14

A party or witness in any proceedings who does not understand or speak the language in which the proceedings are conducted or who is deaf has the right to the assistance of an interpreter.

Article 16

1. English and French are the official languages of Canada and have equality of status and equal rights and privileges as to their use in all institutions of the Parliament and government of Canada.

2. English and French are the official languages of New Brunswick and have equality of status and equal rights and privileges as to their use in all institutions of the legislature and government of New Brunswick.

3. Nothing in this Charter limits the authority of Parliament or a legislature to advance the equality of status or use of English and French.

Article 17

1. Everyone has the right to use English or French in any debates and other proceedings of Parliament.

2. Everyone has the right to use English or French in any debates and other proceedings of the legislature of New Brunswick.

Article 18

1. The statutes, records and journals of Parliament shall be printed and published in English and French and both language versions are equally authoritative.

2. The statutes, records and journals of the legislature of New Brunswick shall be printed and published in English and French and both language versions are equally authoritative.

Article 19

1. Either English or French may be used by any person in, or in any pleading in or process issuing from, any court established by Parliament.

2. Either English or French may be used by any person in, or in any pleading in or process issuing from, any court established by New Brunswick.

Article 20

1. Any member of the public in Canada has the right to communicate with, and to receive available services from, any head or central office of an institution of the Parliament or government of Canada in English or French, and has the same right with respect to any other office of any such institution where

(a) there is a significant demand for communications with and services from that office in such language; or

(b) due to the nature of the office, it is reasonable that communications with and services from that office be available in both English and French.

2. Any member of the public in New Brunswick has the right to communicate with, and to receive available services from, any office of an institution of the legislature or government of New Brunswick in English or French.

Article 21

Nothing in sections 16 to 20 abrogates or derogates from any right, privilege or obligation with respect to the English and French languages, or either of them, that exists or is continued by virtue of any other provision of the Constitution of Canada.

Article 22

Nothing in sections 16 to 20 abrogates or derogates from any legal or customary right or privilege acquired or enjoyed either before or after the coming into force of this Charter with respect to any language that is not English or French.

Article 23

1. Citizens of Canada:

(a) whose first language learned and still understood is that of the English or French linguistic minority population of the province in which they reside, or

(b) who have received their primary school instruction in Canada in English or French and reside in a province where the language in which they received that instruction is the language of the English or French linguistic minority population of the province, have the right to have their children receive primary and secondary school instruction in that language in that province.

2. Citizens of Canada of whom any child has received or is receiving primary or secondary school instruction in English or French in Canada, have the right to have all their children receive primary and secondary school instruction in the same language.

3. The right of citizens of Canada under subsections (1) and (2) to have their children receive primary and secondary school instruction in the language of the English or French linguistic minority population of a province:

(a) applies wherever in the province the number of children of citizens who have such a right is sufficient to warrant the provision to them out of public funds of minority language instruction; and

(b) includes, where the number of those children so warrants, the right to have them receive that instruction in minority language educational facilities provided out of public funds.

Article 55

A French version of the portions of the Constitution of Canada referred by the Minister of Justice of Canada as expeditiously as possible and, when any portion thereof sufficient to warrant action being taken has been so prepared, it shall be put forward for enactment by proclamation issued by the Governor General under the Great Seal of Canada pursuant to the procedure then applicable to an amendment of the same provision of the Constitution of Canada.

Article 56

Where any portion of the Constitution of Canada has been or is enacted in English and French where a French version of any portion of the Constitution is enacted pursuant to section 55, the English and French versions of that portion of the Constitution are equally authoritative.

Article 57

The English and French versions of this Act are equally authoritative.

3.26 CENTRAL AFRICAN REPUBLIC

21 November 1986.

Article 1

... The national language is Sango. The official language is French.

3.27 CHINA

4 December 1982.

Article 4

All nationalities in the People's Republic of China are equal. The state protects the lawful rights and interests of the minority nationalities and upholds and develops a relationship of equality, unity and mutual assistance among all of China's nationalities. Discrimination against and oppression of any nationality are prohibited; any act which undermines the unity of the nationalities or instigates their secession is prohibited.

The state assists areas inhabited by minority nationalities in accelerating their economic and cultural development according to the characteristics and needs of the various minority nationalities.

Regional autonomy is practised in areas where people of minority nationalities live in concentrated communities; in these areas organs of self-government are established to exercise the power of autonomy. All national autonomous areas are integral parts of the People's Republic of China.

All nationalities have the freedom to use and develop their own spoken and written languages and to preserve or reform their own folkways and customs.

Article 19
The state develops socialist educational undertakings and works to raise the scientific and cultural level of the whole nation.

The state runs schools of various types, makes primary education compulsory and universal, develops secondary, vocational and higher education and promotes pre-school education.

The state develops educational facilities of various types in order to wipe out illiteracy and provide political, cultural, scientific, technical and professional education for workers, peasants, state functionaries and other working people. It encourages people to become educated through self-study.

The state encourages the collective economic organisations, state enterprises and undertakings and other social forces to set up educational institutions of various types in accordance with the law.

The state promotes the nationwide use of Putonghua.

Article 121
In performing their functions, the organs of self-government of the national autonomous areas, in accordance with the regulations on the exercise of autonomy in those areas, employ the spoken and written language or languages in common use in the locality.

Article 134
Citizens of all nationalities have the right to use the spoken and written languages of their own nationalities in court proceedings. The people's courts and people's procuratorates should provide translation for any party of the court proceedings who is not familiar with the spoken or written languages commonly used in the locality.

In an area where people of a minority nationality live in a concentrated community or where a number of nationalities live together, court hearings should be conducted in the language or languages commonly used in the locality; indictments, judgments, notices and other documents should be written, according to actual needs, in the language or languages commonly used in the locality.

3.28   COLOMBIA

5 July 1991.

Article 10
Castilian is the official language of Colombia. The languages and dialects of ethnic groups are also official in their territories. Education in communities with their own linguistic traditions shall be bilingual.

Article 13
Everyone is born free and equal before the law and shall receive the same protection and treatment from authorities as well as enjoy the same rights, freedoms and opportunities without any discrimination based on sex, race, national or family origin, language, religion, political or philosophical opinions.

3.29   COMORES

1 October 1978. Modified in October 1982 and January 1985.

Article 2
... The official languages shall be French and Arabic.

Article 30
The utilisation of the official languages and the choice of working languages and languages of instruction shall be established by law.

3.30   CONGO

15 March 1992.

Article 3
... The official language is French. The national vernacular languages are Lingala and Munukutuba.

3.31   COSTA RICA

1975.

Article 75
Spanish is the official language of the nation.

3.32   CROATIA

22 December 1990.

Article 12
The Croatian language and the Latin script shall be in official use in the Republic of Croatia.
In individual local units another language and the Cyrillic or some other script may, along with the Croatian language and the Latin script, be introduced into official use under conditions specified by law.

Article 14
Citizens of the Republic of Croatia shall enjoy all rights and freedoms, regardless of race, colour, sex, language, religion, political or other opinion, national or social origin, property, birth, education, social status or other properties.
All shall be equal before the law.

Article 15
Members of all nations and minorities shall have equal rights in the Republic of Croatia.

Members of all nations and minorities shall be guaranteed freedom to express their nationality, freedom to use their language and script, and cultural autonomy.

Article 17
During a state of war or an immediate danger to the independence and unity of the Republic, or in the event of some natural disaster, individual freedoms and rights guaranteed by the Constitution may be restricted. This shall be decided by the Croatian Sabor by a two-thirds majority of all representatives or, if Croatian Sabor is unable to meet, by the President of the Republic.

The extent of such restrictions shall be adequate to the nature of the danger, and may not result in the inequality of citizens in respect of race, colour, sex, language, religion, national or social origin.

Article 24
... The arrested person shall be immediately informed in a way understandable to him of the reasons for arrest and of his rights determined by law.

3.33   CUBA

24 February 1976, as modified July 1992.

Article 2
El nombre del estado cubano es Republica de Cuba, el idioma oficial es el espanol y su capital es la ciudad de La Habana.

3.34   CYPRUS

6 August 1960.

Article 2
For the purposes of this Constitution:
1. the Greek Community comprises all citizens of the Republic who are of Greek origin and whose mother tongue is Greek or who share the Greek cultural traditions or who are members of the Greek Orthodox Church;
2. the Turkish Community comprises all citizens of the Republic who are of Turkish origin and whose mother tongue is Turkish or who share the Turkish cultural traditions or who are Moslems.

Article 3
1. The official languages of the Republic are Greek and Turkish.
2. Legislative, executive and administrative acts and documents shall be drawn up in both official languages and shall, where under the express provisions of this Constitution promulgation is required, be promulgated by publication in the official Gazette of the Republic in both official languages.
3. Administrative or other official documents addressed to a Greek or a Turk shall be drawn up in the Greek or the Turkish language respectively.

4. Judicial proceedings shall be conducted or made and judgements shall be drawn up in the Greek language if the parties are Greek, in the Turkish language if the parties are Turkish, and in both the Greek and the Turkish languages if the parties are Greek and Turkish. The official language or languages to be used for such purposes in all other cases shall be specified by the Rules of Court made by the High Court under Article 163.

5. Any text in the official Gazette of the Republic shall be published in both official languages in the same issue.

6. (1) Any difference between the Greek and the Turkish texts of any legislative, executive or administrative act or document published in the official Gazette of the Republic, shall be resolved by a competent court.

(2) The prevailing text of any law or decision of a Communal Chamber published in the official Gazette of the Republic shall be that of the language of the Communal Chamber concerned.

(3) Where any difference arises between the Greek and the Turkish texts of an executive or administrative act or document which, though not published in the official Gazette of the Republic, has otherwise been published, a statement by the Minister or any other authority concerned as to which the text should prevail or which should be the correct text shall be final and conclusive.

(4) A competent court may grant such remedies as it may deem just in any case of a difference in the texts as aforesaid.

7. The official languages shall be used on coins, currency notes and stamps.

8. Every person shall have the right to address himself to the authorities of the Republic in either of the official languages.

Article 11

4. Every person shall be informed at the time of his arrest in a language which he understands of the reasons for his arrest and shall be allowed to have the services of a lawyer of his own choosing...

6. The judge before whom the person arrested is brought shall promptly proceed to inquire into the grounds of the arrest in a language understandable by the person arrested and shall, as soon as possible and in any event not later than three days from such appearance, either release the person arrested on such terms as he may deem fit or where the investigation into the commission of the offence for which he has been arrested has not been completed remand him in custody and may remand him in custody from time to time for a period not exceeding eight days at any one time;

Article 12

5. Every person charged with an offence has the following minimum rights:

(a) to be informed promptly and in a language which he understands and in detail of the nature and grounds of the charge preferred against him;...

(e) to have the free assistance of an interpreter if he cannot understand or speak the language used in court.

Article 28

2. Every person shall enjoy all the rights and liberties provided for in this Constitution without any direct or indirect discrimination against any person on the ground of his community, race, religion, language, sex, political or other convictions, national or social descent, birth,

colour, wealth, social class, or on any ground whatsoever, unless there is express provision to the contrary in this Constitution.

Article 30

3. Every person has the right...

(e) to have free assistance of an interpreter if he cannot understand or speak the language used in court.

Article 171

1. In sound and vision broadcasting there shall be programmes both for the Greek and the Turkish Communities.

2. The time allotted to programmes for the Turkish Community in sound broadcasting shall be not less than seventy-five hours in a seven day week, spread to all days of such week in daily normal periods of transmission:

- provided that if the total period of transmissions has to be reduced so that the time allotted to programmes for the Greek Community should fall below seventy-five hours in a seven day week, then the time allotted to programmes for the Turkish Community in any such week should be reduced by the same number of hours as that by which the time allotted to programmes for the Greek Community is reduced below such hours;

- provided further that if the time allotted to programmes for the Greek Community is increased above one hundred and forty hours in a seven day week, then the time allotted to programmes for the Turkish Community shall be increased in the ratio of three hours for the Turkish Community to every seven hours for the Greek Community.

3. In vision broadcasting there shall be allotted three transmission days to the programmes for the Turkish Community of every ten consecutive transmission days and the total time allotted to the programmes for the Turkish Community in such ten transmission days shall be in the ratio of three hours to seven hours allotted to programmes for the Greek Community in such ten transmission days.

4. All official broadcasts in sound and vision shall be made both in Greek and Turkish and shall not be taken into account for the purposes of calculating the time under this Article.

Article 180

1. The Greek and the Turkish texts of this Constitution shall both be originals and shall have the same authenticity and the same legal force.

Article 189

Notwithstanding anything in Article 3 contained, for a period of five years after the date of the coming into operation of this Constitution:

(a) All laws which under Article 188 will continue to be in force may continue to be in the English language.

(b) The English language may be used in any proceedings before any court of the Republic.

3.35 DOMINICA

3 November 1978.

Article 8
Every person who is charged with a criminal offence...
(b) shall be informed as soon as reasonably practicable, in a language that he understands and in detail, of the nature of the offence charged;...
(f) shall be permitted to have without payment the assistance of an interpreter if he cannot understand the language used at the trial.

3.36 ECUADOR

10 August 1979.

Article 1
... The official language is Castilian. Quechua and other indigenous languages are recognised as elements of the national culture.

Article 27
In schools established in areas of predominantly indigenous population, Quechua or the pertinent indigenous language shall be used as the main language of instruction and Castilian as language of intercultural ties.

3.37 EGYPT

11 September 1971.

Article 2
Islam is the religion of the state and Arabic its official language. The principles of Islamic Shari'ah are primary sources of legislation.

Article 40
Citizens are equal before the law. They have equal public rights and duties without discrimination between them on the basis of sex, origin, language, religion or creed.

3.38 EL SALVADOR

20 December 1983.

Article 62
The official language of El Salvador is Spanish. The government is bound to see to its preservation and teaching.
Indigenous languages spoken in the national territory are part of the cultural heritage and are to be preserved, used and respected.

3.39   EQUATORIAL GUINEA

3 August 1982.

Article 1
The official language of the Republic of Equatorial Guinea is Spanish. The aboriginal languages are recognised as integral to the national culture.

Article 20
3. All discrimination by reason of ethnic background, race, sex, language, religion, filiation, political or any other kind of views, social origin, economic position, or birth, is prohibited.

3.40   ESTONIA

28 June 1992.

Article 6
The official language of Estonia shall be Estonian.

Article 12
All persons shall be equal before the law. No person may be discriminated against on the basis of nationality, race, colour, gender, language, origin, religion, political or other beliefs, financial or social status, or other reasons.

Article 21
Any person who is deprived of his or her liberty shall be informed promptly, in a language and manner which he or she understands, of the reason for the arrest, and of his or her rights, and shall be given the opportunity to notify his or her immediate family of the arrest...

No person may be held in custody for more than 48 hours without specific permission by a court. Such a decision shall be promptly made known to the person in custody in a language and in a manner he or she understands.

Article 37
All persons shall have the right to an education.

... Parents shall have the final decision in choosing education for their children.

All persons shall have the right to instruction in Estonian. Educational institutions established for ethnic minorities shall choose their own language of instruction.

Article 49
Every person shall have the right to preserve his or her ethnic identity.

Article 50
Ethnic minorities shall have the right, in the interests of their national culture, to establish institutions of self-government in accordance with conditions and procedures established by the Law on Cultural Autonomy for Ethnic Minorities.

Article 51

All persons shall have the right to address state or local government authorities and their officials in Estonian, and to receive answers in Estonian.

In localities where at least half of the permanent residents belong to an ethnic minority, all persons shall have the right to receive answers from state and local government authorities and their officials in the language of that ethnic minority.

Article 52

The official language of state and local government authorities shall be Estonian.

In localities where the language of the majority of the population is other than Estonian, local government authorities may use the language of the majority of the permanent residents of that locality for internal communication, to the extent and in accordance with procedures established by law.

The use of foreign languages, including the languages of ethnic minorities, by state authorities and in court, and pre-trial proceedings shall be established by law.

Article 104

Procedures for the adoption of laws shall be established by the Law on the *Riigikogu* Standing Orders.

The following laws may be adopted or amended only by a majority of the members of the *Riigikogu*...

(10) Law on Cultural Autonomy for Ethnic Minorities;

3.41   FIJI

10 October 1970.

Article 10

2. Every person who is charged with a criminal offence...

(b) shall be informed as soon as reasonably practicable, in a language that he understands and in detail, of the nature of the offence;...

(f) shall be permitted to have without payment the assistance of an interpreter if he cannot understand the language used at the trial of the charge.

Article 56

The official language of Parliament shall be English, but any member of either House may address the chair in the House of which he is a member in Fijian or Hindustani.

3.42   FINLAND

17 July 1919.

Article 14

Finnish and Swedish shall be the national languages of the Republic.

The right of Finnish citizens to use their mother tongue, whether Finnish or Swedish, before the courts and the administrative authorities, and to obtain from them documents in these languages, shall be guaranteed by law; care shall be taken that the rights of the Finnish speaking population and the rights of the Swedish speaking population of the country shall be promoted by the state upon an identical basis.

The state shall provide for the intellectual and economic needs of the Finnish speaking and the Swedish speaking populations upon a similar basis.

Article 22

Laws and decrees as well as bills submitted by the Government to Parliament and the replies, recommendations, and other documents addressed by Parliament to the Government shall be drawn up in the Finnish and the Swedish languages.

Article 50

For the purpose of general administration Finland shall remain divided into provinces, circuits and communes.

Changes in the number of provinces shall be made by law; the Council of State shall decide all other changes concerning administrative divisions, unless otherwise provided by law.

In redrawing the boundaries of the administrative districts, it is to be observed that these shall, as far as circumstances permit, be so constituted as to contain populations speaking only one language, Finnish or Swedish, or to make the language minorities as small as possible.

Article 75

Every Finnish citizen must take part in, or make his contribution to, the defence of the country as prescribed by law.

Every conscript, unless he otherwise desires, shall if possible be enrolled in a military unit of which the rank and file speak his own mother tongue (Finnish or Swedish) and shall receive his training in that language. Finnish shall be the language of command of the Armed Forces.

3.43   FRANCE

4 October 1958. Modified 25 June 1992.

Article 2

The language of the Republic is French.

3.44   GABON

1975.

Article 2

... The Gabonese Republic shall adopt French as the official language.

3.45   GAMBIA

24 April 1970.

Article 15

2. Any person who is arrested or detained shall be informed as soon as reasonably practicable, in a language that he understands, of the reasons for his arrest or detention.

Article 78
   The business of the House of Representatives shall be conducted in English.

3.46   GERMANY

23 May 1949. Amended 1990. English translation provided by the Ministers of the Interior, Justice and Finance.

Article 3
   3. No one may be prejudiced or favoured because of his sex, his parentage, his race, his language, his homeland and origin, his faith or his religious or political opinions.

3.47   GREECE

11 June 1975.

Article 3
   The text of the Holy Scripture shall be maintained unaltered. Official translation of the text into any other form of language, without prior sanction by the Autocephalous Church of Greece and the Great Church of Christ in Constantinople is prohibited.

Article 5
   All persons living within the Greek territory shall enjoy full protection of their life, honour and freedom, irrespective of nationality, race or language and of religious or political beliefs. Exceptions shall be permitted only in cases provided for in international law.

3.48   GUATEMALA

31 May 1985 and 14 January 1986.

Article 18
   In the year following its entry into force, this Constitution will be widely distributed in the Qiche, Mam, Cakchiquel and Kekchi languages.

Article 43
   Spanish is the official language of Guatemala. The vernacular languages are part of the nation's cultural heritage.

Article 58
   Individuals and communities have the recognised right to their cultural identity in conformity with their values, language and customs.

Article 66

Guatemala is formed of various ethnic groups, including the indigenous groups of Maya origin. The state recognises, respects and promotes their life styles, customs, traditions, forms of social organisation, use of indigenous dress for men and women, their language and their dialect.

Article 76

The administration of the educational system shall be decentralised and regionalised.

In schools operating in zones where the indigenous population predominates, teaching should preferably be bilingual.

3.49   GUYANA

6 October 1980.

Article 53

Subject to article 155 a person shall be qualified for election as a member of the National Assembly if, and shall not be so qualified unless, he...

(b) is able to speak and, unless incapacitated by blindness or other physical cause, to read the English language with a degree of proficiency sufficient to enable him to take an active part in the proceedings of the Assembly.

Article 144

2. It shall be the duty of a court to ascertain the truth in every case provided that every person who is charged with a criminal offence:

(a) shall be informed as soon as reasonably practicable, in a language that he understands and in detail, of the nature of the offence charged;

(b) shall be permitted to have without payment the assistance of an interpreter if he cannot understand the language used at the trial of the charge.

3.50   HAITI

March 1987.

Article 5

All Haitians are united by a common language: Creole. Creole and French are the official languages of the Republic.

3.51   HONDURAS

20 January 1982.

Article 6

The official language of Honduras is Spanish. The state shall protect its purity and increase its learning.

3.52 HUNGARY

1990.

Article 65
(1) On terms laid down in the law, the Republic of Hungary ensures the right of asylum for foreign citizens persecuted in their homeland and for those displaced persons who are at their place of stay harassed on grounds of race, religion, nationality, language or political affiliation.

Article 68
(1) The national and ethnic minorities living in the Republic of Hungary share the power of the people; they are constituent elements in the state.

(2) The Republic of Hungary grants protection to national and ethnic minorities, it ensures the possibilities for their collective participation in public life, and enables them to foster their own culture, use the mother tongue, receive school instruction in the mother tongue, and freedom to use their names as spelled and pronounced in their own language.

(3) The laws of the Republic of Hungary ensure representation for the national and ethnic minorities living in the territory of the country.

(4) National and ethnic minorities may set up their own local and national government organisations.

(5) The votes of two thirds of the MPs present are required to pass the law on the rights of national and ethnic minorities.

Article 70/A
(1) The Republic of Hungary guarantees for all persons in its territory human and civil rights without discrimination on account of race, colour, sex, language, religion, political or other views, national or social origins, ownership of assets, birth or any other grounds.

3.53 INDIA

26 January 1950.

Article 29
1. Any section of the citizens of India or any part thereof having a distinct language, script or culture of its own shall have the right to conserve the same.

2. No citizen shall be denied admission into any educational institution maintained by the state or receiving aid out of state funds on grounds only of religion, race, caste, language, or any of them.

Article 30
1. All minorities, whether based on religion or language, shall have the right to establish and administer educational institutions of their choice.

1A. In making any law providing for the compulsory acquisition of any property of an educational institution established and administered by a minority, referred to in clause 1, the state shall ensure that the amount fixed by or determined under such law for acquisition of such property is such as would restrict or abrogate the right guaranteed under that clause.

2. The state shall not, in granting aid to educational institutions, discriminate against any educational institution on the ground that it is under the management of a minority, whether based on religion or language.

Article 120

1. Notwithstanding anything in Part XVII, but subject to the provisions of Article 348, business in Parliament shall be transacted in Hindi or in English:

Provided that the Chairman of the Council of States or Speaker of the House of the People, or person acting as such, as the case may be, may permit any member who cannot adequately express himself in Hindi or in English to address the House in his mother tongue.

2. Unless Parliament by law otherwise provides, this article shall, after the expiration of a period of fifteen years from the commencement of this Constitution, have effect as if the words "or in English" were omitted therefrom.

Article 210

1. Notwithstanding anything in Part XVII, but subject to the provisions of Article 348, business in the Legislature of a state shall be transacted in the official language or languages of the state or in Hindi or in English:

Provided that the Speaker of the Legislative Assembly or Chairman of the Legislative Council, or person acting as such, as the case may be, may permit any member who cannot adequately express himself in any of the languages aforesaid to address the House in his mother tongue.

2. Unless the Legislature of the state by law otherwise provides, this article shall, after the expiration of a period of fifteen years from the commencement of this Constitution, have effect as if the words "or in English" were omitted therefrom:

Provided that in relation to the Legislature of the states of Himachal Pradesh, Manipur, Meghalaya and Tripura this clause shall have effect as if the words "fifteen years" occurring therein, the words "twenty-five years" were substituted.

Article 343

1. The official language of the Union shall be Hindi in Devanagari script.

The form of numerals to be used for the official purposes of the Union shall be the international form of Indian numerals.

2. Notwithstanding anything in clause 1, for a period of fifteen years from the commencement of this Constitution, the English language shall continue to be used for all the official purposes of the Union for which it was being used immediately before such commencement:

Provided that the President may, during the said period, by order authorise the use of the Hindi language in addition to the English language and of the Devanagari form of numerals in addition to the international form of Indian numerals for any of the official purposes of the Union...

8. Notwithstanding anything in this article, Parliament may by law provide for the use, after the said period of fifteen years of:

(a) the English language, or

(b) the Devanagari form of numerals,

for such purposes as may be specified in the law.

Article 344

1. The President shall, at the expiration of five years from the commencement of this Constitution and thereafter at the expiration of ten years from such commencement, by order constitute a Commission which shall consist of a Chairman and such other members representing the different languages specified in the Eighth Schedule as the President may appoint, and the order shall define the procedure to be followed by the Commission.

2. It shall be the duty of the Commission to make recommendations to the President as to:

(a) the progressive use of the Hindi language for the official purposes of the Union;

(b) restrictions on the use of the English language for all or any of the official purposes of the Union;

(c) the language to be used for all or any of the purposes mentioned in Article 348;

(d) the form of numerals to be used for any one or more specified purposes of the Union;

(e) any other matter referred to the Commission by the President as regards the official language of the Union and the language for communication between the Union and a state or between one state and another and their use.

3. In making their recommendations under clause 2, the Commission shall have due regard to the industrial, cultural and scientific advancement of India, and the just claims and the interest of persons belonging to the non-Hindi speaking areas in regard to the public services.

Article 345

Subject to the provision of Articles 346 and 347, the Legislature of a state may by law adopt any one or more of the languages in use in the state or Hindi as the language or languages to be used for all or any of the official purposes of that state:

Provided that, until the Legislature of the state otherwise provides by law, the English language shall continue to be used for those official purposes within the state for which it was being used immediately before the commencement of this Constitution.

Article 346

The language for the time being authorised for use in the Union for official purposes shall be the official language for communication between one state and another state and between a state and the Union:

Provided that if two or more states agree that the Hindi language should be the official language for communications between states, that language may be used for such communication.

Article 347

On a demand being made in that behalf the President may, if he is satisfied that a substantial proportion of the population of a state desire the use of any language spoken by them to be recognised by that state, direct that such language shall also be officially recognised throughout that state or any part thereof for such purpose as he may specify.

Article 348

1. Notwithstanding anything in the foregoing provisions of this Part, until Parliament by law otherwise provides:

(a) all proceedings in the Supreme Court and in every High Court,

(b) the authoritative texts:

(i) of all bills to be introduced or amendments thereto to be moved in either House of Parliament or in the House or either House of the Legislature of a state,

(ii) of all Acts passed by Parliament or the Legislature of a state and of all ordinances promulgated by the President or the Governor of a state, and

(iii) of all orders, rules, regulations and bylaws issued under this Constitution or under any law made by Parliament or the Legislature of a state,

shall be in the English language.

2. Notwithstanding anything in subclause (a) of clause 1, the Governor of a state may, with the previous consent of the President, authorise the use of the Hindi language or any other language used for any official purposes of the state, in proceedings in the High Court having its principal seat in that state:

Provided that nothing in this clause shall apply to any judgement, decree or order passed or made by such High Court.

3. Notwithstanding anything in subclause (b) of clause 1, where the Legislature of a state has prescribed any language other than the English language for use in bills introduced in, acts passed by the Legislature of the state, or in any order, rule, regulation or bylaw referred to in paragraph (iii) of that subclause, a translation of the same in the English language published under the authority of the Governor of the state in the official Gazette of that state shall be deemed to be the authoritative text thereof in the English language under this article.

Article 349

During the period of fifteen years from the commencement of this Constitution no bill or amendment making provision for the language to be used for any of the purposes mentioned in clause 1 of Article 348 shall be introduced or moved in either House of Parliament without the previous sanction of the President, and the President shall not give his sanction to the introduction of any such bill or the moving of any such amendment except after he has taken into consideration the recommendations of the Commission constituted under clause 1 of Article 344 and the report of the Committee constituted under clause 4 of that article.

Article 350

Every person shall be entitled to submit a representation for the redress of any grievance to any officer or authority of the Union or a state in any of the languages used in the Union or inn the state, as the case may be.

Article 350A

It shall be the endeavour of every state and of every local authority within the state to provide adequate facilities for instruction in the mother tongue at the primary stage of education to children belonging to linguistic minority groups, and the President may issue such directions to any state as he considers necessary or proper for securing the provision of such facilities.

Article 350B

1. There shall be a special officer for linguistic minorities to be appointed by the President.

2. It shall be the duty of the special officer to investigate all matters relating to the safeguards provided for linguistic minorities under this Constitution and report to the President upon those matters at such intervals as the President may direct, and the President shall cause all such reports to be laid before each House of Parliament, and sent to the governments of the states concerned.

Article 351
It shall be the duty of the Union to promote the spread of the Hindi language, to develop it so that it may serve as a medium of expression for all the elements of the composite culture of India and to secure its enrichment by assimilating, without interfering with its genius, the forms, style and expression used in Hindustani and in the other languages of India specified in the Eighth Schedule, and by drawing, wherever necessary or desirable, for its vocabulary, primarily on Sanskrit and secondarily on other languages.

Eighth Schedule
1. Assamese. 2. Bengali. 3. Gujarati. 4. Hindi. 5. Kannada. 6. Kashmiri. 7. Malayalam. 8. Marathi. 9. Oriya. 10. Punjabi. 11. Sanskrit. 12. Sindhi. 13. Tamil. 14. Telegu. 15. Urdu.

3.54   INDONESIA

August 1945.

Article 36
The official language shall be the Indonesian language.
In the areas possessing languages of their own which are actively used by the people concerned (for instance, Javanese, Sundanese, Madurese, and so forth), those languages will be respected and also cared for by the state.
Those languages are a part of the living culture of Indonesia.

3.55   IRAN

3 December 1979.

Article 15
The official and common language and script of the people of Iran is Persian. Official documents, correspondence and statements, as well as text books, shall be written in this language and script. However, the use of local and ethnic literature in the schools, together with Persian language instruction, is also permitted.

Article 16
The language of the Koran and Islamic studies and instruction are in Arabic, and Arabic totally permeates Persian literature. Therefore, Arabic must be taught in all classes and areas of study from the time that elementary school is completed until graduation from secondary school.

Article 19
The people of Iran, regardless of their ethnic, family and tribal origins, shall enjoy equal rights. Colour, race, language and the like shall not be cause for privilege.

3.56 IRAQ

16 July 1970.

Article 7
1. Arabic is the official language.
2. The Kurdish language is official, besides Arabic, in the Kurdish region.

Article 19
1. Citizens are equal before the law, without discrimination because of sex, blood, language, social origin or religion.

3.57 IRELAND

1948.

Article 4
As soon as may be after the signature and promulgation of a bill as a law, the text of such law which was signed by the President or, where the President has signed the text of such law in each of the official languages, both the signed texts shall be enrolled for record in the office of the Registrar of the Supreme Court, and the text, or both the texts, so enrolled shall be conclusive evidence of the provisions of such law.

In case of conflict between the texts of a law enrolled under this section in both the official languages, the text in the national language shall prevail.

Article 8
1. The Irish language as the national language is the first official language.
2. The English language is recognised as a second official language.
3. Provision may, however, be made by law for the exclusive use of either of the said languages for any one or more official purposes, either throughout the state or in any part thereof.

Article 18
7. Before each general election of the members of the *Seanad Eireann* to be elected from panels of candidates, five panels of candidates shall be formed in the manner provided by law containing respectively the names of persons having knowledge and practical experience of the following interests and services, namely:
(i) national language and culture, literature, art, education and such professional interests as may be defined by law for the purpose of this panel;

Article 25
4. (3) Every bill shall be signed by the President in the text in which it was passed or deemed to have been passed by both Houses of the *Oireachtas*, and if a bill is so passed or deemed to have been passed in both the official languages, the President shall sign the text of the bill in each of those languages.
(4) Where the President signs the text of a bill in one only of the official languages, an official translation shall be issued in the other official language.

(5) As soon as may be after the signature and promulgation of a bill as a law, the text of such law which was signed by the President or, where the President has signed the text of such law in each of the official languages, both the signed texts shall be enrolled for record in the office of the Registrar of the Supreme Court and the text, or both texts, so enrolled shall be conclusive evidence of the provisions of such law.

(6) In case of conflict between the texts of a law enrolled under this section in both the official languages, the text in the national language shall prevail...

5. (1) It shall be lawful for the *Taoiseach*, from time to time as occasion appears to him to require, to cause to be prepared under his supervision a text, in both official languages, of this Constitution as then in force embodying all amendments theretofore made therein...

(4) In case of conflict between the texts of any copy of this Constitution enrolled under this section, the text in the national language shall prevail.

3.58   ITALY

1 January 1948.

Article 3
All citizens are invested with equal social status and are equal before the law, without distinction as to sex, race, language, religion, political opinions and personal or social conditions.

Article 6
The Republic shall safeguard linguistic minorities by means of special provisions.

3.59   IVORY COAST

1963.

Article 1
... The official language shall be French.

3.60   JAMAICA

6 August 1962.

Article 15
2. Any person who is arrested or detained shall be informed as soon as reasonably practicable, in a language which he understands, of the reasons for his arrest or detention.

Article 20
6. Every person who is charged with a criminal offence
(a) shall be informed as soon as reasonably practicable, in a language which he understands, of the nature of the offence charged;...
(e) shall be permitted to have without payment the assistance of an interpreter if he cannot understand the English language.

3.61   JORDAN

8 January 1952.

Article 2
Islam shall be the religion of the state and the Arabic language shall be its official language.

Article 6
(i) Jordanians shall be equal before the law. There shall be no discrimination between them as regards their rights and duties, on grounds of race, language or religion.

3.62   KAMPUCHEA

Constitution adopted by the Constitutional Assembly, Phnom Penh, 21 September 1993.

Article 5
The official language and script are Khmer.

Article 31
... Every Khmer citizen shall be equal before the law, enjoying the same rights, freedom and fulfilling the same obligations regardless of race, colour, sex, language, religious belief, political tendency, birth origin, social status, wealth or other status.

Article 67
The state shall adopt an educational programme according to the principle of modern pedagogy including technology and foreign languages.

Article 69
The state shall protect and promote the Khmer language as required.

3.63   KAZAKHSTAN

28 January 1993.

EIGHT PREAMBLE
The Kazakh language is the state language in the Republic of Kazakhstan. The Russian language is the language of inter-ethnic communication.
The state guarantees the preservation of the sphere of the use of language of inter-ethnic communication and other languages, and looks after their free development.
Restrictions of the rights and freedoms of the citizens on the basis of incapability to speak the state language or the language of inter-ethnic communication is forbidden.

Article 1
Citizens of the Republic of Kazakhstan are guaranteed equality of rights and freedoms, regardless of race; nationality; sex; language; social, property, and official status; social origin;

place of residence; attitude to religion; convictions; membership in a public association; as well as previously incurred criminal punishment.

Any form of discrimination against citizens is forbidden.

Article 65

The chairman of the Supreme Soviet of the Republic of Kazakhstan is elected by the Supreme Soviet at its first session from the number of deputies of the Supreme Soviet in command of the state language by secret ballot, through the majority of votes from the total number of deputies.

Article 98

The consideration of cases in courts is carried out on the basis of the principles of legality, spontaneity, with observance of the language of legal proceedings, under conditions of openness, contest, equality of rights of all sides, independence of judges, and free evaluation by them of evidence in making judgement.

The consideration of cases in closed session is permitted when public legal proceedings will lead to disclosure of state or commercial secrets, or when the necessity exists to defend the private or family life of citizens from publicity.

Persons participating in a case who do not know the language of legal proceedings are provided with a translator, as well as with the right to speak in the court in their native language.

Article 114

A citizen of the Republic of Kazakhstan, being not younger than 35 years old and not older than 65 years of age, permanently living on the territory of the Republic of Kazakhstan for not less than ten years, who is in perfect command of the state language, can be elected president.

A citizen of the Republic of Kazakhstan, permanently living on the territory of the Republic of Kazakhstan not less than ten years and who is in command of the state language, can be elected Vice President.

The Vice President is elected together with the President of the Republic of Kazakhstan.

Transitional Provisions

Article 4

For the transition period, to create conditions for unlimited and free study of the state language, all the official documents in the Republic of Kazakhstan shall be presented in the Kazakh and Russian languages.

3.64   KENYA

12 December 1963. Amended.

Article 72

2. Any person who is arrested or detained shall be informed as soon as reasonably practicable, in a language that he understands, of the reasons for his arrest or detention.

Article 34
   Subject to section 35, a person shall be qualified to be elected as a member of the National Assembly if, and shall not be qualified unless, at the date of his nomination for election...
   (c) he is able to speak and, unless incapacitated by blindness or other physical cause, to read the Kiswahili and English languages well enough to take an active part in the proceedings of the National Assembly;

Article 53
   1. Subject to the provisions of this section the official languages of the National Assembly shall be Kiswahili and English and the business of the National Assembly may be conducted in either or both such languages.
   2. Every bill, including the memorandum accompanying a bill, every act of Parliament whenever enacted, all other actual or proposed legislation under the authority of an act of Parliament, all financial resolutions and documents relating thereto, and every actual or proposed amendment of any of the foregoing, shall be written in English.
   3. In all proceedings of the National Assembly which involve the discussion of any of the following matters, that is to say a bill, including the memorandum accompanying a bill, any act of Parliament, any other legislation whether actual or proposed, any financial resolution or document relating thereto, or any actual or proposed amendment thereof, the wording of every such matter shall, as occasion requires, be quoted in English.

Article 82
   2. Every person who is charged with a criminal offence...
   (b) shall be informed as soon as reasonably practicable, in a language that he understands and in detail of the nature of the offence charged;...
   (f) shall be permitted to have without payment the assistance of an interpreter if he cannot understand the language used at the trial of the charge.

Article 93
   Any person who...
   (e) satisfied the Minister that he has an adequate knowledge of the Swahili language;
shall be eligible, upon making application in such manner as may be prescribed by or under an act of Parliament, to be naturalised as a citizen of Kenya, and the Minister may grant a certificate of naturalisation to any such person who so applies.

   3.65   KIRGIZSTAN

3 May 1993.

Article 5
   1. The official language of Kirgizstan shall be the Kirgiz language.
   2. Kirgizstan shall guarantee preservation, equal and free development and functioning of the Russian language and all other languages which are used by the population of the republic.
   3. Infringement of the citizens' rights on the ground of absence of knowledge and command of the official language shall not be allowed.

Article 15

3. All persons in Kirgizstan are equal before law and the court.

No person shall be subject to any kind of discrimination, violation of his rights and freedoms on the ground of ethnic origin, sex, race, nationality, language, political and religious convictions, as well as under other conditions and circumstances of private and social nature.

Article 43

3. A citizen of Kirgizstan may be elected President of the Republic if he is not younger than 35 years of age and is not older than 65 years of age, who has command of the official language and has been a resident of the republic for not less than 15 years before the nomination of his candidature to the office of President.

3.66 KIRIBATI

12 July 1979.

Article 10

2. Every person who is charged with a criminal offence...

(b) shall be informed as soon as reasonably practicable, in detail and in a language that he understands, of the nature of the offence charged;...

(f) shall be permitted to have without payment the assistance of an interpreter if he cannot understand the language used at the trial of the charge;

Article 127

The provisions of this Constitution shall be published in a Kiribati language text as well as this English text, but in the event of any inconsistency between the two texts this English text shall prevail.

3.67 KOREA (PEOPLE'S DEMOCRATIC REPUBLIC)

27 December 1972.

Article 46

The state defends our language from the policy of the Imperialists and their stooges to destroy it and develops it to meet present-day needs.

Article 139

Judicial proceedings are conducted in the Korean language.

Foreigners may use their own language in court proceedings.

3.68 KUWAIT

16 November 1962.

Article 82

A member of the National Assembly shall...

(d) be able to read and write Arabic well.

3.69   LEBANON

1943.

Article 11
Arabic is the official national language. The cases in which French may be used shall be determined by law.

3.70   LESOTHO

1983.

Article 8
(b) a person shall be qualified to be elected as a member of the National Assembly if, and shall not be so qualified unless at the date of his nomination for election, he...
(iii) is able to speak and, unless incapacitated by blindness or other physical cause, to read and write the Lesotho language well enough to take an active part in the proceedings of the National Assembly.

3.71   LIBERIA

6 January 1986.

Article 43
The business of the Legislature shall be conducted in the English language or, when adequate preparations shall have been made, in one or more of the languages of the Republic as the Legislature may by resolution approve.

3.72   LIBYA

11 December 1969, amended 2 March 1977.

Article 2
Islam is the religion of the state and Arabic is its official language. The state protects religious freedom in accordance with established customs.

3.73   LIECHTENSTEIN

6 October 1921.

Article 6
The German language is the national and official language.

3.74 LITHUANIA

25 October 1992.

Article 14
Lithuanian shall be the state language.

Article 29
All people shall be equal before the law, the court, and other state institutions and officers.

A person may not have his rights restricted in any way, or be granted any privileges, on the basis of his or her sex, race, nationality, language, origin, social status, religion, convictions, or opinions.

Article 37
Citizens who belong to ethnic communities shall have the right to foster their language, culture, and customs.

Article 45
Ethnic communities of citizens shall independently administer the affairs of their ethnic culture, education, organisations, charity, and mutual assistance. The state shall support ethnic communities.

Article 117
... In the Republic of Lithuania, court trials shall be conducted in the state language.

Persons who do not speak Lithuanian shall be guaranteed the right to participate in investigation and court proceedings through an interpreter.

3. 75 LUXEMBOURG

1979.

Article 29
The law will determine the use of languages in administrative and judicial matters.

3.76 MACEDONIA

1991.

Article 7
The Macedonian language, written using its Cyrillic alphabet, is the official language in the Republic of Macedonia.

In the units of local self-government where the majority of the inhabitants belong to a nationality, in addition to the Macedonian language and Cyrillic script, their language and alphabet are also in official use, in a manner determined by law.

In the units of local government where there is a considerable number of inhabitants belonging to a nationality, their language and alphabet, in addition to the Macedonian language and Cyrillic script, are also in official use under conditions and in a manner determined by law.

Article 48

Members of nationalities have a right freely to express, foster and develop their identity and national attributes.

The Republic guarantees the protection of the ethnic, cultural, linguistic and religious identity of the nationalities.

Members of the nationalities have the right to establish institutions for culture and art, as well as scholarly and other associations for the expression, fostering and development of their identity.

Members of the nationalities have the right to instruction in their language in primary and secondary education, as determined by law. In schools where education is carried out in the language of a nationality, the Macedonian language is also studied.

Article 54

... The restriction of freedoms and rights cannot discriminate on grounds of sex, race, colour of skin, language, religion, national or social origin, property or social status.

3.77   MALAWI

6 July 1964, amended.

Article 23

Subject to section 24, a person shall be qualified to be elected as a member of the National Assembly if, and shall not be so qualified unless, he...

(b) is able to speak and to read the English language well enough to take an effective part in the proceedings of the Assembly;

Article 43

The proceedings of the National Assembly shall be conducted in the English language.

3.78   MALAYSIA

31 August 1957, amended 16 September 1963.

Article 16

Subject to Article 18, any person of or over the age of eighteen years who was born in the Federation before Merdeka Day is entitled, upon making application to the Federal Government, to be registered as a citizen if he satisfies the Federal Government...

(d) that he has an elementary knowledge of the Malay language.

Article 16A

Subject to Article 18, any person over the age of eighteen years who is on Malaysia Day ordinarily resident in the State of Sabah or Sarawak is entitled, upon making application to the

Federal Government before September 1971, to be registered as a citizen if he satisfies the Federal Government...

(d) except where the application is made before September 1965, and the applicant has attained the age of forty-five years at the date of the application, that he has a sufficient knowledge of the Malay language or the English language or, in the case of an applicant ordinarily resident in Sarawak, the Malay language, the English language or any native language in use in Sarawak.

Article 19

1. Subject to clause 9, the Federal Government may, upon application by any person of or over the age of twenty-one years who is not a citizen, grant a certificate of naturalisation to that person if satisfied...

(ii) (c) that he has an adequate knowledge of the Malay language.

2. Subject to clause 9, the Federal Government may, in such special circumstances as it thinks fit, upon application made by any person of or over the age of twenty-one years who is not a citizen, grant a certificate of naturalisation to that person if satisfied...

(c) that he has an adequate knowledge of the Malay language.

Article 152

1. The national language shall be the Malay language and shall be in such script as Parliament may by law provide, provided that:

(a) no person shall be prohibited or prevented from using, otherwise than for official purposes, or from teaching or learning any other language; and

(b) nothing in this clause shall prejudice the right of the Federal Government or of any State Government to preserve and sustain the use and study of the language of any other community in the Federation.

2. Notwithstanding the provisions of clause 1, for a period of ten years after Merdeka Day, and thereafter until Parliament otherwise provides, the English language may be used in both Houses of Parliament, in the Legislative Assembly of every state and for all other official purposes.

3. Notwithstanding the provisions of clause 1, for a period of ten years after Merdeka Day, and thereafter until Parliament otherwise provides, the authoritative texts:

(a) of all bills to be introduced or amended thereto to be moved in either House of Parliament, and

(b) of all acts of Parliament and all subsidiary legislation issued by the Federal Government, shall be in the English language.

4. Notwithstanding the provisions of clause 1, for a period of ten years after Merdeka Day, and thereafter until Parliament otherwise provides, all proceedings in the Federal Court or a High Court shall be in the English language:

Provided that, if the Court and counsel on both sides agree, evidence taken in the language spoken by the witness need not be translated into or recorded in English.

5. Notwithstanding the provisions of clause 1, until Parliament otherwise provides, all proceedings in subordinate courts other than the taking of evidence, shall be in the English language.

Article 161

1. No act of Parliament terminating or restricting the use of the English language for any of the purposes mentioned in clauses 2 to 5 of Article 152 shall come into operation as regards

the use of the English language in any case mentioned in clause 2 of this article until ten years after Malaysia Day.

2. Clause 1 applies:

(a) to the use of the English language in either House of Parliament by a member for or from the State of Sabah or Sarawak; and

(b) to the use of the English language for proceedings in the High Court in Borneo or in a subordinate court in the State of Sabah or Sarawak, or for such proceedings in the Federal Court as are mentioned in clause 4; and

(c) to the use of the English language in the State of Sabah or Sarawak in the Legislative Assembly or for other official purposes, including the official purposes of the Federal Government.

3. Without prejudice to clause 1, no such act of Parliament as is there mentioned shall come into operation as regards the use of the English language for proceedings in the High Court of Borneo or for such proceedings in the Federal Court as mentioned in clause 4, until the act or the relevant provision of it has been approved by enactments of the legislatures of the States of Sabah and Sarawak, and no such act shall come into operation as regards the use of the English language in the State of Sabah or Sarawak in any other case mentioned in paragraph (b) or (c) of clause 2, until the act or the relevant provision of it has been approved by an enactment of the legislature of the state.

4. The proceedings in the Federal Court referred to in clauses 2 and 3 are any proceedings on appeal from the High Court in Borneo or a judge thereof, and any proceedings under clause 2 of Article 128 for the determination of a question which has arisen in proceedings before the High Court in Borneo or a subordinate court in the State of Sabah or Sarawak.

5. Notwithstanding anything in Article 152, in the State of Sabah or Sarawak, a native language in current use in the state may be used in native courts or for any code of native law and custom, and in the case of Sarawak, until otherwise provided by enactment of the Legislature, may be used by a member addressing the Legislative Assembly or any committee thereof.

Article 161E

2. No amendment shall be made to the Constitution without the concurrence of the *Yang di-Perthua Negeri* of the State of Sabah or Sarawak or each of the States of Sabah and Sarawak concerned, if the amendment is such as to affect the operation of the Constitution as regards any of the following matters...

(d) religion in the state, the use in the state or in Parliament of any language and the special treatment of natives of the state;

3.79   MALDIVES

4 June 1964, amended.

Article 63

Compulsory qualifications for members of the Citizens' Majlis and those of the Citizens' Special Majlis...

(e) Shall be a person who can read and write Arabic, Maldivian letters and also cipher.

3.80   MALI

2 June 1974.

Article 1
   ... The Republic guarantees for all equality before the law, without any discrimination as to origin, race, language, sex, religion or belief.
   ... The official language is French.

3.81   MALTA

1961, as amended.

Article 5
   1. The national language of Malta is the Maltese language.
   2. The Maltese and the English languages and such other languages as may be prescribed by Parliament, by a law passed by not less than two-thirds of all the members of the House of Representatives, shall be the official languages of Malta and the Administration may for all official purposes use any of such languages:
   Provided that any person may address the Administration in any of the official languages and the reply of the Administration thereto shall be in such language.
   3. The language of the courts shall be the Maltese language:
   Provided that Parliament may make such provision for the use of the English language in such cases and under such conditions as it may prescribe.
   4, The House of Representatives may, in regulating its own procedure, determine the language or languages that shall be used in parliamentary proceedings and records.

Article 35
   2. Any person who is arrested or detained shall be informed, at the time of his arrest or detention, in a language that he understands, of the reasons for his arrest or detention:
   Provided that if an interpreter is necessary and is not readily available or if it is otherwise impracticable to comply with the provisions of this subsection at the time of the person's arrest or detention, such provisions shall be complied with as soon as practicable.

Article 75
   Save as otherwise provided by Parliament, every law shall be enacted in both the Maltese and English languages and, if there is any conflict between the Maltese and the English texts of any law, the Maltese text shall prevail.

3.82   MAURITANIA

12 July 1992.

Article 6
   National languages shall be Arabic, Poular, Soninké and Wolof; the official language is Arabic.

3.83   MAURITIUS

12 March 1968, as amended.

Article 5
2. Any person who is arrested or detained shall be informed as soon as reasonably practical, in a language that he understands, of the reasons for his arrest or detention...

4. Where a person is detained in pursuance of any such provision of law as is referred to in subsection (1)(k) —

(a) he shall, as soon as is reasonably practicable and, in any case not more than 7 days after the commencement of his detention, be furnished with a statement in writing in a language that he understands specifying in detail the grounds upon which he is detained;

Article 10
2. Every person who is charged with a criminal offence...

(b) shall be informed as soon as reasonably practicable, in a language that he understands and, in detail, of the nature of the offence;...

(f) shall be permitted to have without payment the assistance of an interpreter if he cannot understand the language used at the trial of the offence,...

Article 14
1. No religious denomination and no religious, social, ethnic or cultural association or group shall be prevented from establishing and maintaining schools at its own expense.

Article 15
4. Where any person whose freedom of movement has been restricted in pursuance of subsection 3(a) or (b) so requests —

(a) he shall, as soon as is reasonably practicable and in any case not more than 7 days after the making of the request, be furnished with a statement in writing in a language that he understands, specifying the grounds for the imposition of the restriction;

Article 33
Subject to section 34, a person shall be qualified to be elected as a member of the Assembly if, and shall not be so qualified unless, he...

(d) is able to speak and, unless incapacitated by blindness or other physical cause, to read the English language with a degree of proficiency sufficient to enable him to take an active part in the proceedings of the Assembly.

Article 49
The official language of the Assembly shall be English but any member may address the chair in French.

3.84   MEXICO

1917, amended January 1992.

Article 4

The Mexican nation has a multicultural composition originally based on its indigenous peoples. The law will protect and promote the development of their languages, cultures, usages, customs, resources, and specific forms of social organisation. It will guarantee to members of indigenous peoples effective access to the state's legal system. When indigenous peoples are parties involved in decisions and proceedings relating to agricultural matters, account will be taken of their practices and customs of a legal nature according to the terms established by law.

3.85   MOLDOVA

1992 Draft.

Article 4

2. All citizens of the Republic of Moldova are equal before the Law regardless of their origin, social and patrimonial status, race and nationality, sex, education, language, religion, occupation, place of residence or other circumstances.

Article 11

2. The state recognises and guarantees to persons of other ethnic origin the right to preserve, develop and express their ethnic identity as well as their cultural, linguistic and religious identities.

Article 14

1. The state official language of the Republic of Moldova is the Romanian language.
2. The use of languages on the territory of the Republic of Moldova is regulated by a common law.

Article 39

2. Education is carried out in the Romanian language. Education of the citizens of the Republic of Moldova in other languages is determined by law.

Article 76

2. Candidates to the post of the President of the Republic of Moldova can be the citizens of the Republic who have attained the age of 35 years and have been residents of the country for at least 10 years and who speak the state language. The law will determine the procedure for nomination of the candidates.

Article 113

1. The judicial processes are carried out in the Romanian language.
2. Persons of other ethnic origin as well as persons who don't understand or speak the Romanian language have the right to use an interpreter in order to make themselves familiar with all the instruments and proceedings of their dossier as well as to speak or make a conclusion.

3.86   MONACO

17 December 1972.

Article 8
The French language is the official language of the state.

3.87   MONGOLIA

6 July 1960.

Article 69
Court proceedings are conducted in the Mongolian language; persons not knowing that language are guaranteed the right to acquaint themselves fully with the material of the case through an interpreter and likewise the right to use their own language in court.

Article 83
... Any direct or indirect restriction of the rights of citizens on account of their nationality or race and the advocacy of the ideas of chauvinism or nationalism are forbidden by law. The Mongolian People's Republic ensures representatives of all nationalities living on the territory of the Republic the opportunity to develop their national culture and to receive tuition and conduct business in their native language.

3.88   MOZAMBIQUE (FUMO)

25 June 1975, amended.

Article 8
All citizens are equal before the law and no one shall be privileged or disabled because of social condition, ancestry, birth, sex, race, language, origin, religion or religious convictions.

3.89   NAMIBIA

20 March 1990.

Article 3
1. The official language of Namibia is English.

2. No provision of this Constitution shall prohibit use of any other language as medium of instruction in private schools or in schools financed or supported by the state, providing conditions that may be required by law in order to ensure knowledge of the official language or for educational reasons are respected.

3. No part of paragraph 1 above will supersede an act of Parliament permitting the use of any language other than English for legislative, administrative or judicial affairs, in regions or areas where this other language is spoken by a substantial segment of the population.

Article 8
Every person has a right to enjoy, practice, profess, maintain and promote any culture, language, tradition or religion subject to the terms of this Constitution, and further subject to the condition that the rights protected by this article do not impinge upon the rights of others or the national interest.

3.90   NAURU

29 January 1968.

Article 10
3. A person charged with an offence...
(b) shall be informed promptly in a language that he understands and in detail of the nature of the offence with which he is charged;...
(d) shall be permitted to have without payment the assistance of an interpreter if he cannot understand or speak the language used at the trial of the charge;

3.91   NEPAL

16 December 1962.

Article 4
The national language of Nepal is the Nepali language in the Devanagari script.

Article 8
2. Laws to be made in pursuance of clause 1 shall, *inter alia*, stipulate that a foreigner may qualify for the acquisition of citizenship if:
(a) he can read and write in the national language of Nepal;

3.92   NICARAGUA

January 1987.

Article 11
Spanish is the official language of the state. The languages of the communities on the Atlantic Coast of Nicaragua will also be official in the cases determined by law.

Article 27
All persons are equal before the law and have the right to equal protection. There shall be no discrimination for reasons of birth, nationality, political belief, race, sex, language, opinions, origins, economic position or any other social condition.

Article 33
2. Any person detained has the right:

(a) to be informed without delay, in a language he understands and in detail of the reasons for his detention and of the offence with which he is charged;

Article 90
The Atlantic Coast communities have the right to the freedom of expression and to preserve their languages, art and culture. The development of their culture and values enriches the national culture. The state will set up special programmes for the exercise of these rights.

Article 91
The state has the obligation of adopting laws that will ensure no Nicaraguan will be the victim of discrimination because of his language, culture or origin.

Article 121
Access to education is free and equal for all Nicaraguans. Basic education is free and mandatory. Atlantic Coast communities will have in their region access to education in their mother tongue up to the levels determined by national plans and programmes.

Article 128
The state protects the archaeological, historical, linguistic, cultural and artistic heritage of the nation.

Article 180
The communities of the Atlantic Coast have the right to live and develop according to the forms of social organisation that correspond to their historical and cultural traditions.
... The state also guaranties the preservation of their cultures and languages, religions and customs.

Article 197
This Constitution shall be widely distributed in the official language of the country; it will also be distributed in the languages of the Atlantic Coast communities.

3.93   NIGER

8 November 1960.

Article 1
The official language shall be French.

3.94   NIGERIA

1 October 1979, amended.

Article 5
3. Every person who is arrested or detained shall be informed in writing within 24 hours, and in a language that he understands, of the facts and grounds for his arrest or detention

Article 6

Every person who is charged with a criminal offence shall be entitled:

(a) to be informed promptly in the language that he understands and in detail of the nature of the offence;...

(f) to have without payment the assistance of an interpreter if he cannot understand the language used at the trial of the offence.

Article 19

4. Government shall promote the learning of indigenous languages.

Article 53

The business of the National Assembly shall be conducted in English, and in Hausa, Ibo and Yoruba when adequate arrangements have been made therefore.

Article 95

The business of a House of Assembly shall be conducted in English, but the House may in addition to English conduct the business of the House in one or more other languages spoken in the state as the House may by resolution approve.

3.95 NORTHERN CYPRUS (TURKISH REPUBLIC OF NORTHERN CYPRUS)

1983.

Article 2

2. The official language is Turkish.

Article 16

5. Every person arrested or detained shall be informed at the time of his arrest or detention in a language which he understands of the reasons for his arrest or detention, and shall be allowed to have the services of a lawyer of his own choosing or chosen by his relatives.

Article 17

4. Every person has the right...

(d) to have the free assistance of an interpreter if he cannot understand or speak the language used in court.

Article 18

5. Every person charged with an offence has the following minimum rights:

(a) to be informed in a language which he understands of the nature and grounds of the charge preferred against him;...

(d) to have the free assistance of an interpreter if he cannot understand or speak the language used in court.

3.96   NORWAY

17 May 1814, amended.

Article 92
Only Norwegian citizens, men and women, who speak the language of the country, shall be appointed to official posts of the state,...

Article 110A
The state authorities have a duty to create conditions in order to make the Sami population able to secure and develop its language, culture and social life.

3.97   PAKISTAN

10 April 1973.

Article 28
Subject to Article 251, any section of citizens having a distinct language, script or culture shall have the right to preserve and promote the same and, subject to law, establish institutions for that purpose.

Article 251
1. The national language of Pakistan is Urdu, and arrangements shall be made for its being used for official and other purposes within fifteen years from the commencing day.
2. Subject to clause 1, the English language may be used for official purposes until arrangements are made for its replacement by Urdu.
3. Without prejudice to the status of the national language, a provincial assembly may by law prescribe measures for the teaching, promotion and use of a provincial language in addition to the national language.

Article 255
1. An oath required to be made by a person under the Constitution shall be made in a language that is understood by that person.

3.98   PANAMA

11 October 1972. Modified April 1983.

Article 7
El espanol es el idioma oficial de la Republica.

Article 10
Pueden solicitar la nacionalidad panamena por naturalizacion:
1. Los extranjeros con conco anos consecutivos de residencia en el territorio de la Republica si, despues de haber alcamzado su mayoria de edad, declaran su volontad de naturalizarse, renuncian expresamente a su nacionalidad de origen o a la que tengan y comprueban que

poseen el idioma espanol y conocimientos basicos de geografia, histoira y organizacion politica panamenas.

Article 78
El Estado velara por la defensa, difusion y pureza del idioma espanol.

Article 84
Las lenguas aborigenes seran objeto de especial estudio, conservacion y divulgacion y el Estado promovera programas de alfabetizacion bilingue en las comunidades indigenas.

Article 86
El Estado reconoce y respeta la identidad etnica de las comunidades indigenas nacionales, realizara programas tendientes a desarrollar los valores materiales, sociales y espirituales propios de cada una de sus culturas y creara una institucion para el estudio, conservacion, divulgacion de las mismas y de sus lenguas, asi como para la promocion del desarrollo integral de dichos grupos humanos.

Article 96
La educacion se impartira en el idioma oficial, pero por motivos de interes publico la Ley podra permitir que en algunos planteles esta se imparta tambien en idioma extranjero.

3.99   PAPUA NEW GUINEA

16 September 1975.

Article 37
4. A person charged with an offence...

(b) shall be informed promptly in a language which he understands, and in detail, of the nature of the offence with which he is charged; and...

(d) shall be permitted to have without payment the assistance of an interpreter if he cannot understand or speak the language used at the trial of the charge;

Article 67
2. To be eligible for naturalisation, a person must...

(c) unless prevented by physical or mental disability, speak and understand Pisin or Hiri Motu, or a vernacular of the country, sufficiently for normal conversational purposes;

Article 68
2. Without limiting the matters that may be taken into account in deciding on the application for naturalisation, under Section 67, the following matters shall be taken into account in deciding on an application that is made during the first eight years after Independence Day...

(h) the applicant's knowledge of Pisin or Hiri Motu or of a vernacular of the country;

3.100   PARAGUAY

20 June 1992.

Article 12
Nadie sera detenido ni arrestado sin orden escrita de autoridad competente, salvo caso de ser sorprendido en flagrante comision de delito que mereciese pena corporal. Toda persona detenida tiene derecho a:
(4) que disponga de un interprete, si fuese necesario...

Article 77
La ensenanza de los comienzos del proceso escolar se realizara en la lengua oficial materna del educando. Se instruira asimismo en el conocimiento y en el empleo de ambos idiomas oficiales de la Republica.

En el caso de las minorias etnicas cuya lengua materna no sea el guarani, se podra elegir uno de los dos idiomas oficiales.

Article 140
El Paraguay es un pais pluricultural y bilingue.

Son idiomas oficiales el castellano y el guarani. La Ley establecera las modalidades de utilizacion de uno y otro.

Las lenguas indigenas, asi como las de otras minorias, forman parte del patrimonio cultural de la Nacion.

3.101   PERU

28 July 1980.

Article 2
Every person has the right...
2. to equality before the law, without any discrimination by virtue of sex, race, religion, opinion, or language.

Article 35
The state promotes the study and knowledge of indigenous languages. It guarantees the right of the Quechua, Aymara, and other native communities to also receive primary education in their own dialect or language.

Article 83
Spanish is the official language of the Republic. Quechua and Aymara are also in official use in the areas and form provided by law. The other indigenous languages also make up the nation's cultural heritage.

3.102 PHILIPPINES

2 February 1987.

Article 14
6. The national language of the Philippines is Filipino. As it evolves, it shall be further developed and enriched on the basis of existing Philippine and other languages.

Subject to provisions of law and as the Congress may deem appropriate, the Government shall take steps to initiate and sustain the use of Filipino as a medium of official communication and as language of instruction in the educational system.

7. For the purposes of communication and instruction, the official languages of the Philippines are Filipino and, unless otherwise provided by law, English.

The regional languages are the auxiliary official languages in the regions and shall serve as auxiliary media of instruction therein.

Spanish and Arabic shall be promoted on a voluntary and optional basis.

8. This Constitution shall be promulgated in Filipino and English and shall be translated into major regional languages, Arabic and Spanish.

9. The Congress shall establish a national language commission composed of representatives of various regions and disciplines which shall undertake, coordinate, and promote researches for the development, propagation, and preservation of Filipino and other languages.

3.103 PORTUGAL

26 April 1976, amended.

Article 13
2. No one may be privileged, benefited, damaged, deprived of any right or exempt from any responsibility by virtue of influence, sex, race, language, territory of origin, religion, political or ideological convictions, education, economic or social status.

Article 74
3. In the implementation of an educational policy, the state is obliged...
(h) to provide instruction in the Portuguese language and access to Portuguese culture to the children of immigrants.

3.104 QATAR

2 April 1970.

Article 1
Qatar is an independent sovereign Arab state and a member of the Union of Arab Emirates. Its religion is Islam, and Islamic Shari'ah law shall be a fundamental source of its legislation. Its regime is democratic and its official language is Arabic.

Appendix

3.105   ROMANIA

21 November 1991.

Article 4
2. Romania is the common and indivisible homeland of all its citizens, without any discrimination on account of race, nationality, ethnic origin, language, religion, sex, opinion, political adherence, property or social origin.

Article 6
1. The state recognises and guarantees the right of persons belonging to national minorities, to the preservation, development and expression of their ethnic, cultural, linguistic and religious identity.

2. The protecting measures taken by the Romanian state for the preservation, development and expression of the persons belonging to national minorities shall conform to the principles of equality and non-discrimination in relation to the other Romanian citizens.

Article 7
The state shall support the strengthening of links with the Romanians living abroad and shall act accordingly for the preservation, development and expression of their ethnic, cultural, linguistic and religious identity, under observance of the legislation of the state of which they are citizens.

Article 13
In Romania, the official language is Romanian.

Article 23
5. Any person detained or arrested shall be promptly informed, in a language he understands, of the grounds for his detention or arrest, and notified of the charges against him, as soon as practicable; the notification of the charges shall be made only in the presence of a lawyer of his own choosing or appointed *ex officio*.

Article 32
2. Education of all grades shall be in Romanian. Education may also be conducted in a foreign language of international use, under the terms laid down by law.
3.   The right of persons belonging to national minorities to learn their mother tongue, and their right to be educated in this language are guaranteed; the ways to exercise these rights shall be regulated by law.

Article 59
2. Organisations of citizens belonging to national minorities, which fail to obtain the number of votes for representation in Parliament, have the right to one Deputy seat each, under the terms of the electoral law. Citizens of a national minority are entitled to be represented by one organisation only.

Article 127
1. Procedure shall be conducted in Romanian.

2. Citizens belonging to national minorities, as well as persons who cannot understand or speak Romanian have the right to take cognisance of all acts and files of the case, to speak before the Court and formulate conclusions, through an interpreter; in criminal trials, this right shall be ensured free of charge.

Article 148
1. The provisions of this Constitution with regard to the national, independent, unitary and indivisible character of the Romanian state, the Republican form of government, territorial integrity, independence of the judiciary, political pluralism and official language shall not be subject to revision.

3.106   RUSSIA

12 December 1993.

Article 19
2. The state shall guarantee the equality of rights and liberties regardless of sex, race, nationality, language, origin, property or employment status, residence, attitude to religion, convictions, membership of public associations or any other circumstance. Any restrictions of the rights of citizens on social, racial, national, linguistic, or religious grounds shall be prohibited.

Article 26
2. Everyone shall have the right to use his native language and to freely choose the language of communication, education, training and creative work.

Article 29
2. Propaganda or inciting social, racial, national, or religious hatred and strife is impermissible. The propaganda of social, racial, national, religious, or linguistic supremacy is forbidden.

Article 68
1. The state language of the Russian Federation throughout its territory shall be the Russian language.
2. The republics shall have the right to institute their own state languages. They shall be used alongside the state language of the Russian Federation in bodies of state power, bodies of local self-government and state institutions of the republics.
3. The Russian Federation shall guarantee all its peoples the right to preserve their native language and to create the conditions for its study and development.

Article 69
The Russian Federation guarantees the rights of numerically small indigenous peoples in accordance with the generally recognised principles and norms of international law and the international treaties of the Russian Federation.

3.107   RWANDA

17 December 1978.

Article 4
The national language is Kinyarwanda.
The official languages are Kinyarwanda and French.

3.108   SAINT LUCIA

22 February 1979.

Article 25
Subject to the provisions of section 26 of this Constitution, a person shall be qualified to be appointed as a Senator if, and shall not be so qualified unless, he...

(c) is able to speak and, unless incapacitated by blindness or other physical cause, to read the English language with sufficient proficiency to enable him to take an active part in the proceedings of the Senate.

Article 31
Subject to the provisions of section 32 of this Constitution, a person shall be qualified to be elected as a member of the House if, and shall not be so qualified unless, he...
(c) is able to speak and, unless incapacitated by blindness or other physical cause, to read the English language with a degree of proficiency sufficient to enable him to take an active part in the proceedings of the House.

3.109   SAINT KITTS AND NEVIS

19 September 1983.

Article 5
2. A person arrested or detained shall be informed within a reasonable delay, and in any event no later than forty-eight hours after his arrest and detention, in a language he understands and in detail, of the reasons for his arrest and detention; reasonable measures will be undertaken to permit him to communicate, in private, with a lawyer of his choice and, in the case of a person aged under eighteen years, with his parents or tutor.

Article 10
2. A person charged with a criminal offence...
(b) will be informed as soon as is reasonable to do so, in a language he understands and in detail, of the nature of the offence with which he is charged;...
(f) shall be permitted to have without payment the assistance of an interpreter if he cannot understand or speak the language used at his trial.

Article 17
1. Notwithstanding Article 5 but in conformity with Article 16, the following provisions will apply when a person is detained under emergency measures:
(a) the person shall be informed within a reasonable delay, and in any event no later than seven days after the start of his detention, in a language he understands and in detail, of the reasons for his detention; he will be given a written declaration in English explaining in detail these reasons.

3.110 SAINT VINCENT AND THE GRENADINES

27 October 1979.

Article 25
1. Subject to the provisions of section 26 of this Constitution, a person shall be qualified to be elected as a representative if, and shall not be so qualified unless, he...
(c) is able to speak and, unless incapacitated by blindness or other physical cause, to read the English language with a degree of proficiency sufficient to enable him to take an active part in the proceedings of the House.

3.111 SENEGAL

3 March 1963, amended.

Article 1
... The official language of the Republic of Senegal is French. The national languages are Diola, Malinké, Poular, Sérère, Soninké and Wolof.

Article 3
Political parties shall contribute to the expression of suffrage. They shall be required to respect the Constitution and thus the principles of national sovereignty and democracy. They are prevented from identifying themselves by race, ethnicity, sex, religion, sect, language or region.

3.112 SEYCHELLES

5 June 1979.

Article 4
The official languages of Seychelles are English, French and Creole, but the President may, by regulations made under this section, prescribe the occasions when one, or more than one, of these languages shall be used and, if he does so, the other languages or language shall not be used on the prescribed occasions.

3.113   SIERRA LEONE

14 June 1978.

Article 7
2. Any person who is arrested or detained shall be informed as soon as reasonably practicable, in a language which he understands, of the reasons for his arrest or detention.

Article 13
5. Every person who is charged with a criminal offence:
(a) shall be informed as soon as reasonably practicable, in the language which he understands and in detail, of the nature of the offence charged;...
(e) shall be permitted to have without payment the assistance of an interpreter if he cannot understand the language used at the trial of the charge;

Article 44
Subject to the provisions of section 45 any person who...
(e) is able to speak and to read the English language with a degree of proficiency sufficient to enable him to take an active part in the proceedings of Parliament,
shall be qualified for election or appointment as such a member of Parliament...

Article 61
The business of Parliament shall be conducted in the English language.

3.114   SINGAPORE

3 June 1958, amended.

Article 44
2. A person shall be qualified to be elected as a member of Parliament, if:
(e) he is able, with a degree of proficiency sufficient to enable him to take an active part in the proceedings of Parliament, to speak and, unless incapacitated by blindness or other physical cause, to read and write at least one of the following languages, that is to say English, Malay, Mandarin and Tamil;

Article 53
Until the Legislature otherwise provides, all debates and discussions in Parliament shall be conducted in Malay, English, Mandarin or Tamil.

Article 127
1. Subject to clause 4, the government may, upon application made by any person of, or over the age of, twenty-one years who is not a citizen of Singapore, grant a certificate of naturalisation to that person if the government is satisfied...
(c) that he has an adequate knowledge of the national language.

Article 152

2. The government shall exercise its functions in such manner as to recognise the special position of the Malays, who are the indigenous people of Singapore, and accordingly it shall be the responsibility of the Government to protect, safeguard, support, foster and promote their political, educational, religious, economic, social and cultural interests in the Malay language.

3.115   SLOVAKIA

3 September 1991.

Article 6

1. Slovak is the official language of the Slovak Republic.
2. The use of languages other than the official language in official communications shall be determined by law.

Article 12

2. Fundamental rights shall be guaranteed in the Slovak Republic to every person regardless of sex, race, colour, language, faith, religion, political affiliation or conviction, national or social origin, nationality or ethnic origin, property, birth or any other status, and no person shall be denied their legal rights, discriminated or favoured on any of these grounds.

Article 26

5. Government authorities and public administration shall be obligated to provide reasonable access to the information in the official language of their work. The terms and procedures of execution thereof shall be specified by law.

Article 33

Membership in national minority or ethnic group may not be used to the detriment of any individual.

Article 34

1. Citizens of national minorities or ethnic groups in the Slovak Republic shall be guaranteed their full development, particularly the rights to promote their cultural heritage with other citizens of the same national minority or ethnic group, receive and disseminate information in their mother tongue, form associations, and create and maintain educational and cultural institutions. Details thereof will be determined by law.
2. In addition to the right to learn the official language, the citizens of national minorities or ethnic groups shall, under conditions defined by law, also be guaranteed:
   (a) the right to be educated in a minority language,
   (b) the right to use a minority language in official communications,
   (c) the right to participate in decision-making in matters affecting the national minorities and ethnic groups.

Article 47

2. Every person shall have the right to counsel from the outset of proceedings before any court of law, or a governmental or public authority as provided by law...

4. A person who claims not to know the language used un the proceedings under section 2 of this Article shall have the right to an interpreter.

3.116 SLOVENIA

1991. Reprinted from *Butlletí del Centre "Mercator Dret i Legislació Lingüístics"*, No. 8, September 1993.

Article 11
The Slovene language shall be the official language in Slovenia. In the communes with Italian or Hungarian populations, the Italian or Hungarian language shall also be the official language.

Article 61
Everyone has the right to freely express his belonging to his nation or nationality, to develop and express his culture and to use his language and alphabet.

Article 62
Everyone has the right, in the exercise of the rights and duties as well as in proceedings before state organs and public authorities, to use his own language and alphabet, in the manner determined by law.

Article 64
The autochthonous Italian and Hungarian ethnic communities and their members are entitled freely to use their ethnic symbols in order to preserve their ethnic identity, they are entitled to establish organisations, develop economic, cultural, scientific and research activities, and activities in the fields of mass media and publishing. Further they are entitled, as determined by law, to education in their language or to bilingual education. Regions where bilingual schools are compulsory shall be determined by law. The two ethnic communities and their members are entitled to cultivate the relations with their two parent nations and their respective states. The state shall support the implementation of the aforementioned rights financially and morally.

In order to exercise their rights, the members of the two ethnic communities will establish their own self-managing community councils in the regions where the two ethnic communities live. On their proposal, the state shall authorise such self-managing community councils to perform specific functions which are now within the competence of the state, and provide for funds required for the implementation of such functions.

The two ethnic communities are directly represented in the representative bodies of local self-management and in the State Assembly.

The status, and the mode of exercising of the rights, of the Italian and Hungarian ethnic communities in the regions where they live, the obligations of the self-managing local community councils regarding the implementation of the foregoing rights, and those rights which are exercised by the members of these ethnic communities also beyond the above mentioned regions shall be regulated by law. The rights of the two ethnic communities and their members are guaranteed regardless of the number of members of the two communities.

Laws, other regulations, and general acts relating exclusively to the implementation of the constitutional rights and status of the two ethnic communities, may not be adopted without consent of the representatives of the ethnic communities.

Article 80
The State Assembly is composed of representatives of Slovenia's citizens and counts 90 representatives.
The Italian and Hungarian national community shall each have one representative elected to the State Assembly.

3.117   SOLOMON ISLANDS

7 July 1978.

Article 10
2. Every person who is charged with a criminal offence...
(b) shall be informed as soon as reasonably practicable, in detail and in a language that he understands, of the nature of the offence charged;...
(f) shall be permitted to have without payment the assistance of an interpreter if he cannot understand the language used at the trial of the charge;

Article 20
4. The information required to be contained in an application for the purposes of this section is as follows...
(f) a declaration by the applicant of his allegiance to Solomon Islands and his respect for the culture, the language and the way of life of Solomon Islands;

3.118   SOMALIA

23 September 1979.

Article 3
2. Somali is the language which all Somalis speak and through which they recognise each other; Arabic is the language which links the Somali people with the Arab nation, of whom they are an integral part, and the two languages shall constitute the official languages of the Somali Democratic Republic.

Article 6
All citizens regardless of sex, religion, origin and language shall be entitled to equal rights and duties before the law.

3.119   SOUTH AFRICA

28 January 1994.

Article 3
1. Afrikaans, English, isiNdebele, Sesotho sa Leboa, Sesotho, siSwati, Xitsonga, Setswana, Tshivenda, isiXhosa and isiZulu shall be the official South African languages at national level,

and conditions shall be created for their development and for the promotion of their equal use and enjoyment.

2. Rights relating to language and the status of languages existing at the commencement of this Constitution shall not be diminished, and provision shall be made by an Act of Parliament for rights relating to language and the status of languages existing only at regional level, to be extended nationally in accordance with the principles set out in subsection 9.

3. Whenever practicable, a person shall have the right to use and to be addressed in his or her dealings with any public administration at the national level of government in any official South African language of his or her choice.

4. Regional differentiation in relation to language policy and practice shall be permissible.

5. A provincial legislature may, by a resolution adopted by a majority of at least two-thirds of all its members, declare any language referred to in subsection 1 to be an official language for the whole or any part of the province and for any or all powers and functions within the competence of that legislature, save that neither the rights relating to language nor the status of an official language as existing in any area or in relation to any function at the time of the commencement of this Constitution, shall be diminished.

6. Wherever practicable, a person shall have the right to use and to be addressed in his or her dealings with any public administration at the provincial level of government in any one of the official languages of his or her choice as contemplated in subsection 5.

7. A member of Parliament may address Parliament in the official South African language of his or her choice.

8. Parliament and any provincial legislature may, subject to this section, make provision by legislation for the use of official languages for the purposes of the functioning of government, taking into account questions of usage, practicality and expense.

9. Legislation, as well as official policy and practice, in relation to the use of languages at any level of government shall be subject to and based on the provisions of this section and the following principles:

(a) The creation of conditions for the development and for the promotion of the equal use and enjoyment of all official South African languages;

(b) the extension of those rights relating to language and the status of languages which at the commencement of this Constitution are restricted to certain regions;

(c) the prevention of the use of any language for the purposes of exploitation, domination or division;

(d) the promotion of multilingualism and the provision of translation facilities;

(e) the fostering of respect for languages spoken in the Republic other than the official languages, and the encouragement of their use in appropriate circumstances; and

(f) the non-diminution of rights relating to language and the status of languages existing at the commencement of this Constitution.

10. (a) Provision shall be made by an Act of Parliament for the establishment by the Senate of an independent Pan South African Language Board to promote respect for the principles referred to in subsection 9 and to further the development of the official South African languages.

(b) The Pan South African Language Board shall be consulted, and be given the opportunity to make recommendations, in relation to any proposed legislation contemplated in this section.

(c) The Pan South African Language Board shall be responsible for promoting respect for and the development of German, Greek, Gujerati, Hindi, Portuguese, Tamil, Telegu, Urdu and other languages used by communities in South Africa, as well as Arabic, Hebrew and Sanskrit and other languages used for religious purposes.

Article 8
1. Every person shall have the right to equality before the law and to equal protection of the law.

2. No person shall be unfairly discriminated against, directly or indirectly, and, without derogating from the generality of this provision, on one or more of the following grounds in particular: race, gender, sex, ethnic or social origin, colour, sexual orientation, age, disability, religion, conscience, belief, culture or language...

4. *Prima facie* proof of discrimination on any of the grounds specified in subsection 2 shall be presumed to be sufficient proof of unfair discrimination as contemplated in that subsection, until the contrary is established.

Article 25
1. Every person who is detained, including every sentenced prisoner, shall have the right:
(a) to be informed promptly in a language which he understands of the reason for his or her detention;...

2. Every person arrested for the alleged commission of an offence shall, in addition to the rights which he or she has as a detained person, have the right:
(a) promptly to be informed, in a language which he or she understands, that he or she has the right to remain silent and to be warned of the consequences of making any statement;...

3. Every accused person shall have the right to a fair trial, which shall include the right:...
(i) to be tried in a language which he or she understands or, failing this, to have the proceedings interpreted to him or her;

Article 31
Every person shall have the right to use the language and to participate in the cultural life of his or her choice.

Article 32
Every person shall have the right:
(a) to basic education and to equal access to educational institutions;
(b) to instruction in the language of his or her choice where this is reasonably practicable; and
(c) to establish, where practicable, educational institutions based on a common culture, language or religion, provided that there shall be no discrimination on the ground of race.

Article 107
1. A party to litigation, an accused person and a witness may, during the proceedings of a court, use the South African language of his or her choice, and may require such proceedings of a court in which he or she is involved to be interpreted in a language understood by him or her.

2. The record of the proceedings of a court shall, subject to section 3, be kept in any official language: Provided that the relevant rights relating to language and the status of languages in this regard existing at the commencement of this Constitution shall not be diminished.

Article 141
1. A law of a provincial legislature referred to in section 140(2) shall be enrolled of record in the office of the Registrar of the Appellate Division of the Supreme Court in such official South African languages as may be required in terms of section 3, and copies of the law so enrolled shall be conclusive evidence of the provisions of such law.

Article 164
3. In carrying out its functions the Commission [on Provincial Government] shall, *inter alia*, take into consideration...
(k) cultural and language realities.

Article 232
1. Unless it is inconsistent with the context or clearly inappropriate, a reference in a law referred to in section 229...
(d) to an official language or to both official languages, shall be construed, with due regard to section 3, as a reference to any of the official South African languages under this Constitution.

3.120 SPAIN

29 December 1978.

Article 3
1. Castilian is the official Spanish language of the state. All Spaniards have the duty to know it and the right to use it.
2. The other languages of Spain will also be official in the respective autonomous communities, in accordance with their statutes.
3. The richness of the linguistic modalities of Spain is a cultural patrimony which will be the object of special respect and protection.

Article 148
1. The Autonomous Communities may assume jurisdiction in the following matters...
(17) assistance to culture, research and, as the case may be, for the teaching of the language of the Autonomous Community;

3.121 SRI LANKA

31 August 1978.

Article 12
2. No citizen shall be discriminated against on the grounds of race, religion, language, caste, sex, political opinion, place of birth or any one of such grounds:
Provided that it shall be lawful to require a person to acquire within a reasonable time sufficient knowledge of any language as a qualification for any employment or office in the public, judicial or local government service, or in the service of any public corporation, where such knowledge is reasonably necessary for the discharge of the duties of such employment or office:
Provided further that it shall be lawful to require a person to have a sufficient knowledge of any language as a qualification for any such employment of office where no function of that employment or office can be discharged otherwise than with a knowledge of that language.
3. No person shall, on the grounds of race, religion, language, caste, sex or any one of such grounds, be subject to any disability, liability, restriction or conditions with regard to access to

shops, public restaurants, hotels, places of public entertainment and places of public worship of his own religion.

Article 14
1. Every citizen is entitled to...
(f) the freedom by himself or in association with others to enjoy and promote his own culture and to use his own language;

Article 18
1. The official language of Sri Lanka shall be Sinhala.
2. Tamil shall also be an official language.
3. English shall be the link language.

Article 19
The national languages of Sri Lanka shall be Sinhala and Tamil.

Article 20
A member of Parliament or a member of a local authority shall be entitled to perform his duties and discharge his functions in Parliament or in such local authority in either of the national languages.

Article 21
1. A person shall be entitled to be educated through the medium of either of the national languages:
Provided that the provisions of this paragraph shall not apply to an institution of higher education where the medium of instruction is a language other than a national language.
2. Where one national language is a medium of instruction for or in any course, department or faculty of any university directly or indirectly financed by the state, the other national language shall also be made a medium of instruction for or in such course, department or faculty for students who prior to their admission to such university, were educated through the medium of such other national language:
Provided that compliance with the proceeding provisions of this paragraph shall not be obligatory if such other national language is the medium of instruction for or in any like course, department or faculty either at any other campus or branch of such university or any other like university.

Article 22
1. The official languages shall be the language of administration throughout Sri Lanka:
Provided that the Tamil language shall also be used as the language of administration for the maintenance of public records and the transaction of all business by public institutions in the Northern and Eastern Provinces.
2. A person, other than an official acting in his official capacity, shall be entitled:
(a) to receive communications from, and to communicate and transact business with, any official in his official capacity, in either of the national languages;
(b) if the law recognises his right to inspect or to obtain copies of or extracts from any official register, record, publication or other document, to obtain a copy of or an extract from such register, record, publication or other document or a translation thereof, as the case may be, in either of the national languages; and

(c) where a document is executed by any official for the purpose of being issued to him, to obtain such document or a translation thereof, in either of the national languages.

3. A local authority in the Northern and Eastern Provinces which conducts its business in either of the national languages shall be entitled to receive communications from, and to communicate and transact business with, any official in his official capacity, in such national language.

4. All orders, proclamations, rules, bylaws, regulations and notifications made or issued under any written law, the Gazette and all other official documents including circulars and forms issued or used by any public institution or local authority, shall be published in both national languages.

5. A person shall be entitled to be examined through the medium of either of the national languages at any examination for the admission of persons to the public service, judicial service, local government service, a public corporation or statutory institution, subject to the condition that he may be required to acquire a sufficient knowledge of the official language within a reasonable time after admission to any such service, public corporation or statutory institution where such knowledge is reasonably necessary for the discharge of his duties:

Provided that a person may be required to have a sufficient knowledge of the official language as a condition for admission to any such service, public corporation or statutory institution where no function of the office or employment for which he is recruited can be discharged otherwise than with a sufficient knowledge of the official language.

Article 23

1. All laws and subordinate legislation shall be enacted or made, and published, in both national languages together with a translation in the English language. In the event of any inconsistency between any two texts, the text in the official language shall prevail.

2. All laws and subordinate legislation in force immediately prior to the commencement of the Constitution, shall be published in the Gazette in both national languages as expeditiously as possible.

3. The law published in Sinhala under the provisions of paragraph 2 of this article shall, as from the date of such publication, be deemed to be the law and supersede the corresponding law in English.

Article 24

1. The official language shall be the language of the courts throughout Sri Lanka and accordingly their records and proceedings shall be in the official language:

Provided that the language of the courts exercising original jurisdiction in the Northern and Eastern Provinces shall also be Tamil and their records and proceedings shall be in the Tamil language. In the event of an appeal from any such court, records in both national languages shall be prepared for the use of the court hearing such appeal:

Provided further that:

(a) the Minister in charge of the subject of Justice may, with the concurrence of the Cabinet of Ministers, direct that the record of any such court shall also be maintained and proceedings conducted in the official language; and

(b) the record of any particular proceeding in such court shall also be maintained in the official language if so required by the judge of such court, or by any party or applicant or any person legally entitled to represent such party or applicant in such proceedings, where such judge, party, applicant or person is not conversant with the Tamil language.

2. Any party or applicant or any person legally entitled to represent such party or applicant may initiate proceedings, and submit to court pleadings and other documents, and participate in the proceedings in court, in either of the national languages.

3. Any judge, juror, party or applicant or any person legally entitled to represent such party or applicant, who is not conversant with the language used in a court, shall be entitled to interpretation and to translation into the appropriate national language, provided by the state, to enable him to understand and participate in the proceedings before such court, and shall also be entitled to obtain in either of the national languages any such part of the record or a translation thereof, as the case may be, as he may be entitled to obtain according to law.

4. The Minister in charge of the subject of Justice may, with the concurrence of the Cabinet of Ministers, issue directions permitting the use of a language other than a national language in or in relation to the records and proceedings in any court for all purposes or for such purposes as may be specified therein. Every judge shall be bound to implement such direction.

Article 25
The state shall provide adequate facilities for the use of the languages provided for in this chapter.

Article 28
1. All laws and subordinate legislation shall be enacted or made and published in both national languages together with a translation in the English language. In the event of any inconsistency between any two texts, the text in the official language shall prevail.

2. All laws and subordinate legislation in force immediately prior to the commencement of the Constitution, shall be published in the Gazette in both national languages as expeditiously as possible.

3. The law published in Sinhala under the provisions of paragraph 2 of this article shall, as from the date of such publication, be deemed to be the law and supersede the corresponding law in English.

3.122 SUDAN

12 April 1973.

Article 10
The Arabic language shall be the official language of the Democratic Republic of Sudan.

Article 38
All persons in the Democratic Republic of Sudan are equal before courts of law. The Sudanese have equal rights and duties, irrespective of origin, race, locality, sex, language or religion.

Article 139
The deliberations of the People's Assembly, business of its committees and its correspondence shall be conducted in Arabic. Nevertheless, any language other than Arabic may be used with the permission of the Speaker or Chairman of Committees.

3.123   SURINAME

1982, amended.

Article 2
2. No one may be discriminated because of his birth, sex, race, language, religion, origin, education, economic position or social condition or any other status.

3.124   SWEDEN

1 January 1975.

Article 8
In the exercise of their functions the courts and administrative authorities shall maintain objectivity and impartiality. They may not without legal grounds treat persons differently by reason of their personal conditions such as faith, opinions, race, skin colour, origin, sex, age, nationality, language, social status, or financial circumstances.

3.125   SWITZERLAND

29 May 1874, amended.

Article 107
1. The members and temporary appointees of the Federal Tribunal are nominated by the Federal Assembly, which will take due care that the three official languages of the Confederation are represented.

Article 116
1. German, French, Italian and Romansh are the national languages of Switzerland.
2. German, French and Italian are declared to be the official languages of the Confederation.

3.126   SYRIA

12 March 1973.

Article 4
The Arabic language shall be the official language.

3.127   TRINIDAD AND TOBAGO

1974, amended.

Article 3
3. Any person who is arrested or detained shall be entitled:

(a) to be informed promptly, and in a language he understands, of the reasons for his arrest or detention;

Article 4

3. Every person who is charged with a criminal offence shall be entitled:

(a) to be informed as soon as practicable, in a language which he understands and in detail, of the nature of the offence charged; ...

(e) to have without payment the assistance of a competent interpreter if he cannot understand the English language.

Article 5

2. Without prejudice to subsection 1, but subject to this chapter and to section 54, Parliament may not...

(g) deprive a person of the right to the assistance of an interpreter in any proceedings in which he is involved or in which he is a party or a witness, before a court, commission, board or other tribunal, if he does not understand or speak English;

3.128   TUNISIA

1976.

Article 1

Tunisia is a free state, independent and sovereign; its religion is Islam, its language is Arabic, and its regime is the republic.

3.129   TURKEY

7 November 1982.

Article 3

The Turkish state, its territory and nation, is an indivisible entity. Its language is Turkish.

Article 10

All individuals are equal without any discrimination before the law, irrespective of language, race, colour, gender, political opinion, philosophical belief, religion and sex, or any such considerations.

Article 14

None of the rights and freedoms embodied in the Constitution shall be exercised with the aim of violating the indivisible integrity of the state, its territory and nation, of endangering the existence of the Turkish state and the Republic, of destroying fundamental rights and freedoms, of placing the government of the state under the control of an individual or a group of people, or establishing the hegemony of one social class over others, or creating discrimination on the basis of language, race, religion or sect, or of establishing by any other means a system of government based on these concepts and ideas.

Article 26
No language prohibited by law shall be used in the expression and dissemination of thought. Any written or printed documents, phonograph records, magnetic or video tapes, and other means of expression used in contravention of this provision shall be seized by a duly issued decision of judge or, in cases where delay is deemed prejudicial, by the competent authority designated by law. The authority issuing the seizure order shall notify the competent judge of its decision within twenty-four hours. The judge shall decide on the matter within three days.

Article 28
The press is free and shall not be censored. The establishment of a printing house shall not be subject to prior permission and to the deposit of a financial guarantee.
Publication shall not be made in any language prohibited by law.

Article 42
... No language other than Turkish shall be taught as mother tongue to Turkish citizens at any institution of training or education. The law shall determine the foreign languages to be taught in institutions of training and education, and the rules to be followed by schools conducting training and education in a foreign language. The provisions of international treaties are reserved.

Article 134
The "Atatürk High Institution of Culture, Language and History" shall be established as a public corporate body, under the moral aegis of Atatürk, under the supervision and with the support of the President of the Republic, attached to the office of the Prime Minister, and composed of the Atatürk Centre of Research, the Turkish Language Society, the Turkish Historical Society, and the Atatürk Cultural Centre, in order to conduct scientific research to produce publications and to disseminate information on the thought, principles, and reforms of Atatürk, Turkish culture, Turkish history, and the Turkish language.
The income of the Turkish Language Society and Turkish Historical Society, bequeathed to them by Atatürk in his will, is reserved and shall be allocated to them accordingly.
The establishment, the organs, operating procedures, and personnel matters of the Atatürk High Institution of Culture, Language and History, and its authority over the institutions within it, shall be regulated by law.

3.130   TURKMENISTAN

18 May 1992.

Article 13
The state language of Turkmenistan shall be the Turkmen language.
All citizens of Turkmenistan shall be guaranteed the right to use their native language.

Article 17
Turkmenistan shall guarantee the equality of the rights and freedoms of citizens, as well as the equality of citizens before the law irrespective of nationality, origin, property status or official position, place of residence, language, attitude towards religion, political beliefs, or party membership.

Article 28

Citizens shall have the right to create political parties and other public associations operating within the framework of the Constitution and the laws.

The creation and activity of political parties and public organisations that have the goal of forcible change in the constitutional structure, allow violence in their activity, act against the constitutional rights and freedoms of citizens, propagandise war or racial, national, social, or religious hostility, or that encroach on the health and morality of the people, and also the creation of militarised associations and political parties on a national or religious basis shall be forbidden.

Article 106

Judicial procedure shall be conducted in the state language. Persons participating in the case who do not speak the language of the judicial procedure shall be ensured the right to acquaint themselves with the materials of the case and to participate in judicial action, and also the right to testify in court in their native language.

3.131   TUVALU

1 October 1978.

Article 5

2. Any person who is arrested or detained shall be informed as soon as reasonably practicable, and in a language that he understands, of the reasons for his arrest or detention.

3.132   UGANDA

8 September 1967.

Article 10

2. Any person who is arrested, detained or restricted shall be informed as soon as reasonably practicable, in a language that he understands, of the reasons for his arrest, detention or restriction...

5. Where a person is detained or restricted by virtue of such law as is referred to in paragraph (j) of clause 1 of this article or of paragraph (c) of clause 3 of article 19 of this Constitution, the following provisions shall apply, that is to say:

(a) he shall, not more than twenty-eight days after the commencement of his detention or restriction, be furnished with a statement in writing in a language that he understands specifying the grounds upon which he is detained or restricted and shall be afforded an opportunity of making representations in writing to the authority by which his detention or restriction was ordered;

Article 15

2. Every person who is charged with a criminal offence...

(b) shall be informed as soon as reasonably practicable, in a language that he understands, of the nature of the offence charged;...

(f) shall be permitted to have without payment the assistance of an interpreter if he cannot understand the language used at the trial of the charge.

Article 21

6. (a) he shall, as reasonably practicable and in any case not more than two months after the commencement of his detention, be furnished with a statement in writing in a language that he understands specifying the grounds upon which he is detained;

Article 41

Subject to the provisions of Article 42 of this Constitution, a person shall be qualified to be a member of the National Assembly if, and shall not be so qualified unless,...

(b) he is able to speak and, unless incapacitated by blindness or other physical cause, to read the official language well enough to take an active part in the proceedings of the Assembly.

3.133   UKRAINE

Draft of 27 June 1993.

Article 7

The state language of Ukraine is the Ukrainian language.

In areas of dense concentration of one or several national groups, along with the state language, one may also use, as an official language in state bodies, organisations and institutions, the accepted language of the majority of the population of the particular area.

Article 8

The state encourages the consolidation and development of the Ukrainian nation, its historic consciousness, traditions and cultures, the development of ethnic, cultural, language and religious identities of all the national minorities.

Ukraine fosters the satisfaction of the national-cultural, spiritual, and linguistic needs of Ukrainians who are living beyond the borders of the state.

Article 15

The citizens of Ukraine have equal constitutional rights and freedoms and are equal before the law regardless of their origin, social and economic status, office, sex, race, nationality, language, religion, political and other convictions, occupation, or place or residence, participation in citizens' affiliations and other circumstances.

Article 80

The state shall ensure conditions for free, universal multi-faceted development of education, science and culture, familiarisation with the spiritual heritage of the Ukrainian people, world culture and its development.

The law guarantees to all national minorities the right to: use and to study in their native language or to study their native language in state educational institutions or through national cultural societies; develop national cultural traditions; celebrate national holidays; profess their faith; create national cultural and educational institutions; and perform any other activities, in the national and cultural sphere, which do not contradict the law.

Article 110

The Constitution and laws of Ukraine have exclusivity over the following matters...

4. rights of national minorities;
5. status of languages;

Article 142
The President of Ukraine is the head of state and acts on its behalf.

The President of Ukraine is elected by citizens of Ukraine on the basis of universal, equal and direct suffrage by secret ballot for a term of five years.

The procedure of elections of the President of Ukraine is established by the Law on the Election of the President of Ukraine.

A citizen of Ukraine, who has the right to vote, is at least thirty-five years of age, has lived on the territory of Ukraine for no less than 10 years, speaks the state language and is in good health, enabling him or her to fulfil presidential responsibilities, may be President

Article 174
Legal proceedings are conducted in the state language. In places of dense concentration of one or several national groups, legal proceedings may be conducted in the language spoken by the majority of the population of the particular locality.

Individuals, who participate in the case and who are not fluent in the language of the judicial proceedings, are guaranteed the right of full access to the materials of the case, participation in the court proceedings through an interpreter and the right to speak before the court in one's native language.

Article 181
Ukraine is a unified and unitary state. The territorial structure of Ukraine is based upon the principles of integrity of state territory, integrated socio-economic development and administration of its parts taking into account their economic, historic, geographic, and demographic peculiarities, ethnic and cultural traditions.

3.134 UNITED ARAB EMIRATES

2 December 1971.

Article 6
The Union shall be part of the Great Arab Nation, to which it is bound by the ties of religion, language, history, and a common destiny. The people of the Union shall be a single people, and shall be part of the Arab Nation.

Article 7
Islam shall be the official religion of the Union. The Islamic Shari'ah shall be a principle source of legislation in the Union. The official language of the Union shall be Arabic.

3.135 UZBEKISTAN

Draft of 28 September 1992.

Article 4
     The official language of the Republic of Uzbekistan is Uzbek.
     The Republic of Uzbekistan ensures a respectful attitude toward the languages, customs, and traditions of the peoples which live on its territory and the creation of the conditions for their development.

Article 18
     All citizens have identical rights and liberties and are equal before the law without distinction as to sex, race, language, religion, social origin, beliefs, and personal and social position.

Article 89
     A citizen of the Republic of Uzbekistan not less than 35 years of age, fluent in the official language, and a permanent resident of the territory of Uzbekistan for no fewer than 10 years directly preceding the elections may be elected president of the Republic of Uzbekistan.

Article 114
     Judicial proceedings in the Republic of Uzbekistan are conducted in Uzbek and Karakalpac or in the language of the majority of the population of a given locality. Persons involved in proceedings who do not know the language in which the judicial proceedings are being conducted are assured the right of full familiarisation with the material of the case, participation in the judicial actions via an interpreter, and the right to speak in court in their native language.

     3.136   VANUATU

30 July 1980.

Article 3
     1. The national language of the Republic is Bislama. The official languages are Bislama, English and French. The principal languages of education are English and French.
     2. The Republic shall protect the different local languages which are part of the national heritage, and may declare one of them as a national language.

Article 5
     2. Protection of the law shall include the following...
     (c) everyone charged shall be informed promptly in a language he understands of the offence with which he is being charged;
     (d) if an accused does not understand the language to be used in the proceedings, he shall be provided with an interpreter throughout the proceedings;

Article 28
     1. The National Council of Chiefs has a general competence to discuss all matters relating to custom and tradition and may make recommendations for the preservation and promotion of Vanuatuan culture and languages.

Article 62
1. A citizen of Vanuatu may obtain, in the official language that he uses, the services which he may rightfully expect from the Republic's administration.

Article 84
A bill for an amendment of a provision of the Constitution regarding the status of Bislama, English and French, the electoral system, the powers and organisation of regional councils or the parliamentary system, passed by Parliament under Article 83, shall not come into effect unless it has been supported in a national referendum.

3.137   VENEZUELA

23 January 1961.

Article 6
The official language is Spanish.

3.138   VIETNAM

18 December 1980.

Article 5
... All the nationalities have the right to use their spoken languages and scripts, and to preserve and promote their fine customs, habits, traditions, and cultures.

Article 134
The People's Courts shall ensure to the citizens of all nationalities in the Socialist Republic of Vietnam the right to use their own spoken languages and scripts before the courts.

3.139   WESTERN SAMOA

1 January 1962.

Article 9
4. Every person charged with an offence has the following minimum rights:
(a) to be informed promptly, in a language which he understands and in detail, of the nature and cause of the accusation against him; ...
(e) to have the free assistance of an interpreter, if any doubt exists as to whether he can understand or speak the language used in court.

Article 15
2. Except as expressly authorised under the provisions of this Constitution, no law and no executive or administrative action of the state shall, either expressly or in its practical application, subject any person or persons to any disability or restriction or confer on any person or persons

any privilege or advantage on grounds only of descent, sex, language, religion, political or other opinion, social origin, place of birth, family status, or any of them.

Article 54

1. All debates and discussions in the Legislative Assembly shall be conducted in the Samoan language and the English language.

2. The minutes and the debates of the Legislative Assembly, every bill introduced therein, every paper presented thereto, and all minutes of the proceedings, minutes of evidence and reports of committees of the Assembly, shall be in the Samoan language and the English language.

Article 112

The Samoan and English texts of this Constitution are equally authoritative but, in case of difference, the English text shall prevail.

3.140   YEMEN

28 December 1970.

Article 2

Islam is the religion of the state and Arabic is its official language.

Article 43

The state has no right to impose distinction in human rights due to religion, colour, sex, language, natural origin, or profession.

3.141   YUGOSLAVIA

21 February 1974.

Article 154

Citizens shall be equal in their rights and duties regardless of nationality, race, sex, language, religion, education or social status.

All shall be equal before the law.

Article 170

Citizens shall be guaranteed the right to opt for a nation or nationality and to express their national culture, and also the right to the free use of their language and alphabet.

Article 171

Members of nationalities shall, in conformity with the Constitution and law, have the right to use their language and alphabet in the exercise of their rights and duties, and in proceedings before state agencies and organisations exercising public powers.

Members of the nations and nationalities of Yugoslavia shall, on the territory of each republic and/or autonomous province, have the right to instruction in their own language in conformity with the law.

Article 214

Ignorance of the law in which proceedings are conducted shall not be an obstacle to the defence and the realisation of the rights and justified interests of citizens and organisations.

Every person shall have the right to use his own language in proceedings before a court of law or before other state agencies, organisations of associated labour and other self-managing organisations and communities which in exercising public powers decide on a citizen's rights and obligations, and to be informed in his own language of the facts in the course of the proceedings.

Article 243

The equality of languages and alphabets of the nations and nationalities of Yugoslavia shall be ensured in the Armed Forces of the Socialist Federal Republic of Yugoslavia, in conformity with the Socialist Federal Republic of Yugoslavia Constitution.

In matters of command and military training in the Yugoslav People's Army, one of the languages of the nations of Yugoslavia may be used, and in parts of the country, the languages of the nations and nationalities, in conformity with federal statute.

Article 246

The languages of the nations and nationalities and their alphabets shall be equal throughout the territory of Yugoslavia. In the Socialist Federal Republic of Yugoslavia the languages of the nationalities shall be used in conformity with the present Constitution and federal statute.

The realisation of the equality of languages and alphabets of the nations and nationalities regarding their official use in areas populated by individual nationalities shall be ensured and the way and conditions for its realisation regulated by statute, the bylaws of the socio-political communities, and by self-management enactments of organisations of associated labour and other self-managing organisations and communities.

Article 247

In order to ensure that its right to express its nationality and culture shall be realised, each nationality shall be guaranteed the right freely to use its language and alphabet, to develop its culture and for this purpose to set up organisations and enjoy other constitutionally established rights.

Article 271

... The principle of the equality of languages of the nations of Yugoslavia, and analogously the principle of the equality of languages of the nations and nationalities, shall be applied in international communication.

When international treaties are drawn up in the languages of the signatory countries, the languages of the nations of Yugoslavia shall be equally used.

3.142 ZAMBIA

25 August 1973.

Article 15

2. Any person who is arrested or detained shall be informed as soon as reasonably practicable, in a language that he understands, of the reasons for his arrest or detention.

Article 27
1. Where a person's freedom of movement is restricted or he is detained under the authority of any such law as is referred to in Article 24 or 26, as the case may be, the following provisions shall apply:
(a) he shall, as soon as is reasonably practicable and in any case not more than fourteen days after the commencement of his detention or restriction, be furnished with a statement in writing in a language that he understands specifying in detail the grounds upon which he is restricted or detained;

Article 67
Subject to the provisions of Article 68, a person shall be qualified to be elected or nominated as a member of the National Assembly if, and shall not be qualified to be so elected or nominated unless...
(d) he is literate and conversant in the official language of Zambia;

3.143 ZIMBABWE

21 December 1979.

Article 13
3. Any person who is arrested or detained shall be informed as soon as reasonably practicable, in a language that he understands, of the reasons for his arrest or detention and shall be permitted at his own expense to obtain and instruct without delay a legal representative of his own choice and to hold communication with him.

Article 18
3. Every person who is charged with a criminal offence...
(b) shall be informed as soon as reasonably practicable, in a language that he understands and in detail, of the nature of the offence charged; ...
(f) shall be permitted to have without payment the assistance of an interpreter if he cannot understand the language used at the trial of the charge.

Article 82
1. A person shall not be qualified for appointment as a judge of the High Court unless:
(a) he is or has been a judge of a court having unlimited jurisdiction in civil or criminal matters in a country in which the common law is Roman-Dutch or English, and English is an official language; or
(b) he is and has been for not less than seven years, whether continuously or not, qualified to practise as an advocate:
(i) in Zimbabwe;
(ii) in a country in which the common law is Roman-Dutch and English is an official language; or
(iii) if he is a citizen of Zimbabwe, in a country in which the common law is English and English is an official language.

Article 87
4. A tribunal appointed under subsection 2 or 3 shall consist of not less than three members

selected by the President from the following...

(b) persons who hold or have held office as a judge of a court having unlimited jurisdiction in civil or criminal matters in a country in which the common law is Roman-Dutch or English, and English is an official language;

***

BIBLIOGRAPHY

Books and Printed Reports

The Aboriginal Language Policy Study — Phase II: Implementation Mechanism (1988), National Indian Brotherhood, Ottawa.

Aboriginal Peoples and the Law: Indian, Metis and Inuit Rights in Canada (1985), B.W. Morris (ed.), Carleton University Press, Ottawa.

Aboriginal Self-Determination (1991), Frank Cassidy (ed.), Oolichan Books, Lantzville, B.C. and The Institute for Research on Public Policy, Halifax, Canada.

Acuña, Ramon Luis (1993), *Las tribus de Europa*, Ediciones B, Barcelona.

Adeyemi, O. A. (1972), "A Day in the Criminal Court", in T.O. Elias (ed.), *The Nigerian Magistrate and the Offender*, Ethiope, Benin City, Nigeria.

An Agenda for Peace: Preventive Diplomacy, Peacemaking and Peacekeeping — Report of the Secretary-General (1992), United Nations Publications, New York.

Agreement-in-Principal Between the Inuit of the Nunavut Settlement Area and Her Majesty in Right of Canada (1990), Department of Indian Affairs and Northern Development, Ottawa.

Alderman, Geoffrey (1993), *Governments, Ethnic Groups and Political Representation*, Dartmouth Publishing, Aldershot, United Kingdom.

Alexander, Neville (1989), *Language Policy and National Unity in South Africa/Azania*, Buchu Books, Cape Town.

Alexander, Neville (1989), "The Language Question", in *Critical Choice for South African Society*, Institute for the Study of Public Policy, Johannesburg, pp. 3-9.

Alfredsson, Gudmundur (1990), *Report on Equality and Non-Discrimination: Minority Rights*, Council of Europe, Strasbourg.

Ammoun, Charles D. (1957), *Study of Discrimination in Education*, United Nations Publications, New York.

Assembly of First Nations Education Secretariat (1991-92), *Annual Report*, Assembly of First Nations, Ottawa.

Australia's Language: The Australian Language and Literacy Policy (1991), Australian Government Publishing Service, Canberra.

Australian Indigenous Languages Framework (1993), Australian Indigenous Languages Project, Wayville, South Australia.

Avis sur d' éventuelles modifications à la Charte de la langue française (1993), Bibliothèque nationale du Québec, Québec.

Barendt, Eric (1993), *Broadcasting Law — A Comparative Study*, Clarendon Press, Oxford, United Kingdom.

Baron, Dennis E. (1990), *The English-Only Question: An Official Language for Americans?*, Yale University Press, New Haven, USA.

Barrow, R. H. (1949), *The Romans*, Penguin Press, Baltimore, USA.

Bayly, John (1991), "Unilingual Aboriginal Jurors in a Euro-Canadian Criminal Justice System: Some Preliminary Views of the Northwest Territories Experience", in *Proceedings of the VIth International Symposium*, Commission on Folk Law and Legal Pluralism, Ottawa, pp. 306-319.

Beardsmore, H. Baetens (1991), "L'aménagement linguistique à Singapour", in J.-J. Symoens and J. Vanderlinden (eds.), *Symposium : Les langues en Afrique à l'horizon 2000*, Institut Africain and Académie Royale des Sciences d'Outre-Mer, Bruxelles, pp. 211-224.

Blache, P. and Woehrling José (1988), *L' accord Meech-Langevin et les compétences linguistiques du Québec*, Éditeur officiel du Québec, Québec.

Blaustein, Albert P. and Epstein, Dana Blaustein (1986), *Resolving Language Conflicts: A Study of the World's Constitutions*, US English, Washington, D.C.

Blaustein, Albert F. and Flanz, Gilbert H. (1988), *Constitutions of the Countries of the World*, Oceana Publications, Dobbs Ferry, New York.

Bokatola, Isse Omanga (1992), *L'Organisation des Nations unies et la protection des minorités*, Établissements Émile Bruylant, Bruxelles.

Borgmann, A. (1974), *The Philosophy of Language: Historical Foundations and Contemporary Issues*, Martinus Nijhoff, Dordrecht, Netherlands.

Bossuyt, Marc (1976), *L'interdiction de la discrimination dans le droit international des droits de l'homme*, Établissements Émile Bruylant, Bruxelles.

Bossuyt, Marc J. (1987), *Guide to the Travaux Préparatoires of the International Covenant on Civil and Political Right*, Martinus Nijhoff, den Haag, Netherlands.

Bot Ba Njock, Henri Marcel (1987), "Planification linguistique au Cameroun : De l'aménagement linguistique à la politique linguistique", in Lorne Laforge (ed.), *Proceedings of the International Colloquium on Language Planning*, Les Presses de l'Université Laval, Québec, pp. 204-222.

Braën, André (1981), *La santé au Nouveau-Brunswick : Quelques aspects juridiques et linguistiques*, Société des Acadiens du Nouveau-Brunswick, Petit-Rocher, Canada.

Braan, Conrad B. (1978), *Multilinguisme et éducation au Nigéria*, International Centre for Research on Bilingualism, Québec.

Braan, Conrad B. (1983), *Language Policy, Planning and Management in Africa: A Select Bibliography*, International Centre for Research on Bilingualism, Québec.

Braan, Conrad B. (1991), *Official and National Language in Africa: Complement or Conflict?*, International Centre for Research on Language Planning, Québec.

Brown, David (1994), *The State and Ethnic Politics in Southeast Asia*, Routledge, London.

Brownlie, I. (1990), *Treaties and Indigenous Peoples*, Clarendon Press and Oxford University Press, London.

Brunton, Brian and Colquhoun-Kerr, Duncan (1984), *The Annotated Constitution of Papua New Guinea*, University of Papua New Guinea Press, Port Moresby.

Bulletin pour minorités nationales et ethniques en Hongrie (1993), Nemzeti és Etnikai Kisebbségi Hivatal, Budapest.

Bullivant, B.M. (1984), *Pluralism: Cultural, Maintenance and Evolution*, Clevedon, Avon, United Kingdom.

Burnaby, Barbara (1989), "Language Policy and the Education Of Native Peoples: Identifying the Issues", in David Schneiderman (ed.), *Language and the State: The Law and Politics of Identity — Proceedings of the Second National Conference on Constitutional Affairs* (1989), Les Éditions Yvon Blais, Cowansville, Québec, pp. 279-289.

Burrows, F. (1987), *Free Movement in European Community Law*, Clarendon Press, Oxford, United Kingdom.

Canadian Bar Association (1984), *Current Issues in Aboriginal and Treaty Rights*, Ontario Continuing Legal Education, Ottawa.

Calvet, Louis-Jean (1987), *La guerre des langues et les politiques linguistiques*, Payot, Paris.

The Canadian Charter of Rights and Freedom (1989), Gérald A. Beaudoin and Ed Ratushny (eds.), Carswell, Toronto.

Canadian Institute for the Administration of Justice (1993), *Discrimination in the Law and the Administration of Justice*, Éditions Thémis, Montréal.

Capotorti, Francesco (1979), *Étude des droits des personnes appartenant aux minorités ethniques, religieuses et linguistiques*, United Nations Publications, New York.

Cassidy, F. and Bish, R.L. (1989), *Indian Government: Its Meaning in Practice*, Oolichan Books, Lantzville B.C. and The Institute for Research on Public Policy, Halifax, Canada.

Cerexhe, Étienne (1982), *Le droit européen : La libre circulation des personnes et des entreprises*, Nauwelaerts, Bruxelles.

Charte européenne des langues régionales ou minoritaires : Traités et rapports (1993), Council of Europe, Strasbourg.

Chaszar, Edward (1988), *The International Problem of National Minorities*, Indiana University of Pennsylvania, Indiana.

Chomsky, Noam (1988), *Language and Politics*, Black Rose Books, Montréal.

Clark, B. (1992), *Native Liberty, Crown Sovereignty: The Existing Aboriginal Right of Self-Government in Canada*, McGill-Queen's University Press, Montréal and Kingston.

Cobarrubias, Juan and Garmendia Lasa, Carmen (1987), "Language Policy and Language Planning Efforts in Spain", in Lorne Laforge (ed.), *Proceedings of the International Colloquium on Language Planning*, Les Presses de l'Université Laval, Québec, pp. 60-67.

Commission of the European Communities (1986), *Linguistic Minorities in Countries Belonging to the European Community*, Office for Official Publications of the European Communities, Strasbourg.

Commission européenne pour la démocratie par le droit (1991), *Rapport explicatif relatif à la proposition pour une convention européenne pour la protection des minorités*, Council of Europe, Strasbourg.

Commissioner of Official Languages (1994), *Annual Report 1993*, Minister of Supplies and Services, Ottawa.

Les compétences linguistiques du Québec après l'Accord du Lac Meech (1977), Conseil de la langue française, Québec.

Connor, Walker (1984), *The National Question in Marxist-Leninist Theory and Strategy*, Princeton University Press, Princeton, USA.

Consejo de Organizaciones Mayas de Guatemala (1991), *Derechos Específicos del Pueblo Maya*, Editorial Cholsamaj, Guatemala.

Conseil de la langue française (1986), *Le libre échange Canada-États-Unis et la langue française au Québec*, Bibliothèque nationale du Québec, Québec.

Conseil de la langue française (1987), *La place du français dans les écoles de langue française à clientèle pluriethnique de l'île de Montréal*, Bibliothèque nationale du Québec, Québec.

Conseil de la langue française sur la francisation des entreprises (1986), *Les enjeux actuels de la francisation des entreprises*, Bibliothèque nationale du Québec, Québec.

Coulmas, Florian (1991), "European Integration and the Idea of the National Language", in Florian Coulmas (ed.), *A Language Policy for the European Community*, Mouton de Gruyter, Berlin, pp. 1-43.

La crise des langues (1985), Jacques Maurais (ed.), Conseil de la langue française, Québec.

Crawford, James (1992), *Hold Your Tongue: Bilingualism and the Politics of English-Only*, Addison-Wesley, Reading, USA.

Cruse, H. (1987), *Plural but Equal — A Critical Study of Blacks and Minorities and America's Plural Society*, William Morrow and Company, Inc., New York.

Cummins, Jim (1984), "The Minority Language Child", in Stan Shapson and Vincent D'Oyley (eds.), *Bilingual and Multicultural Education: Canadian Perspectives*, Clevedon, Avon, United Kingdom, pp. 71-89.

Daes, Erica-Irène (1992), *Discrimination Against Indigenous Peoples*, United Nations Publications, New York.

de Balogh, Arthur (1930), *La protection internationale des minorités*, Éditions internationales, Paris.

De Bandt, Jean-Pierre (1988), "Commentary", in Robert A. Goldwin, Art Kaufman, and William A. Schambra (eds.), *Forging Unity out of Diversity: The Approaches of Eight Nations*, American Enterprise Institute for Public Policy Research, Washington, D.C., pp. 135-137.

Décisions sur la langue de travail (1991), Office de la langue française, Bibliothèque nationale du Québec, Québec.

Delrieu, Jacqueline (1984), "Scolarisation des enfants de migrants et enseignement des langues d'origine. Les textes officiels et leurs applications dans le premier degré", in *Status of Migrants' Mother Tongues*, European Science Foundation, Strasbourg, pp. 23-29.

Demoz, A. (1991), "Report on Ethiopia", in J.-J. Symoens and J. Vanderlinden (eds.), *Symposium: Les langues en Afrique à l'horizon 2000*, Institut Africain and Académie Royale des Sciences d'Outre-Mer, Bruxelles, pp. 141-163.

Derecho Indigena y Derechos Humanos en América Latina (1988), Rodolfo Stavenhagen (ed.), Instituto Interamericano de Derechos Humanos and El Colegio de México, México.

Desai, Zubeida and Trew, Robin (1992), "Comments on the ANC Language Policy", in *National Education Policy Investigation (NEPI) Working Paper*, Pretoria, pp. 1-7.

Dessemontet, François (1984), *Le droit des langues en Suisse*, Éditeur officiel du Québec, Québec.

de Tocqueville, Alexis (1969), *Democracy in America*, Doubleday Anchor, New York.

Deutsch, K. A. (1975), "The Political Significance of Linguistic Conflicts", in Jean-Guy Savard and Richard Vigneault (eds.), *Les États multilingues*, Presses de l'Université Laval, Québec.

Deutsch, Karl (1979), *Tides Among Nations*, Free Press, New York.

de Varennes, Fernand (1996), *Language Conflicts in Eastern European and Central Asian States: Preliminary Report on Early Warning and Resolution Mechanisms*, Foundation on Inter-Ethnic Relations, den Haag, Netherlands.

de Witte, Bruno (1989), "Droits fondamentaux et protection de la diversité linguistique", in P. Pupier and J. Woehrling (eds.), *Language and Law: Proceedings of the First Conference of the International Institute of Comparative Linguistic Law*, Wilson & Lafleur, Montréal, pp. 91-126.

de Witte, Bruno (1990), "Educational Equality for Community Workers and their Families", in Bruno de Witte (ed.), *European Community Law of Education*, Nomos Verlagsgesellschaft, Baden-Baden, pp. 71-79.

de Witte, Bruno (1991), "The Impact of European Community Rules on Linguistic Policies of the Member States" in Florian Coulmas (ed.), *A Language Policy for the European Community: Prospects and Quandaries*, Mouton de Gruyter, Berlin, New York, pp. 163-177.

de Witte, Bruno (1992), "Conclusion: A Legal Perspective", in Sergij Vilfan (ed.), *Comparative Studies on Governments and Non-Dominant Ethnic Groups in Europe 1850-1940*, New York University Press, New York, pp. 303-314.

de Zayas, Alfred-Maurice (1993), "The International Judicial Protection of Peoples and Minorities", in Peoples and Minorities in International Law, Catherine Brölmann, René Lefeber, and Marjoleine Zieck (eds.), Martinus Nijhoff, Dordrecht, Netherlands, pp. 253-287.

Dhar, T.N. (1987), "Language Planning and Development: Problems of Legislation Amidst Diversity", in Lorne Laforge (ed.), *Proceedings of the International Colloquium on Language Planning*, Les Presses de l'Université Laval, Québec, pp. 238-254.

Didier, Emmanuel (1990), *Langues et langages*, Wilson & Lafleur, Montréal.

Dinstein, Yoram (1993), "The Degree of Self-Rule of Minorities in Unitarian and Federal States", in Catherine Brölmann, René Lefeber and Marjoleine Zieck (eds.), *Peoples and Minorities in International Law*, Martinus Nijhoff, Dordrecht, Netherlands, pp. 221-235.

Documents on Autonomy and Minority Rights (1993), Hurst Hannum (ed.), Martinus Nijhoff, Dordrecht, Netherlands.

Les droits des autochtones au Canada : Du défi à l'action (1988), Canadian Bar Association, Ottawa.

Dua, Hans R. (1987), "Comments on Brian Weinstein's Paper: Language Planning and Interests", in Lorne Laforge (ed.), *Proceedings of the International Colloquium on Language Planning*, Les Presses de l'Université Laval, Québec, pp. 60-67.

Edmondson, Jerold A. (1990), "China's Minorities", in Florian Coulmas (ed.), *Linguistic Minorities and Literacy: Language Policy Issues in Developing Countries*, Mouton Publishers, Berlin, pp. 63-75.

Ellegärd, Alvar (1973), "Study of Language", in Philip P. Wiener (ed.), *Dictionary of the History of Ideas — Studies of Selected Pivotal Ideas, Volume II*, Charles Scribner's Sons, New York.

Enrique Hamel, Rainer (1989), "Politiques et droits linguistiques des minorités indiennes au Mexique" in P. Pupier and J. Woehrling (eds.), *Language and Law: Proceedings of the First Conference of the International Institute of Comparative Linguistic Law*, Wilson & Lafleur, Montréal, pp. 445-456.

Epstein, Erwin H. (1970), *Politics and Education in Puerto Rico: A Documentary Survey of the Language Issue*, Scarecrow Press, Metuchen, New Jersey.

Ermacora, Felix (1964), *Der Minderheitenschutz in der Arbeit der Vereinten Nationen*, Wilhelm Braumüller, Vienna.

Ercamora, Felix (1993), *Grundrechte der Europaischen Volksgruppen*, Wilhelm Braumüller, Vienna.

Ericksen, Thomas Hylland (1991), *Languages at the Margins of Modernity — Linguistic Minorities and the Nation-State*, International Peace Research Institute, Oslo.

¿ Un Estado, una lengua ? La organización política de la diversidad lingüística (1994), Albert Bastardas and Emili Boix (eds.), Octaedro Universidad, Barcelona.

The Ethnic Dimension in International Relations (1993), Bernard Schechterman and Martin Slann (eds.), Praeger, Westport, Connecticut.

Ethnic Groups and Language Rights, Comparative Studies on Governments and Non-Dominant Ethnic Groups in Europe 1850-1940 (1990), Sergij Vilfan (ed.), European Science Foundation, New York University Press, New York.

Ethnic Groups and the State (1985), Paul Brass (ed.), Croom Helm, Beckenham, United Kingdom.

Ethnic Groups in International Relations: Comparative Studies on Governments and Non-Dominant Ethnic Groups in Europe, 1850-1940 (1991), Sergij Vilfan (ed.), European Science Foundation, New York University Press, New York.

L'Europe centrale et ses minorités : vers une solution européenne? (1993), André Liebich and André Reszler (eds.), Presses Universitaires de France, Paris.

European Community Law of Education (1990), Bruno de Witte (ed.), Nomos Verlagsgesellschaft, Baden-Baden, Germany.

Falch, J. (1973), *Contribution à l'étude des langues en Europe*, Les Presses de l'Université Laval, Québec.

Fierman, William (1991), *Language Planning and National Development: The Uzbek Experience*, Mouton de Gruyter, Berlin.

Fishman, Joshua (1972), *The Sociology of Language*, Newbury House Publishers, Rawley, Massachusetts.

Fishman, Joshua A. (1972), *Language and Nationalism*, Newbury House Publishers, Rawley, Massachusetts.

Fishman, Joshua A. (1985), *The Rise and Fall of the Ethnic Revival: Perspectives on Language and Ethnicity*, Mouton Publishers, Berlin.

Fishman, Joshua A. (1989), *Language and Ethnicity in Minority Sociolinguistic Perspective*, Clevedon, Avon, United Kingdom.

Fleiner, Thomas (1988), "Commentary", in Robert A. Goldwin, Art Kaufman, and William Schambra (eds.), *Forging Unity out of Diversity: The Approaches of Eight Nations*, American Enterprise Institute for Public Policy Research, Washington, D.C., pp. 239-254.

Foreign Workers Problems: Japan and the US, Shigenori Matsui and Susumu Noda (eds.), Centre for Japan-United States Exchange in the Humanities and Social Sciences, Osaka.

Forging Unity out of Diversity: The Approaches of Eight Nations (1988), Robert A. Goldwin, Art Kaufman, and William Schambra (eds.), American Enterprise Institute for Public Policy Research, Washington, D.C.

Fosty, Anne (1985), *La langue française dans les institutions communautaires de l'Europe*, Éditeur officiel du Québec, Québec.

Foucher, Pierre (1990), "Les droits linguistiques en 1990", in Ryszard I. Cholewinski (ed.), *Les droits de la personne au Canada : Dans les années 1990 et au-delà*, University of Ottawa, Ottawa, pp. 131-153.

Foulkes, David (1991), "The Status and Use of the Welsh Language", in J.-J. Symoens and J. Vanderlinden (eds.), *Symposium : Les langues en Afrique à l'horizon 2000*, Institut Africain and Académie Royale des Sciences d'Outre-Mer, Bruxelles, pp. 179-210.

The Future of Cultural Minorities (1979), A.E. Alcock, B.K. Taylor and J.M. Welton (eds.), MacMillan Press Ltd, London.

Gambier, Yves (1986), *La Finlande bilingue : histoire, droit et réalités*, Éditeur officiel du Québec, Québec.

Gellner, Ernest (1983), *Nations and Nationalism*, Blackwell, Oxford, United Kingdom.

General Comment on Non-Discrimination (1989), United Nations Publications, New York.

Getches, David and Wilkinson, Charles (1986), *Federal Indian Law — Cases and Materials*, West Publishing, St. Paul, Minnesota.

Goffin, Roger (1987), "Le statut des langues et les stratégies linguistiques dans les services de traduction des communautés européennes", in Lorne Laforge (ed.), *Proceedings of the International Colloquium on Language Planning*, Les Presses de l'Université Laval, Québec, pp. 365- 376.

Grandguillaume, Gilbert (1983), *Arabisation et politique linguistique au Maghreb*, Éditions G.-P. Maisonneuve et Larose, Paris.

Grau, Richard (1981), *Le statut juridique de la langue française en France*, Éditeur officiel du Québec, Québec.

Grau, Richard (1985), *Les langues et les cultures minoritaires en France : une approche juridique contemporaine*, Éditeur officiel du Québec, Québec.

Gray, Tracy (1987), "Language Policy and Educational Strategies for Language Minority and Majority Students in the United States", in Lorne Laforge (ed.), *Proceedings of the International Colloquium on Language Planning*, Les Presses de l'Université Laval, Québec, pp. 255-276.

Greece — Country Reports on Human Rights Practices for 1993 (1994), US State Department, Washington, D.C.

Griffiths, Stephen Iwan (1993), *Nationalism and Ethnic Conflict: Threats to European Security*, Oxford University Press, London.

Grofman, Bernard, Handley, Lisa, and Niemi, Richard G. (1992), *Minority Representation and the Quest for Voting Equality*, Cambridge University Press, Cambridge.

Groupement pour les droits des minorités (1985), *Les minorités à l'âge de l'État-nation*, Fayard, Paris.

Haarmann, Harald (1986), *Language in Ethnicity: A View of Basic Ecological Relations*, Mouton de Gruyter, Berlin.

Hagège, Claude (1992), *Le souffle de la langue : voies et destins des parlers d'Europe*, Éditions Odile Jacob, Paris.

Halim, Amran (1987), "Language Planning in Indonesia", in Lorne Laforge (ed.), *Proceedings of the International Colloquium on Language Planning*, Les Presses de l'Université Laval, Québec, pp. 96-102.

Hannum, Hurst (1989), *The Limits of Sovereignty and Majority Rule: Minorities, Indigenous Peoples, and the Right to Autonomy*, University of Pennsylvania Press, Philadelphia.

Hannum, Hurst (1990), *Autonomy, Sovereignty, and Self-Determination*, University of Pennsylvania Press, Philadelphia.

Hastings, William K. (1988), *The Right to an Education in Maori: The Case from International Law*, Victoria University Press, Wellington, New Zealand.

Haugen, Einar (1981), "Language Fragmentation in Scandinavia", in Einar Haugen, Derrick McClure and Derick Thomson (eds.), *Minority Languages Today*, Edinburgh University Press, Edinburgh.

Héraud, Guy (1966), *Peuples et langues d'Europe*, Éditions Denoël, Paris.

Héraud, Guy (1967), *Qu'est-ce que l'ethnisme?*, Éditions I.J.D., Charleroi, France.

Heuberger, Valeria (1991), "European Gypsies and Minority Rights: A Hungarian Case Study", in *Proceedings of the VIth International Symposium*, Commission on Folk Law and Legal Pluralism, Ottawa, pp. 437-445.

Heugh, Kathleen (1987), *Trends in Language Policy for a Post-Apartheid South Africa*, University of Cape Town, Cape Town, pp. 206-220.

Hobsbawm, Eric (1990), *Nations and Nationalism since 1780*, Cambridge University Press, Cambridge.

Horowitz, Donald L. (1985), *Ethnic Groups in Conflict*, University of California Press, Berkeley, USA.

Hourani, Albert (1991), *A History of the Arab Peoples*, Warner Books, New York.

Human Rights in International Law: Legal and Policy Issues (1984), Theodor Meron (ed.), Clarendon Press, Oxford, United Kingdom.

Hunczak, Taras (1993), "Ukraine 1993 — A Multinational State", in *Report on an Expert Consultation in Connection with the Activities of the CSCE High Commissioner on National Minorities*, Foundation on Inter-Ethnic Relation, den Haag, Netherlands, pp. 55-62.

Huta-Mukana, Mutombo (1991), "Les langues au Zaïre à l'horizon 2000", in J.-J. Symoens and J. Vanderlinden (eds.), *Symposium: Les langues en Afrique à l'horizon 2000*, Institut Africain and Académie Royale des Sciences d'Outre-Mer, Bruxelles, pp. 84-107.

Indigenous Peoples: Living and Working Conditions of Aboriginal Populations in Independent Countries (1953), International Labour Organisation, Geneva.

Innis, Harold A. (1986), *Empire and Communications*, Press Porcépic, Victoria, Canada.

International Centre for Research on Bilingualism (1978), *Linguistic Minorities and Interventions, Towards a Typology*, Les Presses de l'Université Laval, Québec.

The International Centre on Censorship (1990), *Freedom of Information and Expression in Canada*, Article 19, London.

International Conference on Provision for Minority Languages (1989), Western Isles Islands Council, Isle of Lewis, Scotland.

International Protection of Minorities (1986), S. Chandra (ed.), Mittal Publications, Delhi.

Isajiw, Wsevolod W. (1985), "Learning and Use of Ethnic Language at Home and School: Sociological Findings and Issues", in M.R. Lupul (ed.), *Ukrainian Bilingual Education*, Canadian Institute of Ukrainian Studies, Edmonton, Canada, pp. 225-230.

Karakwas Stacey-Diabo, Carol (1990), "Les droits linguistiques des autochtones dans les années 1990", in Ryszard I. Cholewinski (ed.), *Les droits de la personne au Canada: Dans les années 1990 et au-delà*, University of Ottawa, Ottawa, pp. 155-184.

Karpat, Kemal H. (1982), "Millets and Nationality" in Benjamin Braude and Bernard Lewis (eds.), *Christians and Jews in the Ottoman Empire: The Functioning of a Plural Society*, Holmes & Meier, New York.

Kaufman, Otto K. (1988), "Swiss Federalism" in Robert A. Goldwin, Art Kaufman, and William A. Schambra (eds.), *Forging Unity out of Diversity: The Approaches of Eight Nations*, American Enterprise Institute for Public Policy Research, Washington, D.C., pp. 206-237.

Kerr, Donal, Breuer, Mordechai, Gilley, Sheridan, and Suttner, Ernst Christopher (1994), *Religion, State and Ethnic Groups*, Dartmouth Publishing, Aldershot, United Kingdom.

Khamisi, Abdul (1987), "Language Planning Strategies in Tanzania", in Lorne Laforge (ed.), *Proceedings of the International Colloquium on Language Planning*, Les Presses de l'Université Laval, Québec, pp. 194-201.

Klein, G. (1986), *La politica linguistica del facismo*, II Mulino, Bologna.

Kloss, H. (1971), *Les droits linguistiques des Franco-Américains aux États-Unis*, Les Presses de l'Université Laval, Québec.

Koch, Harald (1991), "Legal Aspects of a Language Policy for the European Communities: Language Risks, Equal Opportunities, and Legislating a Language", in Florian Coulmas (ed.), *A Language Policy for the European Community*, Mouton de Gruyter, Berlin, pp. 147-161.

Krstitich, Dragolioub (1924), *Les minorités, l'État et la communauté internationale*, Librairie Arthur Rousseau, Paris.

Kymlicka, Will (1989), *Liberalism, Community and Culture*, Clarendon Press, Oxford, United Kingdom.

Labrie, Normand (1993), *La construction linguistique de la communauté européenne*, Honoré Champion, Paris.

Lador-Lederer, J.J. (1968), *International Group Protection*, A.W. Sijthoff, Leiden, Netherlands.

Language and Culture: A Matter of Survival (1992), Australian Government Publishing Service, Canberra.

Language and Law: Proceedings of the First Conference of the International Institute of Comparative Linguistic Law (1989), P. Pupier and J. Woehrling (eds.), Wilson & Lafleur, Montréal.

Language in Australia (1991), Suzanne Romaine (ed.), Cambridge University Press, Cambridge.

Language of Inequality (1985), N. Wolfson and J. Manes (eds.), Mouton Publishers, Berlin.

Language Planning and Language Education (1983), Chris Kennedy (ed.), Unwin Publishers, London.

Language Problems of Developing Nations (1968), Joshua A. Fishman, Charles A. Ferguson and Jyotirinda Das Gupta (eds.), John Wiley & Sons, New York.

Language and Society in Africa (1992), Robert K. Herbert (ed.), Witwatersrand University Press, Witwatersrand, South Africa.

Language and the State: The Law and Politics of Identity — Proceedings of the Second National Conference on Constitutional Affairs (1989), David Schneiderman (ed.), Les Éditions Yvon Blais, Cowansville, Québec.

La langue catalane aujourd'hui (1992), Generalitat de Catalunya, Barcelona.

Les langues autochtones du Québec (1992), Jacques Maurais (ed.), Les Publications du Québec, Québec.

Langues et constitutions (1993), François Gauthier et al. (eds.), Les Publications du Québec, Québec.

Lapierre, Jean-William (1988), *Le pouvoir politique et les langues*, Presses Universitaires de France, Paris.

Laponce, Jean A. (1984), *Langue et territoire*, Les Presses de l'Université Laval, Québec.

Laponce, Jean A. (1987), *Languages and Their Territories*, University of Toronto Press, Toronto.

Laponce, Jean A. (1992), "Language and Politics", in *Encyclopedia of Government and Politics, Volume 1*, Routledge, London, pp. 587-602.

Laponce, Jean A. (1992), "L'heure du fédéralisme personnel est-elle arrivée?", in Jean Lafontant (ed.), *L'État et les minorités*, Éditions du Blé, Saint-Boniface, Canada, pp. 55-65.

Lasok, D. and Bridge, J.W. (1991), *Law and Institutions of the European Communities*, Butterworths, London.

Leclerc, Jacques (1989), *La guerre des langues dans l'affichage*, V.L.B. Editions, Montréal.

Leibowitz, Arnold H. (1982), *Federal Recognition of the Rights of Minority Language Groups*, National Clearinghouse for Bilingual Education, Rosslyn, Virginia.

Lerner, Nathan (1991), *Group Rights and Discrimination in International Law*, Martinus Nijhoff, Dordrecht, Netherlands.

Lerner, Nathan (1992), "The 1989 ILO Convention on Indigenous Populations: New Standards?", in Yoram Dinstein and Mala Tabory (eds.), *The Protection of Minorities and Human Rights*, Martinus Nijhoff, Dordrecht, Netherlands, pp 213-231.

The Lesser Used Languages — Assimilating Newcomers (1992), Llinos Dafis (ed.), Joint Working Party on Bilingualism in Dyfed, Dyfed, Wales.

Lewis, E. Glyn (1978), "Bilingualism in Education in Wales", in B. Spolsky and R. Cooper (eds.), *Case Studies in Bilingual Education*, Newbury House, London, pp. 249-290.

Linde, Enrique, Ignacio Ortega, Luis, and Sanchez Moron, Miguel (1979), *El sistema europeo de protección de los derechos humanos*, Editorial Civitas, Madrid.

Linguistic Minorities and Literacy: Language Policy Issues in Developing Countries (1990), Florian Coulmas (ed.), Mouton Publishers, Berlin.

Linguistic Minorities, Policies and Pluralism (1984), John Edwards (ed.), Applied Language Studies, Harcourt Brace Jovanovich, London.

Linguistic Rights of Minorities (1994), Frank Horn (ed.), Northern Institute for Environmental and Minority Law, University of Lapland, Rovaniemi, Finland.

Linz, Juan J. (1988), "Spanish Democracy and the Estado de las Autonomias", in Robert A. Goldwin, Art Kaufman, and William A. Schambra (eds.), *Forging Unity out of Diversity: The Approaches of Eight Nations*, American Enterprise Institute for Public Policy Research, Washington, D.C., pp. 260-303.

Lo Bianco, Joseph (1987), *National Policy on Languages*, Australian Government Publishing Service, Canberra.

Lucas, J. O. (1964), *Yoruba Language*, Ore Kigbe Press, Lagos, Nigeria.

Macartney, C.A. (1968), *National States and National Minorities*, Russell and Russell, New York.

Maintenance and Loss of Minority Languages (1992), Willem Fase, Koen Jaspaert and Sjaak Kroon (eds.), John Benjamins Publishing Co., Amsterdam/Philadelphia.

The Main Types and Causes of Discrimination, Memorandum submitted by the Secretary General (1949), United Nations Publications, New York.

Mannheim, Bruce (1984), *Una nación acorralada: Southern Peruvian Quechua Language Planning and Politics in Historical Perspective*, Cambridge University Press, Cambridge.

Martel, Angéline (1991), *Les droits scolaires des minorités de langue officielle au Canada : De l'instruction à la gestion*, Office of the Commissioner of Official Languages, Ottawa.

Marti-Rolli, Christine (1978), *La liberté de la langue en droit suisse*, Juris Druck and Verlag, Zurich.

Matsui, Shigenori (1993), "Aliens under the Japanese Constitution", in Shigenori Matsui and Susumi Noda (eds.), *Foreign Workers Problems: Japan and the US*, Center for Japan-US Exchange in the Humanities and Social Sciences, Osaka, pp. 85-116.

Mattera, Alfonso (1988), *Le marché unique européen, ses règles, son fonctionnement*, Jupiter, Paris.

Maw, Joan (1991), "Multilingualism in Tanzania", in J.-J. Symoens and J. Vanderlinden (eds.), *Symposium: Les langues en Afrique à l'horizon 2000*, Institut Africain and Académie Royale des Sciences d'Outre-Mer, Bruxelles, pp. 165-179.

Mazrui, Ali A. (1977), *A World Federation of Cultures*, Free Press, New York.

McDonald, Laughlin and Powell, John (1993), *The Rights of Racial Minorities*, Southern Illinois University Press, Carbondale and Edwardsville, USA.

McDougal, M.S., Lasswell, H.D. and Chen, Lung-chu (1980), *Human Rights and World Public Order*, Yale University Press, New Haven, USA.

McGoldrick, Dominic (1991), *The Human Rights Committee: Its Role in the Development of the International Covenant on Civil and Political Rights*, Clarendon Press, Oxford, United Kingdom.

McKean, Warwick (1983), *Equality and Discrimination under International Law*, Clarendon Press, Oxford, United Kingdom.

McNeill, William H. (1967), *Essays in the Liberal Interpretation of History*, University of Chicago Press, Chicago.

McRae, H., Nettheim G. and Beacroft L. (1991), *Aboriginal Legal Issues: Commentary and Materials*, The Law Book Company Limited, Sydney, Australia.

McRae, Kenneth D. (1983), *Conflict and Compromise in Multilingual Societies: Switzerland*, Wilfrid Laurier University Press, Waterloo, Canada.

McRae, Kenneth D. (1986), *Conflict and Compromise in Multilingual Societies: Belgium*, Wilfrid Laurier University Press, Waterloo, Canada.

Meillet, A. (1928), *Les langues dans l'Europe Nouvelle*, Payot, Paris.

Melucci, Alberto and Diani, Mario (1992), *Nazioni senza stato : I movimenti ethnico-nazionali in Occidente*, Feltrinelli, Milano.

Memorandum of Safeguards for Linguistic Minorities (1956), Ministry of Home Affairs, New Delhi.

Meuleau, Maurice and Pietri, Luce (1971), *Le monde et son histoire — Le monde Antique et les débuts du Moyen-Âge*, Éditions Bordas and Robert Laffont, Paris.

Milian i Massana, Antoni (1992), *Drets lingüístics i Dret fonamental a l'educació. Un estudi comparat: Itàlia, Bèlgica, Suïssa, el Canadà i Espanya*, Generalitat de Catalunya, Barcelona.

Mill, John Stuart (1946), *On Liberty and Considerations of Representative Government*, Blackwell, London.

Mini-Guide to the Lesser Used Languages of the European Community (1993), European Bureau for Lesser Used Languages, Dublin.

Ministerio de Gobierno, Dirección General de Asuntos Indígenas (1993), *De Los Territorios Indígenas A Las Entidades Territoriales Indígenas — Participación y Autonomía*, Ministerio de Gobierno, Santafé de Bogotá, Colombia.

Les minorités en Europe : droits linguistiques et droits de l'Homme (1992), Henri Giordan (ed.), Éditions Kimé, Koln.

Minorités et État (1986), Pierre Guillaume et al. (eds.), Presses Universitaires de Bordeaux, Bordeaux.

Minorities and the Law (1972), Mohammed Imam (ed.), Indian Law Institute, New Delhi.

Minorities: Community and Identity (1983), C. Fried (ed.), Springer-Verlag, Berlin.

Minorities in Central and Eastern Europe (1993), Minorities Rights Group, London.

Minority Languages Today (1981), Einar Haugen, J. Derrick McClure and Derick Thomson (eds.), Edinburgh University Press, Edinburgh.

Minority Rights in Europe: Policies and Practices in CSCE Participating States (1991), Minority Rights Group, London.

Modeen, T. (1969), *The International Protection of National Minorities in Europe*, Åbo Akademi, Åbo, Finland.

Modern Law of Self-Determination (1993), Christian Tomuschat (ed.), Martinus Nijhoff, Dordrecht, Netherlands.

Morrisson, Clovis C. (1981), *The Dynamics of Development in the European Human Rights Convention System*, Martinus Nijhoff, den Haag, Netherlands.

Multilingual Political Systems Problems and Solutions (1975), Jean-Guy Savard and Richard Vigneault (eds.), Les Presses de l'Université Laval, Québec.

Nariman, Fali Sam (1988), "The Indian Constitution: An Experiment in Unity amid Diversity", in Robert A. Goldwin, Art Kaufman, and William A. Schambra (eds.), *Forging Unity out of Diversity: The Approaches of Eight Nations*, American Enterprise Institute for Public Policy Research, Washington, D.C., pp. 7-35.

Nation-States and Indians in Latin America (1991), Greg Urban and Joel Sherzer (eds.), University of Texas Press, Austin, USA.

National Policy on Education, Ministry of Education and Social Welfare (1968), Government of India, New Delhi.

National Separatism (1982), Colin H. Williams (ed.), University of British Columbia Press, Vancouver.

Nazione, etnia, cittadinanza in Italia e in Europa (1992), G.E. Rusconi (ed.), La Scuola, Brescia, Italy.

New Directions in Human Rights (1989), Ellen L. Lutz, Hurst Hannum and Kathryn J. Burke (eds.), University of Pennsylvania Press, Philadelphia.

Nisan, Mordechai (1991), *Minorities in the Middle East: A History of Struggle and Self-Expression*, McFarland & Co., Jefferson, USA

Nowak, Manfred, "The Evolution of Minority Rights in International Law", in Catherine Brölmann, René Lefeber and Marjoleine Zieck (eds.), *Peoples and Minorities in International Law*, Martinus Nijhoff, Dordrecht, Netherlands, pp. 103-118.

O'Bryan, K.G., Reitz J.G. and Kuplowska O.M. (1976), *Les langues non officielles : Étude sur le multiculturalisme*, Supply and Services Canada, Ottawa.

O Màille, Tomas (1990), *The Status of the Irish Language — A Legal Perspective*, Bord na Gaeilge, Dublin.

Organization of American States (1993), *Annual Report of the Inter-American Commission on Human Rights 1992-1993*, General Secretariat, Washington, D.C.

Oyelaran, Olasope O. (1991), "Language in Nigeria Towards the Year 2000", in J.-J. Symoens and J. Vanderlinden (eds.), *Symposium : Les langues en Afrique à l'horizon 2000*, Institut Africain and Académie Royale des Sciences d'Outre-Mer, Bruxelles, pp. 109-139.

Palley, Claire (1978), *Constitutional Law and Minorities*, Minority Rights Group Report, London.

Peoples and Minorities in International Law (1993), Catherine Brölmann, René Lefeber, and Marjoleine Zieck (eds.), Martinus Nijhoff, Dordrecht, Netherlands.

Petschen Verdaguer, Santiago (1990), *Las minorías lingüíticas de Europa occidental: Documentos 1491-1989*, Eusko Legebiltzarra, Vitoria-Gasteiz, Spain.

Des peuples enfin reconnus (1994), Marie Léger (ed.), Éditions Écosociété, Montréal.

Phillipson, Robert (1992), *Linguistic Imperialism*, Oxford University Press, Oxford, United Kingdom.

Piatt, Bill (1990), *¿Only English? Law and Language Policy in the United States*, University of New Mexico Press, Albuquerque, USA.

Piatt, Bill (1993), *Language on the Job: Balancing Business Needs and Employee Rights*, University of New Mexico Press, Albuquerque, USA.

Pizzorusso, Alessandro (1975), *Il pluralismo linguistico in Italia fra Stato nazionale e autonomie regionali*, Pacini, Pisa, Italy.

Plourde, Gaston (1972), *Options politiques fondamentales de l'État plurilingue*, Les Presses de l'Université Laval, Québec.

Plourde, M. (1988), *La politique linguistique du Québec, 1977-1987*, Institut québecois de recherche sur la culture, Québec.

Pluralisme en Europe et au Canada — Perspectives de recherche (1986), J.-D. Gendron and P. H. Nelde (eds.), Research Centre on Multilingualism, Bruxelles.

Le plurilinguisme européen (1994), Claude Truchot (ed.), Honoré Champion, Paris.

Poulin, Richard (1984), *La politique des nationalités de la République populaire de Chine : de Mao Zedong à Hua Guofeng*, Éditeur officiel du Québec, Québec.

Prasad, Nawal (1979), *The Language Issue in India*, Leeladevi Publications, Delhi.

Proceedings of the International Colloquium on Language Planning (1987), Lorne Laforge (ed.), Presses de l'Université Laval, Québec.

Proceedings of the Sixth International Colloquy about the European Convention on Human Rights (1986), Directorate of Human Rights (ed.), Martinus Nijhoff Publishers, Dordrecht, Netherlands.

A Profile of Aboriginal Languages in the Yukon (1988), Yukon Executive Council Office, Whitehorse, Canada.

The Protection of Ethnic and Linguistic Minorities in Europe (1993), John Packer and Kristian Myntti (eds.), Institute for Human Rights, Åbo Akademi University, Åbo, Finland.

The Protection of Minorities and Human Rights (1992), Yoram Dinstein and Mala Tabory (eds.), Martinus Nijhoff, Dordrecht, Netherlands.

The Protection of Minorities — Special Protective Measures of an International Character for Ethnic, Religious or Linguistic Groups (1967), United Nations Publications, New York.

Le quadrilinguisme en Suisse — présent et futur (1989), Département fédéral de l'intérieur, Bern.

Québec-Communauté française de Belgique : autonomie et spécificité dans le cadre d'un système fédéral (1991), Wilson & Lafleur, Montréal.

Rapport mondial sur le développement humain (1994), Programme des Nations unies pour le développement, Economica, Paris.

Readings in the Sociology of Language (1968), Joshua A. Fishman (ed.), Mouton and Co. N.V. Publishers, den Haag, Netherlands.

Recueil des législations linguistiques dans le monde — Tome V : L'Algérie, l'Autriche, la Chine, le Danemark, la Finlande, la Hongrie, l'île de Malte, le Maroc, la Norvège, la Nouvelle-Zélande, les Pays-Bas, le Royaume-Uni, la Tunisie, la Turquie, l'ex-URSS (1994), Jacques Leclerc and Jacques Maurais (eds.), International Center for Research on Language Planning, Québec.

Recueil des législations linguistiques dans le monde — Tome VI : La Colombie, les États-Unis, le Mexique, Porto Rico et les traités internationaux (1994), Jacques Leclerc and Jacques Maurais (eds.), International Center for Research on Language Planning, Québec.

Renard, R. (1991), "Éléments d'une problématique de l'aménagement linguistique en Afrique", in J.-J. Symoens and J. Vanderlinden (eds.), *Symposium : Les langues en Afrique à l'horizon 2000*, Institut Africain and Académie Royale des Sciences d'Outre-Mer, Bruxelles, pp. 43-49.

Renaud, P. (1991), "Essai d'interprétation des pratiques linguistiques au Cameroun : Les données, les choix et leur signification", in J.-J. Symoens and J. Vanderlinden (eds.), *Symposium : Les langues en Afrique à l'horizon 2000*, Institut Africain and Académie Royale des Sciences d'Outre-Mer, Bruxelles, pp. 51-83.

Report of the CSCE Meeting of Experts on National Minorities (1991), CSCE Secretariat, Washington, D.C.

Report of the Human Rights Committee Vol. II (1990), United Nations Publications, New York.

Report of the Māori Language Commission for the Year Ended 30 June 1992 (1992), Government Publications Service, Wellington, New Zealand.

Report of the Working Group on Indigenous Populations on its Tenth Session (1992), United Nations Publications, New York.

Report on Behalf of the Committee on Petitions on Languages in the Community and the Situation of Catalan (1990), European Parliament Session Documents, Strasbourg.

Report on the Rights of Minorities (1990), Council of Europe Parliamentary Assembly Document, Strasbourg.

Rey-Von Allmen, Micheline (1983), "Le statut des langues d'origine dans les pays d'accueil", in *Status of Migrants' Mother Tongues*, European Science Foundation, Strasbourg, pp. 17-22.

Richstone, Jeffrey (1989), "La protection juridique des langues autochtones au Canada", in P. Pupier and J. Woehrling (eds.), *Language and Law: Proceedings of the First Conference of the International Institute of Comparative Linguistic Law*, Wilson & Lafleur, Montréal, pp. 259-278.

The Rights of Indigenous Peoples (1990), United Nations Publications, Geneva.

The Rights of Indigenous Peoples in International Law (1987), Ruth Thompson (ed.), University of Saskatchewan Native Law Centre, Saskatoon, Canada.

Robert, Jacques and Oberdorff, Henri (1989), *Libertés fondamentales et droits de l'homme : Textes français et internationaux*, Montchrestien, Paris.

Robinson, O.F., Ferguson, T.D., and Gordon, W.M. (1985), *An Introduction to European Legal History*, Professional Books, Trowbridge, United Kingdom.

Rosseel, E. (1980), *L'éducation des enfants de travailleurs migrants en Europe occidental — Bibliographie sélective*, International Centre for Research on Bilingualism, Québec.

Rubin, J. (1968), *National Bilingualism in Paraguay*, Mouton, den Haag, Netherlands.

Saint-Germain, Michel (1988), *La situation linguistique en Haïti : bilan et perspectives*, Université d'Ottawa, Ottawa.

Salomone, Rosemary C. (1986), *Equal Education under Law: Legal Rights and Federal Policy in the Post Brown Era*, St. Martin's Press, New York.

Santa Cruz, Hernàn (1977), *La discrimination raciale*, United Nations Publications, New York.

Schermerhorn, R.A. (1978), *Ethnic Plurality in India*, The University of Arizona Press, Tucson, USA.

Scholsem, Jean-Claude (1992), "Faut-il protéger les minorités?" in *Présence du droit public et des droits de l'Homme*, Université Libre de Bruxelles, Bruxelles, pp. 1167-1178.

Schooling, Educational Policy and Ethnic Identity (1991), Janusz Tomiak (ed.), New York University Press, New York.

Sherman Swing, E. (1980), *Bilingualism and Linguistic Segregation in the Schools of Brussels*, International Centre for Research on Bilingualism, Québec.

Siguan, Miguel (1990), *Linguistic Minorities in the European Economic Community: Spain, Portugal, Greece*, Commission of the European Communities, Bruxelles.

Simard, Carole, Bélanger, Sylvie, Lavoie, Nathalie, Polo, Anne-Lise and Turmel, Serge (1991), *Minorités visibles, communautés ethnoculturelles et politique canadienne : La question de l'accessibilité*, Supply and Services Canada, Ottawa.

Sinnadurai, Visu (1988), "Unity and Diversity: The Constitution of Malaysia", in Robert A. Goldwin, Art Kaufman, and William A. Schambra (eds.), *Forging Unity out of Diversity: The Approaches of Eight Nations*, American Enterprise Institute for Public Policy Research, Washington, D.C., pp. 327-341.

Situation of Human Rights in Estonia and Latvia — Report of the Secretary General (1993), United Nations Document, New York.

The Situation of Regional or Minority Languages in Europe (1994), Council of Europe, Strasbourg.

Skutnabb-Kangas, Tove (1981), *Bilingualism or Not: The Education of Minorities*, Clevedon, Avon, United Kingdom.

Skutnabb-Kangas, Tove (1990), *Language, Literacy and Minorities*, Minority Rights Group, London.

Skutnabb-Kangas, Tove and Bucak, Sertaç (1994) "Killing a Mother Tongue — How the Kurds are Deprived of Linguistic Human Rights", in T. Skutnabb-Kangas and R. Phillipson (eds.), *Linguistic Human Rights: Overcoming Linguistic Discrimination*, Mouton de Gruyter, Berlin, pp. 347-370.

Smith, Anthony D. (1981), *The Ethnic Revival*, Cambridge University Press, Cambridge.

Smolicz, J.J. (1988), *Australia's Language Policies and Minority Rights: A Core Value Perspective*, Centre for Intercultural Studies and Multicultural Education, University of Adelaide, Adelaide.

Sociolinguistics: Proceedings of the UCLA Sociolinguistics Conference (1966), William Bright (ed.), Mouton, den Haag, Netherlands.

South African Law Commission (1991), *Project 58, Group and Human Rights — Interim Report*, University of the Witwatersrand, Johannesburg.

Southerland, J. Alfred (1987), *National Origin Discrimination Based on Accent or Manner of Speaking*, Prentice-Hall Information Services, Paramus, New Jersey.

Sparer, Michel (1986), *Libre-échange et droit linguistique*, Conseil de la langue française, Québec.

Srivastava, R.N. (1990), "Literacy Education for Minorities: A Case Study from India", in Florian Coulmas (ed.), *Linguistic Minorities and Literacy: Language Policy Issues in Developing Countries*, Mouton Publishers, Berlin, pp. 39-55.

The Status of Minorities and Ethnic Groups in the Member States of the Council of Europe (1988), Council of Europe, Strasbourg.

Stavenhagen, Rodolfo (1990), *The Ethnic Question: Conflicts, Development and Human Rights*, United Nations University Press, Tokyo.

Stavenhagen, Rodolfo (1990), "Linguistic Minorities and Language Policy in Latin America: The Case of Mexico", in Florian Coulmas (ed.), *Linguistic Minorities and Literacy: Language Policy Issues in Developing Countries*, Mouton Publishers, Berlin, pp. 56-62.

Stubbs, Michael (1991), "Educational Language Planning in England and Wales: Multicultural Rhetoric and Assimilationist Assumptions", in Florian Coulmas (ed.), *A Language Policy for the European Community*, Mouton de Gruyter, Berlin, pp. 215-239.

Study of Equality in the Administration of Justice, Mohammed Ahmed Abu Rannat, Special Rapporteur (1972), United Nations Publications, New York

Study of the Problem of Discrimination Against Indigenous Populations, José R. Martinez Cobo, Special Rapporteur (1987), United Nations Publications, New York.

Study of the Right of Everyone to be Free from Arbitrary Arrest, Detention and Exile (1965), United Nations Publications, New York.

Study on the Rights of Persons belonging to Ethnic, Religious and Linguistic Minorities, Francesco Capotorti, Special Rapporteur (1979), United Nations Publications, New York.

Sub-Commission on Prevention of Discrimination and Protection of Minorities, Working Group on Indigenous Populations (1983), *Consideration of the Evolution of Standards Concerning the Rights of Indigenous Populations*, United Nations Publications, New York.

Sun, Hong-kai (1987), "An Outline of Language Planning in China", in Lorne Laforge (ed.), *Proceedings of the International Colloquium on Language Planning*, Les Presses de l'Université Laval, Québec, pp. 115-131.

Sundberg, Jacob W.F. (1992), "Intent or Effect — A Look at Legislative Intent", in *Présence du droit public et des droits de l'homme - Mélanges offerts à Jacques Velu*, Université Libre de Bruxelles, Bruxelles, pp. 1235-1252.

Svensson, Tom (1991), "The Attainment of Limited Self-Determination Among the Sami in Recent Years", in *Proceedings of the VIth International Symposium*, Commission on Folk Law and Legal Pluralism, Ottawa, pp. 28-38.

Symposium : Les langues en Afrique à l'horizon 2000 (1991), J.-J. Symoens and J. Vanderlinden (eds.), Institut Africain and Académie Royale des Sciences d'Outre-Mer, Bruxelles.

Tabouret-Keller, Andrée (1991), "Factors of Constraints and Freedom in Setting a Language Policy for the European Community: A Sociolinguistic Approach", in Florian Coulmas (ed.), *A Language Policy for the European Community*, Mouton de Gruyter, Berlin, pp. 45-57.

Taylor, Charles (1985), *Human Agency and Language — Philosophical Papers I*, Cambridge University Press, Cambridge.

Taylor, Charles (1992), *Rapprocher les solitudes : Écrits sur le fédéralisme et le nationalisme au Canada*, Les Presses de l'Université Laval, Québec.

Tetley, W. (1986), *Les droits linguistiques et scolaires au Québec et au Canada*, International Centre for Research on Bilingualism, Québec.

Thornberry, Patrick (1991), *International Law and the Rights of Minorities*, Clarendon Press, Oxford, United Kingdom.

Thornberry, Patrick (1991), *Minority and Human Rights Law*, Minority Rights Group, London.

Tollefson, James W. (1991), *Planning Language, Planning Inequality*, Longman Inc., New York.

Tomas y Valiente, Francisco (1988), "Commentary", in Robert A. Goldwin, Art Kaufman, and William A. Schambra (eds.), *Forging Unity out of Diversity: The Approaches of Eight Nations*, American Enterprise Institute for Public Policy Research, Washington, D.C., pp. 304-314.

Tomuschat, Christian (1983), "Protection of Minorities under Article 27 of the International Covenant on Civil and Political Rights", in *Völkerrecht als Rechtsordnung Internationale Gerichtsarbeit Menschenrechte*, Springer, Berlin, pp. 949-979.

Tosi, Arturo (1984), *Immigration and Bilingual Education*, Pergamon Press, Oxford, United Kingdom.

Trudel, Pierre and Abran, France (1991), *Droit de la radio et de la télévision*, Éditions Thémis, Montréal.

Tsuda, Yukio (1986), *Language Inequality and Distortion in Intercultural Communication. A Critical Theory Approach*, John Benjamins Publishing Company, Amsterdam/Philadelphia.

Tucker, G. Richard (1984), "The Future of Language Policy in Education", in Stan Shapson and Vincent D'Oyley (eds.), *Bilingual and Multicultural Education: Canadian Perspectives*, Clevedon, Avon, United Kingdom, pp. 143-153.

Turcotte, D. (1981), *La politique linguistique en Afrique francophone : Une étude comparative de la Côte d'Ivoire et de Madagascar*, Les Presses de l'Université Laval, Québec.

Turcotte, D. (1982), *Politique linguistique et modalités d'application en Polynésie française : Vers l'implantation du bilinguisme officiel français-tahitien*, International Centre for Research on Bilingualism, Québec.

Turcotte, D. (1982), *Composition ethnique et politique linguistique en Nouvelle-Calédonie : Adoption, implantation et diffusion du français comme langue officielle et véhiculaire unique*, International Centre for Research on Bilingualism, Québec.

Turcotte, D. and Aubé H. (1983), *Lois, règlements et textes administratifs sur l'usage des langues en Afrique occidentale française (1826-1959)*, Les Presses de l'Université Laval, Québec.

Turi, Giuseppe (1977), *Les dispositions juridico-constitutionnelles de 147 États en matière de politique linguistique*, International Centre for Research on Bilingualism, Québec.

The Use of Vernacular Languages in Education (1953), UNESCO, Paris.

Vanderlinden, Jacques (1988), "Communities, Languages, Regions, and the Belgian Constitution, 1831-1985", in Robert A. Goldwin, Art Kaufman, and William A. Schambra (eds.), *Forging Unity out of Diversity: The Approaches of Eight Nations*, American Enterprise Institute for Public Policy Research, Washington, D.C., pp. 109-133.

Van Dyk, P. and Van Hoof, G.J.H. (1990), *Theory and Practice of the European Convention of Human Rights*, Kluwer Law and Taxation Publishers, Deventer-Boston.

Van Dyke, Vernon (1985), "Human Rights, Ethnicity, and Discrimination", in *Contributions in Ethnic Studies*, Greenwood Press, Westport, Connecticut, USA., pp. 3-77.

Verdoodt, Albert (1963), *Naissance et signification de la Déclaration universelle des droits de l'homme*, Nauwelaerts, Louvain-Paris.

Verdoodt, Albert (1985), *Les droits linguistiques des immigrants*, Éditeur officiel du Québec, Québec.

Vers la réconciliation? La question linguistique au Canada dans les années 1990 (1992), D. Bonin (ed.), Queen's University, Kingston, Canada.

Vierdag, E. (1973), *The Concept of Discrimination in International Law*, Martinus Nijhoff, den Haag, Netherlands.

Vikør, Lars S. (1993), *The Nordic Languages: Their Status and Interrelations*, Novus Press, Oslo.

Wadhwa, Kamlesh Kumar (1975), *Minority Safeguards in India*, Thompson Press (India), Delhi.

Waite, Jeffrey (1992), *Aoteareo: Speaking for Ourselves — A Discussion on the Development of a New Zealand Languages Policy, Part B*, Ministry of Education, Wellington, New Zealand.

Weill, Georges (1930), *L' éveil des nationalités et le mouvement libéral 1815-1848*, Librairie Félix Alcan, Paris.

Weinstein, Brian (1987), "Language Planning and Interests", in Lorne Laforge (ed.), *Proceedings of the International Colloquium on Language Planning*, Les Presses de l'Université Laval, Québec, pp. 34-57.

Wildsmith, B.H. (1988), *Aboriginal Peoples and Section 25 of the Canadian Charter of Rights and Freedoms*, University of Saskatchewan Native Law Centre, Saskatoon, Canada.

Woehrling, José (1993), "L'article 1 de la Charte canadienne et la problématique des restrictions aux droits et libertés : l'état de la jurisprudence de la Cour suprême" in *Droits de la personne: l'émergence de droits nouveaux*, Éditions Yvon Blais, Cowansville, pp. 3-34.

Woehrling, José (1993), *La conformité de certaines modifications projetées au régime linguistique de l'affichage public et de la publicité commerciale découlant de la Charte de la langue française avec les chartes des droits et libertés — Annexe à l'Avis sur d'éventuelles modifications à la Charte de la langue française*, Bibliothèque nationale du Québec, Québec.

Woehrling, José (1993), "Politique linguistique et libre-échange : l'incidence de l'Accord de libre-échange entre le Canada et les États-Unis sur la législation linguistique du Québec" in *Contextes de la politique linguistique québécoise*, Publications du Québec, Québec, pp. 79-123.

Wolff, Philippe (1970), *Les origines linguistiques de l'Europe occidentale*, Hachette, Paris.

Wolfrum, Rüdiger (1993), "The Emergence of New Minorities as a Result of Migration", in Catherine Brölmann, René Lefeber, and Marjoleine Zieck (eds.), *Peoples and Minorities in International Law*, Martinus Nijhoff, Dordrecht, Netherlands, pp. 153-166.

Woodward, J. (1989), *Native Law*, Carswell, Vancouver.

Woolner, A. C. (1938), *Languages in History and Politics*, Oxford University Press, London.

World Directory of Minorities (1990), Minority Rights Group (ed.), Longman, Harlow, United Kingdom.

Zepeda, Ofelia and Hill, Jane H. (1991), "The Condition of Native American Languages in the United States", in R.H. Robins and E.M. Uhlenbeck (eds.), *Endangered Languages*, New York, pp. 135-155.

Articles

A. B. et al. v. Italy, South Tyrol Case (1991), in *Human Rights Law Journal*, Vol. 12, N° 1-2, 25.

Adams, Charles F. (1973), "Citado a Comparecer: Language Barriers and Due Process — Is Mailed Notice in English Constitutionally Sufficient?", in *California Law Review*, Vol. 61, 1395-1421.

Ajulo, S. B. (1985), "Law, Language and International Organisations in Africa: The Case of ECOWAS", in *Journal of African Law*, Vol. 29, N° 1, 1-24.

Albanese, Ferdinando (1991), "Ethnic and Linguistic Minorities in Europe", in *Yearbook of European Law*, Vol. 11, 313-337.

Alexander, Yonah (1993), "Editor's Note", in *International Journal on Group Rights*, Vol. 1, N° 1, 1-5.

Alfredsson, Gudmundur and de Zayas, Alfred (1993), "Minority Rights: Protection by the United Nations", in *Human Rights Law Journal*, Vol. 14, 1-8.

Andress, Judith L. and Falkowski, James E. (1980), "Self-Determination: Indians and the United Nations — The Anomalous Status of America's Domestic Dependant Nations", in *American Indian Law Review*, Vol. 8, 97-116.

Andrews, J.A. and Henshaw, L.G. (1983-85), "The Use of the Welsh Language in The Courts", in *Cambrian Law Review*, Vol. 14-16, 13-30.

Andrews, J.A. and Henshaw, L.G. (1983), "The Irish and Welsh Languages in the Courts: A Comparative Study", in *Irish Jurist*, Vol. 18, 1-22.

Anghie, Antony (1992), "Human Rights and Cultural Identity: New Hope for Ethnic Peace?" in *Harvard International Law Journal*, Vol. 33, N° 2, 341-352.

An-Na'im, Abdullahi A. (1987), "Religious Minorities under Islamic Law and the Limits of Cultural Relativism", in *Human Rights Quarterly*, Vol. 9, 1-18.

Annis, Melissa (1982), "Indian Education: Bilingual Education — A Legal Right for Native Americans", in *American Indian Law Review*, Vol. 10, 333-360.

Asch, Michael (1992), "Aboriginal Self-Government and the Construction of Canadian Constitutional Identity", in *Alberta Law Review*, Vol. XXX, N° 2, 465-491.

The Austrian State Treaty and Human Rights (1956), in *International and Comparative Law Quarterly*, Vol. 5, 265-274.

Avila, Joaquin (1984), "Equal Educational Opportunities for Language Minority Children", in *University of Colorado Law Review*, Vol. 55, 559-569.

Baetens-Beardsmore, Hugo (1993), "Multilingual Concepts in the Schools of Europe — Belgium", in *Sociolinguistica*, Vol. 7, 12-21.

Bahnev, Yulii (1990), "Non-Discrimination Against and Protection of Minorities under Contemporary International Law", in *Plural Societies Research Papers*, Vol. XXI, 109-127.

Barsh, Russel Lawrence (1983), "Indigenous North America and Contemporary International Law", in *Oregon Law Review*, Vol. 62, 73-125.

Barsh, Russel Lawrence (1986), "Indigenous Peoples: An Emerging Object of International Law", in *American Journal of International Law*, Vol. 80, 369-385.

Bates, D. L. (1991), "Maori Language: Some Observations Upon its Use in Criminal Proceedings", in *New Zealand Law Journal*, February, 55-60.

Beloff, Michael (1987), "Minority Languages and the Law", in *Current Legal Problems*, Vol. 40, 139-157.

Bendjedid, Chadli (1992), "Algérie — Généralisation de l'utilisation de la langue arabe", in *Revue de droit international et de droit comparé*, N° 1, 70-76.

Berger, Thomas R. (1984), "Native Rights and Self-Determination: An Address to the Conference on the Voices of Native People", in *University of Western Ontario Law Review*, Vol. 22, N° 1, 1-14.

Berkey, Curtis (1989), "Indian Nations under Legal Assault — New Restrictions on Native American Sovereignty: Are they Constitutional? Are they Moral?", in *Human Rights*, Vol. 16, N° 9, 18-23.

Berkey, Curtis G. (1992), "International Law and Domestic Courts: Enhancing Self-Determination for Indigenous Peoples", in *Harvard Human Rights Journal*, Vol. 5, 65-94.

Berman, Nathaniel (1992), "A Perilous Ambivalence: Nationalist Desire, Legal Autonomy, and the Limits of the Interwar Framework", in *Harvard International Law Journal*, Vol. 33, N° 2 353-379.

Berman, Nathaniel (1993), "But the Alternative is Despair: European Nationalism and the Modernist Renewal of International Law", in *Harvard Law Review*, Vol. 106, 1792-1903.

Bernier, Chantal (1984), "La négociation de l'autonomie politique des autochtones du Québec et le droit international", in *Revue québecoise de droit international*, Vol. 1, 359-372.

Bilingual Education and Desegregation (1978-79), in *University of Pennsylvania Law Review*, N° 4-6, 1564-1606.

Bistline, Andrea L. (1993), "Preferential Admissions Policies and Single-Minority Scholarships: The Legal Implications of Race-Preference in Higher Education", in *Dickinson Law Review*, Vol. 97, 283-303.

Black Grubb, Erica (1974), "Breaking the Language Barrier: The Right to Bilingual Education", in *Harvard Civil Rights-Civil Liberties Law Review*, Vol. 9, 52-94.

Boisson de Chazournes, Laurence (1988), "Publicité commerciale et liberté d'expression dans le cadre du Conseil de l'Europe", in *Revue générale de droit international*, Vol. 92, 929-960.

Borrows, John J. (1992), "A Genealogy of Law: Inherent Sovereignty and First Nations Self-Government", in *Osgoode Hall Law Journal*, Vol. 30, N° 2, 291-353.

Bossuyt, Marc (1990), "The United Nations and the Definition of Minorities", in *Plural Societies Research Papers*, Vol. XXI, 129-136.

Bouchard, Josée (1992), "Aperçu comparatif du concept d'égalité en droit constitutionnel américain et canadien", in *Canadian Journal of Women and the Law*, Vol. 5, 87-117.

Brace, Kimbal, Grofman, Bernard, Handley, Lisa and Niemi, Richard (1988), "Minority Voting Equality: The 65 % Rule in Theory and Practice", in *Law and Policy*, Vol. 10, 43-71.

Breitenmoser, Stephan and Richter, Dagmar (1991), "Proposal for an Additional Protocol to the European Convention on Human Rights Concerning the Protection of Minorities in the Participating States of the CSCE", in *Human Rights Law Journal*, Vol. 12, N° 6-7, 262-265.

Brett, Nathan (1991), "Language Laws and Collective Rights", in *Canadian Journal of Law and Jurisprudence*, Vol. IV, N° 2, 347-360.

Buergenthal, Thomas (1991), "The CSCE Rights System", in *George Washington Journal of International Law and Economics*, Vol. 25, 334-386.

Bullier, Antoine J. (1991), "Le cas de la Colombie britannique : Le procès criminel en français, convention ou concession?", in *Revue de science criminelle et droit pénal comparé*, Vol. 2, 311-323.

Campbell, Archie (1979), "Les services judiciaires en Ontario", in *La revue de l'Université de Moncton*, Vol. 12, N° 2-3, 163-167.

Campbell, Gordon Scott (1993), "Language, Equality and the Charter: Collective Versus Individual Rights in Canada and Beyond", in *National Journal of Constitutional Law*, Vol. 4, 29-73.

Capotorti, Francesco (1986), "Les développements possibles de la protection internationale des minorités", in *Les Cahiers de Droit*, Vol. 27, N° 1, 239-254.

Carbonneau, Thomas E. (1981), "Linguistic Legislation and Transnational Commercial Activity: France and Belgium", in *American Journal of Comparative Law*, Vol. 29, 393-412.

Chabot, Marie-France (1991), "Le Tribunal Waitangi et les droits des autochtones", in *Les Cahiers de Droit*, Vol. 32, 59-85.

Chavers, D. (1973-74), "Indian Education: Failure for the Future?", in *American Indian Law Review*, Vol. 1-2, 61-84.

Chill, Adam J. (1992), "The Fourteenth and Fifteenth Amendments with Respect to the Voting Franchise: A Constitutional Quandary", in *Columbia Journal of Law and Social Problems*, Vol. 25, 645-678.

Cholevinski, Ryszard (1988), "State Duty Towards Ethnic Minorities: Positive or Negative?", in *Human Rights Quarterly*, Vol. 10, 344-371.

Clasby, Sarah B. (1991-92), "Understanding Testimony: Official Translation and Bilingual Jurors in Hernandez v. New York", in *Inter-American Law Review*, Vol. 23, N° 2, 515-537.

Clyne, Michael (1991), "Australia's Language Policies: Are We Going Backwards?", in *Current Affairs Bulletin*, Vol. 68(6), 13-20.

Commission européenne pour la démocratie par le droit (1991), "Proposition d'une Convention pour la protection des minorités", in *Revue universelle des droits de l'homme*, Vol. 3, N° 5, 189-192.

Conference on Security and Cooperation in Europe — Report of the CSCE Meeting of Experts on National Minorities (1991), in *International Legal Materials*, Vol. 30, 1692-1702.

Conference on Security and Cooperation in Europe — Report of the CSCE Meeting of Experts on National Minorities (1991), in *Human Rights Law Journal*, Vol. 12, N° 8-9, 332-334.

Conférence pour la paix en Yougoslavie (1992), in *Revue générale de droit international public*, Vol. 96, 264-269.

Cordero, Laura (1990), "Constitutional Limitations on Official English Declarations", in *New Mexico Law Review*, Vol. 20, 17-53.

Coronado Suzán, G. (1992), "Educación Bilingüe en México: Propósitos y Realidades", in *International Journal of the Sociology of Language*, Vol. 96, 53-70.

Côté-Harper, Gisèle (1986), "Introduction : Les minorités et le droit à l'égalité", in *Les Cahiers de Droit*, Vol. 27, N° 1, 135-143.

Cronheim, Alan J. and Schwartz, Andrew H. (1976), "Non-English-Speaking Persons in the Criminal Justice System: Current State of the Law", in *Cornell Law Review*, Vol. 61, 289-311.

Crouch, Alan (1985), "The Way, the Truth and the Right to Interpreters in Court", in *Law Institute Journal*, Vol. 59, N° 7, 687-691.

Crowe, David (1988), "Minorities in Hungary since 1948", in *Nationalities Papers*, Vol, XVI, N° 1, 22-35.

Cumming, Peter and Ginn, Diana (1986), "First Nations Self-Government in Canada", in *Nordic Journal of International Law*, Vol. 55, 86-116.

Daes, Erica-Irène (1986), "Native People's Rights", in *Les Cahiers de Droit*, Vol. 27, N° 1, 123-133.

Decentralization and Regional Autonomy in the Nordic Countries (1988), in *Regional Contact*, N° 2, 48-69.

Declaration on Principles of International Law Concerning Friendly Relations and Co-operation among States in Accordance with the Charter of the United Nations (1970), in *International Legal Materials*, Vol. 9, 1292-1297.

Declaration on the Rights of Persons Belonging to National or Ethnic, Religious and Linguistic Minorities (1993), in *Human Rights Law Journal*, Vol. 14, N° 1-2, 54-56.

de la Garza, Rodolfo O., and DeSipio, Louis (1993), "Save the Baby, Change the Bathwater, and Scrub the Tub: Latino Electoral Participation After Seventeen Years of Voting Rights Act Coverage", in *Texas Law Review*, Vol. 71, 1479-1523.

Delaporte, Vincent (1976), "La loi relative à l'emploi de la langue française", in *Revue critique de droit international privé*, 447-476.

Delgado Cintrón, Carmelo (1991), "La Declaración Legislativa de la Lengua Española como el Idioma Oficial de Puerto Rico", in *Revista Jurídica Universidad de Puerto Rico*, Vol. 60, 587-631.

Delpérée, Francis (1988), "Les politiques linguistiques en Belgique", in *Revue générale de droit*, Vol. 19, 255-267.

Demengeaux, James Harvey (1986), "Native-Born Acadians and the Equality Ideal", in *Louisiana Law Review*, Vol. 46, 1151-1195.

de Montigny, Yves (1978), "L'O.N.U. et la protection internationale des minorités depuis 1945", in *Revue juridique Thémis*, Vol. 13, N° 2-3, 389-447.

El derecho de aviso — Due Process and Bilingual Notice (1973), in *Yale Law Journal*, Vol. 83, 384-400.

Deschênes, Jules (1986), "Qu'est-ce qu'une minorité?", in *Les Cahiers de Droit*, Vol. 27, N° 1, 255-291.

de Varennes, Fernand (1992), "Langue et discrimination au Canada", in *Canadian Journal of Law and Jurisprudence*, Vol. V, N° 2, 321-355.

de Varennes, Fernand (1994), "Language and Freedom of Expression in International Law", in *Human Rights Quarterly*, Vol. 16, N° 1, 163-186.

de Varennes, Fernand (1994), L'article 35 de la Loi constitutionnelle de 1982 et la protection des droits linguistiques des peuples autochtones", in *National Journal of Constitutional Law*, Vol. 4, N° 3, 265-303.

de Witte, Bruno (1985), "Linguistic Equality: A Study in Comparative Constitutional Law", in *Revista de Llengua i Dret*, Vol. 3, 43-126.

de Witte, Bruno (1990), "The Position of Linguistic Minorities in Italy", in *Plural Societies Research Papers*, Vol. XXI, 51-65.

de Witte, Bruno (1991), "Minorités nationales : reconnaissance et protection", in *Revue française d'études constitutionnelles et politiques*, 113-127.

Dinstein, Yoram (1976), "Collective Human Rights of Peoples and Minorities", in *International and Comparative Law Quarterly*, Vol. 25, 102-120.

Educational Choice in a Multi-Cultural Society: Analysis (1992), in *Public Law*, Winter, 522-533.

Eide, Asbjørn (1991), "Minority Situations: In Search of Peaceful and Constructive Solutions", in *Notre Dame Law Review*, Vol. 66, 1311-1346.

Equality of Language in South Africa Must be Enshrined (1992), in *CSD/SWO Bulletin*, June, 14-15.

Farago, Bela (1993), "La démocratie et le problème des minorités nationales", in *Le débat*, N° 76, 6-24.

Fettes, Mark (1994), "The International Context of Aboriginal Linguistic Rights", in *Canadian Centre for Linguistic Rights Bulletin*, Vol. 1, N° 3, 6-11.

Folsom, Roy D. (1975), "Equal Opportunity for Indian Children — The Legal Basis for Compelling Bilingual and Bicultural Education", in *American Indian Law Review*, Vol. 3, 51-82.

Fortier, D'Iberville (1986), "Les droits linguistiques canadiens en évolution", in *Les Cahiers de Droit*, Vol. 27, N° 1, 227-238.

Foster, Elizabeth (1989), "Les droits à l'instruction dans la langue de la minorité à la lumière des décisions des Cours d'appel de l'Ontario et l'Alberta", in *Les Cahiers de Droit*, Vol. 30, 777-799.

Foucher, Pierre (1992), "Droits linguistiques : à l'image des cercles concentriques", in *University of New Brunswick Law Journal*, Vol. 41, 171-176.

Francis, Marc Douglas (1985), "The Constitutional Future of the All-English Ballot", in *Pacific Law Journal*, Vol. 16, 1029-1043.

Fritz, Ronald (1994), "Effective Representation Denied: MacKinnon v. Prince Edward Island", in *National Journal of Constitutional Law*, Vol. 4, 207-222.

Gallo, Wayne (1989), "Discrimination — Ancestry — An Unpersuasive Overruling of 42 U.S.C. Section 1981 to Include Private Alienage Discrimination", in *Suffolk Transnational Law Journal*, Vol. 12, 479-490.

Garcia, Franco (1974), "Language Barriers to Voting: Literacy Tests and the Bilingual Ballot", in *Columbia Human Rights Law Review*, Vol. 6, 83-106.

Gibson, Dale (1990), "Section 27 of the Charter: More Than a «Rhetorical Flourish»", in *Alberta Law Review*, Vol. XXVIII, N° 3, 589-603.

Goldberg-Ambrose, Carole (1991), "Not «Strictly» Racial: A Response to Indians as Peoples", in *University of California in Los Angeles Law Review*, Vol. 39, 169-190.

Gonzalez Cedillo, Ricardo (1983), "A Constitutional Analysis of the English Literacy Requirement of the Naturalization Act", in *St. Mary's Law Journal*, Vol. 14, 899-936.

Grabau, Charles M. and Williamson, David-Ross (1985), "Language Barriers in our Trial Courts: The Use of Court Interpreters in Massachusetts", in *Massachusetts Law Review*, Vol. 70, 108-114.

Grammond, Sébastien (1991), "La protection constitutionnelle des droits ancestraux des peuples autochtones et l'arrêt Sparrow", in *McGill Law Journal*, Vol. 36, 1382-1415.

Grammond, Sébastien (1992), "Les effets juridiques de la Convention de la Baie James au regard du droit interne canadien et québécois", in *McGill Law Journal*, Vol. 37, 761-800.

Green, L.C. (1983), "Aboriginal Peoples, International Law and the Canadian Charter of Rights and Freedoms", in *The Canadian Bar Review*, Vol. 61, 339-353.

Green, Leslie (1987), "Are Language Rights Fundamental?", in *Osgoode Hall Law Journal*, Vol. 25, N° 4, 639-669.

Groisser, Debra (1980), "A Right to Translation Assistance in Administrative Proceedings", in *Columbia Journal of Law and Social Problems*, Vol. 16, 469-520.

Gromacki, Joseph P. (1992), "The Protection of Language Rights in International Human Rights Law: A Proposed Draft Declaration of Linguistic Rights", in *Virginia Journal of International Law*, Vol. 32, 515-579.

Guerra, Sandra (1988), "Voting Rights and the Constitution: The Disenfranchisement of Non-English Speaking Citizens", in *Yale Law Journal*, Vol. 97, 1419-1437.

Guinier, Lani (1993), "Groups, Representation, and Race-Conscious Districting: A Case of the Emperor's Clothes", in *Texas Law Review*, Vol. 71, 1589-1642.

Guitart i Agell, Joan (1987), "Linguistique de l'enseignement en Catalogne", in *Perspectives*, Vol. XVII, N° 2, 319-326.

Gustavsson, Sven (1990), "Socialism and Nationalism: Trends and Tendencies in the Language, Nationality and Minority Policy of the Socialist Countries in Post-War Europe", in *Sociolinguistica*, Vol. 4, 50-83.

Haft, Jonathan D. (1983), "Assuring Equal Educational Opportunity for Language Minority Students: Bilingual Education and the Equal Educational Opportunity Act of 1974", in *Columbia Journal of Law and Social Problems*, Vol. 18, 209-293.

Hailbronner, Kay (1991), "The Legal Status of Population Groups in a Multinational State under Public International Law", in *Israel Yearbook on Human Rights*, Vol. 20, 125-149.

Hall, John A. (1993), "Nationalisms: Classified and Explained", in *Dædalus - Journal of the American Academy of Arts and Sciences*, Vol. 122, N° 3, 1-28.

Halvorsen, Kate (1990), "Notes on the Realization of the Human Right to Education", in *Human Rights Quarterly*, Vol. 12, 341-364.

Hamilton, Ian (1989), "Nationality and Regional Identity in the Soviet Union", in *Regional Contact*, N° 2, 46-51.

Hannum, Hurst (1988), "New Developments in Indigenous Rights", in *Virginia Journal of International Law*, Vol. 28, 649-678.

Hannum Hurst (1993), "The Second Amsterdam International Law Conference: Peoples and Minorities in International Law", in *International Journal on Group Rights*, Vol. 1, N° 1, 45-50.

Herz, Richard (1993), "Legal Protection for Indigenous Cultures: Sacred Sites and Communal Rights", in *Virginia Law Review*, Vol. 79, 691-716.

Hetmar, Tytte and Jørgensen, J. Normann (1993), "Multilingual Concepts in the Schools of Europe — Denmark", in *Sociolinguistica*, Vol. 7, 79-89.

Hofman, Julien (1991), "Official Languages for a New South Africa: Article 5 of the ANC's Draft Bill of Rights", in *Stellenbosch Law Review*, Vol. 3, 328-338.

Hosein, Hanson R. (1992), "Distorted: A View of Canadian Multiculturalism Within a Bilingual Framework", in *Alberta Law Review*, Vol. XXX, N° 2, 597-624.

Hupchick, Dennis P. (1993), "Orthodoxy and Bulgarian Ethnic Awareness under Ottoman Rule, 1396-1762", in *Nationalities Papers*, Vol. XXI, N° 2, 75-93.

Human Rights in the Republic of Estonia, Raimo Pekkanen and Hans Danelius, Special Rapporteurs (1991), in *Human Rights Law Journal*, Vol. 13, N° 5-6, 236-256.

Hvenekilde, Anne (1993), "Multilingual Concepts in the Schools of Europe — Norway", in *Sociolinguistica*, Vol. 7, 174-186.

Igartua Salaverria, Juan (1989-90), "Nación, Cultura, Lengua", in *Revista de la Facultad de Derecho de la Universidad Complutense* 451.

Les inégalités historiques et certains faits (prospection de pétrole et de gaz) plus récents, menaçant le mode de vie et la culture de la bande du lac Lubicon, violent les droits des minorités (1991), in *Revue universelle des droits de l'Homme*, Vol. 3, 69-74.

Inter-American Court of Human Rights (1984), Amendments to the Naturalization Provisions of the Constitution of Costa Rica, Advisory Opinion, in *Human Rights Law Journal*, Vol. 5, N° 2-4, 161-190.

International Labour Organisation Revised Convention (No. 169) Concerning Indigenous and Tribal People in Independent Countries (1989), in *International Legal Materials*, Vol. 28, 1382-1392.

Isaac, Thomas (1992), "Individual versus Collective Rights: Aboriginal People and the Significance of Thomas v. Norris", in *Manitoba Law Journal*, Vol. 21, N° 1, 618-630.

Isaac, Thomas (1992), "The Nunavut Agreement-in-Principle and Section 35 of the Constitution Act, 1982", in *Manitoba Law Journal*, Vol. 21, N° 3, 390-405.

Isaac, Thomas (1992), "The Storm Over Aboriginal Self-Government: Section 35 of the Constitution Act, 1982 and The Redefinition of the Inherent Right of Aboriginal Self-Government", in *Canadian Native Law Reporter*, Vol. 2, 6-24.

Jaccoud, Mylène (1992), "Processus pénal et identitaire : le cas des Inuit au Nouveau-Québec", in *Sociologie et sociétés*, Vol. XXIV, 26-43.

Jenkins, Elwyn (1992), "Gathering of the Dugmore Clan", in *Contact*, Vol. 2, N° 16, 17-19.

Johnson, Sheri Lynn (1993), "The Language and Culture (not to say Race) of Peremptory Challenges", in *William and Mary Law Review*, Vol. 35, 21-92.

Juteau, Danielle (1992), "Projet national, immigration et intégration dans un Québec souverain", in *Sociologie et sociétés*, Vol. XXIV, N° 2, 161-180.

Kamasinski c. l'Autriche — Article 6 de la Convention pris isolément ou combiné avec l'article 14 (1991), in *Revue trimestrielle des droits de l'Homme*, N° 6, 217-240.

Karmis, Dimitrios (1993), "Cultures autochtones et libéralisme au Canada : les vertus médiatrices du communautarisme libéral de Charles Taylor", in *Canadian Journal of Political Science*, Vol. XXVI, N° 1, 67-96.

Kaufman, Eileen R. and Schwartz, Martin A. (1988), "Civil Rights in Transition: Sections 1981 and 1982 Cover Discrimination on the Basis of Ancestry and Ethnicity", in *Touro Law Review*, Vol. 4, 183-254.

Keotahian, Avak (1985-86), "National Origin Discrimination in Employment: Do Plaintiffs Ever Win?", in *Employee Relations Law Journal*, Vol. 11, N° 3, 467-492.

Kingsbury, Benedict (1992), "Claims by Non-State Groups in International Law", in *Cornell International Law Journal*, Vol. 25, 481-513.

Kirgis, Frederic L. (1994), "The Degrees of Self-Determination in the United Nations Era", in *American Journal of International Law*, Vol. 88, 304-310.

Kiss, Charles Alexandre (1986), "Le concept d'égalité : définition et expérience", in *Les Cahiers de Droit*, Vol. 27, N° 1, 145-153.

Kitis, Eliza (1993), "Multilingual Concepts in the Schools of Europe — Greece", in *Sociolinguistica*, Vol. 7, 119-134.

Klebes, Heinrich (1993), "Draft Protocol on Minority Rights to the ECHR Adopted by the Parliamentary Assembly of the Council of Europe", in *Human Rights Law Journal*, Vol. 14, N° 3-4, 140-148.

Kline, Marlee (1992), "Child Welfare Law, Best Interest of the Child, Ideology, and First Nations, in *Osgoode Hall Law Journal*, Vol. 30, 375-397.

Kloss, Heinz (1971), "Language Rights of Immigrant Groups", in *International Immigration Review*, Vol. 5, 250-267.

Kovacs, Peter (1993), "La protection des langues des minorités ou la nouvelle approche de la protection des minorités ?", in *Revue générale de droit international public*, Vol. 93, N° 2, 411-418.

Kronowitz, Rachel San, Lichtman, Joanne, McSloy, Steven Paul and Olsen Matthew G. (1987), "Toward Consent and Cooperation: Reconsidering the Political Status of Indian Nations", in *Harvard Civil Rights-Civil Liberties Law Review*, Vol. 22, 507-622.

Lacasse, Jean-Paul (1993), "Les droits linguistiques des autochtones du Québec", in *Bulletin du Centre canadien des droits linguistiques*, Vol. 1, 11-13.

Language, Politics and Electoral Rights in Belgium (1987), in *European Law Report*, Vol. 12, 398-400.

Language Rights and the Legal Status of English-Only Laws in the Public and Private Sector (1992), in *North Carolina Central Law Journal*, Vol. 20, 65-91.

Laponce, Jean A. (1993), "Do Languages Behave Like Animals?", in *International Journal of the Sociology of Language*, 19-30.

Larson, David (1991), "Title VII Compensation Issues Affecting Bilingual Hispanic Employees", in *Arizona State Law Journal*, Vol. 23, 821-830.

Lawrey, Andrée (1990), "Contemporary Efforts to Guarantee Indigenous Rights Under International Law", in *Vanderbilt Journal of Transnational Law*, Vol. 23, N° 4, 703-777.

Lebel, Michel (1974), "Le choix de la langue d'enseignement et le droit international", in *Revue Juridique Thémis*, Vol. 9, N° 2, 221-248.

LeBouthillier, Yves (1990), "L'Affaire Mahé et les droits scolaires", in *Ottawa Law Review*, Vol. 22, N° 1, 77-137.

LeBouthillier, Yves (1993), "Le droit à l'instruction en français dans les provinces canadiennes à majorité anglophone : le statut des enfants de parents immigrés", in *Revue générale de droit*, Vol. 24, 255-268.

Legault, Michel (1993), "Le défi de l'intégration", in *Justice*, Vol. XV, N° 1, 10-15.

Leibowitz, Arnold H. (1969), "Literacy: Legal Sanction for Discrimination", in *Notre Dame Law Review*, Vol. 45, 7-67.

Leibowitz, Arnold H. (1970), "English Literacy: Legal Sanction for Discrimination", in *Revista Juridica de la Universidad de Puerto Rico*, Vol. XXXIX, N° 1, 313-400.

Leslie, Peter M. (1986), "L'aspect politique et collectif", in *Les Cahiers de Droit*, Vol. 27, N° 1, 161-170.

Leuprecht, Peter (1986), "Le Conseil de l'Europe et les droits des minorités", in *Les Cahiers de Droit*, Vol. 27, N° 1, 203-213.

Levin, Betsy (1983), "An Analysis of the Federal Attempt to Regulate Bilingual Education: Protecting Civil Rights or Controlling Curriculum?", in *Journal of Law and Education*, Vol. 12, 29-60.

Lindsey Jr., Edward (1983), "Linguistic Minority Educational Rights in Canada: An International and Comparative Perspective", in *Georgia Journal of International and Comparative Law*, Vol. 13, 515-547.

Lochak, Danièle (1987), "Réflexions sur la notion de discrimination", in *Droit Social*, N° 11, 778-790.

Lowrey IV, Frank M. (1992), "Through the Looking Glass: Linguistic Separatism and National Unity", in *Emory Law Journal*, Vol. 41, 223-319.

Lüdi, Georges (1990), "Les migrants comme minorité linguistique en Europe", in *Sociolinguistica*, Vol. 4, 113-135.

Lüdi, Georges (1993), "Conceptions plurilingues dans l'enseignement européen — Suisse", in *Sociolinguistica*, Vol. 7, 32-48.

Lyon, Noel (1992), "A Perspective on the Application of the Criminal Code to Aboriginal Peoples in Light of the Judgement of the Supreme Court of Canada in R. v. Sparrow", in *University of British Columbia Law Review, Special Edition*, 306-312.

Macklem, Patrick (1992), "Aboriginal Peoples, Criminal Justice Initiatives and the Constitution", in *University of British Columbia Law Review, Special Edition*, 280-305.

Macklem, Patrick (1993), "Distributing Sovereignty: Indian Nations and Equality of Peoples", in *Stanford Law Review*, Vol. 45, 1311-1367.

Magnet, Joseph E. (1982), "Minority Language Educational Rights", in *Supreme Court Law Review*, Vol. 4, 195-216.

Malinverni, Giorgio (1991), "The Draft Convention for the Protection of Minorities: The Proposal of the European Commission for Democracy Through Law", in *Human Rights Law Journal*, Vol. 12, N° 6-7, 265-269.

Malinverni, Giorgio (1991), "Le projet de Convention pour la protection des minorités élaboré par la Commission européenne pour la démocratie par le droit", in *Revue universelle des droits de l'Homme*, Vol. 3, N° 5, 157-165.

Mallya, Lynne (1992), "Deportation and Due Process: Does the Immigration and Naturalization Act or the Fifth Amendment Provide for Full Interpretation of Deportation and Exclusion Hearings?", in *Law and Inequality*, Vol. 11, 181-208.

Mandell, Louise (1986), "Indian Nations: Not Minorities", in *Les Cahiers de Droit*, Vol. 27, N° 1, 101-121.

Manwaring, Melissa (1993), "A Small Step or a Giant Leap? The Implications of Australia's First Judicial Recognition of Indigenous Land Rights: Mabo and Others v. State of Queensland", in *Harvard International Law Journal*, Vol. 34, N° 1, 177-191.

Marasinghe, M.L. (1988), "Ethnic Politics and Constitutional Reform: The Indo-Sri Lankan Accord", in *International and Comparative Law Quarterly*, Vol. 37, 551-587.

Margulies, Peter (1981), "Bilingual Education, Remedial Language Instruction, Title VI, and Proof of Discriminatory Purpose: A Suggested Approach", in *Columbia Journal of Law and Social Problems*, Vol. 17, 71-78.

Martel, Normand (1988), "Le recours aux traités relatifs aux droits et libertés de la personne aux fins d'interprétation de la législation québécoise: la jurisprudence relative à la Charte de la langue française", in *Revue québécoise de droit international*, Vol. V, 255-271.

Massey, Calvin R. (1992), "Hate Speech, Cultural Diversity, and the Foundational Paradigms of Free Expression", in *University of California in Los Angeles Law Review*, Vol. 40, 103-153.

Mathieu, Daniel (1990), "L'exercise en français de la profession d'avocat au Manitoba", in *Manitoba Law Journal*, Vol. 14, 5-30.

Matsuda, Mari J. (1991), "Voices of America: Accent, Anti-Discrimination Law, and a Jurisprudence for the Last Reconstruction", in *Yale Law Journal*, Vol. 100, 1329-1407.

McAll, Christopher (1992), "Langues et silence : les travailleurs immigrés au Québec et la sociologie du langage", in *Sociologie et sociétés*, Vol. XXIV, N° 2, 117-130.

McDougal, Myres et al. (1976), "Freedom from Discrimination in Choice of Language and International Human Rights", in *Southern Illinois University Law Journal*, Vol. 1, 151-174.

McFadden, Bernard (1983), "Bilingual Education and the Law", in *Journal of Law and Education*, Vol. 12, 1-27.

McGoldrick, Dominic (1991), "Canadian Indians, Cultural Rights and the Human Rights Committee", in *International and Comparative Law Quarterly*, Vol. 40, 658-669.

McHugh, Paul (1986), "Aboriginal Rights and Sovereignty: Commonwealth Developments", in *New Zealand Law Journal*, Vol. 57, N° 7, 57-63.

McLean, Daryl (1991), "Language Policy in a New South Africa: A Mild Form of Oppression?", in *Rhodes Review*, 17-18.

McMahon, Bryan M.E. (1990), "Case 379/87, Groener v. Minister for Education and the City of Dublin Vocational Education Committee CDVEC, Judgement of 28 November 1989", in *Common Market Law Review*, Vol. 27, 129-139.

McNamara, Luke (1992), "Aboriginal Human Rights and the Australian Criminal Justice System: Self-Determination as a Solution", in *Manitoba Law Journal*, Vol. 21, N° 3, 544-617.

McNamara, Luke (1992), "Aboriginal People and Criminal Justice Reform: The Value of Autonomy-Based Solutions", in *Canadian Native Law Reporter*, Vol. 1, 1-12.

Mealey, Linda (1989-90), "English-Only Rules and Innocent Employers: Clarifying National Origin Discrimination and Disparate Impact Theory under Title VII", in *Minnesota Law Review*, Vol. 74, 387-436.

Melkevik, Bjarne (1991), "Autochtones et droit : le nouveau droit norvégien des Samés (Lapons)", in *Les Cahiers de Droit*, Vol. 32, 33-57.

Melkevik, Bjarne (1992), "L'organisation de l'autonomie politique autochtone : l'exemple des Samés (Lapons) de Norvège", in *Manitoba Law Journal*, Vol. 21, N° 3, 406-425.

Mendes, Errol P. (1992), "Two Solitudes, Freedom of Expression and Collective Linguistic Rights in Canada: A Case Study of the Ford Decision", in *National Journal of Constitutional Law*, Vol. 1, N° 3, 283-313.

Mentzell, Peter (1993), "The German Minority in Inter-War Yugoslavia", in *Nationalities Papers*, Vol. XXI, N° 2, 129-143.

Message of His Holiness Pope John Paul II for the Celebration of the World Day of Peace (1989), in *Regional Contact*, N° 1, 5-12.

Milian i Massana, Antoni (1984), "La regulación constitucional del multilingüismo", in *Revista Española de Derecho Constitucional*, Vol. 4, N° 10, 123-154.

Milian i Massana, Antoni (1992), "Droits linguistiques et droits fondamentaux en Espagne", in *Revue Générale du Droit*, Vol. 23, 561-581.

Modeen, Tore (1970), "The Situation of the Finland-Swedish Population in the Light of International, Constitutional and Administrative Law", in *McGill Law Journal*, Vol. 16, N° 1, 121-139.

Mönch-Bucak, Yayla (1990), "The Kurdish Language in Turkey Between Repression and Resistance", in *Plural Societies Research Papers*, Vol. XXI, 75-87.

Moran, Rachel F. (1988), "The Politics of Discretion: Federal Intervention in Bilingual Education", in *California Law Review*, Vol. 76, 1249-1352.

Moran, Rachel F. (1993), "Of Democracy, Devaluation and Bilingual Education", in *Creighton Law Review*, Vol. 26, 255-319.

Morgan, Edward M. (1984), "Self-Government and the Constitution: A Comparative Look at Native Canadians and American Indians", in *American Indian Law Review*, Vol. 12, 39-56.

Morris, Sally (1991-92), "One More Battle in the Ongoing War over Affirmative Action: Metro Broadcasting, Inc. v. FCC", in *New England Law Review*, Vol. 26, 921-961.

Mullerson, Rein (1993), "Minorities in Eastern Europe and the Former USSR: Problems, Tendencies and Protection", in *Modern Law Review*, Vol. 56, 793-811.

Munday, Roderick (1985), "Legislation in Defence of the French Language", in *Cambridge Law Journal*, 218-235.

Naidu, Arjuna (1987), "The Protection of Human Rights in Sri Lanka: Some Lessons for South Africa?", in *South African Journal on Human Rights,* Vol. 3, 52-67.

Nakatsuru, Shaun (1985), "A Constitutional Right of Indian Self-Government", in *University of Toronto Faculty of Law Review*, Vol. 43, 72-99.

Neate, Graeme (1981), "Legal Language Across Cultures: Finding the Traditional Aboriginal Owners of Land", in *Federal Law Review*, Vol. 12, 187-211.

Nettheim, Garth (1987), "Indigenous Rights, Human Rights and Australia", in *Australian Law Journal*, Vol. 61, 291-300.

Neumeier, Richard L. (1992), "Civil Rights Act of 1991: What Does it do? Is it Retroactive?", in *Defense Council Journal*, October, 500-510.

Newman, Terri Lynn (1984), "Proposals: Bilingual Education Guidelines for the Courts and the Schools", in *Emory Law Journal*, Vol. 33, 577-629.

The NHLAPO-Alexander Proposal for the Harmonisation of Nguni and Sotho Languages in South Africa (1991), in *Language Project's Review*, Vol. 5, N° 4, 2-3.

Norton, Robert L. (1991), "The New Disparate Impact Analysis in Employment Discrimination: Emanuel v. Marsh in Light of Watson, Antonio, and the Failed Civil Rights Act of 1990", in *Missouri Law Review*, Vol. 56, 333-352.

Nowak, Manfred (1993), "The Right of Self-Determination and Protection of Minorities in Central and Eastern Europe in Light of the Case-Law of the Human Rights Committee", in *International Journal on Group Rights*, Vol. 1, N° 1, 7-16.

O'Brien, Sharon (1991), "Tribes and Indians: With Whom Does the United States Maintain a Relationship?", in *Notre Dame Law Review*, Vol. 66, 1461-1494.

Official English: Federal Limits on Efforts to Curtail Bilingual Services in the States (1987), in *Harvard Law Review*, Vol. 100, 1345-1362.

Ong Hing, Bill (1993), "Beyond the Rhetoric of Assimilation and Cultural Pluralism: Addressing the Tension of Separatism and Conflict in an Immigration-Driven Multiracial Society", in *California Law Review*, Vol. 81, 863-925.

Ouane, Adama (1990), "Langues nationales, Langues maternelles", in *Le courrier de l'Unesco*, July, 27-29.

Paradis, Jerome B. (1970), "Language Rights in Multicultural States: A Comparative Study", in *Canadian Bar Review*, Vol. XLVIII, 651-697.

Patenaude, Pierre (1992), "Les droits linguistiques au Canada : de l'intolérance à l'utopie", in *University of New Brunswick Law Journal*, Vol. 41, 159-165.

Patry, Réjean (1983), "Le bilinguisme dans les juridictions fédérales", in *Les Cahiers de Droit*, Vol. 24, 69-79.

Paxman, John T. (1989), "Minority Indigenous Populations and Their Claims for Self-Determination", in *Case Western Reserve Journal of International Law*, Vol. 21, 185-202

Pepper, Mary (1993), "Linguistic Justice in Canada's North", in *Circuit*, March, 12-14.

Perea, Juan F. (1990), "English-Only Rules and the Right to Speak One's Primary Language in the Workplace", in *Journal of Law Reform*, Vol. 23, 265-318.

Perea, Juan F. (1992), "Demography and Distrust: An Essay on American Languages, Cultural Pluralism, and Official English", in *Minnesota Law Review*, Vol. 77, 269-373.

Perea, Juan F. (1992), "Hernandez v. New York: Courts, Prosecutors, and the Fear of Spanish", in *Hofstra Law Review*, Vol. 21, 1-61.

Perea, Juan F. (1994), "Ethnicity and Prejudice: Re-evaluating National Origin Discrimination under Title VII", in *William and Mary Law Review*, Vol. 35, 805-870.

Phillipson, Robert and Skutnabb-Kangas Tove (1994), "English, Panacea or Pandemic?", in *Sociolinguistica*, Vol. 8, 73-87.

Piatt, Bill (1984), "Linguistic Diversity on the Airwaves: Spanish-Language Broadcasting and the FCC", in *La Raza Law Journal*, Vol. 1, N° 2, 101-119.

Piatt, Bill (1986), "Toward Domestic Recognition of a Human Right to Language", in *Houston Law Review*, Vol. 23, 885-901.

Polack, Kenneth and Corsellis, Ann (1990), "Non-English Speakers and the Criminal Justice System", in *New Law Journal*, Vol. 140, N° 23, 1634-1636, and Vol. 140, N° 30, 1676-1677.

Pollis, Adamantia (1994), "The Greek Concept of National Identity", in *ASEN Bulletin*, N° 7, 11-14.

Pratt, Alan (1992), "Aboriginal Self-Government and the Crown's Fiduciary Duty: Squaring the Circle or Completing the Circle?", in *National Journal of Constitutional Law*, Vol. 2, 163-195.

Primera consulta sobre el contenido de un futuro instrumento jurídico interamericano sobre los Derechos Humanos de los Pueblos Indígenas (1992), in *Revista del Instituto Interamericano de Derechos Humanos*, Vol. 15, 264-273.

Proposals by the CSCE High Commissioner on National Minorities, Mr Max van der Stoel, Upon his Visits to Slovakia and Hungary (1993), in *Human Rights Law Journal*, Vol. 14, 224-225.

Proyecto de Declaración Universal Sobre Los Derechos de Los Pueblos Indígenas (1992), in *Revista del Instituto Interamericano de Derechos Humanos*, Vol. 15, 241-250.

Prujiner, Alain (1992), "Territorialité et personnalité des droits linguistiques", in *University of New Brunswick Law Journal*, Vol. 41, 166-170.

Ramcharan, B.G. (1993), "Individual, Collective and Group Rights: History, Theory, Practice and Contemporary Evolution", in *International Journal on Group Rights*, Vol. 1, N° 1, 27-43.

Ramga, Philip Vuciri (1992), "The Bases of Minority Identity", in *Human Rights Quarterly*, Vol. 14, 409-428.

Reagan, T. G. (1986), "Language Ideology in the Language Planning Process: Two African Case Studies", in *South African Journal of African Languages*, Vol. 6, N° 2, 94-97.

Réaume, Denise and Green, Leslie (1989), "Education and Linguistic Security in the Charter", in *McGill Law Journal*, Vol. 34, N° 4, 777-816.

Recommendations by the CSCE High Commissioner on National Minorities, Mr Max van der Stoel, upon his Visits to Estonia, Latvia, and Lithuania (1993), in *Human Rights Law Journal*, Vol. 14, 216-223.

Reeber, Christopher (1972), "Linguistic Minorities and the Right to an Effective Education", in *California Western International Law Journal*, Vol. 3, 113-132.

Reid, Euan (1993), "Multilingual Concepts in the Schools of Europe — Great Britain and Northern Ireland", in *Sociolinguistica*, Vol. 7, 110-118.

Renaud, Jean (1992), "Un an au Québec : La compétence linguistique et l'accès à un premier emploi", in *Sociologie et sociétés*, Vol. XXIV, N° 2, 131-142.

The Role of Language in Achieving National Reconciliation (1991), in *Language Projects' Review*, Vol. 6, N° 3-4, 16-17.

Roos, Peter D. (1978), "Bilingual Education: The Hispanic Response to Unequal Educational Opportunity", in *Law and Contemporary Problems*, Vol. 42, N° 4, 111-140.

Rosenbaum, Stephen (1981), "Educating Children of Immigrant Workers: Language Policies in France and the USA", in *American Journal of Comparative Law*, Vol. 29, 429-465.

Rosenberg, Dominique (1992), "Le peuple Touareg, du silence à l'autodétermination", in *Revue belge de droit international*, Vol. XXV, 5-39.

Rosenfeld, Michel (1991), "Metro Broadcasting Inc. v. FCC: Affirmative Action at the Crossroads of Constitutional Liberty and Equality", in *University of California in Los Angeles Review*, Vol. 38, 583-635.

Roth, Stephen (1991), "Comments on the CSCE Meeting of Experts on National Minorities and its Concluding Document", in *Human Rights Law Journal*, Vol. 12, N° 8-9, 330-331.

Roth, Stephen (1991), "Toward a Minority Convention: Its Need and Content", in *Israel Yearbook on Human Rights*, Vol. 20, 93-107.

Rwezaura, B. (1993), "Constraining Factors to the Adoption of Kiswahili as a Language of the Law in Tanzania", in *African Law Journal*, Vol. 37, 30-45.

Ryavec, Karl (1993), "Slovenia and Independence: An Early Assessment", in *Analysis of Current Events — Association for the Study of Nationalities*, Vol. 5, N° 8, 1-3.

Safford, Joan Bainbridge (1977), "No Comprendo: The Non-English-Speaking Defendant and the Criminal Process", in *Journal of Criminal Law and Criminology*, Vol. 68, 15-30.

Salter, Michael (1992), "Laws of Language in Hegel's Semiology", in *International Journal for the Semiotics of Law*, Vol. 14, 165-180.

Salvatore, Vincenzo (1992), "Quotas on TV Programmes and EEC Law", in *Common Market Law Review*, Vol. 29, N° 5, 967-990.

Savage, Kin (1992), "Lack of Bilingual Services at Social Security Offices: Why Non-English-Speaking Clients Are Not Getting Help", in *Clearinghouse Review*, Vol. 26, N° 8, 911-919.

Savino, Vic and Schumacher, Erica (1992), "Whenever the Indians of the Reserve Should Desire it: An Analysis of the First Nation Treaty Right to Education", in *Manitoba Law Journal*, Vol. 21, N° 3, 476-497.

Scanlon, T. (1978-79), "Freedom of Expression and Categories of Expression", in *University of Pittsburgh Law Review*, 519-543.

Schifter, Richard (1991), "To Hate All the People Your Relatives Hate", in *Human Rights Law Journal*, Vol. 12, N° 8-9, 327-330.

Schmid, Carol (1987), "Language and Education Rights in the United States and Canada", in *International and Comparative Law Quarterly*, Vol. 36, 903-908.

Schulman, Michael B. (1993), "No Hablo Inglés: Court Interpretation as a Major Obstacle to Fairness for Non-English Speaking Defendants", in *Vanderbilt Law Review*, Vol. 46, 176-196.

Schwartz, Benjamin I. (1993), "Culture, Modernity, and Nationalism — Further Reflections", in *Dædalus — Journal of the American Academy of Arts and Sciences*, Vol. 122, N° 3, 207-226.

Scott, Andrew (1990), "Language Policy and the Law", in *Witwatersrand University Student Law Review*, Vol. 2, 33-53.

Shapiro, Howard M. (1984), "The Constitutional Imperative of Proportional Representation", in *Yale Law Journal*, Vol. 94, 163-208.

Shockley, Evelyn Elayne (1991), "Voting Rights Act Section 2: Racially Polarized Voting and the Minority Community's Representative of Choice", in *Michigan Law Review*, Vol. 89, N° 1-4, 1038-1067.

Short, David (1981), "Restrictions on Access to English Language Schools in Quebec: An International Human Rights Analysis", in *Canada-United States Law Journal*, Vol. 4, 1-38.

The Situation of Human Rights in Turkey (1992), in *Human Rights Law Journal*, Vol. 13, N° 11-12, 464-480.

Slattery, Brian (1983), "The Constitutional Guarantee of Aboriginal and Treaty Rights", in *Queen's Law Journal*, Vol. 8, 232-273.

Slattery, Brian (1984), "The Hidden Constitution: Aboriginal Rights in Canada", in *American Journal of Comparative Law*, Vol. 32, 361-391.

Slattery, Brian (1987), "Understanding Aboriginal Rights", in *Canadian Bar Review*, Vol. 66, 727-783.

Slattery, Brian (1991), "Aboriginal Sovereignty and Imperial Claims", in *Osgoode Hall Law Journal*, Vol. 29, N° 4, 681-703.

Slattery, Brian (1992), "First Nations and the Constitution: A Question of Trust", in *Canadian Bar Review*, Vol. 71, 261-293.

Smith, Anthony D. (1992), "National Identity and the Idea of European Unity", in *International Affairs*, Vol. 68, 55-71.

Sperling, Jonathan (1994), "Equal Protection and Race-Conscious Reapportionment", in *Harvard Journal of Law and Public Policy*, Vol. 17, N° 1, 283-292.

Spielmann, Alphonse and Frowein, Jochen A. (1993), "Report on Human Rights in Romania for the Parliamentary Assembly of the Council of Europe", in *Human Rights Law Journal*, Vol. 14, N° 3-4, 133-140.

Steele, Graham J. (1992), "Court Interpreters in Canadian Criminal Law", in *Criminal Quarterly*, Vol. 34, N° 2, 218-251.

Stomski, Laura (1991), "The Development of Minimum Standards for the Protection and Promotion of Rights for Indigenous Peoples", in *American Indian Law Review*, Vol. 16, N° 2, 575-591.

The Structure of a Constitution for a Democratic South Africa (1991), in *South African Journal on Human Rights*, Vol. 7, 233-238.

Tabory, Mala (1980), "Language Rights as Human Rights", in *Israel Yearbook on Human Rights*, Vol. 10, 167-223.

Tabory, Mala (1990), "Minority Rights in the CSCE Context", in *Israel Yearbook on Human Rights*, Vol. 20, 197-221.

Tarnopolsky, W.S. (1986), "Ways for Ensuring the Protection of Minorities", in *Les Cahiers de Droit*, Vol. 27, N° 1, 155-160.

Tennant, Chris (1993), "The Rights of Indigenous Peoples in International Law", in *Harvard International Law Journal*, Vol. 34, 277-284.

Thornberry, Patrick (1980), "Is There a Phoenix in the Ashes: International Law and Minority Rights", in *Texas International Law Journal*, Vol. 15, 421-458.

Thornberry, Patrick (1989), "Self-Determination, Minorities, Human Rights: A Review of International Instruments", in *International and Comparative Law Quarterly*, Vol. 38, 867-889.

Timmermans, Isabella (1992-93), "Native American Self-Determination as Affected by Educational Funding and its Sources", in *Idaho Law Review*, Vol. 29, 187-214.

Tingbjörn, Gunnar (1993), "Multilingual Concepts in the Schools of Europe — Sweden", in *Sociolinguistica*, Vol. 7, 207-217.

Torres, Raidza (1991), "The Rights of Indigenous Populations: The Emerging International Norm", in *Yale Journal of International Law*, Vol. 16, 127-175.

Triebold, Ellen L. (1991), "Constitutional Law — The Court Meets Half-Way on Affirmative Action: Metro Broadcasting, Inc. v. Federal Communications Commission", in *Journal of Corporation Law*, Vol. 16, N° 3, 653-691.

Turi, Joseph-G. (1990), "Le droit linguistique et les droits linguistiques", in *Les Cahiers de Droit*, Vol. 31, N° 2, 641-650.

Ugalde, Aileen Maria (1990), "No se Habla Español: English-Only Rules in the Workplace", in *University of Miami Law Review*, Vol. 44, 1209-1241.

Uyttendaele, Marc (1987), "Les obligations linguistiques des mandataires politiques", in *Courrier hebdomadaire du Centre de recherche et d'information socio-politiques*, Vol. 1150, 3-44.

Van Bunnen (1988), "L'emploi des langues dans l'étiquetage et le droit communautaire", in *Journal des tribunaux*, N° 5448, 41-42.

Van Dyke, Vernon (1973), "Equality and Discrimination in Education: A Comparative and International Analysis", in *International Studies Quarterly*, Vol. 17, 375-398.

Vebers, Elmars (1993), "Demography and Ethnic Politics in Independent Latvia: Some Basic Facts", in *Nationalities Papers*, Vol. XXI, N° 2, 179-194.

Veitch, Edward (1990), "Language, Culture and Freedom of Expression in Canada", in *International and Comparative Law Quarterly*, Vol. 39, 101-119.

Veiter, Theodor (1988), "Political Notion of Ethnicity", in *Regional Contact*, N° 2, 70-78.

Veiter, Theodor (1989), "Self-Determination and the Protection of Ethnic Minorities — The Case of the South Tyroleans", in *Regional Contact*, N° 2, 81-90.

Verhoeven, Joe (1970), "L'arrêt du 23 juillet 1968 dans l'affaire relative à certains aspects du régime linguistique de l'enseignement en Belgique", in *Revue belge du droit internationale*, Vol. 6, 353-382.

Violation of Freedom of Expression of English Speaking Citizens of Quebec — McIntyre et al. v. Canada (1993), in *Human Rights Law Journal*, Vol. 14, 171-178.

Walker, Roger (1991), "Federal Bilingual, Bicultural Education: The Failure of Entitlement", in *University of Missouri-Kansas City Law Review*, Vol. 59, 769-800.

Walter, Mark (1992), "British Imperial Constitutional Law and Aboriginal Rights: A Comment on Delgamuukw v. British Columbia", in *Queen's Law Journal*, Vol. 17, 350-413.

Weiner, Richard (1983), "Teaching the Immigrant's Child: A Model Plan for Court-Ordered Bilingual Education" in *Journal of Law and Education*, Vol. 12, 61-85.

Weiner, Richard (1989), "70 Languages Equal and Free? The Legal Status of Minority Languages in the Soviet Union", in *Arizona Journal of International and Comparative Law*, Vol. 6, 73-96.

Weissman, Steven (1980), "The FCC and Minorities: An Evaluation of FCC Policies Designed to Encourage Programming Responsive to Minority Needs", in *Columbia Journal of Law and Social Problems*, Vol. 16, 561-589.

Why is Language Standardisation an Issue for Workers and Peasants? (1991), in *Language Project's Review*, Vol. 5, N° 4, 4-5.

Wickey, Tim (1991), "The FCC's Minority Preference Policies: The Missing Premise, Participation and Control", in *University of Missouri-Kansas City Law Review*, Vol. 59, 1075-1092.

Wildsmith, Bruce H. (1992), "Treaty Responsibilities: A Co-Relational Model", in *University of British Columbia Law Review, Special Edition*, 324-336.

Wittevrongel, Shelley (1990), "Sanchez v. Bond, 110 S.Ct. 275 (1989): Challenge to the Judicial Manageability of the Thornburg v. Gingles Threshold for Determining Minority Vote Dilution", in *Hamline Law Review*, Vol. 13, 127-166.

Woehrling, José (1981-82), "À la recherche d'un concept juridique de la langue : Présence et qualité du français dans la législation linguistique du Québec et de la France", in *Revue Juridique Thémis*, Vol. 16, 457-504.

Woehrling, José (1985), "Minority Cultural and Linguistic Rights and Equality Rights in the Canadian Charter of Rights and Freedoms", in *McGill Law Review*, Vol. 31, 50-92.

Woehrling, José (1986), "La Constitution canadienne et la protection des minorités ethniques", in *Les Cahiers de Droit*, Vol. 27, N° 1, 171-188.

Woehrling, José (1987), "La réglementation linguistique de l'affichage public et la liberté d'expression : P. G. Québec c. Chaussures Brown's Inc.", in *McGill Law Journal*, Vol. 32, 878-894.

Woehrling, José (1992), "Les droits des minorités : La question linguistique et l'éventuelle accession du Québec à la souveraineté", in *Revista de Llengua i Dret*, Vol. 18, 95-153.

Wozniakowski, Waldemar (1993), "Multilingual Concepts in the Schools of Europe — Poland", in *Sociolinguistica*, Vol. 7, 201-206.

Yánez Cossió, C. (1991), "The Implementation of Language Policy: The Case of Ecuador", in *International Review of Education*, Vol. 37, N° 1, 53-66.

Yaown, Zhou (1992), "Bilingualism and Bilingual Education in China", in *International Journal of the Sociology of Language*, Vol. 97, 37-45.

Zierer, Ernesto (1988), "Las Minorías linguisticas en la Constitución política del Peru", in *Revista Juridica del Peru*, Vol. 39, 19-28.

Zolf, Dorothy (1989), "Comparisons of Multicultural Broadcasting in Canada and Four Other Countries", in *Canadian Ethnic Studies*, Vol. XXI, N° 2, 13-26.

Unpublished Papers

Ajayi, Jacob Ade (1993), *Historical Perspectives on Ethnicity and Nationalism in Nigeria*, paper delivered at Conference "Ethnicity, Identity and Nationalism in South Africa: Comparative Perspectives", 20-24 April 1993, Rhodes University, Grahamstown, South Africa.

Broadcasting and Canada's Aboriginal Peoples: A Report to the Task Force on Broadcasting Policy (1985), J. Mark Stiles & Associates, Ottawa.

Cultural Rights of Peoples in Europe (1991), Centre UNESCO de Catalunya, Girona, Spain.

de Varennes, Fernand (1993), *Derechos Humanos y Lengua: La Situación Especial de los Pueblos Indígenas*, paper presented at the XI Congress of the Instituto Indigenista Interamericano, November 22-26 1993, Managua, Nicaragua. Publication forthcoming.

de Varennes, Fernand (1993), *Les droits linguistiques dans une perspective internationale*, paper presented November 6th, 1993, "National Conference on Linguistic Rights", Ottawa, Canada. Publication forthcoming.

de Varennes, Fernand (1993), *Language Rights and the Multiethnic State*, paper presented at Conference "Ethnicity, Identity and Nationalism in South Africa: Comparative Perspectives", 20-24 April 1993, Rhodes University, Grahamstown, South Africa.

de Varennes, Fernand (1994), *Human Rights and Linguistic Minorities: In Search of a Balance for Ethnic Peace*, paper presented at the 15th Conference Europe of Regions "Regionalism and Europe of the Future", 19-22 August 1994, Christiansborg Palace, Copenhagen, Denmark. Publication forthcoming.

de V. Cluver, A. D. (undated), *Language Planning Models for a Post-Apartheid South Africa*, Pretoria, South Africa.

Didier, Emmanuel (1984), *Droit des langues et langues du droit au Canada*, Doctoral Thesis, Université de Paris I - Panthéon Sorbonne.

Enrique Hamel, Rainer (1994), *Droits linguistiques universels et diversité socioculturelle : critères sociolinguistiques*, French translation by Jacques Maurais, to appear in "Langues et sociétés en contact. Mélanges en l'honneur de J.-C. Corbeil", pp. 520-547.

Ghai, Yash (1993), *Legal Responses to Ethnicity in South and South East Asia*, paper delivered at Conference "Ethnicity, Identity and Nationalism in South Africa: Comparative Perspectives", 20-24 April 1993, Rhodes University, Grahamstown, South Africa.

Hann, Chris (1993), *Ethnicity and Language in Northeast Turkey*, paper prepared for conference "The Anthropology of Ethnicity", Amsterdam, Netherlands.

Labrie, Normand (1993), *La protection des minorités de langues officielles au Canada au moyen des accords de réciprocité : Prospectives de l'aménagement linguistique*, paper prepared for "Colloque sur la problématique de l'aménagement linguistique : enjeux théoriques et pratiques", 6 May 1993, Chicoutimi, Canada.

Lee, M. (1991), *Language, Law and Nationalism*, Institute of Commonwealth Studies, London.

Maurais, Jacques (1991), *Language Planning and Human Rights: Some Preliminary Comments*, paper presented at "Symposium on Linguistic Human Rights", 13-15 October 1991, Tallinn, Estonia.

Maurais, Jacques (1994), *The Québec Experience of Language Planning*, paper presented at "Conference on Democracy and Ethnopolitics", 9-11 March 1994, Riga, Latvia.

Mercurio, Antonio, and Amery, Rob (1993), *Can Senior Secondary Studies Help to Maintain and Strengthen Australia's Indigenous Languages?*, paper presented at the World Indigenous Peoples' Conference, 13-17 December 1993, Wollongong, Australia.

Morand, Charles-Albert (1992), *Liberté de la langue et principe de territorialité*, paper presented at the first Ascona Meeting on Multilingualism, 27-29 September 1992, Ascona, Switzerland.

Nahanee, Teressa (1991), *Aboriginal Language Rights in Canada: Considering Sections 2(b), 15 and 35 of the Constitution Act, 1982*, paper prepared for Assembly of First Nations and Professors Mary Ellen Turpel of Dalhousie University Law School and Trisha Monture, University of Ottawa Law School, Ottawa, Canada.

Öhlinger, Theo (1993), *Minority Languages in Austria in the Light of the European Charter for Regional or Minority Languages*, EURORegion National Report, Fribourg, Switzerland.

Pizzorusso, Alessandro (1974), *Tutela Delle Minoranze Linguitiche E Competenza Legislativa Regionale*, paper presented at "Conferenza internazionale sulle minoranze", 10-14 July 1974, Trieste, Italy.

Steiert, Thierry (1993), *La Suisse et la Charte européenne des langues régionales ou minoritaires*, EURORegion National Report, Fribourg, Switzerland.

Tremblay, Josée (1988), *Report on a National Institute for Aboriginal Languages*, paper prepared for the Native Council of Canada, Ottawa, Canada.

Turp, Daniel (1993), *La constatation du Comité des droits de l'homme de l'ONU sur la langue d'affichage et le projet de loi 86 : de l'argumentation déficiente à la discrétion excessive*, Montréal, Canada.

Von Komlossy, Joseph (1994), *Regionalism in the Carpathian Basin — Is it a Vision or a Reality?*, paper presented at the Conference of Europe of Regions "Regionalism and the Europe of the Future", 19-22 August 1994, Copenhagen, Denmark.

INDEX OF CASES

INDEX OF TREATIES AND INTERNATIONAL INSTRUMENTS

GENERAL INDEX

Aborigines: 18, 254-255, 256, 269, *see also Indigenous Peoples, Language*
Aboriginal and Torres Straight Islanders: 256
Achuar: 262
Affirmative Action: 117-120
Afghanistan: 380-381
Africa: 6, 22-23, 251, 252
— Language Policies: 22-23, 108-113, 123, 124-125, 127-128, 175, 197, 208, 215-216
Afrikaans: 177, 208, 216
Åland Islands: 26, 28, 181, 208
Albania: 381
— Minorities Treaty: 26, 133, 153-154, 201, 218-219
Albanian: 222, 226
Alexander the Great: 4
Alfonso X: 12
Algeria: 46, 164-165, 221, 382
— Freedom of Expression: 45, 50, 163, 165, 227
Aliens: 65, 127, 133, 143-144, 243, *see also Non-Citizens*
Allah: 6
Alsace: 17, 220
America: 6-7, 12-13, 71-73, 90, 101
Andorra: 382
Antigua and Barbuda: 124, 382
Arab Conquest: 4
Arabic: 5-6, 13, 22, 45, 50, 101, 105, 106, 149, 159, 162, 164-165, 195, 214, 221, 222, 275
Argentina: 160, 383
Armenian: 5, 7, 19, 171, 251
Asia: 4, 22, 23, 31, 105, 109, 112, 127-128, 251, 261-262
Asia Minor: 4, 5
Assimilation: 5, 10, 18, 20, 90, 134, 135
Atatürk: 22
Austria: 17, 26, 36, 59, 162, 185-188, 202, 383
Austro-Hungarian Empire: 18

Autonomy: 5, 6, 13-14, 17, 22, 26, 31, 94, 98, 130, 170, 181, 202, 250, 263, 265, 266-267, 272-273, 274
Australia: 18, 220, 226-227, 236, 256, 261, *see also Aborigines, Aboriginal and Torres Strait Islanders*
Aymara: 259

Bahamas: 383
Bahasa Indonesia: 111
Bahrain: 383
Baluchis: 251
Bangladesh: 250, 253, 261
Barbados: 383-384
Barbarians: 4, 32
Barrere: 10
Basque: 8, 10, 12, 13, 21, 58, 99, 179, 250
Belarus: 384
Belarussian: 245
Belgium: 17-18, 123, 384-387
— Discrimination: 74-77, 102, 103, 104, 203, 208-209
— Freedom of Expression: 36, 40-41, 42
— Language Policies: 175, 181, 203, 208-209, 221
see also Conflict
Belize: 387-388
Benin: 388
Berber: 6, 165, 221, 227, 250
Bilingualism: 5, 6, 18, 38, 39, 60, 61, 75, 76-77, 78, 88, 97, 98, 116, 175, 176, 178, 179-180, 181, 194, 196, 203, 210-212, 221, 230, 249, 258, 259, 260
Bohemia: 18
Bolivia: 196, 259, 388
Bosnia-Hercegovina: 388-389
Botswana: 389
Brazil: 13, 136, 390
Breton: 10, 12, 20, 38, 45, 94, 186, 187
Breton Cases: 38-40, 45, 70, 78, 82, 86, 94, 154, 186-187
Brunei: 390-391

International Studies in Human Rights

20. A. Bloed and P. van Dijk (eds.): *The Human Dimension of the Helsinki Process.* The Vienna Follow-up Meeting and its Aftermath. 1991   ISBN 0-7923-1337-2

21. L.S. Sunga: *Individual Responsibility in International Law for Serious Human Rights Violations.* 1992   ISBN 0-7923-1453-0

22. S. Frankowski and D. Shelton (eds.): *Preventive Detention.* A Comparative and International Law Perspective. 1992   ISBN 0-7923-1465-4

23. M. Freeman and P. Veerman (eds.): *The Ideologies of Children's Rights.* 1992   ISBN 0-7923-1800-5

24. S. Stavros: *The Guarantees for Accused Persons Under Article 6 of the European Convention on Human Rights.* An Analysis of the Application of the Convention and a Comparison with Other Instruments. 1993   ISBN 0-7923-1897-8

25. A. Rosas and J. Helgesen (eds.): *The Strength of Diversity.* Human Rights and Pluralist Democracy. 1992   ISBN 0-7923-1987-7

26. K. Waaldijk and A. Clapham (eds.): *Homosexuality: A European Community Issue.* Essays on Lesbian and Gay Rights in European Law and Policy. 1993
ISBN 0-7923-2038-7; Pb: 0-7923-2240-1

27. Y.K. Tyagi: *The Law and Practice of the UN Human Rights Committee.* 1993
ISBN 0-7923-2040-9

28. H.Ch. Yourow: *The Margin of Appreciation Doctrine in the Dynamics of European Human Rights Jurisprudence.* 1995   ISBN 0-7923-3338-1

29. L.A. Rehof: *Guide to the* Travaux Préparatoires *of the United Nations Convention on the Elimination of All Forms of Discrimination against Women.* 1993
ISBN 0-7923-2222-3

30. A. Bloed, L. Leicht, M. Novak and A. Rosas (eds.): *Monitoring Human Rights in Europe.* Comparing International Procedures and Mechanisms. 1993
ISBN 0-7923-2383-1

31. A. Harding and J. Hatchard (eds.): *Preventive Detention and Security Law.* A Comparative Survey. 1993   ISBN 0-7923-2432-3

32. Y. Beigbeder: *International Monitoring of Plebiscites, Referenda and National Elections.* Self-determination and Transition to Democracy. 1994 ISBN 0-7923-2563-X

33. F. de Varennes: *Language, Minorities and Human Rights.* 1994.   ISBN 0-7923-2728-4

34. D.M. Beatty (ed.): *Human Rights and Judicial Review.* A Comparative Perspective. 1994   ISBN 0-7923-2968-6

35. G. Van Bueren, *The International Law on the Rights of the Child.* 1995
ISBN 0-7923-2687-3

36. T. Zwart: *The Admissibility of Human Rights Petitions.* The Case Law of the European Commission of Human Rights and the Human Rights Committee. 1994
ISBN 0-7923-3146-X; Pb: 0-7923-3147-8

37. H. Lambert: *Seeking Asylum.* Comparitive Law and Practice in Selected European Countries. 1995   ISBN 0-7923-3152-4

International Studies in Human Rights

This series is designed to shed light on current legal and political aspects of process and organization in the field of human rights.

MARTINUS NIJHOFF PUBLISHERS – THE HAGUE / BOSTON / LONDON